Challenging Boundaries

BORDERLINES

Challenging Boundaries
Global Flows, Territorial Identities

MICHAEL J. SHAPIRO AND
HAYWARD R. ALKER, EDITORS

BORDERLINES, VOLUME 2

 University of Minnesota Press

Minneapolis

London

Chapter 2 first appeared as "Of Incarceration and Enclosure: Neo-Realism and the New/Old World Order," *Millennium: Journal of International Studies* 22:2 (Summer 1993), reprinted by permission of Millennium Publishing Group; chapter 5 first appeared as "Tocqueville, Territory, and Violence," *Theory, Culture, and Society* 11 (1994), reprinted by permission of Sage Publications Ltd.; chapter 7 first appeared in *Alternatives: Social Transformation and Humane Governance* 19:4 (Fall 1994), copyright 1994 *Alternatives*, reprinted by permission of Lynne Rienner Publishers, Inc.; chapter 9 first appeared in *Alternatives: Social Transformation and Humane Governance* 18:4 (Fall 1993), copyright 1993 *Alternatives*, reprinted by permission of Lynne Rienner Publishers, Inc.; chapter 17 first appeared in *Kibbutz Journal: Reflections on Gender, Race, and Militarism in Israel* (Pasadena, Calif.: Trilogy Books, 1995), reprinted by permission of Trilogy Books.

Published by the University of Minnesota Press
111 Third Avenue South, Suite 290
Minneapolis, MN 55401-2520

Book design by Will Powers.
Set in Sabon and Officina types
by Stanton Publication Services, Inc., Saint Paul, Minnesota
Printed in the United States of America on acid-free paper

Library of Congress Cataloging-in-Publication Data

Challenging boundaries : global flows, territorial identities /
    Michael J. Shapiro and Hayward R. Alker, editors.
        p.   cm. — (Borderlines ; v. 2)
    Includes index
    ISBN 0-8166-2698-7 (hc)
    ISBN 0-8166-2699-5 (pbk.)
    1. Sovereignty.   2. Group identity.   3. International relations.
    I. Shapiro, Michael J.   II. Alker, Hayward R.   III. Series: Borderlines
    Minneapolis, Minn.) ; v. 2.
    JC327.C45   1996
    320.1'2—dc20   95-31465

Contents

Preface and Acknowledgments

HAYWARD R. ALKER

At an increasing tempo, theoretical perspectives from the humanities have been challenging entrenched conceptions and interpretations of global political issues. Our dialogue about the significance of these perspectives began when, at the 1991 meeting of the International Studies Association in Vancouver, I served as a commentator on Michael Shapiro's paper, which treated modernity's global dynamics on the basis of the differential forces of sovereignty and exchange.[1] As a result of our continuing exchanges over his analyses, which combined conceptions from both the social sciences and humanities, we developed an interdisciplinary theme for the program of the 1993 International Studies Association meeting in Acapulco.[2] In our summary statement of that program, titled "The Enterprises of the Americas," we emphasized the way that "identity dynamics" as well as the kinds of exchanges treated by conventional international political economists characterize modernity's global flows. We said, among other things, that our program

> invites investigation of the more general dynamics of political and economic "exchange." In this broader, post-modern sense of the term, . . . domestic and international orders are constituted on the basis of symbolic exchanges of recognition as much as of capital, consumer goods, weapons, and political [including territorial] favors. Over time, collective identities are formed, consolidated, developed and dissipated within and across nations. Every system of sover-

eignty—i.e., a system of authority over space and subjects—is based on both an exchange of recognition and on some rules and practices for limiting or enabling exchanges of other kinds. For example, the consolidation and policing of national borders involves limitations on the exchanges of workers as well as of goods and capital investments. Systems of sovereignty and exchange have submerged some cultural identities and political affiliations, e.g., those based on ethnicity or gender or coevolutionary status, while enhancing others, e.g., those based on private property relations, male-dominated families and states, historical conquests, and post-war territorial settlements. Terrorism, illegal drug trade, pre-conquest ethnic identifications, changes in gender relationships, and the demand for sustainable development all challenge prevailing paradigms of sovereignty, national integration, legitimate exchange, and human-nature relationships.

By embracing this broader system of identity dynamics within our entrepreneurial theme, we encourage examination of the continuing ways in which contemporary individual and group selves are being created, challenged, sustained, disintegrated and consolidated in and through their exchanges with others. Apropos of the 500th anniversary of Columbus's voyage, historians, political scientists, anthropologists and literary theorists, among others, have provided significant challenges to the familiar heroic, entrepreneurial narratives of "discovery" and "conquest" of "the new world." Based on such recent, critical orientations, we encourage work that challenges the narratives that have been providing historical/ideational support for the dominant systems of authority, extraction, marginalization and criminalization in modern America.[3]

These concerns prefigure the thematic unity of the present volume: its focus on territorially defined collective identities and authority structures, as well as on the related, boundary-preserving and -transgressing, often violent, flows of human beings, communications, resources, productions, and identity constituents. In this preface, I simply want to situate the contributions here in a broad set of issues surrounding the relations between modernity and identity.

As soon as we recognize that (1) the units in terms of which we describe inter-national relations are changing in ways that affect collective interests, preferences, and actions, that (2) states no longer monopolize or fully control many of the corporately organized production and exchange relationships within and across borders that affect our lives, that (3) politically unified nation-states have become the exception rather than the rule in an era where most violent inter-group conflicts pit peoples versus states, and that (4) personal, occupational, professional, communal, ethnic, or religious group loyalties or responsibilities transcend the boundaries of patriotic obligations, we must admit the need to study identity politics.

In studying identity politics, however, we need to have a view not only of the current spaces within which identity operates but also of the historical legacies lending persistence to some forms of global subjectivity and fragmentation to others. Whether we characterize modernity in terms of the awakened humanist sensitivities and indi-vidualizing achievements of the European Renaissance and Refor-mation, the political-economic practices of a globalizing, wealth-increasing but inequality-accelerating capitalism, the European (re-)discovery, conquest, and exploitation of an anything-but-new "new world," the development of the "Westphalian" system of sov-ereign states more recently populated by more or less democratic nations somewhat likely to war on their nondemocratic peers, the exponential growth in global energy consumption, world popula-tion, weapon lethality, and CO_2 production, or (William Connolly's notion of) the insistent realization of man's incompletely self-reflective desires to take charge of the world, we are faced with challenging problems of modern, late modern, and postmodern identity dynamics.

The studies collected in this volume do not fit within the typical frames of political explanation. The inferences they encourage must be understood more from the point of view of cultural criticism than of accumulation and analysis of scientific information. We neither connect these investigations to specific, technically advanced re-search programs nor appeal to a naturalistic social science more gen-erally, because such a "science" embodies an assumed-to-be-stable, gender-neutral actor as well as a stable model of the spaces of action. Mobile identities and shifting boundaries are the subject matter of the studies in this volume. Moreover, because these mobile aspects of identity and space cannot be subsumed within the dominant, univer-salistic narratives of the contemporary state system, the emphasis is on specific departures from the intellectual abstractions that have helped stabilize political interpretations emerging from that system.

Rather than retreating to abstractions that occult all but the familiar political identities constructed within a geopolitical, sover-eignty-oriented discourse, the arguments and investigations in this volume allow various persons and peoples to emerge by providing a conceptual space to recall their most important symbols and retell the stories that have given their identities coherence. Like the collective identity known as the nation-state, subnational and nonstate identities are narrated.[4] Many of the studies here examine modes of writing because a variety of "literatures"—including the writing of "international relations" as well as those genres traditionally regarded as literature—are involved in the constitution and dissolution of individual and collective identities.

In addition, because the analyses here are critical, much of the focus is on diasporic or migrating identities, on such dynamics, for example, as the ways that those with marginalized sexualities or gender ambiguities are treated differently in the different national societies they encounter. More generally, these investigations locate forms of domination that have not been evident to the disciplinary concerns of mainstream international relations theorists, whose emphases have been primarily on belligerence and commodities crossing national borders.

In short, this is a focused, thematically unified, theoretically and philosophically informed, disciplined yet interdisciplinary work. It builds on previous studies in the humanities as well as in the social sciences. I hope that it will stimulate productive controversy, broaden and make more contentious disciplinary commitments, and, especially, invite into the dialogue on global politics both hemispheric scholars and those from the older "worlds."

The editors extend special thanks to David Campbell, Michael Hardt, and Rob Walker, who supplied valuable reactions to various chapters. We also want to express our gratitude to our editor, Lisa Freeman, her associates at the University of Minnesota Press, especially Todd Orjala and Mary Byers, and the copy editor, Mary Keirstead, all of whom helped turn the efforts of twenty-one authors into a coherent and focused assemblage.

NOTES

1. See Michael J. Shapiro, "Sovereignty and Exchange in the Orders of Modernity," *Alternatives* 16 (1991), pp. 447-77.

2. I served as president of the International Studies Association that year, and Michael Shapiro served as program chair for the annual meeting in Acapulco. My thematic concerns, which provided some of the orientation for the program, are expressed in Hayward Alker Jr., "The Humanistic Moment in International Studies: Reflections on Machiavelli and las Casas," ISA Presidential Address, *International Studies Quarterly* 36 (1992), pp. 347-71.

3. From "Theme Statement: The Enterprises of the Americas," published in the program documents for the 1993 meeting of the International Studies Association, March 1993, Acapulco.

4. See Homi Bhabha, ed., *Nation and Narration* (New York: Routledge, 1990), for a series of studies that emphasize the narrative dimensions of national and other identities.

Introduction

MICHAEL J. SHAPIRO

In recent years, challenges to domestic authority structures and instabilities in global jurisdictions have highlighted inadequacies of traditional political discourses of comparative politics and international relations. It is less the case, however, that these discourses have been made invalid by changes in the political situations to which they referred than it is that their adequacy was always limited. For a while they were adequate to the legitimation needs of the dominant political forces. They contained political conversations within the problematics that served the centralizing authorities of nation-states and the dominance of states in global exchanges.

Nevertheless, those involved in the production of these discourses have largely operated with the illusion that they offer a universal perspective. They have thought of themselves as serving disinterested knowledge rather than dominant tendencies. But the official discourses of the state and their complicit academic echoes have effectively overcoded various social and cultural segments—ethnicities, mobilized women's groups, indigenous peoples, and stateless tribal groups—whose interests, affiliations, resistances, and actions have failed to achieve political articulation. To the extent that these affiliational groupings have appeared in mainstream political discourses, they have usually been quarantined within the administration of "social problems."

What has been attenuated of late is the smugness that has attended the state power configuration. The assumption that bordered state sovereignties are the fulfillment of a historical destiny rather than a particular, and in some quarters controversial, form of political containment has been challenged. The instabilities in global units and their interrelations are an incitement to discourse, an invitation to review the partialities of the voices that have monopolized the interpretation of political identity and space and to create a discursive frame that can enunciate alternatives. To appreciate this invitation, however, it is necessary both to treat more specifically the idea of "political discourse" and to map the sites of alternative voices whose addresses have not appeared in the directories provided by mainstream political science disciplines. Aspects of this mapping are provided in the essays collected in this volume. What this introduction provides is a framing for what the alternative voices imply.

Critical political theorists and analysts have been increasingly attracted to the notion of "political discourse." Among other things, this attraction carries the recognition that the intelligible worlds of objects and events emerge through contentious discursive, as well as material and institutional, practices. But although there is increasing recognition that one cannot wholly separate inquiry into political dynamics from struggles over how they emerge in articulations, there remains wide disagreement over the way to treat the epistemic status and value of a discourse. At a minimum, an effectively politicized approach to political discourse (and hence to the world[s] of politics), cannot avoid metadiscursive issues. Because this anthology is very much involved in a political struggle over both discourse and its metadiscursive predicates, it is important to establish some of the primary linguistic partisanships directing our efforts.

Within the more scientistic and empiricist traditions, discourse has been treated on the basis of the fit between its statements and the referents of those statements. This position is intimately tied to a model in which the value of a discourse is exhausted by its truthfulness, understood as either correspondence or instrumentally mediated validation. Alternatively, within the more familiar hermeneutic or interpretive approaches, discourse has been treated on the basis of its ability to reflect adequately the depth or more fundamental level of meaning of which the discourse's statements are believed to be a reflection. Within this hermeneutic model, truth is again a central concern, but in this case it is construed in expressivist rather than correspondence imagery. For many of those whose inquiries are hermeneutically oriented, the value of a discourse is tied to the success of the disclosure it achieves in application.

The commitment guiding our investigations departs markedly from both of these traditions. From our perspective, discourse is always simultaneously a form of impoverishment, even as it affords value and access. All intelligible oral or textual articulations involve a temporary fix on a meaning at the expense of other possible structures of intelligibility. In the case of those social and political discourses that construct the frames of national and international politics, what is involved is the establishment or reproduction of identities, political space, and consequently the distribution of resources. Certainly intelligibility is better than noncomprehension, but the political sensibility guiding our efforts suggests that intelligibilities do not simply reveal the truth but rather establish one possibility among many. Accordingly, to politicize interpretation, "we must," as Michel Foucault has put it, "make the intelligible appear against a background of emptiness, and deny its necessity. We must think that what exists is far from filling all possible spaces."[1]

It is a short step from this recognition of what might be termed the political economy of intelligibility to the achievement of a politicized view of the value of a discourse. Again, Foucault has provided guidance with specific reference to the failures of empiricist and hermeneutic positions. In one of his earlier statements about analyzing a "discursive formation" he employs an economic rather than an epistemic metaphor. Noting that interpretion can be considered as a response to an "enunciative poverty" with a meaning-producing act, he adds that nevertheless what is produced is not the elimination of poverty—the substitution of meaning for its lack—but an elaboration of the economy of the impoverishment: "To analyze a discursive formation, is to seek the law of that poverty." Continuing with an economic metaphor, he adds that this seeking after the law of a discourse's poverty amounts to a weighing of the "value of statements": "A value that is not defined by their truth,"—here he dismisses empiricism—"that is not gauged by the presence of a secret content"—here he refers to the resort of the hermeneuticist—"but which characterizes their place, their capacity for circulation and exchange, their possibility of transformation, not only in the economy of discourse, but more generally in the administration of scarce resources."[2]

Foucault asserts, then, that the value of a discourse is a function of the power and authority resources it distributes. Control over space and identity within this Foucauldian model derives from effective ownership of enunciation. This form of the exercise of power, the control over discourse, is inaccessible to one's apprehension when discourses are treated referentially or expressively, that is, as directly about *the* world or as disclosures of a true world hidden behind a hieroglyphic expression—a mere appearance. Rather, it must be recognized that discourses are assets.

Two of the essays in this volume provide ready examples, for they are addressed to dramatic changes in the global distribution of discursive assets. Cindy Patton's analysis of "queer peregrinations" shows how the tropes, which occupy the center of the epidemiological discourse that is articulated in the U.S. media's approach to AIDS, have produced a model of disease migration inadequate to the new solidarities of gay people. Epidemiological discourse functions within an anachronistic social imaginary; everyone is simply a citizen, and the newer affiliations, for example, gay communities, are allowed no recognition and effectivity.

Jim George's essay also is addressed to a current situation in which discursive control is contentious. He notes that the distribution of discursive assets has been shifting, for "the traditional hierarchical rituals of global power relations" are no longer controlling the agenda. To develop the implications of this idea at the level of discourse, he summons a remark by Czech President Václav Havel, who has noted that the U.S. strategic elite is now deluded in thinking that it has the "capacity to explain and control everything that exists." This elite has been used to hearing nothing but its own voice, articulating its own problematics. Because the United States had operated from a relatively uncontested frame of reference, it, along with the powerful political units that shaped first the colonial world and then the postcolonial, Cold War world, functioned within a delusional political narrative. It imagined itself as part of a story in which its dominance in the world order is a historic destiny and a utopian end to global political forms.

This political imaginary has been nowhere more apparent than in two very well entrenched domains of political science analysis in the West. One is political psychology and the other comparative politics. Both subdisciplines, which took shape in the aftermath of World

War II, selected as their constituting frame the avoidance of another Adolf Hitler. In the case of political psychology what was enjoined was a search for the fascist personality, understood to be a deviant type susceptible to authoritatian impulses or appeals. This search resulted in, among other canons in political psychology, the authoritarian personality studies of Theodor W. Adorno and his associates, Milton Rokeach's work on open versus closed minds, and H. G. Eysencks addition of a tender-minded versus tough-minded axis of opinion to the study of political ideology.

In the case of comparative politics, the study of political parties has been dominated by a fear of instability and, accordingly, a disparagement of those multiparty systems that allow for the aggregation of extreme or marginalized voices and interests. Those visible eruptions of discontent that do not operate through party politics have become "social movements," the analysis of which has tended to operate within psychologizing rather than politicizing frames. A safe "civic culture," one that would never allow a Hitler to emerge, must have structural impediments to the articulation of extreme appeals in the political process. Such was the anxiety of the imperial center as it produced many of the conceptual commitments of postwar political science.

How else might one construct the Hitler question? One response emerges when we listen to a voice that has been available but unheeded during the construction of the dominant discourses of political science, that of Aimé Césaire, a Black poet from Martinique. Césaire, known primarily for his participation in the anticolonialist, negritude literatures, resisted the treatment of the Hitler phenomenon as simply part of an aberration called Nazism. Instead, he treated it as part of a more general Western European barbarism, arguing that there is a truth that the peoples of Europe have hidden from themselves. What they have failed to understand about the Hitler phenomenon is

> that it is barbarism . . . but before they were its victims, they were its accomplices; that they tolerated Nazism before it was inflicted on them, that they absolved it, shut their eyes to it, legitimized it, because, until then, it had been applied only to non-European peoples; that they have cultivated that Nazism, that they were responsible for it.[3]

He goes on to note that the "European man's" complaint against Hitler is not Hitler's "*crime* in itself, *the crime against man*, it is not *the humiliation of man as such*, it is the crime against the white man, the humiliation of the white man, and the fact that he has applied to Europe colonialist procedures which until then had been reserved exclusively for the Arabs of Algeria, the coolies of India, and the blacks of Africa."[4]

The purpose of this example is not to deepen historical grievances or reinforce particular partisanships but to inquire instead into the levels of institutionalized inattention and forgetfulness that make such a voice so dissonant with established traditions of political analysis.

The political consolidations represented by the state territorial map—the international imaginary—were achieved through violent confrontations. Moreover, although space appears innocent, "the epitome of rational abstraction . . . because it has already been occupied and used, and has already been the focus of past processes whose traces are not always evident in the landscape,"[5] it remains contested. The violence continues as states attempt, physically and discursively, to marginalize or destroy various aspects of centrifugal otherness: ethnic solidarities, reasserted nationalisms, indigenous movements, and draft resistances, all dissonant elements proclaiming the tenuous hold of states over territories and identities.

Although these affronts to the state system do not appear on standard territorial maps or within the conceptual spaces of modernity's dominant political discourses, the challenges they pose have become increasingly registered as the former stabilities of the bordered world become more fragile and states react to reassert control.

The primary contestations in current global instabilities are over identity and spaces. Accordingly, this anthology is aimed at elucidating the current pressures arrayed against the policing of the bordered, Westphalian world of states and their sovereign citizen-subjects and, at the same time, providing critical alternatives to the conceptual commitments that have been accomplices of that policing. As a whole the essays constitute a literary intervention in the process by which all those discourses and systems of intelligibility that fail to contest dominant territorialities have daily helped to reproduce the international imaginary.

We are not claiming to be initiating a resistance, for challenges to the modern geopolitical map have existed in various genres of writing all along. For example, one exemplary challenge has been provided in a novel by Russell Banks. His *Continental Drift* serves as a counterdiscourse to the articulations of international relations and comparative politics because it privileges movement or flows and denigrates border policing. It stands as a striking intervention into the present narration of the United States as static, pacified national space. *Continental Drift* tells the stories of Robert Dubois, an oil-burner repairman from New Hampshire, and Vanise Dorsinville, a political refugee from the Allanche settlement in Haiti in the 1980s. The promise of a better life encourages both of them to move to Florida. Their paths cross when Dubois ends up illegally carrying Haitians to Florida in his charter fishing boat.

Apart from Banks's focus on the prosaics of global events—the specific human consequences of those who profit and those who lose as a result of national and transnational capital flows and the policing of national borders—he constructs spaces and the stories they contain without reproducing the grammar of international discourse. Instead, Banks produces a view of the planet that privileges flows of people rather than the consolidations of states and their practices of inclusion and exclusion. Specifically, he treats human flows as if they were physical, planetary ones:

> It's as if the creatures residing on this planet in these years, the human creatures, millions of them traveling singly and in families, in clans and tribes, traveling sometimes as entire nations, were a subsystem inside the larger system of currents and tides, of winds and weather, of drifting continents and shifting, uplifting, grinding, cracking land masses.[6]

And more specifically, he offers a moral map of the planet that privileges motion:

> Systems and sets, subsystems and subsets, patterns and aggregates of water, earth, fire and air—naming and mapping them, learning the intricate interdependence of the forces that move and convert them into one another, this process gradually provides us with a vision of the planet as an organic cell, a mindless, spherical creature whose only purpose is to be born as rapidly as it dies and whose general principle informing that purpose, as if it were a moral imperative, is to keep moving.[7]

Although Banks's narration focuses primarily on the diasporic lives of individuals, he often intervenes with a more geopolitical discourse on the movements of peoples. For example, he refers to "the stubborn determination of the Somali tribes to find food, water and peace, even though they must cross deserts alone to get there" and to "the Afghans' willingness to face ice and snow and murderous bandits in the high Hindu Kush rather than letting government soldiers enter their villages and shoot them for having given shelter one night to a few ragtag local Muahedeen guerillas."[8]

At all levels, Banks's stories resist the territorially oriented geography followed by Immigration and Naturalization agents, the Internal Revenue Service, and other agencies that firm up boundaries, resist flows, and effectively contain the trajectories of the lives of people like Robert Dubois and Vanise Dorsinville. Significantly, both have surnames of French national origin, representing, at the same time, the historical fact of earlier flows and, in contrast with national legitimating narratives, the arbitrariness of national origin and residence.

The flows of the 1980s that inspire Banks pale in comparison with those of the 1990s. The state system, which Gilles Deleuze and Félix Guattari suggest is characterized by its resistance to flows,[9] is under challenge, not only in terms of its control over territory but also in terms of its capture of cultural imagination and more generally its ability to control the range of felt affiliations. Whereas formerly the state had "overcoded" the subnational affiliations of various cultural segments[10] or, in Arjun Appadurai's terms, had managed to "subvert and annex the primary loyalties attached to more intimate collectivities,"[11] its grip is weakening. What are afoot are increasing postnational mobilizations.[12]

As a result, a primary political dynamic at work is a confrontation between, on the one hand, increasing flows as formerly submerged forces contest jurisdictional boundaries and, on the other, reassertions and consolidations by states to resist these forces. Among the ways that the state strikes back are immigration restriction, refugee repatriation, trade restriction and retaliation, and visa refusals to HIV-positive people. This volume tracks and theorizes many of the global mobilizations that transgress and weaken state boundaries and the reactions that aim at maintaining them. In the process, it foregrounds a global politics of contested spaces and contentious identities.

NOTES

1. Michel Foucault, "Friendship as a Way of Life," in *Foucault Live,* ed. Sylvère Lotringer, trans. John Johnson (New York: Semiotext[e], 1989), p. 209.

2. Michel Foucault, *The Archaeology of Knowledge,* trans. A. M. Sheridan-Smith (New York: Pantheon, 1972), p. 120.

3. Aimé Césaire, *Discourse on Colonialism,* trans. Joan Pinkham (New York: Monthly Review Press, 1972), p. 14.

4. Ibid.

5. Henri Lefebvre, "Reflections on the Politics of Space," *Antipode* 8 (May 1976), p. 3.

6. Russell Banks, *Continental Drift* (New York: Ballantine, 1985), p. 39.

7. Ibid., pp. 44-45.

8. Ibid., pp. 45-46.

9. Gilles Deleuze and Félix Guattari, *The Anti-Oedipus,* trans. Robert Hurley, Mark Seem, and Helen R. Lane (New York: Viking, 1977).

10. Ibid., p. 198.

11. Arjun Appadurai, "Patriotism and Its Futures," *Public Culture* 5:3 (1993), p. 414.

12. Ibid., p. 417.

I

Refiguring "International Relations"

Introduction to Part I

MICHAEL J. SHAPIRO

The global system of sovereign states has been familiar both structurally and symbolically in the daily acts of imagination through which space and human identity are construed. The persistence of this international imaginary has helped to support the political privilege of sovereignty affiliations and territorialities. In recent years, however, a variety of disciplines have offered conceptualizations that challenge the familiar, bordered world of the discourse of international relations.

There are alternative imaginaries that are increasingly salient. For example, seeking to identify alternative "landscapes" that comprise the contemporary global configuration and the corresponding "imagined worlds" that direct human action, Arjun Appadurai has recently specified five dimensions of disjunctive "cultural flows." These he terms ethnoscapes, mediascapes, technoscapes, finanscapes, and ideoscapes.[1]

Appadurai's terms constitute a theoretical opposition to the political discourses that have been insensitive to those flows. Despite the persistence of the international imaginary in international relations discourse, the flows of people, technologies, capital, images, and ideas that are part of rapidly increasing global cultural transactions are creating a different and nonstatic planetary map. It is now the task of critical political discourses to become adequate to these flows.

At a minimum "adequacy" must involve an altered frame of political recognition. As is well known, for example, nonstate peoples and extrastate forces have failed to achieve significant attention in traditional political discourses. The hegemony of the state has existed not only in its political and administrative control over its spaces and populations but also in its privileged place in the discourses and literatures of global representation. David Campbell's essay, which follows immediately, sets the tone for the rest of this volume, for it is a critical appraisal of the state's place in the literature of international relations. Moreover, like Appadurai's conceptual innovations, Campbell's essay provides an alternative focus on people's transactions and the structures that allow global encounters, not effectively coded in state-oriented discourse, to become a part of political circumspection.

Campbell notes that the discipline of international relations has addressed itself vigorously in recent decades to changes in global political life. But he shows effectively how in general the field, which has been dominated by an anachronistic sovereignty problematic, has been conceptually ill equipped to treat the forces of effective global agency. Not content to simply critique the field, Campbell goes on to provide an "interpretive disposition" that exposes dynamics to which the traditional sovereignty discourse is insensitive.

Most significantly, with his genealogical mode of interpretation, Campbell points to the way that collective subjectivities emerging in discourses of global politics are historically produced; they are not essences to be discovered. Once this point is appreciated, the important focus for analysis of global orders becomes those forces at work producing levels of global recognition and creating the spaces within which recognized identities are deployed.In addition, with his emphasis on the political prosaics of global life, Campbell provides a guiding ethos for his analysis. His approach seeks to extend political recognition to peoples and the quotidian facts of their daily lives.

Accompanying Campbell's genealogical interpretive disposition is therefore an ethnographically focused ethos of concern for the multitude of dimensions of global life. Campbell seeks to establish what he terms a "philosophical anthropology of everyday life on a global scale." This commitment is situated not only in Campbell's specific contributions but also in the focus of this volume as a whole.

Jim George's reprise of the realist legacy in the study of international relations provides an effective complement to Campbell's analysis. George exposes the traditions of realism in the study of international relations as complicit with the coercive practices of state power. Operating within the epistemological alibi of objectivity, realist traditions have been driven by a moral fervor disguised as a disinterested and merely analytic geopolitical gaze.

As Harold Garfinkel pointed out in an analysis of a society's gender boundaries, what is taken to be the "normal" is also taken as the morally correct.[2] George brings this insight into the global arena. By theorizing the state sovereignty system as the normal frame for global political life, realists have constructed an "international relations" that is less a science than it is a moral mapping of spaces and identities. Moreover, it is a partisan projection that has closed off effective critique by constructing itself within a scientistic epistemology that radically separates fact and theory, subject and object, and fact and value. With its restriction of global life to state jurisdictions and its dream of a totalizing approach to theory, mainstream international relations theory has been insensitive to the morally driven spatial predicates of its gaze. It has also been temporally insensitive, mistaking a particular historical power configuration for a historical destiny rather than a relatively recent and violently produced system of control.

George's commitment, like Campbell's, is to create a conceptual space to think beyond the world map of sovereign states reproduced in the theorizing of international relations. In his review of critical approaches, which move in the thinking direction he endorses, he sets the stage for the analyses that follow in subsequent sections of this anthology. They all seek to heed George's injunction and "go beyond the dominant rituals of International Relations theory."

NOTES

1. Arjun Appadurai, "Disjuncture and Difference in the Global Cultural Economy," *Public Culture* 2: 2 (1990), pp. 1-23.

2. Harold Garfinkel, "Passing and the Managed Achievement of Sex Status in an Intersexed Person," in *Studies in Ethnomethodology* (Englewood Cliffs, N.J.: Prentice Hall, 1967), p. 116.

Political Prosaics, Transversal Politics, and the Anarchical World

DAVID CAMPBELL

In the documentary photography of Sebastiao Salgado can be found one powerful representation of the multiple realities of world politics. Salgado's depiction of workers at Brazil's Serra Pelda gold mine, in the blazing oil fields of Kuwait, and in the cattle slaughterhouses of South Dakota; his evocative pictures of the "uncertain grace" possessed by the inhabitants of the African Sahel in their struggle with drought and famine; and his empathetic portrayal of the daily lives of people in central and southern America open a window onto what Nietzsche called the rich ambiguity of existence.[1]

Yet Sebastiao Salgado's photographs are not merely representations of individuals; they are testament to the way lives in the modern world are bound and shaped, constrained and constituted, by a complex manifold of social forces often unseen and often from elsewhere. For in the faces of those photographed, and through the environments in which they are situated, flow the many and varied effects of an increasingly globalized political economy in tension with a range of identities and practices.[2] As a *New York Times* critic remarked, the photographs "carry a sense of smoldering energy, of passion too big to be held in check by any body, any job, any relationship or any political system."[3]

Salgado's photographs can thus be read as manifesting what Fredric Jameson has called "the geopolitical aesthetic."[4] For Jameson, our location in what he calls "the new world system of late capitalism"[5] poses innumerable representational problems for politics, principal among them being our "structural incapacity . . . to construct a narrative that can map totality."[6] To come to terms with this challenge, and as a means of fashioning "a conceptual instrument for grasping our new being-in-the-world,"[7] Jameson reads a range of films (such as Pakula's *All the President's Men*) as attempts to figure the intersection of two incommensurable levels of being, the individual subject and the concealed network of the social order in which they can be located.[8] What is being allegorized in Jameson's reading of these films is the way in which "the local items of the present and the here-and-now can be made to express and to designate the absent, unrepresentable totality; how the individuals can add up to more than their sum; what a global or world system might look like after the end of cosmology."[9]

For Jameson, reading films in this light highlights a larger issue, that "all thinking today is *also,* whatever else it is, an attempt to think the world system as such."[10] In this context, Jameson's argument concerning the geopolitical aesthetic is a development of his earlier concern to move toward what he has called "an aesthetic of cognitive mapping—a pedagogical political culture which seeks to endow the individual subject with some new heightened sense of its place in the global system." As Jameson maintains, such a project is anything but a nostalgic call for returning to a "transparent national space." Instead, "the new political art (if it is possible at all) will have to hold to the truth of postmodernism, that is to say, to its fundamental object—the world space of multinational capital—at the same time at which it achieves a breakthrough to some as yet unimaginable new mode of representing."[11]

Jameson's framing of the issue has a number of limitations, perhaps the greatest of which is the reinscription of a new and determinate ground in terms of a conventionally rendered multinational space as the basis for politics.[12] Specifically, Jameson argues that the study of capital "is now our true ontology. It is indeed the new world system, the third stage of capitalism, which is for us the absent totality, Spinoza's God or Nature, the ultimate (indeed, perhaps the only) referent, the true ground of Being of our own time."[13] Such certainty in the face of ambiguity and contingency may be misplaced. As such, reframing Jameson's argument in chronopolitical rather than geopolitical terms (or at least some combination of the two) might be more suggestive.[14] Nonetheless, recognizing both the need for, yet current inability to achieve, the representation of the local and the global, spaces and flows, Jameson has identified a major political problematic.

Moreover, Jameson's argument has (indirectly at least) issued a substantial challenge to the discipline of international relations. As that subfield of the social sciences to which the task of thinking about world politics has either fallen or been arrogated, international relations has a responsibility to consider the best way in which to participate in the project of cognitive mapping in a manner that directly addresses the multiple realities of Salgado's photographs. International relations must address the basic question of whether it is adequate as a mode of understanding global life given the increasing irruptions of accelerated and nonterritorial contingencies upon our political horizons, irruptions in which a disparate but powerful assemblage of flows—flows of people, goods, money, ecological factors, disease, ideas, etc.—contest borders, put states into question (without rendering them irrelevant), rearticulate spaces, and re-form identities.[15]

This essay argues that because of the continued hegemony of spatial modes of representation, specifically the geopolitics of the levels of analysis, international relations is unrealistic. In an effort to point the way to modes of representation that could possibly be considered more adequate, the argument here suggests that a form of inquiry, which might be termed "political prosaics," concerned with the *transversal* (instead of trans*national*) character of politics in an an-archical world (as distinct from anarchy) is worth pursuing.

REPRESENTING TRANSFORMATIONS

The discipline of international relations has not been blind to the increasingly transnational transformations and the theoretical and practical challenges to which they give rise. Indeed, for more than the last two decades, the literature of international relations has made a concerted attempt to come to grips with what it perceives as major changes in world order. Although some have pointed out that this awakening was induced more by the declining fortunes of American power subsequent to the Vietnam War than a disinterested appreciation for the globalization of politics,[16] there can be no doubt that those who have written about transnationalism, interdependence, international regimes, hegemonic stability, and, particularly, international political economy have sought to make more complicated the state-centric view of the world, in which the "billiard ball" model was the metaphor of choice and the levels of analysis were the preferred mode of understanding.

Nonetheless, even a cursory examination of some of these literatures shows—for all the fanfare of theoretical innovation and the claims of cumulative knowledge in the social sciences—some remarkably persistent assumptions about what is significant in international relations/world politics. In particular, even when transformations like those discussed earlier are cited as important, what demands our attention is the way in which the issue has been posed, the question raised, or the problem stated. What we find when these representational concerns are our focus is, first, that these transformations are understood in terms of the rise of "nonstate" actors and, second, that the "nonstate" problematization of the issues does not seek to displace the state from the core of a regulative ideal of interpretation.[17]

A number of textual references from the international political economy literature could be offered in support of this proposition, but an influential argument by Robert Gilpin provides an exemplary illustration. Writing in 1971, Gilpin posed the specific issue of transnational economic actors in terms that are still very familiar:

> In specific terms the issue is whether the multinational corporation has become or will become an important actor in international affairs, supplanting, at least in part, the nation-state. If the multinational corporation is indeed an increasingly important and independent international actor, what are the factors that have enabled it to break the political monopoly of the nation-state? What is the relationship of these two sets of political actors, and what are the implications of the multinational corporation for international relations?[18]

Nearly twenty years later, theorists critical of realism, who drew upon a disparate range of sources divergent from those which underpinned Gilpin's thoughts, put forward similar formulations.[19] Nor is the framing of the debate in terms of state/nonstate the only formulation of interest and concern in these literatures. A number of other related assumptions—especially those concerning autonomy and power—figure often and prominently. For example, in the same year as Gilpin wrote, Joseph Nye and Robert Keohane set forth a world politics paradigm—parts of which they later retracted because it moved too far from the state—in which, because they defined politics "in terms of the conscious employment of resources," they argued that "the central phenomenon [of world politics] is bargaining between a variety of autonomous or semiautonomous actors."[20]

Although far from a comprehensive survey, I will venture to suggest that the literatures of which these formulations might be representative exhibit a number of common assumptions:

> They recur to the presence of certain agents (such as states, corporations, intergovernmental organizations, etc.), thereby exhibiting a preference for a sovereign presence as the organizing principle around which understanding can be constructed.

> Autonomy and semiautonomy are said to be important conditions, such that actors are taken to be separate from and prior to the relationships in which they are implicated.

> The capacity to wield power as a (usually material, though sometimes symbolic) resource over other agents is an important proviso of agency.

> Any complexity surrounding the issue of actors and agency is represented by additional levels of analysis—such as the supplementing of national and international with local and global—rather than by any sustained questioning of the assumptions of agency that might be challenged. This is most obvious in the way that complexity is always anchored in a "something-national" formulation, whether it be "international," "multinational," or "transnational."[21]

Such concerns are, of course, perfectly legitimate, such questions are certainly worth asking, and such formulations make sense given those concerns and questions. The worry is, why have these formulations triumphed over nearly all others as a means of understanding the wide-ranging and truly radical transformations of the global political economy and world order in the postwar period?

Much of the new literature in international relations, especially that concerned with transnational epistemic communities, multilateralism, and the importance of knowledge as a source of power, contains impressive evidence and valuable insights on some of the changes in global life.[22] At least as far as it goes. Which may not be very far—that is, not as far as it either should or could go—given the broader purview of world politics rather than international relations.[23] To illustrate this limitation, I want to consider two valuable and recent contributions to the international relations literature that are both cognizant of these empirical developments and (apparently) open to developments in social and political theory from which others have sought inspiration to raise anew fundamental issues of representation in world politics.

Alexander Wendt, who has argued strongly for the appreciation of the mutually constituted and codetermined nature of agents and structures in international relations,[24] recently concluded that the appropriate research agenda for international relations was a state-centric one. "The significance of states relative to multinational corporations, new social movements, transnationals, and intergovernmental organizations is clearly declining, and 'postmodern' forms of world politics merit more research attention than they have received," he wrote. "But I also believe, with realists, that in the medium run sovereign states will remain the dominant political actors in the international system."[25] Although Wendt did not seek to delegitimize other research concerns, he recognized that the priority he accorded state-centrism would be "depressingly familiar" to many. But what is of particular interest is how Wendt's self-professed modernist constructivism re-endorses state-centric realism, and how this explanation might shed light on the broader issues of this essay.

One possible answer may lie in the often explicit social-scientific preferences exhibited in the argument, most evident in the concern that international relations theorists structure their work in terms of a "research agenda" that can offer "causal" and "empirical" answers.[26] Another important, though related, argument is that for all the effort to go beyond the bounds of the "rationalist problematique" that binds neorealists and neoliberals together,[27] Wendt exhibits an overwhelming but underrecognized commitment to many of the general tenets of that disposition. Wendt wants to maintain that "philosophies of science are not theories of international relations" (hence we should avoid spending too much time on "questions of ontology"),[28] but there seems little escape from the fact that consciously or not international relations theorists are philosophers of knowledge. After all, as Wendt acknowledges, "All theories of international relations are based on social theories of the relationship between agency, process, and social structure."[29] The real question is whether we want to take the constitution and nature of agency seriously—which would by definition require considerable attention to the question of ontology—or whether we are happy in the final instance to merely posit the importance of certain agents. To do the latter involves gliding over a point well made by Judith Butler:

> Agency belongs to a way of thinking about persons as instrumental actors who confront an external political field. But if we agree that politics and power exist already at the level at which the subject and its agency are articulated and made possible, then agency can be *presumed* only at the cost of refusing to inquire into its construction . . . In a sense, the epistemological model that offers us a pregiven subject or agent is one that refuses to acknowledge that *agency is always and only a political prerogative.*[30]

Although Wendt might initially agree that "politics and power exist already at the level at which the subject and its agency are articulated and made possible" (hence his focus on identity- and interest-formation amongst states), a powerful rationalist pull in his argument curtails the logical consequence of pushing the constitutive nature of political agency to its limits. This commitment can be observed at two key points: when the anthropomorphism of the individual-state analogy is defended by Wendt,[31] and when it is argued that the body is the "material substrate of agency" that remains for the individual once the constitutive properties of the self are stripped away.[32] The latter point is particularly telling, on two counts. First, one of the major contributions of recent political theorizing, particularly feminist scholarship, has been to put in question the assumption of pregiven, material bodies as the unproblematic ground for identity and politics.[33] To overlook such arguments in favor of a (seemingly commonsense) resolution of this complex issue forecloses Wendt's potential to come to terms with "postmodern" politics. The second count of interest is that Wendt retreats in the end to the (supposedly) secure foundations of the body politic because of his moral commitment to an "epistemic realism" whereby the world comprises objects independent of ideas or beliefs about them.[34]

Another instance in which a rationalist faith overcomes postmodern potential is John Gerard Ruggie's attempts to problematize modernity in international relations through an analysis of the status of territoriality.[35] Ruggie contends that in the face of developments similar to those outlined earlier, visualizing "long-term challenges to the system of states only in terms of entities that are institutionally substitutable for the state" is evidence of "an extraordinarily impoverished mind-set at work." The inability, Ruggie argues, to even conceive of these developments in terms of "the possibility of fundamental institutional discontinuity in the system of states" is "because, among other reasons, prevailing modes of analytical discourse simply lack the requisite vocabulary."[36]

Few should disagree with such a contention. But from a broader perspective, a tension is evident between this proposition and the manifest limits of Ruggie's own analytical discourse. Like Wendt, Ruggie frames the quest for knowledge in overtly social-scientific terms, with his article marking "a relatively modest and pretheoretical task: to search for a vocabulary and for the dimensions of a research agenda by means of which we can start to ask systematic questions about the possibility of fundamental international transformation today."[37] Pretheoretical. Research agenda. Systematic questions. The rationalist commitment is evident.

Most interestingly, Ruggie reveals that this commitment—which John Lewis Gaddis has argued was utterly incapable of coming to terms with the end of the Cold War (and thus the emergence of the issues driving Ruggie's argument)[38]—is made possible by an irrational fear of the irrational. For what is striking about Ruggie's argument is his disavowal of the possibility that postmodern analytics may have something to say about the cultural category of postmodernity. Arguing via secondhand sources that within international relations postmodern theorizing has been at best "symptomatic" and "preoccupied with style and method" and offers "limited substantive insight," Ruggie attempts to drive the nail into the postmodern coffin by declaring that "the Paul de Man saga, especially the shameful defense of de Man by several leading deconstructivists, shows poignantly how deleterious the political consequences can be that follow from the moral vacuum—if not moral vacuity—the French fries would have us inhabit."[39]

One hardly need be a defender of de Man's offensively fascist and sometimes openly anti-Semitic writings for the (then German-controlled) Belgian newspaper *Le Soir* between December 1940 and November 1942—writings which Derrida painfully noted manifested "an alliance with what has always been for me the very worst"[40]—to recognize the anti-intellectual and highly polemical nature of Ruggie's caricature. It seems to be based upon the dubious proposition that periods in the life of an individual taint irrevocably an intellectual tradition for all subsequent interpreters, an argument which to be sustained would require supreme confidence that one's own theoretical debts were to discourses made possible only by saints. Of course, as Christopher Norris contends, such a defense is no substitute for "serious, responsible debate" *except* in cases of "crude *ad hominem* abuse."[41] But many moments in the controversy surrounding Paul de Man—including David Lehman's book, upon which Ruggie relies for his attack[42]—have been marked by ad hominem arguments. A great deal could and should be said about this debate, for it has many implications for our understandings of ethics, politics, and theory, but given the space here I will restrict my remarks to a couple of observations, worthy of further development, that are relevant to the immediate argument.

The first is that de Man and his wartime writings are taken by the critics (including, it seems, Ruggie) to be indissolubly linked with a body of theory, such that "the primary goal of the rage in question is a settling of accounts with 'deconstruction.'"[43] It is for this reason that the entire first half of Lehman's book is concerned with deconstruction rather than de Man. But logic of this type, even assuming that de Man as a thinker can be said to stand in for a varied tradition assembled under the heading "deconstruction," is far from being shared by all those justifiably critical of the wartime politics of de Man (and Heidegger). With respect to the latter, Jürgen Habermas, certainly no apologist for Heidegger's politics, has argued that "Illumination of the political conduct of Martin Heidegger cannot and should not serve the purpose of a global depreciation of his thought."[44]

At the same time—and somewhat paradoxically—it can be said that deconstruction is not really on trial, for "it has already proved its usefulness, even in the work of many who now attack it."[45] This is, one suspects with unintended irony, abundantly evident in Lehman's book, where for all the lamentations about the perfidious influence of textuality as one of deconstruction's central ideas,[46] the focus of his argument and the target of his wrath are texts and their politics: de Man's wartime writings and the responses of those, like Derrida, who have so outraged the critics.[47] In this vein, it is remarkable that the same angry critics who are so keen to maintain a sharp distinction between the world and the text have no hesitation in referring to de Man as an "academic Waldheim," an act of moral leveling that equates the actions of an officer in a German army unit known for its record of atrocities with the words of a newspaper columnist and reviewer.[48]

More importantly, especially for those prepared to think beyond the fear that the only certain alternative to specific commands of the Enlightenment tradition is a dark period of evil doings, Ruggie's off-the-cuff gestures ignore a growing literature on the ethical character of postmodern theorizing and its political entailments.[49]

Indeed, at one time, it seemed as though Ruggie himself wished to cultivate the interpretive possibilities of postmodern analytics with respect to postmodern politics. Writing during the great European political upheavals symbolized most obviously by the collapse of the Berlin Wall, Ruggie noted that what was most intriguing about the modernity/postmodernity debates in European social theory was how postmodern insights—concerning "detotalized, decentered, and fragmented discourses and practices; multiple and field-dependent referents in place of single-point fixed referents; flow-defined spaces and sequential temporal experiences; the erosion of sovereign or macro powers over society coupled with the diffusion of disciplinary or micro powers within society"—sounded familiar to the student of international political economy sensitive to "certain recently emerged global systems of economic transaction."[50] One should perhaps not overstate Ruggie's seeming interest in the nexus of postmodern inquiry and postmodern practices, for his subsequent questions concerning the issue of authority relations in a global context were still framed in terms of "how states see themselves in relation to one another; how they stand in relation to private actors."[51] Nonetheless the absence of ill-informed characterizations in 1989 is to be contrasted to the calculated closing down and willful writing off of postmodern possibilities a mere four years later. Any number of things could account for Ruggie's change in tone, but perhaps it was an instance of the belief that the accelerating globalization and simultaneous fragmentation of the post–Cold War world order was beyond understanding.

THE PROBLEMATIC OF SOVEREIGNTY

Of course, theorists of Wendt's and Ruggie's caliber do not want to reduce everything to states, territory, or the international system. Yet in framing their concerns in a manner that gives those or other grounds some priority, they seem to be exhibiting a fear, a (Cartesian) anxiety, that if one pushes to the logical conclusions of their arguments, and avoids the defensive maneuvers whose sole purpose is to ward off "foreign" theoretical traditions, no longer will it be possible to speak again of the state, or any other foundation of politics upon which one can ethically secure the good life. I want to argue that what is behind this anxiety and fear is an often unstated yet unequivocal commitment enabled by a narrow rationalism to "the sovereignty problematic" that restricts the interpretive possibilities of world politics understood as international relations.

Sovereignty, as Derrida noted, "is presence, and the delight in presence."[52] The sovereignty problematic is thus an articulation of two of Derrida's central concepts, the metaphysics of presence and logocentrism, whereby order can be said to result from a conformity to first principles, such that we make sense of the world by differentiating and normalizing contingency in terms of a hierarchical understanding of sovereignty/anarchy (or agent/structure, endogenous/exogenous, inside/outside, domestic/foreign, etc.). *Sovereignty* (or the equivalent first term) comes to be thought of as a center of decision presiding over a unitary self, whereas *anarchy* (or the equivalent second term) is that which cannot or will not be assimilated to this prior subjectivity.[53]

The idea of sovereignty, of presence, of the ground of first principles, is closely connected to the metanarrative of subjectivity from which we derive the interpretive resources for making sense of politics and transformations. Identified by Stephen White as the strong tradition of Western thought that is "oriented to the consciousness of a subject (singular or collective) who is faced with the task of surveying, subduing, and negotiating *his* way through a world of objects, other subjects, and his own body,"[54] the metanarrative of subjectivity underpins the way in which, through a proper name ("the keystone of logocentrism"),[55] we turn "dynamic, interconnected phenomena into static, disconnected things."[56]

The desire for presence and the fear of absence favor geopolitical grounds, the levels of rigid political segmentarity that devolve from those grounds, and the presumption of agency. It is because of these interpretive debts that the dynamics of global transformations have been represented through statements—of the sort that pronounce that "Non-state actors such as multinational corporations and banks may increase in importance, but there are few signs that they are edging states from center stage"[57]—that both depend upon and reproduce logocentric vocabularies. These analytic discourses, part of the "extraordinarily impoverished mind-set" that Ruggie decried but did not escape, continually reinscribe three assumptions through their operation: (1) that there is a "center stage" or pinnacle of power from which most if not all relationships can be governed, (2) that the site of power can only ever be occupied by one source of authority, and (3) that the presiding source of authority has to be an easily identifiable, unitary agent, endowed with relative autonomy and capable of purposively wielding material resources. It is in these terms that those international relations literatures that have sought to represent the complexity of world politics have been hampered in their task by a commitment to the problematic of sovereignty.

To this point I have focused on the sovereignty problematic and its assumptions about the centrality of geopolitical space and agency as presence. But inescapably intertwined with this are assumptions about power, because hand in hand with the sovereignty problematic goes an economistic conception of power,[58] whereby power is regarded as a commodity to be wielded by agents. Such a perspective is, however, wholly inadequate as a basis for understanding our postmodern time. Only if we understand power—in a manner that recalls recent observations about corporate structures in the global economy—"as something which circulates, or rather as something which only functions in the form of a chain . . . [as] employed and exercised through a net-like organisation,"[59] can we begin to grasp the economic and political globalization of the last thirty years. As Wendy Brown has observed:

> Postmodern capitalist power, like postmodern state power, is monopolized without being concentrated or centered: it is tentacular, roving, and penetrating, paradoxically advancing itself by diffusing and decentralizing itself . . . Postmodernity decenters, diffuses, and splays power and politics. Postmodern power incessantly violates, transgresses, and resituates social boundaries; it flows on surfaces and irrigates through networks rather than consolidating in bosses and kings; it is ubiquitous, liminal, highly toxic in small and fluid doses.[60]

Moreover, this theorization of power, in combination with the many globalizing tendencies discussed earlier, identifies a powerful reason for the unwillingness-cum-inability of theorists like Wendt and Ruggie, let alone the mainstream of international relations, to go beyond the sovereignty problematic. It is that in a time marked by this "centrifugation of power," a sense of dislocation and homelessness can prevail: indeed, as Brown notes, "we are today very susceptible to getting lost."[61] Or, as Daniel Warner has poignantly suggested, "we are all refugees."[62]

In response to this sense of dislocation and homelessness, identity politics (i.e., understanding and practicing politics in terms of ethnicity, race, gender, sexuality, region, continent, nation, state, etc.) emerges to provide a sense of situation, a feeling of location, and an air of certainty about our place in the world. In Brown's formulation, "Identity politics emerges as a reaction, in other words, to an ensemble of distinctly postmodern assaults upon the integrity of communities producing identity."[63] In this context, international relations as a discipline, because of its propensity to discursively recur to the state as the organizing identity in the face of both empirical and theoretical assaults, might be better understood as a particular though powerful *discourse of identity politics,* writers indebted to the sovereignty problematic might be understood as particular though powerful *theorists of identity politics,* and the state might be understood as a particular though powerful *formation of identity politics.* All of which gives, by definition, only limited purchase on the complexities of world politics.

The issue, then, is, can we represent world politics in a manner less indebted to the sovereignty problematic? What would be highlighted in place of the sovereign presence of agents and the relationships between them? Can we think international relations and world politics beyond the sovereignty problematic?

TOWARD A POLITICAL PROSAICS

The challenge for a mode of representation adequate to our postmodern time is therefore to articulate an understanding of world politics attuned to the need to move beyond the sovereignty problematic, with its focus on geopolitical segmentarity, settled subjects, and economistic power, that appreciates the significance of flows, networks, webs, and the identity formations located therein but does not resort simply to the addition of another level of analysis or of more agents to the picture.

Some attempts in this direction are being made outside of international relations in a burgeoning literature on globalization.[64] What I want to suggest is that thinking in terms of a *political prosaics* that understands the *transversal* nature of politics and the *an-archical* condition of postmodern life is one way of approaching the issue. Such an effort, however, should *not* be thought of in terms of constructing a theory, much less a new theory of international relations. Rather, it is part of an aspiration to encourage genealogically inclined critique of the sort Foucault indicated in his thoughts on Kant and the Enlightenment:

> The critical ontology of ourselves has to be considered not, certainly, as a theory, a doctrine, nor even as a permanent body of knowledge that is accumulating; it has to be conceived as an attitude, an ethos, a philosophical life in which the critique of what we are is at one and the same time the historical analysis of the limits that are imposed on us and an experiment with the possibility of going beyond them.[65]

This ethos begins with the notion of "prosaics," derived from the Russian literary theorist Mikhail Bakhtin, which signifies two associated yet discrete concepts.[66] The first is the antonym of "poetics" and comes from one of the central themes of Bakhtin's work: that the prose of the novel rather than poetics constituted the highest art form, because of the novel's ability to convey what Bakhtin called the heteroglossia of life.[67] This focus upon the contribution of prose to human understanding finds a (perhaps unlikely) resonance in John Lewis Gaddis's argument concerning international relations theory at the end of the Cold War. Faulting the pretensions of social-scientific theory in the discipline—and particularly its failure to offer any insights on the end of the Cold War—Gaddis argues that like historians and novelists, "we 'model' human actions by falling back upon the only known simulative technique that successfully integrates the general and the specific, the regular and the irregular, the predictable and the unpredictable: we construct narratives."[68]

Heteroglossia—the panoply of discordant voices, abundance of disorder, and the clash between centrifugal (unofficial) forces and centripetal (official) forces that, without apparent reason, seek to construct order out of the disorder that is the norm—is the basis for the second of the two notions of prosaics, that which understands these features as part and parcel of an antisystematic philosophy of the everyday and ordinary.[69]

This attitude (in a manner that resonates with Derrida's notion of undecidability) is understood by the "all-purpose carrier" concept of "unfinalizability," which signifies the conviction that the world is a messy, open, and plural place.[70] Concomitant with this is the importance of dialogue as something like a model of the world.[71] But Bakhtin's notion of dialogue (and of dialogism as a nonteleological dialectics)[72] exceeds the idea of argument or debate. Instead, the notion of dialogue brings into question certain assumptions linked to the conventional view of discussion, specifically those of interacting and autonomous monads. For Bakhtin, communication is so central to existence that to separate out particular identities from their conditions of possibility is an instance of "theoretism" (the mistaken belief that events should be understood in terms of rules or structures to which they purportedly conform).[73]

For the conventional modes of understanding world politics these concepts have some significant ramifications. In the first instance, an interpretive disposition indebted to prosaics reverses the burden of proof to focus analysis on the intellectual and political constitution of order rather than disorder, and the constructed rather than discovered character of selfhood and ethics.[74] The presumption of agency and the naturalness of autonomy are thus called into question. But even more importantly, Bakhtin's thoughts—akin again to a Derridean notion, this time of the trace—highlight the way in which individual and collective subjects are "extraterritorial, partially 'located outside' themselves," such that Bakhtin can speak of the " 'nonself-sufficiency' of the self."[75] With respect to individuals, Bakhtin maintains:

> I achieve self-consciousness, I become myself only by revealing myself to another, through another, with another's help. The most important acts, constitutive of self-consciousness, are determined by their relation to another consciousness (a 'thou'). Cutting oneself off, isolating oneself, closing oneself off, those are the basic reasons for loss of self . . . It turns out that every internal experience occurs on the border, it comes across another, and this essence resides in this intense encounter . . . The very being of man (both internal and external) is a *profound communication. To be* means to *communicate* . . . To be means to be for the other, and through him, for oneself. Man has no internal sovereign territory; he is all and always on the boundary; looking within himself, he looks *in the eyes of the other* or *through the eyes of the other* . . . I cannot do without the other; I cannot be-

come myself without the other; I must find myself in the other, finding
the other in me (in mutual reflection and perception).[76]

These thoughts also have important implications for collective
subjects (such as states, etc.), because they point to the limitations of
"territory" and "boundary" as metaphors, stressing that "cultural
entities are, in effect, *all* boundary."[77] As Bakhtin notes, "One must
not, however, imagine the realm of culture as some sort of spatial
whole, having boundaries but also having internal territory. The
realm of culture has no internal territory: it is entirely distributed
along the boundaries, boundaries pass everywhere, through its every
aspect."[78] And without boundaries, rigid segmentarity (the levels of
analysis problem) is no more.

Were one constructing a theory, the next question would inevitably be, How are such concerns to be made more concrete?, or
(even more scientifically) How are these ideas to be operationalized?
But as I am interested in no more than—because it is quite sufficient—a critical attitude or ethos toward our limits and that which
lies beyond them, the animus behind those queries can be answered
by saying "This philosophical attitude has to be translated into the
labor of diverse inquires."[79] And the labor of those diverse inquiries
might be organized around a number of related attitudes that intersect with the ethos of prosaics.

The first would be "philosophical anthropology," a term that
Bakhtin used to encompass his reflections on alterity, being, boundaries, the self, and the other (some of which are presented earlier).
Philosophical anthropology, drawn out by Tzvetan Todorov as that
which holds the key to most of Bakhtin's work, is that ethos which
refers to Bakhtin's "general conception of human existence, where
the *other* plays a decisive role. This is then the fundamental principle: it is impossible to conceive of any being outside of the relations
that link it to the other."[80]

Although Todorov draws attention to a fundamental principle, a
second element of this ethos is that life is not organized in terms of
first principles. An interpretation that moves toward a political prosaics and philosophical anthropology of the postmodern world thus
does more than reverse the priority of sovereignty over anarchy in
conditioning political possibilities. Instead, a political prosaics sub-
verts those terms by thinking of action and agency in terms of anar-

chy, not anarchy in the sense of being without a central authority or existing in a state of nature (its common rendering within international relations) but in terms of its Greek etymology, *an-arche,* that is, being without first principles, foundations, or grounds.[81]

Given life is understood in terms of being without first principles, the ethos articulated here pays particular attention to thinking that presumes the importance of the quotidian facts of daily life. This disposition is found in (among others) the histories of Fernand Braudel, the philosophy of Henri Lefebvre, and the genealogies of Michel Foucault.[82] But this is not to suggest that there exists some sort of positivist level of analysis called "everyday life" to which we can turn for the truth. On the contrary, our "life-world" is one in which competing discourses and interpretations about reality are already folded into the reality we are seeking to grasp.[83] Nor is it to suggest a return to presumptive social atomism and individuation as the basis for everyday life. Instead, and in keeping with Bakhtin's philosophical anthropology, a focus on everyday life depends upon the recognition that "a relation (always social) determines its terms, and not the reverse, and that each individual is a locus in which an incoherent (and often contradictory) plurality of such relational determinations interact."[84]

Likewise, neither is "everyday life" a synonym for the local level, for in it global interconnections, local resistances, transterritorial flows, state politics, regional dilemmas, identity formations, and so on are always already present. Everyday life is thus a *transversal* site of contestations rather than a fixed level of analysis. It is transversal because it "cannot be reconciled to a Cartesian interpretation of space."[85] And it is transversal because the conflicts manifested there not only transverse all boundaries; *they are about those boundaries,* their erasure or inscription, and the identity formations to which they give rise.[86]

In the "labor of diverse inquiries" that might employ such notions, the situation in the former Yugoslavia serves as a powerful example of the limitations and problems associated with international relations' standard modes of representation. Indeed, few instances in recent world politics better illustrate the way in which alterity, boundaries, and questions of self/other erupt in transversal conflicts incapable of being understood in geopolitical terms. Nonetheless, to try and read the Balkan conflict in a conventional manner, many analyses have struggled between understanding the conflict in terms of, on the one hand, "civil war" and, on the other, a "war of aggression," a vacillation made possible by doubts as to whether the war is "internal" or "external" to the space of the former Yugoslavia. In recent times, another sovereign interpretation, the idea that the bloodshed is the natural playing out of ancient animosities formerly suppressed, has stepped to the fore to shore up doubts about what is going on.[87]

The trouble with this perspective, particularly its fatalistic determinism, is that it is ethnographically dubious. Its inattentiveness to history overlooks the important fact that in the federal state of Yugoslavia the communist leadership did not suppress nationalist identifications but rather constitutionally enshrined and utilized them to further its authority. And its inattentiveness to the prosaics of everyday life overlooks the fact that at the same time as news accounts have spread the line on permanent enmity, they have also contained statements from Bosnian residents that speak to the lie of centuries-old hatreds.[88] In one such report, an eighty-two-year-old (Serbian) Bosnian—whose own son, a doctor, was killed by Serb nationalist forces because he refused to join "ethnic cleansing operations"—was mystified at the Vance-Owen plan: "We have lived together for a thousand years . . . Where did they come up with this crazy plan to divide us up? Why don't they come and talk to us?"[89]

A good question, indeed, and one that points to the necessity of understanding the violence as constitutive of, rather than a response to, settled borders and absolute alterity. It is because of instances like this that I contend that for international relations to be about world politics in our postmodern time it should incorporate a prosaics of everyday life and order to replace the Olympian detachment and reifications of the sovereignty problematic, and it should recognize that the an-archical condition of postmodern, globalized life is better represented as a series of transversal struggles rather than as a complex of inter-national, multi-national, or trans-national relations, because of their being modes of representation that have powerful investments in the very borders being questioned. In these terms, international relations—or at least that part of it that wants to understand world politics—might be better understood as a *philosophical anthropology of everyday life on a global scale,* an understanding that is, most surely, incapable of representation in exclusively geopolitical, segmented terms.

NOTES

1. Sebastiao Salgado, *An Uncertain Grace,* essays by Eduardo Galeano and Fred Ritchin (New York and San Francisco: Aperture/San Francisco Museum of Modern Art, 1990), and Salgado, *Workers: An Archeology of the Industrial Age* (New York: Aperture, in association with the Philadelphia Museum of Art, 1993).

2. This location is made explicit in the text accompanying the photographs in Salgado, *Workers.*

3. Matthew L. Wald, "The Eye of the Photojournalist," *New York Times Magazine,* June 9, 1991, p. 58, quoting Michael Brenson.

4. Fredric Jameson, *The Geopolitical Aesthetic: Cinema and Space in the World System* (Bloomington and Indianapolis: Indiana University Press, 1992).

5. Ibid., p. 49.

6. Ibid., p. 41.

7. Ibid., p. 3.

8. Ibid., p. 33.

9. Ibid., p. 10.

10. Ibid., p. 4.

11. Fredric Jameson, *Postmodernism, or The Cultural Logic of Late Capitalism* (Durham: Duke University Press, 1991), p. 54.

12. Jameson, *The Geopolitical Aesthetic,* p. 1.

13. Ibid., p. 82.

14. For a discussion of chronopolitics and international relations, see James Der Derian, *Antidiplomacy: Spies, Terror, Speed, and War* (Cambridge: Blackwell, 1992), especially ch. 6.

15. The literature on these developments is obviously large, but the texts I have found particularly useful include Mike Davis, *City of Quartz: Excavating the Future in Los Angeles* (New York: Verso, 1990); David Harvey, *The Condition of Postmodernity* (Oxford: Basil Blackwell, 1989); Saskia Sassen, *Global City: New York, London, Tokyo* (Princeton: Princeton University Press, 1991); and Timothy W. Luke, "Discourses of Disintegration, Texts of Transformation: Re-Reading Realism in the New World Order," *Alternatives* 18 (1993), pp. 229-58.

16. Robert Cox, "Social Forces, States, and World Orders: Beyond International Relations Theory," in *Neorealism and Its Critics,* ed. Robert O. Keohane (New York: Columbia University Press, 1986).

17. Richard K. Ashley, "Untying the Sovereign State: A Double Reading of the Anarchy Problematique," *Millennium* 17 (1988), especially pp. 244-51.

18. Robert Gilpin, "The Politics of Transnational Economic Relations," in *The Theoretical Evolution of International Political Economy: A Reader,* ed. George T. Crane and Abla Amawi (New York: Oxford University Press, 1991), p. 170.

19. Stephen Gill and David Law, *The Global Political Economy* (Baltimore: Johns Hopkins University Press, 1988), p. 204: "Ultimately, different interpretations of the role and impact of transnationals have to focus on the relationship between these firms and the states they deal with. How far are the policies, strategies and goals of the state influenced by transnationals? How far can states influence the behavior of transnational corporations so as to meet 'national goals.' "

20. Joseph Nye and Robert Keohane, "Transnational Relations and World Politics: A Conclusion," *International Organization* 25 (1971), p. 730. The retraction comes in Keohane and Nye, *Power and Interdependence*, 2d ed. (Glenview, Ill.: Scott Foresman, 1989). As they note in the preface to the first edition (p. vi), "In this book we try to understand world politics by developing explanations at the level of the international system."

21. See, for example, Robert C. North, *War, Peace and Survival: Global Politics and Conceptual Synthesis* (Boulder: Westview, 1990), one of a number of works that has added a fourth (global) tier to the levels of analysis to accommodate recent transformations. This tendency is also succinctly manifested by Rosenau when he writes that the relocation of authority involves movement "both outward toward supranational entities and inward toward subnational groups." James N. Rosenau, "Governance, Order, and Change in World Politics," in *Governance without Government: Order and Change in World Politics*, ed. James N. Rosenau and Ernst-Otto Czempiel (Cambridge: Cambridge University Press, 1992), pp. 2-3. As Walker observes, notwithstanding "the importance of global processes, the spatial imagery of levels necessarily provides an inappropriate guide to what these processes involve." R. B. J. Walker, *Inside/Outside: International Relations as Political Theory* (Cambridge: Cambridge University Press, 1993), p. 206n.

22. See, for example, Peter Haas, ed., "Knowledge, Power, and International Policy Coordination," *International Organization* 46 (1992), pp. 1-390; and "Symposium: Multilateralism," *International Organization* 46 (1992), pp. 561-708.

23. A good illustration of this unrealized potential is James N. Rosenau, *Turbulence in World Politics: A Theory of Change and Continuity* (Princeton: Princeton University Press, 1990). Although the argument, premised on the idea of a new era of "postinternational politics" and sensitive to the limitations of the "non-state actor" mode of representation (see p. 36), seems to want to go beyond the levels of analysis problem, some of its later formulations seem to lapse back into a form of segmented representation. Specifically, the central idea of the "two worlds of global politics" (ch. 10)—i.e., the state-centric world vs. the multi-centric world—depends upon qualitative distinctions between the domains, and thus reinforces the notion of distinct levels, neither of which seems to call into question the other.

24. See Alexander Wendt, "The Agent-Structure Problem in International Relations Theory," *International Organization* 41 (1987), pp. 335-70. For commentaries and criticisms, see David Dessler, "What's at Stake in the Agent-Structure Debate," *International Organization* 43 (1989), pp. 441-73; Richard K. Ashley, "Living on Borderlines: Man, Poststructuralism, and War," in *International/Intertextual Relations: Postmodern Readings of World Politics,* ed. James Der Derian and Michael J. Shapiro (Lexington: Lexington Books, 1989), pp. 276-77; and Barry Buzan, Charles Jones, and Richard Little, *The Logic of Anarchy: Neorealism to Structural Realism* (New York: Columbia University Press, 1993), ch. 6.

25. Alexander Wendt, "Anarchy Is What States Make of It: The Social Construction of Power Politics," *International Organization* 46 (1992), p. 424.

26. Ibid., pp. 425-26. For one discussion of why this stricture is problematic, see the discussion of a similar argument made by Robert Keohane, in Walker, *Inside/Outside,* pp. 99-100.

27. Wendt, "Anarchy Is What States Make of It," pp. 391-92.

28. Ibid., p. 425.

29. Ibid., p. 422.

30. Judith Butler, "Contingent Foundations: Feminism and the Question of Postmodernism," in *Feminists Theorize the Political,* ed. Judith Butler and Joan W. Scott (New York: Routledge, 1992), p. 13.

31. Wendt, "Anarchy Is What States Make of It," p. 397, note 21.

32. Ibid., p. 402.

33. See, in particular, Judith Butler, *Bodies That Matter: On the Discursive Limits of "Sex"* (New York: Routledge, 1993). Of importance here is the writing of Michel Foucault with respect to the concept of "biopower." See Foucault, *The History of Human Sexuality,* vol. 1, *An Introduction,* trans. Robert Hurley (New York: Vintage Books, 1980), part 5. I have attempted to connect some of these insights to the state and foreign policy in David Campbell, *Writing Security: United States Foreign Policy and the Politics of Identity* (Minneapolis: University of Minnesota Press, 1992), especially pp. 8-10, 87-92.

34. Campbell, *Writing Security,* p. 4; and William E. Connolly, "Democracy and Territoriality," *Millennium* 20 (1991), p. 483n.

35. John Gerard Ruggie, "Territoriality and Beyond: Problematizing Modernity in International Relations," *International Organization* 47 (1993), pp. 139-74.

36. Ibid., p. 143.

37. Ibid., p. 144.

38. John Lewis Gaddis, "International Relations Theory and the End of the Cold War," *International Security* 17 (Winter 1992-93), pp. 5-58.

39. Ibid., pp. 145-46. See also the critical remarks concerning so-called "postmodernist epistemologues" at p. 170, where Ruggie protests the "fetishistic parent (he[re]tical) obscurantism" of degenerative postmodernist method (his terms) by offering as evidence—in an argument that praises "straightforward scientific methods"—nothing more than a secondhand bibliography.

40. Jacques Derrida, "Like the Sound of the Sea Deep within a Shell: Paul de Man's War," trans. Peggy Kamuf, in *Responses: On Paul de Man's Wartime Journalism,* ed. Werner Hamacher, Neil Hertz, and Thomas Keenan (Lincoln: University of Nebraska Press, 1989), p. 132.

41. Christopher Norris, *What's Wrong with Postmodernism: Critical Theory and the Ends of Philosophy* (Baltimore: Johns Hopkins University Press, 1990), p. 223.

42. David Lehman, *Signs of the Times: Deconstruction and the Fall of Paul de Man* (New York: Poseidon Press, 1991).

43. Rodolphe Gasché, "Edges of Understanding," in *Responses,* ed. Hamacher et al., p. 208.

44. Jürgen Habermas, "Work and Weltanschauung: The Heidegger Controversy from a German Perspective," *Critical Inquiry,* 15 (1989), p. 433.

45. Gerald Graff, "Looking Past the de Man Case," in *Responses,* ed. Hamacher et al., p. 248.

46. Lehman, *Signs of the Times,* pp. 67, 84-85, 106-7.

47. Derrida's response to the rage is his "Like the Sound of the Sea Deep within a Shell." One can safely say that this is not the critique Ruggie would have written, but one can say with equal assurance that neither is it made possible by a "moral vacuum" let alone "moral vacuity."

48. The comparison was made by Jon Wiener in *The Nation,* and later reprinted in his *Professors, Politics and Pop* (New York: Verso, 1991), p. 3. Critical responses can be found in Gasché, "Edges of Understanding," p. 209; and J. Hillis Miller, "An Open Letter to Professor Jon Wiener," in *Responses,* ed. Hamacher et al., p. 335.

49. See, for example, William Connolly, *The Augustinian Imperative: A Reflection on the Politics of Morality* (Newbury Park, Calif.: Sage, 1993); Drucilla Cornell, *The Philosophy of the Limit* (New York: Routledge, 1992); *Deconstruction and the Possibility of Justice,* ed. Drucilla Cornell, Michael Rosenfeld, and David Gray Carlson (New York: Routledge, 1992); and Simon Critchely, *The Ethics of Deconstruction: Derrida and Levinas* (Oxford: Blackwell, 1992). My attempts to begin thinking about this issue can be found in David Campbell and Michael Dillon, "The Political and the Ethical," in *The Political Subject of Violence,* ed. David Campbell and Michael Dillon (Manchester: Manchester University Press, 1993); and David Campbell, *Politics without Principle: Sovereignty, Ethics, and the*

Narratives of the Gulf War (Boulder, Colo.: Lynne Rienner, 1993), especially ch. 6. For a recognition of the importance to international relations of postmodern theorizing on these issues—even as he takes issue with some of its formulations—see Steve Smith, "The Forty Years Detour: The Resurgence of Normative Theory in International Relations," *Millennium* 21 (1992), pp. 489-506.

50. John Gerard Ruggie, "International Structure and International Transformation: Space, Time, and Method," in Ernst-Otto Czempiel and James N. Rosenau, *Global Changes and Theoretical Challenges: Approaches to World Politics for the 1990s* (Lexington: Lexington Books, 1989), p. 30.

51. Ibid., p. 31.

52. Jacques Derrida, *Of Grammatology*, trans. Gayatri Spivak (Baltimore: Johns Hopkins University Press, 1976), p. 296.

53. See Ashley, "Untying the Sovereign State," p. 230; and Ashley, "Living on Borderlines," pp. 261- 62.

54. Stephen K. White, *Political Theory and Postmodernism* (Cambridge: Cambridge University Press, 1991), p. 6.

55. Geoffrey Bennington and Jacques Derrida, *Jacques Derrida,* trans. Geoffrey Bennington (Chicago: University of Chicago Press, 1993), p. 105.

56. Wolf, *Europe and the People without History,* p. 2.

57. Mark W. Zacher, "The Decaying Pillars of the Westphalian Temple: Implications for International Order and Governance," in *Governance without Government,* ed. Rosenau and Czempiel, p. 64.

58. See Michel Foucault, "Two Lectures," in *Power/Knowledge: Selected Interviews and Other Writings 1972-1977,* ed. Colin Gordon (New York: Pantheon, 1980).

59. Ibid., p. 98.

60. Wendy Brown, "Feminist Hesitations, Postmodern Exposures," *differences: A Journal of Feminist Cultural Studies* 3 (1) 1991, p. 64.

61. Ibid., p.66.

62. Daniel Warner, "We Are All Refugees," *International Journal of Refugee Law* 4 (1992), pp. 365-72.

63. Brown, "Feminist Hesitations, Postmodern Exposures," pp. 66-67.

64. See, for example, *Global Culture: Nationalism, Globalization and Modernity,* ed. Mike Featherstone (London: Sage, 1990); Arjun Appadurai, "Disjuncture and Difference in the Global Cultural Economy," *Public Culture* 2 (spring 1990), pp. 1-24; *Culture, Globalization and the World-System: Contemporary Conditions for the Representation of Identity,* ed. Anthony D. King (Department of Art and Art History, State University of New York at Binghamton, 1991); Ulf Hannerz, *Cultural Complexity: Studies in the Social Organization of Meaning* (New York: Columbia University

Press, 1992). There is not space here to pose the question of whether this literature does in the end exceed the sovereignty problematic, but it is worth asking.

65. Michel Foucault, "What Is Enlightenment?" in *The Foucault Reader,* ed. Paul Rabinow (New York: Pantheon, 1984), p. 50.

66. Although Bakhtin used the notion of prosaic, "prosaics" is a neologism constructed by Morson and Emerson. Gary Saul Morson and Caryl Emerson, *Mikhail Bakhtin: Creation of a Prosaics* (Stanford: Stanford University Press, 1990), p. 15.

67. Ibid., pp. 30, 139-42.

68. Gaddis, "International Relations Theory," p. 56.

69. Ibid., pp. 23-25, 27-30, 32-36.

70. Ibid., pp. 36-40.

71. Ibid., p. 49.

72. Robert Young, "Back to Bakhtin," *Cultural Critique* 2 (1985), p. 76.

73. Morson and Emerson, *Mikhail Bakhtin*, pp. 49-50.

74. See Gary Saul Morson, "Prosaics: An Approach to the Humanities," *American Scholar* 57 (1988), pp. 515-28.

75. Morson and Emerson, *Mikhail Bakhtin*, p. 50. Derrida's notion of the trace accents the way identity is constituted in relation to difference. As Bennington and Derrida argue, "if every element of the system only get its identity in its difference from the other elements, every element is in this way marked by all those it is not: it thus bears the trace of those other elements." Accordingly, "no element is anywhere present (nor simply absent), there are only traces." What this means is that "in referring to a stimulus or a self-presence of the subject, we are not finally referring to a fundamental presence with respect to which we might then comfortably envisage all the ambiguity one might wish, but still to a network of traces." Bennington and Derrida, *Jacques Derrida,* pp. 74-75, 111.

76. Mikhail Bakhtin, "Toward a Reworking of the Dostoyevsky Book," Appendix 2 in his *Problems of Dostoyevsky's Poetics,* ed. and trans. Caryl Emerson (Minneapolis: University of Minnesota Press, 1984), quoted in Tzvetan Todorov, *Mikhail Bakhtin: The Dialogical Principle,* trans. by Wlad Godzich (Minneapolis: University of Minnesota Press, 1984), p. 96. Emphasis in the original.

77. Morson and Emerson, *Mikhail Bakhtin,* p. 51.

78. Quoted in ibid.

79. Foucault, "What Is Enlightenment?" p. 50. As an example of one path such labors might take, consider George E. Marcus, ed., *Perilous States: Conversations on Culture, Politics, and Nation* (Chicago: University of Chicago Press, 1993). In addition, I will furnish my own example later to satisfy this concern.

80. Todorov, *Mikhail Bakhtin: The Dialogical Principle,* p. 94. Todorov's own work has been inspired by this ethos. See especially his *Conquest of America: The Question of the Other,* trans. Richard Howard (New York: Harper and Row, 1984).

81. This theme is central to Reiner Schurmann's, *Heidegger on Being and Acting: From Principles to Anarchy,* trans. Christine Marie Gros in collaboration with Reiner Schurmann (Bloomington: Indiana University Press, 1987). As Schurmann declares, "the turn beyond metaphysics . . . reveals the essence of praxis: exchange deprived of principle" (p. 18). I take the political implications that devolve from this to be radically democratic. See Campbell and Dillon, "The Political and the Ethical," where various readings of Schurmann's argument are discussed.

82. See Fernand Braudel, *Afterthoughts of Material Civilization and Capitalism,* trans. Patricia Ranum (Baltimore: Johns Hopkins University Press, 1977); Henri Lefebvre, *Everyday Life in the Modern World,* trans. Sacha Rabinovitch (New Brunswick, N.J.: Transaction Publishers, 1984); and Lefebvre, *Critique of Everyday Life,* trans. John Moore (New York: Verso, 1991).

83. Edith Wyschogrod, *Spirit in Ashes: Hegel, Heidegger, and Man-Made Mass Death* (New Haven: Yale University Press, 1985), especially pp. 9-24.

84. Michel de Certeau, *The Practice of Everyday Life,* trans. Steven Rendall (Berkeley: University of California Press, 1984), p. xi.

85. Ashley, "Living on Borderlines," p. 296.

86. Ibid., pp. 270, 296-97.

87. Among many examples, see Richard Cohen, "Serbs Savour Ancient Hatreds," *Manchester Guardian Weekly,* December 27, 1992, p. 15; "Hostages to a Brutal Past," *U.S. News and World Report,* February 15, 1993; and "Meddling in the Balkans: A Peril of the Ages," *New York Times,* April 11, 1993, p. E5.

88. For example, "Besieged Muslims Place Their Dignity over Life," *New York Times,* March 7, 1993, p. E3.

89. Maggie O'Kane, "A Public Trial in Bosnia's Sniper Season," *Manchester Guardian Weekly,* March 21, 1993, p. 10.

2

Understanding International Relations after the Cold War: Probing beyond the Realist Legacy

JIM GEORGE

ARTICULATING THE PROBLEM OF UNDERSTANDING IN THE 1990S

Reality it seems is not what it used to be in International Relations.[1] The Cold War is over, and patterns of thought and behavior identified as corresponding with an enduring universal essence of global existence are coming under increasing scrutiny, as old ideological commitments and alliances are reformulated, territorial boundaries are hastily redrawn, and new symbols of identity are constructed and/or resurrected. Integral to the critical reassessments taking place within the International Relations community is the question of how we might now understand global political life in that space beyond the Cold War when, for many, the dominant realist/neorealist perspective has been exposed as a politico-philosophical emperor at best only scantily clad. This is a theme integral also to the argument to follow, which suggests that the theory/practice of realism that invoked a reality of violence, dichotomy, and global containment *as* International Relations after World War II remains a serious impediment to any attempt to understand a complex, changing global environment in the 1990s.

A whole range of commentators have acknowledged this as a crucial issue in attempts to analyze and evaluate any new world order in the last decade of the twentieth century. The Cold War historian

John Lewis Gaddis is one who has recently expressed his disquiet at the current state of affairs.[2] In so doing Gaddis illustrates that the latest articulation of realist grand theory (neorealism) cannot adequately explain that which it assured a generation it understood—the behavior of the Soviet Union as a power-politics actor in the anarchical system. This primarily is because, in any of its guises, realism represents its knowledge of the world in terms of generalized, universalized and irreducible patterns of human behavior, which reduces global politics to the incessant, anarchical power struggle between states, and rational interstate activity to the simple utilitarian pursuit of self-interest. From such a perspective there can be no "rational" explanation for Soviet behavior in peacefully relinquishing its power status and systemic authority, other than in traditional terms. Hence the shrill triumphalism of those invoking the "victory" of the Western superpower in its power struggle with its mortal Cold War enemy. Hence the continuance of "successful" power-politics strategies in the Gulf War.

Like many of the more discerning observers of the post–Cold War era, Gaddis is concerned about the broader implications of this triumphalist tendency and its impact on the capacity of the International Relations community in the United States, in particular, to comprehend and sensitively address complex and volatile global scenarios in the future. He concludes that, at its core, International Relations is beset by a fundamental failure of orthodox theory, which despite its claims for scientific insight has shown itself incapable of detecting momentous changes in global behavior and/or predicting an event as significant as the demise of the Soviet superpower.[3] This concern is shared by Stanley Hoffmann, who has focused on the behavior of the United States and its United Nations allies during the Gulf War as an example of the serious problems of theory/practice facing the International Relations community in the 1990s.[4] In the Gulf, he maintains, the war-fighting policy was derived not from a careful, nuanced appreciation of the particular issue at hand nor from the long-term implications of coercive action but, primarily, from the "doctrines of realism" centered on traditional balance of power dictates and a pragmatic reformulation of collective security themes.[5]

On the specific application of this doctrine in the Gulf War he emphasized that, in strategic terms, the use of overwhelming force seldom works as an instrument of order but more often gives rise to dysfunctional consequences that "punish the innocent even more than the guilty."[6] The relative fate of untold numbers of Iraqi dead and that of Saddam Hussein offer poignant testament to the salience of this insight. There is salience too in the proposition that even when the violence is perpetrated in the name of rational-technical "clean war," the misery is no less tangible for a society suffering in the wake of a devastated health system and the destruction of adequate water and power supplies.

The problem, as Hoffmann acknowledges, goes beyond the immediate issue of strategic "practice" in the Gulf. Rather, it is integral to the basic pattern of realist thinking designed primarily for violent response and big-power coercion rather than for prevention and sensitive negotiation. Hence, in circumstances like the Gulf War—a new world scenario—the United States–led alliance invoked Old World images (e.g., of Hitlerism and the specter of appeasement) and acted in accordance with Old World rituals in accomplishing what Cold War alliances had been unable to accomplish for forty years—that is, actually punish the designated Other without fear of major retaliation.

Ultimately, argues Hoffmann, this traditional doctrine is a recipe for disaster in a post–Cold War future sure to be punctuated by conflicts that defy the kind of simplistic conceptual and strategic responses of the past generation. Consequently, in an emerging age of great dangers, complexities, and opportunities Hoffmann has emphasized the need to go beyond the simple, ritualized re-presentation of traditional theory/practice and begin seriously to question that which for so long has evoked certain, irreducible images of "reality" for the policy and intellectual communities in International Relations.

Lewis Lapham, Tom Post, and Václav Havel have done this in their different ways. Lapham has focused on an intellectual and policy "paralysis" at the core of the International Relations community in the United States as indicative of the general problem of understanding global political life in the 1990s.[7] In particular, Lapham argues, the mainstream International Relations community in the United States is floundering primarily because "[n]obody knows the language in which to ask or answer the questions presented by the absence of the Soviet empire".[8] Nevertheless, in the 1990s, while acknowledging, at one level, the difficulties of retaining its status as

world policeman, the United States continues to articulate its hegemonic ambitions in terms of retaining "the pre-eminent responsibility for addressing selectively those wrongs which threaten not only
our interests, but those of our allies and friends."[9] This situation, for
Lapham, represents something more than the delusions of grandeur
of an American society seeking to buttress a threatened identity in
the post–Cold War void. Rather, and more seriously, it represents the
continuance of a "grotesque" general theory of International Relations that continues to reduce highly complex historico-political phenomena to narrowly focused ahistoric rituals of thought and action,
dominant in the era of imperialist power politics and for four
decades of the "balance of terror."

For Post, the static traditionalism of the 1990s is most tragically
evident in relation to the ethnic wars in the former Yugoslavia and in
particular the plight of Bosnia.[10] He argues, for example, that difficult as it undoubtedly has been for analysts and policymakers, there
is/was nothing inevitable about the Balkan situation that has led to
the chaos of the present. Instead, in a situation that demanded innovative and imaginative thought and action, the Western response to
the disintegration of Yugoslavia was characterized generally by the
paralysis of thought and action noted by Lapham. Consequently, at
that crucial moment in June 1991, when U.S. Secretary of State
Baker was confronted by Bosnian appeals for support in its struggle
for self-determination, his rejection was framed in terms that stressed
traditional notions of sovereignty, security, and status quo order.[11] At
this vital moment in post–Cold War history, accordingly, the Western
superpower effectively informed Serbia and the Yugoslav military
that it could use any means to defend the sovereign state—without
fear of Western intervention. Or, as Post has put it, from the beginning in Bosnia "the West fell back on outmoded diplomacy, insisting
that Yugoslavia stay together. When it didn't, the United States and
most of the European Community acted like an anaesthetized patient,
tuning in and out of the Balkan conflict."[12]

This is not at all to minimize or underestimate the complexities
and dangers of the Balkan situation. Nor is it any simple appeal to
hindsight, suggesting that the United States had clearly defined policy alternatives in the Balkans or that armed with the powers of
some new grand theory of reality it could have avoided the devastation that has eventuated in that troubled region. There is nothing

clear or simple about the Balkans War circa 1992/93. Nor is there any singular, all encompassing grand "theory" of strategic action that can be applied to it in "practice." And yet, in their different ways, commentators as diverse as Gaddis, Hoffmann, Lapham, and Post have recognized precisely this commitment—to simplistic grand theorized patterns of (Cold War) policy practice—as integral to the problems, inadequacies, silences, and omissions in Western, particularly U.S., responses to current global issues.

One final commentary offers a valuable insight into these silences and omissions and orients the discussion more directly to the issues at the core of this essay. It concerns Václav Havel's recent ruminations on the post–Cold War era and the contrast they evoke with orthodox International Relations approaches.[13] From Havel's perspective the demise of the Soviet empire does not, by linear necessity, represent a progressive stage in the movement toward Liberal-capitalist synthesis (e.g., as in the Fukuyama thesis). Rather, it has major implications for the way in which the dominant articulations of modernity, in both the Liberal West and in Communist societies, have been represented as "historical symbol[s] for the dream of reason."[14] Havel's proposal is that instead of understanding the end of the Cold War as the victory of "Western" theory/practice, the time has come for the "victors" to confront those aspects of their own societies that bound them together with their Soviet enemy for so long in "a kind of alliance between the last citadels of the modern era making a common cause against the ravages of time and change . . . [thus] the two self-proclaimed superpowers propped each other up against the storm blowing from the abyss of a world dissolved."[15]

The specific proposition here is one rarely encountered in International Relations literature, notwithstanding its significance for global life. It represents an appeal for serious critical reflection on the fundamental philosophical premises of Western modernity. More precisely, it represents an appeal to the most powerful Western societies at the moment of their greatest triumph to reflect not just on the great achievements of modern political life but also on the dangers, costs, silences, and closures integral to it. Indeed, suggests Havel, the prospects of meaningful democratic change taking place in the wake of the Cold War depend, to a significant extent, on the capacities of the most powerful global actors to confront those aspects of their theory/practice that in the 1990s continue to restrict their understanding of a changing global environment. In particular they must go beyond the "technocratic, utilitarian approach to Being" that characterized superpower theory and practice in the Cold War and profoundly reappraise modern ideologies of power politics based on "the proud belief that man, as the pinnacle of everything that exists, [is] capable of objectively describing, explaining and controlling everything that exists, and of possessing the one and only truth about the world."[16]

This insight on Havel's part is significant because in its representation of dominant modern theory/practice—as the pursuit of objectivity, omnipotence, and control—it helps relocate International Relations as part of a much larger discursive enterprise that has seen a singular, homogeneous, and narrowly focused image of human social life defined, primarily, in terms of the (Western) European Enlightenment become transformed into a universalized and essentialized doctrine of humanity per se. In an International Relations context the result has been a crude (positivist-based) realism that has reduced complex and turbulent global experience to a patterned and rigidly ordered framework of understanding derived from a particular representation of post-Renaissance European history, articulated in orthodox Anglo-American philosophical terms. Under U.S. socialscientific tutelege since World War II, this realism has continued to determine the boundaries of legitimate theory, research, and the "art of the possible" in policy terms.[17]

Only in very recent times has there been a concerted challenge to this perspective pitched at the level insisted on by Havel and (implictly) acknowledged as necessary by as diverse a group of commentators as Gaddis, Hoffmann, Lapham, and Post. This essay seeks to make a contribution to the debate, in these critical terms, and in a manner that complements the general concerns of commentators such as these but that develops and extends their perspectives to take into account an even greater diversity of contemporary critical works on these issues. It does so by suggesting that the silences and omissions of realist theory have some frightening consequences in "practice" for those excluded from the narrow agenda of orthodox "reality" and by bearing in mind a range of contemporary issues that exist beyond the boundaries of the traditional agenda. In this silenced space, for example, one encounters the agony of former "comfort women" brutalized by the Japanese military in World War

II who recently relived their humiliation for the world's media in order that the violence perpetrated on them be no longer rationalized as merely the "spoils of war." Here too are some of the less publicized events at the G7 meeting in Tokyo (1993): those which saw anxiety expressed about Russia's use of the Sea of Okhotsk as a dumping ground for used nuclear reactors, which saw the Prime Minister of Tuvalu seeking help to prevent his island nation being submerged in the event of global warming, and which saw Salman Rushdie's appeal to world leaders against the death sentence imposed on him by an Iranian mullah for denigrating Islam.

These, I suggest, are new world problems that defy Old World responses such as those which, in 1993, saw U.S. helicopter gunships again firing cruise missiles into the suburbs of Baghdad to deter Saddam Hussein from acting in the manner once encouraged in the name of balance diplomacy, and which saw the United Nations in Somalia engaged in another vicious, confusing, and bloody conflict with a people it initially sought to save from the ravages of starvation. The point is that the deep multifaceted problems of the Middle East, of exploding ethnic hatred in the Balkans, of warlordism and famine in the Horn of Africa, and of culture, gender, transmigration, and global economic inequality cannot be solved by recourse to a crude theology of power, nor even to the most fear-inspiring displays of contemporary techno-rationalist savagery (as in the Gulf War 1990-91), for all its laser-directed fascination for some sectors of the community.

I do not suggest for a moment that there are simple answers to problems such as these—the issues at stake are too serious for such simplistic posturing. Rather, in acknowledging the dangers and complexities of the current period, this essay seeks to illustrate how it might be possible to begin to think and act beyond the boundaries of International Relations "reality" and begin to exploit the opportunities for a more tolerant, more inclusive, and less dangerous theory/practice in the final decade of the twentieth century. This essay does so, generally, in relation to a critical social theory literature, which over the past two decades has sought to locate International Relations, and its contemporary politico-strategic problems, as part of a much larger critical debate over dominant approaches to theory and practice in Anglo-American societies in particular.[18] It does so, more specifically, in arguing that questions of ontology and epistemology—of the way we think and act in the world and understand reality—that have either been ignored in International Relations or rendered marginal and barely relevant by its realist mainstream must now be brought to the forefront of the debate over understanding the post–Cold War era. In this regard this essay seeks to illustrate that the issues of political "practice" central to the various introductory commentaries—on U.S. identity, the continuance of stilted traditionalism in thinking on Bosnia and Eastern Europe, and the predictable violence of the Gulf War—are an integral part of that larger and more profound conversation about modern ways of thinking and Being, a conversation effectively closed off within the International Relations community.

The discussion to follow represents an explanation of how and why this closure has occurred and what might be done about it. Initially, it concentrates on some dimensions of the broader closure associated with modern theory/practice per se, and then in more specific terms it considers the analytical implications of this closure within International Relations and among prominent neorealists in particular. Finally, having opened up the debate in a manner that allows for different kinds of questions to be asked of the International Relations orthodoxy, the essay probes beyond the realist legacy and indicates how it might be possible to construct a more comprehensive, sophisticated, and less dangerous understanding of global life in the space beyond the Cold War.

UNDERSTANDING INTERNATIONAL RELATIONS
The Power of the Empiricist Metaphysic
and the Positivist Orthodox Consensus

At the core of International Relation's inadequate understanding of global political life is a dichotomized ontological logic that assumes into ritualized reality a distinction between a realm of empiricist "fact" and a realm of "theorized" knowledge derived in one way or another (i.e., either inductively or deductively) from it. The origins of this assumption arguably reside in the broader dualized tendencies of post-Platonic discourse and have therefore always been intrinsic to (dominant) Western philosophical images of truth, rationality, and reality. The more immediate and explicit origin of the assumption lies in the post-Cartesian age of modern rationality and in crystalized politico-intellectual terms in the empiricist-positivism of the period since the Enlightenment of the eighteenth century.[19] And although since this time the fact/theory dichotomy has been the focus of widespread critique, it has remained a powerful if unstated constant at the core of much mainstream Anglo-American thought— often at its crudest within an "Americanized" International Relations discipline after World War II. The endurance of this dichotomy has little to do with the qualitative merits of its logic, as scholars since Hume have attested. But in an era that has seen modern Western societies represent their achievements and identities as correlative with the successful pursuit of rational-scientific certainty, this dichotomy has accorded a legitimate (albeit paradoxical) logic to that sense of singular unified reality so vital to politico-strategic images of rationalized interstate hierachy and violence, and to "theories" of order congruent with them (e.g., deterrence theory).

In Ernst Gellner's terms this dichotomy represents the most powerful articulation of an empiricist metaphysic that distinguishes between a world of fact "out there" and a cognitive realm of theory that retrospectively orders and gives meaning to the (already existing) factual data.[20] Gellner's commentary in this context is particularly instructive because its focus is the work of Karl Popper and the falsificationist approach to mediated "scientific" knowledge so influential within the disciplinary mainstream since the 1960s. Accordingly, Gellner, like many others, argues that, paradoxically, the falsificationist project retained at its core precisely this (inductivist) image of the knowledge process, articulated as a dualized "conflict between hard fact and logical contradiction." Popper, therefore, was "wrong in repudiating or disassociating himself from positivism."[21]

Max Weber is an important figure in this context also, because, like Popper, he brought a sophisticated European dimension to Anglo-American thinking, effectively mediating its cruder (logical positivist) aspects on the theory/practice conundrum. As Anthony Giddens and others have indicated, however, Weber's contribution, like that of Popper, requires a more critical evaluation than it has received if its influence is to be more profoundly understood at the core of the "orthodox consensus" in Anglo-American social theory, still characterized by logical positivist protocols and a commitment to hypothetico-deductive systems.[22] The recent and very profound connections drawn between Weber and the exemplary International

Relations scholar Hans Morgenthau (and realism generally) make this inquiry even more significant for the present discussion.[23]

The point, in short, is that the sophisticated Weberian image of reality has, if anything, increased the tendency toward positivist closure in International Relations for, as Susan Hekman has explained, in continuing to acknowledge a fundamental ontological assumption, "the opposition of subject and object" (and fact/value, etc.), Verstehen approaches, like Weber's (and Morgenthau's), represent "the other side of the positivist coin" and lie at the heart of the orthodox consensus inherent in realism and the "backward discipline" of International Relations.[24]

Realism and the "Backward Discipline"

The dominant post–World War II approach to International Relations has been centered on one variant or another of a "spectator" theory of knowledge, in which knowledge of the real world is gleaned via a realm of external facts (e.g., of interstate anarchy) that impose themselves on the individual scholar/statesman, who is then constrained by the policy/analytical "art of the possible." In its (mainly) North American variant, infused with (primarily) Popperian insight and behavioralist training rituals since the 1960s, this approach has resulted in a positivist-based realism set on the enthusiastic invocation of falsificationist scientific principles. The (mainly) British alternative, meanwhile, has invoked a species of "intuitionist" inductivism often more sensitive in tone to the various critiques of positivism but, ultimately, no less committed to its perpetuation.

Consequently, two rather primitive subthemes have become integral to the question of political reality in International Relations.[25] The first projects reality as existing "out there" and is articulated through the logic and language of immediacy. The real world, accordingly, is that which is immediately "there," around us and disclosed to us via sensory information. Realism in International Relations thus becomes the commonsensical accommodation to the tangible, observable realities of this (externalized) world. The second primitive realist theme reaffirms the first and by its own logic, at least, grants it greater legitimacy. This is the necessity theme, which confirms the need for accommodation to the facts of reality but accords them greater historical and philosophical status. Reality now becomes the realm of the unchangeable and inevitable, "a world of eternity, objectivity, gravity, substantiality and positive resistance to human purposes."[26] In this manner realism is imbued with moral, philosophical, and even religious connotation in its confrontation with the world "out there." It becomes moral in its observance of certain rules of conduct integral to its understanding of human (power-politics) behavior. It can take on religious dimensions in its accommodations to the realm of inexorable destiny and ultimate necessity. It can represent itself in philosophical terms as, for example, in the serious contemplative manner of the scholar/statesman dealing with the often unpalatable "is" of the world.

All this pretention aside, the end result has been one variant or another of a crude power politics realism that has seen a generation of International Relations scholars and practitioners incarcerated within the narrow confines of an image of global life in which "states [are] involved in an unending struggle with each other (because that is the nature of states in an anarchic world); power is necessary to survive in it or continue to fight [and] all states are potential enemies . . . but the worst might be avoided by clever diplomacy and by virtue of the fact that all alike shared a similar conception of [utilitarian] rational behaviour."[27]

The inadequacies and dangers of this approach were starkly illustrated in a work entirely ignored by mainstream scholarship, John Vasquez's *The Power of Power Politics: A Critique* (1983), which, in the most comprehensive survey of the discipline yet undertaken, indicated clearly enough the problems of understanding and explaining global existence in realist grand theoretical terms. More significantly, it did so in the falsificationist terms that, since 1945, have been dominant at the (North) American disciplinary center.[28] Setting aside the quantitative idiom at the end of his study, Vasquez acknowledged that although a power-politics image is a useful way of understanding some periods of interstate behavior, the realist perspective, overall, actually "promotes certain kinds of [violent] behavior and often leads to self-fulfilling prophecies."[29] Drawing out some of the implications of this situation on the central question of war and peace, Vasquez had a chilling statement to make on the realist answer—the alliance system and balance of power. Here, he maintained, the most likely outcome of a state-centric, anarchical "theory" in power-politics "practice" is *war*, not peace.

For most mainstream scholars, of course, critical perspectives of this kind have at best a fading relevance, and in the wake of the Vietnam War International Relations literature has resonated with claims of having gone beyond (crude) realism and (unreflective) positivism.[30] Indeed, it has been in this period that the realist mainstream has understood itself as engaged in the third major stage of its (rational-progressive) development, centered around its Third "great" Debate and the emergence of neorealism.[31] This "progress," I suggest, is largely illusory, and although some orthodox works have illustrated a capacity for important insight (e.g., Interdependence à la Keohane and Nye), they have, ultimately, closed off our capacity to ask more profound questions and to construct genuinely alternative interpretations about global life in the last part of the twentieth century. Consequently, for all its developmental claims to the contrary, International Relations in the 1990s remains fundamentally incarcerated in the positivist-realist framework that characterized its understanding of the world "out there" in the 1940s and 1950s. This is Mervyn Frost's conclusion also, hence his appeal to realists of all hues to go beyond their positivist bias and confront the underlying (philosophical) problems of the "backward discipline" of International Relations.[32]

This backwardness is not just a matter of Hans Morgenthau orienting a whole generation of scholars toward the "objective laws" of politics at the international level.[33] Nor is it just about that moment of major irony in disciplinary folklore when E. H. Carr attacked the inadequacy of interwar idealism on the basis that it was a narrow, ethnocentric approach, drawn uncritically from Western Enlightenment sources.[34] It concerns too the nominally unrelated proposition of Klaus Knorr and James Rosenau in 1969 that, in the dispute between realists of the second "great debate," one point "command[ed] universal agreement, namely that it is useful and appropriate to dichotomize the various approaches to international phenomena."[35] It is integral also to Michael Sullivan's conclusion that one of the problems with the critiques of realism in the 1970s was that perhaps "their picture of the world . . . [was] at variance with the real world"[36] and to Rosenau's continuing insistence in the mid-1980s on "the basic tenets of empirical science which require that variables be specified and the analyst be ever mindful of the eventual need to observe and measure."[37] And it concerns Kal Holsti's traditionalist commentary, in the same period, which suggested that a new paradigm would not be unwelcome in the discipline if it passed the test that both scientific and classical-realist scholarship had instigated, and that required that any new approach be characterized by "logical consistency, the capacity to generate research, and reasonable correspondence with the observed facts of international politics."[38]

More immediately, this continuing backwardness in International Relations circles is intrinsic to Roger Tooze's insights in 1988 on the state of the intellectual art in contemporary neorealist international political economy, which see "mutual incomprehension, if not antagonism" existing between scholars seeking to go beyond orthodox strictures, and a positivist mainstream for whom "matters of philosophical interest and concern are either defined as not relevant to the individual or group producing knowledge or are left to the provenance of the theorists who . . . [are] inconsequential to the 'real world,' except to provide instrumental frameworks for the selection and ordering of 'the facts.' "[39] More significant still is the backwardness of the most influential neorealist literature of recent years, and it is to some of that literature that the discussion now turns in order to indicate further the scope and danger of incarceration and closure at the very apex of International Relations thought. Initial attention in this regard will be paid to the exemplary figure and text of neorealism—Kenneth Waltz and *Theory of International Politics* (1979).

Neorealism: Waltz and Banal Structuralism

Kenneth Waltz's contribution to International Relations spans four decades. In that time he has added influential dimensions to realist scholarship. Since its publication in 1959, for example, his *Man, the State and War* has been accorded the status of a classical text in the discipline. Moreover, Waltz's *Theory of International Politics* (1979) has been promoted, by Joseph Nye, as the work that manages to reveal the logic of power-politics realism more profoundly than any other.[40] It is difficult to argue with such a view, which, unwittingly and ironically, vindicates the critical attitude taken toward realist and neorealist theory and practice in this essay. My own position on *Theory of International Politics* and (to a lesser degree) *Man, the State and War* is that they stand as major indictments of an International Relations community that, closed to critical reflective capacity for so long, has accorded such high status to works of so little substance. They stand, in this regard, as a testament to the continuing legacy of a closed discourse in the period of realist dominance in International Relations.[41]

The similarities with Waltz's earlier "great text" are clear enough from the outset of *Theory of International Politics*, when Waltz reiterates his intentions to "construct a theory of international politics that remedies the defects of present theories."[42] The basic theoretical defect—reductionism—is here to be superseded by structuralist grand theory. If the implications of Waltz's efforts were not so serious, his attempts to remedy realist theory would, in this way, be an enterprise filled with (unintended) mirth. This is primarily because from the beginning of *Theory of International Politics*, Waltz's antireductionist position is presented in the most *reductionist* of terms—those associated with the singularity of the "unity" of science thesis and Popperian analytical strategies.[43]

In *Theory of International Politics*, for example, Waltz simply follows Popper in contrasting "reductionist" realism (i.e., factgrubbing empiricism) with his deductivist-based structuralism that, it is claimed, acknowledges the "theory" dimension in its search for systemic generalized explanations of reality. Waltz's argument has three basic assumptions: (1) that it is necessary and desirable for International Relations to have a general theory characterized by the logic and rigor of theorizing in the natural sciences, (2) that this general theory could not be achieved while International Relations remained committed to reductionism, and (3) that this general theory was achievable via a systemic order in global politics that could be discovered if scholars thought systematically about "the striking sameness in the quality of international life through the millenia."[44] At this point Waltz appears to be confronting the reductionism of the empiricist metaphysic, noting that classical realism, in particular, "apparently rests on the conviction that knowledge begins with certainties and that induction can uncover them. But we can never say with assurance that a state of affairs inductively arrived at corresponds to something objectively real."[45]

As with much of the moderated neorealist perspective of the 1980s and 1990s (and much "post-positivism" generally), this is fine as far as it goes. The problem is that this *is* as far as it goes. Thus, although (ostensibly) acknowledging the illusory notion of an external real world of "fact," Waltz follows this logic anyway in search of his scientific structuralism. Consequently, he invokes the great dichotomy between "theory" and the "real" world—the former, the realm of (internally) generated "invention"—the latter, the (external) repository of laws that theories (retrospectively) explain, order, and systematize. Ultimately, he proposes that "theory, though related to the world about which explanations are wanted, *always remains distinct from that world."*[46]

The implications of Waltz's positivism are most evident when he moves into an explicit essentialist mode to explain the correspondence between his structuralism and the "real" world. Here, he insists, certain "vague and varying" factors must be omitted from analysis before "useful" structuralist theory can be applied. These factors include "environment, situation, context and milieu." A whole range of questions must also be "left aside" in search of "useful" theory—questions, for example, "about the kinds of political leaders, social and economic institutions, and ideological commitments states may have." Deleted also must be other (presumably) non-useful questions "about the cultural, economic, political and military interaction of states" because only in this way is it possible to "establish structure by abstraction from 'concrete reality.' "[47] This is the basis of a structuralist realism, because "[h]ow units stand in relation to one another, the way they are arranged or positioned, is not a property of the units. The arrangement of the units is a property of the system."[48] The sense of ahistorical staticity engendered here is increased when Waltz outlines what a structuralist approach is set to achieve. Indeed, at this point, a generation of realist conservatism is renewed again in Waltz's "great text" of neorealism, with the proposal that it is "the structure of the system [that] acts as a *constraining and disposing force,* and because it does so, systems theories explain and predict *continuity* within the system."

Above all, therefore, Waltz's structuralism is system oriented because it is "within a system, [that] a theory explains *recurrences and repetitions, not change."*[49]

At about this point the "banality" theme attributed to *Man, the State and War,* by Justin Rosenberg, becomes even more relevant to the neorealism of *Theory of International Politics,* written twenty years later.[50] Unlike in 1959, however, there is no attempt now to embroider the structuralist conservatism in interesting philosophical fabric. In the place of the Rousseauian parable, consequently, there is another—the parable of the capitalist market—presented as a micro-economic analogy for the *endemic anarchy* of the unchanging international system. Rousseau thus meets Adam Smith. The result, rather incongruously represented in this context, is an ahistorical, depoliticized scenario replete with vague references to "spontaneously" generated markets and political structures that mysteriously "emerge."[51] This scenario is the fundament of Waltz's structuralist insight—the intellectual font of a neorealist perspective so inadequate that a generally sympathetic critic like John Ruggie has maintained that it is not only unable to explain historically where individual states came from but also unable to explain how the contemporary state *structure* emerged.[52]

GILPIN, KRASNER, AND KEOHANE AND THE NARROW WORLD OF NEOREALISM

Even when attempts are made to rehistoricize Waltz's neorealism, the positivist-realist discursive legacy continues to dominate proceedings. In Robert Gilpin's *The Political Economy of International Relations* (1987), for example, this legacy is evident within a work presented in the tolerant, moderated tones of the "post-positivist" age in International Relations. But, as Stephen Gill has illustrated, Gilpin's approach is very much of the Old World, representing a synthesis of "institutionalism, utilitarian rational choice analysis and a Realist framework of international relations, which is built upon the insights of Thucydides, E. H.Carr and Hans Morgenthau . . . [Accordingly] he is a methodological individualist who separates 'politics' and 'economics' and his ontology emphasizes states and markets."[53] Gilpin's "theoretical" knowledge, consequently, is *intrinsic* to his power-politics image of contemporary global "practice." Not surprisingly, therefore, the major substantive concern of Gilpin's neorealist perspective is the retention of a particular kind of stability in the international arena in a period of American hegemonic decline. It is via this knowledge/power nexus that Gilpin in *The Political Economy of International Relations* observes the world "from the 'top downward' through the lens of the dominant interest of the largest capitalist nations"—a perspective entirely congruent with Waltz's, which more explicitly seeks the kind of structural order that serves such interests.[54] Like Waltz's too, Gilpin's new/old realism continues to utilize a rational-actor model of state behavior within "given" systemic boundaries. The end result, inevitably, is an anarchic scenario, in which status quo order is the priority, and the pregiven (utilitarian) interests of all actors are calculated as support for the structures and institutional mechanisms (e.g., World Bank, International Monetary Fund) that produce such order and that buttress the position of the United States, the hegemonic "orderer."

Self-proclaimed "modified" neorealist structuralists such as Stephen Krasner and Robert Keohane share these commitments, and their perspectives require some comment. A useful location for this inquiry is that chosen by Krasner as the space in which their so-called "modified" structuralism has shown its new sophistication—in relation to the issue of regimes.[55] Emphasizing the new sensitivity and sophistication on the regime issue, Krasner insists that "the issue is not so much whether one accepts the possibility of principles, norms, rules, and decision making procedures affecting outcomes and behaviour, as what one's basic assumptions are about the normal state of international affairs."[56] This is an insightful proposition and one that invites a critical investigation of Krasner's own "basic assumptions." Once accepted, however, it finds them wanting. The first problem in Krasner's case arises when one ponders his "modified" structuralism, which, he explains, does not accept regime behavior as the fundamental organizing principle of the contemporary international system. Rather, for Krasner, as for realists down the ages, "power-maximizing states acting in an anarchical environment" remain the foundational element of international reality.[57] This being the case, and if regimes, defined by Krasner as "principles, norms, rules and decision making procedures," are *not* fundamental to international life, the question is begged as to the precise nature of this anarchic world.

More precisely, Krasner's position begs two questions. The first, simply put, is this: If contemporary state interaction is not about principles, norms, and decision-making procedures, how precisely does the international system operate? By Krasner's own account, "principles" are "beliefs of fact, causation, and rectitude." Norms of behavior, meanwhile, relate to sets of social "rules and obligations." "Rules" relate to "specific prescriptions or proscriptions for action," whereas "decision making practices" are defined as the "prevailing practices for making and implementing collective choice."[58] In light of this, the proposition that these are *not* fundamental issues in everyday international life becomes more problematic. Indeed it is hard to imagine, theological images aside, how one does come to an understanding of regimes or of anything else, if not through a process such as this. Putting the question a little differently, one would ask Krasner this: If understanding is not derived via "beliefs of fact and causation," if it is not formulated in human societies with "rules and obligations" that mediate, define, and police understanding in terms of sociointellectual "prevailing practices," what on earth is it derived from? *If, in other words, understanding is not derived from human social interaction and knowledge construction, where does it come from?* The answer, in Krasner's terms, is already given—that is, from one's "basic assumptions" about the normal state of international affairs. Which, of course, only serves to beg the second and obvious question concerning the derivative *source* of these "basic assumptions" if they do not emanate from the historical, societal, and philosophical experiences encompassed in regimes.

For neorealists so confidently asserting the "concreteness" of their approach to the world, it is at this point that the commitment to the "empiricist metaphysic" is exposed as part of a still dominant ontology that (like Waltz's and Gilpin's) is paradoxically reductionist—and reliant on positivist premises concerning the anarchic structure that *just exists* (unexplained) "out there." This becomes more evidently Krasner's position when he proposes that the "prevailing explanation" among "modified" structuralists for regime behavior, and indeed all other behavior at the international level, is simply and predictably the utilitarian impulse of the independent actor in the (anarchical) market, "egoistic self-interest . . . [which is] the desire to maximise one's utility function where the function does not include the utility of another party.[59] In short, the "basic (unexplained) assumption" of modified structuralist neorealism is the old interstate anarchy assumption—the same circular, self-enclosed, assumption that has informed Waltz and Gilpin, Carr and Morgenthau, Wight, Bull, Kaplan, and Tucker, and a generation of realists about the real nature of the world "out there." In the era of neorealism, postpositivism and a new sensitivity to economic themes, there has been some attempt to repackage this Old World doctrine, but this has been as superficial within the intellectual community as it has within the New World Order advocates at the policy level.

Robert Keohane is the exemplar of repackaged neorealists, and this was never more evident than the mid-1980s when, in speaking of his own "basic assumptions," he gently chided contemporary policy analysts for thinking that "theory" was irrelevant to the real world of International Relations.[60] Not so, soothed Keohane, because theory can be "useful" in understanding the real world. Indeed, he suggested, "theory does have implications for practice."[61] In outlining some of these implications Keohane concentrates on the distinction between the "theories of world politics on which policymakers and commentators rely" and scientific theories such as Newtonian physics. The essential difference here, he explained, is that whereas the latter provide "powerful, value-free explanations of outcomes," the former are invested with the "scholar's values, and their own personal experiences and temperaments."[62]

In the 1980s it might be expected that the odd policy analyst who has read Thomas Kuhn or pondered Heisenberg's conclusions about the interpretive nature of quantum physics might want to question this particular rendition of a complex issue. But this aside, it is when Keohane turns to the central question of the relationship between theory and reality that the primitiveness of his understanding becomes clearer. Again the tone is moderate and impeccably 1980s, even if the substance reeks of eighteenth-century empiricism. Thus, intones Keohane on the question of understanding reality, "[e]ven if one could eradicate theory from one's mind it would be self defeating to try." Why? Because "reality has to be ordered into categories, and relationships drawn between events."[63]

For Keohane, then, as for so many in the line through Descartes, Locke, Hume, Comte, and Popper, "theory" is represented as a *cognitive reaction to reality* rather than as integral to its construction. "Theorizing," consequently, is understood as the retrospective process by which reality is ordered into (interpretive) categories. "Theory" in this context takes place *after the fact*. "Theory," more explicitly, helps us understand the "relationship between events" that are *prior to theory*. From this position, of course, the really meaningful question becomes that framed by logical positivism, that is, how do we test/verify whether our "theories" are in fact congruent with reality as it is "out there"?[64] The analytical results are, again, entirely predictable. Thus, because the world "out there" is made up of sovereign states following selfish interest, two conclusions must "logically" flow from this: (1) any cooperative/communitarian impulse within the state system is, in reality, an illusion, and (2) all "meaningful" international behavior is, in essence, the pursuit of individual self-interest on the part of sovereign states following classical "self-help" principles. Regime behavior can *only* be understood, therefore, as the pragmatic (rational-actor) response of self-seeking actors to conditions in which utility maximizing is sometimes best served by some sort of collective decision-making scenario.

Change, in other words, as the realist tradition has always asserted, can *only* come from above—from the rational action of the major powers following rational self-interest. The change to regime institutionalism in the post–World War II period, celebrated by some as fundamental change, is, from this perspective, no more than a pragmatic readjustment of power-politics behavior. *Realism is thus saved from critical challenge by neorealism.* The discipline can get on with doing what it has been doing—solving the problems of the world as it really is, not as some casts of reformulated "reflectivists" (idealists) would have it. Thus, in the 1990s, the anarchical world "out there" remains contrasted to the rational, ordered model of domestic life, even while the experience of so many at the domestic level is incontrovertibly and terrifyingly "anarchical." Thus, the enormous complexity and indeterminacy of human behavior, across all its cultural, religious, historical, and linguistic variations, continues to be reduced to the simplicities of utilitarian rational-choice models and reformulated images of "billiard ball" logic. Consequently (and distressingly) in an era that has seen Western images of reality increasingly resisted, and other voices, perspectives, and realities heard in the global arena, International Relations, via its dominant neorealist mainstream, continues to represent the world in (seventeenth-century) metaphysical terms.

In the broader terms established for this essay there is nothing terribly surprising in this situation. Like orthodox responses before, across the social theory spectrum, the neorealist response of the 1980s and 1990s has all the traditional hallmarks of discursive incarceration and closure, albeit in updated and reformulated mode. There has been the resort to an even more precise level of certitude and a narrowing down of the "meaningful" principle (i.e., rational order under anarchy) that would have done the logical positivists proud. And, in replicating earlier paradoxes associated with the postwar "quest for certainty," the neorealism of the present is articulated in exemplary positivist terms, consistent with the behavioralist attempt to make International Relations more "scientific."

Which begs the question of what might be done about this situation and more specifically how might we begin to think and act beyond the realist legacy. This has been the focus of much of the critical social theory literature of recent years, which, resisting the traditional resort to simplistic responses (e.g., show us your alternative "realism") and noting the dangers of such approaches, has sought to readdress some of the silenced questions of Western philosophy, and its disciplinary derivatives such as International Relations, in order that we might begin to understand more profoundly the nature of global life in the 1990s.

PROBING BEYOND THE REALIST LEGACY

Going beyond the "God's-Eye View"

On the age-old quandry "What is to be done?" a critical social theory perspective has emerged that, in a number of different ways, insists that any solving of contemporary problems must emanate from the everyday practices of people's lives rather than from the "god's-eye view" of traditional elite forums. R. B. J. Walker has captured this perspective nicely with the proposal that

> under the present circumstances the question "What is to be done?" invites a degree of arrogance that is all too visible in the behavior of the dominant political forces of our time. The most pressing questions of the age call not only for concrete policy options to be offered to existing elites and institutions but also, and more crucially, for *a serious rethinking of the ways in which it is possible for human beings to live together.*[65]

Jane Flax and the Need for Positive Ambivalence

The sense that something fundamental must change if we are to better coexist as human beings is integral to much feminist scholarship in International Relations.[66] Jane Flax's contribution, for example, speaks very powerfully to International Relations in this context with her observation that

> something has happened, is happening to Western societies. The beginning of this transition can be dated somewhat arbitrarily from after the First World War in Europe and after the Second World War in the United States. Western culture is in the middle of a fundamental transformation: a "shape of life" is growing old. The demise of the

old is being hastened by the end of colonialism, the uprising of women, the revolt of other cultures against white Western hegemony, shifts in the balance of economic and political power within the world economy, and a growing awareness of the costs as well as the benefits of scientific "progress."[Moreover] Western intellectuals cannot be immune from the profound shifts now taking place in contemporary social life.[67]

For Flax this represents a growing recognition that the Enlightenment dream is over, that people everywhere are increasingly awake to dangers of the Enlightenment narrative of reason, knowledge, progress, and freedom. This is an important theme in any context concerned about opening up the incarceration and closure of International Relations because it allows for (effectively) silenced voices to be heard again, including those associated with anti-Enlightenment sentiments, such as Nietzsche. It is important, in this sense, because it acknowledges the nightmarish dimensions of the Enlightenment dream, which, for example, connect the ascent of the modern, rational subject with the experiences of Hiroshima and Auschwitz. The point, of course, is that a celebration of the age of rational science and modern society cannot simply be disconnected from the weapons of mass slaughter, of the techniques of genocide. Nor can the language and logic of liberty and emancipation be easily detached from the terror waged in their names by, for example, the major Cold War foes—each proclaiming itself the natural systemic heir to the Enlightenment dream. And although many in the 1990s celebrate the "end" of the Cold War, as the victory of one Enlightenment-based economic doctrine over another, the other side of this particular coin must also be confronted, in the poverty in so much of the world, and in the growing underclasses in "developed" societies where neoclassical and neo-Marxian "scientific" approaches have dominated the economic debates.

But I offer no grand theorized condemnation of the Enlightenment (or more precisely its dominant scientific project) in favor of some ready-made alternative "realism," unfettered by its distorting influences. Rather, my position is consistent with the Foucault of "What Is Enlightenment?" who, in retaining a deep suspicion of modernist rhetoric and ambition, acknowledges that "the thread that may connect us with the Enlightenment is not faithfulness to doctrinal elements, but rather the permanent reactivation of an attitude—that is of a philosophical ethos that could be described as a permanent critique of our historical era."[68] This perspective, which dissents from the dominant discursive practices of modern life, while acknowledging the positive ontological and social potentials of modernity, connects a "reflectivist" critical social theory approach to the "concrete" policy concerns of Post on Bosnia, Lapham on U.S. strategy, and Havel on Eastern Europe, and distinguishes it from the narrow, abstract "problem solving" rituals of the neorealists. It does so in its understanding of the need to go beyond simple dichotomy, traditional formulas, and respectable polemic. It does so in Flax's terms in its acknowledgment of the need for a positive critical ambivalence to the ambiguities, paradoxes, and uncertainties of everyday realities and the way we understand and cope with them.[69]

This perception, of course, is no source of comfort for contemporary thinkers, critically inclined or otherwise. Indeed, as Flax has put it, "the more the fault lines in previously unproblematic ground become apparent, the more frightening it appears to be without ground."[70] Hence the "intellectual vertigo" she speaks of. There are, however, many who have taken up the challenge of modernity in a positive, constructive manner: they are still suffering from "vertigo" to be sure, still shaken by both the extraordinary achievement and colossal brutality that is their heritage, but they are now no longer willing to celebrate the former while remaining blind to the latter. Their changed perspective has meant more than a surface level consciousness of the need to think and act in more sensitive and tolerant ways. It has meant a more profound willingness to critically confront the way we think and act, to strip bare the very basis of thinking and acting, to reinterrogate its meaning and the ways we legitimate the social and intellectual "givens" that for so long have been reality—the way the world is "out there."

It has resulted in a range of works that resonate with alternative images of global politics derived often from previously alien sources, for example, German critical theory, Gramsci, and varieties of postmodernism.

Critical Theory, Gramsci, and International Political Economy from the Bottom Up

One of the most significant articulations of a (broad) critical theory perspective has come from Robert Cox over the years.[71] In 1981, for example, Cox confronted realism's problem-solving approach with the proposition that it is inadequate because, in focusing its attention on a frozen objectified image of the world "out there," and not reflecting upon the larger process by which that image is theoretically constructed, realism effectively blinded itself to the *prospect of a changing reality,* generated by the dialectical interaction of theory and practice. A critical theory approach is necessary, in this context, precisely because it *does* reflect upon the process of theorizing, in order to "become clearly aware of the perspective which gives rise to theorizing, and its relation to other perspectives."[72] Critical theory, thus, reconnects (theoretical) knowledge to the everyday practice of power and opens up a previously foreclosed debate about the way we "know" and create reality. It does not posit an ahistorical "continuing present" but is oriented toward a "continuing process of historical change." It does not accord existing institutions and power relations the status of "facts" or "givens" but "call[s] them into question by concerning itself with their origins and how and whether they might be in the process of change."[73]

It was in these terms that, in 1981 and in subsequent works, Cox introduced a definably Gramscian tone to his critical theory arguments. This he did in confronting neorealism's approach to international political economy and U.S. hegemony with a series of counterhegemonic propositions centered less on traditional state-centric analysis per se and more on the emancipatory potentials of "social forces."[74] To reconceptualize contemporary international political economy, Cox argues, an alternative (Gramscian) approach to hegemonic power is required, which insists on a dialectic between knowledge and power, between the power structure (the state system) and its "superstructural" elements (e.g., ideological) that help constitute and legitimate that power. The point, he maintains is that neither the structure of state interaction nor the question of hegemony in the international political economy can be understood exclusively in power-politics terms. Rather, to understand systemic and hegemonic power is to understand the "temporary universalization in thought of a particular power structure, conceived not as domination but as the necessary order of nature."[75] This ideological transformation of a particular power structure into a "natural" element of international political economy has, since the nineteenth century, seen universalized capitalist market relations and associated social formations become a "necessity" of international order and progress. The role of the state in this hegemonic discourse is to ensure the necessary (strategic and ideological) conditions for the universalization process to take place.

In this hegemonic context, realism, from its disciplinary center in the United States, has managed to reduce the complex matrix of issues of International Relations and now international political economy to a concern with hegemonic order, an order represented as in the interests of the state system as a whole, as in the interests of the "natural" (modern) order. Any challenge to this order can on this basis be repulsed for the common good of the state system. In this schema, (capitalist, market) economics are accorded a taken-for-granted status, representing an (often) unspoken but powerful ideological commitment within Anglo-American realism and throughout its hegemonic territory. The emergence of a neorealist structuralism (based on microeconomic theory) and hegemonic stability theory is, in this sense, the *explicit* representation of a deep ideological commitment in realism, drawn out by challenges to its hegemonic power.

These challenges do not represent an immediate threat to international capitalism per se, nor, in the short term, to the state system built upon it. Rather, Cox argues, the hegemonic crisis of the United States is, to a large extent, a crisis of hegemonic legitimation, the crisis of a dominant power no longer able to effectively articulate its hegemonic logic.[76] In Gramscian terms this represents a significant historical moment, when the hegemon can no longer project its domination as in line with the "necessary order of [politico-economic] nature." This is not solely or primarily because of the demise of institutions (e.g., Bretton Woods) that acted as major agencies of U.S. hegemonic power, or because of the end of the Cold War, as such, but it has to do with broader structural changes in the international political economy. These are changes that, for all their concern with structural analysis, neorealists cannot adequately deal with *because they are not reducible to simple models of individual state interaction.* Rather, they concern changes in social forces brought on by an internationalized production process and the international division of labor associated with it. It is in this context that U.S. theory and practice is inadequate in confronting "a world order . . . founded not only upon the regulation of interstate conflict, but also upon a globally conceived civil society i.e., a mode of production of a global extent which brings about links among the social classes of different countries. [It is] the global structuring of [these] social forces [that] shapes the different forms of state, while states in turn influence the evolution of the regulatory pattern of the global hegemony."[77]

From Cox's perspective then global change is not explained from the top down (i.e., at the behest of the major states) as in realism, but it occurs as part of a more complex matrix, as changes in social forces help restructure world order and the pattern of global hegemony. It becomes possible, thus, to think of stability, order, and hegemony not, necessarily, in terms of the dominant state, or as a recurring factor in some determined "historical" structure. Rather, history and the international hierarchy of states is understood, always, as part of a dialectic between social and material forces mediated through the political/institutional agencies of the state. And although, like neorealists, Cox is concerned with the question of what comes after U.S. hegemony, his response has not been to proclaim the ungovernability of the system but to examine the possibilities for alternative state formations in the future—and the emancipatory potentials of social forces emerging in the present.[78]

Other significant challenges to orthodox theory and practice have taken a rather different perspective on the emancipatory themes raised by Cox but have nevertheless provided some provocative and stimulating alternative approaches to thinking and acting in the world. Critical social theory scholars of postmodernist dispositions have been at the forefront of these challenges.

Postmodernism: Reconceptualizing International Relations as Discourse

The nature of the postmodernist challenge to International Relations is quite literally spelled out in the title of James Der Derian's and Michael Shapiro's *International/Intertextual Relations: Postmodern Readings of World Politics*.[79] The explicit influences on this work, those of Foucault, Derrida, Lacan, Kristeva, Barthes, and Baudrillard, are, in more than the obvious sense, "foreign" to a discipline dominated from its Anglo-American center. The influences, more generally, are those of discourse analysis, genealogy, deconstructionism, and textuality, and it is in this context that postmodernists have sought to question, critique, and add dimensions to the dominant "reality" of International Relations.

The "foreignness" of the postmodern approach is epitomized in the inclination to "read" the social world as a discursive text, an inclination integral to Derrida's deconstructive philosophy, aimed at logocentric framing practices, and to Foucault's concern with discursive practices generally. The central questions asked by scholars such as these concern notions of "meaning" and "knowing," fundamental concepts in Western philosophical discourse. Or, more precisely, they concern the implication for our dominant forms of "meaning" and "knowing," if the processes integral to the construction of a text are indeed analogous to the process by which social and political reality is constructed. From a postmodernist perspective, the critical task is to illustrate how the textual and social processes are intrinsically connected and to illustrate, in specific contexts, the implications of this connection for the way we think and act in the contemporary world. It is in this way that postmodernism refocuses contemporary analysis on the power/knowledge nexus and, to a greater extent even than critical theory, on theory *as* practice.

In the postmodernist contribution to International Relations, consequently, there has emerged an alternative way of understanding and articulating reality, one focused on intertextuality and sociolinguistic discursive practice, rather than monological literary convention and positivist objectivism and foundationalism.[80] Whatever else this alternative approach achieves, it problematizes the dominant International Relations commitment to a world of given subjects and objects, and all other dichotomized givens. In so doing it reformulates basic *questions* of neorealist understanding in emphasizing not the sovereign subject (e.g., author/independent state) and/or the object (e.g., independent world/text) but, instead, the historical, cultural, and linguistic practices in which subjects and objects (and theory and practice, facts and values) are constructed.

As postmodernist scholarship proliferates in International Relations, the taken-for-granted premises of a generation have come under critical scrutiny. James Der Derian, for example, has sought to reconceptualize the diplomatic process at a time when a sensitive and sophisticated understanding of global life has never been more necessary.

Der Derian: Thinking beyond Traditional "Diplomacy"

Utilizing a (broadly) Nietzschian genealogical approach in *On Diplomacy* (1987) and *Antidiplomacy* (1992), Der Derian's alternative narrative of diplomacy does not add up to the realist "history" of an "essential" diplomatic statecraft unfolding to the present via an increasingly rationalized process of power-politics logic.[81] The history and philosophy of diplomacy is much too complex for such a closed scenario, and in illustrating that there is nothing in the theory and practice of contemporary diplomacy that can be understood by recourse to some essentialized past, or some universalized common sense, or simple "historical" precedent, Der Derian opens up possibilities for thinking beyond the narrow discursive boundaries of the traditional diplomatic corps.

Confronting the complexities surrounding the independence struggles of the Baltic states in 1991, for example, he offers no easy grand theorized solutions but, on the basis of his critical interrogation of traditional diplomatic practice, Der Derian suggests alternative courses of thought and action that, in rapidly changing times, have relevance also for the current Balkan situation and the complexity that is the breakdown of the Soviet Empire.[82] In this regard and on the Baltic quest for self-determination he notes that "one [alternative] historical lesson should have been learned by all Balts: balance of power politics will not do it." He warns, consequently, that to "seek redress in power politics, [is to] leave the court of international law and human rights behind and enter the international free market of threat exchange."[83] This, he suggests, is most likely to lead for the Baltic states in the 1990s where it has led in previous times— to a fate sealed by diplomatic "secret protocol" (e.g., Yalta) and further repression of culture, language, and life opportunity.[84] An alternative possibility, however, might reside in a process of "detente from below" in which Baltic peoples begin to connect with independent, nonaligned movements in the West, in particular, in order to build an alternative diplomatic pressure on ruling elites seeking to replicate Old World orders in their own interests.[85]

Acknowledging the current asymmetries of power in this old/new diplomatic conflict, Der Derian points, nevertheless, to the success of groups such as the European Nuclear Disarmament group in England and the Campaign for Peace and Democracy/East and West in the United States in helping reformulate the realities of political life in recent times, particularly in "demystify[ing] the demonology of the Cold War and . . . opening a discursive space in which alternative strategies for defence and human rights might freely develop."[86]

There is in Der Derian's approach a humility of purpose and sense of political limitation about any alternative future. And although, in some quarters, its positive ambivalence might still be regarded as essentially "reflectivist" and not "concrete" enough, Der Derian's innovative contribution on the diplomacy issue is always about the *theory as practice* of a contemporary diplomatic community, which, in the 1990s, faces an interdependent world economy, massive social inequality, unique ecological dangers, and exploding historico-cultural tensions with a discursive armory primed by the illusory certainty of a seventeenth-century metaphysic-cum-realist ritual.

Reconceptualizing the Sovereign State: Ashley and the Anarchy Problematique

At the core of the diplomatic narrative investigated by Der Derian is the notion of the sovereign state—still the foundational systemic premise in Realism in the 1990s—albeit in more explicit utilitarian terms. In postmodernist literature in International Relations, however, the sovereign state is now understood in radically different terms and with a radically different sense of its nature and role in contemporary global life. To appreciate the postmodern perspective on the state is to appreciate its relocation as part of the much larger discourse of rationality associated with the post-Kantian sovereign "man"—the modern "heroic figure" invested with the will and capacity to emancipate humankind from those objective forces that were (traditionally) thought to determine "meaning" and restrict "knowing." In this context, as Richard Ashley explains, the problem for sovereign "man" is that "upon exercising his powers of reason, [he] sees plainly that that he is enmeshed in language and in history, indeed that he is an object of language and history. [Further] if man is the transcendental condition of the possibility of all knowledge, he also knows himself to be an empirical fact among facts to be examined and conceptualized."[87] This is the dilemma of the modern man/god, the creator of "knowing" and "meaning" who, knowledgeable of his limitations, must seek to overcome them and fulfill his potential as the maker of history, the shaper and controller of human and material destiny. This becomes both the driving force of the "will to knowledge" in modernity and, in the attempt to impose/apply that knowledge, of the will to certainty, to control, and to power.

Modern traditions of theory/practice have been founded upon

this figure of sovereign man, the "heroic figure" of modernity seeking to deal with the constraints on his capacity to remake the world in his image.[88] But it is with the modern *fusion* of the (theory of) sovereign man and the (practice of) sovereign state that the "will to knowledge" and the "will to power" have found their most powerful form and institutionalized modern forum. The state, in this sense, is the site of reasoning man's knowledge and meaning, and, simultaneously, the major resource by which the constraints upon reasoning man can be controlled, disciplined, and punished.

This is a crucial theme in a Foucauldian-based re-reading of the sovereignty issue, and in International Relations generally, because it prefigures the modern logic of power politics and the state-centric view of an anarchical world of Otherness. In Ashley's terms, it gives *identity* to the state, as a "time and place set in opposition to a region of anarchy—a region of historical contingency and chance that refuses to submit to the sovereign truth of reason."[89] It is in this sense that, for all the differences of the International Relations literature, the basic questions (war, peace, security, power, hegemony, justice) remain framed in a modernist (e.g., realist) discourse, which *opposes* a realm of sovereignty, identity, and reasoned understanding against a realm of anarchical Otherness—that realm that refuses to accept the reality of "history," of power, of structural necessity. Herein, lies an explanation (never forthcoming from mainstream literature) of the foundation of International Relations theory *as* practice. And herein lies an explanation of its inadequacy—an explanation that proposes that International Relations realism can never understand a world it claims to know in "reality" until it acknowledges that *its "practical" answers merely replicate the limitations of its "theoretical" questions.* Until it does this, realism cannot begin to think and act outside the caricatured and ritualized boundaries of "recurrence and repetition," the "security dilemma," "hegemonic stability," and the banality of the anarchical structuralism discussed earlier.

In short, it is in the context of Ashley's anarchy problematique that the primitivism of Cold War realism is replicated by neorealists in the 1990s, in terms of an "unproblematic rational presence already there, a sovereign identity that is the self sufficient source of international history's meaning."[90] The state, in this equation, is not privileged as it once was when it was represented as the only sovereign figure in realist analysis. Rather, the state is now projected as one sovereign actor among a multiplicity of sovereign actors (including nonstate actors), and the new "realism" in International Relations is simply calculated (in Weberian terms) as the sum of the rational decisions made by all (recognized) sovereign actors.

The foundations of contemporary International Relations theory and practice are in this manner shown to be problematic indeed in that the sovereign state central to it can be understood as "never more than effects of practices of representation that [can] be made to work only so long as competing voices of an always equivocal culture [can] be excluded or silenced."[91] Understood this way the anarchy problematique acts to empower ruling elites by silencing differences, discontinuities, and conflicts *within* "domestic" states, and converting them into the anarchical basis of conflict *between* states. It is in this sense that, for postmodernism, International Relations is exposed as a powerful site of modernist discursive struggle—the struggle to impose a dominant discourse of "meaning" and "knowing"—the process of theory as practice, of a particular *representation* of the world *as* International Relations. And with the struggle now out in the open, as it were, scholars like Ashley with his concept of the anarchy problematique are beginning to open up a different set of questions integral to International Relations and its reality.

U.S. Foreign Policy as the Politics of Representation

Some of these questions are now central to postmodernist works on U.S. foreign policy. Michael Shapiro, for example, has investigated the politics of representation in regard to "Central America" and U.S. foreign policy toward seemingly insignificant actors such as "Guatemala."[92] Which begs the question of what precise danger a small state like Guatemala could pose to the United States and its "domestic" way of life. The answer, as Shapiro explains, is intrinsic to the way in which a realist discourse constitutes its identity/difference dichotomy. Thus, if self-identity is construed in terms of contemporary security discourse and the anarchy problematique, then *all* other actors in the discursive system will be located on an "axis of threat" in relation to that identity. If, as in the case of the United States, the self is represented in terms of the contemporary heroic figure most obliged to ward off the anarchical threat, then states such as Guatemala are identified as "indirect threats" whose *potential* for disorder must be disciplined and controlled.[93] Moreover, if identity is understood, in this sense, as a moral/grammatical code of meaning in the world, then there is an added (Western, ethnocentric) dimension to the security discourse concerning Central American states such as Guatemala, because "to the extent that the Other is regarded as something not occupying the same natural/moral space as the self, conduct towards the Other becomes more exploitative."[94]

At the core of its thinking on Central America then U.S. foreign policy remains constricted within the static confines of a security discourse bounded by the anarchy problematique and modernist notions of sovereign self and threatening Other. And, emphasizes Shapiro, this theory *as* practice has some frightening implications for the region in the future if U.S. policymakers, failing to reflect on the way they represent the reality of Central America, continue to *respond* to that politics of representation in traditional fashion. Indeed, he concludes, the representation of Guatemala and Central America in U.S. security discourse in the late 1980s "provides the general rationale for the already-in-place policy of active economic and civilian/military intervention to help the not-yet-perfected Central American Others."[95]

David Campbell has developed these themes from a different angle in looking at some of the implications of U.S. foreign policy continuing in the 1990s to conceptualize the world in terms of modernist sovereignty and the anarchy problematique.[96] Campbell has focused, in particular, on an issue central to the early discussions in this essay, that is, the demise of the major Cold War Other and the tendency toward triumphalism on the part of the "victors." More precisely, Campbell's works go to the core of the issue of what the end of the Cold War might mean for an American identity framed by the reality of its anarchical opposite, the Soviet Other. As the organizing principle of U.S. foreign policy, this dichotomized representation of global reality *became* the absolute "realm of necessity" for U.S. scholars and policymakers.[97] The critical task for Campbell in the 1990s is to show that U.S. foreign policy is constituted by dimensions other than "external" necessity in order both to expose its limits and problematize any future reading of new world orders in traditional terms.[98] Understood in this broader context, U.S. foreign policy is constituted by the "disciplining of the ambiguity and contingency of global politics by dividing it into inside and outside, self and other, via the inscription of the boundaries of the state."[99]

In this way the sovereign state (the U.S.A.) can be understood to have constructed its global identity in terms of the discourse of anarchy and danger "external" to it. Its foreign policy, consequently, is accorded an irreducible logic that privileges the theory and practice of power politics in its efforts to respond to the anarchical world it must control for the sake of systemic order. Similarly, a hierarchy of meaning and relevance is established that expunges from the legitimate analytical task questions concerning the "internal" self and all matters of interpretive ambiguity concerning the self/Other, identity/difference theme. But, Campbell insists, these are questions that must be explored if we are not to further close off the possibilities for sensitive and more appropriate foreign policy in the future. Most importantly, the United States must begin to critically reflect upon itself, to reflect that its identity, framed in relation to danger *between* states in an anarchical world, is part of a much larger regime of discursive framing concerned with the disciplining of dangers *within* the state.

Understood in these terms, of course, the Cold War can be understood not as the only "realistic" response to anarchical necessity but as a "disciplinary strategy that was global in scope but national in design."[100] More precisely the Cold War and orthodox readings of it can be understood as another site at which the anarchy problematique was invoked to provide a sovereign, foundational presence from which the threat of (internal) "difference" and Otherness could be rendered unified and controllable.

From different angles, the works of Shapiro and Campbell have focused postmodernist attention on a core element in International Relations, the discourse of strategy and security that has been central to realist representations of the "is" of the world since 1945. A number of postmodernists have sought, more directly, to reconceptualize the "meaning" of security and strategy in the era that has seen the demise of its Cold War raison d'être.

Rethinking Security and Strategy after the Cold War

Attention here has been focused on the growing sense of *insecurity* concerning state involvement in military-industrial affairs and the parlous state of the global ecology. Questioned, too, has been the fate of those around the world rendered insecure by lives lived at the margins of existence, yet unaccounted for in the statistics on military spending and strategic calculation. In this regard, the postmodernist critique of realist strategic/security discourse, succinctly articulated by Bradley Klein in terms that have a more generalized appropriateness in postmodernist scholarship, is *"to give power no [theoretical] place to hide."*[101] To understand the potentials and dangers of the post–Cold War era in these terms is to understand the Cold War experience as part of a larger process of constructing identity in Western modernity, one that privileges a particular way of life *as* International Relations. What is at stake here then is not just the future of NATO as the strategic mainspring of Western power and order since World War II, but the very framework of "real" knowledge about International Relations that has given "meaning" to the identity of NATO and Western power and order in that period. This is why the issue is exciting so much attention among postmodernists, because the space opened now is that which leaves exposed and vulnerable a process that for so long has represented a particular image of humanity as the unproblematic "is" of the world, the unifying, sovereign presence that "we" must defend, to the point of genocide if necessary, against "them." The process of meaning-making, in other words, is exposed as *process*. Exposed, in particular, is the (representational) process by which the meaning of reality has been made in the period of realist dominance of International Relations.

This exposure, for scholars such as Dillon, Klein, Walker, Ashley, Campbell, Shapiro, and Der Derian (and for a critical theorist such as Cox), does not evoke concern over hegemonic decline and the restoration of traditional order but stimulates suggestions for alternative political formations, for more tolerant, more inclusive forms of human society. This, it must be stressed, is no reiteration of traditional progressivism—the intellectual legacy of Nietzsche and Foucault eschews such a position.[102] Rather, it is the acknowledgement of the space for resistance to power politics and imposed identity in a contemporary Europe now engaging every day in the actual process of remaking its meaning.

All this, of course, needs to be kept in perspective. The war in the Persian Gulf (1990-91), its addendum in 1993, and the emergence of figures such as Zhirinovsky in Russia are evidence enough that the traditional doctrine of power politics remains a ubiquitous and dangerous factor in a world seeking to understand the extraordinary global events of the past few years. On the other hand, the increasingly widespread tendency of communities around the world to question the meanings and boundaries of their lives is a theme of obvious significance for postmodernists. This theme has excited the interest of R. B. J. Walker, who in *One World, Many Worlds*, for example, explores some of the major themes of the genre—sovereignty, textuality, representationalism, the anarchy problematique, and the limitations of strategic/security discourse—from the point of view of the marginalized, the silenced, the omitted, those whose lives, cultures, and histories have for so long been read out of the power-politics narrative.

One World, Many Worlds: Toward a Democratic Politics of Resistance?

The immediate locus of Walker's attention is those critical social movements around the world, ranging from the conventional social movements in Western industrialized societies organizing to resist nuclear weapons, militarism, environmental degradation, and gendered politics to the movements in Eastern Europe and throughout the third world engaged in similar struggles, to those over specific issues of ecology (e.g., pollution, deforestation) and broader struggles for a more secure, peaceful, and dignified life. The significance of these movements for Walker is that although they, inevitably, are part of a global struggle in one (interdependent) world, they represent also a politics of difference, the articulation of the many worlds of people's experiences and aspirations, which cannot, and should not, be constrained by the dictates of a particular meaning of reality as projected in the traditional discourse of International Relations.

Their significance is enhanced in this latter regard by many of their practices, which defy traditional grand theorized strategies of revolutionary thought and behavior in favor of creative, innovative resistance, established and carried out in specific sites of struggle. Those involved in these movements are, in this sense, activating in their everyday lives and struggles the concerns of critical social theorists seeking to challenge dominant discourses of power and closure in other contexts. These activities, consequently, are acknowledged as part of "a transformative assault on our inherited notions of authority, legitimacy and power" that "carries the possibility of reconstructing the conditions for a decent life from the bottom up, without waiting for elites to become enlightened or replaced by still more elites."[103]

The struggles of critical social movements represent an important new dimension of dissent for postmodernists, suspicious of all traditional claims for emancipation on behalf of *the* people, *the* class, *the* common interest, and sceptical of all singular, homogenized images of "reality," "liberty," "freedom," of all "isms" proclaiming post-Enlightenment visions of *the* good life. This is not a perspective that denies the desirability of seeking greater democratic participation globally. On the contrary, it is a perspective that cares enough about the possibility of meaningful democratic life to warn of the dangers of once again abrogating responsibility for radical change to another vanguard, another realism, another tradition, another religion, another philosophy, another rational-scientific panacea for modernity's ills. Accordingly, although there is no sense of reification or idealization of critical social movements in Walker's work, there is an appreciation of their struggles and aspirations as providing a sense of what a postmodern politics of democratic resistance might look like, as a counter to the traditional theory/practice and a realist dominated International Relations.

More explicitly than anywhere else in the postmodernist critique of International Relations, Walker's *One World, Many Worlds* articulates the critical social movements' challenge to modernism and realism, as part of a politics, not just of difference, but of postmodern resistance. It is *postmodern* resistance in the sense that although it is directly, sometimes violently, engaged with modernity, it seeks to go beyond the *dominant* (repressive) ways of thinking, speaking, and acting in modernist political society. It is, therefore, not a resistance of traditional grand-scale emancipation, or of conventional radicalism imbued with the authority of one or another sovereign presence. It is, nevertheless, a resistance that must include an opposition to all processes that restrict peoples lives to misery and basic survival, and to "any autocratic presumption of the right to rule, whether this presumption is defended with crude force or by appeal to some natural superiority given by gender, race, class or expertise."[104]

Just as importantly, a postmodern resistance is active at the everyday, community, neighborhood, and interpersonal levels, where it confronts those processes that close off potential for people to give meaning to their lives, and to change that meaning; which, anywhere and at any level, systematically exclude people from making decisions about who they are and what they can be. It is at this level that power politics operates most insidiously and potently, and if there is one lesson to be learned from the activities of critical social movements, at this level, it is that people, given the opportunities to understand the processes by which they are *constituted* (as, for example, passive subjects in an objective world of anarchical power politics), can become aware that they can change those processes and the realities derived from them. In such circumstances, as peoples around the planet have illustrated in recent times, it becomes possible to say *no,* to ask *why;* to understand *how.*

Critical social movements are of particular importance, in this context, because their practices deal with the world not as "a future abstraction but as a process in which to engage wherever one is."[105] This is an important theme in any discussion of postmodernism, because it locates a postmodernist politics of resistance, be it articulated at the dissenting margins of academic life or as part of a more direct social movement of change, as fully engaged with the everyday language, logic, and power relations of modernity, not as (somehow) detached from the modern world, part of Peter Dews's "philosophy of the avant garde."[106]

QUO VADIS INTERNATIONAL RELATIONS?

Given the nature of the earlier discussion, there should be no surprise about the fact that postmodernists are at the forefront of a proliferating critical social theory literature aimed at the primitive reading/writing practices of neorealism. Nor is it surprising that as critical literature of this kind becomes more widely available the responses of an entrenched mainstream are exposed as primitive to increasing numbers of International Relations scholars in the current generation. It has been in this context, therefore, and to a greater extent than other critical social theory approaches, that postmodernism has exposed International Relations for what it is: a textual tradition *become* "reality"; a particular reading of (Western) philosophy and history, *become* transhistorical/transcultural "fact"; a way of framing "meaning" and "knowing" shaped by Newtonian physics and Cartesian rationalism, *become* meaning and knowing in the world of nuclear weapons, AIDS, and ozone depletion. What postmodernism has exposed, more directly, is International Relations as a discursive process: a process by which identities are formed, meaning is given, and status and privilege are accorded; a process by which threats to identity and its meaning are both disciplined and punished; a process of knowledge *as* power.

This exposure of International Relations as a discursive process is what is at stake in the broader critical social theory challenge to International Relations in the 1990s. Effective political intervention is blocked when those whose identities (literally and figuratively) are dependent upon the traditional knowledge *as* power seek to exclude critical social theory perspectives from serious analysis, marginalize the significance of its arguments, and/or ridicule its attempts to go beyond the boundaries of traditional concepts and language. In this context what is at stake in the post–Cold War period is that "something" that Jane Flax pointed to in *Thinking Fragments*—that which is happening in the late-modern period, *whether International Relations realists like it or not*. This "something" involves a generation experiencing the death throes of a particular "shape of life," centered on a post-Enlightenment dream and the largely unquestioned hegemony of a modernist discourse that is the source of its power and legitimation.[107]

At a more prosaic level—the level of International Relations scholarship—what is at stake, in Kal Holsti's terms, is the demise of a "three centuries long intellectual consensus" in International Relations about what is "real" in the world.[108] This essay has sought to illustrate that for all our sakes, and particularly for those excluded from the benefits of this illusory "reality," we must seek to go beyond the dominant rituals of International Relations theory and practice and confront the great dangers and opportunities of the post-Cold War period in a manner that facilitates intellectual and political openness, and resistance at all levels to the practices of incarceration and closure. And for those still convinced that such a course of action is either impossible, and/or undesirable, this essay has sought also to illustrate some of the rather daunting implications of not making the attempt.

NOTES

1. The term International Relations in its capitalized form refers to the conventional way in which global life has been studied and understood in Western (primarily Anglo-American) universities and policy sectors. In this context it represents a particular kind of theory as practice designated as realism by its advocates that has become synonomous with a universalized, essentialized "reality" of global life for mainstream scholars and policy-makers.

2. John Lewis Gaddis, "International Relations Theory and the End of the Cold War," *International Security* 17 (3) 1992/93, pp. 5-58.

3. Ibid., p. 31.

4. Stanley Hoffmann, "Delusions of World Order," *New York Review of Books,* April 9, 1992, pp. 37-42.

5. Ibid., p. 38.

6. Ibid., p. 41.

7. Lewis Lapham, "Apes and Butterflies," *Harpers,* May 1992, p. 8.

8. Ibid., p. 8.

9. Ibid., p. 8.

10. Tom Post, "How the West Lost Bosnia: Four Missed Opportunities on the Road to Chaos," *Bulletin/Newsweek,* November 3, 1992.

11. Ibid., p. 60.

12. Ibid., p. 60.

13. This was a speech titled "The End of the Modern Era," given in Switzerland in early 1992 and cited in Lapham, "Apes and Butterflies."

14. Cited in Lapham, "Apes and Butterflies," p. 8.

15. Ibid., p. 12.

16. Ibid., p. 8.

17. Many of the themes touched on here are discussed, in more nuanced form, in my *Discourses of Global Politics: A Critical (Re) Introduction to International Relations* (Boulder, Colo. and London: Lynne Rienner and Macmillan's, 1994).

18. For a useful overview of these works see Jim George and David Campbell, "Patterns of Dissent and the Celebration of Difference: Critical Social Theory and International Relations," *International Studies Quarterly,* 34 (3) (1990), pp. 269-95.

19. The debate over the relationship between empiricism and positivism is too complex to engage here. The notion of empiricism/positivism used here owes most to the work of Leszek Kolakowski in *Positivist Philosophy from Hume to the Vienna Circle* (Harmondsworth: Penguin, 1972). In this sense positivism is perceived neither as scientific methodology nor a theory of knowledge per se. Rather it is understood as the major contemporary philosophical expression of an empiricist methodology, synthesized in its

most sophisticated and "sceptical" form by David Hume, and articulated in a variety of forms since then. For a fuller discussion of its (often hidden) influence in International Relations, see my "International Relations and the Positivist/Empiricist Theory of Knowledge: Implications for the Australian Discipline" in Richard Higgott, ed., *New Directions in International Relations: Australian Perspectives* (Canberra: ANU Press, 1988), pp. 65-143.

20. Ernst Gellner, *Legitimation of Belief* (Cambridge: Cambridge University Press, 1974), p. 175.

21. Ibid., pp. 174-77.

22. Anthony Giddens, *Profiles and Critiques in Social Theory* (London: Macmillan, 1982), p. 3. For an updated confirmation of this position, see Giddens and J. Turner, *Social Theory Today* (Cambridge: Polity Press, 1987).

23. See Regis Factor and Stephen Turner, *Max Weber and the Dispute over Reason and Value* (London: Routledge and Kegan Paul, 1984), which argues that this connection goes well beyond any generalized intersection of Anglo-American and Germanic influences in Morgenthau's approach, to the extent that every major idea in Morgenthau's power politics is derived from Weber's hermeneutic perspective. This, of course, to some extent explains the tensions in Morgenthau's work, in which he crudely propounds the existence of "objective laws" at one moment and at another engages in more subtle hermeneutic tones on the issue of textual interpretation.

24. On Weber, Mannheim, and the "other side" of the positivist coin more generally, see Susan Hekman, "Beyond Humanism: Gadamer, Althusser and the Methodology of the Social Sciences," *Western Political Quarterly* 36 (1983), pp. 98-115; and Hekman, *Hermeneutics and the Sociology of Knowledge* (Cambridge: Polity Press, 1986). On the "backward discipline" theme, see Mervyn Frost, *Toward a Normative Theory of International Relations* (Cambridge: Cambridge University Press, 1986).

25. For a broader discussion of these subthemes see R. N. Berki, *On Political Realism* (London: J. M. Dent, 1981).

26. Ibid., p.8.

27. See Robert Rothstein, "On the Costs of Realism," *Political Science Quarterly* 87 (3) (1972), pp. 348-62, at p. 351.

28. On the issue of falsificationist influence generally, see Stanley Hoffmann, "An American Social Science," and for updated confirmation of its continuing influence, Hayward Alker and Thomas Beirsteker, "The Dialectics of World Order: Notes for a Future Archaeologist of International Savoir Faire," *International Studies Quarterly* 28 (2) (1984), pp.121-42.

29. John Vasquez, *The Power of Power Politics: A Critique* (London: Frances Pinter, 1983), p. 216.

30. From a number of angles, see R. Maghoori and B. Ramberg, eds., *Globalism versus Realism: International Relations' Third Debate* (Boulder:

Westview Press, 1982); W. C. Olson and N. Onuf, "The Growth of a Discipline: Reviewed," in *International Relations: British and American Perspectives*, ed. S. Smith (Oxford: Basil Blackwell, 1985); Michael Banks, "The Evolution of International Relations Theory," in *Conflict in World Society: A New Approach to International Relations*, ed. M. Banks (Sussex: Wheatsheaf Books, 1984); M. Sullivan, "Competing Frameworks and the Study of Contemporary International Politics," *Millennium* 7 (1978), pp. 93-110; Robert Keohane and Joseph Nye, *Power and Interdependence: World Politics in Transition* (Boston: Little, Brown, 1977); Robert Keohane, *After Hegemony: Cooperation and Discord in the World Political Economy* (Princeton: Princeton University Press, 1984); Roger Tooze, "The Unwritten Preface: International Political Economy," *Millennium* 17 (2) (1988), pp. 285-93; and Kal Holsti, *The Dividing Discipline: Hegemony and Diversity in International Theory* (Winchester, Mass.: Allen and Unwin, 1985).

31. Some contributors to the Third Debate argue that substantial change has occurred as philosophy of science perspectives begin to appear in International Relations literature. See Y. Lapid, " 'The Third Debate': On the Prospects of International Theory in a Post-Positivist Era," *International Studies Quarterly* 33 (3) (1989), pp. 325-54. There is little doubt that International Relations now articulates its arguments differently because of influences from this and other quarters. The issue is whether the substance of the debate has changed. The discussion to follow argues that it has not. See my "International Relations and the Search for Thinking Space: Another View of the Third Debate," *International Studies Quarterly* 33 (3) (1989), pp. 269-79. On neorealism see Robert Keohane, ed., *Neorealism and Its Critics* (New York: Columbia University Press, 1986); Kenneth Waltz, *Theory of International Politics* (Reading: Addison-Wesley, 1979); Robert Gilpin, *War and Change in World Politics* (Cambridge: Cambridge University Press, 1981); John Ruggie, "Continuity and Transformation in the World Polity: Towards a Neorealist Synthesis," *World Politics* 35 (1983), pp. 261-85; and most incisively Richard Ashley, "The Poverty of Neorealism," *International Organization* 38 (2) (1984), pp. 225-86.

32. Frost, *Towards a Normative Theory of International Relations,* p. 10.

33. Hans Morgenthau, *Politics among Nations: The Struggle for Power and Peace,* 5th ed. (New York: Alfred Knopf, 1978), pp. 4-5.

34. E. H. Carr, *The Twenty Years Crisis: 1919-1939,* 3d ed. (New York: Harper and Row, 1964), chapters 3 and 4 in particular.

35. Klaus Knorr and James Rosenau, *Contending Approaches to International Relations* (Princeton: Princeton University Press, 1969), pp. 13-14.

36. M. Sullivan, "Competing Frameworks and the Study of Contemporary International Politics," *Millennium* 7 (1987), pp. 93-110, at p. 108.

37. This is Rosenau's view in "Before Cooperation: Hegemons, Regimes, and Habit Driven Actors in World Politics," *International Organization* 40 (4) (1986), pp. 849-94, at p. 853.

38. Kal Holsti, *The Dividing Discipline*, p. vii.

39. Roger Tooze, "The Unwritten Preface: International Political Economy and Epistemology," *Millennium* 17 (2) (1988), pp. 285-93, at p. 286.

40. Joseph Nye, "NeoRealism and NeoLiberalism," *World Politics* 40 (1988), pp. 235-51, at p. 235.

41. The differences between the two works are ultimately more a matter of tone and attitude than analytical quality. *Man, the State and War* had a certain charm and intellectual width, manifestly lacking in the later work, and in 1959, at the height of realist confidence and influence, Waltz was willing to ventilate at least some of the philosophical and analytical givens of the realist "catechism." Two decades later, however, in less favorable circumstances for U.S. foreign policy and realist theory, his mood and ambition were narrower, more constrained, and less philosophically tolerant. See also Justin Rosenberg, "What's the Matter with Realism?" *Review of International Studies* 16 (4) (1990), pp. 285-303. The banality theme comes from this work.

42. Kenneth Waltz, *Theory of International Politics* (Reading, Mass.: Addison-Wesley, 1979), p. 1.

43. I refer here to Popper's strategy during the positivist dispute of the 1960s, when he defended his critical rationalism as nonpositivist by (re)defining positivism as the narrow inductivism of logical empiricism. On the Popperian strategy, see Popper, *The Logic of Scientific Discovery* (London: Hutchinson, 1968), pp. 34-54. For an overview, see N. Stockman, *Antipositivist Theories of the Sciences: Critical Rationalism, Critical Theory and Scientific Realism* (Dordrecht: D. Reidel, 1983).

44. Waltz, *Theory of International Politics*, p. 66.

45. Ibid., pp. 4-5.

46. Ibid., p. 6.

47. Ibid., p. 80.

48. Ibid., p. 80.

49. Ibid., p. 69, emphasis added.

50. Rosenberg, "What's the Matter with Realism?"

51. The point here is that like many neoconservatives seeking to fuse a minimalist reading of Smith with a rigid Conservative traditionalism, Waltz does no justice to either discourse by depoliticizing and dehistoricizing them.

52. See J. Ruggie, "Continuity and Transformation in the World Polity"; and Alexander Wendt's commentary in "The Agent-Structure Problem in International Relations Theory," *International Organization* 41 (1987), pp. 335-70.

53. Gill, "Two Concepts of International Political Economy," *Review of International Studies* 16 (1990), pp. 369-81, at p. 369.

54. Ibid., p. 370.

55. Stephen Krasner, "Structural Causes and Regime Consequences: Regimes as Intervening Variables" in *International Regimes,* ed. Krasner (Ithaca: Cornell University Press, 1983).

56. Ibid., p. 10.

57. Ibid., p. 2.

58. Ibid., p. 2.

59. Ibid., p. 11.

60. Keohane, "Realism, Neorealism and the Study of World Politics," in *Neorealism and Its Critics,* ed. Keohane, pp. 1-3.

61. Ibid., pp. 2-3.

62. Ibid., pp. 4-5.

63. Ibid., p. 4.

64. Here again the issue of major International Relations unselfconsciousness is evident given that Keohane is seeking to *distinguish* his theory from the scientific model derived from Newtonian physics. This, however, is an issue that presumably does not warrant the attention of a "real world" researcher.

65. R. B. J. Walker, *One World, Many Worlds* (Boulder, Colo.: Lynn Rienner, 1988), p. 7 emphasis added.

66. For a variety of perspectives, see J. Anne Tickner, "On the Fringes of the World Economy: A Feminist Perspective" in *The New International Political Economy,* ed. Murphy and Tooze (Boulder: Lynne Rienner, 1991); Cynthia Enloe, *Bananas, Beaches and Bases: Making Feminist Sense of International Politics* (Berkeley: University of California Press, 1989); V. Spike Peterson, "Transgressing Boundaries: Theories of Knowledge, Gender and International Relations," *Millennium* 21 (1992), pp. 183-206; Christine Sylvester, ed., "Feminists Write International Relations," Special Issue of *Alternatives* (February 1993); and "Women and International Relations," Special Issue *Millennium* 17 (1988).

67. Jane Flax, *Thinking Fragments: Psychoanalysis, Feminism, and Postmodernism in the Contemporary West* (Berkeley: University of California Press, 1990), p. 5.

68. Michel Foucault, "What Is Enlightenment?" in *The Foucault Reader,* ed. Paul Rabinow (New York: Pantheon Books, 1984), p. 42.

69. See Flax, *Thinking Fragments,* p. 6.

70. Ibid., p. 6.

71. For example, "Social Forces, States and World Orders: Beyond International Relations Theory," Millennium 10 (2) (1981), pp. 126-55; "Production and Hegemony: Toward a Political Economy of World Order," in

The Emerging International Economic Order, ed. H. Jacobsen and D. Sub-
yanski (California: Sage, 1982); "Gramsci, Hegemony and International Re-
lations," *Millennium* 12 (2) (1983), pp. 269-91; and *Power, Production and
World Order: Social Forces in the Making of History* (New York: Columbia
University Press, 1987). There have been some other good contributions in
this genre, particularly by Stephen Gill; see, for example, "Two Concepts of
International Political Economy," and Gill and D. Law, *The Global Political
Economy* (Baltimore: Johns Hopkins University Press, 1989); see also Craig
Murphy and Roger Tooze, eds., *The New International Political Economy.*

72. Cox, "Social Forces," pp. 126-29.

73. Ibid., p. 129.

74. The issue of social forces in Cox's work is an interesting one and it
represents an attempt to go beyond the conventional Marxist notion of the
"social relations of production," although this clearly is its conceptual
source. As Cox explains, a social forces approach is concerned with the in-
terconnection of three dimensions of power: (1) over the productive process;
(2) social power—the relations between classes, and (3) control over the
state—political power. It is from this power matrix, he argues, that particular constellations of social forces emerge. In an interdependent world economy and with the impact within and on the power matrix of monopoly capital and an internationalized production process, there are, suggests Cox,
possibilities for change as new constellations of social forces become evident
around the world. See "Production and Hegemony"; and *Power, Production
and World Order,* chapters 1 and 10 in particular.

75. Cox, *Power, Production and World Order,* p. 38.

76. Here the influence of Habermas is evident also in terms of his arguments in *Legitimation Crisis,* trans. T. McCarthy (Boston: Beacon Press,
1973).

77. Cox, "Production and Hegemony," p. 45.

78. In *Production, Power and World Order* (1987) Cox approached
this issue by developing a complex sociohistorical schema set within patterns of production relations and their attendant social forces. This discussion was complemented by another, outlining various historical forms of the
state characterized by their politico/institutional structures.

79. See James Der Derian and Michael Shapiro, eds., *International/
Intertextual Relations: Postmodern Readings of World Politics* (Lexington,
Mass.: Lexington Books, 1989).

80. In other words where real meaning is derived from the interrela-
tionship of texts rather than from some objectified external source. This is
what Barthes was getting at with his notion of "intertext" as "a multi-
dimensional space in which a variety of writings, none of them original,
blend and clash," cited in Der Derian, "The Boundaries of Knowledge and

Power in International Relations," in *International/Intertextual*, ed. Der Derian and Shapiro, p. 6. In the same volume, see Michael Shapiro, "Textualizing Global Politics"; and William Connolly's discussion of the "discovery" of America in intertextualist terms in "Identity and Difference in Global Politics." The language issue in postmodernism is influenced (as well as by Wittgenstein) by the critical reaction to the structuralism of Saussurian linguistics by scholars like Derrida and the understanding of language and discourse that flows from this debate. Thus, instead of language being an asset employed by a pre-existing subject, or a constraint imposed on that subject, language comes to be seen as the medium through which the social identity and existence of that subject is made possible.

81. See Der Derian, *On Diplomacy: A Genealogy of Western Estrangement* (Oxford: Basil Blackwell, 1987) and *Antidiplomacy: Spies, Terror, Speed and War* (Cambridge: Blackwell, 1992) in which the influences of Virilio are increasingly evident.

82. In *Antidiplomacy*, chapter 7.

83. Ibid., p. 155.

84. Ibid.

85. Ibid., p. 153-54.

86. Ibid., p. 154.

87. See Richard Ashley, "Living on Borderlines: Man, Poststructuralism, and War" in Der Derian and Shapiro, eds., *International/Intertextual Relations*, pp. 259-322, at p. 265.

88. Ibid., p. 267. For "market" Liberalism, accordingly, the modern historical narrative is that of the possessive individual of civil society, struggling (in the general/national interest) to break down constraints upon free choice and natural competition. For Marxism, it is the narrative of the class conscious oppressed, struggling to break down the constraints on their potential as fully conscious human beings. In each case the narrative is framed in terms of a "given" sovereign subject, privileged (via logocentric reasoning) over a world of objectified limitations/constraints.

89. Ibid., p. 268.

90. Ashley, "Untying the Sovereign State: A Double Reading of the Anarchy Problematique," *Millenium* 17 (1988), pp. 227-63, at p. 231.

91. Ibid., p. 252.

92. Michael J. Shapiro, "The Constitution of the Central American Other: The Case of 'Guatemala,'" in *The Politics of Representation* (Madison: University of Wisconsin Press, 1988). Postmodern perspectives are now appearing in the literature on the third world and development studies; see, for example, Arturo Escobar, "Discourse and Power in Development: Michel Foucault and the Relevance of His Work to the Third World," *Alternatives* X (1984-85), pp. 377-400; and more recently Marc Dubois, "The

Governance of the Third World: A Foucauldian Perspective on Power Relations in Development," *Alternatives* 16 (1991), pp. 1-30.

93. Ibid., p. 102.

94. Ibid.

95. Ibid.

96. David Campbell, *Writing Security: United States Foreign Policy and the Politics of Identity* (Manchester: Manchester University Press, 1992); and "Global Inscription: How Foreign Policy Constitutes the United States," *Alternatives* XV (1990), pp. 263-86.

97. This is from Colin Gray, *The Geopolitics of Superpowers* (1988) cited in Campbell, "Global Inscription," p. 282. On this issue also see Charles Nathanson, "The Social Construction of the Soviet Threat: A Study in the Politics of Representation," *Alternatives* 13 (1988), pp. 443-83; and Simon Dalby, "Geopolitical Discourse: The Soviet Union as Other," *Alternatives* 13 (1988), pp. 415-42.

98. Campbell, "Global Inscription," p. 264.

99. Ibid., p. 270.

100. Ibid., p. 283.

101. Bradley Klein, "Strategic Discourse and Its Alternatives," Occasional Paper No. 3 (New York: Center on Violence and Human Survival, John Jay College of Criminal Justice, 1988), p. 5.

102. For some, still restricted by a crude commitment to logical positivist protocols, this emancipatory impulse can only be a "contradiction" in postmodern thinking, reflecting the very Kantianism they seek to deny. It is only a "contradiction," however, from a perspective that designates "meaning" in singular, correspondence rule terms. If, on the other hand, one acknowledges the contributions of Wittgenstein, Sassure, and a generation of analytical philosophers, it is clear enough that "meaning" is interpretively made, and not (foundationally) given. Thus, terms like emancipation are not restricted to a single, essential (e.g., Kantian) meaning, and there is therefore nothing necessarily contradictory about emancipatory tendencies in this context. This is an issue that postmodern scholars do have to confront, particularly in relation to the Hegelian influences in Nietzchean-based analysis, but a complex issue is not enhanced much by works such as Roger Spegele's "Richard Ashley's Discourse for International Relations," *Millennium* 21 (2) (1992), pp. 147-82. On other charges leveled at postmodernism (relativism, subjectivism, apolitical, etc.) see my *Discourses of Global Politics*.

103. Walker, *One World, Many Worlds,* p. 8. The claim here is not that critical social movements explicitly articulate postmodernist principles of critique, nor does Walker make such a claim. The point rather is that their theory and practice can be interpreted in this way and some extrapolations can be drawn from these interpretations. I am perhaps taking a few more in-

terpretive liberties here than Walker did in *One World, Many Worlds* under the auspices of the Committee for a Just World Peace.

104. Ibid., p. 159.

105. Ibid., p. 157.

106. Peter Dews, *The Logic of Disintegration: Post-Structuralist Thought and the Claims of Critical Theory* (London: Verso Books, 1987). This is a tendency undoubtedly evident in some postmodernist perspectives. An example is that of J. F. Lyotard, *The Postmodern Condition: A Report on Knowledge* (Minneapolis: University of Minnesota Press, 1984). It is, fortunately, not evident in the transference of postmodernist themes to International Relations scholarship by those discussed in this essay.

107. Flax, *Thinking Fragments*, p. 7.

108. Holsti, *The Dividing Discipline*, p. 1.

II

Realisms

Introduction to Part II

MICHAEL J. SHAPIRO

The study of "international relations" is, among other things, a disciplinary orientation. Within the mainstream epistemological assumptions of this discipline (elaborated in Jim George's essay in part I) is a tendency to focus primarily on the objects of analysis and the instrumentalities through which those objects are apprehended. In addition to being a discipline, "international relations" is a literature. Unlike the sensibilities attached to explicitly literary practices, however, international relations theorists have paid relatively little attention to the meaning-producing effects of their writing practices. Thus, although what is "real" in this discipline is a function of its representational practices—specifically, its sovereignty-oriented cartography, evolutionary historical narratives, and state-centric grammar of agency—the epistemological commentary that attends its various studies implies that the world is wholly responsible for what international relations theorists discover.

Literary genres in general have exercised a monopolistic control over meanings when they have dominated a field of articulation. Thus, for example, the poet Aimé Césaire, attempting to evoke meanings and experiences of his native land (Martinique) said, "I became a poet by renouncing poetry," for it was the only way "to break the stranglehold the accepted French form held on me."[1] Struggling for an independent voice, he became interested in surrealism as a way to work within a language while at the same time exploding it.[2] Surrealism, with its way of reproducing the familiar with such a hyperinflated level of attention to seemingly trivial detail that the so-called real is made bizarre, provided Césaire with a means of summoning an African consciousness and thereby achieving what he called a "disalienation."[3]

More generally, to avoid the intellectual barrenness of scientistic realism, literary genres have evoked a variety of defamiliarizing modes for challenging the various forms of the real perpetuated in dominant discourses. For example, Césaire produced his intellectual corpus in what Gilles Deleuze and Félix Guattari were to later call a "minor literature," one that "doesn't come from minority language; it is rather that which a minority constructs within major language."[4] Minor literatures are highly politicized, for they are collectively aimed attempts at identity assertion within the cramped conceptual spaces of a dominant system of meaning. Writers of minor literatures seek to become strange within the language of domination in order to open a space for political resistance.

Magic realism provides a similar escape route from governing systems of intelligibility. Although magic realism has been more characteristic of the fiction written in nations on the periphery of global power, it can be found also in the more dominant nation-states. With its mixing of what is taken as the dominant "real" with the seemingly magical or fantastic, it highlights the contradictions in social and political life that fantastical fantasies seek to transcend or oppose. For some time, much of social theory has been aimed at showing how representations produced within realist genres are always partial and misleading, how all ambitions of conceptual mastery are fantastic. The literary genre of magic realism enacts this insight by uncritically mixing the fantastic with the familiar and expected, thereby showing how all forms of the so-called real are simply the result of a more concerted and institutionalized set of fantasies. It also disrupts the spaces within which the real is represented. Magic realist fiction constructs the policed boundaries of social and political administration with impertinent metaphors and counternarrations. It provides unfamiliar spatiotemporal coordinates so that the fixities within which territories ordinarily operate become destabilized.

Folke Lindahl's focus on Caribbean writing relies on both the conceptions of minority literature and magic realism with special emphasis on postcolonial discourse. He effectively provides a reencounter with the Caribbean that serves as an antidote to the initial European encounters. Beginning with the proleptic constructions of Columbus, the Caribbean was constructed as a savage land. Indeed the initial encounter produced the very notion of the cannibal. Most significantly, the Caribbean developed an identity from what Peter Hulme has called a "European monologue," which has dominated its global standing ever since.[5] Lindahl helps to speak back to that monologue by situating Caribbean voices and literatures in a way that challenges the civilizational cartography that has historically locked the Caribbean into a silent periphery. His text mobilizes identities within a reading of the "real" that exposes some long-standing partisanships in the imperial center that have passed as unproblematic descriptions. Most significantly, by foregrounding the identity assertions in the Carribean, which emerge from literary genres, Lindahl seeks not to substitute an identity discourse made in the Caribbean for one imposed from the imperial center but to locate all identity inscriptions within an unstable political agonistic.

The focus on magic realism in writing primarily situated in the first world by Bruno Bosteels, Loris Mirella, and Peter Schilling highlights additional literatures and voices that have provided a counterpolitical sphere to that constructed within familiar political discourses. The emphasis on individual lives rather than political allegory or international events in the fiction they analyze enacts the emphasis on prosaics called for in David Campbell's essay in part I. The significance of this level of analysis is not its refocusing from collectivities to individuals but its identification of the plurality of consequences, registered in different lives, that become available when descriptions of the intersections of different flows of activities are allowed to displace the official language of the order.

In addition, the magic realist literatures they bring to our attention provide a heterogeneity of narrative spaces. The juxtaposition of these literatures with the literature of "international relations" helps to make evident the legitimating forces of literatures and voices that have narrated a world of states and administered a silence with respect to the heterogeneousness of individual, cultural, and collective experiences within a frame in which only consensual citizen bodies are counted as relevant.

NOTES

1. Aimé Césaire, *Discourse on Colonialism,* trans. Joan Pinkham (New York: Monthly Review Press, 1972), p. 67.

2. Ibid., p. 68.

3. Ibid.

4. Gilles Deleuze and Félix Guattari, *Kafka: Toward a Minor Literature,* trans. Dana Polan (Minneapolis: University of Minnesota Press, 1986), p. 16.

5. Peter Hulme, *Colonial Encounters: Europe and the Native Caribbean, 1492-1797* (New York: Methuen, 1986), p. 20.

3

Rewriting the Caribbean: Identity Crisis as Literature

FOLKE LINDAHL

At the historical moment when the search for identity and the celebration of multiculturalism have turned into political myths and ideological tools for various causes and groups, it might be both appropriate and useful to reflect on a more postmodern conception of identity, as well as read an example of the literature that reveals the tension inherent in such projects as finding one's self, discovering one's roots, and establishing one's authentic identity—whether the latter is understood inside a racial, ethnic, religious, gender, or class nomenclature.

The focus of my reflection is itself a "problem" of identity and difference: the Caribbean as a place, and Caribbean writing as a body of literature—both realms concerned with their own self-understanding, both representing or expressing what (somewhat ironically) could be labeled an "identity crisis." It is the products as well as the productiveness of this crisis that can be said to be the theme of this essay. Underlying my interest is a tentative broad hypothesis that the Caribbean region and its literature have something to teach us about the futility of trying to stabilize and authenticate an identity (to form a solid identity, as it were). Or, to put it differently, we learn from the polyglot Caribbean voices to better understand the paradox in the quest for an exclusive, often pious, identity (there is something exclusive about all identities), a paradox because this supposedly true identity creates, through a politics of difference, an "other," an "outsider," that immediately threatens to destabilize what was thought to be a solid and "authentic" self.[1] In a more general and grandiose formulation, I would like to show the quintessentially late- or postmodern nature of the social and literary identities of the Caribbean.

The argument will initially be made with reference to two rhetorical positions on Caribbean identity, the first being rather rigid and limited, the second being a productive and necessary reaction to the first. The former will be presented as more traditional and conventional—more ideological because more univocal—than the latter which is, from my perspective, less ideological because indeterminate and open-ended and therefore also persuasive and attractive. (I am aware that "more" ideological and "less" ideological in these formulations pose theoretical problems since they imply the possibility of a nonideological position on Caribbean identity. Although this is not possible in a strict sense of the word, I still want to argue that an open-ended, pluralistic conception of identity can be said to be less committed to a specific political ideology than a univocal, specific political or cultural identity. Of course, a commitment to pluralism, whether in relation to cultural and/or political identities is itself a form of "ideology.")

In an essay titled "Order, Disorder, Freedom, and the West Indian Writer," Maryse Condé has criticized the tendency in twentieth-century Caribbean literature, criticism, and intellectual life in general to command and police the rules of writing, to try to set the boundaries and enforce an order for what passes for acceptable writing in the Caribbean setting. She is asking "whether it is possible to hope for an era of freedom in West Indian writing." She quotes several slogans from the 1920s and 1930s as examples of the narrow understanding of what writing is and should be: "Literature is the cry of a people who want to say what boils within them" (from a Haitian group proclamation in the journal "La Trouee"). "Literature must be black and proletarian" (Jacques Roumain, "the mulatto and upper bourgeois writer"). Finally Condé quotes Aimé Césaire as summing up these ideas in his *Return to My Native Land*: "My mouth will be the mouth of those who have no mouth, my voice the voice of those who despair."[2] All of this, Condé argues, adds up to a set of rules in the tradition of social(ist) realism. She presents these rules as follows:

1. Individualism was chastised. Only the collectivity had the right to express itself.
2. The masses were the sole producers of Beauty, and the poet had to take inspiration from them.
3. The main, if not the sole, purpose of writing was to denounce one's political and social conditions, and in so doing, to bring about one's liberation.
4. Poetic and political ambition were one and the same.[3]

Although politically a bit surprising, perhaps, this list is all too familiar to anybody vaguely acquainted with the typical intellectual discussions of literature in the 1930s in both Europe and the Americas. (It is an interesting aside that the early Caribbean literary debate follows a parallel pattern to the western European discourse in its concern for social realism and committed art. We are from the outset in a cross-fertilization situation: the Caribbean was always a collection of hybrid cultures, often taking clues from the European imperial centers, but was also always somehow transforming and creolizing the metropolitan messages.)

In any case, Condé's lamentation over the straitjacket and piousness of social realism is as justified in the Caribbean case as it always was in the European or North American context. She argues that in its obvious rigidity and exclusiveness this "order" outlaws a whole range of themes, genres, styles, and topics. Celebrations of natural beauty, descriptions of nature, "psychological turmoil," "exoticism," and "individual love," all form part of what becomes forbidden, forced outside of the legitimate Caribbean discourse and identity.

We have here the beginning of the negative side of my argument: the attempt to create an authentic Caribbean identity through an ideological literary strategy of inclusion and exclusion, the constitution of an otherness that does not belong, that is not supposed to feel at home in the Caribbean situation. It comes as no surprise that the demands for this order are not limited only to literature and poetry. "It also affected history, sociology, and philosophy. West Indian society was not studied per se, as an autonomous object. It was always seen as a result of the slave-trade, slavery, and colonial oppression. This past was the cause of every social and cultural feature and thus explained everything: the relationships between men and women, the family system, as well as oral traditions or popular music."[4] Fortunately, as we shall see, this authoritarian order cannot be maintained; it cracks and leaks; it is too limited and too narrow of a political and literary space to hold together; it invites its own destruction and decentering.

Before turning to the active undermining of this model through literature, we have to elaborate this dominant and stable identity further. Condé gives an example of a novel in this genre, *Masters of the Dew* by Jacques Roumain. She presents this work as "a sacred text, a fundamental text." It "established a model which is still largely undisputed to this day." Condé's characterization of this model is illuminating (and not without its own ideological elements):

1. The framework should be the native land.
2. The hero should be male, of peasant origin.
3. The brave and hardworking woman should be the auxiliary in his struggle for his community.
4. Although they produce children, no reference should be made to sex. If any, it will be to male sexuality.
5. Of course, heterosexuality is the absolute rule.
6. Society should be pitied but never criticized. All its errors should be redeemed by the male hero. In *Masters of the Dew*, Manuel has been compared to a black Christ giving his life for the small community of "Fonds Rogues."[5]

This model, together with the previously quoted "rules," adds up to an identity (literary and political) that obviously invites problematization, destabilization, and transgression. However, we need first to qualify and complicate the scenario in a couple of ways. It should be noted that Condé's argument contains its own rhetorical, and even political, strategy. She has clearly selected elements that add up to an all too coherent and easily targeted identity, and she has done this in the name of an alternative identity that is broader, more complex—it invites more voices to be heard—and more open-ended, for sure, but nevertheless limited in its way and with its own rhetorical delineations. This is inevitable and unavoidable. To see why, we must consider Condé's strategy.

We need to be sensitive to the necessarily selective reading involved in Condé's creation of her target. All Caribbean literatures, except possibly the crudest expressions, lend themselves to readings that would move beyond the model and rules we have just reviewed. There are elements and dimensions in every novel that would encourage the careful reader to see beyond the more obvious political and ideological intentions, especially if we are already aware of the latter and therefore more attentive to those aspects that do not fit the established model. There is invariably an "other" inside the firmly delineated identity. The difference between a conventional work following the traditional model and the type of literature that Condé seems to encourage is that the latter consciously invites heterogeneity, transgression, and the creation of other identities, whereas in the former the reader has, so to speak, to search actively for these features against the explicit and more obvious meaning of the work. It is fair to say that Condé chooses to ignore this more subversive reading of the established Caribbean canon; instead she interprets this tradition according to its own rules and rigid self-understanding.

The important point here, however, remains the extent to which a work actively invites transgression and problematization of a dogmatic identity, as opposed to the extent to which other works attempt to solidify and reify a specific identity. Nevertheless, there is no doubt an element of paradox in all identities in the sense that we cannot do without them, but we need to be aware of their constructed and exclusive qualities. Let it be said, from the outset, that this is not meant to imply that the destabilization of established identities is an easy or simple task; on the contrary. William Connolly has provided an impressive analysis of this process without underestimating the almost insurmountable difficulties involved. His outline of the critical response to firm identities is applicable to our case. This response must involve, he argues, "a problematization of the tactics by which established identities protect themselves through the conversion of difference into otherness, an identification of ambiguities in the identity I and we have become, an ironization of some dimensions in my own identity, a politicization of established naturalizations of identity."[6] Corresponding to this broad response is also a general political direction: "to affirm the indispensability of identity while contending against the dogmatism of identity; to cultivate care for the agonism of life by disclosing contingent elements in any specific identity; to politicize the ambiguity in human being."[7] My argument is that Caribbean identities, through their creolized multiplicity and complexity, are particularly "unstable" and invite the often ironical transgressions that undermine dogmatism and reification. In a sense, the multiple and loose late-modern Caribbean identities are case studies of Connolly's antidogmatic, contingent, and politically ambiguous "program." From one perspective this can be seen as a Caribbean "identity crisis," but from another it is exactly the "crisis" that harbors all the creative possibilities. These possibilities are never completely open-ended; they occur within specific, limited territories and contexts, and they harbor specific ambiguities and tensions that can be mapped out and delineated, but always as part of a contestable political process. Condé, again: "West Indians should be as changing and evolving as the islands themselves. Above all, creativity is a complex process which obeys no rules."[8]

Condé's intentions are clearly to encourage an attitude of experimentation toward literature that transcends explicit rules and models, and she concludes by endorsing the following motto of Maurice Blanchot: "The essence of literature is to escape any fundamental determination, any assertion which could stabilize it or even fix it. It is never already there, it is always to be found or invented again."[9] She also makes the obvious and persuasive argument that there can be no demands for "realism" in literature; dreams and fantasies are of course just as legitimate as concrete descriptions of cultural habits and everyday village life. Real as it may seem, the latter too is "imaginary." In fact, in her novels Condé makes explicit use of what we can refer to as "magical" or "fantastic" textual strategies. They bring to mind the discussion of the use of "magic realism" especially in Latin American fiction but also the claim that it is a hallmark of postcolonial literature in general. The debate over magic realism parallels several substantive points of Condé's perspective on Caribbean literature, as well as her aesthetic strategies in her novels.

It is sometimes claimed that "magic realism" has developed in postcolonial regions as a literary strategy in opposition to the mainstream genres of Western literature, that it is a strategy curiously suited for a literature on the margin, a literature that can also be called, to use Gilles Deleuze and Félix Guattari's expression, a "minor literature."[10] This form of literature is sometimes presented as expressing an implicit political practice that locates it in opposition to "imperial" traditions. "Magic realism," from this perspective, becomes a literary strategy "closely linked with a perception of 'living on the margin,' encoding within it, perhaps, a concept of resistance to the massive imperial centre and its totalizing systems."[11] Although unable to live up to such a billing, it is nevertheless fruitful to think of magic realism as capable of expressing different and otherwise silenced voices through a range of literary devices that are in opposition, if not to all mainstream genres, certainly to conventional realism.

Among the various differences or oppositions between realism and magic realism, the following are particularly relevant for Condé and the Caribbean: history versus myth/legend; mimetic versus fantastic; familiarization versus defamiliarization; empiricism/ logic versus mysticism/magic; closure-ridden versus open-ended; naturalism versus romanticism.[12] When formulated in terms of these stark contrasts, it is easy to see the opportunities and complexities that open up with magic realism. (It is equally clear why the latter cannot be viewed as belonging solely to literature on "the margins.")

Although it has been argued that magic realism is a literary strategy to bring the reader closer to "reality"—"through a process of supplemental illusions, these textual strategies seem to produce a more realistic text"—this can only be maintained *as a form of illusion.*[13] If the desire is to "capture" reality, to get closer to "life," then all signifying attempts will fail due to "the deficiencies which any sign system presupposes."[14] In other words, if magic realism is seen as reflecting or rather as compensating for a frustrating "*lack* in communication," then all attempts to close this gap must still be viewed as a stylistic or aesthetic strategy, that is, as a rhetorical trick on the part of the author to seduce the reader into experiencing the "closeness" to "real life." As Scott Simpkins puts it: "Perhaps the problem with this type of supplementation is really nothing more than that of a rigorous, but overwhelmingly frustrated, endeavor to increase the likelihood of *complete* signification through magical means, to make the text—a decidedly unreal construct—become real through a deceptive seeming."[15] Both author and reader can of course be more or less aware of this deceptiveness, although it is difficult to imagine genuine ignorance of this strategy on the part of the author, and, in our late- to postmodern world, to an increasing degree even on the part of the reader. (This argument should not be interpreted as having addressed the far more enigmatic and perplexing question of the relationship between literature—the text—and the indeterminate "life.")[16]

More productive and significant for Caribbean literature is the linking between magic realism and postcolonial discourse. Without by any means accepting this link as belonging exclusively to postcolo-

nial literature, one finds nevertheless something suggestive and persuasive about the connection between colonial and postcolonial
Caribbean experiences and the elements of magic realism identified
through the oppositions to realism listed earlier. This connection is
not just literary; it is historical, social, and geopolitical as well. After
all, the Caribbean societies are through their polyglot cultural
heritages permeated by a wide variety of myths, legends, mysticism,
and magic from African, East Indian, European, and Amerindian
traditions. In addition, all these mixtures of traditions are further defamiliarized and scrambled through massive external and internal
migrations and a long historical process of creolization. This radical
and unique uprootedness and the intermingling of cultures make the
Caribbean, including its literature(s), a postmodern symbol not just
for postcolonial creolized societies but also for the world as whole
as it is developing at the end of the twentieth century. In Condé's
discussion of *Eloge de la Créolité,* a manifesto by three creole writers
who call themselves "Le Groupe de la Créolité," she moves beyond
understanding "créolité" as merely a call for a rehabilitation of creole
as a language: "It is the reappropriation of oneself, of that 'formida-
ble migan' which created the West Indian personality. It is an aesthetic. Moreover, it is the future of the world. 'The world is moving
towards a state of *créolité.*'"[17] Given the characteristics of magic
realism, it is, from this angle, a Caribbean postmodern, postcolonial
genre par excellence. The stories and narratives searching for multiple Caribbean or Creole identities are thus what Michael Shapiro
would call "profound media events" that disrupt settled and entrenched spiritual and cultural economies, that defamiliarize, territorialize, and desacralize established historical and literary grand
narratives, and that anticipate and prepare us for an increasingly creolized world.[18] Through this unsettling process, narratives and genres
that have laid claim to being "true" or realistic are defetishized and
revealed as being just as imaginary as, for example, the various narratives of magic realism.

   Stephen Slemon argues that the social relations of postcolonial
cultures find their thematic expression in magic realist works in
three ways:

> The first involves the representation of a kind of transcendent or
> transformational regionalism so that the site of the text, though de-
> scribed in familiar and local terms, becomes a metonomy of the post-

colonial culture as a whole. The second is the foreshortening of history so that the time scheme of the novel metaphorically contains the long process of colonization and its aftermath. And the third involves the thematic foregrounding of those gaps, absences, and silences produced by the colonial encounter and reflected in the text's disjunctive language of narration. On this third level, the magic realist texts tend to display a preoccupation with images of both borders and centres, and to work toward destabilizing their fixity.[19]

All three elements highlight general aspects of Caribbean postcolonial literature, notwithstanding Condé's criticism. (More importantly, they apply to the narrative structure of Condé's own *Tree of Life*, which I will turn to later.) There is no doubt that "the Empire writes back to the centre"[20] in the Caribbean setting; the region is populated virtually in its entirety by peoples whose ancestors "originated" from somewhere else in the world; they often came to the Caribbean through "forced" (as opposed to voluntary) migration; and they have continued to move back and forth from the Caribbean to the various (neo)colonial centers: Miami, New York, Toronto, London, Paris, and so on. Emigration, immigration, an intense regionalism mixed with an equally significant cosmopolitanism, and uprootedness in general are typical themes in Caribbean novels. The history of the region, especially the background of slavery or indentured laborers, the struggle for emancipation and independence, and postcolonial crisis return as variations on familiar themes, both in sociopolitical and literary narratives. And, finally, new and previously silenced voices, a heterogeneous cast of new characters, and new geographic and linguistic spaces are being occupied and invented through the diverse islands, languages, dialects, religions, and races. That nothing too stable or too fixed can emerge out of all this should not come as a surprise. What can be said to characterize all the new myths, legends, histories, and stories from the postcolonial Caribbean region as a whole are fragmentation, heterogeneity, and pluralism.

There is a peculiar dialogue with history in this situation, a "revisioning" of a history that belonged to the legacy of colonialism and its dominant modes of discourse. This new "dialogue" produces two vague but nevertheless distinct results that find expression in the new literature: on the one hand, it involves "the recuperation of lost voices and discarded fragments, those elements pushed to the margins of consciousness by imperialism's centralizing cognitive structures," and, on the other hand, a pluralization of origins that prevents or "annihilates the privileging or monumentalizing of any one of them and suggests that the 'shreds and fragments' that come down from them in distorted form are our real historical legacy."[21] Various metanarratives are thus democratized and pluralized, and exist side by side without a clear hierarchy and without a dominant or privileged version as ultimate authority or as master code.

Here we need to keep in mind Condé's criticism of the reified model of Caribbean literature: there is a danger that Slemon's somewhat ideological and romantic claims concerning postcolonial literature can themselves turn into dominant guideposts that inhibit pluralism, experimentation, and the questioning of established styles and voices within the postcolonial setting. A danger, in other words, that Caribbean literature turns too univocal. Although Condé's indictment might be too harsh, Slemon's anti-imperial stand might be too romantic and naive. If the former seems to perhaps underestimate the plurality of literary voices present in the Caribbean, the latter is unaware of the ability of a counterideology to turn itself into a form of pious orthodoxy. Slemon also seems to attach a specific political project to the role of postcolonial literature in general and of magic realism in particular. He concludes: "Read as post-colonial discourse, then, magic realism can be seen to provide a positive and liberating response to the codes of imperial history and its legacy of fragmentation and discontinuity."[22] As long as this is not a call for a new ideology of identity in search of wholeness, holiness, and community, we can of course agree with the conclusion, but judging from Condé's argument, this is exactly the case. What must be stressed is the need to continue to innovate and to challenge *all* established voices and narratives, to see the literary and political futility in the attempt to replace the old imperial and fetishized identity with a new, equally fetishized "authentic" native or postcolonial identity. One strength in the new postcolonial identities seems to lie precisely in their fragmented and discontinuous quality.

Because of the tendency to understand the political dimension of postcolonial literature in too narrow or dogmatic a fashion, it might be fruitful to see how "the political" can be understood without reducing it to the straitjacket model that Condé attacks, and without compromising the aesthetic aspects of literature. Deleuze and Guattari's discussion of "minor literature" is helpful in this regard. Minor literature is defined as "that which a minority constructs within a major language."[23] It is thus, among others, the literatures of former colonies—for example, the Caribbean English literature of Trinidad, Barbados, and Guyana; the creolized French novels of Guadeloupe and Haiti; and the Spanish writings of Cuba, Puerto Rico, and Dominican Republic, just to mention a few. Deleuze and Guattari show how Kafka's Prague German belongs to a minor literature in this sense. Another characteristic of minor literature, according to the two authors, "is that everything in them is political."[24] Whereas in major literatures, the social and political environment can easily become mere background for individual concerns, this is not the case in minor literature: "its cramped space forces each individual intrigue to connect immediately to politics. The individual concern thus becomes all the more necessary, indispensable, magnified, because a whole other story is vibrating within it."[25] In addition, minor literature, because of its political or politicized context, connects and expresses a collective value; it belongs to a collectivity, even if an imagined or unrealized one. "It is literature that produces an active solidarity in spite of skepticism; and if the writer is in the margins or completely outside his or her fragile community, this situation allows the writer all the more the possibility to express another possible community and to forge the means for another consciousness and another sensibility."[26]

Taken together with the remarks on magic realism, these elements of a minor literature show us how we can perceive "the political" and "politics" in Caribbean literature without insisting on particular models, ideologies, and positions. It is a politics of language, history, context, and form, not content or political correctness. It is a politics achieved through using local dialects, Caribbean English, and French patois against (or, for that matter, mixed with) the dominant forms of the ("imperial") language. It is by writing different versions of the colonial and postcolonial histories that there is a politics of the context in postcolonial literature; there is a politics in these works by the mere fact that a different story inevitably emerges when the context is rewritten from the local and previously silenced perspectives and voices—here is also where new collectives and identities are formed (written). It is through experimentation with new forms of narratives, including magic realism, that the Caribbean gets rewritten and defamiliarized. Inevitably a different politics, too, gets articulated, for example, by politicizing aspects that previously fell outside the realm of political discourse, or by changing emphasis on aspects that are political in all too familiar ways. But this is the politics of permanent questioning and defamiliarization processes, not the politics of "the peasants," "the oppressed," or "the People." It can of course be that too, but, as Condé shows, that is now part of the dominant Caribbean discourse and literary identity, and an obstacle to an aesthetics (or politics) of experimentation and innovation.

Condé's criticism is only incompatible with a politics of the narrower and more familiar type, while nothing she argues should be viewed as an attack on a politics in the broader sense. As we will see, *Tree of Life* contains all the elements just discussed with reference to both Deleuze and Guattari and magic realism. Condé is explicitly making the dreamed and the "unreal" part of her literary politics and call to arms: "A writer confined to a small and isolated village of the West Indies is free to dream of 'Another Land' and make of it the subject of his/her fiction. Creative imagination goes beyond the limits of reality and soars to areas of its own choice. In fact, dream is a factor which has always been neglected in West Indian literature. It constitutes the object of some of the most magnificent writings of the world."[27] And she ends this segment of her criticism with the following political question with regard to the role of the dream: "Does its power frighten the West Indian writer?"[28]

So much for Condé as literary critic. If we now turn to her family tale *Tree of Life,* we can reflect on the actual expression of some of these ideas through fiction itself.[29] Spanning four generations of a Guadeloupean family, taking the reader from Guadeloupe to Jamaica, from Panama to California, to Europe and Harlem, this is a grand epic, fantastic and realistic, political and erotic, all in a style somewhere in between (and beyond) Mann's *Buddenbrooks* and García Márquez's *Hundred Years of Solitude*. It also contains elements that are surprisingly consistent with the views discussed earlier.

It is a novel that through paradoxes, ironies, and striking shifts in perspectives creates, re-creates, and undermines identities. The book takes us through some of the familiar territories, themes, and characters of Caribbean history, for example, the building of the Panama Canal, Marcus Garvey, migration, race and miscegenation, Rastafarians, colonial politics, voodoo, and, of course, sun and sex. But in each instance of these hallmarks there is an unfamiliar twist or turn in perspective that gives the traditional view a jolt from which it will hardly recover. New voices are heard, and old familiar historical fragments are rewritten and reinvented. The Caribbean landscape is radically transformed and defamiliarized through this imaginative, rich, sensuous, and original tale.

Toward the very end of the story, in a passage that Condé also quotes approvingly in her own critical essay, Coco, the young female narrator, states:

> Would I perhaps have to recount this story? At the risk of displeasing and shocking, would I in my turn perhaps, have to pay my debt? It would be a story of very ordinary people who in their very ordinary way had nonetheless made blood flow. . . . I would have to tell it and it would be a memorial monument of my own. A book quite different from those ambitious ones my mother had dreamed of writing: *Revolutionary Movements of the Black World* and all the rest. A book with neither great tortures nor lavish martyrdoms. But one that would still be heavy with its weight of flesh and blood. The story of my people.[30]

The book that the reader is just about to finish is this story. And it is certainly a book very different from her mother's political project, which, characteristically, never gets completed. The story begins with Albert Louis, Coco's earliest "forebear," who walks off a plantation in Guadeloupe and shortly finds himself working for the American Canal Company in Panama.

From the outset, Condé shows that she is not going to follow the conventional "model" or adhere to "the rules" outlined earlier; it is not going to be the conventional story of oppression, colonialism, poverty, and racism. Although this story is there as well, it is always told with a surprising edge of irony and an astonishing imagination. For one thing, throughout the narrative, no political or racial commitment and no political or racial identity are sufficiently endorsed or idealized that they can be seen as "correct" or "natural." On the contrary, each character that harbors the dream or illusion that his or her political convictions are True, or that he or she has finally found his/her authentic and genuine identity soon gets these illusions shattered, either by events or by the views or actions of a close family member. What Derek Walcott asserted two decades ago is revealed throughout Coco's story of her own people: "Once we have lost our wish to be white we develop a longing to become black, and those two may be different, but are still careers."[31] Careers, costumes, masks, circumstantial and contingent identities—but no less capable of setting the tone of the lives for the ensemble of characters. When Albert Louis has established himself as an undertaker in Colon and is getting rich off the deaths from the brutal conditions of the Panama Canal construction, Marcus Garvey arrives to give inspiring speeches to the unhappy workers. Albert is swept away by Garvey's ideas and begins to read his works and listen to his speeches any chance he gets. He tries hesitatingly to meet Garvey, but Garvey is out of his office. Still the reader expects that a meeting is inevitable and it will no doubt change Albert's life even more than the reading. But class turns out to be mightier than race:

> Yet Marcus Garvey could not fail to notice the large black Negro with the white mane, silent and somber, dressed with an elegance in sharp contrast to the Canal workers' mud-covered appearance. For Albert was beginning to display that dandified air that so struck everyone who came in contact with him. When Garvey asked about him, his entourage replied that he was a man from Guadeloupe, the partner of an American exploiter who was making his fortune from sickness and death. So Marcus Garvey completely lost interest in him, and the conversation that might have changed my forebear's fate never took place.[32]

Nevertheless, Albert's life is changed because of Garvey's writings, and Albert's favorite quote, "I shall teach the Black Man to see the beauty in himself," becomes a slogan that reverberates down the generations in the Louis family; these reverberations have various implications, positive and negative, serious and ironic, depending on each individual's temperament and interpretation of his or her context. The point is not that this sentence is a meaningless orì true call to action or arms but that it pushes the person who is attracted to its sound in directions unforeseen, unpredictable, and unintended. There is obviously no *core* or *essential* meaning to this sentence. Nor is it the basis for a uniform political perspective; on the contrary, it sparks a broad range of political reactions, all of which further underscore the indeterminate quality of its multiple appeals.

After various mishaps and tragic events in Panama, Albert finds himself, together with his friend Jacob, on a boat to San Francisco, or Yerba Buena as it was first called in the stories about this promised city that Albert listened to in Panama. Entrepreneur that he is, Albert soon finds himself making money in Chinatown. I will quote the page setting the tone for this event merely as an illustration of the flavor of Condé's prose and perspective.

There were many Chinese in Panama. So Albert and Jacob did not feel out of their element among those furtive, courteous men, eyes lowered, pate shaved—a glistening, fat serpent nestled between the shoulder blades! On the contrary. And it was quite natural to find themselves engaging in a conversation with a certain Chi Lu Lee. He was a large, mustachioed Chinese in a brocaded gown who turning and turning his bowl in his hands told them a story that woke more than a few echoes in Albert's mind. Was this not his own tale? And was he not himself, a Chinese?

One knows only one's own troubles and those of ones's kin. One is unaware that other, almost identical troubles lay shriveled: cow dung beneath the harsh sun of unhappy lands. There, too, an ocean away, men's hearts were the same!

"My father, my grandfather, and my grandfather's father before him grew rice in Kwang-Tung Province, whose capital is Guang-zshou, which the American call Canton. From this came their bowed backs, calloused hands, and life empty of its best hopes from the moment of birth. I, too, began as they did, in the green hell of the rice fields. And then one day I had enough of it. I lifted my face toward the sun, saying: 'Do you not shine for me, also? Then give me the strength. I want no more of this life.' I borrowed money and took the boat for Kum Shan . . . "

"Kum Shan?"

"Yes, it is how San Francisco is called in my country. When I have made my pile of green cash, I will go home. I have a wife waiting for me, and a child too. A boy!"

One thing leading to another, Chi Lu Lee invited Albert and Jacob home to smoke some opium.

The next day, leaving Albert immersed in a blissful torpor and determined to find Macon Dennis's boarding-house, Jacob left the home of Chi Lu Lee in the morning fog. As for Albert, he had already made his decision: He would not leave Chinatown. It was the belly in whose depths he would be reborn. He would stay there. He would take a room looking out over the bay, on the second floor of a wooden house with balconies and a carved railing under a pagoda roof. He would breathe in that odor of ginger, or rotting fish and green onions. He would cradle himself in those high and mysteriously friendly voices. He would never weary of the hieroglyphs on the shop fronts.

When Jacob returned with Macon Dennis, a carpenter whose business was not doing badly, Albert refused outright to go with them.

Some time later Albert entered into partnership with Chi Lu Lee, the proprietor of a laundry on Washington Street. The entire trade of washing and ironing laundry was run by the Chinese, who trotted from house to house, their baskets on their backs. But Albert had ideas. It was not for nothing that he had gotten the hang of such things in Panama! He pushed Chi Lu Lee into buying a horse, all skin and bones, and a cart for delivering the laundry; now they were always ahead of their competitors, and the city's leading citizens took notice of this. Chi Lu Lee employed three "brothers," paying each one no more than a bowl of rice and five bowls of tea. Albert took on three more, and eliminated the rice.

The partners became rich.[33]

(The fact that three names—San Francisco, Kum Shan, Yerba Buena—have been introduced to designate the city reminds us of its complex historical creolization; no wonder Albert felt at home!) Not only did Albert and Chi Lu Lee share their leave-taking from treacherous and monotonous labor; their solidarity toward "their people" never interfered with the urge to make money. This urge was another trait that characterized both Albert and later generations of the family: the desire to accumulate wealth was stronger than the identification with the oppressed. It was also to be one of the reasons that kept both Albert and his son Jacob out of politics, in spite of their more spiritual commitment to the aforementioned phrase.

Albert's somewhat split personality on the question of race was to have serious implications especially for his firstborn son, also named Albert, but soon called Bert by the family. Bert was born in Panama but, because of his mother's tragic and mysterious death at childbirth, had been sent to be raised in Guadeloupe, first by Albert's mother and subsequently, once Albert had returned, by Albert and Elaise, Albert's newfound Guadeloupean wife. Given Albert's by now gloomy view of the human condition, Bert was raised according to some peculiar tenets:

> Bert was brought up according to strict principles that had the particularity of never being stated but nonetheless were to guide him like so many invisible signs.
>
> One was to frequent neither whites nor mulattoes, the whites being natural enemies and the mulattoes despicable bastards who had

inherited the arrogance of their fathers and forgotten that they came from the bellies of Negro women.

But above all, one was to avoid other Negroes. For from time immemorial Negroes had hated their fellows and sought with all their might to do them harm!

Therefore one was to live alone. Superbly alone.

And so, Bert took refuge in reading.[34]

Not surprisingly, not only does Bert find a mulatto as a best friend, he also marries a white French working-class woman after she becomes pregnant. This event leads to Bert's "disappearance" from the family and (in)directly to his premature death in France. Bert becomes a mystery for the family, and his fate is unknown until Coco uncovers the true chain of events toward the end of the book.

Another intellectual family feud or generational dispute begins when an illegitimate daughter of one of Albert's sisters marries a member of the local bourgeoisie, a Camille Desir, the head tutor at the lycée, and also "a member of the Elect of the Occidental Lodge." At the wedding—held at Albert's house, "which on that day took its place among the notable houses of the city"—Albert withdraws to his office to get away from the wedding party.

Having made up his mind about the man based on the calumnies he had heard about him, Camille Desir went to join him there and found Albert with his shirt collar open, drinking from a bottle of rum. A friendship mysteriously sprang up between these two men, apparently so little made for understanding each other and so separated by age. From that day on, Camille Desir took up his duties as confidant and mentor.

"I don't fit in with these smokers of Havana cigars," said Albert, "these embellishers of French-French and marriers of light-skinned women! I am a Grosse Caye yam, black as the earth it comes from. I love my race and I want to carry it on . . . "

"Nor do I, no matter what you may think. I don't feel like them. I am a communist. Have you read Marx?"

Albert had never heard the name and incredulously listened to himself being informed that race did not count, only class. He shook his head vigorously:

"No, no, no! They hate me because I'm a Negro!"

That was to be the beginning of endless arguments between the two men.

For the time being, they christened their newborn friendship with fermented rum, and Camille Desir came downstairs dead drunk to take possession of his new wife. Not without having listened to a long speech about Marcus Garvey.

"That man there said things I never heard said by anybody. 'I shall teach the Black Man to see beauty in himself.' Do you know English? Do you know what that means? That the black race is beautiful. That it is great. That it will astound the world."

Camille shrugged his shoulders.

"What are you talking about? It's the proletariat of every color that one day will take their revenge and astound the universe!"[35]

Thus, the thorny topic of race or class enters the family clan; this time not merely in practice but also in theory. The practice was, after all, already established: Albert was a true capitalist who made money off the poor of his own race, not only in Panama, but now in Guadeloupe, where he had built a tenement yard that he rented out, at exploitative levels, to former plantation workers who had moved to the city. To heighten the impact of this momentous event and intellectual conflict, Albert's mother Theodora dies two days after the wedding. Coco, the narrator, comments laconically:

Theodora's old heart could not withstand the pride caused by her granddaughter's marriage to a man equipped with such intellectual baggage. It gave way. Two days after the wedding she fell across her bed and could not rise again.[36]

It should also be noted that at about this time one more intellectual "identity" question touches Albert's mind, and, in spite of Albert's own relative indifference to questions of roots and ancestry, it too becomes part of the family "heritage." To the unstable questions of race and class is added the equally controversial problem of "origin."

A controversy, about which the local papers published a great many articles, rekindled the fire of Albert's hope, rendering him surly and indifferent to everyone but himself. The black American intellectual Du Bois, the Senegalese deputy Blaise Diagne, and a deputy from Guadeloupe were arguing over how much support should be given to the ideas of Marcus Garvey. Marcus Garvey! It is thus that Albert learned his idol was alive, still alive! All the rest was of little importance; the question of whether the so-called Pan-African Congress should be held in London, Brussels, or Paris; the torrents of flattery being poured on the deputy from Guadeloupe ("leader of black Frenchmen"), and so on and so forth. Only this news counted: Marcus Garvey was alive in New York. Albert pressed Camille Desir to gather more information from his contacts in the world of politics. Desir discovered that Garvey was publishing a newspaper called *The Negro World* and even procured Albert a copy; he also learned that Garvey was owner of a steamship line that was to take all the Negroes to Africa.

At this point in the conversation Albert blinked:

"To Africa? Why?"

Camille Desir raised his eyes to the heavens:

"Is it not the land from where our ancestors came? Your Mr. Garvey, who I've heard said is a dangerous fanatic, naively forgets that three centuries have passed and a lot of water has flowed under the bridge!"

To tell the truth, Albert did not burden himself with these considerations. He was carried away on the tide of his own joy.[37]

All these quotations are merely a sample, and all belong to the first quarter of the book, but they might give a sense of the tone and style of the novel, as well as provide some idea of both how its political irony is expressed and how conventional and reified historical and personal identities are questioned and destabilized.

Needless to say, the ideological battles and the overtly political controversies are mostly background and only on occasion the foreground of the complex narrative. The purpose of this exposition is just to illustrate a few of the ways in which Condé deviates from "the rules" and "the model" outlined earlier, how she creates new identities by treating the conventional, the seemingly "natural" ones as open to obvious contestations and ironical interrogations. She shows how politics and history do not contain orderly and clear-cut issues with obvious meanings, truths, or directions. And she challenges the established rules and identities by turning them back on themselves.

For example, the rule against individualism is violated from the outset: Albert is what in a different context would be called "a self-made man," a rugged (an understatement) individualist who nonetheless harbors a collective ambition and dreams of a fixed, "true" collective identity through Garvey's teachings and the favorite phrase. (The fact that Jacob, Albert's son and heir to the import-export business that Albert has built up in Guadeloupe, is described as "unrelievedly ugly" adds irony to the slogan that he too will make his own.)

If there is a collective urge expressing itself in Condé's book, it is an ambiguous or multiple one—to say the least—revealed in Coco's quoted proclamation about telling "the story of my people." On the one hand, this can be read as the story of the family, a family chronicle, the story of the rise of a (petit) bourgeois family comparable, literature-wise, to a *Buddenbrooks;* on the other hand, it can also be read as telling the story of a much broader notion of a "people"— perhaps a story of the people of Guadeloupe, maybe the people of the Caribbean, maybe even a version of the story of all so-called colonized peoples? In any case, whichever story one hears (i.e., reads), it is a story that challenges what we can label two dominant "metanarratives."

Like all "minor literature," Condé's novel is explicitly a critique of the "central" literature of the colonizer, a literature that deterritorializes and decenters the colonial voice, a literature that does not include the perspective of the colonized; Condé's story is in numerous and obvious ways a challenge to European-, French-, white-, imperial-centered voices. In fact, the voices heard in all of Condé's novels are voices that have been historically silenced but are now themselves part of postcolonial literatures. This is a self-conscious strategy, one which of course comes, so to speak, naturally to anybody who grew up in colonies or former colonies. Today, this is such a well-established literary perspective or genre that it might not even be particular perceptive to label this form of literature protest literature, or literature of the oppressed, or whatever. It is simply the literary strategy or perspective that becomes the dominant one in the postcolonial world once a local tradition or minor literature has established itself. That this is now a rather large, varied, and rich genre in itself is self-evident.

More importantly, however—and this is partly the result of the success and impressive output of the postcolonial literatures— Condé, as we have already seen, writes against the grain of this established postcolonial tradition, a tradition that she obviously experiences as already all too predictable and conventional. She uses her own version of magic realism against what we can now call the entrenched postcolonial "realism." The latter has replaced the imperialist ideology that dominated the colonial period. Condé's critique, both through her fiction and her literary criticism, undermines all "realistic" ideologies—the colonial and the postcolonial. She shows how all forms of realism are "imaginary," and through her writing encourages a disruption of this seemingly endless reproduction process that is wedded to an imperialist code, even in its anti-imperialist opposition. This is one reason why generalizations with regard to both form and content of "postcolonial" or "minor" literatures are hazardous, to say the least. At best, so-called postcolonial or magic realist literature is an imaginative genre that reveals all forms of realism as equally "imaginary" and thus defetishizes any established realist genre, this time, not in the name of a new, improved version of the real but in the name of the imaginary itself.

Tree of Life also violates the rule endorsing writing as a critique of certain social and political conditions and as a means to "liberation." For sure, a politicized discourse is present throughout the book, and social and political conditions are criticized from a variety of angles, but always in a skeptical and ironical tone; the call for "liberation" is, if not ridiculed, certainly treated as a highly questionable and indeterminable idea. If politics in general and concepts like "liberation" in particular are defetishized all through the narrative, this is done for both reasons of aesthetics and "life." Condé's book is a work of fiction and it delivers no coherent political or social "truths" or ideology. There is no invitation to draw specific political "conclusions," and there is no attempt made to present political solutions in this work—still, as the quotations have illustrated, there is politics here, in all forms, shapes, and varieties, even to such an extent as to present (not without irony) both Albert's and Jacob's final decline as due to the reception by the Guadeloupean (white and mulatto) elites to their attempts at starting a Black political party. Albert's and Jacob's political dreams drown in the murky waters of race and class. Condé's subversive magic thus operates in a truly postmodern and postcolonial form: it treats both colonialism and anticolonialism as fetishized, realistic genres and ideologies in need of ironization and destabilization.

As Condé shows, even one of the most prominent themes in the postcolonial genre, the search for identity, has to be decoded, transformed, and rewritten. In fact, the theme gets reworked in Condé's novel to the point where the entire identity premise—whether authenticity, homecoming, or political truth—is revealed, often humorously, as somewhat of a tired ideological rhetoric. After all, Condé's narrator Coco sets out to tell her story in explicit opposition to her mother's unwritten "Revolutionary Movements of the Black World," and her tale remains enigmatically open-ended.

Throughout the book, "the same" political circumstances and events generate different reactions and produce different views in the family members. The futility of the fixation on and of identity is repeatedly revealed. The book shows how (political) identities are constituted through a combination of, on the one hand, world historical elements, political ideologies and myths, regional peculiarities, and local politics and, on the other hand, a mishmash of personal impulses, desires, prejudices, and contingencies. Out of this cacophony of voices, perspectives, and ideologies can only come an equally wide and diverse range of fleeting, shifting, and multiple identities. The strength of these varied identities might lie exactly in their weakness, in their lack of stability, in their indeterminable character, in short, in their perpetual crisis.

NOTES

1. This process is analyzed in excellent detail in William E. Connolly, *Identity/Difference: Democratic Negotiations of Political Paradox* (Ithaca, N. Y.: Cornell University Press, 1991).

2. As quoted in Maryse Condé, "Order, Disorder, Freedom, and the West Indian Writer," in *Post/Colonial Conditions: Exiles, Migrations, and Nomadisms,* vol. 2, *Yale French Studies,* No. 83 (New Haven: Yale University Press, 1993), p. 122.

3. Ibid., p. 123.

4. Ibid., p. 124.

5. Ibid., p. 126. Condé also includes Aimé Césaire's *Return to My Native Land* as an example of this sacred text.

6. Connolly, *Identity/Difference,* p. 159.

7. Ibid.

8. Condé, "Order, Disorder, Freedom," p. 130.

9. Maurice Blanchot, as quoted in ibid., p. 134.

10. The expression is explained in Gilles Deleuze and Félix Guattari, *Kafka: Toward a Minor Literature,* trans. Dana Polan (Minneapolis: University of Minnesota Press, 1986), esp. ch. 3, pp. 16-27.

11. Stephen Slemon, "Magic Realism as Post-Colonial Discourse," *Canadian Literature* 116 (spring 1988): 10. Slemon attributes this argument to Linda Kenyon and Robert Kroetsch.

12. These oppositions are adopted from Scott Simkins, "Magical Strate-

gies: The Supplement of Realism," *Twentieth Century Literature* (summer 1988): 141.

13. Ibid., p. 145.

14. Ibid., p. 149.

15. Ibid., p. 143.

16. For an illuminating and Nietzschean discussion of the use of "life" as an "indispensable, nonfixable marker," see the epilogue to William E. Connolly, *Political Theory and Modernity* (Ithaca, N. Y.: Cornell University Press, 1993), pp. 194-95.

17. Condé, "Order, Disorder, Freedom," p. 129. "Migans": "a breadfruit hush or mush, staple of the West Indian diet, made of breadfruit, onion, bacon pig's tail, cloves, garlic, ham, parsley, chili pepper and aromatics." From glossary in Maryse Condé, *Tree of Life,* trans. Victoria Reiter (New York: Ballantine Books, 1992), p. 370.

18. Michael J. Shapiro, *Reading the Postmodern Polity: Political Theory as Textual Practice* (Minneapolis: University of Minnesota Press, 1992), p. 60. See also Michael J. Shapiro, *Reading "Adam Smith": Desire, History and Value* (Newbury Park, Calif.: Sage Publications, 1993), p. xxvi.

19. Slemon, "Magic Realism," pp. 12-13.

20. The phrase is Salman Rushdie's, but is used both in the title and as the main theme in Bill Ashcroft, Gareth Griffiths, and Helen Tiffin, *The Empire Writes Back: Theory and Practice in Post-Colonial Literatures* (London: Routledge, 1989).

21. Slemon, "Magic Realism," pp. 16-17.

22. Ibid., p. 21.

23. Deleuze and Guattari, *Kafka: Toward a Minor Literature,* p. 16.

24. Ibid., p. 17.

25. Ibid.

26. Ibid.

27. Condé, "Order, Disorder, Freedom," p. 130.

28. Ibid.

29. Maryse Condé, *Tree of Life,* trans. Victoria Reiter (New York: Ballantine Books, 1992).

30. Ibid., p. 357.

31. Derek Walcott, *Dream on Monkey Mountain and Other Plays* (New York: Noonday Press, 1970), p. 20.

32. Condé, *Tree of Life,* pp. 33-34.

33. Ibid., pp. 43-45.

34. Ibid., p. 69.

35. Ibid., pp. 82-83.

36. Ibid., p. 83.

37. Ibid., pp. 85-86.

4

The Politics of Totality in Magic Realism

BRUNO BOSTEELS, LORIS MIRELLA,
AND PETER A. SCHILLING

POLITICIZING THE "REAL"

Fictional genres share with the more analytic writings in the social
sciences and other explicitly knowledge-producing disciplines the
condition that what they generate are narrative enactments that address and shape understandings. As such, they propose frames of reference for experiences that, even if fictive, are at least shared and
common. In the case of magic realism, however, its common, if not
stereotypical, affiliation with the literary traditions of Latin America
often serves to obscure this social function, especially for readers in
the United States, where magic realism tends to be reduced to the
aesthetic expression of an exotic otherness. In contradistinction to
this aestheticization, we claim that, especially in the present context
of late capitalism, the fiction of magic realism provides a different set
of both epistemological and ontological parameters, the narrativity
of which replaces the analytical categories of philosophy in the evaluation of experience, truth, and reality. In this sense—the first one in
which we derive political and ideological significance from the phenomenon—magic realism helps to provide what Michel Foucault has
proposed to call a "critical ontology of ourselves."[1]

Produced in any setting, magic realist fiction thus provides a per-
vasively politicizing perspective. But, as we have noted, the tendency
has been to ascribe it, as a genre, to the "otherness" of Latin America.[2] When this happens, the fictitiousness of magic realism is not re-

garded as symptomatic of a global and intercultural ideological environment but is instead grasped and marketed as an essential version of Latin American identity: magic realism as one more category of literary consumption.[3] For this reason, our readings turn to texts other than the best-selling novels from Latin America. As a mode of political interpretation and critique, magic realism is no less applicable to our examples by Canadian and first-world minority authors than to those produced elsewhere.[4]

In addition, to retrieve a political and ideological impetus behind magic realism, we evoke the Marxist idea of totality. The political function of magic realism is to show that the various components of reality, which are often contradictory or incommensurate, can be made to add up to a totality, at least narratively. Magic realism thus takes the lived experience of contradiction in a way that preserves and aestheticizes the dislocation without resolving it. The amalgamation of the real and the magical, which leads to the genre's characteristic heterogeneity of narrative spaces, cultural forms, and political and religious traditions, thereby becomes the source of both the radicality of magic realism (inscribing contradiction as unresolvable) and its passivity (projecting sheer aesthetic paradox and indeterminacy). Thus, for example, magic realism has been shown both to engage with history, by manipulating narrative conventions as symbolic acts of cultural resistance or empowerment, and to reject history for a more static vision, by resisting precisely an engagement with the political.

What is raised in analyzing magic realism's relationship to incommensurability is the issue of whether it is possible to provide a complete, aesthetic account of experience. In this respect, magic realism's rendering of totality is an inversion of Theodor W. Adorno's observations about naturalism.[5] Various commitments to naturalism were aimed at revealing the world through an unmediated representation. In general, naturalism's claims were for no style, no form, only the content. Yet precisely in the breach between object and representation that naturalism nonetheless necessarily allows, Adorno finds the moment of nonidentification that generates the possibility of truth. Adorno's point is that the social totality can be grasped only as the dialectical effect of the incompleteness of representation. To aspire to completeness is to aspire to falsity. Magic realism amounts to the treatment of this epigram as an assertion rather than as a caution.

In registering the difference between various cultures and sociopolitical economies, for example, magic realism demonstrates that totality is a fantastical and impossible contradiction unless it is presented as a fable. As Slavoj Zizek puts it, in a more or less Lacanian frame, "truth has always the structure of a fiction."[6] Thus, magic realism not only accepts the incommensurability of contradictory phenomena but seeks aesthetically to posit a notion of the whole that is both true to the contradictory nature of individual experience and unified and made sense of somewhere before or beyond it.

Whether a meaningful whole is posited either before or beyond the contradictory world of everyday life is thus a fundamental distinction necessary to interpret the politics of magic realism. In Europe, for example, magic realism has often taken the form of an intuitive, spiritual, parapsychological, metaphysical, or even mystical quest for a preternatural realm, an a priori ground posited before or hidden within the world of everyday phenomena. Flemish magic realists like Johan Daisne and Hubert Lampo are strongly influenced, for instance, by the archetypical approach to culture of Jungian ascendancy, and by the quest for a Bergsonian *élan vital*. On the other hand, among Latin American authors such as Miguel Angel Asturias, Alejo Carpentier, Arturo Uslar Pietri, Gabriel García Márquez, and Isabel Allende, the uncovered totality tends to be couched historically, ethnologically, and anthropologically in terms of the mythical and autochthonous substrata partially or wholly extirpated in the processes of colonization and modernization.

The resulting contradictory reality of social life, then, is what magic realism allows articulation of by mediating between various levels of lived experience: on a basic level, between different cultures (indigenous and foreign), between different modes of production (communal, feudal, and capitalist), and ultimately between various national cultures and the primary antagonistic culture, the United States, which today represents both "foreign" culture as such and the entire economic field on which all culture is defined. Here, though, the notion of a meaningful whole is not only nostalgically retrojected onto an essential and pregiven realm that has subsequently been lost; the vision of totality also points, however indirectly, toward other, even utopian possibilities projected onto the future, wherein lies the emancipatory trajectory of its ideology.

A major theoretical force behind this utopian reevaluation of magic realism has come from Marxist cultural theorists, especially Fredric Jameson. For Jameson, the utopian potential of magic realism, as a contemporary expression of the persistence of romance, corresponds to the exhaustion of older paradigms of realism to which Marxism traditionally has had recourse. As he writes in *The Political Unconscious:* "It is in the context of the gradual reification of realism in late capitalism that romance once again comes to be felt as the place of narrative heterogeneity and of freedom from that reality principle to which a now oppressive realistic representation is the hostage. Romance now again seems to offer the possibility of sensing other historical rhythms, and of demonic or Utopian transformations of a real now unshakably in place."[7] Magic realism, then, becomes to Jameson what realism was to Georg Lukács, just as the latter's critical rejection of the historical avant-garde corresponds to the former's polemical and mostly negative interpretation of postmodernism.

Magic realism offers, according to Jameson, the possibility of "some new historicism," or "some constitutive and privileged relationship with history grasped and sensed in a new way, radically different from the chronologies of the historical novel and the fashion plates of nostalgia films alike."[8] Whereas the all-pervasive logic of late capitalism has erased nearly every possibility of historical and critical distance from the hegemonic cultural codes, magic realism promises to offer an answer to the postmodern canon to the extent to which the internal heterogeneity and disjunction of narrative layers also marks the presence of other cultural and ultimately socioeconomic modalities. Jameson thus presents the following, admittedly provisional hypothesis:

> The possibility of magic realism as a formal mode is constitutively dependent on a type of historical raw material in which disjunction is structurally present; or, to generalize the hypothesis more starkly, on a content which betrays the overlap or the coexistence of precapitalist and nascent capitalist or technological features. On such a view, then, the organizing category of magic realist film is not the concept of the generation (as in the nostalgia film), but rather the very different one of modes of production, and in particular of a mode of production still locked in conflict with traces of the older ones (if not foreshadowings of the emergence of a future one).[9]

Here, in other words, the totality that magic realism allows to subsist beneath or beyond the fractured and scarred world of everyday existence is framed as the global backdrop of the history of modes of production, as the historical forms in which people live their lives. The fact of this traditional conceptual framework having fallen into desuetude is, of course, part of the problem Jameson seeks to redress, and it proves less the insufficiency of his interpretation than the success of capitalism. And yet, as is the case with most other features of magic realism, the overlap or coexistence of various modes of production still does not guarantee a critical, let alone utopian, potential. Complacency in the face of capital's expansion, or even complicity, might well be a hidden motivation behind the appeal of magic realism.

In the following three blurbs from publicity for Mexico's national airline, for example, the intended effect seems to be to attract tourism by appeasing any fears of discomfort or culture shock:

> Ixtapa is a place of magic and enchantment which offers visitors the hospitality of the people from Guerrero as well as modern tourist complexes for relaxation and diversion.

> Only Cancún can offer you the modernity of its enormous hotel zone together with the Mayan past and the turquoise beauty of the sea.

> In Oaxaca's streets and little squares, in its craftsmanship, and in the surrounding ruins, one respires the calm and joy of this city which has never ceased to be indigenous, and which begs modernity to delay itself in order to continue the conversation with the most ancient traditions.[10]

These little vignettes should warn all soothsayers against the perils involved in an overboldly utopian reading of magic realism. Radicality and passivity, as mentioned earlier, stubbornly remain the twin expressions of the ideological and political force of magic realists—be they novelists, painters, filmmakers, or ghostwriters for the tourism industry.

The central question here is how "successful" tourists or readers of magic realism will be in blending the modern and the indigenous, or in shuttling back and forth from their modern hotel zone to the Mayan ruins. The slightest disjunction of experience, in fact, might foreground the narrative framing devices without which no meaningful involvement with the world would be possible at all. In this sense, the critical and utopian functions of magic realism are again not merely epistemological but ontological. Thus, like a dysfunctional tool, the heterogeneity of magic realism might be seen as rendering conspicuous the "worldhood" of the world, that is, the horizon against which the whole of inner-worldly experience first becomes meaningful, and against which criticism becomes possible. The vocabulary of modes of production, then, is only another, more specifically socioeconomic way of interpreting this untranscendable ontological horizon.[11]

In sum, the political function of magic realism becomes critical-utopian primarily as the effect of a dysfunction. The sense of the social whole provided by the genre is immanently linked to a sense of incompleteness, to the limits and gaps in experience that form at once the impulse behind the various attempts at a narrative synthesis and the cause of their breakdown. Between part and whole, between form and content, magic realism thus acknowledges the forces of indeterminacy and incommensurability, while at the same time finding a moment of truth in the limits of those framing devices aimed at constructing a coherent picture of the world of lived experience.

In the next two sections, we illustrate the political impetus of magic realism in a variety of first-world venues and in a way that takes account of the gendered aspect of a novel's political orientation.

MAGIC REALISM AND FIRST-WORLD MINORITIES

Most readers have little trouble finding in the manifest plots and characters of the canonical novels of Latin American magic realism (which, with the exception of Isabel Allende, are mostly authored by men), as well as those of such non–Latin American authors as Salman Rushdie, Ben Okri, Tahar Ben Jelloun, and Milan Kundera, at times only a thin allegorical screen for national and international political scenarios. But no understanding of magic realism should be limited only to these texts and their techniques. In first-world countries, contemporary women novelists also bring together the magical with the real in order to force readers to reinterpret the present world as well as their understanding of the past. Gloria Naylor's *Mama Day,* Toni Morrison's *Beloved,* and Keri Hulme's *The Bone People,* among other novels by minority women (Louise Erdrich, Paule Marschall, Maxine Hong Kingston), distinguish themselves, however, from their male contemporaries by foregrounding the lives of individuals. Only behind or beyond these specific men and women can readers glimpse traces of larger political issues.[12]

In *Mama Day* Naylor follows the path of Carpentier's *The King-dom of This World* as she starkly opposes the practical applications of voodoo and herbalism with the ineffective procedures and prac-tices of the dominant society. The misguided representative of the es-tablishment, though African American, is an engineer who bears the name of the home where he was raised as a ward of state. As far as George Andrews is concerned, his progenitors are the salaried em-ployees of a bureaucracy. The island of his life is New York City; his culture, a professional football team; his faith, self-reliance; and his heart, congenitally defective. In pointed contrast to George, Naylor offers the Mama Day of the title. A benevolent conjure woman and the matrilineal descendent of a succession of spiritual benefactors, Mama Day lives on Willow Springs, an island off the coast of both Georgia and South Carolina, though the territory of neither state.

Mama Day's great-niece Cocoa marries George, and self-consciously becomes an African-American woman living between worlds. When the couple leaves New York City and spends a sum-mer holiday on Willow Springs, George attempts rationally to dis-miss Mama Day's abilities and thereby avoid admitting that he has no way of understanding them. But at the moment of crisis—to save the life of his wife poisoned by a jealous woman—George has to accept Mama Day and her power, through his confusion and with-out understanding but with trust. By submitting, his heart bursts and he dies.

In *Beloved,* Toni Morrison retells the 1855 Ohio case of a fugitive slave. Sethe, an African-American woman, has just escaped from the slave state of Kentucky to the free state of Ohio. When a bounty hunter, a sheriff, and her former owner track her and her four chil-dren to the home of her free mother-in-law, Sethe herds her children into an empty woodshed. Neither immobilized by the fear of return-ing to Kentucky nor incapacitated by the thought of her children growing up slaves, Sethe acts in the only way she can. Loving her children, she rips a saw across the throats of her two sons and her just-crawling daughter. As she swings the head of her newborn daughter toward the wall of the shed, the white men stand numbed by the clarity of her love and their cruelty. Another freed slave catches the baby's unsmashed skull.

The two boys live, and the infant joins Sethe in prison. When the magistrate allows Sethe to leave jail and attend the burial of her other daughter, she hears the minister say only the words "Dearly Beloved." Released from prison years later, Sethe prostitutes herself for a rose-colored headstone, though the stone carver will inscribe only the one word: "Beloved." Finally named, the dead daughter begins to haunt the house of Sethe, her mother-in-law, and the three other children—the children fearing that whatever made their mother try to kill them may once return. Instead, the dead daughter returns as a young woman with smooth hands, unworn shoes, and a scarred neck. Demanding all of Sethe's attention, she calls herself "Beloved."

In *The Bone People,* New Zealand's Keri Hulme is not or cannot be as sure of good and evil as Naylor and Morrison. In a contemporary setting, Hulme follows but redraws paths long mapped by an older type of political literature. In *Beowulf,* for instance, Grendel, Beowulf, and Hrothgar all need one another not only to define their respective positions in the political spectrum but also to delineate the boundaries of the political ideologies they represent. The relationship between the three helps readers understand the interaction between various modes of existence, further suggesting that violence will be the cost of stability. Like the authors of *Beowulf* and *Mama Day,* Hulme concocts a triad to depict and hopefully to resolve the conflict.

As *Beowulf* documents the transition from the Norse to the Christian world, and *Mama Day* contrasts the engineer with the conjure woman, so *The Bone People* represents the internal and external conflicts between the descendants of Anglo-Saxon settlers and the displaced indigenous Maori. Joe, the mostly Maori "broken man," who has tried the European colonizers' religion, education, and factory work, has found only a road leading toward the cliff's edge of despair. No longer caring, he throws himself off—only to be rescued by a waiting Maori priest. From this old guardian of one of the Maori deities, Joe comes to understand his past as well as his future.

Kerewin, the mostly white "digger," has wealth but no love. An artist who can no longer paint, whose encyclopedic knowledge does not include happiness, Kere has built herself a tower that has become her prison. No crucifix, no biorhythm chart, no yarrowsticks, no Japanese martial arts have brought freedom any nearer to Kere. She, too, is prepared to die, until a spirit of the land calls a welcome to her.

And Simon, "the stranger," the flax-haired sun child tossed on the shore by a raging sea, who shares a strange scar across his throat with Kere. At once innocent, victim, urchin-Beowulf from across the sea, and gap-toothed monster for whom violence is the only remedy, Simon hears the music of the wind, and at night watches soul-shadows. Mutely and violently, Simon forces all three to touch the essential spirituality of the places so that growth is possible. As the voice of Kerewin in Simon's haunted imagination says, they are "the waves of future chance" (395). But they have to be together.

In ways reminiscent of Miguel Angel Asturias's *Hombres de maiz*, E. M. Forster's *A Passage to India*, and more recently Salman Rushdie's *Satanic Verses*, Hulme, Naylor, and Morrison reiterate that the political domination of the empowered over the powerless is deeply and personally damaging. Yet in each novel political institutions seem absent, even though a long political history has situated the characters in a country in which they are unable to live. *The Bone People* especially never directly discusses the political forces that choke the lives of its characters.

Morrison, Naylor, and Hulme focus primarily on the lived experience of individuals, rather than on political allegory or global political events. Morrison's story, for instance, is that of a small family group escaping from slavery and then trying to survive the post–Civil War Reconstruction. At its base, it tells of a former slave who, though nominally free, bears the scars of her beatings like a tree etched into her back. Sethe turns what Kierkegaard would call the ethical world on its head, but unlike her predecessor Abraham, who is prepared to kill his child because of his faith in a higher world, Sethe kills her daughter because she has no faith in her immediate world.

Starting from a similar lack of faith, and again with no apparent political conflict, Hulme's well-drawn characters live in New Zealand as crossbred descendants of colonists and colonized, "husks, aping the European manners and customs" (359). As individuals, the discontinuities between their lives and the spirit of the land have rendered them impotent. They know that they are lost in the way they live, and that the available structures of Western thought allow them no cure. But Hulme suggests a remedy: subtly at first, she offers the many-chambered, spiraled nautilus shape as a sheltering, all-inclusive alternative to the methodologically straight, domineering Anglo-Saxon line. The helix shapes found in floor designs, staircases, and the narrative's own structure eventually lead all three characters back again to the indigenous culture, the "Maoritanga," which the European colonizers attempted to eradicate militarily, economically, intellectually, and emotionally, but could not kill. And yet, only the horror of immediate and excruciating pain—inflicted and inflicted upon—can bring the characters to take this route.

In these three novels, in sum, the primary locus of action is the family or the relations between two or three persons, whereas the larger sociopolitical context is most definitely implicated but is not the principal manifestation. This strategy distinguishes the magic realism of these first-world minority women from the genre's use by more canonical writers in Central and South America and the Caribbean, as well as by Rushdie, Kundera, and others. In contrast to these male-authored novels, in which political situations are often the principal focus, the present works foreground the social whole only indirectly. Thus, whenever the narrative logic is disrupted by otherwise unaccountable and disruptive events in an individual's life, especially by extreme physical violence, a larger frame of reference must be presupposed, pointing toward a social whole in which the events become, if not immediately meaningful, at least partially understandable. Paradoxically, then, magic realism reemerges as a potentially critical rather than complacent political force whenever the genre's synthetic devices fail or succeed only partially. To the extent to which the magic realist synthesis succeeds, a healing process is effectively allowed to begin. But unless this process leads to a situation of self-congratulatory forgetfulness, critical magic realism will force the reader again and again to consider the social and political conditions, leaving a whole range of contradictions unresolved.

CANADA AND ITS OTHERNESS

Unlike Latin American magic realism, literature from Canada, as the ally and partner of the United States, is not usually mistaken for an exotic other. Although Canada shares with the countries of Latin America a clearly subservient relation to its hegemonic hemispheric neighbor, it manages to view this relationship as a partnership between social and cultural equals. What the use of magic realism in Canada proves, however, is that the experience of this relationship is otherwise. How, then, does magic realism negotiate the intricacies of this particular relationship, and what is the larger cultural problematic that this use of magic realism entails?

Defining a distinctive Canadian identity has always been a problem. When describing Canadian culture, the immediate, ground-clearing impulse for many Canadians is always to begin with the self-effacing claim that it is not British, not French, and, most vehemently, not American culture. This vigorous beginning, however, often constitutes the entirety of the definition; in other words, there is nothing to grasp in Canadian identity, except this difference from others. The tendency to define and describe oneself strictly in terms of "others" produces, when examined directly, an effacement of that self.[13]

Two novels by the Canadian writer W. P. Kinsella, *Shoeless Joe* and *The Iowa Baseball Confederacy,* bear out this analysis of the connections between narrative genre and cultural identity.[14] Both novels scrupulously avoid any mention of Canada, both are set in the United States, and both are written in the genre of magic realism to treat the most American of pastimes: baseball. Just as with the "serious" component of playfulness, baseball here becomes the form through which to articulate and define the contemporary social and political reality. Baseball has traditionally been recognized as a legitimate venue for discussing metaphysical and philosophical issues. *Shoeless Joe* is no exception to this tradition. As one character in the novel explicitly points out, to talk of baseball is to talk "of love, and family, and life, and beauty, and friendship, and sharing" (*SJ* 215). However, the employment of the genre of magic realism to discuss the experiences of baseball adds a dimension to the pat identification of baseball and the United States, imprinting within the narrative the relationship between the United States and Canada.[15]

In these novels Kinsella takes the necessary fictitiousness of magic realist narratives and applies it to baseball, which turns out to be particularly susceptible to such treatment. The game is so conventional, so rule-bound and tradition-bound, so meticulously recorded down to the most obscure statistics, that even to write about it produces an unimpeachable reality effect, a recognizably separate world with its own logic and demands.

Like fiction, baseball is not subject to time because its duration is governed internally. It is played by men who are the eternal "boys of summer" represented by icons such as "shoeless" Joe Jackson. Baseball has developed a metaphysical mystique related to its peculiar properties. As Ray points out to J. D. Salinger, a character in *Shoeless Joe,* baseball and writing are both rituals. Baseball is the most statistic-bound of all sports. All significant actions are reduced to records, which are inscribed in the *Baseball Encyclopedia,* where the fetish of numbers immortalizes achievements in this sport's equivalent of both the Domesday Book and a Borgesian encyclopedia. Stories can be generated simply from the listing noted in the *Baseball Encyclopedia.* For example, a character named Moonlight Graham is created and included in *Shoeless Joe* because, despite his single, inauspicious appearance in a big-league game in 1908, he has become part of the seamless fabric of baseball. Within the world of baseball, there are no contradictions or anomalies; what links the players is the game, and that is sufficient.

We can also apply to baseball the rules of fiction with their seductive elegance and orderliness that stand as a tempting counterpart to sordid reality. In *Shoeless Joe,* the protagonist Ray muses, "baseball is the most perfect of games, solid, true, pure and precious as diamonds. If only life were so simple. . . . If only there was a framework to life, rules to live by" (*SJ* 78). Also like fiction, the possibilities within the parameters of the game are endless. Because baseball is the only sport that is not subject to time, there is always the possibility that the game may never end, which is the premise of *The Iowa Baseball Confederacy.* Nor is the game limited by spatial boundaries: nothing, theoretically, is excluded. The character Ray again: "Within the baselines anything can happen. Tides can reverse; oceans can open up. . . . Colors can change, lifes can alter, anything is possible in this gentle, flawless, loving game" (*SJ* 78). Finally, this possibility of infinite potential, like that of fiction or storytelling, enmeshes the world in one paradigm: "And the field runs to infinity. . . . The foul lines run on forever, forever diverging. There's no place in America that's not part of a major-league ballfield: the meanest ghetto, the highest point of land. . . . " The conclusion is inescapably logical: "Hell, there's no place in the *world* that's not part of a baseball field" (*IBC* 41).

Having said this, the statement about the purity of baseball turns out to be as false as the claim made for the purity of fiction. In Kinsella's magic realist treatment, baseball presents a symbol of history, figured in the icon of the diamond, as a flawless creation only marginally but imperviously affected by the "impurities" of class, gender, or racial struggles. Yet in that very purity it speaks to a history of violence, degradation, misery, alienation, and meaninglessness. Even the "purified" past of baseball is darkened and called into question, in *Shoeless Joe* by the Black Sox scandal, and in *Confederacy* by the legacy of white settlers' injustice in their dealings with Native Americans.[16]

The game of baseball today is played by highly paid professionals, mainly indoors, in climate-controlled stadiums, under artificial lights, and on artificial soil. But this too is part of Kinsella's theme. Baseball sustains its own myths, but not under conditions of its own choosing. The history of those conditions is also the history of the United States. The claims made for baseball's pristine, unstained traditions are nothing if not also ideological claims about the United States and its history. If in *Shoeless Joe* this history can be read (though not necessarily) as a pleasurable fiction, immersed in a gentle pastime, *The Iowa Baseball Confederacy* clearly reveals that baseball's harmonic hermeticism, like fiction's, is motivated, conditioned, and dialectically informed by external social conditions.

Kinsella's novels apply the unique logical possibilities of magic realism to the demands of time and space. It is not accidental that both of these novels present baseball in a rural setting, mainly in Iowa, breadbasket of the United States. Evoking the American heartland, baseball is supposed to represent the oldest American pastime with its simplicity and innocence. The action of these novels is located either in the farmland of Iowa or in the past; in other words, it is dislocated away from the obvious centers of political and economic power. But the very act of dislocation reorganizes space and time, overdetermining them with meaning, forcing an awareness that the particular space and time represented by rural Iowa are a microcosm for greater social forces. In discussions of Canadian magic realism, the relationships of power are described as an antagonism between heartland and hinterland, a variant of the core and periphery opposition that on a global scale encompasses also the relations between the first and third worlds.

The charged and animate landscape of magic realism is not fantastical for its own sake. Rather, it is the trace and register of social practice itself, infused with significance without being fetishized or alienated. The dislocation of space and time is analogous to Michel de Certeau's distinction between place and space.[17] There is not a distinction between the natural land and the cultural practice on it, say between subsistence farming and corporate farming. Rather, it is a distinction between a dominant practice of the land (how it fits smoothly in with all the other land) and a rupture in that unbroken practice: an "improper" use that draws attention to the "proper" use. Place is the "proper" organization of positions that is transformed by practice into space. For Certeau, what is "proper" is inert and stable, undermined when "space" is produced, which literally marks the "proper" as a foreign space. The setting of *Shoeless Joe* in rural Iowa draws attention to the overwhelming presence of land, and the checkerboard farm fields are almost an overdetermined version of Certeau's "proper" space.

Kinsella's second baseball novel, *The Iowa Baseball Confederacy*, treats space not as layered but as jagged and discontinuous, a messy grinding that generates both history and forgetting. Instead of the assault by urban and corporate interests on the farming heartland, we now have a tale that addresses the original transformation of the land. Certeau's "space" is historicized in a new way.

The narrative deals with a small-town insurance salesman from Onamata, Iowa, Gideon Clark, who tries in vain to prove the existence of a baseball league that existed in Iowa in the first decade of the twentieth century. Moreover, an all-star team from this league played a game of biblical proportions against the then professional league-leading Chicago Cubs. For some reason the game has been wiped from any record or memory and exists only in the mind of Gideon's father. The original town of Big Inning and the events that took place in that town only retain existence in his father's mind, who then spends a lifetime trying to convince others of its existence, including petitioning the main figures in the league and writing a dissertation that is rejected as outrageous fabrication (but is recommended for a degree in creative writing). Upon the suicidal death of his father from despair, Gideon imbibes instantaneously from him the knowledge of the complete history of the no longer existent league and town, as well as the quest to prove its existence. On the eve of a July Fourth, birth date of the nation, Gideon goes back in time to the "birth" of Onamata, which is also the "death" or disappearance of Big Inning.

At stake behind the actual game is the effort of an Indian named Drifting Away, who haunts the land to reclaim his love, Onamata, who was killed by white settlers. The game was dreamed by Drifting Away early in his life and becomes fulfilled as a spiritual test, lasting over forty days in torrential rain, which ends with the town of Big Inning disappearing and being replaced by the town of Onamata. The practice of the land is literally deconstructed in this story, as we see it revert to its original name with the accompanying historical guilt of white settlement. Big Inning is the completion of the nineteenth-century settlement of the West; the name changes to Onamata early in the twentieth century, the birth of the modern era.

To replay this baseball game is at once an act of memory and a fiction. The reenactment becomes a way to revisit the historical site of a trauma of the social psyche. The change in name from the original Big Inning to Onamata is an attempt to forget the past as it was lived, to rewrite the unevenness of the historical change as a continuity, and to efface the guilt of that discontinuity. The new name, Onamata, Drifting Away's murdered wife, becomes a signifier both of history and of traumatic displacement. *Confederacy* treats the past as a text to be resuscitated, brought to life, and assimilated into experience. And baseball provides the framework that allows this consciousness to be actuated, as J. D. Salinger, the character, says to Ray: "I don't have to tell you that the one constant through all the years has been baseball. America has been erased like a blackboard, only to be rebuilt and then erased again. But baseball has marked time [while] America has rolled by like a procession of steamrollers" (*SJ* 213).

In fact, beyond the libidinal "space," in Certeau's sense, of the immediate farm, which is crossed with the history of settling it, from ranchers to farmers and now potentially corporations, the wider cultural "place" of the United States is also made significant. The baseball odyssey undertaken by Ray in *Shoeless Joe*, during which he visits several major league parks on his quest, offers a depressing image of the American cultural landscape. Each of the stadiums Ray visits, in Chicago, Cleveland, and Boston, is located in the middle of a bleak, violence-permeated, run-down neighborhood. Baseball is a tremendously expensive sport that, in its present incarnation, can take place only in major metropolitan centers. Baseball stands as the interface between a model of history as a timeless paradigm of practice and the social contingency of everyday life. Thus, baseball in these stories not only mediates between fluffy fantasy and hard reality, firm timeless structure and grimy transitory chaos, but also presents an escapist world as one that to get to, literally requires a willful blindness and an acceptance of guilt. *Confederacy*'s narrative articulates this theme forcefully and systematically with the disappearance and reappearance of the small town. Moreover, in *Confederacy*, the big city is kept offstage. The Cubs arrive from Chicago, from where telegrams and orders are also received, but we never see the city or any part of the outside world. It is pointedly eliminated to highlight the importance of time (history) rather than of space.

For this reason *Confederacy* relies more on the biblical evocations, introducing the apocalyptic into the game, not only in the forty-day span of the game but also in the Black Angel who plays in the game, and players who are struck by lightning or carried away by the flood. In *Shoeless Joe,* the world of baseball is distinguished more as the privileged mode of fiction. Its critique of cultural values is consciously presented as an amalgamation of prototypical American stories, juxtaposing textualities to create a fictional space.[18] Together, these apparently unrelated narratives form a patchwork quilt of shiny fantasy, eager innocence, hauntingly accurate depiction of experience, and murderous violence. In Certeau's terms, Kinsella's narrative transforms the "proper" use of literature, creating the "improper" network that defines magic realism.

The same is more subtly presented by the epigraph of *Shoeless Joe,* which is a quote from Bobby Kennedy: "Some men see things as they are, and say why, I dream of things that never were, and say why not." The ethos of magic realism contained in this statement is undercut only by the historical knowledge of what happened to Kennedy (and, perhaps, to the sixties), and the knowledge that what always lies behind dreaming, or baseball, the conditions that determine and infuse its provocative power, are money and power. The death of Kennedy also signifies the end of a certain moment of politics, and although this quote celebrates the liberating power of dreaming, it also alerts us to the conditions of violence and injustice that call it forth in the first place.

The final question is, what does any of this have to do with Canada or Canadian concerns, given that this section has centered on two novels about the American game, set in the heartland of America, featuring the personal struggles of a few not even remotely Canadian characters? But although Canada is not even mentioned, the use of magic realism is itself a genre that inscribes Canada–

United States relations. These novels present baseball as a cultural paradigm that must be experienced at one remove from daily life, mediated by various circumstances, most prominently (and probably most fundamentally in an absolute schema of consciousness) those of time and space themselves. The magically and historically charged settings of *Shoeless Joe* and *Confederacy* confront the reader with a different world presented as the same. In effect, the magic realist treatment of baseball in these novels creates the distancing from American culture that is concretely in place in the Canadian experience of American culture: we can call this the materiality of being Canadian. For Canadians, after all, the workings of American culture are both familiar and foreign, something to contemplate without necessarily identifying with (much like Ray's relationship with Shoeless Joe himself).

Confederacy does not allow this point as clearly as *Shoeless Joe*. *Confederacy*'s ripping open of history in the treatment of Native Americans by the United States holds true for Canada's treatment of its native population, so the distinction between the United States and Canada would be irrelevant in this case. Both are implicated in the same eradication of memory, the difference being that in Canada the eradication has been more successful.

But *Shoeless Joe* establishes such a position clearly. The narrator, Ray Kinsella, namesake of the author, is also given an identical twin brother, Richard, who cannot in any way be distinguished from Ray. He looks the same down to a scar over one eye. From the outside, they look completely alike, but somehow they are not. Both exist on the margins, connected in some way to the end of the cultural spectrum associated with the spectacle: Ray as a farmer with a magical baseball game and Richard as part of a circus. But their relationship to this aspect of culture is different. Richard, in his role of circus barker, describes the nature of his kind of cultural practice: "This is carnival. People pay to be disappointed" (*SJ* 175). Diametrically opposed to this image of degraded and alienated magic is Ray's hallowed baseball field and game. The only difference between these identical twins is that Ray can see the magical baseball game that takes place in his cornfield every evening, whereas Richard cannot. There is more at stake, however, than baseball holding out the nonalienated alternative space to the consumer-oriented spectacle represented by the circus.

The relationship between the two brothers, or rather the difference in their experiences and perceptions, stands as emblematic of the relationship between the United States and Canada. It would not be fair to locate the Canadian content of Kinsella's novels in the unfallen world of Ray's backyard ballpark. In the end, moreover, the magical field rather lamely becomes the means to save Ray's farm, as people come to visit the ballpark and spend money, unconsciously guided by deep, unspoken urgings. Thus the magical world folds back into the degraded world of consumerism. The (almost) unperceivable difference between the two brothers, however, is part of the same thematic of dislocation and distantiation that runs through both stories. To name explicitly the violence at the edge of magic is to be positioned in an outsider's perspective, like the Canadian perspective on American culture. Magic realism, then, is the generic device to register the experience of difference in a situation where there is no apparent difference, inscribing what can only be acknowledged as fiction, in the double sense of constructed and nonexistent. Magic realism in Canada is the means to formulate a critical distance that just does not appear to be there; it produces not only a charged and libidinized space but also a language for accounting for something that is not seen but is nonetheless experienced and known.

CONCLUSION

In the two series of texts under discussion here, the function of magic realism as a genre or narrative mode seems to be inverted. In Kinsella's novels, the magic realist treatment of baseball provides a framework of gentle and loving, almost unreal perfection, only surreptitiously undercut by the return to memories of violence and exploitation. In the novels of Morrison, Hulme, and Naylor, on the contrary, excruciating physical violence is everywhere only precariously tempered by the attempts at harmony of magic realism. Taken together, both cases in fact represent the inevitable double bind behind the politics of magic realism, which oscillate between passivity and radicality, criticism and complacency. This common double bind is emblematically inscribed in these novels through a phenomenon that becomes something of an incarnation of magic realism's role in the articulation of identity and difference in relation to some notion of totality: the scar.

What might be needed, then, to understand the political and ideological functions of magic realism is a poetics of the scar. A visible, physical trace of past wounds suffered by the body, the scar always represents the site of an in-between: above all, between nature and history, and between past and present. Tokens of inscription, scars literally define what is the body politic. Like magic realism, scars also bind together the natural and the supernatural, as in the case of the stigmata, which mark at once the boundary and the point of contact between mortals and immortals, the secular and the divine. Finally, scars serve the purpose of establishing both continuity and identity, as in the scene of recognition at the end of the *Odyssey*, when the house nurse Euryclea identifies the stranger as Odysseus through the presence of a scar on his thigh.[19]

Indissociable from the wounds of the flesh, scars embody individual and historical memory. Unlike symptoms, moreover, scars never lie, even though their meaning is susceptible to continuous reinterpretations. At the same time, they also mark the beginning and partial completion of a healing process. The inscription of scars thus sketches out the possibility of a meaningful totality, without erasing the historical traces of underlying rifts.[20]

Like the scars of Beloved, Simon, and Kerewin, magic realism is a tender suture that enables the wounded to look forward to a different future while remembering the painful distress of the past. According to whether the main focus is the scar, the wound, or the healing that has already taken place between them, the political stand inherent to magic realism would then be either critical or mystificatory, or both at once. The critical value of magic realism is lost precisely when a person or social group loses sight of the scars, pretending as if there never even had been so much as a wound. This is what happened in Hollywood, for example, to the twin brothers Ray and Richard: in Kinsella's *Shoeless Joe*, they are indistinguishable except for Richard's scar, whereas in the American film version, *Field of Dreams*, by an uncannily accurate instinct, Ray's scarred brother has been eliminated altogether.

130   ·   BRUNO BOSTEELS, LORIS MIRELLA, AND PETER A. SCHILLING

NOTES

1. Michel Foucault, "What Is Enlightenment?" trans. Catherine Porter, *The Foucault Reader,* ed. Paul Rabinow (New York: Pantheon Books, 1984), p. 47.

2. Among Latin-Americanists, the debate has largely been confined to the generic issue. The definitive collection of essays here is *Otros mundos, otros fuegos: Fantasía y realismo mágico en Iberoamérica,* ed. Donald A. Yates (East Lansing: Michigan State University, Latin American Studies Center, 1975).

3. For similar criticisms against the identification of third-world literature with magic realism, and of the latter with Latin America, see Gayatri Chakravorty Spivak, *Outside in the Teaching Machine* (New York: Routledge, 1993), pp. 57-59.

4. A detailed comparative account of magic realism in a wide variety of places is the collection *Le réalisme magique: Roman, Peinture et cinéma,* ed. Jean Weisgerber (Lausanne: L'Age d'Homme, 1987). For painting, see also Seymour Menton, *Magic Realism Rediscovered 1918-1981* (Philadelphia: The Art Alliance Press-Associated University Presses, 1983).

5. Theodor W. Adorno, *Minima Moralia,* trans. E. F. N. Jephcott (London: Verso, 1974), p. 142.

6. Slavoj Zizek, *Everything You Always Wanted to Know about Lacan (But Were Afraid to Ask Hitchcock)* (London: Verso, 1992), p. 261.

7. Fredric Jameson, "Magical Narratives: On the Dialectical Use of Genre Criticism," in *The Political Unconscious: Narrative as a Socially Symbolic Act* (Ithaca: Cornell University Press, 1981), p. 104. In the genealogy of romance that Jameson outlines in cursory fashion (ibid., pp. 130-35), magic realism would be, like the modern fantastic, our time's answer to "the question of what, under wholly altered historical circumstances, can have been found to replace the raw materials of magic and Otherness which medieval romance found ready to hand in its socioeconomic environment" (ibid., p. 131). For an excellent study of the persistence of romance in Latin America, see Doris Sommer, "Irresistible Romance: The Foundational Fictions of Latin America," in *Nation and Narration,* ed. Homi K. Bhabha (London: Routledge, 1990), pp. 70-98, and *Foundational Fictions: The National Romances of Latin America* (Berkeley: University of California Press, 1991).

8. Jameson, "On Magic Realism in Film," in *Signatures of the Visible* (New York: Routledge, 1990), p. 150. This essay was originally published in *Critical Inquiry* 12 (1986): 301-25. A more recent statement is to be found in Jameson's essay "On Soviet Magic Realism," in *The Geopolitical Aesthetic: Cinema and Space in the World System* (Bloomington: Indiana University Press, 1992), pp. 87-113.

9. Jameson, "On Magic Realism in Film," p. 138. In this sense, too, magic realism is a contemporary variant of romance, whose "ultimate condition of figuration . . . is to be found in a transitional moment in which two distinct modes of production, or moments of socioeconomic development, coexist. Their antagonism is not yet articulated in terms of the struggle of social classes, so that its resolution can be projected in the form of a nostalgic (or less often, a Utopian) harmony" ("Magical Narratives," p. 148).

10. An excellent summary of the formal and ontological presuppositions behind magic realism, the cover of this glossy brochure, *The Great Plan: Holidays guaranteed by Aeroméxico* (*Gran Plan: Vacaciones con la garantía de Aeroméxico*), shows two parallel pictures of a young couple standing next to a small hut and palm trees, looking over to the horizon, which becomes visible only at the left end of the pictures on the back cover: the first picture is called "Illusion" (*La ilusión*), the second, "Reality" (*La realidad*). With only a thin strip of white space separating them, both pictures are, of course, exactly identical. Or, is one of them, perhaps, like Menard's *Quixote*, almost infinitely richer? On the cover, in any case, the viewer is teased into detecting a disjunction where none seems to exist; once inside the brochure, on the contrary, interested tourists are made to believe that none of the existing disjunctions will disrupt their joyful holiday experience.

11. Jameson, "Magical Narratives," pp. 111-12. This hypothesis is informed by Martin Heidegger's analysis of the "worldhood of the world" in *Being and Time,* trans. John Macquarrie and Edward Robinson (New York: Harper & Row, 1962), pp. 102-7.

12. Gloria Naylor, *Mama Day* (New York: Ticknor and Field, 1988); Toni Morrison, *Beloved* (New York: Alfred A. Knopf, 1987); Keri Hulme, *The Bone People* (Baton Rouge: Louisiana State University Press, 1983). Subsequent references will be given in the text.

13. This uneasy relationship with the self is reflected in Canadian literature and film, not only thematically but also formally, through specific generic strategies used to inscribe cultural experience. In painting, for example, the use of photorealism by artists such as Alex Colville and Ken Danby carefully eliminates any trace of human intervention or involvement. The same point can be made about the dominant film practice in Canada: the documentary tradition, for which Canadians are recognized internationally, is a genre based on the objective presentation of material, which accepts as one condition of its validity the minimal noninterference of the filmmaker with the material. Both these cultural forms share an impulse toward the effacement of agency or protagonist in favor of an uncentered effort to record. What the following discussion of magic realism shows is that the Canadian cultural impulse toward the effacement of agency is a dialectical articulation of the social, political, and historical conditions that enjoin effacement.

14. W. P. Kinsella, *Shoeless Joe* (Boston: Houghton Mifflin, 1982), and *The Iowa Baseball Confederacy* (Boston: Houghton Mifflin, 1986). Subsequent references will be given in the text (*SJ* and *IBC*). For further analyses, see, for example, the special issue of *Modern Fiction Studies* 33 (1987) dedicated to modern sports fiction, especially Richard Alan Schwartz, "Postmodern Baseball" (pp. 135-49), and Neil Randall, "*Shoeless Joe*: Fantasy and the Humor of Fellow-Feeling" (pp. 173-82). More recent expressions of magic realism in Canada are the focus of *Magic Realism and Canadian Literature: Essays and Stories* (Waterloo, Ontario: University of Waterloo Press, 1986).

15. This may be a good place to illustrate this theme. Last year's World Series was won by the Toronto Blue Jays, the first non-U.S. team to win the treasured American prize. The significant fact lies not in the status of Toronto as a Canadian city but in the lack of any Canadian players on the team. In actuality, much of the team's strength comes from recruitment in the Dominican Republic, proof that baseball links the various nations of the Americas together. In general, only a very small percentage of that Toronto team (whether non-American or American players) could name the capital of Canada.

16. An earlier short story by Kinsella called "The Battery" is a magic realist baseball tale set in the Dominican Republic. This story reminds us that the interests of big business carry over into the imperialistic oppression of the impoverished inhabitants of the other American countries from which baseball draws players. The concerns articulated through the discussion of baseball impact on the social field. Baseball is a fiction or construct, but it is also a model of social and political interaction.

17. Michel de Certeau, *The Practice of Everyday Life*, trans. Steven Rendall (Berkeley: University of California Press, 1984), p. 117.

18. These are *The Wizard of Oz*, a political allegory set in a children's story, complete with a movement from rural Kansas to sophisticated Emerald City. Salinger's *The Catcher in the Rye*, perhaps the definitive story of growing up in America, is a story of youth and loss ironically appropriate to an evocation of baseball, but a story that has transcended its boundaries to be mistaken frequently for reality; therefore it is a touchstone for the theme. Salinger himself is made present as a tribute to his skill, but he disappears with the players at the end (as a reminder that this is a fiction). And Truman Capote's *In Cold Blood* is a story of calculated violence and invasion by irrational forces into the countryside, which impressed its original audience with its gripping authenticity.

19. The classical reading of this scene is of course Erich Auerbach's "Odysseus' Scar," in *Mimesis: The Representation of Reality in Western Literature*, trans. Willard R. Trask (Princeton: Princeton University Press,

1953), pp. 3-23. Upon reading Auerbach's explanations about "the basic impulse of the Homeric style," namely, "to represent phenomena in their fully externalized form, visible and palpable in all their parts, and completely fixed in their spatial and temporal relations," the reader might perceive uncanny proximities with magic realism, especially with the original "new objectivity" of magic realist paintings described by Franz Roh.

20. A scar is in this sense comparable to the word used by Martin Heidegger to describe the origin of the work of art: *Riß,* meaning both "rift" and "outline," at once incommensurable "crack" and informal "sketch." See "The Origin of the Work of Art," in *Basic Writings,* ed. David Farrell Krell (New York: HarperCollins, 1993), pp. 143-212.

III

Boundary Anxieties

Introduction to Part III

MICHAEL J. SHAPIRO

Although the thinkers comprising the political theory canon from the seventeenth through nineteenth centuries have been largely complicit in the production of a state sovereignty political discourse, they have nevertheless often expressed significant ambivalence about political boundaries. They have recognized, as William Connolly's essay in this section shows, that boundaries both secure protection from violence and constitute a form of violence. Emphasizing Tocqueville's struggle with his ambivalence toward boundaries, Connolly suggests that it provides an exemplary and edifying case of the limits of a traditional pluralist imagination. Tocqueville ultimately resolves his ambivalence in favor of the European destruction of indigenous peoples.

After reviewing this catastrophic resolution, Connolly's text reasserts the nomadic, boundary-challenging tendencies that are subdued in Tocqueville's text. Especially important is Connolly's treatment of Thoreau's attempt to become bicultural. To extend Thoreau's incomplete appreciation of indigenous culture, Connolly produces an imagined encounter between Thoreau and William Apess, the son of Pequots, who articulated a political statement for nomadic indigenes against the civi-territorial discourses of the conquering Europeans.

Connolly makes clear that a politics of democratic pluralization must deterritorialize and refigure the civi-territorial, bordered world instead of simply practicing tolerance within its jurisdictions. His gestures toward a conceptual unmapping of the political world invented in Europe and shaped in the United States is pursued in Kennan Ferguson's analysis of U.S. foreign policy. With the disintegration of the political cartography of the Cold War period, global cultural mapping is becoming increasingly salient.

Ferguson shows that the dominant multiculturalism discourses of academia and the media have tended to re-create the geostrategic map rather than producing a cultural pluralism capable of unmapping the traditional global imaginary of U.S. dominance. Like Connolly, Ferguson seeks to introduce a more pervasive political pluralism into the global map. Among other things, this requires a resituating of the concept of aesthetics. For a culture to be given significant political recognition, it must be understood that people's artistic expressions do not simply decorate a world that precedes them; they make the world.

Sankaran Krishna's essay echoes a theme central to Ferguson's, the anxiety that attends instabilities in national and global cartographies. In the United States, cartographic anxiety is tied to the disappearance of the Soviet Union and therefore to the dissolution of an unambiguous security problematic. In India, it is part of a contestation over boundaries that has persisted since nationhood. The Indian civic body has never been stabilized or domesticated. Krishna's treatment makes evident the centrality of cartography or imagined political space to national politics. In India, as elsewhere, current turbulence involves nothing less than the morphology and destiny of the national body.

As a result of all three essays in this section, we are able to see global space as ambiguous, contested, and temporally unstable. Modern maps are wholly inadequate to such comprehensions. Ironically, the maps of various tribes of indigenous peoples of the Americas, peoples whom the conquering Europeans failed to recognize as coherent cultures, were dynamic rather than static. They included pictorial narratives that demonstrated the contested history of spaces rather than fetishizing victories with the fixed jursidictional lines common to present maps.[1] The essays in this section are functional equivalents of such indigenous cartographies, for they render mobile, fragile, and contestable what traditional political discourses tend to naturalize, pacify, and dehistoricize.

NOTES

1. Gordon Brotherston, *Book of the Fourth World* (New York: Cambridge University Press, 1993).

5

Tocqueville, Territory, and Violence

WILLIAM E. CONNOLLY

THE AMBIGUITY OF BOUNDARIES

Boundaries abound. Between humanity and the gods. Between human and animal. Between culture and nature. Between sexual intercourse and rape. Between genders, nations, peoples, times, races, classes, and territories. But boundaries have also become problematic today, perhaps more so than before. In a world experienced by many to be without a natural design to which we might conform, the function of boundaries becomes highly ambiguous. Boundaries form indispensable protections against violation and violence, but the divisions they sustain in doing so also carry cruelty and violence. Boundaries provide preconditions of identity, individual agency, and collective action, but they also close off possibilities of being that might otherwise flourish. Boundaries both foster and inhibit freedom; they both protect and violate life.

The political question is how to come to terms with the ambiguity of boundaries, how to fight against their sacrifices and violences without sacrificing their advantages altogether.

Moses, in *The Book of J* version of Exodus, struggles with the ambiguity of boundaries. He must respect the boundary between himself and Yahweh while bridging it to represent the word of Yahweh to his people, indeed bridging the boundary in order to help constitute his people. And he must represent Yahweh authoritatively to consolidate his people. It seems clear that Yahweh too struggles with the ambiguity

141

of boundaries. "The houses of Egypt will be full, their floors will be one with the land: hidden under flies. That day I will distinguish the borders of Goshen—the land my people squat upon—to be untouched by flies, so you may know I am Yahweh, here on earth. I will put borders between your people and mine—by tomorrow this marking will be plain."[1] The flies at once mark the boundary between two peoples, the power of Yahweh over humanity, the Egyptians as a people selected for special punishment, and the Israelites as the people of Yahweh. Does the very awesomeness of the power required to establish these boundaries testify to their artificial, precarious, ambiguous character?

The most dangerous moment for boundaries may occur when Yahweh descends to Mount Sinai and Moses ascends to meet him. A gift is being transmitted, but its mode of transmission threatens to destroy it. The line between the giver and the recipient must be sacred, for this is the source, the law of laws, upon which laws are grounded. But the division between the sacred and the mundane must also be breached if the sacred gift is to be transmitted. Yahweh becomes nervous and demanding at this moment:

> Descend, hold the people's attention: they must not be drawn to Yahweh to destroy boundaries. Bursting through to see, they will fall, many will die.[2]

Moses, this ambiguous carrier of sacred gifts who speaks with a stammer and bears an Egyptian name, is well equipped to appreciate the ambiguity of boundaries. He responds to the ambiguity of boundaries first by accepting the gift from Yahweh, then by smashing it against the mountain, and then by accepting it again. He responds to his people first by leading, then by repudiating, and then by leading again. His recognition of ambiguity takes the form of discrete acts separated by time, two for and one against. It is when we collapse this temporal boundary between acts that we can discern ambiguity in the reception of boundaries. Is there a better way to respond to the ambiguity of boundaries?

Rousseau, writing centuries later, honors Moses as one of three "legislators" in history who knew how to found a people (Numa and Lycurgus are the other two). Moses is the most admirable of the three according to Rousseau's backhanded compliment, for he founded a people "out of a swarm of wretched fugitives" who did not yet inhabit a territory they could call their own:

He founded the body of a nation, using for his materials a swarm of wretched fugitives who possessed no skills, no arms, no talents, no virtues and no courage, and who without an inch of territory to call their own, were truly a troop of outcasts upon the face of the earth. Moses made bold to transform this herd of servile emigrants into a political society, a free people; at a moment when it was still wandering about in the wilderness . . . Even today, when that nation no longer exists as a body, its legislation endures and is as strong as ever.[3]

Rousseau, who recognizes the fundamental ambiguity involved in the founding of a people,[4] is nonetheless reluctant to emphasize its continuing effects once a good founding has occurred. His drive to political unity discourages him from politicizing the ambiguity he recognizes all too well. Indeed, in the essay on Poland where Moses is introduced, Rousseau is hell-bent on separating the people now in question—the Poles—as thoroughly as possible from other peoples. He wants the strategies of "Moses"—roughly, weighing the people "down with rites and peculiar ceremonies" and "countless prohibitions"[5]—to be combined with the advantage of inhabiting a common territory. He wants, that is, to overcode the difference between the Poles and other peoples—to do so in order to make them a free people. It is good that the Poles have a large territory to themselves:

But so large a country, and one that has never had much intercourse with its neighbours, must have developed a great many usages that are its very own, but are perhaps being bastardized, day in and day out, in line with the Europe-wide tendency to take on the tastes and customs of the French. You must maintain or revive (as the case may be) your ancient customs and introduce suitable new ones that will also be purely Polish. Let these new customs . . . even have their bad points; they would, unless bad in principle, still afford this advantage: *they would endear Poland to its citizens and develop in them a distinctive distaste for mingling with the peoples of other countries.* I deem it all to the good, for example, that the Poles have a distinctive mode of dress.[6]

The line of correspondences is clear: to be free you must belong to a people; to be a people you must have a common identity burned into you; to be a flourishing people you must exclusively inhabit a contiguous territory; to flourish freely as a territorialized people you must stringently limit contact with the foreign. Wandering, disturbance, and plurality must be repressed along a variety of dimensions.

Rousseau underlines the centrality of territory to the constitution and protection of a people in *The Social Contract:*

> It is understandable how the combined lands of private individuals become public territory, and how the right of sovereignty, *extending from the subjects to the ground they occupy,* comes to include both property and persons . . . This advantage does not appear to have been well understood by ancient kings who, only calling themselves kings of the Persians, the Scythians, the Macedonians, seem to have considered themselves leaders of men rather than masters of the country. Today's kings more cleverly call themselves Kings of France, Spain, England, etc. *By thus holding the land, they are quite sure to hold its inhabitants.*[7]

This series of correspondences between people, territory, state, unity, freedom, and legitimacy has been fractured in recent centuries through the international commerce of people, things, and ideas, but it has yet to be reconfigured significantly in either the dominant theories of politics circulating through Western states or in the political cultures prevailing in them. In fact, the accelerated circulation of people, communications, cultural dispositions, things, and currencies across state boundaries often fosters reactive movements of nationalism and fundamentalism that are extremely violent toward heterogeneity inside and outside their regimes.

Evidence of the violence in these inscriptions keeps returning, even in the etymology of territory. "Territory," the *Oxford English Dictionary* says, is presumed by most moderns to derive from *terra. Terra* means land, earth, nourishment, sustenance; it conveys the sense of a sustaining medium, solid, fading off into indefiniteness. But the form of the word, the *OED* says, suggests that it derives from *terrere,* meaning to frighten, to terrorize. And *territorium* is a "a place from which people are warned." Perhaps these two contending derivations continue to occupy territory today. To occupy a territory is to receive sustenance and to exercise violence. Territory is land occupied by violence.

THE CIVI-TERRITORIAL COMPLEX

Alexis de Tocqueville is a Rousseauian pluralist.[8] As pluralist, he celebrates an un-Rousseauian diversity. As Rousseauian, he insists that underlying this diversity must be a common identity, a fixed "civilization" burned into the mores of the people. As pluralist, he is more alert than Rousseau to violences engendered by boundaries; as Rousseauian, he becomes resigned to these violences by de-moralizing them. Tocqueville in these ways registers latent ambiguities residing in those forms of pluralism preceding and succeeding him in the West.

Let us concentrate on the "Indian" in Tocqueville's "America."[9] Tocqueville knows that the North American continent was not devoid of human life before Europeans arrived. Consider a couple of statements:

These vast wildernesses were not completely unvisited by man; for centuries some nomads had lived under the dark forests or the meadows of the prairies.

The Indians occupied but did not possess the land. It is by agriculture that man wins the soil.

North America was only inhabited by wandering tribes who had not thought of exploiting the natural wealth of the soil. One could still properly call North America an empty continent, a deserted land waiting for inhabitants.[10]

If the nomads merely visited the land, if isolated tribes wandered on its surface under the forest wilderness, if they occupied but did not possess the land upon which they wandered, if they failed to win it through agri-culture, to master the land or to exploit its natural wealth, then it is *proper* "to call North America an empty continent, a deserted land *waiting* for *inhabitants*." Civilization and territory thus become intercoded through Tocqueville: agri-culture, mastery, possession, exploiting natural wealth, and applying the experience of fifty centuries to the land constitute crucial elements of civilization, and civilization establishes itself by taking possession of a contiguous territory and becoming possessed by it. Tocqueville registers, then, in carefully crafted language, the construction of "America," a civi-territorial complex in which the crucial dimensions of territory and civilization reinforce each other until they accumulate enough force together to propel the "triumphal progress of civilization across the wilderness."[11] What of those wandering nomads who are, well, not dispossessed from territory they never possessed but displaced from a wilderness upon which they wandered? Tocqueville disposes of them sadly and regretfully.

Christian monotheism provides the cultural glue binding the civi-territorial complex together. It does not matter whether everyone truly believes the Christian faith, only that it is professed generally:

> In the United States it is not only mores that are controlled by religion, but its sway extends over reason . . . [T]here are some who profess Christian dogmas because they believe them and others do so because they are afraid to look as though they did not believe in them. So Christianity reigns without obstacles, by universal consent; consequently, as I have said elsewhere, everything in the moral field is certain and fixed, although the world of politics seems given over to argument and experiment.[12]

Tocquevillian pluralism floats on the surface of the civi-theo-territorial complex. There is a mild pluralization of ethnic groups, religious congregations within Christianity, local customs, and forms of governance. And democratic politics forms the only positive no-madic element in the Tocquevillian world. But politics is free to dance lightly on the surface of life only because everything fundamental is fixed below it. The American imaginary is determined outside of politics. "Thus while the law allows the American people to do everything; there are things which religion prevents them from imagining and forbids them to become . . . Religion, which never intervenes directly in the government of American society, should therefore be considered as the first of their political institutions."[13]

Separation of church and state does not render the state neutral with respect to religion, nor does it sanction significant religious diversity. The superficial faiths of the nomads, for instance, remain outside this zone of tolerance. So does the profession of atheism, which, as Tocqueville notes without dismay, effectively rules one out of public office, probably because those who contend "that everything perishes with the body . . . must be regarded as the natural enemies of the people."[14] Rather, the separation of church and state allows monotheism to install its effects in the hearts of the people and the presumptions of their institutions below the threshold of political debate. The mores of civilization precede, ground, pervade, and confine politics.

Once patriotism is tracked onto religion, mores, reason, imagination, civilization, and territory, the terrain upon which pluralist democracy moves has been fixed. One can also locate the spaces through which democratic sovereignty circulates. "The principle of sovereignty of the people, which is always to be found, more or less, at the bottom of almost all human institutions, usually remains buried there."[15] In most cultures, prior to America, sovereignty appeared to reside in the king while it "more or less" flowed to the king from its hidden source in the people. Sovereignty, that is, was located nowhere exactly but circulated secretly and uncertainly between its official site and its unofficial source. In the new American pluralism this uncertainty remains, but now sovereignty circulates uncertainly between the will of the people and the civi-theo-territorial complex that constitutes them. For "the people" can be officially sovereign in America only because those human beings who diverge from the essence of civilization have been displaced from the land they previously wandered over and because the territorialization of civilization itself sets the parameters of popular sovereignty. The exact site of sovereignty (the people or the civilization that shapes its imagination) remains as uncertain in Tocqueville's America as it does in every theory or culture preceding and succeeding him; it is the spaces through which this uncertainty circulates that have shifted.

The historical consolidation of the civi-territorial complex requires the elimination of the Indian. Because this complex sets conditions of possibility of morality itself, Tocqueville finds it impossible to judge the extermination/colonization of the Indian to be immoral. He has not acquired the powers of imagination, best exemplified by Nietzsche, to probe the "injustice in justice" or the "immorality of morality." How, then, does Tocqueville come to terms with this violence that is both undeserved and exceeds the territory of morality? Tocqueville implicitly struggles with this dilemma by repeatedly using phrases such as "ill-fated," "unfortunate people," "unlucky people" to characterize the victims of this cultural violence. He also repeatedly regrets the "inevitable destruction" bound up with the "stubborn prejudices" of the "savages" and the "chance" that "has brought" two diverse "stocks together on the same soil."[16] This slippery language of regret without moral indictment and, more significantly, of the recognition of undeserved suffering without a plan to curtail it in the future places a heavy burden on this staunch defender of a civilization of moral uprighteousness, solid mores, and deep convictions. For this violence must not be defined as unjust even though it cannot be defined as just. Anything that sets the preconditions of moral virtue must not itself be immoral, according to the implicit dictum guiding Tocqueville's prose. The drive to struggle against the injustice in justice, at any rate, remains outside both the moral imagination of Alexis de Tocqueville and the culture registered through his imagination. The Indian is thus simultaneously the first Other of the civi-territorial complex, the first sign of violence inscribed in its boundaries, and the first marker of how violence is obscured by the complex that requires it.

Tocqueville, I have already suggested, cautiously vindicates a nomadic movement inscribed in the *politics* of pluralism itself. But before this modest nomadism can be installed, the fundamental nomadism of the Indian must be purged. What happens, though, when Tocqueville encounters new nomadic elements *within* the civilization he admires, modes of mobility that are both indispensable to the civilization he celebrates and dangerous to the boundaries it requires? What about money, goods, labor, capital, and entrepreneurial activity, for instance? These mobile media flow across territorial boundaries rather freely; they exceed the effective control of sovereign power, even while it depends on them to provide it with material sustenance. I suspect that the very pressures toward centralization of the state Tocqueville decries so much in volume 2 of *Democracy in America* flow from attempts by the state to control those internal (and yet also external) nomadic elements it cannot expel from the civilization. And I suspect that Tocqueville's later pessimism about the future of democracy is bound up with his inability to imagine a viable response to forms of nomadism that are neither eliminable by, nor very consonant with, the civi-territorial complex he imagines. I will not pursue these latter suspicions. Rather, I will ask, What orientation to the boundaries of pluralism and the pluralism of boundaries might be more responsive in the future to the nomadic element in politics? Is it possible to imagine boundaries to pluralism that are not impelled to eliminate the Indians they engender?

TOCQUEVILLE, THOREAU, APESS

Have I wrenched Tocqueville "out of context"? (As if a context were not always the dissonant conjunction of contemporary issues and the time and place interrogated.) Consider, in the context of my concerns, Henry Thoreau, a nineteenth-century citizen in this same civi-mono-national-territorial complex. In "The Allegash and East Branch," written a couple of decades after *Democracy in America*,

Thoreau reviews his canoeing trip with an Indian guide, Joe Polis. "Polis" or "the Indian"—the two labels through which Thoreau identifies the guide—seems to fit Tocqueville's characterization when Thoreau and he negotiate on the white man's ground. And Thoreau could still identify him in Tocquevillian terms once they arrived at "the wilderness." At first Polis was quiet, stolid, almost "mild and infantile." Then Polis became active, skillful, engaging, and indispensable to the project they pursued together.

Thoreau and Polis, meeting on an ambiguous space neither wholly within nor wholly outside Tocquevillian civilization, both work to extend the cultural imagination through which each engages the other. For example, when Thoreau, the naturalist, discovers the fluorescent light that "dwells in the rotten wood" of one kind of tree, the Indian tells him that the light is called *Artoosoqu'*, and that "his folks sometimes saw fires passing along at various heights, even as high as the trees."[17] This leads to a discussion of Indian gods. Thoreau engages "the Indian" not as he might have been before the arrival of the "white man" (Polis's handle for Thoreau and his type) nor simply as constituted by the white man at that time. Rather, Thoreau engages Polis as the other whose mode of being crosses his own at crucial points and who is central to the ethical sensibility Thoreau himself seeks to cultivate. Polis turns out to be both irreducible to the cultural categories through which the Anglo-American culture receives him and unsusceptible to a characterization that reduces him to a white man with a "red skin." The white man and the Indian, on this journey on the edge of "civilization," forge an operational relationship of dissonant interdependence in which each maintains a certain distance from the other while selectively drawing sustenance from him.[18]

Once, as the conversation wanders toward religion, Polis professes to be a Protestant while nonetheless telling stories reflecting commitments from other times. Thoreau professes to be a Protestant too, while confessing (to the reader) that this profession exaggerates. It is the relation Thoreau seeks to establish that contrasts sharply with Tocqueville: "I have much to learn of the Indian, nothing of the missionary. I am not sure but all that would tempt me to teach the Indian my religion would be his promise to teach me *his*."[19]

The white man finds that the Indian brings out—through terse assertions during conversation that he does not "know" how he guides himself through the forest or stalks game—a strand of tacit skill also flowing silently through the white man's large inventory of explicit, formal knowledge:

> Often when an Indian says 'I don't know,' in regard to the route he is to take, he does not mean what a white man would mean by those words, for his Indian instinct may tell him as much as the most most confident white man knows. He does not carry things in his head, nor remember the route exactly, like a white man, but relies on himself at the moment. Not having experienced the need of the other sort of knowledge, all labelled and arranged, he has not acquired it.[20]

Thoreau, the naturalist who labels and orders everything, does so in part to encounter those experiences that exceed his comprehension. He strives to *cultivate* a generous ethical sensibility that becomes an instinctive disposition to life; he strives, through such journeys as this one in Maine, to detach himself from a set of settled conventions to enable himself to recognize and resist hidden violences in them. Polis thereby helps Thoreau to recognize a subterranean, fugitive strain in his own culture and to modify the (socially crafted) instincts through which he engages difference. Thoreau, who seeks to become bicultural, eventually glimpses how bicultural Polis has become: Polis avails himself "cunningly of the advantages of civilization without losing any of his woodcraft."[21] And Thoreau conveys in his notebooks how the (Tocquevillian/American) perception of "the Indian" as nomadic hunter is belied by the agricultural traditions of many American peoples in corn, melons, squash, tobacco, and other crops. This white man draws sustenance from Polis by appreciating how his own categories of experience never suffice to grasp the other and by cultivating numerous connections enabled by the multiple friction points between them. The pathos of distance between Thoreau and Polis clarifies through amplification a profound element in the ethical relation suppressed by the American/Tocquevillian rendering of civilizational morality.

Still, Thoreau's engagements with Polis precede the invention of anthropology, they occur on a space where politics is circumvented, and they relate to an individual more than a culture. What if Thoreau, while pursuing the trail we have reviewed, had also encountered William Apess, the son of Pequot parents in New England, Christianized by a series of white couples who adopted and abandoned him? This ambiguous Pequot, educated briefly in New England schools, eventually became a leader and spokesman for the Mashpee, a small tribe fighting to protect its land and culture on Cape Cod during the 1830s. Apess, as we can see retrospectively through Barry O'Connell's collection of his essays, became a fierce political leader and effective polemicist, drawing critical resources from the Christianity of his Christian oppressors. Apess crosses the border between two cultures inhabiting the same territory, revealing as he proceeds how these borders have already become blurred and how the dominant party in border building is hell-bent on reconstructing them. Apess, and the peoples he draws sustenance from, disrupts the territorialization of civilization marked by Tocqueville; he crosses that border glimpsed by the Thoreau-Polis encounter.

In his essay on "Indian Nullification of the Unconstitutional Laws of Massachusetts Relative to the Mashpee Tribe; Or the Pretended Riot Explained," Apess explains how he and his band were arrested and jailed for "rioting" when they prevented white poachers from taking wood from their land. He uses this event to publicize the case for a coalition of Indians and whites against the the oppressive practices of the commonwealth. Apess here writes to at least three possible audiences: to those Mashpee and associated peoples touched by this struggle, to a possible minority of white Christians (as he labels them) in New England who might respond to the justice of their claims, and to a generalized posterity that might profit in yet unknown ways from the words of a literate, Christianized, politicized, Pequot, Mashpee not supposed to be able or willing to encompass such a combination. We can merely sample here the prose of this hybrid activist, writing during the time of *Democracy in America:*

> I ask: What people could improve under laws which gave such temptation and facility to plunder? . . . If the government of Massachusetts do not see fit to believe me, I would fain propose to them a test of the soundness of my reasoning. Let them put our white neighbors in Barnstable County under the guardianship of a board of overseers and give them not privileges other than have been allowed to the poor, despised Indians. Let them inflict upon the said whites a preacher whom they neither love nor respect and do not wish to hear. Let them, in short, be treated just as the Mashpee tribe have been; I think there will soon be a declension of morals and population. We shall see if they are able to build up a town in such circumstances.

Any enterprising men who may be among them will soon seek another home and society, which it is not in the power of the Indians to
do, on account of their color . . . The laws were calculated to drive the
tribes from their possessions and annihilate them as a people . . . [22]
    Why should not this odious, and brutifying system be put an end
to? Why should not the remaining Indians in this Commonwealth be
placed upon the same footing as to rights of property, as to civil privileges and duties, as other men? Why should they not *vote*, maintain
schools . . . and use as they please that which is their own? If the contiguous towns object to having them added to their corporations, let
them be incorporated by themselves: let them choose their officers;
establish a police, maintain fences and take up stray cattle. I believe
the Indians desire such a change. I believe they have gone as far as
they are allowed to introduce it. But they are fettered and ground to
the earth.[23]

Suppose the contingencies of time and circumstance had spawned
an encounter between the Thoreaus and the Mashpee of this day (as
well as with, in different combinations, say, the Cherokee in the
South and the Sioux in the Midwest). Is it not *possible* that the former, with their fugitive attractions to "paganism," might have overcome their instinctive aversion to politics, and that the latter, with
their ambiguous "Christianization," might have been drawn into a
new political alliance? In this unactualized space of political conjunction between two types we now know to live in their time we
can glimpse unpursued political possibilities. Within this unex-
ploited space of conjunction resided the possibility for an alliance to
pluralize America in new ways, compromising the hegemony of the
Anglo/American/Christian/national/civilizational complex on behalf
of new permutations of being.
    Identification of a possible conjunction between a few thousand
"Thoreaus" and "Apesses" on the land of "New England" thus presses
people today either to endorse those violences more nakedly or to
participate in struggles against their contemporary effects. We in-
dulge this critical nostalgia for a past that never was to fan sparks of
possibility in the present. For more of the present than we normally
think is bound up with circumstances that might have been otherwise. We are the result of contingent historical arrangements sedimented into complex contemporary constellations, much more than
of civilizational necessities set in the cement of intrinsic cultural

identities. When we excavate past violences, pressing against the self-protective naturalizations and ontologizations in which they have been set, we discern new possibilities of pluralization in the present.

DETERRITORIALIZATIONS OF ARBOREAL PLURALISM

In what follows I explore elements in a contemporary pluralist imagination that scrambles the hegemony of the civi-territorial complex. The intention is not to focus on the economic conditions of pluralist politics, a task pursued elsewhere.[24] Rather, I elaborate some of the political conditions of multifarious pluralism. These pluralizations of pluralism do not issue in a pluralism without boundaries, for no such beast is possible. Nor do they dismantle the territorial state in prose, for such an intervention would be self-destructive even if it succeeded in the late-modern age. They support, rather, a dis-nationalist, late-modern pluralism in which the overcoded boundary of the civi-territorial state is translated into multiple lines of division that do not correspond to one another on the same plane. We seek, then, a more mobile pluralist imagination in which the spirit of nomadism inhabits multiple sites and issues appropriate to the late-modern time.

The Insufficiency of Statist Politics

The formation of cross-national, nonstatist political movements designed to challenge state priorities with respect to refugees, immigration, ecology, geographical units of economic development across state borders, women's rights, sexual diversity, extension of religious diversity, and so on, can have the effect of pluralizing vertically, as it were, sites of collective political identification. Such vertical pluralizations, where a plurality of political identities are formed below the state, through the state, and across states, compromise the state as the final site of collective political identity. They enlarge the number of sites and identities through which individuals and groupings might participate politically. They amplify a plurality of voices in selves and institutions by enabling them to find multiple sites of political expression and action. They maintain the democratic state as one apparatus of action and electoral accountability while challenging violent tendencies to fundamentalize the state into a communal-nation-state in which a single people invests its highest or final identity. The proliferation of nonstatist, cross-national social movements scrambles the experience of correspondence between a nation and a state; it thereby encourages cultivation of multifarious points of contact and negotiation with other identities, including those that exceed the unity of a nation-state.[25] But such cross-state, non-national movements require other supporting conditions.

The Nomadic Element in the Democratic State

If you define the root idea of democracy, vaguely as any root idea must be, to be *rule* by a unified *people* of *itself,* you bring under arrest twice the nomadic element circulating through the ethos of democracy. For that definition impels you to ask first, How can a people become unified enough to rule itself? and last, How can rule reproduce the unity of the people? Your thinking is likely to oscillate between the statist (im)possibilities of a general will, a rational consensus, a Schmittian decisionism, or the arboreal pluralism of Tocqueville, where diversity consists of several limbs stretching out from the (civi-territorial) trunk that provides them with support and nourishment. But if you treat the key theme of democracy to be the more protean idea that those affected have a hand and voice in modeling mulitiple cultures that constitute them, the insufficiency of the politics of rule comes more prominently into view.

On this reading, political rule is always pertinent to a democratic ethos, but so is the question of how to loosen, challenge, or interrupt sedimented cultural presumptions about identity, nature, gender, morality, nationality, divinity, civilization, and the global environment that enter into ruling. A democratic ethos now becomes, among other things, a setting in which nomadic *movements* periodically interrupt centered cultural presumptions so that the element of power, artifice, and contingency in these all too readily naturalized norms becomes more palpable, so that voices defined as (interior, internal, external) others in the established order of things can locate cultural space to contest some of these definitions, so that new combinations emerging out of these disturbances can develop agonistic respect for one another in changing contexts of interdependency.

Tocqueville, of course, makes a certain contribution to this productive ambiguity in a pluralist democracy. But he never encourages disturbance to flow into the sacred trunk of civilization itself. Hence his demoralization of violence against the Indian.

The Ethos of Enactment

The most fragile and indispensable element in a pluralizing democracy is an ethos of responsiveness in relations between identities, an ethos that opens up cultural space through which new possibilities of being can be enacted.

A pluralizing ethos is one that risks the production of new challenges to established cultural constellations in a variety of domains; it then strives to explore how and to what degree it is possible, as each unpredictable enactment begins to crystallize into a new relational identity, to negotiate new terms of intersection and coexistence in the modified cultural constellation. When a cultural ethos of generosity is reasonably intact, the political generation of a new possibility out of old injuries renders palpable both the crucial role of enactment in the politics of freedom and the hidden element of contingency and power in established constellations of identity/difference. The cumulative effect of such enactments links a culture of democracy, first, to appreciation of the fundamental contingency of things, second, to acknowledgment by more people in more settings of the role power plays in the naturalization of cultural boundaries, and, third, to enhanced cultural responsiveness to the call to open up room for new possibilities to crystallize out of the energies and injuries of difference.

The politics of enactment is, though, so fragile, risky, deniable, and crucial that it is necessary to revitalize periodically opportunity and responsiveness in this domain. The risk resides partly in the chance a new enactment will turn out to jeopardize the ethos of responsiveness itself, partly in the chance it will be suppressed to protect the self-confidence of identities disturbed by the threat it poses to their claims to self-certainty, but mostly in the probability it will be defined automatically to fall into the first category by those whose self-certainty is shaken by its very appearance.

We caught a glimpse of the politics of enactment in the terms of interaction between Henry Thoreau and Joe Polis and, more significantly, in that hypothetical alliance between nineteenth-century Thoreaus and Apesses. We also saw through Tocqueville's delineation of the Indian how vulnerable such a movement is to reactive violence in the name of civilization or intrinsic morality or Christian universalism or consensual rule or territorial integrity closed up beyond the (always debatable) point of necessity.

Numerous political movements enacting new possibilities of being are discernible in America's recent past: in a thwarted black power movement that revealed a religious universalism and institutional racism running deeper than prejudice, in a feminist movement that cracked open the existing rule of gender hierarchy, and in multiple ethnic movements forged out of the experience of devalued immigrant nationalities. Perhaps the most revealing moment, though, is when a movement still remains poised on that precarious threshold of enactment prior to its crystallization into a new form. This is the moment when it remains all too vulnerable to dismissal or repression by those responding to it through the very categories it seeks to contest. There are several recent or current examples of such moments in "America": as when sexual minorities fight through injuries imposed on them by medicalization of the hetero/homosexual hierarchy to generate lesbian/gay rights movements pluralizing the possibilities of positive sexual identity and extending the operational space in which rights may be claimed, as when feminists proceed through the fight against gender *hierarchy* to a struggle for a pluralization of gender performances exceeding gender *duality* itself, as when citizens of a state risk the charge of treason or irresponsibility by extending their political affiliations beyond the boundaries of the territorial state, and as when carriers of nontheistic reverence for being struggle to pry open space between the conventions of theism and secularism to place a new possibility on the political scale of the sacred.

Each of these pluralizing movements is precarious at a critical historical moment. Each can all too readily be drawn back into the regulatory discourse of the homo/hetero hierarchy, intrinsic gender duality, the nation-state/world anarchy duo, or the monotheist/secular combo in ways that maintain each attempt at pluralization below the threshold of rights and justice.

How does the struggle to enactment function if and when it breaks into being? What paradoxes does it contain? What does success reveal? What modes of critical responsiveness are appropriate to it? What limits are necessary to it?[26]

A successful enactment fosters freedom by propelling a new possibility into established cultural constellations; its success thereby reveals retroactively, as it were, power and arbitrariness circulating through suffering and injuries previously interpreted as unavoidable or morally justified. What the enactment uncovers, though, is not exactly a fixed identity already existing just beneath the veil of ideology, underdeveloped reason, restricted convention, or a hypocritical practice of universal rights. Those cover-ups do occur, of course. But when a new enactment succeeds, neither the carriers, the respondents, nor the discourses through which their relations are represented remain what they were before it began. For example, in the United States of 1960 the "homosexual" suffered either from a disorder in need of treatment, the wrong choice in need of censure, an inflamed imagination in need of containment, or all three in some variable combination. But later, if and as the lesbian/gay rights movements advance, he or she *will have suffered* from the arbitrary naturalization of heterosexuality, and the heterosexual *will have denied* the element of contingency in what it is. A condition previously existing in that nether world below the threshold of rights and justice is transformed through political action into a new identity eligible to make claims against the (now) injustices it suffers.

Let us trace one hypothetical possibility in this domain, even before it has reached that point where retrospective appraisal is feasible. Suppose a political movement is launched, looking as ineligible or irrelevant to many today as the Mashpee revolt did in the nineteenth century, or as feminism did to most American men and women in the early 1960s, or as the gay/lesbian movement did to many psychiatrists of homosexuality during the same period. This movement strives to pluralize existing spaces of moral/religious identity. It thereby challenges the sufficiency of the existing cultural field, marked by fundamentalist Christianity, moderate Protestant, Catholic, and Jewish monotheisms, post-Christian moral secularisms such as Kantianism and utilitarianism, and atheism. (But, of course, this field delineation is *already* retrospective, already formed from a point of view that marks its boundaries in a specific way. We always run ahead of ourselves in telling the kind of story I have in mind.)

Initially, those challenging the established field of sacred/secular discourse resist conventional definitions of themselves as relativistic, anarchistic, nihilistic, atheistic, or textualistic, insisting that these articulations function as self-reinforcing negations of the protean movement advanced by a temporary alliance of conventional theisms and secularisms. Each of the latter constituencies reinforces the insistence of the others that they together exhaust the range of viable possibilities in this domain. Eventually, through a series of distinctive interventions into issues of gender, race, sexuality, and ecology, many agents of resistance to mono-moralism begin to define themselves, retrospectively as it were, as carriers of nontheistic reverence for the rich diversity of being. They ground a positive ethos of critical diversity in appreciation of a world governed by no prior design or principle of universal identity. These post-secularists, as we may now call them, open up new ethical space between monotheists, mono-Kantians, and mono-secularists, a space that heretofore had existed mostly as a mélange of official negations on one side and vague, unarticulated experiences of injury and limitation on the other. These monsters, fools, or carriers of freedom through cultural pluralization—take your pick—now advance new possibilities of pluralization against which old forms of intrinsic identity, command morality, purposive nature, and arboreal pluralism are to be assessed. They prize the excess of life over identity and the sense, experienced again and again retroactively as new identities are propelled into being, that life, bodies, and the earth persistently exceed cultural articulations of them. They refuse to devalue these retroactive experiences by investing a God, law, or intrinsic purpose into these fugitive sites. They insist on a recovery of reverence connected neither to a set of commands nor to traditional piety. If and when nontheistic reverence for the diversity of being becomes installed as an active competitor on the cultural field, the old cultural oligopoly (as we can now call it) will find itself faced with new questions and challenges. And many of these moral oligopolists will appear, from this perspective, to be too comfortable in what they are, too closed in their universalism, too unalert to injuries lodged in the paradoxical relation between hegemonic identities and the differences through which they become solidified, too oriented to the past alone in their appreciation of the possibilities of pluralization, and too tone deaf to muffled cries of arbitrariness circulating through Christian/secular practices of morality. The issue for them will not so much be if they concur with this unexpected entry into the moral oligopoly, though that may become an issue for some, but what relationship they will seek to establish with this perspective that pluralizes the grounds and codes of ethics.

Would such a postsecular reverence draw new sustenance from American peoples who preceded Christian America? Would political enactment of such a possibility reveal strains in pre-Christian conceptions of gods, life, and the earth heretofore unsusceptible to sensitive appreciation within the Christian/secular/moral complex? Perhaps. But we have already proceeded farther down this hypothetical trail than we could possibly be justified in going now. We can only say that the contemporary promise of such an aggregation is to open up possibilities of pluralization closed down by the Tocquevillian constellation. Its contemporary risk is to spur fundamentalist reactions among a set of moral/religious inheritors of the Tocquevillian model of civilization who insist upon the right to oligopolistic control over the cultural currency of ethics.

The element of paradox in the politics of enactment is that before success the new movement will be judged in those terms through which it is already depreciated, and that after success a new identity will emerge that exceeds the very energies and identifications that spurred it into being. The paradox of enactment of a new possibility within a pluralist ethos thus repeatedly reenacts at a microcosmic level the macroparadox Rousseau identified in the politics of founding a new republic. Such a paradoxical element in enactment creates political binds that a pluralist culture must seek to become sensitive to.

We are primed to expect a new identity to precede our recognition of it, and we tend to judge inchoate claims upon us now through the terms of recognition already installed in our culture. An ethos of responsiveness to the politics of enactment would relax both this expectation and that standard of judgment. It would appreciate how something new and valuable can be enacted out of nothing, where nothing signifies not a void but a set of injuries, energies, and desires yet to be crystallized into an identity susceptible to rigorous judgment.

To become sensitive to the ambiguous politics of enactment is, then, to respond to forms of civilizational violence that may operate below the current threshold of positive identities and that, therefore, fall below those received categories of rights and justice through which they could make claims upon the larger culture. That is why genealogy, deconstruction, political disturbance, and the micropolitics of desire are important components in the life of a pluralizing culture. Cultivation of responsiveness to the binds of political enactment, to binds that show the options between discovery or creation to be too crude to capture their shape, forms the linchpin of a democratic, pluralizing ethos. Those who affirm the politics of enactment to be crucial will seek, first, to enliven awareness of contingency in established constellations of identity and difference; second, to subdue that sense of threat arising when a new movement disturbs the sense of completeness, naturalness, or necessity in what you are; and, third, to cultivate new possibilities of coexistence and interaction between new formations and old forms shaken and moved by them. They will also understand how pluralization is never complete: a pluralist culture, at its best, is always coming into being across one dimension or another, because the existing field of diversities is likely to conceal injuries today to be recognized tomorrow as unnecessary to morality or civilization as such.

It is when a culture appreciates simultaneously inchoate currents of energy flowing through its solid formations, the value amidst the risk of new enactments, and the inability of new enactments to represent perfectly the energies that propelled them into being, that it most actively embodies a democratic ethos. A democratic ethos would be one in which agents of enactment exercise a certain *forbearance* in pressing their claims, and agents of reception exercise a reciprocal *generosity* in responding to those productions that disturb what they are. This agonistic reciprocity *is* the pathos of distance in politics.

Once a new social identity has been consolidated, its indebtedness to cultural differences that endow it with specificity, and its attunement to traces of difference that continue to flow through the identity it now embodies can engender a certain empathy for what is not. This element of empathy across the space of difference and contestation provides the cultural currency of a democratic ethos; it sustains the cultural condition for a pathos of distance, for agonistic respect by each collective identity (identities are always collective or general), for differences giving it definition, even while some of these very differences threaten its drives to self-sufficiency and self-certainty.

The combination of presumptive forbearance and presumptive generosity that constitute the pathos of distance in politics, then, gains its power from political interruptions in established economies of identity/difference, from reciprocal cultivation of empathy toward what you are not, and from prudence today toward the adversary you may need to align with tomorrow for other purposes.[27] Each of these precarious conditions must be operative to sustain the ethos of pluralization, and none is *ever* as secure as it must be.

THE LIMITS OF PLURALIZATION

There are limits, that is, boundaries and exclusions, that must be placed around such a democratic ethos of pluralization. For instance, a pluralizing, democratic regime would tolerate fundamentalisms that insist that what they are is true, intrinsic, or self-sufficient, but it would have to resist their drives to impose themselves too actively upon other segments of the culture. The problem is that the fundamentalist drive to universalize what it is might take over any identity, even one that had recently profited from a general ethos of responsiveness to propel itself into being. A fundamentalist drive to universalization often gives itself the appearance of intrinsic truth and self-sufficiency by struggling to translate the cultural differences through which it has become crystallized into intrinsic evils to be punished or assimilated. The Augustinian translations of Greek religions into paganism and contending interpretations of Christianity into heresies provide a paradigm of how this conversion process proceeds. There are surely other evils in a pluralizing culture, but the evil that requires the most attention and the most sensitive political response is exactly this tendency by old and new identities to fundamentalize what they are by demonizing what they are not.

Once these elementary points are granted, and once one grants that it is often difficult to ascertain when, where, and how democratic exclusions must be enforced, the foremost democratic challenge today still remains to multiply boundaries in imperfect correspondence with one another so that lines of division across one dimension do not mesh too closely with those across others, so that cultural spaces for political enactment are opened up, so that a pathos of distance flowing from the difference within to the difference without circulates more actively through the general culture, and so that the political imperative to general enactments through state assemblages propels negotiation between disparate constituencies connected by multifarious threads of strife and interdependence.

These are impossible conditions of democratic pluralization, in that they have never been fully intact anywhere and never could be combined perfectly in any one time. Multifarious pluralism, therefore, is a valuable cultural impossibility that, even under favorable conditions, is always coming into being across one dimension or another. In pointing persistently toward a multifarious condition always in formation, it foments political possibilities of enactment, responsiveness, and intersection exceeding Tocqueville's America. It reminds us that because politics itself consists of several dimensions that do not coexist perfectly, there is always more political work to be done. And it sustains standards of action and critical judgment more generous than those territorialized by the Tocquevillian imagination.

NOTES

1. *The Book of J,* translated by David Rosenberg and interpreted by Harold Bloom (New York: Grove Weidenfeld, 1990), p. 149. I select the Rosenberg translation partly because being the latest in a very long line of translations, it calls our attention to the unavoidability of translation in this domain and the incorrigible moment of interpretation in every translation, and partly because the Rosenberg translation highlights the question of boundaries I want to consider. Robert Alter, in *The World of Biblical Literature* (New York: Basic Books, 1991), pp. 153-61, argues that the Rosenberg translation is defective and that its attribution of some sections to "J" is questionable. I am sure he is right about the second point, and I am unqualified to judge the first. But Alter's presentation of this issue seems to presuppose the availability of a neutral translation not itself deeply invested with a particular interpretation. This seems dubious to me. And his critique of Bloom's projection of "J" as a woman with an ironic sensibility seems to forget how this very projection functions in Bloom's reading. Bloom invests this reading of "J," partly to give coherence to his reading and partly to underline the inevitability and contestability of some such set of projections in every reading of the text. Bloom's ironic projection, although he takes it seriously, is also in the service of self-modesty in the very act of interpretation.

2. *The Book of J,* p. 162.

3. Jean Jacques Rousseau, *The Government of Poland,* trans. Willmoore Kendall (New York: Bobbs-Merrill Co., 1972), p. 6.

4. See my "Democracy and Territoriality," Millenium (winter 1991), pp. 463-83, where I discuss Rousseau's recognition of the "paradox of politics." The present essay seeks to continue a line of inquiry launched in that one.

5. *The Government of Poland,* p. 6.

6. *The Government of Poland,* p. 14, my emphasis.

7. Rousseau, *On the Social Contract,* trans. Roger Masters (New York: St. Martin's Press, 1978), p. 130.

8. Although Rousseau is not a pluralist in *The Social Contract,* he be-

comes one of sorts in *The Government of Poland*. The first ideal may be actualizable nowhere, whereas the ideal projected for Poland is more likely to be approximated somewhere. The Rousseauian element in Tocquevillian pluralism is suggested in the following formulation: "the laws of a democracy tend toward the good of the greatest number, for they spring from the majority of all citizens, which may be mistaken but which cannot have an interest contrary to its own." *Democracy in America,* trans. George Lawrence (New York: Anchor books, 1969) p. 234. My reading of Tocqueville has affinities to those by Thomas Dumm, *Democracy and Punishment* (Madison: University of Wisconsin Press, 1987), ch. 5, and Stephen Schneck, "Habits of the Head: Tocqueville's America and Jazz," *Political Theory* 17, no. 4 (November 1989), pp. 638-62. I am also indebted to participants in a fall 1992 seminar David Campbell and I co-taught at Hopkins on "Sovereignty and Democracy." Tocqueville's *Democracy in America* was a central object of discussion. Those who have encountered Campbell's *Writing Security* (Minneapolis: University of Minnesota Press, 1992) will detect similarities between this presentation of Tocqueville's "America" and Campbell's general presentation of how foreign policy constitutes American political identity.

9. I will continue to use the term "Indian" throughout this essay, partly to follow Tocqueville's usage, partly to emphasize how we receive this diverse set of indigenous inhabitants as presented to us by a European theorist and a European civilization.

10. Alexis de Tocqueville, *Democracy in America,* 2 vols., trans. George Lawrence (New York: Harper and Row, 1969), pp. 27, 30, 280.

11. *Democracy in America,* p. 280.

12. *Democracy in America,* p. 292.

13. *Democracy in America,* p. 292.

14. *Democracy in America,* pp. 543-44.

15. *Democracy in America,* p. 58.

16. The last formulation comes from p. 317 of *Democracy in America.*

17. "The Allegash and East Branch," in Joseph Moldenhauer, ed., *The Maine Woods* (Princeton: Princeton University Press, 1972), p. 182. My reading of Thoreau is indebted to Jane Bennett, who emphasizes his strategies to cultivate a responsive sensibility through his encounters with nature. See *Henry David Thoreau: A Reading from the Wild* (Newbury Park: Sage Press, 1994).

18. This journey is completely male. And the larger world Thoreau and Polis evoke together seems to be male centered as well. The pathos of distance they engender together may produce another other, but that must remain a topic for another discussion.

19. "The Allegash and East Branch," p. 181.

20. "The Allegash and East Branch," p. 185. For the role such a tacit knowledge plays in the ethical sensibility Thoreau himself strives to develop and the complex relation of Thoreau to nature, see Jane Bennett, "On Being a Native: Thoreau's Hermeneutics of Self," *Polity* 22, no. 4, (summer 1990), pp. 559-80. My reading of Thoreau is indebted to this essay.

21. "The Allegash and East Branch," p. 201.

22. *On Our Own Ground: The Complete Writings of William Apess, A Pequot,* edited with an introduction by Barry O'Connell (Amherst: University of Massachusetts Press, 1993), p. 212.

23. *On Our Own Ground,* p. 216.

24. I explore the economic conditions of a pluralizing culture in the middle chapters of *Politics and Ambiguity* (Madison: University of Wisconsin Press, 1987) and in ch. 3 of *Territorializations: Reworking the Pluralist Imagination* (Ithaca: Cornell University Press, forthcoming).

25. I have discussed this dimension elsewhere, most extensively in "Democracy and Territoriality," and I will not pursue it further here.

26. It is abundantly clear that not every new enactment proves to be compatible with a democratic ethos. That reality forms part of the fragility of democracy. But let us not jump to this defense of existing boundaries prematurely, for that is exactly the strategy by which the exploratory dimension of a democratic ethos is stifled in the name of a civi-territorial complex that de-democratizes democracy in the name of saving it.

27. This, obviously, means that a democratic ethos requires certain economic preconditions, where none is so poor she has to sell herself and none so rich she can buy another. I have responded to them in *Politics and Ambiguity.* The point to emphasize now is that, even while the reduction of economic inequality is crucial to a culture of pluralization, it is by no means sufficient to it. It is important both how equalization is pursued and what other elements in the political culture intersect with it.

6

Unmapping and Remapping the World: Foreign Policy as Aesthetic Practice

KENNAN FERGUSON

CARTOGRAPHIC RESONANCES

It is by now a truism that the dissolution of the Soviet Union has radically changed the world. It is obvious why the dissolution has affected those who lived within its cartographic confines; it is less obvious why it has so deeply affected those who lived elsewhere. The shock waves and emanations from this transformation are numerous but not easily traced, because the changes that have taken place are not changes in physical space but changes in a way of comprehending the globe; what has changed the world is less the shift in state boundaries and specific enmities than the modifications of imaginative mapping. The ways the world is expressed have been transformed, and in the process global subjectivities are transfigured.

These alterations and the mechanisms by which those in the United States are trying to overcome them emerge through the cartographic practices that have served as a sense-making machinery for the United States and other geopolitical entities in the form of the taxonomies that make placing the American self in the world possible. It is these judgments and practices, not what normally passes for geopolitics, that make the demise of Western state-sponsored communism so important to the United States.

That the Soviet threat was easy to locate in the world and was ideologically stable and comprehensible currently pass as the sole reasons that its disappearance destabilizes. Yet these reasons do not

stand up to historical scrutiny. The Soviet Union itself was geographically bounded, but communism was avowedly international. It was
less, not more, recognizable than previous national threats of immigration, gender, and race. Communism could come in disguise: Reds,
unlike "Red Indians," could walk invisibly amongst the American
populace.[1] Nor was the identification of communism limited to ideological location. Long-contested issues in American politics—issues
of gender, race, sexuality, even literary interpretation—became inex-
tricably intertwined with the "threat" of communism. Examples
abound: the speech of the nuclear age is an aggressively masculine
one, and notions of masculinity and femininity were deeply coded
into the arms race.[2] Martin Luther King Jr. was considered a communist by the U.S. security apparatus as a result of his work for civil
rights. The 1964 "Jenkins Affair," wherein the chief of staff of the
Johnson administration was arrested for "indecent gestures" in a
YMCA men's room, soon became rife with metaphors of social in-
festation and civic danger, positioning homosexuality as a risk to be
combated through increased state surveillance.[3] William Epstein describes how even the study of eighteenth-century poetry began to
take its leads from Cold War rhetorical formations.[4] The containment of communism as a dangerous pollutant has been central to
United States culture for half a century.[5]

   The consternation and difficulty the USSR's demise has caused
among those working hardest to cause it is not therefore attributable
to the conventional reasons of interstate relations. Communism has
been animate at levels more important and more immediate. Precisely because so much work has gone into the particular positioning
of the world order of the past fifty years (especially for Americans,
for whom the order was increasingly fixed and settled), its dissolution unmaps the world. The United States's imaginary in the twentieth century was conceivable primarily in reference to the communist
"threat." A world was designed where the geographic and the ideological could be superimposed on one another to create a powerful
map with both horizontal perception and interpretive depth, explaining what the world meant as well as how it looked. Mapping
serves a powerfully personal function, producing the world as understandable as its discursive productions provide guides for certain
modes of travel and highlight sights and sites of importance. Mapping also serves a powerfully collective function, furnishing coher-

ences that make people into a singular people: defining certain sets of persons as unified through borders and districts. To map is to engage in a procedure of identity creation at the individual and group level; it is, bluntly, to produce the world.[6] To have a map as powerful as the bipolar geopolitical conception suddenly revoked is a supremely unsettling occurrence.

The Soviet Union's disintegration disrupted American cultural life even more than it disrupted geopolitical presumptions, thus clearly exhibiting the centrality of communism and anticommunism to cultural practices. As David Campbell has argued, the relation of U.S. identity to its construction of otherness is strong, especially because of the constant foregrounding of America as a postulated, idealized space rather than as a historically grounded one, and because of its special status as a nation of constantly shifting boundaries.[7] The instability of its own geographic identity, its plurality of history, and its character as a method of thought rather than an ideologically secure territory have long provoked a strong need to map. Yet simultaneously, these characteristics have allowed a plurality and an instability of mappings, an often swift response to changes irrelevant to geographic borders. The Cold War American understanding of the Soviet Union was a "strategy associated with the logic of identity whereby the ethical powers of segregation constitute the identity of the agent in whose name they operate, and give rise to a geography of evil."[8]

The dominant political discourse of the United States positioned it as the custodian of identity, policing and locating allies and enemies, threats to, and infections of the American body politic. Given that American governmental organizations have been organized around this custodial orientation, they find themselves now needing to fabricate a new form of geopolitics. An endangered U.S. subjectivity seeks alternative oppositions to shore up the threatened moral distinctiveness. In a statement at his confirmation hearing in early 1993, Secretary of State Designate Warren Christopher candidly recognized this current dilemma: "The unitary goal of containing Soviet power will have to be replaced by more complex justifications to fit the new era. We need to show that, in this era, foreign policy is no longer foreign."[9] Christopher effectively places quotation marks around the generally unproblematic abstraction "foreign policy" and troubles the concepts of external and internal political spaces, recognizing that states and borders have shifted from stable to variable. His imperative tone makes clear the need for a reassertion of oppositions in order that foreign policy can continue unchanged.

Les Aspin, a primary architect of the new territoriality as the chairman of the House Armed Services Committee (before his brief tenure as the secretary of defense), was even clearer about the need for opposition in order to persist in identity. In 1992, he released a paper titled "National Security in the 1990s: Defining a New Basis for U.S. Military Forces," which argued, in short, that "there is no alternative to a threat-based force structure, that is, one that is sized and shaped to cope with the 'things' that threaten Americans. During the Cold War, it was clear to all Americans what that 'thing' was—the Soviet Union. In the post-Soviet world, it is not so clear."[10] For Aspin, the "things" float; that is, it is more important that "things" exist than what they specifically are. Christopher, Aspin, and others who are searching for ways to use a newly changed political system to continue the relative stabilities of the world and to rationalize traditionally militarized policies are predominantly interested in fashioning the new "things" that perpetuate and consolidate U.S. identity.

These abstract difficulties do not correspond well with the bureaucratic discourse that has reified political space since its Westphalian beginnings. The rapid reconfiguration of meaning-space and its disruption of a particularly strong national identity cause great difficulty for those who operated comfortably within the old discursive framework. It becomes necessary to theorize such change to understand the vague anxiety it produces as well as to see the possibilities and dilemmas it generates. Gilles Deleuze and Félix Guattari have invented an appropriate language to interpret this remapping, a terminology of "territorialization." For them, the earth is always coded: territory never just is, but always means. This coding, in their understanding, is primarily a process of creating/separating peoples, most clearly demarcating the civilized and the barbaric.[11]

Deleuze and Guattari understand the modern world to be perpetually in various processes of territorialization and deterritorialization. Societies territorialize when they delimit the earth, when they fragment land and pretend that those boundaries—between states and between people—are in some way natural or true. Land becomes manifest; it is controlled and regimented in various administrative functions. When a bureaucratic entity controls transportation, water, and trade, it creates a socius. Borders and bodies are defended, maintained, policed.[12] The United States government can change entirely from decade to decade, but the need to make Americans, out of a land called America, continues in new and unexpected forms.

The violence done throughout this process is masked. William Connolly refers to the production of the "civi-territorial complex": the location and creation of civilization in a specific consumption of the land, as well as the subsequent delegitimation of those with different conceptions of it.[13] The use of land in a particular way—agrarian for an extended period but more recently referring to industrialized development—justifies the claim of civilization and forms the foundation for denying the nomadic people previously occupying the land any claim to the earth. It is cultural judgment realized through the imaginary of terrain. This conviction is not limited to nineteenth-century America; the civi-territorial complex continues to code the world as Occident and Orient, developed and un(der)developed, first and third world.

Between the singular interpretation of a territory and the plurality of possibilities latent within it lies an inherent instability; Deleuze and Guattari refer to active and continuing territorialization rather than simple and stable expropriation. Land must be coded, and overcoded, for alternative possibilities are to be discerned not only as improbable but as impossible. The territorialization, deterritorialization dynamic holds not only for the state itself but for its understanding of the rest of the world. Ultimately, this is the definitive purview of state organization: the state is the agent by which the meaning of territories is controlled and regulated. In its broadest sense (including organs of financial control, land management, and pedagogical dissemination) the state gives meaning to the land, engineering, regulating, mapping.

There are conventions to these processes. For the past half-century, both the United States and the Soviet Union corresponded in their territorialization: the globe was mapped on a grid of ideology. Who a person or a people were meant their ideological affiliation or lack thereof; narratives of identity were modeled on theoretical correlation. The identity of "Nicaraguan," for example, was not enough: any Nicaraguan must be located as Sandanista or Samozan, communist or capitalist. The study of politics became an acceptance of this mapping, focused primarily on political ideologies because ideology was understood to be the primary determinant of a person. The differences between a small Caribbean nation and an Eastern European country were seen to be, for the most part, far less significant than the sort of political doctrines that informed the structure of each government. Both were coded by the geopolitical discourse in the same way. The map of the world has been a geopolitical configuration with doctrinal coloring: a color-coding for vital ideological difference.

Antithetical to codings, argue Deleuze and Guattari, are flows. Capital, cultures, identities, human bodies—all flow over the surface of the earth in assorted ways and at various speeds. Each is motile, and each resists the inscriptions that states want and need to force upon them. Nomads follow and exhaust flows; the socius tries to capture and contain them (148). Society codes imposing meanings to control and delimit these flows (185). Mappings are forms of overcoding cultures, of trying to freeze them into societies. The state's role is to rivet flows, to try to attach them to whatever can serve as an anchor. Territorialization, in other words, is the attempt to control, limit, and affix meaning to flows.

BUILDING NEW IDEOGRAPHS

Deleuze and Guattari argue that any process of deterritorialization entails a concomitant reterritorialization: "If it is true that the function of the modern State is the regulation of the decoded, deterritorialized flows, one of the principal aspects of the function consists in reterritorializing, so as to prevent the decoded flows from breaking loose at all the edges of the social axiomatic" (258). As certain sense-making machines become obsolete, new ones are constructed. They argue that this is the paramount function of the state in the modern world: as flows break free from territory, they must be remapped. Governments, in encoding and enforcing borders, are literally encoding and enforcing spatiality.[14] The fragmentation of the map of the contemporary world does not mean that cartography itself stops; instead it means that the state must reconstruct its nation and its people with new meaning. It is the process of reterritorializing the world.

Of course, it is always easier to move within territories than without them: this is what maps are for. Discursive maneuvering is simpler when a clear ideograph is in place. The price of this clarity, however, is interpretive containment, the re-inscription and regulation of narratives of meaning. When one views the world in terms of alliance and enmity, for example, one cannot attend to more nuanced relationships: cultural practices, historical attachments, linguistic subtleties. As reterritorialization constructs new possibilities, it simultaneously limits potential freedoms. Like maps, ideographs serve both to make sense of current terrain and to predict the terrain to come. Yet prediction is also blinding: that which is unexpected is often ignored, or more commonly, made to fit previously existing categories. The current transition between modes, the period of reterritorialization, is thus a moment of relative freedom, a time that allows plural interpretations that can call into question both the fading and emerging normative standards.

Therefore the question: What is replacing the previous ideological affiliation in the identity narratives of the United States? To return to Aspin's recapitulation of the world, he places the old and the new worlds side by side, literally charting the differences. For example, where the "old" state is described as attending to "Soviet Military Power; Deliberate Soviet Attack; Economic Power Assumed," the "new" is concerned with "Spread of Nuclear Weapons, Terrorism, Regional Thugs, Drug Traffickers; Instability in the Former Soviet Republics; Japanese Economic Power."[15] Where the first set is understood at the level of doctrinal competition, the second set is found at a cultural level: each of the "new" categories is understood as located in an understanding of people acting for cultural interests rather than rational or doctrinal benefit. In other words, the United States has begun to search for political meaning in the "nature of a people" rather than the doctrines of their governments.

This process of remapping the political world has begun in earnest not only by politicians but by academics. Samuel P. Huntington, for example, agrees that conflict will no longer be intrinsic to a bipolar system. Instead, he argues, upcoming conflicts will be cultural rather than ideological or economic.[16] Like the Clinton administration, Huntington constructs a crude map of culture to narrate and chronicle. Conflicts "are" in themselves; one must merely apply the correct model. Culture, not the defunct theory of ideology, will be the means by which the world will mean. The loci of identity-constituting threats are no longer ideological; now true, significant identification is found in the cultural sphere. This change is not a rejection of the practice of trying to locate the "truth" of a country; instead it is a shift to material grounds.

As theorists like Edward Said have argued, the "West" constitutes itself in response to representations of culture.[17] Arjun Appadurai describes these various representations as overlain systems of images by which the world is understood, the concatenation of "multiple worlds which are constituted by the historically situate imaginations of persons and groups spread around the world."[18] The territories of Deleuze and Guattari follow not singular and total codes but multiple and overlapping ones. The world is interpreted in disjointed ways, some overcoding others, some contesting others. Media, finances, technology, and ethnography all provide worldwide organizations of meaning, all in various ways. Primary to these overlapping "deeply perspectival constructs"[19] is the concept of cultural difference.

Yet rather than recognizing cultural landscapes as enabling new possibilities for understanding the world as political, Huntington wants to remap the world along the old configurations of "nation-states" (a terminology already inattentive to the differences between people and administration). Culture as a code of mapping is depoliticized. Cultures cease to exist as a practice of lives, with all the plurality, ambiguity, and wonder that life entails, and instead become no more than a positivist descriptive category. Hence a clear and disturbing complicity between academic and bureaucratic discourses to simplify and flatten culture, to make ethnographic differences serve only as the ideograph of geopolitical mapping.

Cultures always speak in multiplicitous ways; the political question is how they are heard, or how the depth and complexity of this speech are ignored. As the discursive instabilities about what Americanness means change from ideological to cultural grounds, the issue becomes how other cultures manifest themselves in American life. This is not to talk of these other peoples as identical to states or nations, except indirectly.[20] It is instead to discuss the ways that these certain discourses are involved with their representation, how particular cultural illustrations work in mapping the world. It is to discuss the problems and the politics of cultural interpretation, for example, to show the ways in which perception of Japanese cultural practices and artifacts informs depictions of Japanese economic and political practices.

The trepidation with which the United States is trying to remap the world is less about the world than about the United States itself. It is trying to make itself, as a government and a nation, comprehensible once again. What seems like considerable change in the geopolitical world masks other, more important ways in which the world is mapped and thus controlled: the cultural models that Aspin and Huntington wish to bring to the fore. Because identity is the predicate with which all political enactment functions, the politicization of culture is the necessary precondition to make sense of ideographic territorialization. Yet culture is commonly understood as outside the realm of the political. It is depoliticized by being placed in private and personal space, spaces that are called aesthetic rather than political. There are two major ways this aesthetic interaction with the world is depoliticized: either by concretizing human relationships with things (assigning value) or by individualizing these relationships (claiming tastes). The effects of both these are to continue to experience the world as open to desires, desires uncritically accepted as natural.

This is the topic of exploration for the remainder of this essay, a topic that will unfold in three stages: first, to enjoin the contemporary contestation in American theory concerned with the "foreignness" of its internal culture, a debate usually labeled "multiculturalism," to see how such a debate polarizes and thus flattens aesthetic judgments; second, to try to establish a theory of aesthetics that problematizes and repoliticizes aesthetics as a matter of engagement with and habituation in the world, as a method of mapping the exoteric; and finally, to explore the ways in which aesthetics works as a policy of the foreign, to show how systems of taste and value judgment shape, define, and limit encounters with alterity.

THE POLITICS OF THE MULTICULTURAL

As identity space is recontextualized globally, American identity struggles become increasingly candid about the location of cultures and aesthetics in the attempts to establish a universalized and pervasive identity. Yet to understand the bases of an argument as aesthetic is not to mean that it is apolitical. Instead, it is to politicize notions of the aesthetic: to understand the global ramifications of identity constitution, to see how aesthetics are not isolated and detached from other networks of sense-making but are instead an important dimension of the multiplicitous global flows that form relationships of identity. It is to risk the possibility that we are constantly social actors, even in personal tastes and discernments. Most importantly, it is to require of the self a deep and abiding modesty, the acceptance of a lack of transcendental being, and thus a recognition of spacial and cultural location. That is, to acknowledge that no particular person nor culture has the ability, let alone the right, to appropriate all other cultures into universalized representation.

Most of the debate about "multiculturalism" versus "Western culture" denies the capacities of this politico-aesthetic, being instead predicated on the assumption that those arguing the relative merits of each category can and do have complete access to these cultures. The disagreement has to do with the kind of culture that should be the national trademark, as it were, but it is also one of how the "not us" is understood, the ways we interact with foreign systems of meaning. Each question concerns the nature of representing and appropriating other cultures into a preexisting intellectual/aesthetic system.

What is most important in the debate between the multi- and uniculturalists are the uses to which these conceptions of culture are put. Both uses are appropriations within the American cultural sphere; both uses are subject to the logics of the often hegemonic American social space. The relationships of American cultures to these cultural practices are thereby formed as a mechanism of cultural consumption, a mechanism which must be ignored to work. In fact, those who most assiduously argue the case of multiculturalism are usually those who most tenaciously deny that any cultural/aesthetic regulation is taking place in their multicultural applications: authors and composers who wrench artistic practices from historical and cultural contexts, collectors who use curios as markers of their global mobility, and pedagogues who believe that cultures can be staticly taught without being lived. In other words, this is part of the struggle for global "identity space," where the ways peoples represent themselves are peremptorily challenged.

The debate over multiculturalism in the United States has broken down along somewhat traditional lines: most conservatives and moderates have seen the introduction of other cultures as a threat to American identity; most liberals have seen it as a correction to the previous exclusions of various non-Northern European cultures.[21]

The stage is thereby set as one of clear contention: should cultures that are "other" to the United States be recognized, emphasized, and taught? In other words, should U.S. culture be understood as one affected by other cultures or not?

This disagreement is not as fundamental as those who argue it wish to assert. Such contention is already located within a discursive framework that is itself seen as natural.[22] The first part of this framework assumes that cultures are static, autonomous, and removed from representation, that cultures naturally represent themselves. This view denies that these alterior cultures serve various purposes, that they are formulated in different ways, by different interests, for different purposes. Cultural representation, therefore, disappears as a political problem for both sides of the debate; the questions of *whose* other-cultural representations are being privileged are never asked.

The second part of the framework of this disagreement is one of location: it presupposes that all the participants have control over the cultural practices discussed, that current understandings of them are adequate and appropriate. It assumes that the participants have access to these cultures, whether monetarily, aesthetically, linguistically, and/or historically, that (our) access to (their) culture is an unproblematic and natural stance. And it accepts that those with resources to understand and access other cultures have a right to sort between them, to reject or accept different aspects, practices, and aesthetics—in short, to shop. The result of this framework is the reinforcement of already existing mechanisms of cultural consumption.

Both these contentions are inherently problematic. To claim that culture is static is to make it artifactual and categorical, and thus to position culture as something to be controlled, dominated, and studied. It is to deny that culture is constantly and actively constituted by a people, sometimes self-consciously. It is to refuse to recognize the political debts of culture: the reliance on discursive stereotyping, the constant positioning of difference as defect, and the necessary contingency of community and identification.[23] To claim the equality of all participants is to deny difference in access and resources. Also, it is to deny that accessing a culture enforces certain kinds of changes in that culture. Together these claims and denials make possible colonial tourism, aesthetic domination, and the "Disnification" of cultural behaviors. They enable a new way of mapping the world, of representing and controlling meanings as reality, of authorizing particular valuations and tastes.

Take, as an exemplar of the "promulticultural" flattening of difference, Fredric Jameson's famous essay "Third-World Literature in the Era of Multinational Capitalism."[24] Jameson argues that all literature of the third world (a term he uses unproblematically) is at some basic level the same; that is, these works are different from Western literature in their common history of imperial domination and colonialism and, because of this common history, are analogous. His conclusions, such as "All third world texts are necessarily . . . allegorical"(69) and "We sense, between ourselves and this alien text, the presence of another reader, of the Other reader" (66), imply a facile proposition: from comparable material circumstances must come comparable work. In these conclusions, Jameson's fallacies here seem to be threefold. First, a book can speak only to us; second, a book can speak to only us; and third, a book can only speak to us. That is, that a text for whom the "we" (a group that Jameson keeps separate from the "they") is not the primary audience is at some basic level useless. That a text's meanings must be intelligible to the Western reader in order to be a text. That a text's sole purpose is to speak in an unmediated way to each reader without the reminder that it is produced and constructed. Aijaz Ahmad's critique of Jameson points to the ways Jameson's aesthetics rely "upon a suppression of the multiplicity of significant differences among and within both the advanced capitalist countries and the imperialized formations" and "demands from us that we narrate ourselves through a form commensurate with [Jameson's] ideal-type."[25]

Jameson unwittingly reestablishes the same geopolitical map as those he is ostensibly writing against: that cultures are understandable, that they completely represent peoples, and that they are bifurcated into the West and the not-West, two incommensurate and totally self-contained systems that owe nothing to one another. Two assumptions enable this recurrence. The first, as Ahmad points out, is a drastic conflation of all that is Western and all that is not Western: to Jameson as well as the cultural purists, there is little important difference between, for example, Jamaican and Balinese literature. The second is a continuing denial of debt to alterity, an image of both the self and the other as independent, self-constituting identities. For Jameson's argument, the West must be entirely intelligible on its own terms, must have no need of otherness to place itself in a world cartography. Aesthetic judgment and culture in general then become no more than coalition calculation; one can only be for or against "third world literature," because all non-Western literature can only stand as interchangeable allegories of national cultures.

This is not to say that all apprehension of other cultures is pernicious, of course; only that such apprehension is never mere apprehension. It is always politically constituted and is therefore never politically inert. Familiarity with other cultures enables exploration of inconsistencies in and alternatives to one's own culture. However, a necessary precondition to such a use is a recognition of the situated nature of cultural understanding and to the processes by which these maps are produced. Without an understanding of the political nature of apprehension, cultural apprehension becomes cultural consumption.

The next section attempts to explore this process of becoming. The first part answers the obvious question as to why a political perception of other cultures can be understood as a question of aesthetics, problematizing the traditionally unproblematic ways in which individuals locate themselves in questions of valuation and taste. It then locates these conceptions in practices in the United States, specifically insofar as American cultural networks evaluate non-American cultural artifacts and practices. For an American to know Peruvian art often has little to do with Peru, and much to do with that person's social position in the United States. Finally, this section examines the practice of multiculturalism in the cultural relationships between the United States and European and non-European countries to show how the "multicultural" is tyrannized by a specifically Western social logic and is thereby transformed into the very thing that its promulgators believe they oppose: cultural consumption under the pretense of understanding. Ownership of a Mexican masque not only positions the owner in the United States but also places and encourages a certain aesthetic and set of social logics of Mexico. To put it another way, it is a map of the world.

SOCIAL AESTHETICS

Mapping is representation—creation as much as discovery. Understanding other cultures has traditionally been seen as merely Kantian ascertaining, where understanding denotes a kind of transparency between cultures. This arises from a relatively unproblematic picture of the connection between humans and things, with understanding simply the mental re-creation of what is experienced. For Kant, perception, even mental perception, is still experiential and representational even if he does understand it as in some way mediated.[26] Understanding is thus neither more nor less than clarity of rational representation.

Cultures, in this traditional sense, are no more than systems to be mastered, rules to be determined rather than experiences to be lived. Understanding is seen as a basically mentalistic activity: foreign cultures are objects of study; if they are opaque, it is only because of a lack of adequate methods of conversion to other systems of meaning.[27] Foreign cultures are fit into certain frameworks supplied by disciplines like foreign policy and international relations. The efficacy of these frameworks is the degree to which they make cultures sensible, how they enable systematic representations of societies. These frameworks are considered successful precisely insofar as they can model that which resists modeling. This is a totalizing conception: all practices through which alterity is encountered are bracketed by this Kantian paradigm.

It is no coincidence that this model of representational knowledge has its greatest difficulties with aesthetics. The Kantian cognitive apparatus is stymied, in part, by the recognition that judgments can be subjective, as questions of taste necessarily are.[28] Culture and aesthetics are more properly relational. An alternative conception of culture is Heideggerian: that what "being-human" means is constituted every day, all the time, by humans' relationships to the things around them, not merely when in reflection on those things. Heidegger, for example, understands the Nietzschean will to power as primarily artistic, creative, and constitutive: "Art and Truth, creating and knowing, meet one another in the single guiding perspective of the rescue and configuration of the sensuous."[29] What is true and what is aesthetic are one and the same: to be in the world is to make rather than to discover.

Questions of cultural judgment, such as value and taste, are thus creations rather than discoveries. Algirdas Julien Greimas centers the act of valuing as constitutive of the cognitive apparatus rather than the other way around. In exploring the semantic structuration that enables evaluation, he describes the ways in which the concept of value is only possible in the narrative structure that conjoins subject to object, showing that value arises only when the possibility of this conjunction exists.[30] To Greimas, valuation is constitutive of both the object and the subject; it is the realization of value that creates these identities. "The subject is, therefore, semantically determined through its relation with the value."[31] In the semiotic production of identity, it is the narrative schemata that "call the subjects and objects into a semiotic existence" (90).

At the global level, Homi Bhabha calls this "narrating": the articulation and concretization of a people as a people. The subjects and objects called into existence as the world is mapped are the people of the world, the mappers as much as the mapped. The difference between the two is that those who do not take part in the mapping, whether through choice, distance, or exclusion, have their identities constituted for them. As value is positioned, relationships between peoples are established. Bhabha politicizes the global narrations as "a form of temporality that is open to disjunction and discontinuity and sees the process of history engaged . . . in the framing and naming of social reality."[32] In other words, to map is to "do" politics: to make political judgments, to place people in different worlds, to grant and deny opportunities—but also to attempt to depoliticize and naturalize these judgments. Only when aesthetic judgment is understood as partial, fragmentary, and temporally located, when it can be seen as a conflictual narrative rather than a stable truth, can it be resisted and re-created.

Placing the narrativity of valuation at the center of cultural analysis brings forth multiple avenues by which value is composed. The constructions of the subject and identity are contingent on national and international narratives of value. These narratives of value are less theoretically and more succinctly recognizable in the contemporary conservative jeremiads about the loss of an allegedly core set of American values. The concept of a multicultural United States society is threatening to both the national narrative that depends on a stability of values and to the individuals constituted in such a system. It is the multiplicity of valuation in multiculturalism that is the most provocative: the conception that value is fixed and inherent has been the prerequisite to standardizing values and a necessary condition for stabilizing moral identities. Cultural pluralism—a relation to cultural alterity not harnessed to the desire to control or possess—contests the tendency for culture to naturalize itself as reality rather than contingency, to be unreflective of its own placement as only one possible practice of life. For example, as the Americas are first being generated by Europe, Columbus fails to understand value as it takes place in different cultures. That the Americans find glass as fascinating and valuable as gold coins, or that they cannot tell the difference between coins of different denominations, is clear evidence to Columbus of their inability to understand the truth of value.[33] He thus places them outside the realm of civilization.

Where valuation has been depoliticized through assertions of concrete significance, taste (its mirror image in aesthetic judgment) has been depoliticized by being characterized as the unfettered preferences of atomized individuals. Pierre Bourdieu demonstrates that taste, far from being merely a personal, disassociated choice, is actually a representation of the dense networks of class.[34] What have traditionally been understood as isolated preferences are in fact highly dependent on the positioning of the social structures that locate the individual. Aesthetic affiliations, displayed in taste, demonstrate solidarity with a social group. Taste both creates the conceptions of legitimacy and is the source of symbolic authority for the classes that control capital. By avowing the separateness of taste and the socially determined, classes can continue to identify unproblematically with determined choices while denying that these choices have any social or political design.

To map is to designate members of social classes (in the broadest sense of that term), as well as national peoples, through an aesthetic discrimination in relation to others. These Heideggerian paradigms enable a different model of the ways in which we understand foreign cultures. The traditional Kantian mentalistic direct representation (e.g., the way people are described in a textbook) becomes far less important than the constitution of selves in relation to incarnations of other cultures in everyday life. The immediate and commonplace aspects of cultural items—the things valued—augment relations with alterity; the artifactual is far more important than the intellectual in determining these relations. To determine the American understanding of Africa, for example, most academics study canonical texts of foreign policy like state department bulletins or administration policy statements. These are not unimportant sources, but they are insignificant and tangential to Americans' common lives. More germane to the U.S. comprehension of other peoples are the aesthetic associations with them, the everyday relationships between our lives and other cultures: using African clothing styles, displaying native crafts, wearing handmade jewelry, or viewing imagery of their ways of life in *National Geographic*.[35] Through these cartographic creations, Africans, for example, become objects of a zoological gaze, curiosities of the world rather than significant players in issues of international affairs. Paul Simon is thus a far more important American-international diplomat than whoever happens to be the American representative to the United Nations at a particular time, because he has far more control over representations of "Africanness." It is as important to examine everyday interactions with aesthetic judgments of other cultures as to study the ways those cultures are represented by disciplines like international relations.[36]

The study of the transmission of cultural taste and value is neither a prosaic version of comparative politics nor a study comparing transmissions between different cultures. One cannot compare culture in general without oversimplification, eventually, like Jameson, representing all nonwhite countries as "third world" or "underdeveloped." Yet personal interactions with cultural products do exactly that: they act as cultural markers that both reinforce positions of authority within the United States and connote representational facility with the cultures symbolized. When foreign cultures are introduced into a cultural economy, they are dealt with by the cultural residents through various strategies, which extend from disinterest and dismissal to acceptance and practice, and permutations in between. Each of these strategies is a reaction to a perceived cultural challenge: having been brought up outside a culture, one can only perceive that culture through methods of representation.[37] The study of one culture's (in this case, the United States') reactions to and interpretations of the multicultural is not in fact a study of all the cultures that are affecting the dominant culture, but is a study of a specific aspect of the dominant culture. This interpretation is homologous to an individual psychological one: a person is understood by examining the ways in which he or she identifies and copes with threats, or challenges, or different methods of learning.

It is irrelevant whether the ideology of a culture is homogenous (such as Germany's) or heterogenous (such as the United States'). Not only is such a self-reading likely to be misleadingly partial (the United States is far from the egalitarian "melting pot" it represents itself as, whereas Germany's "monolithic" culture is a compendium of radically different historical practices), but its self-interpretations can easily be rationalizations for inconsistent behaviors. It is difficult, for example, to reconcile America's conception of itself as tolerant and welcoming to other cultures with its historical relations with cultures that challenged the American cosmology or with cultures that were deliberately eliminated, such as Native American or African.

The analysis of aesthetic alterity must discuss the ways in which practices are assimilated (or not, as the case may be) into American practices of cultural representation, in much the way that Said's *Orientalism* is about the West's hegemonic apperception of its "other." Orientalism is the poverty of this apperception, the lack of its reflexivity, how it is controlled (whether as ideological, intellectual, or economic) and the production and dissemination of forms of knowledge about the other. In the cultural sphere, the same problems arise: cultural understanding is one-dimensional, produced through set methods, and uncomprehending of the positionings of the self in the relationship. The process by which this other-cultural knowledge becomes valuable is a particular one, but not particular to the twentieth century. A survey of nineteenth-century cultural valuation in America shows the same kinds of tastes, from Thoreau's obvious pride in being able to quote Confucius and Hindu poetry to the trendiness of Hawaii in the 1890s, tastes often mingled with a history of colonization and imperialism.[38]

If indeed the sense that aesthetics are divorced from interaction with and creation of the world is rejected, it follows that it is no longer possible to treat relationships—be they global or personal in nature—as if they are merely cognitive. Exploring the heterogeneity and variety of world aesthetics is crucial to understanding what the "foreign" in foreign policy (let alone the "inter" in international relations) can suggest. Yet this is singularly difficult terrain with historically loaded maps already in existence.

AESTHETICS AS FOREIGN POLICY

To understand specific means by which bureaucratizing discourses map the world, I turn to an exemplary site of cultural illustration, where the questions of value are most explicitly raised: the modern museum. The museum works as a microcosm of foreign representation for the United States, positioning different sets of humans as objects of knowledge rather than actors and creators of cultures. As a site of knowledge, it delineates and charts peoples and places, rendering their cultural practices intelligible at a glance. As a diorama, it freezes, fixes, displays them. The space of the museum has traditionally been used as a cultural *ur*text: it teaches cultures and communities how to read culture, what paradigmatic interpretations to apply. In its representation of art, cultures, science, and history, a museum is intended to be a total repository of those aspects of interpretation: to be, as Donna Haraway points out, both complete and perfect in its representation.[39]

In placing peoples as objects to be viewed and classified, museums epitomize the teaching of cultures as zoological tableaux. They encourage a reading of alterity that is acquisitive, lacks self-reflection, and depoliticizes otherness. James Clifford has written extensively on the relative meaning systems inherent in such classifications: for example, why aspects of some cultures tend to be represented as aspects of nature whereas aspects of others are determined to be examples of art, ostensibly man's highest calling.[40] The systems of value that determine placement in a hierarchical catalog of culture, however, are not limited to museums. They also exist within the mappings of cultures and nations discussed earlier, following from and augmenting museological representation.

The strategy of reading peoples that American museums provide becomes replicated at the international level, in general placing those cultures found most "premodern" (viz., un-Western) in the natural history museums. In this reading, those cultures represent the evolutionary stages of man, as "he" gradually becomes different from animals. Therefore, these native peoples, not quite human, are classified with the animals, as "natural" in their history.[41] The Europeans, and a few other "cultured" nationalities, are represented as historical or artistic, or are omitted from overt representation entirely. In other words, the French do not need to be represented as a unified people in a museum, because their culture is, it is assumed, far more accessible or even so much a given that in a sense the world provides access to French culture.

Museological understandings of culture reproduce the aesthetic as pregiven, apolitical, and consumable and thus confirm alterior peoples as the same. The museological understanding of cultures constructs the "foreign world" as a display, a performance, an exhibit.

The world is a presentation for us; the only voices that count are the ones to which we are attuned. The Western viewpoint is privileged as the omniscient narrator and interpretive authority, when in fact it is merely un(self-)reflective as to its own subjective positionings.

Americans' perception of culture depends on a homologous organon of difference; dissimilarity and culture are strongly correlated. All cultures are not created equal: some (the British and the Germanic) are seen as much more "advanced" than others (the Colombian or the Vietnamese). This perception follows a persistent set of overlapping motifs, partly colonial, partly racial. It is no coincidence, however, that the latter cultures are more foreign, perceived as more "other." The cultural representations held in high esteem in the United States tend to share the value systems of Western, "first-world" countries, and thus are better able to be mapped within already existing structures of interpretation. The culture systems of "third-world" countries, on the other hand, have different systems of valuation, and the cultures themselves are devalued in the international hierarchy. This is the legacy of museological perception.

The specific cultural logics of American perception and valuation of these cultures follow a familiar pattern. Although most Americans ignore the cultures of non-European countries, especially compared to the value they place on the obvious repositories of European culture like France, Britain, and Germany, those with cultural capital tend to highly value cultures of the "third world." The aforementioned clothing trends, the repeated appropriation of Latin American and African musical styles by the musically elite, and the collection of cultural artifacts (linguistically constituted as "artifacts," not art) are all examples of the transfer of culture from "third-world" countries to the United States.

Only certain aspects of the non-European cultures are valued in the United States. In European artifacts, what is valuable to Americans tends to be that which is already valued in the European culture from which it emanates: artistic works, pop or classical music, forms of philosophical discourse, cinema, and so on, reflecting and reinforcing the systems of European value. On the other hand, many non-European peoples evaluate culture differently from the Americans' dominant paradigm. The items valued by those in the United States are not those that appear to be poor copies of Western civilization; instead, the cultural capitalists value that which over-represents and confirms the otherness of the culture: items like handmade pottery, woven cloths, and tribal rhythms. North American tastes are radically different from the established tastes of these countries; rather than accepting the other culture's definitions of valuable and valueless culture, Americans apply criteria external to the society, thereby redetermining cultural value. Appropriation disregards the culture's own evaluations between, for instance, high and low, instead applying its own. This is the logic of cultural consumption and commodification: a redetermination that adjudicates new cultural valuation, emphasizing cultural practices that fit predetermined prejudices. Unsurprisingly, what those tastes esteem in an "underdeveloped" country is what they are conditioned by cultural prejudices to esteem: those aspects of the culture that are the most different, more "uncivilized," closest to nature. The value of these cultural practices is greatest, to us, where modernity has tread lightest.

Tending to devalue these cultures in the cultural sphere, and still needing a distinctive stance, such consumption ends up privileging the aspects of the cultures that are the most difficult to access. As a result, by inverting these tastes, American consumption delegitimizes the structures, often modeled quite explicitly after Western ones, that assign value. By covertly telling countries that the greatest cultural treasures they possess are the ones that are the least Western, the implication is that the teleology of their cultural position is one of doomed inferiority. This is cultural hegemony in its strongest sense: the structures of evaluation for cultural commodities accentuate the perception of "backwardness," the "underdeveloped" aspects of these cultures.

Such hierarchical evaluation is pernicious in many ways: it assesses that which is incompletely understood, it judges the alterior only according to its own precepts, it is incapable of recognizing cultural plurality in the world, and it lacks political recognition of its own cultural positioning as historically and spatially located. Yet it informs the entire procedure of global mapping that constitutes many Western forms of identity.

The ostensible interest in nativist aspects of other cultures, usually presented as culturally freeing (the project of cultural diversity), is actually a way of remapping the world as a system of dominance. When tourists display Caribbean souvenirs, when American musicians use the rhythms of African *mbanqua*, when college students buy Chilean peasant shirts, even when Roland Barthes uses Asian art to develop his concept of *ecriture*—each is appropriating cultural commodities and continuing a kind of tyranny of intercultural taste.[42] Museological representation impoverishes our understanding of the world by dividing the world into the "civilized" and the "natural," by categorizing "art" and "artifact" in racially coded ways, and by the very process of laying out a smorgasbord of cultures from which the passive viewer picks and chooses.

Geopolitically, this domination is replicated at the level of political representation. Cultural dissimilarities become celebrated in such a way as to delegitimate the societies from which they emanate. The songlines of Native Australians, an alternative mapping of the world, identify them as "primitive," unable to represent space in its modern, truthful form.[43] Difference in political or juridical systems is seen as illustrative of an inherent, unbroachable structure of differences in identities. Hence the worldview common to many of the multiculturalists as well as the antimulticulturalists: that which is not understood by us cannot be understood, those that do not speak to us do not speak, they who do not act for us do not act. Multiculturalism is far too often merely a camouflage for an imperious exploitation of difference for the sake of difference rather than a genuine appreciation of specific dissimilarities or even acknowledgment that it is possible for people to exist in ways that can be neither experienced nor understood. Culture, as an exemplifying category, does not contest the basis of "foreignness" as difference or as alterity; it is merely a contention about what is and is not foreign. Museological representation encourages a lack of political reflection in avowing the truth of its portrayals and denying the evanescence of our particular viewing.

This is precisely why culture, in its current understanding, is such a problematic ground to use to map the world. A foreign policy based on cultural distinction will simplify the world as immediately comprehensible, easily probed, radically alterior, and excessively singular. Not that it is possible for foreign policy not be aesthetic: knowledges and judgments are always intertwined. But it is desirable to be aware of and able to theorize the complexity of relationships to alterity as it is confronted. To deny the political nature of such a confrontation is to deny the violence done through simplistic representations and to obstruct its contestation.

David Campbell enacts such a politicization in foregrounding the interrelationships of foreign policy, identity, and alterity. He explains that the "constant (re)writing of the character of U.S. society in the Foreign Policy texts suggests . . . that the practices of foreign policy serve to enframe, limit, and domesticate a particular identity."[44] As its character is rewritten once again, it is important to pay attention to how it rewrites others.

The first step is to reject the story of the Cold War territorialization as a victory over alterity, the final achievement of a world without a dangerous enemy, which ignores "the debt that subjectivity owes to otherness and the role the requirements of identity play in giving rise to discourses of danger."[45] Yet even the rejection of this allegorical depiction of recent history is ineffectual unless it encourages a critical reading of our continuing remapping of the world, a remapping that seeks new methods of territorialization and takes advantage of powerful old ones, wherein everyday cultural representations of peoples are among the most time-honored and have a continuing robustness.

American identity is reliant on conceptions of the other; the domestic self is opposed to foreign ones. Yet these selves are always complex and multivarious, represented in only a few of an infinite variety of possibilities. Campbell's understanding of the American relation of identity and difference focuses on only one of these, a predominantly oppositional one, that originates primarily from the aspects and foci of the field of foreign policy qua state security. Campbell is not himself responsible for placing threat at the center of foreign policy, of course; danger has long been the dominant way for American bureaucratic discourses to map the relation of the United States to the world. But to focus exclusively on threat and security is to miss a larger sense of the ways in which the foreign and the domestic are intermingled, that is, not only in the reaction to and construction of external and internal threats, but in the aforementioned construction of, and reactions to, ways of dwelling both external and internal.

In the aftermath of the Soviet Union's disintegration, threat continues to direct U.S. foreign policy. But foreign policy continues in other directions as well, and though drugs and trade (the threats Campbell picks as likely to continue the discourses of danger) are important components of present American policy, they are less powerful and ubiquitous than the more prosaic ways in which alterity is experienced (viz., our cultural mapping of the world). It remains important to pay attention to these other long-standing and newly reemergent territorializations that serve to make "coherence and necessity out of accident and contingency."[46] More important, in fact, than the traditional geopolitical territorialization, because the establishment of foreign states in a geopolitical sphere is more readily recognized as a political process than is the establishment of aesthetic connotations.

The USSR was an exemplary state; ideology more readily lent itself to a cognitivist frame because it enforced an internal logical coherence. "State" and "ideology" correspond well: the territories of each are relatively fixed and stable. Culture, on the other hand, is a plurality of flows and meanings, meanings no less powerful for their incoherence within fixed logical systems.[47] For example, the U.S. imaginary of its "Indians" as simultaneously noble primitives and bloodthirsty savages has certainly been no less potent for its logical inconsistencies. Integral to the remapping of alterity by contemporary bureaucratic and academic discourses are a simplification and denial of plurality of newly established territories. The museological cultural map attempts to replace ideology with cultures in just such an exemplary way.

NOTES

1. Michael Rogin, "Kiss Me Deadly: Communism, Motherhood, and Cold War Movies," *Representations* 6 (1984), p. 2.

2. Carol Cohn, "Sex and Death in the Rational World of Defense Intellectuals," *Signs* 12, no. 4 (1987), pp. 687-718.

3. Lee Edelman, "Tearooms and Sympathy, or, The Epistemology of the Water Closet," in *Nationalisms and Sexualities,* ed. Andrew Parker, Mary Russo, Doris Sommer, and Patricia Yaeger (New York: Routledge, 1992), pp. 263-84.

4. William Epstein, "Counter Intelligence: Cold-War Criticism and Eighteenth Century Studies," *English Literary History* 57, no. 1 (spring 1990), pp. 63-99.

5. For additional examples, see Andrew Ross, "Containing Culture in the Cold War," *Cultural Studies* 1, no. 3 (1987), pp. 328-48.

6. As will become clear later, I use the term *mapping* actively; viz., as

something created and produced rather than unearthed and discovered. By using a spatial metaphor, I am trying to foreground the ways in which the political spaces of the world are manufactured, how people are made the objects of social categorizations, not to reify abstract social theory by grounding it in a concrete metaphor. In doing so, I want to emphasize "the imbrication of material and metaphorical space." See Neil Smith and Cindi Katz, "Grounding Metaphor: Towards a Spatialized Politics," in *Place and the Politics of Identity,* ed. Michael Keith and Steve Pile (New York: Routledge, 1993), pp. 67-83.

7. David Campbell, *Writing Security: United States Foreign Policy and the Politics of Identity* (Minneapolis: University of Minnesota Press, 1992), p. 144.

8. Ibid., p. 195.

9. Warren Christopher, statement before the Senate Foreign Relations Committee, Jan. 13, 1993.

10. Les Aspin, "National Security in the 1990s: Defining a New Basis for U.S. Military Forces," presented to the Atlantic Council of the United States, Jan. 6, 1992, p. 6.

11. Gilles Deleuze and Félix Guattari, "Savages, Barbarians, Civilized Men," in *Anti-Oedipus: Capitalism and Schizophrenia,* trans. Robert Hurley, Mark Seem, and Helen R. Lane (New York: Viking Press, 1977), pp. 139-271.

12. Ibid., p. 221.

13. See "Democracy and Territoriality," in *Rhetorical Republic: Governing Representations in American Politics,* ed. Frederick M. Dolan and Tom Dumm (Amherst: University of Massachusetts Press, 1993).

14. See also "Space, Knowledge, and Power," in *The Foucault Reader,* ed. Paul Rabinow (New York: Pantheon, 1984), pp. 239-59.

15. Aspin, p. 18 (table 4: America's Changing Views about Security).

16. Samuel P. Huntington, "The Clash of Civilizations?" *Foreign Affairs* 72, no.3 (1993), p. 22.

17. Edward Said, *Orientalism* (New York: Vintage, 1979).

18. Arjun Appadurai, "Disjuncture and Difference in the Global Cultural Economy," *Public Culture* 2, no. 2 (1990), p. 12.

19. Ibid., p. 7.

20. For example, Benedict Anderson, *Imagined Communities* (New York: Verso, 1991).

21. See, for example, Roger Kimball, *Tenured Radicals: How Politics Has Corrupted Our Higher Education* (New York: Harper and Row, 1990); Arthur M. Schlesigner Jr., *The Disuniting of America* (New York: Norton, 1992); and Charles Taylor, *Multiculturalism and "The Politics of Recognition": An Essay* (Princeton: Princeton University Press, 1992), respectively.

22. Some essayists are beginning to recognize the falseness of this opposition. A particularly germane article is a Marxist analysis of multiculturalism's rôle in expanding global markets. See David Reiff, "Multiculturalism's Silent Partner," *Harper's Magazine* (August 1993), pp. 62-72.

23. An extended critique of these denials of debt at the state level is in William E. Connolly, *Identity/Difference: Democratic Negotiations of Political Paradox* (Ithaca: Cornell University Press, 1991).

24. Fredric Jameson, "Third-World Literature in the Era of Multinational Capitalism," *Social Text* no. 15 (fall 1988), pp. 65-88.

25. Aijaz Ahmad, "Jameson's Rhetoric of Otherness and the 'National Allegory'" *Social Text* (fall 1987), p. 3, 11.

26. For a reading of Kant from a noncognitivist framework, see Heidegger's extended essay on Kant's understanding of our relationships to objects: Martin Heidegger, *What Is a Thing?* trans. W. B. Barton Jr. and Vera Deutsch (Chicago: Henry Regnery, 1968).

27. For a comparison, see Tzvetan Todorov's criticisms of Columbus in *The Conquest of America: The Question of the Other*, trans. Richard Howard (New York: Harper and Row, 1984), pp. 15-50, as being linguistically simplistic: insisting, for instance, that the Amerindians' words for different kinds of rulership be exactly translatable into Spanish political categories.

28. In the section of his *Critique of Judgment* titled "Analytic of the Beautiful," Kant recognizes that some questions of aesthetics cannot, by their very nature, be universal, but he cannot allow that they are not at some level connected to his conception of a "uniform cognitive machine." See Barbara Herrnstein Smith, *Contingencies of Value* (Cambridge: Harvard University Press, 1988) p. 67. See also Paul de Man's discussion of the various rôles that Kant tries to make the sublime fulfill in "Phenomenality and Materiality in Kant," in *Immanuel Kant: Critical Assessments*, vol. 4, ed. Ruth Chadwick and Clive Cazeaux (New York: Routledge, 1992), pp. 334-55.

29. Martin Heidegger, *Nietzsche*, vol. 1, *The Will to Power as Art*, trans. David Farrell Krell (San Francisco: Harper and Row, 1979), p. 161.

30. Algirdas Julien Greimas, *On Meaning: Selected Writings in Semiotic Theory*, trans. Paul Perron and Frank Collins (Minneapolis: University of Minnesota Press, 1987), pp. 84-87.

31. Ibid., p. 87.

32. Homi Bhabha, "The World and the Home," *Social Text* nos. 31-32 (summer 1993) p. 144.

33. Todorov, p. 38.

34. Pierre Bourdieu, *Distinction: A Social Critique of the Judgement of Taste*, trans. Richard Nice (Cambridge: Harvard University Press, 1984).

35. See Catherine Lutz and Jane Collins, *Reading National Geographic* (Chicago: University of Chicago Press, 1993).

36. This is not to argue that the aesthetic should be understood merely through being reduced to some essential nature of capital through the commodification of its sign value: capital holds no materially privileged vantage point from which to understand the nature of the aesthetic (contra Fredric Jameson, *Postmodernism, or the Cultural Logic of Late Capitalism* [Durham: Duke University Press, 1991] and Edward W. Soja, *Postmodern Geographies: The Reassertion of Space in Critical Social Theory* [London: Verso, 1989]). In other words, there is no neutral, evaluative "standard" from which we may judge. I do, however, follow these theorists in noting and rejecting the ways in which Hegelian and Marxist historicism denies differences in space by placing all societies on a singular, temporal progression, in which the West is positioned farther ahead than all others.

37. I of course do not mean to suggest that those who grow up *in* a culture do not rely on representations of that culture as well. In fact, cultural comparison is the only way for an individual to problematize her own culture, to stop seeing it as total and therefore natural.

38. See, for example, throughout *Walden*.

39. Donna Haraway, "Teddy Bear Patriarchy: Taxidermy in the Garden of Eden, New York City, 1908-1936," in Haraway, *Primate Visions* (New York: Routledge, 1991), p. 30.

40. James Clifford, *The Predicament of Culture* (Cambridge: Harvard University Press, 1988).

41. Ivan Karp, "Culture and Representation," in *Exhibiting Cultures: The Poetics and Politics of Museum Display* (Washington, D.C.: Smithsonian Institution Press, 1991), pp. 11-24, at p. 23.

42. Roland Barthes, "Caro Antonioni," *Art & Text* April 1985, p. 45, quoted in Trinh Minh-ha, *When the Moon Waxes Red* (New York: Routledge, 1991).

43. Bruce Chatwin, *The Songlines* (New York: Penguin, 1987).

44. Campbell, *Writing Security*, p. 158.

45. Ibid., p. 249.

46. Pierre Bourdieu, *Outline of a Theory of Practice* (Cambridge: Cambridge University Press, 1987), p. 87.

47. Bourdieu refers to this as "Overdetermination through indetermination" in ibid., p. 110.

7

Cartographic Anxiety: Mapping the Body Politic in India

SANKARAN KRISHNA

The parliamentary elections of May 1991 in India were disrupted by the assassination of former prime minister Rajiv Gandhi. In the aftermath of this event one of the ubiquitous election posters of the Congress (I) party showed a picture of Rajiv Gandhi's identity card. On that card the space allocated for "Religion" was filled by the word "Indian." The not-so-subtle implication was that the slain leader had, in his lifetime, transcended divisive societal identities such as Hindu or Muslim and defined himself primarily as a secular citizen of a nation-state.[1]

The effacement of alternative identities inherent in the filling out of the identity card and their replacement by one based on the modern, sovereign, nation-state (that of "citizen") are interesting. At one level, this action can be seen as an attempt to rewrite India in terms of a univocal narrative of modern nationalism, a nationalism that is supposedly "secular" and hostile to all other forms of identity. The "retrospective illusion"[2] of nationalism renders alternative selves, be they religious, regional, linguistic, or ethnic, as spurious, reactionary, and vestigial. Moreover, modernity comes to be defined in the disciplining of ambiguity and its intolerance for multiple or layered notions of identity or sovereignty: citizenship is invariably an either-or matter.[3]

Yet, at another level, the equation of religion with Indian highlights the fact that terms like nationalism, sovereignty, and citizenship are themselves implicated in practices that are, in their own way, the rituals of a modern "faith." Contemporary nationalism may then, according to this line of thought, be regarded as one in a long line of discourses that have sought to construct social reality and identity for people in a space.[4]

The production of national identity is a contested process everywhere, and the struggle to produce citizens out of recalcitrant peoples accounts for much of what passes for history in modern times.[5] In India, as in many another setting, the process has been accompanied by an enormous degree of violence, both physical and epistemic. This essay looks at one small facet of this ongoing process of nation building in India: that of cartography. By cartography I mean more than the technical and scientific mapping of the country. I use the term to refer to representational practices that in various ways have attempted to inscribe something called "India" and endow that entity with a content, a history, a meaning, and a trajectory. Under such a definition, cartography becomes nothing less than the social and political production of nationality itself. Within this, I am specifically interested in the visual depiction of competing representations of India in public culture, such as the way the country is depicted in political posters, government maps, newspaper and newsmagazine articles, election campaign literature, and other such artifacts that seek to create and reproduce the symbolic universe of the Indian nation.

The argument of this essay can be summarized as follows. In a postcolonial society such as India, the anxiety surrounding questions of national identity and survival is particularly acute.[6] Although this anxiety is writ large over the political culture of the country, its cartographic manifestations are particularly interesting and revealing. Specifically, the ubiquity of cartographic metaphors, the production of inside and outside along the borders of the country, reveals both the epistemic and physical violence that accompanies the enterprise of nation building. At the same time, people who live along borderlines are wont to regard this latest discursive universe of nationality and territoriality as one more minefield to be navigated safely at minimum, and profited from at best. The encounters between the state and the people along the borderlines are suggestive of the contested and tortured production of sovereign identity. Ultimately, cartographic anxiety is a facet of a larger postcolonial anxiety—of a society suspended forever in the space between the ex-colony and not-yet-nation. This suspended state can be seen in the discursive production of India as a bounded, sovereign entity and the deployment of this in everyday politics and in the violent borders. Quotidian life along the borderlines and its micropolitics render transparent the arbitrariness and the violence of the discourse of nationhood. Cartographic anxiety, from this perspective, becomes a prominent signifier of the postcolony.

READING MAPS AS TEXTS

> Maps are too important to be left to cartographers alone.
>
> J. B. HARLEY[7]

Despite his firm belief in the timeless existence of a spiritual and civilizational entity called "India," Jawaharlal Nehru nevertheless felt compelled to begin his appropriately titled *Discovery of India* with a solid and physicalistic description of her "natural" frontiers.[8] Nehru's imaginative geography depicted impassable mountain ranges, vast deserts, and deep oceans that produced a "natural" cradle for what became India. Anxiety regarding the physical boundaries of the nation gets inscribed early in Nehru's *Autobiography*.[9] The narrative script that runs through that definitive work in imagining India clearly traces her downfall to porous frontiers and, more importantly, to an unfortunate timing by which disunited and fragmenting India encountered the cresting and united civilization of the British. The encounter not only produced colonial rule but also with it, Nehru argued, the sources of India's eventual redemption: modernity, science, the rational spirit, and, most importantly, national unity.[10]

The worst fears regarding physical boundaries were realized with the partition of India at independence in 1947 into India and Pakistan. Nehru's recollections of that event are worth quoting:

All our communications were upset and broken. Telegraphs, telephones, postal services and almost everything as a matter of fact was disrupted. Our services were broken up. Our army was broken up. Our irrigation systems were broken and so many other things happened . . . *But above all, what was broken up which was of the highest importance was something very vital and that was the body of India.* That produced tremendous consequences, not only those that you saw, but those that you cannot imagine, in the minds and souls of millions of human beings.[11]

As this creation-by-amputation has attempted to achieve nation-hood, the corporeal element of its existence has remained fore-grounded. It is perhaps unsurprising that this child of partition, India, has cartographic anxiety inscribed into its very genetic code. In the years since 1947, history can be (and often is) read as a series of encounters with this anxiety: if China in 1962 represented a de-moralizing defeat, Bangladesh in 1971 has been recorded as an im-portant victory. Since independence (or since partition), the anxiety has been showcased perfectly in the space of desire called Kashmir. More importantly, "accurate" representations of the body politic in maps and insignia are watched with an intensity that is perhaps un-equaled elsewhere.

In India today, there is an evident obsession with "alien" infiltra-tion, with shadowy "foreign hands" out to destabilize the country, with the need for a blue-water navy to secure the peninsular coast-lines, with plans to construct a fence along the borders with Pakistan and Bangladesh, and with the various threats to the "unity and in-tegrity" of the nation.[12] The prevalence of cartographic themes in po-litical discourse can be seen in the following spectacle. During the Republic Day celebrations in January 1992, the leader of the Bhara-tiya Janata Party (hereafter BJP), Murli Manohar Joshi, embarked on what was described as an "Ekta Yatra" (literally, "Unity Pilgrim-age," note the religious metaphor) to begin at the southern tip of India and to culminate in a grand flag-hoisting ceremony in Srinagar, the capital of the state of Kashmir at the northern end of India. When the "yatra" appeared as if it would be delayed, if not aborted, by avalanches and bad weather, the country was exhorted by the BJP's leaders to draw an outline map of India in the soil nearest them and plant the Indian tricolor on the spot represented by Srinagar.[13]

Cartographic themes were prominent in the elections to the par-liament in 1989, which witnessed an unprecedented use of the mass media to gain popular support. The ruling Congress (I) party, as it has done since at least 1977, played on the fears of impending na-tional disintegration and portrayed itself as the sole party capable of averting balkanization. The party released a series of political com-mercials, published widely in leading newspapers and magazines, including in the regional languages, hammering home this theme of the nation in danger. The series is perhaps best represented by the example in Figure 7.1.[14] The deliberate invocation of the "shape" of India and the notions of anxiety and danger are all too obvious. The conscious use of "heart" inflects the anxiety with connection between blood and soil.

Figure 7.1

As the physical map of India gains ubiquity as an iconic representation of the body politic, it becomes the terrain for competing efforts to define, and possess, the self. In response, the Opposition parties put out their versions of India (Figures 7.2 and 7.3).

Listing a litany of their complaints against the ruling party, these maps are dominated by a narrative that contrasts the normal and the pathological. The utility of such a trope in discussions of the body politic has a long genealogy[15] and is here represented by inscribing the problems of the nation literally all across the map. The BJP's map

Figure 7.2

focuses on all the territorial "losses" of the Congress government, an argument underlain by an implicit reference to the Hindu fundamentalist ideas of "Akhand Bharat" (Greater India).[16] The theme that drives this map is one of the body politic being literally diminished by loss of territory on the one hand and by disease and impurity on the other. Girding the former are the references to "Tibet and Aksai Chin Gifted to China," "Azad Kashmir to Pakistan," whereas the latter is substantiated by references to "infiltration," "fiasco in Sri Lanka," and "terrorism in Punjab." Running down the center of Figure 3 is the theme of corruption and graft literally polluting the nation and hollowing the body politic.

THE CHOICE IS YOURS...

A one-man's corrupt and inefficient rule that has thrown the nation in the grip of . . .	A mature and patriotic leadership that is fully committed to give the nation .

FOR A PEOPLE'S GOVERNMENT

Support

NATIONAL FRONT

VOTE FOR CANDIDATES OF:

	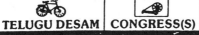		
JANATA DAL	TELUGU DESAM	CONGRESS(S)	DMK

Joint campaign of National Front

Figure 7.3

In contrast, the Congress's map (Figure 1) represents the country in a form of pristine solidity, with the state boundaries within the map adding a further element of veiled threat: it is not just the distant international borders that are in danger but also the intranational borders, which have often been subject to violent renegotiation in India's recent history.

At a societal level, the perceived indispensability of "secure" or "inviolate" borders for national development, in fact for nationality itself, is a recurring theme. A typical comment regarding borders runs as follows:

> According to political scientists one of the prerequisites for the ordered growth of a modern nation state is settled boundaries. Once a

country has well defined borders, the planned development of the various sectors of the economy becomes easier and predictable. Also, as a member of the comity of nations it will have more credibility, if not confidence, in its relations with other nations when it knows that its internationally accepted borders cannot draw it into the mire of territorial chauvinism . . . After almost 40 years as an independent country, India still has undefined borders with two of its neighbours.[17]

The theme of being somewhat less than a nation in the absence of secure borders is repeated in news reports and editorials. Physical preservation of the borders has become metonymous with the state of the union.

What these invocations regarding the sanctity of the body politic usually push to the margins is the violence that produces the border. A classic instance of just such a production of borders is ongoing in the conflict between India and Pakistan over the Siachen Glacier. Interestingly, this part of the Indo-Pakistan border was left unmapped at Partition because the cartographer felt it unnecessary: the terrain was so incredibly inhospitable and the details so sketchy that he never anticipated it would become a matter of contention.[18] Since April 1984, the two sides have lost well over 2,000 soldiers, 97% of them killed by the "weather and the terrain" and 3% by enemy fire. The Siachen glacier begins at 12,000 feet above sea level in the Saltoro Range in the Himalayas and reaches 22,000 feet at its apex. (By way of comparison, Mount Everest, the highest point on earth, is a little over 29,000 feet high).

Although most of the Indian soldiers are in the *Base Camp* (the Pakistani soldiers being in the valley below), they take turns serving at the forward posts, which are situated between 18,000 and 22,000 feet on the glacier. One in two soldiers posted to Siachen will die, and at any point in time, over 2,000 men are stationed at Siachen. The average soldier, if he returns alive, will have lost between 7 to 12 kilograms during his three-month-long stint and undergone one of the most harrowing physical and psychological experiences conceivable. The following lengthy excerpt conveys some of the surreal violence at this borderline:

> Last fortnight, we were witness to the funeral of the latest victim, Chandra Bhan, 28, a sepoy of the Rajput Regiment stationed at the forward post of *Pahalwan* (20,000 feet) which often comes under concentrated Pakistani artillery fire. Bhan, however, did not die be-

cause of enemy action. The cause of death was pulmonary embolism—a blood clot in the lungs caused by the rarefied air. . . . Bhan had actually died 18 days earlier. His body was laboriously carried down the steep snow-covered slope to *Zulu* (19,500 feet), the only post in the area with a helipad . . . Eventually, pilots . . . braved gusty tail winds of over 60 kmph to land the fragile Cheetah helicopter on the narrow, snow-covered helipad. Bhan's body proved too big for the Cheetah. His legs had to be broken to ferry it to *Base Camp*. . . . Bhan's widow—expecting his third child—will get only an urn of her husband's ashes and his ribbons, including a grey and white one awarded to all Siachen veterans. She is fortunate. Many others won't even get that. The bodies of their menfolk—who were trapped in crevasses, buried under avalanches, or lost in blizzards—have never even been recovered.[19]

The Indo-Pakistan border, here as elsewhere, is literally being drawn in blood. Such violence is routinely finessed in news reports about life on the borderlines, which rewrite them into a moral economy of sacrifice for the good of the nation. As Jean Elshtain has noted, "To preserve the larger civic body, which must be 'as one,' particular bodies must be sacrificed."[20]

Operating out of this exculpatory narrative, a retired Indian diplomat averred: "The public will have to be educated into understanding that the bloody war . . . and the miscellaneous frontier clashes which have led to the loss of life would be amply recompensed if India can be assured of secure and inviolable borders in the decades to come."[21] In recent times, the anxiety over incursions from Pakistan has reached a new high. Subversives are allegedly trained in Pakistan to foment unrest in India's provinces of Punjab and Kashmir. To circumvent the erosion of its borders with Pakistan, India has created a scheme for a "security belt" along the entire northwestern and northeastern frontiers of the nation. And in May 1993, the Union Cabinet approved a plan to issue identity cards to all border area residents in 33 districts in 9 states.

A leading newspaper revealed a schizoid reading of this plan, supporting it at the beginning of an editorial but ending on a pessimistic note:

On the face of it the Centre's decision to issue identity cards to people living in 33 border districts bordering Pakistan and Bangladesh will help remove a thorn in the side of India's body politic. On the western

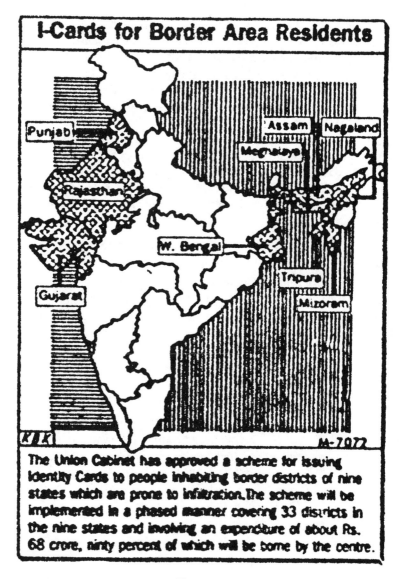

Figure 7.4

border the cards will be a deterrent to the infiltrator armed with guns
and secessionist thoughts. In the east the card is expected to help stem
the tide of millions of Bangladeshi immigrants flowing into India. . . .
Cards are likely to be just another unsuccessful, largely symbolic ex-

ercise in futility like the planned border fence and the odd police combing operation. Without more imaginative administrative thinking and greater political will the identity card will be little more than an expensive successor to the ration card.[22]

In a way, this contradictory reading is a result of the narrow discursive space within which most news coverage of security matters in India operates. The concluding invocations of "political will" and "imaginative administration" reveal a chafing at the limits of this space, without the vision or the vocabulary to transcend it. In this, as in many other instances, the hegemony of realpolitik literally narrates the nation.

The preoccupation with borders and with "alien" infiltration sounds especially disingenuous when India is faced with numerous secessionist threats from within the country. Many of these ethnic, linguistic, and religious movements can hardly be wished away as arising solely out of "external" meddling in "domestic" affairs. The operation of the inside/outside antinomy serves not so much to prevent "foreign infiltration" as it does to discipline and produce the "domestic(ated) self."

Responding to periodic instances of cartographic violations, the Indian state has felt compelled to seal the leaking vessel of sovereignty by releasing yet another map. This one was inscribed with a finality that few dare alter. For those who would hold that this discussion of maps and boundaries is epiphenomenal to ground-level realities, the state's warning effaces the space between that ground and its representations. In a (postmodernist) equivalencing of reality and representation, the state reminds us that a map with "incorrect boundaries of the country indirectly questions the frontiers and challenges the territorial integrity of the nation."[23]

EVERYDAY LIFE ALONG THE BORDERLINES

What the map cuts up, the story cuts across.
MICHEL DE CERTEAU[24]

"Once upon a time, the world was not as it is."[25] Despite the efforts of states and theorists of politics to present the post-Westphalian world of territorially sovereign nation-states as a timeless essence, it is a historically contingent, violently produced, and contested world order. Along the borders of India, Pakistan, and Bangladesh are people

MAKE SURE THE BOUNDARIES ARE CORRECT

DO YOU KNOW ?

The publication of maps of India depicting incorrect boundaries of the country indirectly questions the frontiers and challenges the territorial integrity of the nation.

This is a criminal offence which is punishable with imprisonment which may extend to six months or with fine or both and in case, the publication is of foreign origin it may be banned from entry into India.

• Make sure before publishing any map in newspapers, periodicals, advertisements, books, calendars, chart displays, exhibitions, hoardings and video cassettes etc., that it conforms completely to the map released by Survey of India.

• You can obtain maps of India in different sizes from the Offices of Survey of India at nominal cost.

Figure 7.5

whose lives are abstracted by the discourses of citizenship, sovereignty, and territoriality. Their recalcitrances and compromises are
not to be read exclusively in a register of heroism or romantic eva-
sions, or even as instances of everyday resistance. Rather, quotidian
realities can reveal how cartography produces borders, the arbitrariness involved in the creation of normality, and the fluid definitions of
space and place that prevail in the midst of efforts to hegemonize territory.

Consider the following vignette from everyday life along the Indian
border with Bangladesh, which was reported in a Calcutta newspaper:

Hoseb Ali, a resident of Nabinnagar village in Nadia (a district in West Bengal, India), sat in his courtyard, lit a *bidi* and gently tossed the matchstick away. The matchstick, still smouldering, landed in Bangladesh. "Uncle, come over, I have something to tell you," he shouted.[26]

Hoseb Ali was calling his maternal uncle, Emdadul, to discuss the upcoming village-level administrative elections being held in the state of West Bengal. They were neighbors, but it so happened that the international boundary between India and Bangladesh cut across their courtyard, rendering them citizens of different countries. The "border" at this point consisted of a makeshift fence that was a nuisance more than any barrier. At various other points, the border was a three-foot-tall bamboo fence, and elsewhere there was not even that. Emdadul was irritated by the efforts of the Border Security Force (an Indian paramilitary organization) and the Bangla Desh Rifles to keep the border a reality at least for the duration of the local village elections. He asked querulously, "How can you segregate us? We have grown up together and belong to the same family. We will cross what you people call the 'border' and visit each other. Can the BSF or the BDR keep a constant watch on us?" The Sector Commander of the BSF, Balbir Singh Shahal, was irritable as well. He asked, "How can we stop the infiltration? We do not understand Bengali. These people speak the same language, wear similar clothes and look no different. It is impossible to differentiate between a Bangladeshi and an Indian. Also, many live in houses adjacent to each other."

The arbitrary and violent production of a "border" by the Border Security Force is transparent here. In the face of a reality that does not allow him to distinguish a "Bengali Indian" from a "Bengali Bangladeshi," the Commander is forced to rely on the production of an alternative border, that of the nation-state and of citizenship. Shahal angrily concludes that "Indians should be issued identity cards immediately." Given the impossibility of producing difference out of religious, regional, linguistic, and physical characteristics, Shahal opts for nationality. Yet, in the subcontinent (as elsewhere), the differentiation of nations supposedly rests upon some combination of precisely these "essentialized" characteristics.[27]

In the meantime, people on both sides were operating within a moral economy that had comfortably internalized the border into their everyday lives. This was evident in the panchayat elections in

Figure 7.6

Petrapole village. All three candidates vying for the last gram pan-chayat seat in this village on the Indo-Bangla border were well-known smugglers whose main trade was in illegal immigrants. Chitta Sardar was the Congress (I) candidate, Khagen Mistry repre-sented the BJP, and Atiar Sheikh represented the Communist Party of India (Marxist) [CPI (M)]. In a very matter-of-fact way, Sardar laid out his main difference with Sheikh: "Just because his family owns the land right on the border we have to pay him 'ghat duty' (a transit fee—SK) to transport Bangladeshis," he complained. Mistry noted that up to 1,000 Bangladeshis a day could be transported across the border, at a cost of Rs 30 per person. Mistry's problem was that al-though they did all the work, Sheikh gave them only 10% of the pro-ceeds and kept the rest for himself. Winning the gram panchayat elections was thus mainly a matter of controlling the smuggling operation.[28]

The organization supposedly charged with maintaining the bor-der, the BSF, is also thoroughly implicated in this economy. The local bank officer who operates all the accounts of the BSF personnel divulges the fact that their repatriation of earnings to home villages far exceeds their salaries. In other words, transgressing the border is good business for the BSF. Meanwhile, Mudafat village has seen many Bangladeshi Hindus cross over and settle in this predomi-nantly lower-caste area. Amal Sarkar, a resident of the village noted that there is no tension among the residents, and in fact their panchayat had been adjudged the best for the 1990-91 year in its district for their implementation of various poverty alleviation schemes.[29] Mudafat effortlessly gives lie to the discourse of danger that invariably accompanies reports on Bangla "infiltration" into India.

Even the armed forces of the two countries have become somewhat domesticated in this context. In the neighboring state of Tripura (which also shares a border with Bangladesh), at Akhaura, the BSF checkpost stands alongside that of the BDR. Every morning and evening, the flags of both countries go up or come down at a single command issued by personnel on either side of the border. Trade in staples such as fish, eggs, and clothing routinely moves uninterrupted across the border, and marriages between parties on either side are quite frequent. As the reporter notes, "The bridegroom's party, accompanied by band music, crosses the border without hindrance and goes back with the bride and presentations. Sometimes it's the other way about."[30]

Far across India, on the sandy desert frontier with Pakistan, the BSF enlists the help of a *khoji* (a spooring expert) in following some camel tracks that originated across the border and seem suspicious:

> In the desert the terrain is against man: chill at night and scorching and shadeless during the day. But the dunes are a blessing in disguise to the BSF. Every camel tells the story of its travel. A *khoji* . . . would know if the camel is loaded or not and also the camel's age and sex. A good *khoji* can even say if it comes from a nearby waterhole. He also knows how old the track is. Imprints on the footprints by other desert creatures, like termites and bugs, tell their own tales which the tracker can unravel. If a wind blows sand over the spoor, yet another sand dune protects it down the line, to be revealed to the sharp-eyed BSF men. It is a question of time before the sands reveal their secret.[31]

The skill of the *khoji* is one that arises from a sensuous relationship with the land typical of nomadic and itinerant peoples. Their identity has depended on mobility rather than settlement. The *khoji* equates life and purpose with travel, not with arrival. The enlistment of the *khoji* to maintain and preserve the border, a notion that is supremely an artifact of immobile and settled societies, is deeply ironic.

Running through all these vignettes of daily life along the borderlines are the recurring themes of discipline and abstraction. The vignettes serve to acquaint us with a part of the world we have pulverized in our minds into a space dominated by "the border." Overcoded with the discourses of citizenship, geopolitics, and sovereignty, life here is abstract in the most violent sense of that word.[32] Contrast the tactile relationship with the land entailed in the craft of the *khoji* with its inevitable rescripting into the sterile "Situation Reports" that the BSF has to file every morning with headquarters. As Certeau notes in the context of the transition from the detailed and sensuous medieval tours and itineraries to the modern ensemble of abstract places, "[T]he map, a totalizing stage on which elements of diverse origin are brought together to form the tableau of a 'state' of geographical knowledge, pushes away into its prehistory or into its posterity, as if into the wings, the operations of which it is the result or the necessary condition. It remains alone on the stage. The tour describers have disappeared."[33]

The Indian state attempts, with its maps and its various surveillances, the production and dissemination of this geopolitical second nature against the unconsciously recalcitrant practices of people in the borderlines. The status of these peoples gets rewritten in the defence of the country. An example of such a rewriting, with an interesting reversal in the valorization of human and material "resources," is seen in the following extract on border management:

> For effective border management it is essential that the people staying in border areas be firmly integrated with the rest of their countrymen and function like the eyes and ears of the paramilitary forces/army entrusted with guarding the frontiers. Only then will it be possible to effectively monitor our borders without incurring infrastructural expenditure, which only diverts the precious resources of the country.[34]

Rendered as synecdochical organs on a larger body politic (the "eyes and ears"), people in the border areas are thus literally reduced to abstractions less than human.

CARTOGRAPHIC ANXIETY AND THE ILLUSION OF POSTCOLONIALITY

Every established order tends to produce . . .
the naturalization of its own arbitrariness.
PIERRE BOURDIEU[35]

A recent collection of essays on issues of postcoloniality points to the degree to which Orientalist essentializations underlie both the colonial regime and the "independent" states of South Asia.[36] The derivative discourses of nationality have, even as they rail against Orientalism, relied upon it for their own ammunition and for their desired visions of the future. A crucial question that emerges is this: is there anything "post" about the postcolony at all? If we examine the degree of anxiety revealed by the state over matters of cartographic representation—in the inordinate attention devoted to notions of security and purity; in the disciplinary practices that define "Indian" and "non-Indian," patriot and traitor, insider and outsider, mainstream and marginal; in the physical and epistemic violence that produces the border—the answer to this question is negative.

Cartographic anxiety may be described then as one, of many, symptoms of a postcolonial condition. This preoccupation with a national space and with borders can only approximate a historical original that never existed except as the telos of the narrative of modernity: a pure, unambiguous community called the homeland. In this sense, postcoloniality may be defined as a condition marked by the perpetual effort of colonized societies to catch up with the putative pasts and presents of colonizing societies who never realized they were in a race in the first place. Hence, we are back in the realm of the ironic: the definitive marker of the postcolonial society is that of one trapped in time, post-colony but pre-nation. And yet, the way to modern nationhood can only be through the complete colonization of the self. Thus, to decolonize the self may mean denationalizing the narratives that embody space and time.

NOTES

For their comments and encouragement on previous drafts, I would like to thank, among others, Michael Shapiro, Carol Breckenridge, Itty Abraham, Rob Walker, and Ena Singh. The usual disclaimers apply.

1. In the political universe of contemporary India, the Congress (I) (the "I" standing for the late Indira Gandhi) has portrayed itself as the champion of "secularism" against the explicitly Hindu Bharatiya Janata Party (BJP). The BJP has seen a sharp improvement in its electoral fortunes, going from a relatively insignificant share of the popular vote in the elections of 1980 and 1984 to the largest Opposition party in the parliament following the general election of 1991. Although the religious, indeed the fundamentalist, charac-

ter of the BJP is of little doubt, the Congress (I) party's real commitment to secularism has been an issue of much contention in recent times.

2. Etienne Balibar, "The Nation Form: History and Ideology," trans. Chris Turner, in *Race, Nation, Class: Ambiguous Identities,* Etienne Balibar and Immanuel Wallerstein (London: Verso, 1991), pp. 86-106.

3. It is the dichotomous nature of this choice that led me, among other reasons, to title this piece "Cartographic Anxiety." The direct referent is Richard Bernstein's notion of "Cartesian Anxiety," which he defines as follows: "*Either* there is some support for our being, a fixed foundation for our knowledge, *or* we cannot escape the forces of darkness that envelop us with madness, with intellectual and moral chaos" (emphasis original). Richard Bernstein, *Beyond Objectivism and Relativism: Science, Hermeneutics, and Praxis* (Philadelphia: University of Pennsylvania Press, 1985), p. 18. Foucault aphorized this famously as the "blackmail of the Enlightenment," and it is a particularly appropriate notion in the context of discourses of citizenship. In the modern world system, nationality exhausts the discursive space of identity and impoverishes our imagination for alternative, multiple, or layered understandings of selves. Hence, the sterile choices presented are invariably of the order of inside/outside, patriot/traitor, nationalist/communalist, and so on.

4. Studies that depict the emergence of the modern world of sovereign nation-states and the accompanying ideologies of nationalism, citizenship, sovereignty, and security have long commented on the metonymously religious or eschatological character of these "newest" faiths. Certainly Marx, Durkheim, and Weber, to mention only three, were cognizant of this aspect of the discourse of statism and *citoyen.* (For a superb discussion, see Derek Sayer, *Capitalism and Modernity: An Excursus on Marx and Weber* (New York: Routledge, 1991). In the specific context of India, the following quote from Ashis Nandy makes my point with brevity: "Certainly in India, the ideas of nation-building, scientific growth, security, modernization and development have become parts of a left-handed technology with a clear touch of religiosity—a modern demonology, a *tantra* with a built-in code of violence . . . To many Indians today, secularism comes as a part of a larger package consisting of many standardized ideological products and social processes—development, mega-science and national security being some of the most prominent among them. This package often plays the same role vis-a-vis the people of the society—sanctioning or justifying violence against the weak and the dissenting—that the church, the *ulema,* the *sangha,* or the Brahmans played in earlier times." Ashis Nandy, "The Politics of Secularism and the Recovery of Religious Tolerance," in *Contending Sovereignties: Redefining Political Community,* ed. R. B. J. Walker and Saul Mendlovitz (Boulder, Colo.: Lynne Rienner Press, 1990), p. 134.

5. A superb work that presents a genealogy of the contested production of the terrain called Siam (Thailand) can be found in Winichakul Thongchai, *Siam Mapped: A History of the Geo-Body of the Nation* (Honolulu: University of Hawaii Press, 1994); and an exemplary account of this process in France can be found in Eugen Weber, *Peasants into Frenchmen: The Modernization of Rural France, 1870-1914* (Stanford, Calif.: Stanford University Press, 1976). For a rendition of nation-state building in terms of its affinity to organized crime, see Charles Tilly, ed., *The Formulation of Nation States in Western Europe* (Princeton, N.J.: Princeton University Press, 1975); and Tilly, *Capital, Coercion, and European States, AD 990-1990* (Oxford, England: Blackwell, 1990). For a recent discussion of the production of national boundaries via a dialectic between the local and the national, see Peter Sahlins, *Boundaries: The Making of France and Spain in the Pyrenees* (Berkeley and Los Angeles: University of California Press, 1989). The definitive work on the spatialization of power and the power of space remains Henri Lefebvre, *The Production of Space,* trans. Donald Nicholson-Smith (Cambridge, Mass.: Blackwell, 1991).

6. For discussions that discuss postcoloniality in terms of its continuity with the colonial/imperial project, see Arjun Appadurai, "Number in the Colonial Imagination," in *Orientalism and the Postcolonial Predicament: Perspectives on South Asia,* ed. Carol A. Breckenridge and Peter van der Veer (Philadelphia: University of Pennsylvania Press, 1993), pp. 314-39; and David Ludden, "Orientalism Empiricism: Transformations of Colonial Knowledge," in Breckenridge and Peter van der Veer, pp. 250-78.

7. J. B. Harley, "Deconstructing the Map," in *Writing Worlds: Discourse, Text and Metaphor in the Representation of the Landscape,* ed. Trevor J. Barnes and James S. Duncan (London: Routledge, 1992), p. 231.

8. Jawaharlal Nehru, *The Discovery of India* (1946; reprint, Delhi: Oxford University Press, 1982).

9. Jawaharlal Nehru, *An Autobiography* (London: John Lane, 1939).

10. The ambivalent discourse of anticolonial nationalism is superbly discussed by, among others, Ashis Nandy, *The Intimate Enemy: Loss and Recovery of Self under Colonialism* (Delhi: Oxford University Press, 1983); and Partha Chatterjee, *Nationalist Thought and the Colonial World: A Derivative Discourse* (Delhi: Oxford University Press, 1986). For a discussion focusing on Nehru and the production of national identity, see Sankaran Krishna, "Inscribing the Nation: Nehru and the Politics of Identity in India," in *The Global Economy as Political Space,* ed. Stephen Rosow, Naeem Inayatullah, and Mark Rupert (Boulder, Colo.: Lynne Rienner, 1994), pp. 189-202.

11. Jawaharlal Nehru, *Independence and After: A Collection of Speeches 1946-1949* (New York: John Day, 1950), p. 247; emphasis mine.

12. As an illustration, just consider the following collage of newspaper

212 · SANKARAN KRISHNA

and magazine headlines: "We will not cede an inch: PM," "To seal a porous border," "Bangla infiltration worries Center," "Identity-Cards for Border Area Residents," "Special ID cards soon on 33 border districts," "Border-line Case," "Laying Down the Line," "'Live Borders' of the North-East," "The Border Security Belt," "Charting India," "The Border Security Force: battling at the sandy frontier." These headlines were taken at random from various recent issues of the *Statesman* and the *Telegraph* (both Calcutta-based English language newspapers) and *Frontline*, a newsmagazine published in Madras.

13. The yatra, and its quixotic (in the original sense of that term) finale, was well covered by Indian newspapers. See especially the *Statesman,* January 25, 26, and 27, 1992.

14. For the whole series of advertisements, see Dilip M. Sarwate, *Political Marketing: The Indian Experience* (New Delhi: Tata-McGraw Hill Publishing Co., 1990), pp. 157-63. The ads, designed by a leading agency, Rediffusion (which was headed by an alumnus of Rajiv Gandhi's alma mater, the exclusive Doon School), drew the wrath of many for their elitism, pretentiousness, and highly melodramatic tone. Needless to say, Indian cartoonists had a field day and parodied the ads mercilessly. Sarwate's book includes some choice selections of these ripostes as well.

15. For an excellent discussion of the notions of the normal and the pathological in discussions centering on the body politic, see David Campbell, *Writing Security: United States Foreign Policy and the Politics of Identity* (Minneapolis: University of Minnesota Press, 1992), pp. 85-101.

16. In the BJP's desired cosmology, India's frontiers extend all the way up to Afghanistan in the west and Burma in the east and would include Nepal, Bhutan, Tibet, and sundry other neighboring countries. Maps of "Akhand Bharat" served as the frontispiece for their main publication "The Organiser" and are regularly used in their pamphlets, posters, and party literature. "Akhand Bharat" is the invariable benchmark from which the BJP criticizes the Congress Party and (in an earlier time) was the reason for assassinating Gandhi. For an insightful analysis of the Hindu right's origins and its hyper-masculinity as a complete internalization of the values and pathology of the colonizer, see Ashis Nandy, *At the Edge of Psychology: Essays in Politics and Culture* (Delhi: Oxford University Press, 1980).

17. Appan Menon, "Time for political solution," *Frontline* (Madras), May 16-19, 1987, p. 14.

18. Ravi Rikhye, *The Militarization of Mother India* (Delhi, Chanakya Publications, 1990), pp. 24-27.

19. This, and much of the information in this section, is taken from "Siachen: the forgotten war," a report by W. P. S. Sidhu and Pramod

Pushkarna in *India Today*, May 31, 1992, pp. 58-71. Siachen, incidentally, means "Rose Garden."

20. Jean Bethke Elshtain, "Sovereignty, Identity, Sacrifice," *Millenium* 20, no. 3 (1991), p. 397.

21. N. B. Menon, "Laying down the line," *Frontline*, August 8-21, 1987, p. 40.

22. See the editorial "Borderline Case" in the *Telegraph*, dated May 27, 1993.

23. This map (figure 5) was printed by the Survey of India in a number of leading newspapers and magazines in early 1992. The provocation for it came from an advertisement by Hitachi Ltd. (Japan) that showed a map of India in which all of Kashmir was "ceded" to Pakistan. The company and the newspaper that first published the advertisement, *The Times of India*, were hit with a lawsuit and were forced to publish retractions and apologies.

24. Michel de Certeau, *The Practice of Everyday Life*, trans. Steven Rendall (Berkeley and Los Angeles: University of California Press, 1988), p. 129.

25. R. B. J. Walker, *Inside/Outside: International Relations as Political Theory* (New York: Cambridge University Press, 1993), p. 179.

26. From Aloke Banerjee's report in the *Statesman*, May 29, 1993, titled "Where two nations slip into each other." The next three paragraphs rely heavily on this report.

27. In 1905, the British colonial administration unwisely decided to partition the presidency of Bengal (which was then comprised of contemporary West Bengal and Bangladesh) and triggered off a political movement of such proportions that they had to hastily retract the partition. West and East Bengal wound up in separate countries after August 1947. Since then, the relationship between the two Bengals has been an extraordinary one, revealing all the complex imbrications of language, culture, and religion inflected with geopolitical and national compulsions. For a sensitive tracking of the notion of "Bengali identity" through these vicissitudes, see Subrata Dhar, "The Protean Character of Bengali Identity" (Ph.D. dissertation, University of Hawaii at Manoa, Honolulu, 1994).

28. See the report titled "3 Smugglers fight for panchayat seat," filed by Diptosh Majumdar in the *Telegraph*, May 27, 1993.

29. Pijush Kundu, "Decadence, privation and politicking," report filed in the *Statesman*, May 19, 1993.

30. See Anil Bhattacharjee, "Indo-Bangla Border," in *Frontline*, May 3-16, 1986.

31. Mahesh Vijapurkar, "BSF: Battling at the sandy frontier," a *Frontline* essay, February 8-21, 1986, pp. 38-49.

32. Lefebvre, *The Production of Space*. Consider Lefebvre's expansion

on this theme: "*there is a violence intrinsic to abstraction. . . .* abstraction's *modus operandi* is devastation, destruction . . . The violence involved does not stem from some force intervening aside from rationality, outside or beyond it. Rather, it manifests itself from the moment any action introduces the rational into the real, from the outside, by means of tools which strike, slice and cut—and keep doing so until the purpose of their aggression is achieved" (p. 289; emphasis in original).

33. Certeau, p. 121.

34. A. V. Liddle, "The Role of Locals in Border Management," in *India's Borders: Ecology and Security Perspectives,* ed. D. V. L. N. Ramakrishna Rao and R. C. Sharma (New Delhi: Scholars' Publishing Forum, 1990), p. 204.

35. Pierre Bourdieu, *Outline of a Theory of Practice,* trans. Richard Nice (Cambridge, England: Cambridge University Press, 1977), p. 164.

36. Carol A. Breckenridge and Peter van der Veer, eds., *Orientalism and the Postcolonial Predicament: Perspectives on South Asia* (Philadelphia: University of Pennsylvania Press, 1993).

IV

Modernity's Identity Spaces

Introduction to Part IV

MICHAEL J. SHAPIRO

As cartographies become increasingly unstable, so do the human identities that are historically tied to the normative practices of space. Just as political subjectivities such as nationalities are tied to historical narratives, they are also dependent on the spaces and demarcations that provide systems of inclusion and exclusion, separating one identity from an-Other. As modernity's relatively stable, geopolitical structure has become increasingly unsettled by indigenous movements and reasserted nationalisms, as well as by capital, technological, and human flows across boundaries, identity spaces are being rapidly reconfigured.

This section begins with a focus on the temporal boundary existing at the outset of modernity. Abbas Milani's tale of an "oriental despot's" encounter with modernity and ultimately his self-colonization is exemplary. It shows how the identity spaces of modernity have emerged through movements, accommodations, differentiations, and domestications, as encounters across boundaries have produced new political configurations and have accordingly shaped identities as well as spaces.

The modernity that Nasir al-Din Shah brought to Iran, a deterritorialization of traditional kingly and clerical sacred space, was always already reterritorialized in the reformulations of its effects that he had imposed. Milani shows therefore why the modernity now under challenge was never a completed, ecumenically imposed project. History, as Fernand Braudel has argued, is "conjunctural" rather than linear.[1] As in the domain of analysis of Braudel, the history of economy, so in the domain of political identity—older forms have persisted alongside newer ones. Milani offers us a glimpse of the forces of persistence as older identity forces have resisted or domesticated newer ones.

By contrast, Nicholas Xenos and Jonathan Friedman focus on the forces reshaping the unstable world of postmodernity. Although still not effectively coded in the dominant discourse of sovereignty, refugees and indigenous peoples are increasingly salient political identities. In the case of refugees, Xenos points out, they have become objects in political struggles between states. But it is also the case that they are shaping the contemporary political condition. They are among the primary human flows challenging previously established territorialities as well as established political identities. They are involved in nothing less than a struggle against "the reductionism of national identity."

Friedman takes up another pervasive challenge to modernity's identity spaces, the identity reassertions of indigenous peoples. As these peoples strive to reestablish cultural identities and thereby deterritorialize the nation-state sovereignty system, attempts at reterritorialization take the form of delegitimating the authenticity of cultural affiliations. To challenge the delegitimation of the claims of cultural groups to historical continuity in mainstream nationalist narratives, Friedman provides an effective narration of the emergence and decline of nation-oriented control over identity space.

Against those interpretations that would dismiss or marginalize the de-hegemonizing forces changing contemporary identity spaces, Friedman shows the continuities and coherences of the new (or reasserted old) sources of extrastate models of the self. He indicates how active and alternative destabilizing orders have always been very much alive within what was thought to be a quiescent global order.

NOTES

1. Fernand Braudel, *Afterthoughts on Material Civilization,* trans. Patricia M. Ranum (Baltimore: Johns Hopkins University Press, 1977).

8

Narratives of Modernity:
Perspective of an Oriental Despot

ABBAS MILANI

"Writing," according to Claude Lévi-Strauss, is a means "to facilitate the enslavement of other human beings."[1] In their interrogation of the genealogies of "the Barbaric Despotic Machine," Gilles Deleuze and Félix Guattari proclaim that "it is the despot who establishes the practice of writing."[2] Evidence for these claims can be found not just in the forests of Brazil or the intellectual salons of Paris but also in Nasir al-Din Shah's narratives of his travels to Europe.

Nasir al-Din Shah ruled Iran for nearly half a century. He came to power in 1848, when he was only seventeen years old. An assassin's bullet ended his reign in 1896. Iran's first serious encounters with modernity began under his rule. His coterie of courtiers included both reformist zealots and incorrigible despots. The tremors that ultimately erupted into Iran's Constitutional Revolution (1905-07) began under his reign.

The onslaught of modernity shook to the core the existing Iranian sense of cultural identity and community. With the "overlap and displacement of domains of difference," what Homi Bhabha calls "the fixity and fetishism"[3] of cultural identities began to crack. A new "cultural hybridity"[4] seemed all but imminent.

In this context, new competing and conflicting cultural "strategies of self-hood"[5] began to emerge. Religious forces, reticent of change, advocated social and spiritual autarky. Only a culture enveloped in divine wisdom, they argued, can survive the satanic verses of modernity. Comprador modernists, those advocates of "cultural transubstantiation," encouraged a total submersion of Iranian culture into the "Paradise of European civilization."

And thus, the primitive despotic machine of Nasir al-Din Shah was "forced into a bottleneck." It felt what Deleuze and Guattari call "the dread of flows of desire that would resist coding"; it recognized the necessity for the "establishment of inscriptions . . . that makes desire into the property of the sovereign."[6] Nasir al-Din Shah's travelogues are an early testimony to this desperate attempt at an "inscriptional" process.

The king's idle curiosities, his insatiable desire for frivolities, his "addiction"[7] to travel, his attempt to consolidate his relationship with European powers, his greed for gold, hand in hand with the designs of his reformist courtiers to "enlighten"[8] the king, and finally the colonialists' attempts to enlist his favors led to his decision to travel to Europe and shaped the rubrics of the new "coding" regime. Out of a labyrinth of conflicting desires and designs came a project that laundered a quixotic narrative of despotism as a journey of discovery.

On three occasions, in 1873, 1878, and 1889, each time for about four to five months, the king, along with nearly all of the country's political elite, traveled to Europe. All the customary pomp surrounding an exotic "Oriental" surrounded his entourage.[9]

As was his habit in nearly all his trips, Nasir al-Din Shah decided to write an account of his travels.[10] In the genealogy of their form and the morphology of their content, these travelogues are a fascinating arena in which different cultures and sensibilities, competing orders of "coding" and "overcoding" cohabit and contradict one another.[11] The tensions and pretensions of the text are a metaphor for the historical dilemma of modernity in Iran. Indeed, the texts of the travelogues, as well as the context and the subtext of their production and dissemination betray a fierce battle between competing centers of political power and their incumbent discourses.

In a sense, every political discourse is ultimately also an attempt to "dis-course" alternative claims (or structures) of power. It is, to use Fredric Jameson's words, a narrative in the service of "an imaginary resolution of a real contradiction."[12] In other words, like all other cultural objects, it "brings into being that very situation to which it is also, at one and the same time, a reaction."[13] Nasir al-Din

Shah's narrative is no exception. The "political Unconscious" of his texts betrays a desire to domesticate aspects of modernity amenable to the needs of his despotic rule and subvert those he finds dangerous. To use Mary Louise Pratt's apt metaphor, Iran was then a "contact zone,"[14] a social space where "asymmetrical relations of domination and subordination"[15] between the colonized and the colonizer, as well as between the despot and his subjects, raged on. The narrative of the royal sojourn to Europe was part of his strategy to maintain hegemony in this "contact zone."

Confounding the battle was the peculiar problematic of modernity in Iran. If in the West the battle between the ancients and the moderns was in a sense a bipolar problematic, in Iran the fight was, every step of the way, overshadowed by the enormous complexities of the colonial question. Russia and England fought for hegemony, while lesser European powers each struggled for a smaller piece of the pie. On the one hand, the ferocity of this colonial fight ensured at least the nominal independence of Iran. On the other hand, all aspects of what Hannah Arendt calls "the Social Question"[16]—all the social issues modernity hurls into the public domain—were invariably ensnared with colonial politics. In Naser al-Din Shah's convoluted vision of Europe, in his mutilated narrative of discovery, in his peculiar acts of omission and commission, we see all the perils and the paradoxes of this entanglement.

In the place of the will to know, or possess—the engines of modernity's discourse of discovery[17]—here we find the will to pleasure and the will to contain. Instead of "theoretical curiosity," which in Hans Blumenberg's view is a cardinal element of modernity's epistemology,[18] we have here at best a politically neutered and often frivolous inquisitiveness. Throughout its tropes of concealment and containment, the royal text tries to subvert the subversive potentialities of modernity's discourse by appropriating some of its formal characteristics. The narrative's manner of production and dissemination is also emblematic of modern Oriental despots' elective affinities with modernity.

Before Nasir al-Din Shah, Iran's despots were often oblivious if not in fact haughtily disdainful of the West. In annals of history we read of Iranian kings who, less than one hundred years before Nasir al-Din Shah, received Western envoys in their pyjamas and showed a defiant, if not quixotic, haughtiness in their dealing with the West.[19]

With Nasir al-Din Shah, the tide began to turn. Colonial hegemony was beginning to bloom. Henceforth Iranian despots were in awe of the West; their sense of political security was more dependent on the pulse of Western powers and public opinion than on the opinions of their own "subjects." At great cost, they tried to cultivate a "modern image" of themselves in the eyes of the West. Early signs of this development can be seen in the fate of Nasir al-Din Shah's royal narrative.[20] Their Ecoian "model reader"[21] seemed as much European as Iranian. In fact, the travelogues were immediately ordered by the king to be translated and published in English. Throughout the last decade of the nineteenth century, they were read and discussed in English intellectual circles.[22]

Of course, every narrative is, in the words of Hayden White, "not merely a neutral discursive form . . . but rather, entails ontological and epistemic choices with distinct ideological and even specifically political implications."[23] What then is the way of political life insinuated in the Shah's narrative?

To begin, the privileged position of writing over orality and the nearly fetishistic preoccupation with memory[24] are of course both important signs of modernity in the West. The dearth of autobiographies and travelogues and the near complete absence of official records from Iran's past contrast sharply with the Shah's desire to write and record. At the same time we can speak of Nasir al-Din Shah as the author of these logs only in a Foucauldian sense. In other words, he was not "an individual who pronounced or wrote a text" but rather embodied "a principle of groupings of discourse."[25] The texts he authored were only in a *formal* sense a replica of modernity's privileged attitude toward writing. For him the act of writing was more royal theater than a simple individual discursive practice; it embodied what Certeau calls "scriptural operations" wherein words are orally performed in the "presence of officially sanctioned recorders."[26] Such is the king's description of one of these "scriptural operations":

> Bashi was holding the inkwell; Akbari the candelabra; Amin Khabar holding a notebook, ready to write; Etemad-Al Saltaneh holding a Western newspaper, ready to read; Mirza Muhamad Khan holding a candelabra for him; Majd-l Dowleh, Abbol Hassa Khan, Mardak, Mohhamad Al Khan, Muhamad Hassan Miraza, Adib Joojeh, Karim Khan, Agha Dai all standing, Taghi Khan holding water.[27]

With such a large constellation of courtiers in attendance, some enjoying their aristocratic titles (like *Eteme al Sataneh,* "the trustee of the king"), others suffering belittling, diminutive labels (like *Mardak,* "little man" or *Akbar Joojeh,* "Akbar the chicken"), the king trotted around dictating entries that he expected supplicant scribes would accurately transcribe into a text. If it can be said that the notion of an individual author only rose on the ruins of the idea of God as the master narrator, here we have a godlike distance from the act of creation comingled with authorial pretensions. On rare occasions, the Shah would deign to jot down a few words himself. Textual differences between different "editions" of the logs indicate a certain degree of expected scribal corruption.

The king not only had peculiar notions about the value of writing, but his sense of the mimetic principle implied by the travelogue as a genre is equally ambivalent. For instance, we read, "I said my prayers in the Kremlin, then I had the photographer take a portrait of me, then we went and visited the museum. Now that Abul Hassan Khan is writing these words, I haven't taken any pictures yet, nor have I visited the museum. Maybe there won't even be a picture-taking or a visit to the museum."[28]

The epistemic contract implied in this passage, with repercussions for the whole of the text, seems at once unusually avant-garde and dangerously despotic. The form of the narrative is in some complex and confusing way "modern." It resembles moments in modern novels when the novelist, in the process of writing, engages in a deconstructive act by exposing the fictive nature of the narrative. Like Chaucer's Pardoner, the king exposes the tricks of his narrative, yet unlike the modern novelist, he expects us to suspend disbelief. Whereas in the hands of novelists the deconstructive act serves to demonstrate the permeable boundaries between what Vladimir Nabokov calls "the facts of fiction and the fiction of facts," the tone of the king's narrative leaves no doubt that he expects the reader never to doubt the facticity of his fiction.

From what the narrative betrays, the king travels not just to discover the West as the dreaded and desired "Other," but also to reinvigorate his own waning powers at home. In almost every page, we are treated to elaborate, repetitious details about the pageantry of his visit, the power of his presence among powerful Western politicians and kings, and the "unbelievable, uncontrollable" surge of popular enthusiasm for His Majesty. On all such occasions, the narrative is suffused with the kind of familiar honorifics that Iranian courtly discourse was commonly studded with. If in the Shklovskian trope of "defamiliarization,"[29] the familiar is rendered strange, the Shah's linguistic tropes try to tame and familiarize the unfamiliar. Repeatedly, the king insinuates the vocabulary of despotic power and traditional forms of authority into descriptions of what would have been an unfamiliar world of Western European politics.

The point is nowhere more evident than in the king's narrative of his trip to England. Queen Victoria was the monarch then. In spite of common diplomatic rules of decorum, the queen did not go to meet the visiting king at the port of entry, but forced the Shah to travel to Windsor Palace. Not only does the king make absolutely no mention of this clear diplomatic slight, but he instead waxes eloquent about all the respect afforded him during the visit.

But there was an even more serious problem. Victoria was a woman. To circumvent what the Shah felt to be the embarrassing and potentially dangerous idea of a ruling woman monarch, he chose to essentially hide from any but his most astute readers the gender of Victoria.[30] Throughout the text he repeatedly refers to her using the Persian word *Padshah,* a word that clearly implies the idea of a male ruler. He thus eschews another clearly understood and commonly used word *Malekeh,* which in Persian signifies a woman ruler. When referring to the safe distance of the sixteenth century, the Shah had no compunction about referring to Elizabeth as *Malekeh.* His linguistic preferences here are a fascinating example of the kind of ambivalence of language that Bhabha calls the "language of archaic belonging," a language that attempts to "marginalize" the "present of Modernity."[31]

In fact, the "woman question" permeates, often in a tragicomical manner, much of the fiber of the text. The king was renowned for his insatiable desire for women. By the time he died, he had legally wed eighty-five women. To be bereft of female companionship for the duration of the trip was of course unthinkable. To take all (or even some of) his *harem* proved logistically impossible, and politically embarrassing. Improvisation was in order.

On one trip, he took along a young boy with whom he had fallen in love. Throughout the three logs, the only time the language of the text becomes emotionally charged and resonates with human passion is when the king discusses his young beloved. At the same time, during the same trip, he ordered his ambassador to the Ottoman court to dispatch for the king a fourteen-year-old white slave girl.[32] With the arrival of the girl, the scene of the entourage seems nothing short of a Shakespearean comedy of errors.

The king's description of the affair is at the same time poignantly revealing of his own disturbed sense of self. In these descriptions, we get a rare glimpse of the rather mutilated sense of self, of that Fanonesque masque[33] of a pompous political persona behind which hides a man of pitiable insecurity. In describing the girl, he writes:

> I had asked for a girl from Istanbul. Last night when we were asleep, she arrived. Agha [the eunuch of the entourage] broke the good news of her arrival. We had ordered that her hair be cut so that she could look like a man.
>
> When I saw her today, she smiled. From her laughter, I gathered that when they told the girl that We were taking you for the Persian King she must have had strange ideas in her mind. She must have thought: What kind of a creature is this King of Persia? Does he have horns? In her mind, she conjured the image of a man with heavy, long pointed beard, with seven manes reaching the earth, a thick moustache curled around his head, a lanky jaundiced face, shining, bulging yellow eyes, big mouth, rotten teeth, with a couple of ugly canine teeth protruding, a foul-smelling mouth, long hat on his head, and so short-tempered that whomsoever he meets he slaps so hard that blood gushes from their nostrils.[34]

Aside from the fact that the depicted image bears a frightening resemblance to actual pictures of the Shah's father and grandfather, the passage is particularly significant for what it reveals about the fractured identity the king harbored beneath the facade of royal grandeur. This ambivalence of identity is, I think, at the core of the problematic relationship of many Iranians with Western powers. Whereas xenophobic nationalists and religious fundamentalists harbor narcissistic illusions of ethnic or religious grandeur and perfection, comprador modernists foster a cult of self-denigration and illusory notions about the "perfect West." To fashion a self free from both delusions and abnegations is one of the most central and daunting tasks facing the once colonized peoples of the world today.

Of course none of these competing narratives of submission or segregation, or conflicting tropes of "encoding," have ever succeeded in becoming a totalizing narrative, leaving a window of opportunity for other, more autonomous cultural strategies for selfhood.

As despots are wont to do, the Shah tried to turn necessity into virtue and to launder his constant preoccupation with women as sexual objects into a positive quality. In fact, he claims to have discovered the key to Europe's success, for he writes, "I met the Foreign Secretary of Holland. It has become apparent to me that all these Westerners are whoremongers and lechers. The Foreign Secretary was constantly looking at women. The reason the Westerners are so powerful is that they are constantly in pursuit of pleasure."[35]

Delusive distortions are not of course the only revealing textual strategy employed by the monarch. Implicit in every text is an epistemic hierarchy that helps categorize certain facts as relevant and important, and thus a necessary part of the narrative, and dismisses others as irrelevant. A crucial element of this implicit taxonomy is the presumed boundaries between the realm of the public and the private.[36] If we accept the notion that modernity transforms politics from the private arena monopolized by the elite to the public theater wherein the masses are legitimate players, then the Shah's narrative of discovery seems archaically premodern. Pages after pages of the text are given to descriptions of zoos and hunting trips, with scant allusion to the political structure of Europe. He writes repeatedly of his desire "to buy" the beautiful women he meets.[37] His crude flirtations with a Russian woman—whom he has to give up because she, he finds out, is a Jew[38]—is treated with far more fanfare and in far more detail than the famous London, Paris, and Moscow world exhibits he visits. Indeed, in writing about the exhibit in Moscow, he comments only on "the beautiful women visiting the exhibit," lamenting the fact that he could not get his hand on any of them.[39]

Every day's entry begins with a repetitious reference to the fact that His Majesty woke up, ate, and went out, but there is hardly any allusion to any of the political discussions he engaged in throughout his trip. Nearly all references to such discussions are limited to a curt refrain to the tune of "Some good discussions were held."[40] In all such cases, the implicit tone is one of disdain. It exudes a sense of dismissiveness toward the reader. It implies in no uncertain terms that politics is not the business of the public, and, by extension, we the readers.

Ironically, although the king insists on preserving for himself the privileged monopoly of politics, he accepts no responsibility for the consequences of his own past political decisions. In parts of these three narratives, he uses an eerily cold and distant language to describe the miseries he witnesses in Iranian cities and villages. With no sense of shame, remorse, or responsibility, he writes of emaciated, hungry faces, derelict buildings, and bad roads. In one instance, traveling through one of the villages of his domain, he muses, "it is as if the Mongol hordes have ravaged the land."[41] The tone resembles one of an innocent traveler to a benighted land, not of its absolute ruler, who with his dynasty had by then ruled Iran for nearly a century.

By the third trip the king had also become overtly disdainful of the political atmosphere of Europe. Describing a meeting with Bismarck and the kaiser, he writes:

> I came down into the room and sat down. The Kaiser came too. We would sit, stand up, walk around, eat something, sit down again. The generals were also walking around. Some sat down. There was freedom. There stood one general, smoking, with his ass to the Emperor. Another was sitting yonder with his ass also to the Emperor. One of them had his ass toward me. In a word, there was freedom.[42]

Not all aspects of modernity were of course as disturbing to the king. His eclectic affinity with certain aspects of what he saw in Europe seems emblematic of many other "third-world" leaders' piecemeal appropriation of modernity. Modernity's never-ending fever for exchange fit perfectly with Nasir-al-Din Shah's insatiable personal greed.[43] He was more then willing to auction off Iran's sovereignty for paltry personal gains. Indeed during his reign, eighty-three concession treaties and economic pacts were signed with European powers. Of these, thirty-five were signed by the king before even looking at the details. As a recompense for his blind trust, he received payoffs from European powers.[44]

For a while, after his first two trips, he went into a frantic, often crazy search for gold in Iran. He also appreciated Europe's system of tax collection. With glee he writes about the system of income and property taxes he saw there and adds that "even animals are taxed separately."[45] He approved of the militarist air of Bismarckian Prussia. There even children, he reports, wear military uniforms and learn the habits of army life.[46] He relished the stores filled with commodities—and the enormously long list of his purchases is as impressive in its size as it is embarrassing in its kitsch quality. He liked Western guns. But most of all, he liked modernity's system of social control. During his first visit, he hired an Austrian count to establish a modern police force for Iran. The blueprint the count—who had by then become Tehran's chief of police—prepared[47] reads like pages from Foucault's *Discipline and Punish*. He suggests a new regime of surveillance, based not only on the panoptic principle but also on permanent registration of the population, standardization of weights, and crowd-control techniques. Every teahouse, the traditional hub of neighborhood life and political gossip, was to have a police detachment. The Shah immediately approved the blueprints and ordered their implementation. They heralded the dawn of a new age that is, in a sense, shared by most third-world countries in their early encounters with modernity. It is an age where the despotism of individualized, tyrannical authority combines with the hegemonic force of panoptic surveillance.

There is yet another gradual change evident in the progression of the three narratives. Between the first and third logs, a definite linguistic change creeps into the texts. When talking about Iran, the king uses increasingly more hostile and disparaging adjectives and metaphors. To him Iran had come to look more arid, faces more vacuous, cities more decrepit. On the other hand, descriptions of European nature are more ebullient. On all too numerous occasions, the metaphor of "paradise" is invoked to describe a European garden or a forest. In fact, by the third trip, the word *Farangi*, the Persian word for the "Franks" or Europeans, had become for the king synonymous with higher and more noble qualities. On the eve of his third trip, Tehran, the capital city, was decorated with lights and flags. In praise of the city, Nasir-al-Din Shah writes, "the streets had so much glamour that they hardly looked like Tehran. They looked like European cities. There was grandeur to them."[48]

The royal lexicon is also transformed in the course of the three travelogues. In later writings, the king peppers his discourse with French words. Sometimes these words are by necessity used to refer to concepts still then alien to the Persian language. Oftentimes, however, he seems to derive a sense of personal pride in his newfound linguistic prowess. His linguistic proclivity has all the characteristics of what Pratt calls "autoethnography," or more specifically a "partial collaboration with and appropriation of the idioms of the conqueror."[49] Other accounts left by his courtiers support this perception. The king was always wont to pretend more comprehension of foreign languages than was warranted by his abilities.

Colonial hegemony is always interlaced with the waning aura of the native tongue and a near magical legitimization afforded to the colonizing language. What usually further complicates the picture is that inevitably in the marketplace of ideas and knowledge, these colonial languages are the common currency of exchange. Thus not only comprador modernists but genuine modernists as well have become party to this auratic transformation. And this transformation is a key ingredient in the sense of undermined cultural sovereignty and damaged self-esteem so often found in colonized lands. In terms of the royal texts, these transformations reflected, as well as reinforced, the kind of social and psychological changes that ultimately shaped the Iranian Constitutional Revolution.

Sometimes metaphors of reality are more powerful than any aesthetic construct. At the end of his first trip, in spite of his fear of the open seas, the Shah boards a ship on the Russian side of the Caspian Sea and heads home. If the sea is to be mythically understood as the metaphor of utopia and change, then the Shah's fear of the sea poetically fits his aversion to social change. Near the Iranian port, a storm sets in. He writes, "I descended from the deck. It was impossible to stand there. I went to my room, took off my clothes, and in melancholy, waited to see what Fate had in store for Us."[50] At the end of the second trip, once again near the same port, another storm threatens: "The horizons are bleak, winds are blowing, dark clouds appear. A storm seems imminent."[51] As Fate would have it, history, the Machiavellian *Fortuna* of modern times, had social revolution in store. The "inscriptional overcoding" proved ineffective. Desire for change would not remain "the property of the sovereign" and tore through the "nets of the despotic state."[52] Not long after the sea storms ended, political storms began at home.

NOTES

I am grateful to Jean Nyland, Parvis Shokat, Farzaneh Milani, and Kamal Azari, who read and commented on early drafts of this essay. The idea for the essay came out of a discussion with Mike Shapiro some three years ago. But my debt to him is far greater than his role in the genealogy of this essay.

In a sense, there is a bit of him in everything I have written over the past twenty years.

1. Claude Lévi-Strauss, *Tristes Tropiques*, trans. John Russell (New York: Viking Penguin, 1991), p. 192.

2. Gilles Deleuze and Félix Guattari, *Anti-Oedipus: Capitalism and Schizophrenia*, trans. Robert Hurley, Mark Seem, and Helen R. Lane (Minneapolis: University of Minnesota Press, 1993), p. 202.

3. Homi K. Bhabha, *The Location of Culture* (New York: Routledge, 1994), p. 9.

4. Ibid., p. 4.

5. Ibid., p. 1.

6. Deleuze and Guattari, *Anti-Oedipus*, p. 199.

7. Ehsan Yarshater, "Observations on Nasir-al-Din Shah," in *Qajar Iran: Political, Social and Cultural Change*, ed. Edmund Bosworth and Carole Hellenbrand (Edinburgh: University of Edinburgh Press, 1983), p. 8.

8. Fereydoun Adamiyat, *Andisheye Taragui* (Tehran: Kharazmi, 1972), p. 259.

9. Vita Sackville-West describes how Nasir-al-Din Shah "used to startle Europe by his arrival in her capital with his Oriental accoutrements and the black moustachios like a scimitar across his face." See Vita Sackville-West, *Passenger to Tehran* (New York: Harper Perennial, 1992), p. 138. See also Zeynek Celik, *Displaying the Orient: Architecture of Islam at Nineteenth Century World's Fairs* (Berkeley: University of California Press, 1992), pp. 34-36 and pp. 120-22.

10. In spite of their singular significance in understanding Iran's encounter with modernity, no scholarly edition of these texts has yet been published. Except for parts of the logs for the third trip, recently reissued in a critical, annotated edition, I have relied on reproductions of the handwritten originals. See Nasir-al-Din Shah, *Safar Nameye Nasir-al-Din Shah* (Tehran: Charg, 1964); Nasir-al-Din Shah, *Safar Nameye Farangstan* (Tehran: Charg, 1963); Nasir-Al-Din Shah, *Rooznameye Khaterat Nasir-Al-Din Shaha Dar Safar Sevum Farang* (Tehran: Resa, 1990).

Parts of each of these travelogues were published in English almost immediately after the trips. They were part of the king's attempt to forge a "modern" image for himself. Many oriental despots at the turn of the last century were caught in the frenzy of appearing modern (See Edward Said, *Culture and Imperialism* [New York: Alfred A. Knopf, 1993], pp. 110-35).

11. Deleuze and Guattari, *Anti-Oedipus*, pp. 199-224.

12. Fredric Jameson, *The Political Unconscious: Narrative as a Socially Symbolic Act* (Ithaca: Cornell University Press, 1981), p. 77.

13. Ibid., p. 82.

14. Mary Louise Pratt, *Imperial Eyes: Travel Writing and Transcultura-tion* (New York: Routledge, 1992), p. 4.

15. Ibid., p. 4.

16. Hannah Arendt, *Between Past and Future: Eight Exercises in Political Thought* (New York: Penguin, 1983), pp. 41-80.

17. Stephen Greenblatt's *Marvelous Possessions* is an insightful look into the two types of medieval and modern curiosities, or "wonders," and their corresponding representational practices (see Stephen Greenblatt, *Marvelous Possessions: The Wonder of the New World* [Berkeley: University of California Press, 1991]). For a broader articulation of modernity's "regime of truth," see Michel Foucault, *The Archeology of Knowledge and the Discourse on Language*, trans. A. M. Sheridan Smith (New York: Pantheon, 1982).

18. For a dazzling discourse on modernity's "theoretical curiosity," see Hans Blumenberg, *The Legitimacy of the Modern Age*, trans. Robert M. Wallace (Cambridge: MIT Press, 1983), pp. 229-437.

19. Rustam-al-Hokama, *Rustam-al-Tavarikh* (Tehran: Amir Kabir, 1972).

20. Said, *Culture and Imperialism*, pp. 110-15.

21. Every text, Eco reminds us, has at the moment of its inception a "model reader" in mind. The relationship between the text and this reader is reciprocal. The text at once shapes and is shaped by the model reader. Eco writes that "every text is a syntactic-semantical-pragmatic device, whose foreseen interpretation is part of its generative process." See Umberto Eco, *The Role of the Reader: Explorations in the Semiotics of Text* (Bloomington: Indiana University Press, 1979), p. 11.

22. Sackville-West, *Passenger to Tehran*, pp. 130-40.

23. Hayden White, *The Content of the Form: Narrative Discourse and Historical Representation* (Baltimore: Johns Hopkins University Press, 1987), p. ix.

24. Michel de Certeau, *The Writing of History*, trans. Tom Conley (New York: Columbia University Press, 1988), p. 210.

25. Michel Foucault, "What Is an Author?" in D. F. Boncard, ed., *Language, Counter-Memory, Practice* (Ithaca, N.Y.: Cornell University Press, 1977), pp. 125-27.

26. Certeau, *The Writing of History*, p. 212.

27. Nasir-al-Din Shah, *Rooznameye Khaterat*, p. 17.

28. Ibid., p. 138.

29. Victor Shklovsky, "Art as Technique," in *Russian Formalist Criticism*, trans. Lee T. Lemon Maron (Lincoln: University of Nebraska Press, 1965), p. 13.

30. It is only many pages after recounting the meeting that the king, in passing, mentions the fact that the British monarch had had a husband. Reference to this fact is the only clue to Victoria's gender.

31. Homi K. Bhabha, "Dis-semination: Time, Narrative, and the Margins of the Modern Nation," in *Nation and Narration,* ed. Homi K. Bhabha (London: Routledge, 1990), p. 317.

32. For a discussion of this episode, see Yarshater, "Observations of Nasir-al-Din Shah," pp. 6-9.

33. For a discussion of the impact of the colonial experience on the psyche of the colonized people, see Franz Fanon, *Black Skin, White Masks* (London: Pluto, 1986); and Franz Fanon, *The Wretched of the Earth* (Harmondsworth: Penguin, 1967).

34. Nasir-al-Din Shah, *Rooznameye Khaterat,* p. 17.

35. Ibid., p. 286.

36. For a discussion of the dialectics of the public and the private, see Richard Rorty, *Contingency, Irony, and Solidarity* (Cambridge: Cambridge University Press, 1989), pp. 1-95.

37. Nasir-al-Din Shah, *Rooznameye Khaterat,* p. 130.

38. Ibid., p. 128.

39. Ibid., p. 162.

40. Ibid., p. 17.

41. Ibid., p. 70.

42. Ibid., p. 220.

43. For a discussion of the dialectics of sovereignty and exchange, see Michael J. Shapiro, "Sovereignty and Exchange in the Orders of Modernity," *Alternatives* 16 (1991), pp. 447-75.

44. Nazem Al-Islam Kermani, *Tarikh Bidari Iranian* (Tehran: Agah, 1970), p. 143.

45. Nasir-al-Din Shah, *Safar Nameye Farangstan,* pp. 190-91.

46. Nasir-al-Din Shah, *Safar Nameye Nasir-al-Din Shah,* p. 75.

47. For a detailed account of this blueprint, see Morteza Tafrashi, *Nazm va Nazmiyeh Dar Doreye Ghajar* (Tehran: Neghah, 1973), pp. 53-90.

48. Nasir-al-Din Shah, *Rooznameye Khaterat,* p. 18.

49. Pratt, *Imperial Eyes,* p. 7.

50. Nasir-al-Din Shah, *Safar Nameye Nasir-al-Din Shah,* p. 250.

51. Nasir-al-Din Shah, *Safar Nameye Farangstan,* p. 257.

52. Deleuze and Guattari, *Anti-Oedipus,* p. 224.

9

Refugees: The Modern Political Condition

NICHOLAS XENOS

*Apparently nobody wants to know that contemporary history has
created a new kind of human beings—the kind that are put in concentration camps by their foes and in internment camps by their friends.*
HANNAH ARENDT, *"We Refugees"* (1943)

Having promised during his 1992 campaign for the presidency to de-
vote his attention to domestic issues and to shun the foreign-affairs
focus said to have characterized the Bush administration's period in
office, Bill Clinton took the oath of office amid a controversy of his
own creation that transgressed the domestic/foreign border. Along
with invitations to various balls and parties, preparations for the
inaugural included the dispersal of thousands of leaflets in Haiti intended to dissuade would-be refugees from attempting the hazardous journey to Florida in anticipation of a more lenient asylum
policy from the new president than had been afforded by his Repub-
lican predecessor. For good measure, Coast Guard vessels were dis-
patched to enforce a cordon sanitaire off the coast of that woeful
country. The press, temporarily disdainful of the etiquette of political honeymoons, was quick to point out that another campaign
promise had apparently gone awry, because candidate Clinton had
clearly indicated that he would jettison the Bush administration's
collective ban on Haitian refugees. Score one for *realpolitik*.

President Clinton's change of heart clearly had a foreign-policy side to it. The Haitian boat people had, after all, become pawns in a stalemated game of strategy played out between Washington and Port-au-Prince. On the one hand, the fact of thousands of people fleeing Haiti was bad for the international image of the post-Aristide regime, and by signaling his apparent intention to accept them, candidate Clinton was expressing his political hostility to that regime. But on the other hand, the military government in Haiti had to be well aware that the refugees were unwelcome in the United States for reasons of domestic politics. The social tensions attendant upon economic recession dictated against allowing thousands of potential job seekers into Florida, tensions only exacerbated by the race factor. The government in Port-au-Prince apparently calculated that to forestall the influx of unwanted black asylum seekers, Washington would ease up on sanctions against the military-backed regime in order to ameliorate economic conditions at least to a sufficient degree to stanch the flow of boat people. This strategy was based on the warranted assumption that Washington policymakers would interpret the boat people as economic rather than political refugees. Indeed, the justification for the blanket ban on Haitians arriving illegally in the United States was based on the summary judgment that there was no political repression in Haiti, an argument that became more difficult to make after the coup against Aristide, but one to which the State Department continued to cling nevertheless, despite a federal appeals court ruling in the summer of 1992 that ruled the Bush policy in violation of the Refugee Act of 1980. By backing off from his proposal to change U.S. policy toward the Haitian boat people, President Clinton tacitly acknowledged that his foreign policy initiative had gotten tangled up in his principal promise to ameliorate economic conditions "at home."

That people wishing to flee one country in favor of another should become weapons in a struggle between states is of course nothing new, and there are many other recent examples. In 1991, the Albanian government allowed thousands to sail to Italy in the apparent hope that the Italian government, overwhelmed by the sheer magnitude of the exodus, would bring pressure on the European Community to grant economic aid to Tirana. That the government in Rome was prepared to accept the political costs of televised images of Italian paramilitary forces literally pushing the Albanians back into the sea is evidence of just how transparent the strategy behind the boat people's sudden appearance was. Nevertheless, the Italian government soon increased its foreign aid to Albania. The Romanian governments of Nicolae Ceaușescu and his successors, meanwhile, have long made a business out of selling refugees. Ethnic Germans were allowed to emigrate to West Germany and Jews to emigrate to Israel in exchange for aid during the Ceaușescu regime. In the fall of 1992 the German government reached an agreement with Ceaușescu 's successors in Bucharest to return thousands of Gypsies who had fled Romania and had become targets of anti-immigrant violence in the newly unified Germany. In a reversal of its earlier ventures, the Romanian government was now to be paid for taking people back who were unwanted in the first place.

These examples of strategic human flows could easily be expanded to include those of the Vietnamese boat people, Mexicans seeking work in the United States, the Cubans who fled their country following the fall of Batista as well as those who were allowed to leave in the Mariel boat lift of 1980, and others. One central fact that they point toward is the political context of the refugee question. A great deal of the controversy concerning the movement of people is focused on the definition of a refugee, and in this regard there are two basic principles that have governed the treatment of refugees in international agreements: first, the definition of a refugee has been established on a very narrow basis; second, the case for refugee status has been limited to individuals, rather than groups. But as all of these examples also demonstrate, in practice, both of these conditions have been manipulated in accordance with specific state interests in particular contexts.

The principal document governing the definition and treatment of refugees is the 1951 United Nations Convention on Refugees together with the 1967 Protocol, which expanded the convention by removing limitations on time and geography.[1] The convention defined a refugee as follows:

> The term "refugee" shall apply to any person who . . . owing to a well-founded fear of being persecuted for reasons of race, religion, nationality, membership of a particular social group or political opinion, is outside the country of his nationality and is unable or, owing to such fear, is unwilling to avail himself of the protection of that country; or who, not having a nationality and being outside the coun-

try of his former habitual residence as a result of such events, is unable or, owing to such fear, is unwilling to return to it.[2]

The convention was originally intended to apply to émigrés from Soviet-imposed governments in central and eastern Europe, and the USSR and its subject allies never accepted the convention or the protocol.[3] Western governments were therefore within the bounds of an international pact in refusing to repatriate immigrants from the east, while the Soviet bloc continued to emphasize its right to control the emigration of its subjects.

During the Cold War period, Washington routinely accepted claims to refugee status from persons fleeing westward, thereby dispensing in practice with the individual-case-oriented definition of the convention, just as it has attempted to do with Haitians today, only with the opposite intention. Similarly, a new asylum law introduced in Germany in 1993 allows for the listing of countries where no political repression is deemed to be taking place, thus ruling out, a priori, individual claims to refugee status for persons from those countries.[4] In addition, although the convention's language makes it possible to exclude those who flee a country because of intolerable economic conditions from the safety net of refugee status, during the Cold War western governments chose to relax this restriction because the economic conditions prevalent in the east were thought to be politically generated. Because collectivized, command economies were imposed by so-called totalitarian governments, lack of economic opportunity could be interpreted as a political problem. By contrast, would-be refugees from third-world countries who are deemed to be escaping economic deprivation are rejected, which is a reflection of the view that market economies are natural, not political arrangements.[5]

The 1951 convention therefore lays down general guidelines, but the interpretation of those guidelines remains the prerogative of individual states because there is no authoritative sanctioning body to impose a particular interpretation of the language of the convention. At the same time, although over one hundred governments have signed on to these agreements preventing the return of what are interpreted to be legitimate refugees, the United Nations has been unable to broker a similar agreement guaranteeing the right to asylum. The reason for this failure is clear: immigration policy, which is entailed in the question of asylum, is considered to be sacrosanct to the maintenance of state sovereignty. All states treat absolute control of territory to be an essential element of the claim to sovereignty, and so although governments are willing to consider agreements setting out the normative terms for the treatment of persons fleeing the jurisdiction of other states, few are willing to consider norms that would compromise their own territorial control. And although some states do have a history favoring the granting of asylum, they insist that such acts are at the discretion of the state and not a matter of an individual's right to asylum.[6]

The problem of refugees, their identity, and their fate is thus a complicated problem that has the question of sovereignty at its core. By reflecting on this problem, we can perhaps gain some insight into the nature of the sovereign power of nation-states today.

In many respects, the twentieth century has been the century of the refugee. Previously, migration had been fairly unregulated. Before the beginning of this century, those who sought refuge from political persecution tended to be not refugees but exiles. In the early and middle nineteenth century, such figures as Alexander Herzen, Karl Marx, and Guiseppe Mazzini represented the archetype of individuals who had chosen their place of refuge because of their political activity and who were of little concern to their host countries. By the end of the century, however, others joined them who were not destined to become famous: those who were displaced by the German wars of unification, Jews escaping the pogroms of Czarist Russia, and Armenians fleeing the massacre perpetrated upon them by the Ottomans. Later still, the Balkan wars produced a constant flow of people sent on the move by religious, ethnic, linguistic, and national struggles.[7] With the turmoil of the First World War, the Russian Revolution, and the dissolution of the Hapsburg and Ottoman Empires, the number of people who had become refugees in the accompanying process of new-state formation grew precipitously. The peace treaties that followed the war deployed two terms, one German and one French, to designate these refugees. The French word was *apatrides,* or stateless; the German word was *Heimatlosen,* or homeless.

That these two terms could be taken to be synonymous is instructive and helps us to understand Hannah Arendt's assertion that stateless persons form "the most symptomatic group in contemporary politics."⁸ The notion that one's state is equivalent to one's home is not etymologically obvious. *Heimat* connotes both home and a native place. It is related to the English word *hamlet* and survives in the English suffix *ham*, as in Nottingham or Birmingham. In fact, the word *home* originally referred in its earliest, fourteenth-century usage to a native place in the form of a collection of houses, or a village.⁹ In other words, to be *heimatlose* or homeless could signify to be without a native place, understood to be a community. That this community should be conceptualized as a state tells us a great deal about the social and political situation that forms the general background to the emergence of refugees as a modern phenomenon.

The political upheavals that generated the movement of peoples at the beginning of this century were phenomena associated with the consolidation not of states but of nation-states. That is, the modern state, with a few important exceptions, is an association that claims not only territorial integrity but also a specific national identity.¹⁰ In this claim, the French nation-state has been the archetype. The notion of sovereignty had been applied since at least the sixteenth century in debates over the power of the emerging state and its relationship to multiple competing sources of power within European societies, debates that were bound up with, among other things, questions of religious toleration. It was in Catholic France, however, that a sea change occurred in June 1789 when the representatives of the Third Estate, in what amounted to a coup d'état, declared themselves the National Assembly. The full import of this move became apparent two months later when, in the Third Article of the Declaration of the Rights of Man and Citizen, it was asserted that "the source of all sovereignty resides essentially in the nation." In one stroke, the National Assembly had shifted the battle lines for the control of state power to the terrain of national identity: henceforward, those who were able to impose their version of who the nation was could claim to represent the national will and to direct the state. Aristocrats, the clergy, the monarchy, and anyone deemed in opposition to the revolution, including virtually the entire population of the Vendée, were among those who were at one time or another written off the roles of national membership.¹¹

The development of the nation-state in accord with the French model came to be all about borders. These demarcations were inscribed both on maps and in the souls of citizens. The nation-state had to have its territorial identity marked off against other nation-states without as well as against the others within, those whose physical presence within the mapped borders belied an alien identity. The French Revolution thus had to fight wars on two fronts. Along the internal borders, first the Reign of Terror and then the levée en masse helped to create an "us"—le peuple—doing battle with "them"—the aristos and their brethren. State-directed festivals and, later, educational uniformity also contributed to the purposive construction of a national identity. Preservation of the nation's spatial territory meant an aggressive war against real or imagined threats beyond geographical contingencies that began to take on a new significance—the Pyrenees, the Alps, the Rhine, or the Channel. The sometimes paradoxical result of these wars to defend the sovereign nation and its state was the stimulation of newly discovered national identities elsewhere in Europe (and, to the horror of the metropolitan French nation, in Haiti). Out of the French revolutionary experience was born the nineteenth-century pattern of nations looking for their states (Italy, Greece, Germany, Hungary). This pattern reached its apogee in the aftermath of World War I, when the idea of the sovereign nation-state was codified in the peace treaties,[12] only the old pattern was asked to solve problems for which it had not been cut.

The process of national state formation in Europe before this century had consisted mostly of assimilation rather than expulsion, the French Terror remaining something of an exception. However, in central, eastern, and southeastern Europe, in the Caucasus and Asia Minor, where nation-states were formed out of the breakup of far-flung empires, the process of nation-state formation took the form of exclusion and expulsion. A particularly poignant example is the forcible exchange of populations that took place between Greece and Turkey as a result of the Greco-Turkish war of 1919-22 and its settlement in the Lausanne Convention of 1923. The war, which was initiated by the Greek government of Eleuthérios Venizélos with the intent of extending Greek political control wherever ethnic Greeks resided in the eastern Mediterranean, ended in a Turkish victory. At Lausanne, it was agreed that there would be "a compulsory exchange of Turkish nationals of the Greek Orthodox religion established in Turkish territory and of Greek nationals of the Muslim religion established in Greek territory."[13] Over 1.5 million people were forcibly exchanged, with close to a million entering Greece. In this instance, since "Turkish" and "Greek" populations had been territorially mixed in the area for millennia, religious practices were the only practicable means for distinguishing between them. By expelling Muslim and Orthodox practitioners, the Greek and Turkish governments, respectively, were able to establish what they considered to be homogeneous national populations under uniform territorial control. The same process is occurring in the Balkans today in what was for a time intended to be the national state of the southern Slavs, the former Yugoslavia. There, too, religious practices are being used to sort out what will count as national identity in the now notorious process of "ethnic cleansing."

In the example of the population exchanges between Greece and Turkey, and in the transfers entailed in the partition of India and Pakistan as well as in the example of the less legalistic transfer of populations in Croatia and Bosnia today, the conflation of notions of state and home becomes more clearly discernable. By the logic of the nation-state, people must leave their homes in order to come home; they must sever their connection to whatever other community or communities they belong in order to become members of the only community that counts—the nation with its own state. In these examples, that severance and that joining entail physical upheaval and resettlement. The home is exchanged for the homeland, which exists as an imagined necessity rather than as a lived or historical contingency.

For those who find themselves excluded from the national identity amidst which they live, this exclusion is a perilous one because homelessness is the constant threat, no matter how long they or their ancestors have been resident in a particular bit of geography. In Europe, Jews and Gypsies have represented peoples with homes but no homeland. It is in this sense that Karl Jaspers and Hannah Arendt, in an exchange of letters, agreed that the Zionist movement, which aimed to establish Palestine as a Jewish nation-state, represented the true assimilation of the Jews, the end of their "chosen" self-identity and transformation into a national people like any other.[14] For the Gypsies, assimilation into the world of nations appears to be impossible—they are perpetual refugees.

Although the examples I have so far given have all involved physical displacement, the idea that the modern nation-state requires the loss

of a home in order to find one in the homeland is an all-encompassing one and includes instances where no physical change of location
occurs. This movement, which is characteristic of the formation of
national identity through assimilation in western Europe and to
which I referred earlier, is part of the general phenomenon of modernity that Simone Weil called "uprootedness." "To be rooted," Weil
argued,

> is perhaps the most important and least recognized need of the
> human soul. It is one of the hardest to define. A human being has
> roots by virtue of his real, active, and natural participation in the life
> of a community, which preserves in living shape certain particular
> treasures of the past and certain particular expectations for the
> future. This participation is a natural one, in the sense that it is auto-
> matically brought about by place, conditions of birth, profession, and
> social surroundings. Every human being needs to have multiple roots.
> It is necessary for him to draw well-nigh the whole of his moral, intel-
> lectual, and spiritual life by way of the environment of which he
> forms a natural part.[15]

To be rooted, in Weil's sense, seems to signify something like what I
have indicated by the term *home*. It is only partly, and not most importantly, a geographically centered notion. It is, rather, a complex
set of relationships that make acting possible, which is summarized
in Weil's use of the term *community*. Among the forces at work in
modernity that act to uproot us are two principal ones: the market
economy and the nation-state. The first of these Weil interprets in
terms reminiscent of Marx's analyses of estrangement and of the
reification of commodities. In many of Weil's writings she pays particular attention to the effects of unemployment on the lives of the
working class, but she is also attentive to the general effects of mon-
etized social relations upon culture in general. The emphasis here is
on inducements to short-term interests, which has the cultural effect
that "each thing is looked upon as an end in itself. Uprootedness,"
she concludes, "breeds idolatry."[16]

Idolatry is also the temptation presented by the nation-state. In
her interpretation of French history in *The Need for Roots*, Weil re-
hearses the manner in which the process of nation building over a
period extending from the thirteenth century through the French
Revolution gradually supplanted complex, fragmented, sometimes
overlapping local identities in favor of a single, undifferentiated na-

tional identity.[17] This is a history of struggle, of conquest and assimilation of Corsicans, Bretons, Burgundians, Basques, Alsatians, and
so on. It culminated in the doctrine of the sovereign nation in 1789,
a doctrine that paradoxically predicated national identity upon a
radical break with the past.[18] The result, Weil claims, is that the nation-state, having supplanted all other communities, stands alone as
the loveless object of devotion.[19]

Weil's narrative of French national construction could be replicated for Britain or Spain, the two other archetypes of western European nation-states.[20] What it calls to attention is the degree to which
subjects of the nation-state are always already uprooted. Weil's use
of an organic metaphor also calls to attention the artificial, constructed character of identity in modernity. It would be tempting to
dismiss her concerns as those of an outmoded, naturalistic essentialism, but Weil herself proposed a series of steps to be taken for the
growing of new roots in a postwar France. It is not artifice, as such,
that is the target of her scorn but the reduction of complex communities to a singular devotional object that renders "participation in
the life of a community" meaningless.

Weil's notion of rootedness may help us to think about the meaning of statelessness today when interpreted in conjunction with the
concept of home as it is found in fragments of writing by two other
authors. The first is Václav Havel, who, in a letter from prison written to his wife says this:

> A theme I wanted to write about: what is home? A certain concrete
> horizon to which one relates. . . . The hiddenness of that horizon. The
> more urgently one relates to it as a result. The outline of this horizon
> changes (sometimes it is created by mountains, at other times by an
> urban skyline), the arrangement of people, relationships, milieus, tra-
> ditions, etc. changes, but the horizon "as such" remains. As some-
> thing absolute. Something that merely assumes different concrete
> forms. The paper has run out—[21]

Here, too, I would emphasize in the notion of the "horizon" the geographically indeterminate character of the concept of home. In
Havel's rendering, the concept transcends and contains the quotidian
particularities of lived experience and allows that experience to be
rendered meaningful. It is therefore akin, I think, to the concept of
home I find in Hannah Arendt. In her discussion of the condition of

refugees at the end of World War II, of stateless people who were without the protection of state-guaranteed rights, Arendt writes:

> The first loss which the rightless suffered was the loss of their homes, and this meant the loss of the entire social texture into which they were born and in which they established for themselves a distinct place in the world. This calamity is far from unprecedented; in the long memory of history, forced migrations of individuals or whole groups of people for political or economic reasons look like everyday occurrences. What is unprecedented is not the loss of a home but the impossibility of finding a new one. Suddenly, there was no place on earth where migrants could go without the severest restrictions, no country where they would be assimilated, no territory where they could found a new community of their own. This, moreover, had next to nothing to do with any material problem of overpopulation; it was a problem not of space but of political organization.[22]

What is important to Arendt in her understanding of what it means to be homeless is not the loss of a particular place but of the possibility of being at home anywhere. And home here signifies a place in the world insofar as such a place makes acting in the world possible, that is, makes action meaningful through shared understandings and a shared interpretation of action.[23] More clearly than Weil's organic "roots," Arendt's conception of home is to be distinguished from what I earlier referred to as the homeland, because it is something explicitly made, the product and precondition of political life. It is, I think, something that retains its character even as its concrete manifestations are mobile. Homelands are places that are unchanging and to which one must return, no matter how hostile they may be to the returnee. Homes can be made and remade, if there is space for them.[24]

As Arendt indicates, that space is not really geographical but rather political. The problem of refugees in our time is a symptom of the uprootedness or homelessness of the modern age. It is a phenomenon of the era of nation-states and of the international political economy, and it is a problem not insofar as the refugee is denied a homeland but insofar as he or she is denied the possibility of establishing a home. The system of nation-states systematically denies that possibility through its insistence upon the principle of sovereignty and the state's hegemony over questions of identity. The principles of human rights, by contrast, are meant to create that space and that possibility, but as long as those rights are interpreted and enforced by nation-states, there will be no uncontrolled space. Refugees thus represent the contemporary political identity crisis. In their homelessness as statelessness they are the often unwitting representatives of a cosmopolitan alternative to the idea of a homeland. Such an ideal can be seen as an unrealizable ideal,[25] or recognized as the site for a struggle against the reductionism of national identity and for the making of a home.

NOTES

This paper was originally presented at the 34th Annual Convention of the International Studies Association in Acapulco, Mexico, in March 1993. An earlier version was subsequently published in the journal *Alternatives*. My thanks to Jean Bethke Elshtain, Kiaran Honderich, James Der Derian, J. Timothy Cloyd, R. B. J. Walker, Daniel Warner, and Michael Shapiro for their thoughtful comments.

1. The 1951 Convention on Refugees was limited to Europe and to persons whose status was determined by events preceding January 1, 1951. Leon Gordenker, "The United Nations and Refugees," in Lawrence Finkelstein, ed., *Politics in the United Nations System* (Durham: Duke University Press, 1988), p. 276.

2. Quoted in ibid., p. 199.

3. David P. Forsythe, "The Political Economy of UN Refugee Programmes," in David P. Forsythe, ed., *The United Nations in the World Political Economy: Essays in Honour of Leon Gordenker* (New York: St. Martin's Press, 1989), p. 132.

4. Stephen Kinzer, "Rights Groups Attack German Plan on Refugees," *New York Times,* February 7, 1993, p. L11.

5. For the politics of U.S. refugee policy, see Gil Loescher and John A. Scanlan, *Calculated Kindness: Refugees and America's Half-Open Door, 1945 to the Present* (New York: Free Press, 1986).

6. Latin American states have shown a particular predilection for granting asylum. For a discussion of the UN's failure to secure an agreement on this issue, see Louise W. Holborn, *Refugees: A Problem of Our Time,* 2 vols. (Metuchen, N.J.: Scarecrow Press, 1975), pp. 228-32. The jealously guarded prerogatives of state power are described by Gordenker, "The United Nations and Refugees," p. 280, as follows: "[The United Nations High Commissioner for Refugees] may recognize that an individual is a

refugee and request a government to issue internationally recognized travel documents to that person, but the ultimate protection of the rights of such a person, his admission to asylum, the physical receipt of a travel document, or his permission to return to his point of departure depend on national priorities."

7. For this background, see Michael R. Marrus, *The Unwanted: European Refugees in the Twentieth Century* (New York: Oxford University Press, 1985), ch. 1.

8. Hannah Arendt, *The Origins of Totalitarianism,* new ed. (New York: Harcourt, Brace & World, 1966), p. 277.

9. *The Oxford Dictionary of English Etymology,* ed. C. T. Onions (Oxford: Oxford University Press, 1969).

10. The exceptions would appear to be in North and South America and Australia, i.e., in states where indigenous peoples have been shunted aside in favor of polyglot immigrant settlers. However, Benedict Anderson has argued that it was in such areas—most importantly in Central and South America—that nationalism first arose. See Benedict Anderson, *Imagined Communities: Reflections on the Origin and Spread of Nationalism,* rev. ed. (London: Verso, 1991).

11. For a fuller discussion of the implications of this development, see Nicholas Xenos, "The State, Rights, and the Homogeneous Nation," *History of European Ideas* 15, nos. 1-3 (1992): 77-82.

12. See Anthony Giddens, *The Nation-State and Violence: Volume Two of a Contemporary Critique of Historical Materialism* (Berkeley and Los Angeles: University of California Press, 1987), pp. 257-66.

13. Quoted in Marrus, *The Unwanted,* p. 102. My discussion of this episode is drawn from ibid., pp. 97-106.

14. Hannah Arendt and Karl Jaspers, *Correspondence: 1926-1969,* ed. Lotte Kohler and Hans Saner, trans. Robert and Rita Kimber (New York: Harcourt Brace Jovanovich, 1992), pp. 94-99. Jaspers, p. 95, writes that the Jewish state "threatens to reduce the Jewish people to the level of 'nations' and so make them unimportant for the spiritual development of things."

15. Simone Weil, *The Need for Roots: Prelude to a Declaration of Duties toward Mankind,* trans. Arthur Wills (New York: Harper Colophon, 1971), p. 43.

16. Ibid., p. 69.

17. Ibid., pp. 99-184.

18. Ibid., p. 110.

19. Ibid., p. 114.

20. Cf. Linda Colley, *Britons: Forging the Nation 1707-1837* (New Haven: Yale University Press, 1992), who argues that British national identity, dependent on its imperial success, was never as successfully assimila-

tionist as the French and that distinct Welsh, Scottish, English, and Irish identities continued to exist within it.

21. Václav Havel, *Letters to Olga, June 1979-September 1982,* trans. Paul Wilson (New York: Knopf, 1988), p. 120.

22. Arendt, *Origins of Totalitarianism,* pp. 293-94.

23. Ibid., p. 296: "The fundamental deprivation of human rights is manifested first and above all in the deprivation of a place in the world which makes opinions significant and actions effective. Something much more fundamental than freedom and justice, which are the rights of citizens, is at stake when belonging to the community into which one is born is no longer a matter of course and not belonging no longer a matter of choice, or when one is placed in a situation where, unless he commits a crime, his treatment by others does not depend on what he does or does not do. This extremity, and nothing else, is the situation of people deprived of human rights. They are deprived, not of the right to freedom, but of the right to action."

24. Because the phenomenological conception of home I am sketching out here is future oriented, I think it escapes the Nietzchean criticism of "homesickness" elaborated by William E. Connolly, *Political Theory and Modernity* (Oxford: Basil Blackwell, 1988), ch. 5. At the same time, the distinction between a homeland and a home is intended to make possible a critique of the nationalism Nietzsche abhorred while acknowledging that some form of collective identity is necessary to political action. That identity, I would argue, is formed in the action itself.

25. Arendt expressed this ideal in a letter to Jaspers written from New York and dated June 30, 1947 (Hannah Arendt and Karl Jaspers, *Correspondence,* p. 91): "What I would like to see and what cannot be achieved today would be such a change in circumstances that everyone could freely choose where he would like to exercise his political rights and responsibilities and in which cultural tradition he feels most comfortable. So that there will finally be an end to genealogical investigations both here and in Europe."

10

The Implosion of Modernity

JONATHAN FRIEDMAN

THE EMERGENCE AND DECLINE OF MODERNITY
AS AN IDENTITY SPACE

Mainstream political discourses continue to cleave to their concern with national identity, but it is increasingly obvious that the present state of affairs involves the following kinds of phenomena as well:

1. Immigrants in the West are gaining in strength of identity at the same time as their hosts are becoming more ethnic themselves, leading to direct confrontations described as racism.
2. Indigenous peoples living on the margins of national states, for example, Sami, American Indians, Maori, South and Southeast Asian tribal minorities, are finding their rights to land and to both political and cultural autonomy on the agenda of the United Nations.
3. Older ethnic subdivisions in Europe, both west and east, are coming to life once more. A process that has been going on in western Europe—Bretagne, Occitanie, Lombardia, Cornwall, Ireland, Scotland, Wales, Catalonia, Basque country, Corsica—for almost a decade has been overshadowed in the media by the ethnic explosion occurring with the dismemberment of the empire to the east.

Cultural identity is the most general rubric that can be used to categorize the welter of phenomena that confront us. The term refers to a social identity that is based on a specific cultural configuration of a conscious nature. History, language, and race are all possible bases for cultural identity, and they are all socially constructed realities. This does not make them false or ideological if we recognize the degree to which all identity is constructed. Identity is only false for those who feel alienated enough from any particular identity that they could never dream of participating in what appears as quasi-religious mystification. But very many have, from being extremely modern and cynical with respect to ethnicity, returned to ethnic roots with a vengeance.

The structure of modernity as an identity space is the foundation for any understanding of the present state of affairs. The dominant structure of this space is modernism, predicated on the disintegration of former holistic structures of identity in which the subject was integrated in a larger field of organized forces that were constitutive of selfhood. It is in modernity that the self is separated from these larger cosmological structures. This is a modernity that has surely emerged in previous commercial civilizations but that, in our own era, appears in the eighteenth century with the breakdown of older ascriptive hierarchies of aristocratic Europe.

Modernity is, in a fundamental way, the emergence of "alterity" as a permanent condition of existence. Where the self is never defined, where there are always other possibilities of identity and existence. This is a world in which private becomes the real, and public the artificial or constructed, in which the notion of civilization is equivalent to artifice. The word *negligee* was first used to refer to all apparel worn in the privacy of the home, *negligee* because natural, nonconstructed. The opposition between the private and the public took on its specific form in this period.

Alterity, in its turn, implies that the social self is neither natural, necessary, nor ascribed. Rather it is achieved, developed, constructed. Alterity, thus, harbors a tendency to change, to "develop," it might be said. Combined with the principle of trial and error, alterity yields progress, or evolution—going on, learning more, becoming better, more efficient, more intelligent. Here we have the key to what might be called modernism. Goethe's *Faust,* part 2, contains the essence of the strategy of modernism, the principle of movement in and for itself. Faust combines the anguish of being alone with the driving desire to move on to greater heights. The cosmology of modernism is evolutionism. The cosmology of the previous holism is best expressed in the notion of the "great chain of being," a universal hierarchy stretching from God through the angels, to man, to animals, and in some versions to the devil, a hierarchy in which every separate form of existence has its established place. Now, if one were to take such a hierarchy and turn it on its end, making it into a horizontal chain called time's arrow, one would have transformed the great chain of being into an evolutionary scheme. Evolution is essentially the result of the temporalization of the "great chain of being." It occurs when biological and social positions in the world are no longer definable in terms of relative nearness to God. This transformation is also a temporalization of space. That which is "out there," from reptiles to apes (Rousseau was convinced that recently discovered apes were in fact humans that had been disqualified by an act of racism), from the Bushmen to the Inca, were forerunners of the modern and civilized state of the world, that is, back then.

DISORDER AND POSTMODERNISM

Modernism as the dominant figure of hegemonic power in the global system orders the world in a hierarchy of developmental stages. It orders the public sphere according to the dictates of civilizational authority. Although it does not really homogenize the world, its pretensions in that direction generate a more/less hierarchy that is the essence of evolutionary thought. A decline of hegemonic centrality is simultaneously the rebirth of cultural autonomies, a general liberation of formerly contained and encompassed identities. The breakup of modernity is the dissolution of its principles of organization. The individualist component of modernity, the separation of the subject from any particular identity, is also the autonomization of the activity of understanding as a public discourse and consequent capacity to replace one complex of propositions about the world by another. This paradigm is purified in Popperian and related models of scientific praxis and the evolution of theory. It relies ultimately on the separation of the individual theory maker from the product of his activity, even if this separation is rarely attained other than in certain of the natural sciences. What becomes clear in the crisis of modernity is the degree to which scientific activity is a social project and not a natural faculty or self-evident procedure for the production of truth. The dissolution of the rational-scientific paradigm is the breakdown of the public sphere of scientific activity, the arena of theory and falsification, of the evolution of knowledge. In its place is substituted wisdom, "edifying conversation," and a pluralism of cultural worlds, a complete relativization of possible world-proposing discourses. If there is disorder here, it is the lack of any principle of order connecting propositions and discourses, that is, the absence of criteria of discrimination. The criteria of discrimination inherent in the public sphere of modernism rank propositions in terms of truth value. But these criteria also ensure the replacement of highest ranked propositions by more adequate propositions. Where such criteria are eliminated, the formerly ranked space is flattened out and its voices take on equal value with respect to one another. This proliferation of potential voices is thus parallel to the proliferation of identities referred to earlier. Other medicines, holistic wisdoms, other understandings of nature, gemeinschafts, all invade the former self-cleansing field of rational thought and modernist developmentalist identity.

The global connection here relates the crisis of hegemony to the crisis of modernism, its dominant ideology, to the emergence of postmodernism, the fragmentation of the former, its multiculturalization. In terms of representations of science, postmodernism is a relativization of scientific knowledge, internally and externally: internally a neutralization of the procedure of falsification, and externally a relativization of scientific knowledge with respect to other forms of knowledge. All knowledge is thus translated into one or another corpus of culturally specific propositions about the world, corpora that are ultimately incommensurable and for which there are, thus, no criteria of comparison or evaluation.

The disordering of the world can be seen as a systematic fragmentation among a number of parallel processes:

scientific knowledge	incommensurable cultural corpora
modernist identity	multicultural rooted identity
political and economic hegemony	multicentric politics and economic accumulation
modern ego formation	narcissistic dissolution

THE FRAGMENTATION OF THE PERSON AND THE DECLINE OF MODERNISM

As we have described the emergence of modernity, the establishment of a specific form of individualized experience plays a central role. It is one in which the body becomes the container of a self-organizing person whose project is disconnected from any larger project in principle, that is, a state in the body. The project of this individualized person is crystallized in the modernism itself, the essence of continuous movement and self-development. It is a fragile identity, constructed on the principle of alienation from all that has been previously attained, on the always felt possibility of being other than what one is at present. It is thus predicated on the absolute separation of self from social identity. This can only be overcome, as Dumont has suggested, by the practice of cultural ascription, which in modernity can only take the form of an essentializing racism.[1] I shall argue here that the essentializing of personhood need not take the form of explicit racism or biological reductionism. In fact, both the latter as well as other forms of ascriptive identification are generated when the ego structure is threatened with dissolution, that is, where the support mechanisms of modern existence fail.

The logic that we have outlined is one that leads from de-hegemonization at the global level to economic decline in the center. This is followed by a dissolution of the modernist project and a crisis of personhood in general, and finally by the advent of depression, as the world no longer conforms to the subject's structure of desire. Ultimately there ensues an unbearable "depressive overload"[2] that threatens psychic survival. It is in this state that clinical narcissism looms large, a situation in which the person becomes increasingly dependent on the "gaze of the other" to ensure his very existence. In such states, a number of solutions appear:

1. The narcissistic state can become relatively stable, however conflict filled.
2. Depression can turn into despair and mental collapse. This is also a tendency in the previous situation.
3. The nascent state: psychic salvation by means of submitting oneself to a larger project, "greater than oneself." This is the core of Francesco Alberoni's "Falling in Love" and of his view of social movements in general.[3]

THE PROCESS OF DISORDERING AND REORDERING THE SOCIAL FIELD

The process of disordering in global systems is not a question of randomization or of increasing entropy. It is, as I have suggested, a process of decentralization that is quite intensive, even explosive at times, and that harbors a tendency to reorganization or at least the strengthening of social forms at more local levels.[4] The individual subject and his emergent strategies and practices play a crucial role in understanding this process. It is the subject that sustains the conditions of social disintegration, and it is the subject's desire for self-maintenance and integration that is the driving force in the process of reordering.

Recent works in France by authors such as Alain Touraine, François Dubet, and Pierre Bourdieu[5] have repeatedly stressed the importance of considering the subjective conditions of action. Dubet, in particular, has in a study of the very large relatively new class of marginalized youth in France demonstrated the ways in which social and personal disintegration are linked to one another and how the latter in its turn produces a specific set of possible courses of action. His work concentrates on the formation of what might be called a culture of violence, a "violence without object" and the way in which it has stabilized by means of the reproduction of identical conditions of existence over a couple of decades. Although this study concentrates essentially on structurally unemployed youth in the deindustrializing north of France, other studies have concentrated on ethnic strategies, the explosive increase in Islamic identity among formerly secularized North Africans. Dubet insists on the nonethnic character of the youth groupings he has studied, not their transethnic but their nonethnic character. The latter criteria appear to be irrelevant in their self-identification. But at the same time and in the same period, the number of mosques in Paris has increased from approximately 10 to over 1,000,[6] and there has been a great deal of alarm concerning a new religious militancy in the country. The recruitment to this emergent reidentification is primarily from the structurally marginalized youth described by Dubet. The two descriptions do not contradict one another but report different phases or perhaps aspects of the same process of disordering/reordering. A systemic aspect of this process, as I have suggested, is that disorder in a social field may produce increasing order within the components of that field. This is what fragmentation is all about. And from the point of view of the subject it is quite reasonable that reidentification and existential engagement are more satisfactory than continuous desperation and anguish. This process reinforces the fragmentation by generating a set of viable boundaries and projects that become increasingly independent of the projects of the larger system. In formal terms this kind of situation can be likened to a "catastrophe," a field in which several solutions may reinstate equilibrium, described in theoretical language as points of bifurcation, trifurcation, and so on.

The outlines of the processes discussed here can be represented as in figure 1. This diagram refers only to the center of a modern global system in conditions of decentralization and decline. Processes in the peripheral sectors necessarily have a different character to the extent that identity is constructed differently there, thus producing a different set of motives and strategies. If there is a rough similarity in the parallel processes of disorganization, ethnic conflict, religious developments, and balkanization, this has to do with the more general properties of social disorder and even personal disorder. Thus, it has been forcefully argued that what appears as ethnic warfare in Sri Lanka is not founded on the same kinds of strategies as Western ethnic conflict.[7] Bruce Kapferer argues that ethnicity is not constructed in the same kinds of terms but is closely related to a self whose identity is bound up with the Buddhist state. Singhalese attack Tamils because of the way they disrupt the hierarchical order of the state, and thus of the individual, whose entire existence is predicated on the maintenance of the state as a cosmological entity. For Singhalese, cultural identity is not born within the body any more than the individual bears his own personal life project. Both are defined as external to the subject, so that the latter practices a form of selfhood that is an expression of the larger totality. But the fact of identity, that is, of identifiable people, no matter what the criteria of identification, the experience of fragmentation and of loss of power, desperation, and anguish, and so on, are common to both this situation and to Western modernity. In the West, ethnicity is sustained within the body, defined as a substance that is passed on from one generation to the next, reducible ultimately to the biological concept of race. In such terms it might be argued that ethnicity does not exist as such in South and Southeast Asia. But as a social construction of identity it is highly variable. Migration in and to Europe, which has become a mass phenomenon in the past few years, is, of course, not a new phenomenon. But in periods of expansion, or at least in periods when modernist identity functions adequately, immigrants are integrated via a process of assimilation or of ranking that places them in one way or another in an unambiguous position. It is only in periods

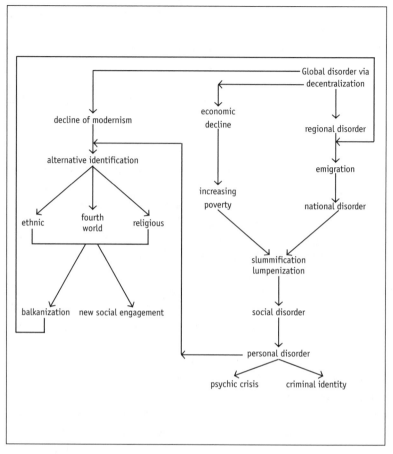

Figure 10.1. Global order/disorder in the center of the system

when the hegemony of central identity declines that multiculturalism emerges, and when, as a consequence, ethnicity, not only of immigrants but of indigenous populations, regional populations, and national populations, becomes salient.

CONCLUSION: THE TWIN PEAKS OF CULTURAL FRAGMENTATION

Salvation and the euphoria of cultural identity, or death metal and ethnic cleansing. These are not two alternatives that have emerged in the contemporary situation, but two intimately related aspects of the process of reidentification in this age of fragmentation. For those who see in all of this a gigantic process of hybridization, I would caution that such a view combines a certain wishful thinking with an entirely external perspective that charts the origins of things rather than the actual structures of practice in the world. It is, furthermore, a view of those who can afford such an external perspective, the various, often short-lived, global elites or professionals whose calling it is to represent the state of the world to others. The literature of the diaspora is a literature of conflict, often insurmountable, often bloody. And here too, the transnational, transethnic, and transcultural are products of intellectual distancing rather than lived experiences. The invasion of those forces that are usually held at a distance by modernist identity appears to pervade every aspect of the contemporary condition. This invasion combines a certain exhilaration, the exhilaration of newfound meaning, and fear, the fear of the outsider, of treachery, and of violence. The invasion is not merely geographic, the implosion of "the others," but internal as well, the implosion of formerly repressed psychic desires, the surfacing of the other within. It is this process that would appear to underlie not only the explosive nature of contemporary conflict as well as its intensity, but also the massive increase of literary, film, and other representations of the combined loss of control of self and others. On the positive side, the exhilaration of violent engagement is, furthermore, a solution to the fear, and the two terms form a system or unity that is difficult to break without changing the circumstances in which it develops. When marginalized youth without any hope in the future are offered drugs and arms to engage in mass murder, we find ourselves in a world in which interlocking processes spin off viciously positive feedback cycles of violence that take on their own momentum and may even become lifestyles and cultures. Today's ethnic wars may well be the sporadic expressions of the more generally seething forces in the global arena.

I have sought here to connect processes that occur at the highest levels of global systems to those that occur within individual subjects. I have implied throughout that these different levels are best understood not as separate entities but as properties or aspects of life processes and that the latter are indeed observable. I have also suggested, implicitly perhaps, that any understanding of cultural production and identity formation in the world today is dependent on insights into the way in which global processes ultimately affect social experience, because it is out of the latter that cultural forms are generated. I have, finally, implied throughout that it is via a concept of identity space that we can grasp the logic of variation in cultural dynamics, one that might allow us to understand how ethnic wars can suddenly burst forth where there was previously no apparent basis for conflict founded on cultural identity. This kind of perspective is not a mere theoretical problem but one that may, hopefully, throw light on some of our major contemporary problems.

NOTES

1. Louis Dumont, *Essais sur l'indivualisme* (Paris: Seuil, 1983).

2. Francesco Alberoni, *Movement and Institution* (New York: Columbia University Press, 1984), pp. 52-83.

3. Alberoni, *Movement and Institution*.

4. The discussion throughout most of this essay concentrates on so-called modern sectors of the global system and is not applicable in the same way to sectors organized on more "holistic" lines.

5. See Alain Touraine, *Critique de la modernité* (Paris: Fayard, 1992); Francois Dubet, *La Galère. Jeunes en survie* (Paris: Fayard, 1987); and Pierre Bourdieu, ed., *La misère du monde* (Paris: Seuil, 1993).

6. Gilles Kepel, *Les banlieus d'Islam* (Paris: Seuil, 1987).

7. Bruce Kapferer, *Legends of People, Myths of State* (Washington, D.C.: Smithsonian Institution, 1988).

Transversal Flows

Introduction to Part V

MICHAEL J. SHAPIRO

The discourse of international political economy has focused primarly on capital exchanges and has paid little attention to the cross-border movement of bodies. Moreover, as Jan Pettman points out, even when labor movement is addressed, it is rarely treated with a gender-sensitive eye. Pettman highlights especially the "traffic in women's bodies" that ranges from an increasingly feminized labor force in degrading jobs to the trade in sexual labor that is an increasing effect of sex tourism.

Most significantly, in treating the variety of identity politics of various marginalized groups—women, indigenous peoples, and refugees—affected by the combination of border policing and the forces of international political economy, Pettman challenges the tendency of mainstream international relations discourses to privilege borders and ignore migrations.

Nevzat Soguk's chapter also is concerned with border crossing. Focusing on the human flows across the U.S.–Mexican border, he provides a palpable political challenge to the traditional sovereignty model of space. However, Soguk adds a dimension to this challenge that has been underappreciated. Rather than simply treating the way that marginalized people have had their identities scripted by dominant statist institutions, he provides counterscripts, largely from the individual narratives with which migrants and refugees articulate the meanings of their experiences.

Whatever might be the state's plans for managing alien populations, these peoples have their "strategies of living." By including their voices within his text, Soguk alters the frame within which border crossings and their consequences have been understood. Instead of a legalistic or sovereignty-oriented frame, he offers a frame that foregrounds cultural encounters so that it becomes evident how places are transformed by these human flows. In bringing an ethnographic imagination and set of methods to his analysis, Soguk allows for increased comprehension of lives and perspectives involved in a struggle for recognition. And he highlights a territorial dynamic that has been largely uncoded in traditional political discourses.

With Richard Maxwell's analysis, the attention shifts to another border area, that between France and Spain. This vicinity, as much as any, testifies to the wisdom of separating the concepts of state and nation. The Basque nation, which spreads across the French-Spanish border, has never been subjugated, and Basque peoples and practices continue to stand as a challenge to those whose image of global politics recognizes states rather than nations or peoples.

Maxwell's analysis, however, is not simply a discursive reassertion of Basque identity politics. His analysis brings us into a rarely glimpsed world of media struggles, showing how the Basque technologies of articulation work to unite them and, at the same time, resist the attempts of state-dominated media to contain them. It is a contention between forces and counterforces involved in what Maxwell calls a dynamic of "containment and trespass," a struggle over various broadcast technologies affecting dynamics of identity politics ranging across the Spanish border and centered in the Basque nation. Electronic signals cross policed borders more easily than visible bodies. The media technology struggle associated with containment and trespass therefore summons issues and insights often neglected when the political focus is on struggles between bodies.

11

Border Crossings/Shifting Identities: Minorities, Gender, and the State in International Perspective

JAN JINDY PETTMAN

This essay looks at the drawing, contesting, and defending of borders, and at border crossings. It focuses on "the wandering people"[1]—colonizers, migrants, migrant laborers, and refugees, whose movements and associations reflect and shape shifting political identities. In turn, national and minority politics and related citizenship politics undermine classic international relations distinctions between the inside and the outside, between the "domestic" and the foreign.[2] This essay elaborates some issues concerning boundaries and minorities in state and global politics. Alongside, it reveals another borderline, as I gender the account. I suggest another kind of international politics—an international political economy of (gendered) bodies.[3]

MAKING THE WORLD: THE STATE SYSTEM

The year 1492 was a crucial moment signaling the "discoveries" and the process of coloniality through which "the world" was incorporated into a single system.[4] That system was a hierarchy of states and colonies, a hierarchy preserved with the universalization of states through decolonization in recent decades. The rules and functioning of the modern state system hinge on notions of sovereignty and particular understandings about "international relations" that were spread, with much else, through "the continuous expansion of a modernist, secular and materialist social system, spanning the globe . . . perhaps the key motor force in contemporary history."[5] This system is also patriarchal, constructed in part through a public/private dichotomy that routinely relegates women away from "the political," including the international political.

The Australian state is a product of this expansion and statisation. It is a settler state, one created by colonization, but where settlers quickly outnumbered as well as outgunned "the natives," where decolonization established a European state far from "home," and which later lost the European empire buffer between it and newly independent "third-world" states. This has left "Australia" with a profound sense of insecurity and an identity crisis in international relations that continues to inform definitions of security and danger in foreign policy and defence, as well as in immigration and citizenship debates.[6]

Insecurity may stem in part from "the spectre of Truganini,"[7] the echoes of the violent invasion, conquest, and dispossession of Aboriginal people that lie at the heart of Australia's state and nation building, leaving a first-nation people stranded in the margins of the settler state. Insecurity is more often articulated in terms of a conflict between our history and our geography,[8] with interesting questions about who "we" are in this counterpoising. Here History lies still in Europe and especially in Britain and Ireland, while we are misplaced far away on the edges of the Asia-Pacific region. This region is represented as dense, teeming, violent, threatening, and thoroughly "other." Now, too, it is seen as an engine of economic growth that might overwhelm us. From this looking place, Australia is caught in the in-between (in a non-place?),[9] between the margins of Europe and the margins of Asia.

Such representations are a reminder that the global spread of states was a part of colonization, migration, and decolonization, which constituted "race" as a central category in the hierarchy of states and in different political identities in international relations. These political identities are infused with notions of otherness, borders of difference that are often racialized. The clusters of identities and categories that are common currency in international relations—the West, the Free World, the Third World, Islam—frequently conflate spatial and relational identities with associations of cultural and bodily difference. Australia occupies ambiguous terrain here, caught between the north and the south. Long part of the West and the Free World, its living standards and self-image of first-world urbanity pull against its physical location in the south and its farm, mine, and tourist-site economy.

MAKING THE WORLD: GLOBAL CAPITALISM AND THE NEW INTERNATIONAL DIVISION OF LABOR

"The New World Order—an imperialist and capitalist world-system—is from any internationalist or postcolonial perception disturbingly reminiscent of the old world order. . . . [I]t is necessary to insist both upon the sustained globality of capitalism, and upon the unevenness of development at the level of the world-system."[10]

The global economic system is irretrievably capitalist and imperialist. All states are now incorporated—unequally—into this economy. Here we can trace the interlocking historical processes of colonization, capitalism, and immigration, shaping among other things an international division of labor both between states and between different regions, fractions of classes, and so on. Much of the international political economy literature lately admitted to international relations is of the liberal or nationalist states-and-markets kind, or else a world systems view, attending in different ways to the recurrent crises and dramatic restructuring of the last twenty years.[11] Here recession, growing internationalization of production, and increasing globalization of finance, with state and financial market deregulation and pressure toward increasing export-orientation, all suggest states with less control than ever over their economies. Of particular interest to international relations then is the apparent contradiction between increasingly globalized economy and the maintenance of states and sovereignty for the political organization of international relations.[12]

Australia is far from immune to this restructuring, which also profoundly affects the welfarist state and the class trade-off and corporatist labor politics of the postwar decades. Organized labor is split, increasingly besieged and disorganized, with a labor aristocracy dealing with government and business to deliver "efficiency," productivity, and "international competitiveness."

Restructuring affects different segments of the labor market differently and reveals a labor force that is segmented along "race" and ethnic lines. Thus in Australia the immigrant factory fodder of the

1950s and 1960s is concentrated in aging manufacturing industries, now increasingly moving offshore. Among those especially hard hit are footware, clothing, and textile workers, who are mainly ethnic minority women.[13] The international political economy of labor migration reveals its particular ironies. Australia's crossover from a labor shortage to a labor surplus economy in the early 1970s coincided with the elimination of racially and culturally restrictive immigration criteria, allowing "in" migrants from the Asia-Pacific region under increasingly selective skills criteria. As a result, nonrefugee Asian migrants' class, education, and occupation profile is on average above those of English-speaking and Australian-born background. Although still supposedly nondiscriminatory in terms of "race" and country of origin, immigration is now pressed back in numbers. Even then immigration can be targeted in election campaigns that tap into anxiety about where we are in the world, and into popular associations of rising unemployment with the arrival of larger numbers of conspicuously different immigrants.

These threads between the international political economy and the state labor market, between restructuring and cutbacks to welfare and social rights provision, and between these and immigration and citizenship policies and racialized politics, remind us of the impossibility of separating out foreign and domestic, political, economic, and social. They also remind us that the increasingly global economy shapes the new international division of labor along state, national, racialized, ethnicized, and gender divides.

AN INTERNATIONAL POLITICAL ECONOMY OF BODIES?

The international political economy of migrant labor is a part of this division of labor and a core motive in the huge population movements of contemporary times. Much of current international political economy literature privileges an international political economy of trade and finance, with labor often receiving less attention.[14] The very unevenness of different states' incorporation into the global economy and the changing needs and nature of capital shape flows and patterns of both employment and migration.

The extraordinary movements of people within and across state and other political boundaries in the past five hundred years include different forms of labor—the slave trade, indentured labor, "free" labor.[15] People moved initially largely from the centers or between colonies, then from 1945 increasingly from the margins to the centers, and most recently from poorer regions to the oil-rich Middle East, to Japan, and to the newly industrialized countries. Contemporary forms of international traffic including migrant labor, legal and illegal, refugees, tourists, and students are often obscured or erased within mainstream international relations. At the same time, the margins themselves are spatially and politically shifting and changing. Colonization and migration, and the unequal impact of the global economy, give us a first world in many thirds, and growing third worlds in the firsts.[16]

A striking feature of the new global division of labor is an increasingly marginalized, casualized, and feminized labor force, sought out in the competition for cheaper labor. The new international labor migrant is now often a (young) woman. Young women[17] are also often the laborers in factories or sweatshops, or they do piecework at home, in a global assembly line especially evident in, for example, textiles and electronics in both first and third worlds.[18] Their labor is cheapened,[19] and they are even more marginalized, often than male workers, by their construction and treatment as female workers. Ideologies of femininity[20] construct "women's work" as temporary and supplementary, even though many are single mothers and heads of households and many more are the sole income earner for their family. Their labor is classified as unskilled even when they do work that is designated skilled when men do it. They are seen in their racialized womanliness as nimble fingered, good at routine and boring tasks, more docile and less likely to unionize and demand than male workers are. These stereotypes persist despite many women's organizing and acting politically.[21] Indeed when they do so, they are frequently represented as stooges and dupes of men or of western feminism, or their leaders are defeminized—and sacked.

Mainstream international relations usually fails to pursue migration including labor migration except sometimes as a foreign policy issue, or, for example, when "refugees" enter the United Nations agenda. International relations and its international political economy brothers are even less likely to analyze other kinds of female work whose forms are increasingly internationalized. Women work on the streets or in bars in a sex industry that is international both in military and tourist prostitution and in the importation of "exotic" foreign women to work the local scene. Women are part of an international trade in bodies that sees governments turn a blind eye to sex tourism and base abuse, at least until AIDS threatens either the tourist dollar or the local men. Here some states, like Thailand and the Philippines, become sex tourist destinations or exporters of "mail-order brides," whereas others, like Australia, provide the men who exploit this trade in women's—and children's—bodies.[22] They exploit others' poverty or lack of options in the patriarchal political economy of their home states. They also exploit racialized gender stereotypes that represent "Asian" women as passive, meticulous, and sexually subservient and performative.

The traffic in women's bodies takes a different but related form in racialized international domestic service, as "maids" from Bangladesh, the Philippines, and Sri Lanka go to work in Middle Eastern or Japanese households, for example.[23] Recent scandals involving two of Clinton's possible cabinet appointments, both women who had employed "illegals" as nannies, show another aspect of this trade.[24] These scandals were fueled by growing African American and Hispanic resentment against "illegals" as unfair competition for jobs. Again it becomes very difficult to separate out international, state, local, and personal politics.

The family location of domestic work, the sexual politics of domestic labor generally, and the "race," cultural, class, and often age differences between the employing and employed women in the household remind us, too, of another margin: those supposedly "private" parts of life that political science and international relations have long excluded from their view/s.[25] They remind us further of women's frequent entrapment in the dependent side of the dangerous protector/protected relationship. Women who work in sex, household, outwork, or family businesses are often dependent on a boss-protector and vulnerable to exploitation and abuse from their supposed protectors. This situation is especially present where "foreign" women's home states seek their export in return for remittances from overseas workers and foreign aid from oil-rich states, and are reluctant to take up their nationals' rights or act to supervise recruitment activities.

Lack of international relations attention to this trade in bodies led to commentators' surprise at both the numbers of overseas workers and the large numbers of women caught in the cross fire in the recent

Gulf conflict.[26] Yet the international traffic in women is the focus of concern of many women's organizations in exporting states, and some commentators suggest that this traffic is currently more lucrative than the arms trade.[27]

MINORITIES IN THE MARGINS AND THE CENTERS

Tracking the "wandering people"[28] dislodged by war, political violence, and the uneven workings of the global economy reveals exiles, diasporas, "aliens," and others whose rights of residence or citizenship in what are now their living places are often insecure.[29] In current restructuring, with many, including first-world states, facing large-scale unemployment and welfare cutbacks, women have been called on to make an "invisible adjustment" to cope with growing family stress and to compensate for reduced social provision. At the same time, these pressures lead states to discourage immigration and to restrict citizenship, while perceived outsiders are often blamed for the troubles. Other international politics also heighten the vulnerability of those in the margins. Thus black, migrant, refugee, and human rights groups organize across state borders in the likelihood of exclusionary or underclass implications of the moves toward the European community.[30]

Increasing state defensiveness and redrawing of citizenship boundaries are partly a response to the perceived threat of difference after decades of importation of migrant workers, and to fears of growing numbers of "illegals" and refugees. These others are often racialized, as are Turkish guest workers in the former West Germany and Vietnamese guest workers in the former East Germany. So too are "black" and "Asian" British-born citizens in the United Kingdom. Here the politics of identity and the construction of minorities speak clearly to a history of colonization, racialization, and unequal development globally, and to the effects of discrimination and citizenship politics within particular states. Once again it is simply not possible to draw the line between international and domestic politics.

These borderline politics are a reminder that the state never just is.[31] It is always in the process of becoming, as is the nation, its people. State and national borders are defended through immigration and citizenship politics as well as "foreign" policy and defence. Indeed, "floods" of refugees, an "immigrant invasion," "our culture" under siege from both numbers and "foreign bodies," the body politic vulnerable to pollution,[32] to being eaten away from within, display a militarized language of security and danger deployed in discourses around immigration.

These debates about who belongs and who does not, about who we are and who threatens us, reveal large groups of people who may be inside the state but outside the nation, whose rights to residence, family reunion, access to social resources, or a job are vulnerable at best.[33] Again the inside and the outside are unclear and are fought over. Here we watch the construction and play of new political identities and categories in the resurgence of nationalisms and ethnic/racialized conflicts globally. These conflicts often crystallize over competition for control of the state or in protests against particular minorities' unequal access to the state and its resources.

Here we can distinguish between hegemonic or dominant group nationalisms, or "reethnicizations" as older, for example, European, nationalisms react against perceived strangers within,[34] and mobilizations of minority identities in the face of displacement, discrimination, or exploitation.[35] In the process, these political identities and their borderlines, membership, and presumed associations shift and are context specific. Thus "Asian" in the United Kingdom mainly means South Asian and homogenizes and encloses groups and communities, including some locked in bitter ethnicized strife "at home"; whereas "Asian" in Australia used to be a code word for Southeast Asian or for Vietnamese/refugee, but in the wake of growing numbers of Hong Kong Chinese migrating to Australia is increasingly being read as "Chinese."

Nationalisms and ethnicities are not necessarily progressive or reactionary in themselves—though the dangers and damage of boundary making are dreadfully evident at present. But although both hegemonic and minority identities mobilize around notions of a shared past, they are patently modern identities, generated by international and intrastate political and economic changes. Here too we see the ironies in global politics of apparent trends toward both integration and disintegration.[36] Transformations toward globalism themselves appear to trigger rising awareness of and organization around difference/s. This contradiction is itself informed by the spread of ideas and languages circulating across state borders, and by contingent and shifting political identities within as well as between states.

THE STATE AND MINORITY MAKING IN AUSTRALIA

This year (1993) is the Year of Indigenous People. Australia is a settler state containing within it a first-nation/fourth-world people. The Australian state is responsible for administration of "the Aboriginal problem."[37] Indeed, the state is partly responsible for "the making of the Aborigines,"[38] in a complex play between state management, Aboriginal resistance to and claim on the state, and state response in attempts to incorporate and domesticate Aboriginal protest.[39] All this occurs against an international backdrop where Aboriginal people make use of international forums and linkages, and the Australian state seeks to shed its reputation in its region and within the United Nations as colonialist and racist. Here minority politics within the state are part of hierarchically organized international processes and of the transnational politics of new social movements and emerging global norms around human rights.[40]

Here, too, are the difficulties for settler-state nationalism in dealing with an indigenous minority that continues to call attention to the dubious moral bases of the state. One Aboriginal community leader declared on Australia Day 1992, "Your continuing failure over the past 200 years to treat with us as equals will condemn you, all of you, as a community of thieves in the eyes of your children's children, and the rest of the world. We are your only true connection to this continent, to this entire region. We are the land, and we are here forever."[41] Some non-Aboriginal Australian political leaders have acknowledged the theft, most strongly the present prime minister, Paul Keating, who marked the beginning of the Year of Indigenous Peoples by declaring "We took the traditional lands . . . We committed the murders . . . We practised discrimination and exclusion," a construction of a non-Aboriginal collectivity in unreconciled relation of ongoing domination with those here before. This assertion of responsibility is part of a wider political project, the reconstitution of a new, modern, and more appropriate Australian nationalism in three parts: detachment from an anachronistic and infantilizing imperial maternal connection with the British crown, a reorientation toward Asia, and a reconciliation with those who paid the violent cost of the establishment and consolidation of a white settler state.

More often, a strategy of appropriation and domestication is deployed, where, for example, Aboriginal designs are used as "local color" and a marker of difference from old Europe, while Aboriginal people are simultaneously contained within the "cultural," the "traditional," and away from politics and contending nationalisms. This move is strongly resisted by many Aboriginal groups. Their counter histories in the brief space created by the 1988 bicentenary "celebrations" declared "White Australia has a Black History," and "You're on Aboriginal land, so pay the rent!" In a calculated challenge to statist claims to singular authority and representation, Aboriginal people use the language of sovereignty, claiming "sovereignty unceded" in the absence of negotiations or treaties through which they might be seen to "make over" their land or authority to the settlers/invaders. These claims disrupt the play of statism/sovereignty to "cohere" the domestic community against an anarchy outside the borders. They highlight difference and unauthorized power in domination practices within the state territory and its body/politic.

Aboriginal discourses draw attention to Aboriginality as ongoing presence. This presence as subjects and landowners is called up in essentialized spirituality [42] constructed as both not- and anti-West/materialist/capitalist, as well as not-White. Aboriginal presence/land is given a "beyond" quality in both difference and abidingness, as in the recurring imaging "Always Was—Always Will Be." [43] Aboriginal people define themselves against the settlers/invaders, seen as unrooted, uncomprehending, superficial—despite the horrific violence and pain inflicted on Aboriginal bodies and land over two hundred years.

Aboriginal people's particular construction of time/place/people as theirs, in forever/land/indigenous associations, mocks the very recent and palpably from-somewhere-else nature of settler-state nationalism. For two hundred years, that state attempted to erase the indigenous presence in the doctrine of terra nullius—effectively, unoccupied land—which entailed legal constitution of settler colonies and then the federal state through denial of Aboriginal people and cultures. Against this symbolic and legal/ized violence, Aboriginal people claim identity and sovereignty. In the process, "race," nation, culture—and "blood"—are conflated, the last a metaphor of survival in the face of extraordinary state disciplining practises directed at Aboriginal bodies and difference over generations.

In June 1992, the High Court ruled that some Aboriginal people might claim native title, effectively disrupting the moral and legal bases of "Australia."[44] This decision has regenerated heated argument about indigenous rights, about whose country it is, and who should have what rights within it.[45] Aboriginal national energies rapidly moved to reconstruct a language of self-government and compensation claim in a new cooperation among usually disparate groups, communities, and organizations. Against this, a powerful alliance of state developmentalist politicians, mining companies, and forces for obliteration of Aboriginal difference assert conventional notions of sovereignty and the individuated citizen.

Aboriginal people draw a clear borderline between themselves and "the rest," even where they too have white ancestry and/or are engaged in family and close social relations with non-Aboriginal people. The identity and rights of different Aboriginal people are also contested from the outside and managed by the state, lately privileging self-identification. Aboriginal people may live in and identify with different kinds of associations and communities, but one common/izing feature is their identification and treatment as Aboriginal by the state.[46]

A MULTICULTURAL AUSTRALIA?

Over long periods, Aboriginal people's experience of the state has brought violence and terror. Some non-Aboriginal people have come to Australia to escape other forms of state violence and terror. They are now reconstituted as different within state discourses of multiculturalism and ethnicity, which speak to other conflicts around identity and the boundaries of political community. They are associated in particular with the long processes of immigration and in particular the widening sources of immigration to Australia since 1947. Now, twenty-three percent of Australians are overseas born, and Australia is second only to Israel in the numbers and diverse origins of its current population.

Before 1947, Australia's national political project was defined in racially and culturally exclusivist language, literally as "Australia for the white man." Within this project, white women were occasionally visible as breeders of the white race.[47] After 1947, the combined pressures to "populate or perish," for labor and a domestic market for industrialization, and reduced interest in migrating among those from the United Kingdom and Ireland forced a widening definition of those who were seen as assimilable to include people from southern Europe, then from the Middle East, and in the 1970s from the local Asia-Pacific region.[48]

A remarkable shift in the terms of the national political project has occurred over the past twenty-five years.[49] In the postwar period, the condition of entry was that immigrants become like us, become "New Australians." But the very numbers of "them" and the beginnings of both a left-labor ethnic rights movement and a restless ethnic middle class prompted official declaration of Australia as a multicultural society in the early 1970s. This led to the construction of ethnicity as a way of managing minority mobilization and claims against the state. The borrowing of the new language of intergroup or community relations, especially from Canada, again reflected an international circulation of ideas about difference.

Multiculturalism is based on a pluralist model of society, so the Australian society is a mosaic of differences, held together by an assertion of "core values" that leave power relations and structured inequalities unavailable for political critique. Multiculturalism reflects the state's attempts to defuse the radical possibilities of identity politics into special needs or administrative category politics.[50] In the process, ethnicity is depoliticized, made into something "cultural," a relegation of difference into "tradition." It becomes a way of primitivizing Others, relegating them out of the mainstream of supposedly rational, modern, and secular politics, which is thus preserved for elite men.

Here there is a double move. The first establishes the state and its "domestic" politics as safe, knowable, and orderly, against a disorder of the international/outside. The state polices its borders through defence, immigration, and customs and conducts an elaborate selection and admissions policy that is reinforced by island-occupation and the state's territorializing control. Those different others who are admitted entry are expected to become citizens of a public politics and are subject through this to state disciplining by/through the dominant culture. Beyond the body politic, they are allowed a private or domesticated sphere in which they may still be different, but they may not bring other than sanitized lifestyle differences into performance in the public domain. This is the condition of their belonging, a test of their citizenship, of being Australian. Nostalgia, difference, concern for "there," may thus activate dominant group anxieties about the alien, the foreign, the disorderly within. Here is another inside/outside borderland, where minorities, Aboriginal or ethnic, have an ambiguous nationality. Legally citizens, they are widely seen as not really belonging, marked by a difference that is potentially dangerous and somehow unpatriotic. Such conditionality became clear when Arab and Muslim Australians were asked during the Gulf War to demonstrate that they were really loyal Australians, and were targets of racist violence, even though Australia had gone to the aid of Arab allies (and the United States).[51]

In the borderlands, too, is the threat of homeland wars. While the United Kingdom and Ireland remain the main sources of immigrants, many other migrants and especially refugees reflect troubled times and wars elsewhere. Australia has accepted 420,000 refugees since 1945, including some 100,000 Vietnamese people since 1975.[52] More recently numbers of Central and South American refugees have arrived, coming from both the left and the right in bitter wars, and yet put together in hostels and English language classes.[53] They come too with personal and family histories of violence and torture, with fear, grief, and sometimes guilt about others left behind.

Australia's "ethnic" television channel, SBS, notes its news as "bringing the world back home." For many, it brings "home" back "here." At times, momentous events "at home" will shatter local peace/pieces and force personal, family, and community redefinition of identity and alliance. Thus the breakup of Yugoslavia and the mobilization of the large Australian Croation community against Serbian moves and of the smaller Australian Serbian one in defence of a bad press locally made life especially difficult for those of the second-generation whose identities had been nationalized, as Yugoslav and/or as Australian, and for those in "mixed" families. Meanwhile, rapid changes in Eastern Europe and the former Soviet empire have affected older, virulently anticommunist migrants from those parts and reopened traffic between here and there for many individuals. At the same time, "they" are urged to leave "the past," and "home," behind—usually by the same patriots and zealots who bewail current moves toward an Australian republic as betrayal of "our" history and culture.

World media reporting of homeland wars is a reminder of a body/politics in its most physical and immediate forms. Migrants and those they left behind have often felt the full force of war, persecution, state violence, intercommunal strife, or economic exploitation, even while many of them attempted defence, resistance, change. International processes are played out on and through bodies—classed, racialized, gendered bodies. Their treatment, options, and status reflect their past and present locations in the margins or in safer climes.

DOUBLE DISPLACEMENT/S: WOMEN SUBSUMED

The multilayered, shifting texture and connections of this world/ these worlds[54] are hard to plot, especially given the political, administrative, and academic predilection to binaries and territorial boundaries. In Australia, for example, a complex politics of identity is reduced to a pluralist and relativist form of identity politics. Here we see a reification of categories for easy distinction between them and us, and for managing the minorities. The multitude of potential categories are posited as alternative identities. So we have Aborigines *and* Australians, migrants *and* Australians (though some migrants are more migrant than others), Aborigines *or* migrants *or* women. Along these simple fault lines, multiple identities, political alliances, and intermarriages[55] are obscured, and differences within the homogenized categories are erased.[56]

Here a double displacement frequently occurs.

The mainstream international relations distinction between the inside and the outside disguises differences/minorities/margins within the territorial state. It disguises the ambiguities and contests around citizenship. But when attention is given to the minorities, they are often located in terms of another inside/outside split, and identified primarily in terms of cultural difference or lack of fit with the dominant/normalized/naturalized nation/state. Where they are formally recognized or offered a place within the state, it is often in welfare, education, or special needs servicing, away from the main business of the state in its powerful economic, legal, foreign, and defence functions.

Women in the minorities experience a double displacement, for they are on the margins—or the inner, private recesses—of the minorities.

Women have long been relegated into the private, away from the public/political in Western political thought. Women's ambiguous relations with the state, for example, as mothers of citizens[57] and as those to be protected by their men/state against other men/states, casts them as dependents, as primarily involved in the family, unable to claim full citizenship.[58] But the state does treat different women differently, for example, as legal citizens or not, as members of the dominant culture or not.[59] Here women are frequently subsumed within their dominant or minority group, and minority women especially are assumed cultural or communal first and gendered second.

In times of crisis, community or nationalist struggles are privileged above women's emancipation.[60] Indeed, minority status or struggles for national liberation may be what most crucially locate women in their treatment by the state. But women experience category privilege or danger in terms of their "race," culture, nationality, ethnicity—along with class, age, and so on—differently from "their" men.[61]

Gender is a constitutive part of multiple and possibly conflicting identities. Being oppressed in terms of national or ethnic background, for example, does not remove oppressive relations within the group.[62] There is no necessary virtue in oppression or shared interest or empathy with other oppressed. Minority women are often spoken for by "their" men. But such dis/placement also occurs when some dominant-group feminists speak for "women." A group of Aboriginal academic women recently addressed white Australian feminist academics with the caution, "Just because you are women doesn't mean you are necessarily innocent. You were, and still are, part of that colonising force."[63] So, white, dominant-group women in settler states like Australia need to attend to their/our complicity or privilege in terms of a structure of race power that is still with us.[64] This requires commitment to antiracist and progressive struggles as women's struggles, and to "owning" our own social experiences, even while struggling to change the social relations that inform them.

Women have long been invisible, or occasionally stereotypically represented as victims, in international relations, a discipline that has proved especially resistant to feminist critiques.[65] Over the past twenty years feminist scholarship in related areas, in political theory and sociology concerning the nature of the state and citizenship, in history documenting women's lives in wars, liberation movements, and migrations, for example, reveals women in the borderlands in national/state/international politics. A growing feminist international relations literature[66] critiques foundation texts and key concepts and categories in international relations, and demonstrates that gender is a structuring relation in global, state, and local politics. Citizenship, nationalist movements, war, development, the labor market are all experienced in gendered forms. We can know little of the world if we theorize it in terms of (elite) men's experiences only.

Nation, race, and community are gendered social categories that materialize among other ways in the policing of women's movements, bodies, and relations—especially sexual relations—with "others."[67] "Tradition" pertains mainly to women, who are used symbolically to mark the boundaries of otherness and belonging. They are seen as the bearers of cultural authenticity, the ones responsible for the physical and cultural reproduction of the "race" or community. They are the mothers of the nation, whose birthing—and having the "right" children—becomes, literally, part of nation building, especially under siege.[68]

Women's roles in boundary politics, and as possessions of "their" community/men, make them especially vulnerable to particular forms of violence and danger—from other men and also from their own.[69] The "comfort women" used by the Japanese military and the systematic rape of Bosnian Muslim women as part of a Greater Serbian political project are disruptions to an international relations discourse that does not address issues of sexuality and sexualized violence.[70] Nor does it usually ask, whose security? against whom? in terms of women's experiences of violence and danger.[71] So the politics of identities, of centers and margins, of borderline conflicts can be revisioned as a body politics, in which the sexed body is central.

CONCLUDING

There is more movement on the ground than in the academy, as many women's organizations work to bring women's rights and voices to the international political arena. Women's nongovernmental organizations were particularly active around the Rio Earth Summit and the Vienna World Conference on Human Rights, documenting abuses against women but moving beyond women-as-victim images to a robust body politics. Here the shifting and mutually constituted politics of identity/ies become clearer, though women's voices are still largely contained and recognized only, if at all, as sectional or special interests.

A world or state politics that aims to make a space for other voices is complicated by the ways in which women's own embodied experiences and resistances are often erased or else spoken for by male elite members of their group, or by outsiders, including academic women. The politics and ethics of voice require constant attention to, who speaks? and who is being heard? in a situation where spokesmen, usually, of the more organized minorities may effectively silence other voices within the margins.

Where to then from here? Beyond statism, recognizing increasingly transnational/global politics, economy, ideas, and associations across the territorial boundaries of the state, differences within the presumed nation-state, and the complex human traffic and body politics within and across state borders. Beyond an ahistorical essentialism, peopling world politics in ways that avoid replacing a homogenized state with a plurality of homogenized "communities." Beyond a false universalism, to recognize the double displacement that frequently renders women invisible, even within attempts to give voice to those in the margins. And beyond international relations, to locate different local, national, state, and wider political identities within structures of power that are increasingly global in nature and effect.

NOTES

1. Homi Bhabha, ed., *Nation and Narration* (London: Routledge, 1990).

2. Earlier versions of this essay were presented at the International Studies Association conference at Acapulco in 1993, and the State in Transition conference at LaTrobe University in 1993.

3. I develop this notion further in my forthcoming book, *Worlding Women* (Sydney: Allen & Unwin).

4. Anibal Quijano and Immanuel Wallerstein, "Americanity as a Concept, or the Americans in the Modern World-System," *International Social Science Journal* 134, pp. 549-57.

5. Stephen Gill, "Reflections on Global Order and Sociohistorical Time," *Alternatives* 16 (1991), p. 276.

6. Jan Jindy Pettman, "Security and Identity," in *Threats without Enemies*, ed. StJohn Kettle and Gary Smith (Sydney: Pluto, 1992).

7. Truganani is referred to as "the last of the Tasmanian Aborigines," but she is succeeded by many Tasmanian Aboriginal people descended, for

example, from Aboriginal women and white sealers and sailors; see Lynall Ryan, "Aboriginal Women and Agency in the Process of Conquest," *Australian Feminist Studies* 2 (1986), pp. 35-43. Much popular and some academic racist representation constructs "real" Aboriginal people as "fullblood" and "traditional," and denies those who are paler, "educated," urban, radical, or otherwise not contained within a spiritualizing gaze and outback location their Aboriginality, even as they discriminate against these same people as Aborigines; see Marcia Langton, "Urbanising Aborigines: The Social Scientists' Great Deception," *Social Alternatives* 2, no. 2 (1981), pp. 16-22; and David Hollingsworth, "Discourses on Aboriginality and the Politics of Identity in Urban Australia," *Oceania* 63, no. 2 (1992), pp. 137-55.

8. Henry Reynolds, "Catching Up with Our Geography," *Australian Society* April 1991, pp. 28-30.

9. Richard K. Ashley, "Living on Borderlines: Man, Poststructuralism and War," in James Der Derian and Michael J. Shapiro, eds., *International/Intertextual Relations* (Lexington, Mass.: Lexington Books, 1989), pp. 259-322.

10. Neil Lazarus, "Doubting the New World Order: Marxism, Realism and the Claims of Postmodernist Social Theory," *differences* 3, no. 3 (1991), p. 95.

11. Ralph Pettman, *International Politics* (Melbourne: Longman Cheshire, 1991); J. Ann Tickner, *Gender in International Relations* (New York: Columbia University Press, 1992).

12. See, for example, Robert Cox, *Production, Power and World Order: Social Forces in the Making of History* (New York: Columbia University Press, 1987); and Gill, "Reflections on Global Order and Sociohistorical Time," p. 276.

13. Barbara Misztal, "Migrant Women in Australia," *Journal of Intercultural Studies* 12, no. 1 (1991), pp. 15-31.

14. This may be changing. A number of papers on migrant labor were presented at the 1993 International Studies Association conference at Acapulco.

15. Lydia Potts, *The World Labour Market: A History of Migration* (London: Zed Books, 1990); Robert Miles, *Capitalism and Unfree Labour: Anomaly or Necessity?* (London: Tavistock Publications, 1987); Robin Cohen, "East-West Migration in a Global Context," *New Community* 18, no. 1 (1991), pp. 9-26.

16. Swasti Mitter, *Common Fate, Common Bond: Women in the Global Economy* (London: Pluto, 1986).

17. And children. Children's labor, including forced family and bonded labor, is becoming visible in some human rights, women's and labor organization literature. Although still very quiet about women, international relations is almost silent on children and young people; see Alex Fyfe, *Child*

Labour (Cambridge: Polity Press, 1989); and UNICEF, *The State of the World's Children* (New York: UNICEF, 1992).

18. Ibid.; Cynthia Enloe, *Bananas, Bases and Beaches: Making Feminist Sense of International Relations* (London: Pandora, 1990), ch. 6.

19. Cynthia Enloe, "Silicon Tricks and the Two Dollar Woman," *New Internationalist* January 1992, pp. 12-14.

20. Connections between ideologies of femininity and women's work are beyond the scope of this paper. They include, for example, definitions of women's roles, ideologies of seclusion and control that limit women's mobility, and their access to certain kinds of work and to social resources; see Haleh Afshar, *Women, State and Ideology: Studies from Africa and Asia* (New York: State University Press, 1987). Both the nature of women's work and their vulnerability to bodily abuse are related to the construction of women as "nature," there for the taking; see Maria Mies, *Patriarchy and Accumulation on a World Scale* (London: Zed Books, 1986); V. Spike Peterson, ed., *Gendered States: Feminist (Re)Visions of International Relations* (Boulder, Colo.: Lynne Rienner, 1992).

21. Mitter, *Common Fate, Common Bond;* Women Working Worldwide, *Common Interests: Women Organising in Global Electronics* (London: Women Working Worldwide, 1990).

22. Des Cahill, *Intermarriage in International Contexts* (Quezon City: Scalabrini Migration Centre, 1990); Melba Marchison, "Filipina Migration and Organisation in Australia," *Lilith* 7 (1991), pp. 11-24.

23. Special issue of *Asian Migrant* on Migrant Women Workers, 4, no. 2 (1991).

24. Jeffrey Rosen, "Good Help: Race, Immigration and Nannies," *New Republic* 15/2 (1993).

25. Gayle Rubin, "The Traffic in Women: Notes on the Political Economy of Sex," in *Towards an Anthropology of Women,* ed. Rayna Reiter (New York: Monthly Review Press, 1975); Enloe, *Bananas, Bases and Beaches;* Heidi Tinsman, "The Indispensable Service of Sisters: Considering Domestic Service in Latin America and United States Studies," *Journal of Women's History* 4, no. 1 (1992), pp. 37-59. See also Wendy Brown, "Where is the Sex in Political Theory?" *Women and Politics* 7, no. 1 (1987), pp. 3-24.

26. Cynthia Enloe, "The Gulf Crisis: Making Feminist Sense of It," *Pacific Research* November 1990, pp. 3-5.

27. Kay Murray, "The Asia Pacific Regional Human Rights Conference," *Womanspeak* June/July 1993, p. 29.

28. Bhabha, *Nation and Narration.*

29. Nira Yuval-Davis, "The Citizenship Debate: Women, Ethnicity and the State," *Feminist Review* 39 (1991), pp. 58-68.

30. Mirjana Morokvasic, "Fortress Europe and Migrant Women," *Fem-*

inist Review 39 (1991), pp. 69-84; A. Sivanandan, "New Circuits of Imperialism," *Race and Class* 3, no. 4 (1989), pp. 1-19.

31. Charles Tilly, "War Making and State Making as Organised Crime," in *Bringing the State Back In*, ed. Peter Evans, Dietrich Rueschemeyer, and Theda Skocpol, eds. (New York: Cambridge University Press, 1985); Pettman, *International Politics;* Peterson, *Gendered States.*

32. Adam Lerner, "Transcendence of the ImagiNATION," paper presented at the 32nd Annual International Studies Association Convention, Vancouver, B.C., March 1991.

33. Stuart Hall and David Held, "Left and Rights," *Marxism Today* June 1989, pp. 16-21; Yuval-Davis, "The Citizenship Debate"; Jan Jindy Pettman, "Security and Identity."

34. Benedict Anderson, "The New World Disorder," *New Left Review* 193 (1992), p. 3-14.

35. Homi Bhabha and Bhikhu Parekh, "Identities on Parade," *Marxism Today* June 1989, pp. 24-29.

36. Fred Halliday, "International Relations: Is There a New Agenda?" *Millennium* 20, no. 1 (1990), pp. 249-59; Anderson, "The New World Disorder"; Roland Robertson, *Globalization: Social Theory and Global Culture* (London: Sage, 1992).

37. Jeremy Beckett, "Aboriginality, Citizenship and the Nation-State," *Social Analysis* 24 (1988), pp. 3-18.

38. Bain Attwood, *The Making of the Aborigines* (Sydney: Allen and Unwin, 1989).

39. Jan Jindy Pettman, *Living in the Margins: Racism, Sexism and Feminism in Australia* (Sydney: Allen and Unwin, 1992).

40. R. B. J. Walker, One World/Many Worlds (Boulder, Colo.: Lynne Rienner, 1988); Pettman, *International Politics.*

41. Shirley Smith, "Mum Shirl," as quoted in Ann Curthoys, "Feminism, Citizenship and National Identity," *Feminist Review* 44 (1993), p. 19.

42. Providing interesting ethical and political challenges for social scientists of modernist or postmodern inclination. Aboriginal identity and constructions of self/other as essential warn "hands off" to outside "experts" long authorized to represent "Aborigines," and authorize insider-knowledges on the bases of experience and belonging which, by definition, outsiders are not privy to.

43. See, for example, Jackie Huggins, "Always Was, Always Will Be," *Australian Historical Studies* 25, no. 100 (1993), pp. 459-64.

44. David Mercer, "Terra Nullius, Aboriginal Sovereignty and Land Rights in Australia," *Political Geography* 12, no. 4 (1993), pp. 299-318; Jan Jindy Pettman, "Australia," in *Beyond Dichotomies: Gender, Ethnicity,*

Race and Class in Settler Societies, ed. Daiva Stasiulis and Nira Yuval-Davis (London: Sage, forthcoming).

45. Irene Watson, "Has Mabo Turned the Tide for Justice?" *Social Alternatives* 12, (1993), p. 1; Tim Rowse, "Mabo and Moral Anxiety," *Meanjin* 52, no. 2 (1993), pp. 229-52.

46. Beckett, "Aboriginality, Citizenship and the Nation-State"; Jan Jindy Pettman, *Living in the Margins.*

47. Marie de Lepervanche, "Breeders for Australia: A National Identity for Women?" *Australian Journal of Social Issues* 24, no. 3 (1989), pp. 163-81; Marilyn Lake, "Mission Impossible: How Men Gave Birth to the Australian Nation," *Gender and History* 4, no. 3 (1992), pp. 305-22; Jan Jindy Pettman, *Living in the Margins.*

48. Stephen Castles, Mary Kalantzis, Bill Cope, and Michael Morrissey, *Mistaken Identity: Multiculturalism and the Demise of Australian Nationalism* (Sydney: Pluto, 1988).

49. Jan Jindy Pettman, "Australia."

50. Helen Meekosha and Jan Pettman, "Beyond Category Politics," *Hecate* 17, no. 2 (1991), pp. 75-92.

51. Human Rights and Equal Opportunity Commission (HREOC), *Report of the National Inquiry into Racist Violence in Australia* (Canberra: HREOC, 1991).

52. Bureau of Immigration Research, *Australia's Population Trends and Prospects* (Canberra: AGPS, 1990).

53. Beryl Langer, "From History to Ethnicity: El Salvadoran Refugees in Melbourne," *Journal of Intercultural Studies* 11, no. 2 (1990), pp. 1-13.

54. Walker, *One World/Many Worlds.*

55. Charles Price notes that at least 7 million Australians of the total 17 million have three or more ancestries, and 4 million have four or more—though he counts the Welsh and Cornish, for example, as separate ethnic origins; Charles Price, *Ethnic Groups in Australia* (Canberra: Australian Immigration Research Centre, 1989), p. 2.

56. Meekosha and Pettman, "Beyond Category Politics."

57. Kathleen Jones, "Citizenship in a Woman-Friendly Polity," *Signs* 15 (1990), pp. 781-812; Gisela Bock and Susan James, eds., *Beyond Difference and Equality: Citizenship, Feminist Politics and Female Subjectivity* (London: Routledge, 1992); Lake, "Mission Impossible."

58. See Cynthia Fuchs Epstein, "In Praise of Women Warriors," *Dissent* summer 1991, pp. 421-22, for a liberal feminist argument on the need for women to serve equally as warriors in order to claim equal citizenship rights; and Grant, "The Quagmire of Gender and International Security," in Peterson, *Gendered States,* pp. 83-98, on possible implications of increasing

numbers of women in the military, and the push toward women in state combat.

59. Nira Yuval-Davis and Floya Anthias, eds., *Woman/Nation/State* (London: Macmillan, 1989).

60. Maxine Molyneux, "Mobilisation without Emancipation? Women's Interests, the State and Revolution in Nicaragua," *Feminist Studies* 11, no. 2 (1985), pp. 227-54; Kumari Jayawardena, *Feminism and Nationalism in the Third World* (London: Zed Books, 1986).

61. Jan Jindy Pettman, "Women, Nationalism and the State: An International Feminist Perspective," Occasional Paper No. 4, Gender Development Studies Unit, Asian Institute of Technology, Bangkok.

62. Gita Sahgal and Nira Yuval-Davis, eds., *Refusing Holy Orders: Women and Fundamentalism* (London: Virago, 1992).

63. Jackie Huggins, Letters to the Editor, *Women's Studies International Forum* 14 (1991), p. 5.

64. Jackie Huggins, "A Contemporary View of Aboriginal Women's Relationship to the White Women's Movement," in *A Woman's Place in Australia* (Geelong: Deakin University, 1992); Nupur Chandhuri and Margaret Strobel, *Western Women and Imperialism: Complicity and Resistance* (Bloomington: Indiana University Press, 1992); Jan Jindy Pettman, "Gendered Knowledges: Aboriginal Women and the Politics of Feminism," *Journal of Australian Studies* 35 (1992), pp. 120-32.

65. Fred Halliday, "Hidden from International Relations: Women and the International Arena," in *Gender and International Relations*, ed. Rebecca Grant and Kathleen Newland (Bloomington: Indiana University Press, 1991); Peterson, *Gendered States;* Jan Jindy Pettman, "Gendering International Relations," *Australian Journal of International Affairs* 47, no. 1 (1993), pp. 47-62. Revealing other margins and contested borderlines, in terms of academic territory/ies and states of mind; Sandra Whitworth, "Gender in the Inter-Paradigm Debate" *Millennium* 18, no. 2 (1989), pp. 265-72; Peterson, *Gendered States;* Pettman, "Gendering International Relations."

66. *Millennium*, special issue on Women and International Relations 17, no. 3 (1988); Enloe, *Bananas, Bases and Beaches;* Grant and Newland, *Gender and International Relations;* Tickner, *Gender in International Relations;* Peterson, *Gendered States.*

67. Tessie Lui, "Race and Gender in the Politics of Group Formation," *Frontiers* 12, no. 2 (1991), pp. 155-65; Andrew Parker, Mary Russo, Doris Sommer, and Patricia Yaeger, eds., *Nationalisms and Sexualities* (London: Routledge, 1992).

68. Yuval-Davis and Anthias, *Woman/Nation/State;* Enloe, *Bananas, Bases and Beaches;* Deniz Kandiyoti, "Identity and Its Discontents: Women and the Nation," *Millennium* 20, no. 1 (1991), pp. 429-43; Jan Jindy

Pettman, "Women, Nationalism and the State." The connections between nationalist and state political projects, immigration and population policies, and differential provision of health and reproductive services to dominant group and minority women is yet another example of the unreality of a separation of international from domestic politics; Barbara Hartmann, *Reproductive Rights and Wrongs: Global Politics of Population Control and Contraceptive Choices* (New York: Harper and Row, 1987); de Lepervanche, "Breeders for Australia"; Gisela Bock, "The Power and Powerlessness of Women," in Bock and James, *Beyond Difference and Equality*.

69. The unequal and dangerous protector/protected relationship between men and women is a key theme in writings on "domestic" violence and in feminist peace research; Judith Stiehm, ed., *Women and Men's Wars* (Oxford, Pergamon Press, 1984); Barbara Roberts, "The Death of Machothink: Feminist Research and the Transformation of Peace Studies," *Women's Studies International Forum* 7, no. 4 (1984), pp. 195-200; Rosemary Ridd and Helen Callaway, eds., *Women and Political Conflict: Portraits of Struggle in Times of Crisis* (New York: University Press, 1987); Jan Jindy Pettman, "A Feminist Perspective on Peace and Security," *Interdisciplinary Peace Research* 4, no. 2 (1992), pp. 58-71. Other feminist writings interrogate gendered international political identities, which in old international relations texts and war tales are naturalized in representations of men as the citizen-warriors. See, for example, Jean Bethke Elshtain, *Women and War* (New York: Basic Books, 1987); Grant, "The Quagmire of Gender and International Security."

70. Brown, "Where is the Sex in Political Theory?"

71. Peterson, *Gendered States*; Pettman, "Security and Identity."

12

Transnational/Transborder Bodies: Resistance, Accommodation, and Exile in Refugee and Migration Movements on the U.S.–Mexican Border

NEVZAT SOGUK

> *If history is to be creative, to anticipate a possible future without denying the past, it should . . . emphasize new possibilities by disclosing hidden episodes of the past when, even in brief flashes, people showed their ability to resist, join together occasionally to win.*
>
> HOWARD ZINN

WHILE INTRODUCING: A LOOSE CONVERGENCE OF IDEAS

The modernist conceptions and taxonomies of people, ideas, identities, and subjectivities are becoming increasingly ineffective in controlling/disciplining the flow of phenomena and in fixing the boundaries of "the meaningful" words, vocabularies and libraries, and proper presents and histories. The global and local interactions and the interplay of peoples are ever more fluid, with their participants exhibiting incessant mobility even in seeming inertia. As Arjun Appadurai put it, people, machinery and money, images and ideas now follow increasingly nonisomorphic paths.[1] Deterritorializing mobility of peoples, ideas, and images plays against the laborious moves of statism to project an image of the world divided along territorially discontinuous (separated) sovereign spaces, each supposedly with homogeneous cultures and impervious essences.

The peculiar dynamics of this process are especially clear in the case of "marginalized peoples" such as refugees and migrants whose larger formations of cultural/political identities are born out of "similar antagonistic relationship to the dominant culture" of territorialization.[2]

This essay investigates the movements of refugees and migrants on the U.S.–Mexican border as being both deterritorializing (resistant) and recuperating (accommodative) of a variety of "sovereignty practices." To illustrate the dynamics of border areas, a critical analysis of the Sanctuary Movement operating on/along/beyond border areas since the early 1980s is undertaken in the last section of the essay. A series of tentative propositions on the phenomenon of "bordering," as well as on the political economy of refugee and migrant movements is offered. The cardinal proposition of the essay is that the refugee and migration movements on and beyond border areas spell out a paradoxical situation as being both resistant and accommodative of territorializing practices of a large variety. In "many realms" of identities and meanings, the activities that intend to discipline and those that are determined to resist and contest cohabit uncertain terrains with ever-shifting possibilities for life expressions, strategies, and practices. The point is emphasized throughout the essay that resistances to the disciplining and territorializing activities are always within reach. The creativity with which the "discipliners" labor to undermine or accommodate the resistances, however, must not be underestimated. After all, still, bullets kill, hunger hurts, schools educate, and the "papers" provide license to be "somebody." Finally, what follows is a loose convergence (a patchwork) of ideas. As such, the ideas are mostly tentative and limited reflections on the indeed very complex and diverse "worlds" we live in.

THE WORLDS WE LIVE IN

In reflecting upon the conditions of local and global interactions, there seems to be a loose convergence around an image that makes it increasingly more problematic to speak of the conditions of local and global life in terms of a Cartesian spatial segmentation built around the image/name of the modern state. This familiar state-oriented practice of territorialization or "the spatial incarceration of peoples,"[3] their images, ideas, and identities within/around the state is beset by challenges from within and without. Increasingly, "pride of place" is attributed to the notion of spatial mobility perceived largely as the movements of peoples, identities, images, ideas, and technologies in a non-Cartesian space through nonisomorphic fashions. Put succinctly, the pervasive activity of the day is the politico-cultural and politico-economic deterritorialization of "life" across the borders and boundaries drawn at the juncture of modernity. It is at this juncture where the notions of nation, the state, sovereignty, identity, and security collapse into one another to create "the myth of the modern" that the dislocations, accelerations, and contingencies of the world gradually inculcate the images and manifest the realities of "many worlds."[4] Thus, the perceptions of the worlds we live in are more diverse than ever before.

These emergent images of the conditions of the global and the local do not point, however, to the demise of the statist activities as territorializing practices. In fact, an economy of statist practices, best conceptualized and understood in the articulation of peculiar sovereignty claims on life expressions and meanings, is a practice prevalent in the terrain of activities, though no more eliciting an axiomatic reverence and approval. In a practical sense, sovereignty claims, connected inescapably to some understanding of space/territory/identity, are territorializing practices in the quest for constructing "representable" essences, meanings, identities, and cultures. In that sense, sovereignty claims over a space/territory/body are engaged not only in the construction of "referable" national physical borders and boundaries but also in the construction of "representable" cultural, political, and economic identities and "essences" (of bodies/spaces) ostensibly overlapping with the physical borders.

These practices are realized through the production and effective circulation of exclusionary definitions of world as consisting of "culture/nation gardens separated by boundary values"[5] and manifested in the state sovereignty. At a more visible level, the most effective of the sovereignty practices is the discursive reinscription onto space/territory dividing lines, imaginary or physical (as in the U.S.–Mexican border), separating those that belong to "us" and those that do not: foreign, unfamiliar, strange, alien, and dangerous.

Still, the emergent images of the global processes suggest that such practices of boundary drawing are never challenge-free under the conditions of global and local interactions of peoples, ideas, images, and identities whose underlying quality is an emergent spatial continuity[6] as opposed to spatial fragmentation (as representing posited national, cultural, political, religious, and even aesthetic essences). There are various ways of articulating the ongoing changes in the understanding of space/movement/identity relationships. A rather bold but incisive interpretation/observation is offered by Arjun Appadurai in an article titled "Disjuncture and Difference in the Global Cultural Economy."[7] In the article, Appadurai speaks of an increasingly complex global cultural economy that should be understood as a disjunctive order. The complexity of the global conditions has to do with certain fundamental disjunctures between economy, culture, and politics. Appadurai locates the disjunctive dimensions of the global/local conditions in the landscapes of persons (Ethnoscapes), media (Mediascapes), images (Ideoscapes), technology (Technoscapes), and money (Finanscapes).[8] He perceptively argues that none of the disjunctures (images of interactions) reflects an objectively given set of relations that look the same from every angle of vision; rather, each represents a plurality of (power) relations "inflected very much by the historical, linguistic and political situatedness of different sorts of actors: nation-states, multinationals, diasporic communities, as well sub-national groupings and movements . . . and even intimate face to face groups such as villages, neighborhoods and families."[9] The cardinal assertion is that the dynamics of these disjunctive dimensions of the global/local occurrences profoundly undermine, if not rupture, the power of the modernist conceptions and assumptions on space/movement/identity. This is ever more the case, for the sheer speed, magnitude, volume, visibility, and vitality of the activities that inhabit these disjunctures are unprecedented. Nor have they ever been so central in global interactions. Deterritorialization, Appadurai suggests, is at the core of the disjunctive global cultural economy. Whether orderly or not, the emergent forms of activities and practices herald the "becoming" of a world where the modernist conceptions of the world, their arbitrariness ever more visible, are fast eroding.

Perceived undermining/displacement of the traditional conceptions of modernity and its peculiar processes, that is, the sovereignty claims of state, with the counter forms of conceptions (called postmodern in some circles and high-modern in others) is also worked upon sharply in the works of many scholars (Spivak, Kristeva, Derrida, Baudrillard, Lyotard, Bourdieu, Foucault, Rorty, Smart, Jameson, Berman, Appadurai, Chakrabarty, Guha, Said, JanMohamed to name some of those that I find interesting). Although there are clearly profound differences in the ideas as well as in the agendas of these scholars, there is among these scholars a "common" occupation with the politics of change as construction of subjectivities away (different) from the modernist conceptions. Interestingly, another common attribute of the works by most of these scholars is the recognition of the impossibility of "producing" a blueprint of subjectivities ranging from "modernist" to "postmodernist" or "high-modernist" or whatever else. In other words, it is not inaccurate to say that modernist strategies of life linger here, are under erasure there, and are still dominant elsewhere. Beginnings and endings to the reflections of many scholars are never fully sure as to the trajectories of "modernist" and "nonmodernist" conceptions of identities and their possibilities. In other words, almost every space/movement/identity is already cohabited by contra-conceptions of life which, old or emerging, exhibit contingent vitality and visibility. To paraphrase Antonio Gramsci, "The old is not yet dying, and the new cannot yet be born." My sense is that it is precisely in the spaces in between as well as in the spaces where the "old" is still resistant and the spaces where the "new" is bold and arresting that the strategies of the conceptualization of life experiences, peoples, their ideas, their images, and their identities are being molded and remolded, perhaps, each time, into something other than the expected, but still "real" like death or hunger or cold or rape.

MIGRATION AND "REFUGEEISM" AS DETERRITORIALIZATION AND RECUPERATION OF STATISM: THEORETICAL VIEWS
Human Vistas from a Personal Memory

Julio is from El Salvador. I talked to him in Casa Companera, a refugee house in Phoenix, Arizona. He told me that his journey to the U.S. took him through Guatemala and Mexico, arriving in Tijuana at the Mexican–U.S. border. During his trip, he endured endless hardships traveling mostly on foot, sometimes on train and sometimes on bus.

Adnan is from Turkish Kurdistan. I met him in *Haji Baba,* a Middle Eastern grocery store in Tempe, where he was working as a cook. He spoke Turkish, Kurdish and Arabic but hardly any English. His reason for leaving Turkey, he said, was the government violence and discrimination toward the "poor" Kurds like himself. He told me after learning that I too am "half-Kurdish," that his wife and their two children had just arrived from Turkey through Canada, but he did not want to reveal how.

Kashyap Nalin Choksi, my office-mate and roommate for two years in Athens, Ohio, is from India, and now a Ph. D. student at Virginia Tech in Blacksburg, Virginia. He used to say that he would never return to India and would quickly add, "After all, I am a first-generation immigrant in search of a proper place to live in." His brother and sister-in-law, both Ph.Ds, are settled in Mesa, Arizona.

Amadeo (I only knew his first name) is from El Salvador. I was introduced to him in 1988 in Athens, Ohio. He spoke very little English, but he was, I was told by Spanish speakers, an eloquent user of Spanish. He was a union organizer in El Salvador and lost many of his companions to violence in that country. He was living with the collaborators of the Sanctuary Movement in Athens, waiting for his papers to move on to Canada where he could receive political asylum. Amedeo made his living painting houses or mowing lawns with Branco Stankovich, a Macedonian immigrant aspiring capitalist.

Zine is from Iraqi Kurdistan from the city of Sulaimania now living in Sweden. I met her in Athens, Ohio, also. She came to the U.S. as a "legal" refugee along with her ten or so family members in 1977. She became a naturalized citizen in 1989 and left for Sweden immediately, where she was to meet her husband and three children. She showed me her U.S. passport and Swedish residency papers and said, "These are instruments of survival and hope."

Harish, who worked in our department's data lab last year, is now in California "making" 40,000 dollars a year. He bought a Nissan car, which cost him 17, 000 dollars. In a "tired" evening last year I ran into him and he offered me a ride home. On the way to my house, he told me leaning against the soft cushion of his seat and with gleeful eyes, "This is what I call life, Nevi, what do you say, huh?" He "made it" in America! How many millions did not?

Eduviques is from Huehuetenango in the Guatemalan highlands. She is sixteen years old. I have not yet met her but heard stories about her through Clare, my wife. Eduviques now lives in Phoenix, Arizona, with Karen who was involved in the Sanctuary Movement. Eduviques's mother also lives in Phoenix and works as "domestic help," which is a euphemism for "colonial servant." Who knows, one of these days, her employer too may be up for the position of Attorney General of the U.S. Eduviques does not want to talk about her "coming" to the U.S.

My sister Gulderen and brother-in-law Ismael, who, for the last 10 years, have been living in Bremerhaven, Germany, have no intention of calling Turkey "home" once again. Despite the threatening specter of racism and neo-Fascism in almost all of Europe, they continue to cultivate vulnerable and ambiguous surfaces on which to maintain a resurgent life.

I watched the evening news on CBS showing groups of "Mixtecs" running into the U.S. through the customs. They were all on the highway in the middle of cars and trucks surely endangering their lives. They waited until the coyotes (people smugglers) gave the signal to run. Upon getting the signal, they simply ran across the border into the United States. For some it is a daily routine, a necessity of living on the borderlines of violence of all sorts, economic political social. One of them later put it to the CBS cameras this way: "I sometimes think that I might die while crossing, but I've just gotta do it."

These human vistas pulled out of a very personal memory are indicative of a general trend of movements by the peoples of the non-Western worlds into the Western geographies in (not so) obscure yet endless streams for a variety of purposes. First and foremost, what characterizes these mass movements is the activity of moving (the bodies) across/from/between spaces. In a world where (the conceptions of) the borders and boundaries of modernity melt into the emergent forms of postmodernity, and then "fold back upon themselves," the common thread that runs through the multiplicity of life activities is the increasing mobility of the actors. Bodies, their images, ideas, and their products are more mobile than ever in simple, yet mysterious ways. Simplicity of mobility is seen in the ever enlarging horizon of individuals and groups as a consequence of the advancements in the technologies of the transportation of bodies, images, and ideas. Yet, the mysteriousness of the mobility baffles the critics in the refusal of such movements to lend themselves to algorithmic interpretations that leave nothing unexplained and ambiguous. The participants of the mobility are conspicuous here and undetected there, desired here and detested there, and resistant here and accommodative and recuperative there. A kaleidoscope of moving bodies with complex subjectivities variegates the global scene.

Of the groups that navigate the politico-cultural and politico-economic terrains in search of "a dream place of rest," refugees and migrants constitute two of the most significant categories in terms of their visibility in the transformation of the conditions in which their activities take place and the implications for the ways of conceptualizing the very activities themselves.[10]

Refugees and immigrants along with "guest workers," exiles, the permanent tourists, and "the displaced" participate in the making of an ongoing revolution of the undermining/displacement of the imagined certainties of "native" places and cultures with the uncertain possibilities of world as nominally fragmented but pragmatically continuous space (where the origins and loyalties of experiences blur due to the complexity and intensity of the crosscurrents and intercurrents of cultural, social, and economic activities). In this continuous space, "everywhere" has the potential for building "home," though the new homes may themselves be seen only as mere imitations of some beginning, original place like India, Turkey, Algeria, or Mexico. Or they might be perceived as new beginnings based on a willingness for a complete "forgetting" of the past. Consider the case of a Kurdish refugee in a ship headed to Sweden, who, upon seeing the Swedish coastline, declared: "When I see the shore of Sweden I think it is my motherland, and the day we arrive, I feel, is my birthday."[11] Still, despite this desire to forget, parts of Berlin, London, and Los Angeles become the imagined microcosms of Istanbul, Bombay, or Mexico City to the extent that the dwellers of Mexico City, Istanbul, or Bombay themselves can imagine these places as "homes" with cultural/social certainties and homogenous identities. Although, there is a quality of "simulacra"[12] to the "transplanting" of imagined homelands to new spaces, lives are lived for "real" and people continue to move, even in their inertia, all across the globe.

The movements of refugees and migrants are motivated by a plethora of reasons that surely deserve careful analyses, if the connections between the histories of the presents and pasts are to be fully established and living strategies for tomorrows formulated. In their "beginnings," the movements of the bodies across borders and boundaries might be no more than the quest for a "better" life, however that "better" is defined in the image of the participants. The realness of the experience of moving the body toward a better life could be seen in an escape from a bullet to the brain or in a piece of corn finding its way to the stomach. The whole objective of the move across the hundreds of miles could be just as simple for those who are participating in it as "dropping an honest day's sweat on the fields" for survival. Yet, as suggested in the aphorism of Michel Foucault, once in circulation in larger contexts, movements of individual bodies have far more important implications (than the participants themselves would care to acknowledge) for the historically contingent practices and processes by which peculiar identities (of community, noncommunity, home, exile, and familiar and strange) are constructed, assigned, negotiated, resisted, and, most importantly, made peculiar to a particular territory, that is, territorialized in the image of the statist practices.

In a fundamental way, there is an amorphously "metamorphosing" quality to the movements of immigrant and refugee bodies. Above all, however, these movements are, for those who are part of them, acts of resistance by which the "moving" people are able to shape their own experiences in ways hitherto unprecedented.

Yet, from the perspective of moving peoples, and the effects of the mass movements on the statist practices of re/presentation, refugees and immigrants spell out a paradoxical situation. On the one hand, as moving peoples, they transgress political and cultural borders and undermine or reaffirm the strategies of exploitation, subjugation, and domination, as well as of resistance. They problematize familiar and comfortable narratives of life and partake in the activities that construct and negotiate new identities and attenuate and resist others. On the other hand, they participate in legal, economic, cultural, political, and even charitable activities married to the techniques and apparatuses of statist practices. I shall call this situation "the economy of refugeeism and migration." By the term *economy*, I refer to a situation where the presence of a group of people or peoples becomes both a problem to be addressed and a resource to be employed in the service of this or that objective. It is at the juncture of being both a problem and a resource simultaneously that refugees and migrants constitute a paradox. Their movements or inertia point to the unsettling of loyalties to familiar identities and localities. Perhaps unwittingly, they contest seemingly axiomatic, atavistic "realities" of life such as a membership in a clan, in a tribe, in a profession, or in a domestic community as constituting a nation. In that way, they unmake the traditional language with which the tales of life are told, thus undermining the territorializing sovereignty practices. Yet their very presence affords opportunities for the participants of territorializing practices and conceptualizations to employ that presence in order to shore up that which is problematized by refugee and migrant movements, namely, for instance, the "natural-ness" of a domestic community of citizens.

Herein lies the significance of the refugee or migrant category use-ful to recuperate all that is fast eroding under pressure from the fluid local and global interactions and interplay of things. Increasingly, refugees and migrants become a series of strategic reference points to which the statist practices refer in order to construct subjectivities and affirm the semblance of continuities. Referentiality of the refu-gees and migrants is achieved through a variety of representational practices by which refugees and migrants become objects of a multi-tude of narratives of inadequacy. For instance, at times refugees and immigrants are re/presented as figures of lack as opposed to the ade-quacy and fullness of the figure of citizen. In such re/presentations, refugee or migrant status is marked as a double signifier. They simul-taneously signify their own void and the completeness of the citizen vis-à-vis a refugee or a migrant.

In other instances, they are written as representing the anarchy of the outside of the domestic sphere. Here, the domain of refugees and migrants becomes a security threat and the signifier of disorderliness, whereas the domestic (inside) sphere is perceived to be the embodi-ment of peace and security. Refugees and migrants are seen to be the transmitters of/from anarchy of the outside. Large influxes are there-fore presented to be a security threat to the peacefulness and the civ-ilization of the inside.[13]

The efforts to construct the citizen (as constitutive of domestic community) by constructing an inadequate refugee or a migrant (a noncitizen) are directed in the final analysis at affirming the "sover-eignty claims" that there exists a coherent domestic community from which the state receives its legitimacy and authority, and on whose behalf the state acts.

As suggested, the very refugee or migrant bodies, which, while at first undermining, for instance, a state's ability to produce the claim that it is in control of its proper territories/borders, at times also be-come a source of re/presentation for the state(ism) whereby the state(ism) poses itself as an ontological necessity (being). I shall call this situation the "paradox of the representable refugee." This para-dox of representability finds use in the movements in overlapping fields of activities. The paradox can be clearly observed in the activities/movements of refugees and immigrants on the U.S.–Mexican border.

TRANSNATIONAL/TRANSCULTURAL BODIES AND THE U.S.–MEXICAN BORDER: DYNAMICS OF MOVING INTO/ACROSS THE SPACE

Now, the question seems to be, How will the movements of the people from Central and Latin America and Mexico fit into this picture of global/local interactions as the sites of these interactions that are also the sites for enacting and reenacting strategies of living? It is at the juncture where the individual and collective experiences of the peoples of the Americas "happily/unhappily" coincide that one can look for tentative answers or suggestions. Our focus here will be on the activities staged on/in/around what is called the "world's busiest illegal border-crossing": the U.S.–Mexican border and its beyond.

In the case of the refugee and migrant movements across the Americas into the U.S.–Mexican border areas, for a long time, streams of "moving peoples" have been conceptualized through a variety of theories ranging from the theory of ethnicity[14] to the theories of pull and push and the third worldization of the first world[15] to the theory of environmental catastrophe.[16] Modernization theories, world system theories, dependency theories, and pull and push migration theories all claim a "legitimate" mastery in the quests to ferret out (to exhaust) reasons behind these movements.

Insightful as they are, the underlying problem with most of these explanations is their intrinsic ontological and methodological tendency to reduce complex sets of problems to one or another factor/reason. This reduction (privileging) has the effect of producing the refugee and the migrant bodies as "spectacles" to be gazed at as objects of desire, anger, hatred, discipline, sympathy, charity, and solidarity that lend themselves to representations of a rich variety. Refugees and migrants turn into either dangerous illegals "stealing our jobs"[17] or foreign bodies "browning" the country.[18] At another level, they are represented as the most desirous and hard-working labor group in search of employment who would "sell its soul" just to get a job. Concomitantly, in the face of this desirous body, the slavelike working conditions could be justified as a natural consequence of supply and demand, pull and push, and so on.

In the final analysis, when the pages are written, books published, images produced, and representational projects get well under way, refugees and migrants appear either as powerless, lacking in constitutive subjectivity, and, as Eric Wolf put it, without a memorable history or as "super-resistant" great heros/heroines of the "underdeveloped worlds" who are now "contra-colonizing" the Western spaces. To the astonishment of the "expectant" scholars in search of a blueprint of salvation for humanity, however, moving peoples do not seem preoccupied with the question of which category of subjectivities and reasons to fit into. Propelled with their "thousand points of moving," they simply are on the move crossing borders of countries and the imagined boundaries of "culture gardens." Still, in the works of the anthropologist-writers, their thousand reasons give way to the prominence of one or two or three reasons, and, most of the time, in imagined oppositions to one another. This, according to Brenda Marshall, is no less than a constitution of a discourse on power with a particular strategy of representation underpinning it. The activity of representation, then, figures as the activity of "controlling who is allowed to speak, for whom and to what purpose."[19]

Aware of the dangers of what Marshall called "imperialism of representation," it is imperative to eschew "writing" the reasons and causes of refugee and migrant movements. For the purpose of this study, it would suffice to suggest that complex configurations of social, political, religious, cultural, and economic forces shape the environment in which peoples' mobility finds relative meanings and possesses utility expectations. In the case of refugee and migrant movements in and across most of Central and North America, "the multiple effects of political and economic crises, civil wars, slow-working societal disjunctures engendering endemic violence and mass poverty and the enticements of the imagined possibilities of 'other homelands' in distant places have transformed [once relatively small traditional internal migration flows in the Americas] into massive displacement and exodus of peoples."[20] Although the final destination for many millions has increasingly become the United States and continues to be so, many hundreds of thousands remain in proximity to their native places. For instance, many Guatemalans and Salvadorans take refuge in Mexico and others move into Honduras or Costa Rica. As for the Mexican migrants, many become part of an internal migratory circuit across different regions including the Maquiladora belt along the U.S.–Mexican border. In the midst of a series of waves that unsettle the certainties of the "many worlds," however, the United States, as "the Disneyland of the Americas," becomes both the centripetal and the centrifugal space due to its imagined and real possibilities, its magical qualities, and real dangers. As a result, millions of people mark their destiny as the United States of America while many others quietly make their ways out to other places. In most cases, however, the lives of the migrants, refugees, and exiles remain in suspense in a politico-cultural and an economic sense. They live what Roger Rouse called "bifocal lives," the dynamics of which must constantly navigate the volatile terrains in between the imagined certainties of the "native" lands and the imagined un/certainties of the "other" worlds.

Since the early 1970s and through the 1980s, millions of Mexicans and Central Americans have been flooding the border areas between the U.S. and Mexico, thus changing the dynamics of life on the border areas and beyond. Although desperately inaccurate, estimates indicate that millions of people have moved into the peripheries/ghettos of the big U.S. cities, with many more millions establishing "marginal lives" on the other side of the border. It is estimated that about a million Salvadorans—one-fifth of El Salvador's population—now live in the United States.[21] Hundreds of thousands of Nicaraguans and Guatemalans live in a belt spanning from Miami to Los Angeles. The numbers of Mexican migrants on both sides of the border are staggering to the degree that their magnitude can only be guesstimated. The magnitude of the cross-border movement is best represented in the 1.62 million people who were arrested trying to cross the border in 1986. In 1991 alone, the border patrol agents apprehended 1.08 million people along the southern border. Armstrong and Dulin for the *Christian Science Monitor* reported the patrol officers as saying that one out of every three "illegal" attempts to cross the border turns successful.[22]

These endless movements of refugees, migrants, and exiles transformed and continue to transform the border and border areas into unique places in/around and beyond which people encounter and/or realize a multitude of life possibilities. They negotiate, resist, compromise, and adapt to the interplay of meanings and identities. They devise and redevise strategies for living. Even in the face of the danger of abortion and failure, they have to face the next day with hope and courage. In an "unhurried manner," they gradually manage to transplant imagined verisimilitudes of the memorable homelands onto and beyond border areas.[23] Cities such as Los Angeles, San Diego, Houston, Miami, San Francisco, Phoenix, Chicago, Tijuana, and Nogales are long incorporated into this ever-growing transnational/ transborder cultural space.

Now, in the face of the recognition and magnitude of the movements of refugees and migrants across local, regional, and international borders, one of the primary questions that intrigues this study is, What are the implications of these movements on various processes of identity building, normalization of life activities, and the disciplining of recalcitrance and resistance? More specifically, in the face of "the state's" claim of (sovereign) supremacy over the activities in the border areas, this question should be posed in terms of the implications of the movements of "alien" or "illegal" peoples, that is, refugees, migrants, and exiles, for the sovereignty practices of the state.

In a general sense, mere movements by the individuals effectively curtail the ability and challenge the capacity of the state to control the "status of the border" in accordance with the modernist conceptions of border as a proper division and/or differentiation of cultures and their meaning systems. In practical terms, this translates into an empowerment of the moving bodies while undermining the government's ability to impose "difference" by patrolling the dynamics of the bodies in border areas. Overall, as Michael Kearney put it, it means the reconstitution of the border areas into a zone where the meanings are continually contested and transformed. It also means the creation of a new border "ethnicity" of a transnational and transborder culture with its peculiar practices and experiences.[24] As noted earlier, in the midst of peculiar culture practices, both the movements of peoples and the sovereignty practices acquire greater mobility and flexibility, each lending itself to one another's projects.

This dynamic "ethnography of the border area" is significant in terms of its power implications for the subaltern groups. Yet, it is equally important for the institutionalized and discursive statist practices in subjectivizing the individuals in/along the border areas. First, the ability of the ordinary people in curbing the "policing" strategies pertinent to the border/body issues demonstrates indeed the dynamics of the power relations that are hardly ever complete and always in flux. The activism of the Central Americans and Mexicans along both sides of the border is a manifestation of the power of the subaltern groups.[25] The paradox of the representable refugee, however, manifests itself in the dynamics of the groups' movements. In a Foucauldian sense, their activism is disruptive of the power relations insomuch as it penetrates and ruptures the legal and juridical networks of power and popular and cultural myths about the essences of the imagined communities. However, the resistant parties to the movements almost always run the risk of recuperating the very juridical and legal system as well as the image of the imagined communities. For instance, they might quite unwittingly reconstitute the proper subject position of a dangerous otherness, an "illegal" migrant or a refugee, thus allowing the system a raison d'être.

The participants of sovereignty practices are ever willing to utilize the opportunities in any way possible. They enact laws (Immigration Reform and Control Act [IRCA]), establish institutions of policing and normalization (Immigration and Naturalization Agency [INS] and the border patrol, detention centers), erect miles of fences to symbolize the presence of the division of space and identities, collaborate with their cohorts across those fences in order to extend their claims to sovereignty into distances (Operation Hold the Line)[26] and offer amnesties to the illegals, thus confirming their (states') "meta-auhority" as the dispenser of "proper" identities. On the other hand, in the face of their clamor to stem the flow, they keep silent as millions move across the border back and forth. This according to some is precisely another way in which the moving bodies become sites of control and exploitation albeit in nondiscursive ways. In their book *Disorganized Capitalism,* Lash and Urry argue to this effect, suggesting that the transborder movements of immigrants and refugees provide the capitalist system with cheap labor.[27]

Although "violated" daily, the significance of the border stems not so much from its ability to be a barrier as from its being a discursive reference around which a multitude of actors, refugees, and immigrants and the state organize their activities. It is the "presence" of the border that makes an economy of activities possible. Put another way, on the one hand, the state activities are dependent on the constructed threat of refugees and immigrants. On the other hand, the particular articulation and activation of migrant and refugee activities are developed as a reaction to the state's claim "to stamp or not to stamp" one's papers, bestowing proper subjectivity. At this level, "the border is a word game"[28] by reference to which a routinization and a ritualization of life activities are achieved. In that sense, the border partially fulfills its promise as a boundary (discourse) of normalization of the expectations and their articulations. So, we have as part of the border scenes the "illegal immigrants (now referred to as the undocumented persons) versus the legal, documented immigrants, coyotes versus the state (border agents), and the imagined peacefulness of the inside versus the imagined anarchy of the outside.[29] In fact, in 1975, Leonard Chapman, an ex-general and then the commissioner of immigration, described the situation as a "vast and silent invasion," predicting that as many as 12 million aliens had taken up residence in the United States. In a more dramatic manner, former CIA director William Colby declared that the immigration from Mexico was a greater threat to the national security of the United States than the Soviet Union was.[30] Nowadays, similar constructions are realized by reference to the bodies of the Haitians.

Curiously, the border as an "everyday affair" that has to be lived in its minutiae is both painfully present and satirically insufficient:

> The boundary between the U.S. and Mexico is in places merely a trace in the dirt. . . . In the cities, the boundary hardens into a steel fence to keep out northbound immigrants, and it does not work. In the open desert, it dwindles to three strands of barbed wire to keep cattle in, and it works better, at least for the cattle. For more than half of its length the border is the Rio Grande, a small swimable river.[31]

If the border is a physical barrier designed to stop the bodies from crossing at will, for all practical purposes, it fails, for when it is a fence, it is cut open, when it is a river, it is swum across, and when it is a barbed wire, it is leaped over or passed through. Consider the border scene in Nogales on the U.S.–Mexican border on a late winter day where I watch a steady stream of people go through a barbed wire (border) laid against the slopes of a hill. Down the hill in the valley is the customs through which thousands pass daily getting their papers stamped. The regularity with which this scene is enacted creates a spectacle that mocks the "fool" who thinks the border is the end of one kind of life and the beginning of another. Consider also, the cases of Mexican-Nogales kids who wait by the revolving door that lets the "privileged," that is, those on the U.S. side, into Mexico without any papers and stamps. As the "privileged" roll their way into

Mexico, the kids get in from the other end into the United States, perhaps on their way to a Burger King or a McDonalds for lunch.

In many ways, the border is an embellished, enhanced spectacle that serves to undergird existing myths as to impervious and homogeneous "culture/nation gardens" or to create new ones. The embellishment of the border is a complex and rather expensive enterprise. It requires an integrated set of activities with sophisticated and not so sophisticated technologies. The wonders of the high-tech era help to create the border as a spectacle for representational practices. Nightscopes, motion sensors, search lights, television cameras, helicopters, spotter planes, and patrols in various kinds of boats and ground vehicles, all coordinated by computers and radio communications, serve the purpose.[32] How do all these fit into the picture in an ordinary border day near Tijuana, Mexico/California? Michael Kearney describes the fit in some border scenes.

> As the afternoon shadows move in to the Canyon the migrants who have assembled eat their last taco, take a final swig of soda pop or beer, and possibly put on new shoes or a jacket that they have just bought. Then in groups of five or may be ten or twelve, they start to head out, up the canyon, and into its side branches. They walk in single file, each little group led by its coyote. . . . When the sun is low, Border Patrol agents, the Migra, are silhouetted on the hills above the canyon. They scurry about in jeeps and motorcycles and horses, responding to the probings of different groups, some of which are serving as diversions to draw the patrols from others. The Migra almost never comes down into the base of the canyon where the migrants congregate, nor does the Unitedstatian government make any attempt to fence off or otherwise close or occupy this staging area. . . .
>
> It is a moonless night. Two sleepy Border Patrol agents sit in an observation post that resembles a gun emplacement. . . . The Border Patrol agents scan the hills around and the fields below them with infrared nightscopes. Peering through these devices they see dozens of human forms, bent over, clutching small bags, parcels and sometimes children silently hurrying along well worn trails through the dry bush. Two days earlier, some eighty miles to the northeast, one of the agents had been sitting on a hilltop with binoculars scanning trails a two day walk from the national boundary line.[33]

The stories about the permeability of the border proliferate. Ethnography of the penetrable border becomes the most generous of the fields of study in that no one returns from the border observations with empty hands/notebooks. Curiously, the "inflation" of the stories about the penetrability of the border is a manifestation of the realness of the experience of penetrating the border. However, the ease with which many overcome the border as a barrier should not push the stories of failures into oblivion. The border on both sides is fraught with dangers for migrants and refugees. For those (especially Central Americans) who are yet traveling toward the United States, dangers are immense and of different variety. For instance, for women, the most typical of the risks is rape, which befalls many. Ted Conover notes the case of two Salvadoran teenagers who, having failed to pay the coyotes, were kept as sex-slaves by the coyotes.[34] It is also no secret that the migrants and refugees fall victim to abuse, thievery, and violence at every step of their journey through Mexico.[35] A variety of dangers lurk all through even after the border is in sight.

In fact, all along the border from Texas to Arizona to California, there have been many deaths among the people trying to cross the border. For instance, the *San Diego Union* reported that in 1991 alone, 49 people drowned trying to swim the Rio Grande.[36] Similarly, many died trying to cross Interstate 5 away from border patrol checkpoints; three deaths occurred on the night of January 17, 1992, alone.[37] Furthermore, abuses, including death, at the hands of the coyotes and the border patrol officers are, at least in some cases, well documented. In late 1992 in Phoenix, the case of a Salvadoran refugee who was shot and (allegedly) left bleeding to death appeared in court, a rare occurrence, thus pointing to the hazardous nature of "moving the bodies" across the border. Similar cases have been continuously brought to light in the San Diego area. In fact, according to Helsinki Watch, the border patrol agents along the U.S.–Mexican border routinely abuse undocumented migrants and sometimes "unjustifiably" shoot, torture, or sexually abuse them. According to the same report, abuses are "serious and systematic. . . . and that even if they are documented, they are covered up by the INS agents and the Justice department and offending officers escape punishment."[38] An earlier, more flexible but bitterly critical report by the American Friends Service Committee pointed to similar problems of abuse by the agents.[39]

Another example of the unique difficulties awaiting refugees and migrants who are entering the country "illegally" is seen in the case of Sabina Rocha, whose sexual assault case made it to the headlines. Interestingly, a civil suit by Rocha against the U.S. government was resolved in a confidential settlement, with Rocha getting "considerably" more than $5,000.[40] How ironic it must have been for the U.S. government to "speak to" the confusing presence (subjectivity) of an "illegal" alien. Imagine also a scene of a "Chicano" neighborhood in Orange County, California, in late 1992, experiencing an immigration raid with hundreds of officers sweeping through the neighborhood in search of illegal migrants. At the end of the raid, 216 had been apprehended and deported to Mexico, most on their own cognizance, perhaps, already planning to make it back to the U.S. side of the border in the next day or so.[41] Within the general economy of statism, the raid is intended to be double signifier. It is both the signified, an activity of the state, and the signifier, an activity that refers to the name of the state. In other words, it is one of the ways in which the participants of the statist discourse are able to invoke/call the name of the state and refer to it as yet the functionally indispensable and necessary element of living.

As expected, life on the U.S. side is replete with everyday "victories" and "defeats" and a diverse set of experiences in between. For many of the migrants and refugees, life that is awaiting on and beyond the border is not an easy one. Death, rape, theft, labor exploitation, and other kinds of abuses continue unabated. Two examples are telling. First is the story of a Ventura County flower-rancher "charged with enslaving hundreds of Mexicans." The rancher agreed to plead guilty to corporate racketeering, and to pay about $1.5 million in back wages to former workers.[42] The second case is the story of a woman in San Diego who was sentenced to three years in prison on a "slavery charge." According to the report, nineteen-year-old Mexican maid Juana Hernandez was imprisoned in the garage and abused by her boss for months at a time over a period of fifteen months.[43] Although individual stories, these might just be telling of the characteristics of larger waves of experiences among the refugee and migrant movements. This general vulnerability of the peoples moving their bodies in search of "better" lives is accentuated in an old Mexican folk song about an illegal immigrant who unsuccessfully pursued his dreams in California. "Goodbye dream of my life, goodbye movie stars, I am going back to my beloved homeland, much poorer than when I came."[44]

Although without announcement to the effect, the focus of this study has already moved to a slightly different terrain in the last couple of paragraphs. This move was made by speaking of activities in border areas rather than border activities as in penetrating the actual border itself. The term *area(s)*, when juxtaposed to the word *border*, takes us into a different terrain, different in the sense that the border as a fence or as a river or a barbed wire ceases to be the dominant spectacle around which activities converge. Rather, although indispensable to the general scene, the border becomes only a part of a terrain called "the border area" in which a multiplicity of activities take place both around and beyond and far from the border as a physical obstacle. Border area activities encompass areas as far south as the highlands of Guatemala and as far north as the interiors of Canada.[45] As with the physical border itself, what is contested is not the border area, the territory, or the soil itself. Instead, armed with a conception of space as a continuous terrain for forging new lives, what is contested is "personal and collective identities, their cognitive maps of movements and the cultural and political hegemonies of peoples."[46] This very activity of contesting is carried out in the discursivity of everyday affairs. At times, the individual participants are more conscious of the activities and more reflexive as to the larger effects of what they do. At other times, the only question that they ask is, Shall I make it to tomorrow? without bothering about the implications of what they do just today, just then, and just there.

Consider the following correspondence between two Mexican women, Angela living in Fresno, California, and Marianna in Guadalajara, Mexico.

> From Angela to Marianna:
> You know what, it has not gone so well for me in the area of work. . . . I met a couple, the man is Italian and the woman is Salvadoran, who wanted me to take care of their children, and they were going to pay me 200 dollars a month but the bad part is I couldn't go to school. I accepted the job, but I could only stand them a week because it was fucked, the woman was really a big "c . . . t," and aside from taking care of their kids I had to clean a huge house, make breakfast and dinner, and go around picking up everything they dropped aside from which the woman is an anti-communist, one of those really rancid ones who goes around looking for communists in her refrigerator even. . . . Right now, I am living with Esther. We live

in a really tiny apartment, six of us here, it has only one bedroom and the living room. . . . We are in this situation because my sister and her husband are illegals, so they are really exploited; they work mountains and they pay them very little, on the pretext that they are illegals. . . . Right now, I'm participating in Radio Bilingue. It is the Hispanic community's radio station. I like going there because you get to know people who are little different, and besides I am in touch more with cultural situations. . . . The thing is that I can't work here, and well, like I can't be here without money. As you can see, I wanted to climb out of one grave in Guadalajara and I came to fall into even deeper one.

From Marianna to Angela:

Your letter sounded down, full of loneliness and very little enthusiasm, since receiving it I have thought constantly about you, about how you must be feeling, and in truth I can't situate you in a good wave, one of the reasons I feel this way is that you don't talk about a single friend, nor anyone else for whom you feel affection, or that someone feels for you. Where your letter picks up a little is where you speak of the English class of the radio, but even there I don't sense the kind of enthusiasm necessary to bear the situation like the one you describe. . . . What I want to say is that for me nothing's worth the trouble if it doesn't have its dose of affection, of love, which is so necessary for a person in a world that's such a motherfucker in that respect. . . . Unfortunately we are not born wise or prophetic and we spend life looking for the ideal, some never find it, others perhaps think they have found it already, but daily existence sets many traps for us and sometimes we don't know how to get around them.[47]

Consider also the case of Amparo Ramirez, who is in Los Angeles, California, writing her daughter in Guatemala:

Rubidia, I am writing you answering the letter you wrote me, the things you sent me arrived but you haven't written telling me about the packages in which I sent your dress and the kids' clothes and the other one in which I sent my mama's dress and other things. I am sending a check with $180 to you there, grab $100 for food, $80 for the clothes you want. In two weeks, I'll send you another $100 for food, because, it almost doesn't stretch for me. . . .

Rubidia. . . . I'll send you your shoes and a paste to clean them with because you don't wash these; with the next trip, I'll send Dennis his shoes and those of the others who are lacking them. The sky blue

pencil holder is Yunem's and the others are one for each one, and I am
sending money by Flores Express the first of April . . . (273)

Ah Rubidia, I don't say going to work is bad, but that I want you
all to prepare yourself so you don't suffer like me. . . . I didn't have
the opportunity to prepare myself and nobody showed me the world
farther away than what I was seeing everyday, and on the other hand
I tell you everything I suffered, and that is why I want you to study,
because a person with no preparation is worth nothing, she is like an
animal or a plant . . . (279)

Rubidia, look I want you to do me a favor, to send me some
smooth mango peels but from the red ones. . . . I am just a bundle of
sickness, and what exasperates me most are my eyes, but anyway
don't worry. . . .

Rubidia, I am sending you some toys, a frog and a dolphin, you
put the battery in its stomach. . . . I wonder if you have been able to
see how the airplanes worked, you all have liked them. . . . Rubidia,
behave yourself and don't go crazy with young guys because people
are going to start making jokes or truths and I wouldn't want to see
you cry tears of pain.

In between the lines of questions, suspicions, love, complacency,
and consistent fears and out of the discursive everyday activities of
peoples like the ones above and many others, what is contested in/by
the movements of migrants and refugees is a variety of disciplining
and normalizing practices in the juridical, the capitalist-economic,
the plutocratic-political, and the bourgeois-cultural fields. Such ac-
tivites of disciplining are there to inscribe and reinscribe "difference"
in the service of the re/production of peculiar power relations,
which, if left unchallenged, have a tendency to engender continuous
poverty for some and unending wealth for the others—just a curious
coincidence of history.

It is precisely in the attempts of contestation that refugees and migrants act both as resistant and accommodative of normalizing activities. Fredric Jameson calls this the power of the unconscious.[48] To
the degree that the refugee and migrant movements are largely discursive without a grand conception as well as consciousness of how
they impact processes, their activities are better suited to escape the
control of normalizing practices into a full discourse with its economy of representation. The "subterranean world" of the migrants
retains enough of its ambiguity, and the ordinary makers and movers
of that world exhibit enough creativity to deflect and subvert the dis-

ciplining activities. In the book *Coyotes,* Ted Conover's ("well-intended") attempts to "fully and authentically narrate" the stories of "just those peoples" meets a similar end. Unable to comprehend, that is, to rationalize many aspects of the activities of Mexican migrant workers, at times Conover resorts to his "American roots" to make sense of the situations. Yet, at each "such" time, he very quickly realizes the futility, if not the utter difficulty of his attempts "to know the Mexican" by constructing him/her in the image of a "blue-eyed world." Mexican migrants retain their ambiguity to the extent that their ambiquity allows them to diffuse Conover's narrative gaze.[49]

Analogically speaking, the contestation of identities and hegemonies in larger fields of activity takes place in a similar fashion. However, the extent to which the participants of the statist disciplining projects (INS, public policies, scholarly works) can create a spectacle out of the discursivity of movements, that is, if they can construct a spectacle of a refugee or a migrant, the effects of resistances are largely accommodated. At the juncture of the resistances and accommodations, the political economy of such activities of contestation might just facilitate the recuperation of otherwise already eroding modernist conceptions of space, community, culture, and authority. But, the chances are that they might also adumbrate the coming of "ends" different than those envisioned in the modernist conceptions.

The border areas witness a routinization of life as carnivalesque. The only permanent fixture is the carnivalesque quality of life activities with uncanny resistances, accommodations, and resilient exiles. People adjust to living as eternal "becoming" through constant change; as times and technologies of control/routinization undergo changes, so do the peoples' (refugees', immigrants') ways of "becoming" this or that, a refugee, an immigrant, an exile, or something else. Although change and "becoming" are permanent conditions in the landscapes of what Appadurai referred to as "the ethnoscapes and the ideoscapes," that does not mean the negation of culture/identity as a perennial "habit of the heart," or in the words of Raymond Williams as an "informing spirit of a whole way of life"[50] that lingers on in metamorphosis. In the acts of eternal becoming, through all kinds of activities, resistance, accommodation, and exile, not-so-ephemeral strategies of becoming (identities) find continuous expression across/within "imagined culture gardens" as perceived in the minds/experiences of an indigenous Guatemalan, a Mixtec, a Chicana, an urbane, a "Unitedstatesian" priest, a lawyer, a student, a homeless person, and so on. As Eric Wolf argues, all human expressions (processes) are historically specific, feeding on knowledges and norms of being and becoming peculiar to specific circumstances, conditions, and times.[51] Despite the ambiguous and fluid nature of these processes, relatively similar positions occupied by peoples help craft "collective identities." The collective identities, though branching out within and permeated by forces from without, nonetheless enable (or even force) people to occupy specific power-positions in particular fields of activity. After all, it is not so difficult to distinguish the similarities of the experiences (also of the identities) of refugees in the orange groves in Arizona or California from the experiences of those "subjects" who are in a position to "employ" them or to apprehend them or in the position of the comfortable scholar to represent them.

These identities could be those of the Mixtecs along the U.S.–Mexican border areas, the "Almanci" Turks and Kurds in Germany, Maghrebis in France and Spain, Sri Lankans in Canada, or the Greeks in Australia. In a sense, I feel, it is almost "natural" that such forces and tendencies are generated. If memory is to tell us anything, it is that the collective experiences, shared expectations, and collectively designed strategies of survival on/beyond the border areas have long been integral parts of the resistances to the policing of the human landscapes. As I discussed at the onset, effective resistance might just necessitate the formation of relatively coherent sets of meanings and the imaginings of identities.[52] On a day to day basis for instance, it is undeniable that a peculiar culture and an orrery of identities, however fluid and contingent, of cross-border activities and movements predominate the border areas where the coyotes, border bandits, Mixtecs, Central Americans, and the border patrol (La Migra) (and also the observant scholar) act out long-routinized deterritorialization/reterritorialization scenes.

In fact, it is these scenes of deterritorializations by the movements of Gabriels, Amedeos, Renees, and Joses that are most telling in terms of their implications on the politico-social and economic culture on the border areas and far beyond.

The movements on/along the U.S.–Mexican border areas exhibit certain characteristics. One of these characteristics is of great importance to us here. It is the ability of the participants of the peoples to forge alliances and coalitions contingent upon the circumstances and conditions.[53] Such alliances and solidarities, although "temporary" as JanMohamed suggests, are crucial in engendering effective resistances. In the same fashion, as transnational and transcultural movements, the significance of the practices/activism of the migrants and refugees around/on the U.S.–Mexican border best manifests itself in the links and connections established with the people on the other side of the border.[54] Implications of these links for the claims of the state to represent a unitary and singular domestic community are unprecedented.

One great example of such links, established out of the encounters of different cultures and peoples, is surely the Sanctuary Movement, which was first founded in Tucson, Arizona, and then spread all over the United States and Mexico. The sanctuary movement will be the subject of the rest of this study in discussing (and illustrating) the power of the movements of ordinary peoples across the borders and boundaries.

The significance of the Sanctuary Movement was that it involved the ordinary peoples across the borders who, it was claimed by the participants of the statist discourses, were the loyal subjects of "culture gardens" with their supposedly pure and unchanging essences. It was expected that they speak to each other after getting their papers stamped by the dispenser of legitimate meanings, that is, the state. But the specific circumstances and spirits in which the Central American refugee experiences encountered or made their ways into specific circumstances and spirits of some people on/along and beyond the U.S.–Mexican border slowly gave rise to a set of experiences that, like many others in other fields of activities, problematized the statist request as to the possession of papers and stamps for legitimacy. In other words, the Sanctuary Movement came as a result of the "problematizing attitude" that saw the particular field of activity as a field of struggle, a field whose content and contours are expressions of a certain economy of power positions. The increasing awareness that this or that way of believing, acting, and thus "becoming" is necessarily conversant, in agreement or disagreement with some power positions but not some others, motivated the people to search for "different" ways of experiencing and encountering the "others."

The determination to live the encounter differently than through papers and stamps has slowly led to the formulation of the strategies of resistance and played against the policing of borders that labors to force life into categories across the spatial and representational lines. The different encounter of the two supposedly distinct peoples has led to the birth of a rather small but a forceful social/political/economic movement that still functions to this day. The transformation of the Sanctuary Movement, its strategies, its objectives, and its participants is telling in terms of the daily practices in the border areas. It is also reflective of the realities of movements whose protagonists are attached to one another not through totalizing and grandiose ideas and images but rather through simple commitments to life's worth, or "God's goodness," or whatever else.

THE SANCTUARY MOVEMENT

I do not want to talk about what you understand about this world. I want to know what you will do about it. I do not want to know what you hope. I want to know what you will work for. I do not want your sympathy for the needs of humanity. I want your muscle!

AN UNATTRIBUTED STATEMENT OF COMMITMENT

Human Vistas from Collective Memory

The hot desert wind furled and unfurled the banners painted with signs of hope. A small group of women from the Los Angeles religious community gathered outside El Centro detention center near the Mexican border in southern California. Hundreds of Central American refugees are imprisoned there in the desert behind 10-foot-high Cyclone fences topped with spirals of barbed wire and guarded by the U.S. Immigration and Naturalization Service. As the women vigiled outside, the imprisoned men, awaiting deportation, threw a bed sheet over the barbed wire. The sheet pointed north and bore the words, *En el nombre de Dios, ayudanos* ("In the name of God, help us"), the bright red letters painted with a mixture of punch and their own blood.[55]

December 2, 1982. There were flash floods that night. One major bridge was out and the rain was coming in torrents. The radio was warning everyone to stay at home. But still they came. Over seven hundred persons nearly filled the cathedral of St. John in the heart of Milwaukee to welcome into sanctuary campesinos from El Salvador and Guatemala. That night, St. Benedict the Moor and Cristo Rey became the first Catholic parish in the United States to declare themselves public sanctuaries (11).

On my way to the United States [from Guatemala] I went from Chiapas to Mexico City to Hermosillo and then to Nogales, Arizona. In Nogales I had many problems. It was late at night when we slipped through a hole in the barbed wire. I carried my baby on my back, Guatemalan style. Suddenly a bright light was shining in my eyes and two INS (Immigration and Naturalization Service) agents grabbed my arms (34).

The Quaker had never "conducted" anyone before. A frightened young Salvadoran sat stiffly next to him, his fist gripping the door handle. It was spring 1981 and Jim Corbett was maneuvering his van through the backroads of the Sonora Desert, carefully avoiding the Peck Canyon roadblock (37).

From coast to coast a railroad would extend as far north as Canada and as far east as Boston. . . . the calls came, coded conversations-midnight emergency calls from a Colorado highway driver, from the Rio Grande valley, from a pastor in Ohio, from a Methodist housekeeper in Nebraska, from refugees alone in a room in a dark church, from the clandestine Mexican church, from a Trappist monastery, from an Amerindian tribe in upstate New York. . . . from a farm in Iowa, from a synagogue in Madison, Wisconsin (52-53).

The plan was simple enough. We'd conduct twelve Central American refugees out of Mexico into the U.S.A. Jim and Robin and I would transport them to Mexico City. From there, we would split into two groups (99).

In July of 1980, twenty-six Salvadorans were found in the Arizona desert. Thirteen of them had died from heat exposure, hunger, and thirst. They were deserted by their coyotes who, having collected their fees, had gone off to pick up their next victims. "The remaining Salvadorans were arrested for deportation back to El Salvador as soon as they were well enough to move."[56] These were not the first refugees who had met death in a supposed journey of survival and "hoped" salvation. However, the circumstances surrounding the incident and the number of deaths were too troubling to forget quickly. It was as if they had died just around the corner or in the campground that the family had gone to regularly over the years. Moreover, the numbers of refugees were rising. They were increasingly more visible, failing to confine their bodies to the shadows of groves or the backstreets of the inner cities. The stories that they were telling were "heart-wrenching." So, some "good" people of the area offered their helping hands. This though was not meant to be anything more than supplementing the "proper activities of the proper agencies" as defined by the laws of the national and international culture gardens. "The refugees [had] asked for help—En el Nombre de Dios, ayudanos." The religious community responded with food and shelter, and attempts to work through legal machinery set up by the INS.[57] Soon after the Salvadorans were arrested, a group of people, among whom was Rev. John Fife, started collecting money for bonds to temporarily free the refugees in detention and help them through the legal processes. "They posted bonds to get the refugees out of detention camps, putting up their own cars and homes collateral, but the best they could do was to buy time. After two years of such work, not one of the fourteen hundred refugees they had helped had gained political asylum" (14). The frustration with this "failure" was aggravated as people's sympathy for the Central American refugees increased as it became clear that refugees were legitimately escaping a circle of violence. It was incomprehensible to the "good people" that "their government" would refuse to abide by its very own laws on refugees by a mere play of interpretation of these laws. The almost innocent bewilderment is reflected in *A Justice Ministry,* a guidebook prepared by Chicago Religious Task Force on Central America, in the following words: "Even though Salvadoran and Guatemalan refugees meet the requirement of U.S. Code, Refugee Act of 1980, and are recognized by the UN High Commissioner for Refugees, the U.S. State Department refuses to grant them their proper status."[58] It is at the juncture (where the bodies escaping from violence, peoples who experience constant failure and the activities of the "proper agents" met) that what Michel Foucault called "problematization"[59] of the situation started. The questions of "how" these formulations of the problem (and its possible solutions/responses) came to be, rather than some other formulations and responses, slowly prepared the shifting of grounds in people's thoughts. This "epistemological shift" is observed in the ensuing intense questioning of the issue of legality. For instance, in another guidebook, titled *Sanctuary and the Law,* it was argued that

> the law is a political creature, and is enforced—or not enforced—
> *within the context of the political arena* [my emphasis]. . . . Although
> the criminal liability is a legal question . . . the possibility of prosecu-

tion is a political question which should be evaluated in light of the law, practice, and—most importantly—religious and political conviction. The willingness to risk possible prosecution is a question of conviction, not a matter of law.[60]

The faith in the legal system was short-lasted, for political objectives of the U.S. refugee policies made it simply impossible for the Central American refugees (with the exception of Nicaraguans) to be granted permission to stay in or even entry into the United States Golden and McConnell point out that "it had become clear that the hearing process was not designed to grant justice for immigrants."[61] According to David Matas of the International Commission of Jurists, there are simply dozens of legal/juridical ways of denying a person refugee status if the government agent chooses to use one or the other. Corroborating Matas, Wendy LeWin[62] of the Sanctuary Movement asserts that less than three percent of the asylum-seeking Guatemalans and Salvadorans were granted the refugee status.[63]

As the frustration with the normalizing/disciplining legal framework grew to new highs, Central Americans kept flooding the border areas. Along with the moving bodies of Mexicans, the Central American bodies continued to transform the U.S.–Mexican border into the busiest "illegal" border crossing in the world and the border areas into zones of struggle. Encounters of the Central Americans with the "Unitedstatesians" were now routine, though still largely confined to the framework of the territorializing institutional practices of the governments and their agents. On the U.S. side of the border, however, increasing knowledge of the refugee situation and the continuing hostility of the U.S. government toward refugees further honed the problematizing wills of the individuals like Wendy LeWin, Rev. John Fife, and Jim Corbett. The epistemological shift in the realm of thoughts made it possible for many to perceive the history of the refugee as a category of thought formulation with its unique history and economy of power relations. It also made it possible for the people to formulate "differing" responses to the presence of moving bodies, responses/formulations that were no more perceived to be mere "supplements" to the "proper category" of the state but resistance to it. Out of this process of problematization came the (possibility) formulation of a movement called the Sanctuary Movement.

Two events, the development of the underground railroad by Jim

Corbett and the declaration of public sanctuary by Rev. John Fife and his congregation,[64] became instrumental in the process. The most important factor in the "birth" of the Sanctuary Movement was the realness of the experiences of people in their own locales with everyday details. "The sanctuary movement was born from an encounter of North Americans and Central Americans—not around a conference table but on the road, in the desert, along the barbed wire of border crossings."[65]

On March 24, 1982, the South Side Presbyterian Church in Tucson was declared a sanctuary for the refugees. During the press conference, Rev. Fife read the following, which had already been sent to the U.S. Attorney General as a manifesto:

> "We have declared our church as a Sanctuary for undocumented refugees from Central America. . . . We believe that justice and mercy require that people of conscience actively assert our God-given right to aid anyone fleeing from persecution and murder. The current administration of U.S. law prohibits us from sheltering these refugees from Central America. Therefore, we believe the administration of the law to be immoral as well as illegal."[66]

From the declaration of March 1982, the Sanctuary Movement spread, and spread quickly. As of March 1985, there were 222 declared sanctuaries throughout the United States.[67] The movement grew fast primarily as a grassroots movement, and its organizational structure was loosely put together, thus enabling it to fulfill the strategic exigencies such as the coordination of the transportation of the refugees. This characteristic was key in the preservation of its "democratic" organization. According to Sally Schwartz,[68] a spokesperson for the Sanctuary defendants during their trial in 1986, the participation of the people was largely uncoordinated, and the ways in which it was materialized were generally left to the people themselves in their respective regions. The very basic limitations that were observed were due to the necessities of coordination. "It did not focus on few visible, charismatic leaders. . . . It had no hierarchies, no formal organizations, no regulations regarding membership."[69] In a Sanctuary source book titled *Organizer's Nuts and Bolts,* the very first sentence reaffirms this quality of the movement: "Each local situation is unique and each congregation is different and will have its own ideas about how best to organize and handle its sanctuary ministry."[70] In another guide, prepared by the Unitarian Universalist Service Committee, the importance of the "local" configurations of relationships is emphasized under the subheading "Practical suggestions for working with your congregation." "Know the politics of your congregation," the guide urges the Sanctuary participant who is in search of "connections."[71]

By mid-1985, over three hundred churches were functioning as Public Sanctuaries for the Central American refugees. Another six hundred "co-conspiring" congregations and organizations were also active in aiding the Sanctuary Movement.[72] According to one observer, during the two years from 1985 to 1987, the participants of the Sanctuary Movement helped facilitate the participation of 50,000 to 100,000 people on the U.S. side,[73] whose involvement goes mostly unnoticed by all but the refugees themselves. Here is an example from my personal memory:

> Human Vistas: Paul, or better known as Paublo among the "illegal" refugees is one of the hundreds of volunteers who are active in aiding Central Americans and the Mexicans. He is not at the core of the movement, but is always "on the road." When I went to visit him in Mesa for first time on Christmas 1990, he had four "illegals" in his house who had been living with him for about two years. Paublo's dedication to "the road" is continuous, and he is always on the move. Twice a week, he prepares sandwiches collected from Phoenix churches and individuals and takes them to the fruit groves just outside the city where the "illegals" gather and hide. Once a week a doctor accompanies Paublo who volunteers his services and prescribes donated medicine.

The human connections that the Sanctuary Movement and the moving peoples of the Americas established led well into the territories in Mexico and as far south as the highlands of Guatemala and El Salvador. People like Renny Golden and Robin Lener of the Chicago Religious Task Force and Jim Corbett of Tucson started making regular trips to Mexico and farther south to guide the refugees north, thus establishing another "underground railroad." They also founded links with the Mexican sanctuary movements organized by "the Clandestine Church of Mexico" with strong indigenous roots. People like "Padre Rodolfo" were counterparts of Corbett and the others. Their reasons for involvement in the "illegal" underground railroad were also simple, and not so far removed from those of the Unitedstatesians. An indigenous women put it this way: "We all live under the same sky. I am one hundred percent indigenous. I lived the suffering of the people. I haven't stayed behind. Jesus said to help the sojourner because he was one. Jesus became one with the suffering of the people."[74]

Nowadays, the Sanctuary Movement is more dispersed and loose both organizationally and philosophically. Its participants can be seen on different stages and platforms. For instance, in Arizona, its activities revolve around two loose organizations. The Valley Religious Task Force on Central America could be considered one extension in the Phoenix area, while the Tucson Ecumenical Council is active in Tucson area. Both maintain a minimum level of organizational structure consisting of sanctuary (Casa Companera) and political advocacy (Central American Bureau of Information and Outreach [CAMBIO]). The activities, though still largely focused on Central America, are also involved with the other issues in this hemisphere such as the Haitian (refugee) situation. Volunteers are the backbone of the activities, as the task force in Phoenix has only three full-time staff. Yet hundreds of volunteers who put in a tremendous amount of time and energy "make things happen." For instance, feeding the refugees and migrants in the citrus groves with one meal a day throughout the year necessitates a serious undertaking. Notwithstanding the dangers of "narration," the following is what I experienced in one of the visits to the citrus groves.

> Human Vistas: In late February, I went to the citrus groves with Renee, a Guatemalan refugee turned human rights activist. Renee is in fact one of the first refugees connected with the Sanctuary Movement in the early 1980s. He is now the organizer of a project called *Clinica Caminantea* which serves the "illegals" passing through the Phoenix and Tucson areas. "Welcoming" us in the groves was a group of Central Americans, some playing soccer and others just waiting for the meal of the day to arrive. There were about 150 people, many of whom were teenagers as young as 12 or 13, and also some women with babies. The meal came along with clothes and blankets necessary to spend the cold nights out there. In fact, the same night, Phoenix had one of its heavy desert rains. At the end of the afternoon, everyone had a meal and also a plate of food for later. There were no pretensions as to "feeling sorry" or what not. It was, as if both sides felt (my feelings only) it was simply necessary just to do it. I did not hear anybody suggesting that the "root-causes" of the

problem were thus eliminated by one meal a day. I carried pitchers of hot chocolate around pouring into hundreds of cups, and also had a meal afterwards. At the end, I asked Renee about his personal story; he said that he would "rather not talk about it, for the struggle had moved to another positioning nowadays."

The Sanctuary activities are now well beyond providing refuge for the "illegal" immigrants and refugees. In fact, they have become a catalyst in charting new territories, producing new meanings and images. They have become also a small but telling symbol of solidarity, more than charity according to many participants, between the peoples of different places and times, hopes, and expectations.

From the very beginnings, there were various problems. For instance, the decision-making processes quickly reflected the tendencies of the hegemonic culture to place its "rationals" and its strategies in the center to which the reasonings and rationals of the refugees themselves were expected to submit. Refugees were largely marginalized if not excluded from the decision-making circles. But there were also learning processes by which such reaffirmations of hegemonic culture and its reasonings were problematized, and became suspect. In other words, people strived to experience one another through that which would resist accommodation into the political economy of hegemonic political culture. What happened to these strivings? The terrain of such activities is too complex to map. Nor do I feel certain that one should try to do such a thing. However, the ongoing activities of peoples on and along the border areas are suggestive that the "becoming" as an activity of living is continuing. People continue to become refugees, migrants, exiles, locals, tourists, coyotes, Los Angelesian, Californian, Mexican-American, American, or all of these simultaneously.

Although hardly significant when viewed within the larger picture of the border scenes, of the movements of the bodies and spirits across the borders, the Sanctuary activities constitute one of the many struggles against the disciplinary practices of the state conceived and practiced in accordance with a modernist image of culture/nation gardens. If at all, the significance of the movement should not be "measured" by its size but by its strategic contribution to the effective deterritorialization of the political and cultural spaces straddling the borders and beyond.

It is in fact these greater challenges that triggered a harsh government response to the movement. In 1985, the U.S. government charged the movement with violating the 1980 Refugee Act, indicting sixteen Sanctuary workers and sixty refugees in the Phoenix area. Eventually some were acquitted, and some were imprisoned. It seems that the reaction of the government was one of a calculated practice of asserting its sovereign claim of control (a sovereignty practice) over the events and their symbolic/textual meanings. According to some sanctuary workers, such as Renee, the trial was initiated in order to intimidate its participants as well as sap their energy to go on with the movement.[75] No less than these objectives was the government's objective also to sap the financial resources of the movement. The cardinal objective, however, was to recruit the very presence of the movement in the construction and maintenance of the spectacle of the refugee and/or the migrant as a security threat to the national "culture gardens," and their proper dwellers, that is, the citizens. This trial, along with regionalized ones and other instruments of representation such as the border patrol and the INS, led to a proliferation of writings/readings of the illegal refugee and migrant in INS reports, Congressional hearings, institutional policy outlines, presidential task forces, daily and weekly newspaper and television reports, and so on. In a way, a political economy of refugeeism and migration was created whereby the statist representational practices managed to preserve their profitable positionings in the intersections of life experiences as intertexts.

Ironically, the implications of the trial for the Sanctuary Movement were also rather "positive" because the trial facilitated the publicizing of the movement's objectives, thus attracting more attention and support.[76] Among the sixteen indicted was Wendy LeWin. Wendy, during my interview with her, looked and sounded just as willing as before to work for and with refugees who navigate across interpenetrating sites in search of a "better life," as the Salvadoran refugee Luis put it to me in the Casa Companera.

> Human vistas: Casa Companera is a lively place full with the so-called "illegals." It has seven bedrooms and an entry-level room which is used both as a living room and as an office. The house has also a TV room where the TV is constantly turned to Channel 33, Univision, in Spanish. The food for the house is provided generally through the food-banks and other charities as well as the contributions by the refugees themselves. One way in which to make money

for the house is cooking thousands of tamales in a marathon cooking for four or five days. During one such marathon-cooking, people in the house cooked 2,500 tamales in four days. Last time when I went there, there were about fourteen Central Americans "residing" there "illegally." They were from Honduras, Guatemala, and El Salvador, mostly indigenous people. I asked Jose to tell me how he came to the U.S., quickly assuring him that I have nothing to do with the *La Migra*. He simply told me that his story is not really important to talk about. Luis, who is from El Salvador, agreed to talk to me the following Saturday. When I called him that Saturday, I was told that he had found a day's job in "the fields" and could not come.

During one of my last visits to the *Casa Companera,* as I was talking to Wendy LeWin, a man and a nine- or ten-year-old child came in to "pick up" his W-2 tax forms. I was told that he used to live in the house as an "illegal." However, he is now out there among the taxpaying crowd, getting perhaps upset or perhaps happy, like many (citizens) with proper papers, at the prospects of a tax increase to pay for education or the "national" deficit or building up of "national security." This was a rather strange experience for me, for I thought that the man was both the symbol of the dissolution of the territorializing practices and a participant in the recuperation of those practices here and there. This paradoxical existence, both resistant to and accommodative of statist practices, was clearly manifested by the "loyalty" of the "illegal" to the W-2 tax form. Perhaps his was and is a position of such ambiguity that I can not make sense of his resistances, compromises, or accommodations. On the other hand, perhaps I should not try at all to make "sense," as in a "complete deciphering" of the meanings and intentions of people's activities. Interestingly, at this juncture of migrant identities and curiously shifting loyalties lies (my) personal dilemma yet to be negotiated.

NOTES

1. Arjun Appadurai, "Disjuncture and Difference in the Global Cultural Economy," in *Theory, Culture and Society,* ed. Mike Featherstone (Bristol: J. V. Arrowsmith, 1991), p. 103; Barry Smart, *Modern Conditions, Postmodern Controversies* (New York and London: Routledge, 1992); Jacques Attali, "Lines on the Horizon: A New Order in the Making," *New Perspectives Quarterly* 7, no. 2 (spring 1990).

2. A. R. JanMohamed and D. Lloyd, "Introduction: Toward a Theory of Minority Discourse: What Is to Be Done?" in *The Nature and Context of Minority Discourse,* ed. A. R. JanMohamed and D. Lloyd (New York, Oxford: Oxford University Press, 1990).

3. Arjun Appadurai, "Putting Hierarchy in Its Place," *Cultural Anthropology* 3, no. 1 (1988), pp. 36-49.

4. R. B. J. Walker, "State Sovereignty and the Articulation of Political Space / Time," *Millennium* 20, no. 3 (1991), pp. 445-61.

5. Liisa Malkki, "National Geographic: The Rooting of Peoples and the Territorialization of National Identity among Scholars and Refugees," *Cultural Anthropology* 7, no. 1 (February 1992), pp. 24-44.

6. A. Gupta and J. Ferguson, "Beyond 'Culture': Space, Identity and the Politics of Difference," *Cultural Anthropology* 7, no. 1 (February 1992), pp. 6-23; Malkki, "National Geographic."

7. Appadurai, "Disjuncture and Difference in the Global Cultural Economy."

8. **Ethnoscapes** refers to the landscape of persons who constitute the shifting world in which we live: tourists, immigrants, refugees, exiles, guestworkers, and other moving groups and persons constitute an essential feature of the world.

Technoscapes refers to the global configuration, also ever fluid, of technology, and of the fact that technology, both high and low, both mechanical and informational, now moves at high speeds across various kinds of previously impervious boundaries.

Finanscapes means that the disposition of global capital is now a more mysterious, rapid, and difficult landscape to follow than ever before, as currency markets, national stock exchanges, and commodity speculations move megamonies through national turnstiles at blinding speed.

Mediascapes refers both to the distribution of the electronic capabilities to produce and disseminate information (newspapers, magazines, television stations, film production studios, etc.), which are now available to a growing number of private and public interests throughout the world; and to the images of the world created by these media.

Ideoscapes are often directly political and are variegated by the growing diasporas of peoples who continuously inject new meaning-streams into the discourse of democracy in different parts of the world (Appadurai, "Disjunction and Difference in the Global Cultural Economy," pp. 296-305).

9. Appadurai, "Disjuncture and Difference in the Global Cultural Economy," pp. 296-97.

10. In this study, more often than not, I employ the practice of conflating (using) the two terms together. To the extent that this study is interested in the problematique of space/movement/body/identity, an enterprise in taxon-

omy is unnecessary. In fact, in the following pages, the reader shall read my discomfort in the face of such a task. Moreover, the phrases "migration of refugee" or "forced migration" are yet a further testimony to the ontological intimacy that exists between the life experiences of what are otherwise arbitrarily called "refugees" and "migrants." At the level of praxis, it is almost impossible to distinguish clearly refugees from migrants. Overlaps in terms of experiences are too complex and too many to map a world of refugees that is clearly distinct from the supposed world of migrants. Therefore, my references to refugees and migrants are not meant to reconstruct or reconstitute the conceptions of refugees and immigrants in the modernist image and its categories. Only in the section on the Sanctuary Movement do I start exclusively speaking of refugees just to focus the reading/writing on Central America. And, admittedly, this itself is a move in arbitrariness.

11. Henry Kamm, "People Smugglers' Send New Tide of Refugees onto Nordic Shores," *New York Times,* 15 February 1993, sec. A.1.

12. I am indebted to Baudrillard for the term *Simulacra,* though I may have "strayed" from the intent of the original use.

13. Samuel T. Francis, *Illegal Immigration: A Threat to U.S. Security* (London: The Centre for Security and Conflict Studies, 1986); Richard K. Ashley, "Living on Border Lines: Man, Poststructuralism and War," in *International/Intertextual Relations,* ed. James Der Derian and Michael Shapiro (Lexington, Mass.: Lexington Books, 1989); R. B. J. Walker, "Security, Sovereignty, and the Challenge of World Politics," *Alternatives* 15 (1990), pp. 3-27; R. B. J. Walker, "State Sovereignty and the Articulation of Political Space/Time."

14. Michael Kearney, "Borders and Boundaries of the State and Self at the End of Empire," *Journal of Historical Sociology* 4, no. 1 (March 1991), pp. 52-74; Michael Kearney, "Mixtec Political Consciousness: From Passive to Active Resistance," in David Nugent, ed., *Rural Revolt in Mexico and U.S. Intervention,* Center for U.S.–Mexican Studies, University of California, San Diego, Monograph Series, 27 (1988).

15. N. Hamilton and N. S. Chinchilla, "Central American Migration: A Framework for Analysis," *Latin American Research Review* (1991), pp. 75-109.

16. Jodi Jacobson, "Environmental Refugees: A Yardstick of Habitability," World Watch Paper, 86 (Washington, D.C.: World Watch Institute, 1988).

17. Ellwyn R. Stoddard, "Northern Mexican Migration and the U.S.–Mexico Border Region," *New Scholar* 9, no. 1, 2 (1984), pp. 51-72.

18. Francis, *Illegal Immigration*; Ted Conover, *Coyotes: A Journey through the Secret World of America's Illegal Aliens* (New York: Vintage Books, 1987).

19. Brenda K. Marshall, *Teaching the Postmodern: Fiction and Theory* (New York and London, Routledge, 1992), p. 59.

20. Hamilton and Chinchilla, "Central American Migration."

21. American Broadcasting Company, *Nightline*, 29 January 1992.

22. S. Armstrong and J. Dulin, "Illegal Border Traffic Rising Again," *Christian Science Monitor*, 16 October 1992, p. 7.

23. Kearney, "Borders and Boundaries of the State and Self at the End of Empire"; Conover, *Coyotes*.

24. Kearney, "Borders and Boundaries of the State and Self at the End of Empire."

25. Michael Kearney and C. Nagengast, "Mixtec Ethnicity: Social Identity, Political Consciousness and Political Activism," *Latin American Research Review* 25, no. 1 (1990), pp. 61-91.

26. See Bill Frelick, *Running the Gauntlet: The Central American Journey through Mexico* (Washington, D.C.: The U.S. Committee for Refugees, 1991), for a look into the strategies of cooperation between the U.S. and Mexican governments. The "Operation Hold the Line" is one example of the cooperation between the two governments in the 1980s.

27. S. Lash and J. Urry, *The End of Organized Capitalism* (Oxford: Polity Press, 1987); Kearney, "Borders and Boundaries of the State and Self at the End of Empire"; Ellwyn R. Stoddard, "Northern Mexican Migration and the U.S.–Mexico Border Region," *New Scholar* 9, no. 1, 2 (1984), pp. 51-72; Alex Monto, "Ethnographic Notebook Running the Gauntlet: The Frontier and the Migrants," *Cambridge Anthropology* 14, no. 1 (1990), pp. 67-77; N. Hamilton and N. S. Chinchilla, "Central American Migration: A Framework for Analysis." In almost every piece on international migration and refugee movements, there is extensive analysis from the standpoint of capitalist forces of production and distribution as nondiscursive, all-encompassing factors that define the basic qualities of space as a continuous arena of activity. The dynamics capitalism calls for the movements of peoples, money, goods, and products in accordance not with the expectations of the devout subjects (citizens) of nation-states but with the exigencies of the possible most profitable configuration of productive forces.

28. William Langewiesche, "The Border," *Atlantic Monthly*, May 1992, p. 55.

29. Walker, "State Sovereignty and the Articulation of Political Space/Time"; Ashley, "Living on Border Lines; Leon Gordenker, *Refugees in International Politics* (London: Croom Helm, 1987).

30. Langewiesche, "The Border," p. 68.

31. Ibid., p. 53.

32. Kearney, "Borders and Boundaries of the State and Self at the End of Empire," p. 57; Langewiesche, "The Border," p. 53.

33. Kearney, "Borders and Boundaries of the State and Self at the End of Empire," p. 57.

34. Conover, *Coyotes*.

35. Bill Frelick, *Running the Gauntlet*.

36. *San Diego Union*, "49 die in 91 trying to swim Rio Grande," 12 December 1992.

37. J. M. Gomez and L. Hall, "3 Killed at Border Patrol Checkpoint," *Los Angeles Times*, 18 January 1992.

38. *San Diego Union*, "INS Agents Accused of Abuse," 6 June 1992.

39. Sabestian Rotella, "Despite Figures, Group Claims Abuse Along Border," *Los Angeles Times*, 26 February 1992. Similar abuses were also documented in an Americas Watch report. See Americas Watch, *Brutality Unchecked: Human Rights Abuses Along the U.S. Border with Mexico* (New York: Americas Watch, May 1992).

40. Philip J. LaVelle, "Grand Jury to Hear Border Agent Case, Lawyer Says," *San Diego Union*, 12 March 1992.

41. *San Diego Union*, "Roundup of Migrants in Orange is Protested," 21 November 1992.

42. Daryl Kelley, "Rancher to Pay $1.5 Million Fine in Slavery Case," *Los Angeles Times*, 24 March 1992.

43. Agnes Roletti, "Maid's Boss Gets Three Years in Slavery Case," *San Diego Tribune*, 19 October 1991.

44. Leo Ralph Chavez, *Shadowed Lives: Undocumented Immigrants in American Society* (Fort Worth, Tex.: Harcourt Brace Jovanovich, 1992).

45. Carlos E. Cortes, "Searching for Imaginative Responses to Inevitable Challenges," *New Scholar* 9, no. 2 (1984), pp. 39-50; Robert Alvarez, "The Border as Social System: The California Case," *New Scholar* 9, no. 1, 2 (1984), pp. 119-31.

46. Kearney, "Borders and Boundaries of the State and Self at the End of Empire," p. 55.

47. Larry Siems, *Between the Lines: Letters between Undocumented Mexican and Central American Immigrants and Their Families and Friends* (Hopewell, N.J.: Teco Press, 1992), pp. 95-104.

48. Fredric Jameson, *The Political Unconscious* (London: Methuen, 1981).

49. Conover, *Coyotes*.

50. Raymond Williams, *Culture* (Glasgow: Fontana, 1981).

51. Eric Wolf, *Europe and the People without History* (Berkeley: California University Press, 1982).

52. Lash and Urry, *The End of Organized Capitalism*, p. 291.

53. R. B. J. Walker, *One World, Many Worlds: Struggles for a Just World Peace* (Boulder, Colo.: Lynne Rienner, 1988); JanMohamed and Lloyd, "Introduction: Toward a Theory of Minority Discourse"; Kearney, "Borders and Boundaries of the State and Self at the End of Empire."

54. Kearney, "Borders and Boundaries of the State and Self at the End of Empire."

55. R. Golden and M. McConnell, *Sanctuary: The New Underground Railroad* (New York: Orbis Books, 1986), p. 1.

56. David Matas, *The Sanctuary Trial* (Manitoba: International Commission of Jurists, 1989), p. 47.

57. Golden and McConnell, *Sanctuary,* p. 14.

58. Chicago Religious Task Force on Central America, *Sanctuary: A Justice Ministry* (Chicago: 1986), p. 1.

59. Michel Foucault, *The Foucault Reader,* ed. Paul Rabinow (New York: Pantheon Books, 1984).

60. Chicago Religious Task Force on Central America, *Sanctuary and the Law: A Guide for Congregations* (Chicago: 1986), pp. 2-3.

61. Golden and McConnell, *Sanctuary,* pp. 14, 44-45.

62. Wendy LeWin, interview by author, tape recording, Phoenix, Arizona, 15 and 22 January 1992. Wendy LeWin was one of the defendants in the sanctuary trial in 1986, of which I shall write more in the following pages. I have come to know Wendy LeWin more as I have become more involved in various local organizations such as VRTFCA (Valley Religious Task Force on Central America) and the Amnesty International Phoenix chapter.

63. To a great degree, the attitude of the U.S. government to refugee issues has traditionally been shaped by its ideological/political and racial "positionings" at any particular time or episode concerned. With respect to Central American refugee issues, the ideological preoccupation of the government is clearly revealed by one of its practitioners. Michael Trominski, then the INS district director for Mexico, argued that the INS does not view Central Americans as refugees. "We have interviewed refugee applicants in Central America," said Trominski, "They do not fit the program. It is hard to get a good, solid claim." Of Salvadorans, Trominski commented, "We won't let FMLN types into the United States as refugees" (Frelick, *Running the Gauntlet*, pp. 4-5). Nowadays, it is the Haitians that signify the "FMLN types," although not so much in a political sense as in a racial one. In fact, the treatment of the Haitians might be suggestive of the U.S. government's historical attitude to the influx of "certain" foreign bodies to the United States.

64. Jack R. Ferrell and Gregory L. Wiltfang, "The Sanctuary Movement on Stage: The Politics and Morality of a Central and North American Drama," *Review of Latin American Studies* 1, no. 1 (1988), pp. 11-20.

65. Golden and McConnell, *Sanctuary,* p. 14.

66. Robert Tomsho, *American Sanctuary Movement* (Austin, Tex.: Texas Monthly Press, 1987), p. 31.

67. Ibid., p. 50.

68. Sally Schwartz, interview by author, telephone recording, Phoenix Arizona, 14 January 1992. I contacted her through the VRTFCA (Valley Religious Task Force on Central America).

69. Ignatius Bau, *The Ground is Holy: Church and Central American Refugees* (New York: Paulits Press, 1985), p. 174. Sally Schwartz suggested also that this openness and loose structure was one of the reasons why the government agents were able to penetrate the Sanctuary Movement so easily. One of the interesting strategies employed by the agents of the government was to approach refugees, trying to cajole them to testify against the Sanctuary defendants by offering them lawful stay (residency, etc.) in the United States.

70. Chicago Religious Task Force on Central America, *Public Sanctuary for Salvadoran and Guatamalen Refugees: Organizer's Nuts and Bolts* (Chicago: 1986), p. 2.

71. "Keep the rhetoric to a minimum" the guide continues. "Realize that searching questions or opposition to sanctuary do not constitute a denial of basic religious or ethical values, but may be an honest expression of doubt about the tactics or the ability of your congregation to carry out the proposed sanctuary activities. . . . Know the politics of your congregation. . . . has the congregation ever played a significant role in support of another social cause? what is the relationship of the social concerns committee to the board of trustees and to the congregation? Be sensitive to interpersonal dynamics and spheres of interests ('turf')." Unitarian Universalist Service Committee, *Giving Sanctuary and Refugee Assistance* (Boston: Unitarian Universalist Service Committee, 1988), pp. 23-24.

72. Gary MacEoin, ed., *Sanctuary: A Resource Guide for Understanding and Participation in the Central American Refugees' Struggle* (New York, Cambridge: Harper & Row, 1985), p. 23.

73. Elizabeth G. Ferris, *The Central American Refugees* (New York: Praeger, 1987), p. 128.

74. Golden and McConnell, *Sanctuary*, p. 116.

75. My conversations with Renee are ongoing, as I see him "around" all the time.

76. Ferrell and Wiltfang, *The Sanctuary Movement on Stage*, p. 15.

13

Technologies of National Desire

RICHARD MAXWELL

Welcome to Euskal Telebista,
the youngest TV for the oldest country in Europe.
CORPORATE PR OF THE BASQUE RADIO-TV COMPANY

All nationalisms imagine a communication system fit to a nation. For the philologist Sabino de Arana Goiri (1865-1903), the "apostle of Basque Nationalism," language defined the race, but territory was needed to make the nation. In the 1890s, Arana invented a Basque word to capture the land where Basques lived; he called it *Euskadi.* Before this word, there was no indigenous name that gave earth to a "homeland" of Basque speakers—that is, of the sort identifying "birthplace." The Latin-rooted Vasconia, a country whose children were Vascos, had no equivalent in *euskera* (or *euskara*), the Basque language. Rather, the region was called *Euskal Herria,* meaning, more or less, where euskera speakers live. People of Euskal Herria are *euskaldun*: holders of euskera. *Euskal Herria* signifies, in other words, the presence of the *euskaldun*—it is the vernacular matrix of the Basques. Until Sabino de Arana territorialized this vernacular matrix, the Others for Basques were *erdaldun,* that is, speakers of *er-dara,* or those who speak "half way."[1]

The spatial presence of the *euskaldun,* that is, *Euskal Herria,* had been diminishing steadily since the eighteenth century. By 1863, when Prince Louis Lucien Bonaparte published his study of the main

327

Basque dialects (according to which there are eight, not counting numerous subdialects and isolects), the borders of *Euskal Herria* were coordinated northeast in three French departments of the Atlantic Pyrenees and northwest and southeast in four Spanish provinces that included "large portions of central and eastern Vizcaya, small corners of Alava, the north of Navarre, and, discounting the enclaves, all of Guipúzcoa."² Prior to this time, as far as the records show, the largest contiguous geographical extensions of *Euskal Herria* occurred in the Middle Ages, when the *euskaldun* were found east almost as far as Andorra and south to Burgos. At the end of the nineteenth century, with equal numbers of *erdaldun* and *euskaldun* living within Vasconia, *Euskal Herria* underwent a different kind of diminishment—it was absorbed into something altogether new, something racialized, territorialized, and modern.³

Euskadi was invented in a spirit of nation building at a time when the language of the Other, *erdara*—more precisely, Castilian—was becoming dominant. This place naming hailed a retraditionalized people within an increasingly modernized *erdara* territory. This was a time when nationalism throughout Europe was politicized, when the spreading hegemony of industrial capitalism motivated a nationalized yet modern system of independent nation-states.⁴ *Euskadi* absorbed *Euskal Herria* and rooted *erdaldun* and *euskaldun* alike firmly in the ground of modern cultural sovereignty. There, identity crystalized in the location of a bounded ethnic political space. The Vasconia defined by ancient imperial states became the *Euskadi* defined by a modern desire of national borders. Sabino de Arana valorized this desire with a neologism he engineered from the vernacular matrix.

The value of *Euskadi* was also defined by a nationalist interpretation of the creeping industrialization of Vasconia. Although the regions of Spain were absorbed into the absolutist state by the sixteenth century,⁵ the centralized state system that emerged worked against commercial and industrial capitalism in Spain. Capitalism developed unevenly as a result, and regional economic differentiation eventually assumed political form. Barcelona (Catalonia) and Bilbao (in the Basque province of Vizcaya) were the first sites of capitalist development in Spain, followed by Madrid.⁶ In addition, the *latifundistas* of southern Spain resisted industrialization and with the support of the state opposed the hegemony of an emergent northern bourgeoisie. This tension kept Basque and Catalan capitalists from using the Spanish national economy to become "first comers" of the industrial revolution.[7]

Under these general conditions, however, laborers were encouraged to migrate to the northern zones of industry. There thus emerged in these regions new social demands to accommodate the development of human and technical forces of production for a modern industrial society dependent on population mobilization. Among these demands was a suitable language, that is, a national lingua franca that would articulate the division of labor. Diglossia in southern European capitalism, nonetheless, tended to favor romanized languages, which in turn favored the linguistic providence of the Spanish national state over the emerging urban industrial society (*euskera* has not been traced to any Indo-European root). Immigrants to Vasconia could not learn *euskera* easily, nor could *euskera,* as it was constituted at the time, provide an adequate discourse to coordinate new techniques, material processing, and industrial exchange relations.[8] The language of the dominant national state (Spain) thus tended to be the language best suited to capitalism in Vasconia.

Cultural nationalism developed against the pressures of population mobilization with a distinctly anti-industrial sentiment. It politicized a birthplace identity and enclosed that space with the name *Euskadi.* At the same time, industrialization encouraged a national ideology among the cosmopolitan bourgeoisie of Vasconia, who invoked an older tradition of internal tariffs and taxes to protect what they also interpreted as their national culture—the internal market. Still, this national bourgeoisie was more liberal than the ethnonationalists in attitude and action regarding both the Spanish government and foreign investment and trade (read British capital and read also the Basque bourgeoisie's consciousness of their dependence on imperialism). Typically, it was the growing middle class of administrators, journalists, and professionals (the cultural mass) who adopted the wider repertoire of nationalist symbols in opposition to "Spain" and other "foreign powers."[9]

In the event, Sabino de Arana inspired the rise of Basque nationalism and racialist determinations of Basque nationality. Largely a twentieth-century invention, Basque nationalism drew on myths and legends of invented tradition that became suffused with scientific racism as supports for an ethnically distinct homeland.[10] For his part, Sabino de Arana inveighed against miscegenation, disgusted by "Spanish" immigrants to *Euskadi,* and sought the establishment of a pastoral, Catholic society in which only authentic Basques would live in a separate, preindustrial regime (he designed the Basque flag too).[11]

Euskadi thus forged an ethnic identity by breeding across, as it were, the us/them divide of *euskaldun* and *erdaldun.* Possession of language was still integral to national identity, but now one did not have to be an *euskera* speaker to be Basque. The territorial helix made a nation of a race defined—ironically as in many modern nationalist revivals—by a language that was disappearing. To the extent that a word was necessary for the act of naming a space of difference, and thus territorializing blood ties, language served as a technology of inclusion/exclusion. But when the isoglossic divisions within *Euskal Herria* were suppressed by the new inter-national division upheld by *Euskadi,* the more decisive role of inclusion/exclusion was assumed by the technology of modern politics, by a politics of national movement. The desired ties of blood and tongue found a third term of nation in land. In the wake of capitalist regionalization, modern Basque nationalism was mobilized: where the *euskaldun* once made all the difference, there stood the politics of *Euskadi.*

Nevertheless, the nation thus desired as a political region was coextensive with the vernacular matrix of *Euskal Herria.* As the *euskaldun* receded as the necessary and sufficient marker of identity and difference, the fractured space of *Euskal Herria* was forged into the unified place of *Euskadi.* The vernacular matrix was displaced, in other words, by a territorial object desired by nationalism. This can be seen in the first expression of the political region of *Euskadi*: its map drew together the four Spanish and three French provinces that on their peripheries were at best only a nostalgic home of an *euskaldun* long since gone. A new slogan was created that expressed this nationalist fetish: *Zazpiak Bat,* "Out of Seven, One." Of course, the wishfully thought sovereign (i.e., *Euskadi, Zazpiak Bat*) never materialized. Today, an *Euskadi* smaller than Vasconia of old stands as the official national territory of the Basques in Spain. In Castilian, *el País Vasco,* the Basque Country, is the singular political region representing in realist terms the closest thing Basques have to a sovereign nation.

Today *Euskadi* remains a nation without a state, yet it valorizes the same old object desired by Basque nationalism, even if in name only. *Euskadi* signifies a fantasy about a place coextensive with *Euskal Herria,* the vernacular matrix of the *euskaldun,* but displaces that fantasy onto a territory. It is this national fantasy alone that integrates the fractured space of *Euskal Herria*. What has changed in the hundred years of failed attempts to make a sovereign is the technology that helps reinterpret, and refetishize, the object of national desire. *Euskadi* dreams of *Euskal Herria* today as an electronic region populated by an *audience* collectively tuned into Basque radio and television. Where once a political rhetoric of *Euskadi* sought to identify *erdaldun* and *euskaldun* as children of one home, today Euskal Irrati Telebista (Basque Radio and Television) hails a singular *audience*—an electronic nation of Basques—as one of the decisive, and constitutive, conditions of *Euskal Herria*.

Euskadi displaced *Euskal Herria* but could not root itself to the latter's ancient boundaries, contained as it was by modern political realities. In contrast, the electronic region of nationalist television can trespass the borders imposed by the logic of political regionalization. All nationalisms imagine a communication system fit to a nation, and the nation of *Euskadi* retains an imaginary territory fit, now electronically, to *Euskal Herria*—"the youngest TV for the oldest country." As it tries to make the *audience* in its own image, however, the electronic national fantasy is forced to confront contending interpretations of people as *audience*.

Consider that an audience is an institutional construct of collective taxonomies—we are only audiences to others, never a member of one unless asked to imagine ourselves as such under someone else's institutional labeling. Given this, media audiences are produced not just along one axis of identity, nationality, for example, but are objects sought by contending discourses that include the politics of the larger nation-state, the exchange imperatives of the international media market, or the categories of social science.[12] In the electronic region of Euskal Irrati Telebista, therefore, the national fantasy will intersect with competing valorizations of a national community— that desired object which in one form were the *euskaldun,* in another the citizens of *Euskadi,* and in still another Spanish subjects, and so on. The electronic matrix of this confrontation elides the older vernacular matrix yet revives familiar turf wars as it initiates new ones.

In 1982, a Basque Government, presiding over the autonomous community of the Basque Country within the territorial state of Spain, created a corporation called Euskal Irrati Telebista (EITB), or Basque Radio and TV. This Basque Country, *Euskadi* for better or worse, comprised only three of the seven provinces of *Euskal Herria:* Guipuzcoa, Vizcaya, and Alava. To the east is Navarra, and north of these four peninsular (Spanish) provinces, across the Pyrennees in southern France, lie the three continental provinces of Laburdi, Benabarra, and Zuberoa. The polity of official *Euskadi* formed under the Francoist regime in Spain and in exile; and it emerged in transition to democracy in Spain, redefining the present political region through negotiation among local authorities and the central government.[13] Navarra would not ally itself with this *Euskadi*, nor could the nationalist desire overcome the political attachments of the French Basques to France. The political regionalization of this *Euskadi* was left to contain the official national culture. This official *Euskadi* (Guipuzcoa, Vizcaya, and Alava) was, moreover, as a result of industrialization and its attendant immigration the most multinational and multicultural region of *Euskal Herria*—thus in the electronic province of Euskal Irrati Telebista the *erdaldun* outnumbered *euskaldun* four to one.[14]

Euskal Irrati Telebista was founded as "an essential instrument for the informational and political participation of Basque citizens, and as a fundamental medium of cooperation with our education system to foment and diffuse Basque culture, keeping very much in mind the fomentation and development of *euskara*."[15] This instrument of a Basque nation was restricted by political mandate to operate within the borders of official *Euskadi*. Its language would be *batua,* invented to unite the eight recognized dialects into one national lingua franca. Batua, as the Basque linguist Koldo Mitxelena notes, is a "naturally" expressed desire for unity in those aspects of Basque society where a "supradialectal" or "colorless, odorless, and insipid" prose is most needed. That is, it is an *euskera* that can be revived as a practical language, as Mitxelena insists, everywhere but in literature, poetry, and arts, where expressive differences are desirable—of course, this divide may not hold up well to the ungovernability of popular cultural appropriations of a unitary national grammar.[16] Nevertheless, as a matter of course, batua became the lingua franca of the schools (*ikastolas*) and radio and television—in the same manner that so-called "BBC English" expressed a desired unity of the languages and dialects of Britain. Those who would learn and use batua and the subdialects are the *euskaldun-berri,* or Basques formed by *euskera* as a second language.

The territorial logic of the political region impinges on the electronically expressed nationalist desire for the nation in two ways. First is the presumptive logic that ties broadcasting to a territory of an imagined national community. In Spain, such a logic of national containment first became the sine qua non of radio with Franco's nationalist war against the Second Republic. Second, and indissolubly connected to the first, national containment expressed at once the threshold of communicative trespass. In other words, the political region ends where interpretation of electronic trespass begins. Depending on which side of that border one is, such trespass can be interpreted in two distinct ways. On the one hand, it is the valorization of a national community at the expense of the official political region, what is sometimes called irredentism. So *Euskal Herria* is the desired object, the highly valued irredenta, of nationalist *Euskadi*. As we will see later, Euskal Irrati Telebista electronically connects, and so wishfully redeems, the *euskaldun* within the imaginary space of *Euskal Herria* by trespassing beyond the borders of *Euskadi*. On the other hand, such trespass can be identified as imperious—that is, as an uninvited extension of hegemonic expression, as the cultural imperialism of a foreign subject, or as the social imperialism of a local minority. This has been the case with the anti-*Euskadi* Basques of Navarra who have jammed the signals of Euskal Irrati Telebista, also discussed later. It goes without saying that sometimes there are others out there who may not appreciate such an electronic exchange—whereas others may welcome the projected identification without feeling it as a transgression.

The central presence giving the emotional charge to this electronic dynamic of containment and trespass is the political region. After World War I, the Spanish government coordinated the extension of electronic culture to fit the territorial state but retained a relative respect for local differences. With the nationalist-fascist rebellion, however, the differences among subnational communities were elided by an integrated national radio network. One nation, one electronic region, one state. The technology of radio, and later television, reflected this centralism. The regionalist radio-TV that emerged after the death of the dictatorship defined itself against this center, yet modeled itself paradoxically in the same national-centralist mold (to the disappointment of localists).

Experiments in radiowave communication started early in the

twentieth century. The Spanish government created legislation in
1908 that gave the central state the right to establish and exploit "all
systems and apparatuses related to the so-called 'Hertzian telegraph,' 'ethereal telegraph,' 'radiotelegraph,' and other similar procedures already invented or *that will be invented in the future.*"[17]
The first "legal" radio broadcast began in Barcelona in 1924 and,
like most pre–Spanish civil war radio stations, was started up by private interests to make a profit.[18] In the law on radio broadcasting of
1934, the Second Republic reaffirmed that "the service of national
radio broadcasting is an essential and exclusive function of the
state"; again in 1935, "sounds *and images* already in use or *to be invented in the future*" would be established and exploited by the
state.[19] Nevertheless, the Second Republic demonstrated little interest in centralizing more than the management of spectrum allocation
and of distribution of transmitters. In one of its first decrees, for instance, the government of the Second Republic authorized the instal-
lation of low-power transmitters to promote the growth of radio
with a distinctly local character.[20]

Despite such localism, radio was not attached in any systematic
way to the regionalist projects that emerged under the Second Republic. At the time, the autonomy movement of *Euskadi*, for example, was entangled in other problems related to the purview of its
charter and to financing its new government.[21] Throughout the rest
of the Spanish territory, political authorities had little influence over
the sites of investment in radio or the nature of the programming.
The early development of radio instead followed a pattern of mar-
ket-oriented investment, with multiplication of stations in urban
zones and only one private chain of any significance, the Unión
Radio, showing signs of concentration.

Still, some urban radio stations operated with wider regionalist
intentions, like the Radio Emisora Bilbaina, a private station in Bilbao. In the 1930s, Radio Emisora Bilbaina broadcast Basque language lessons as part of an educational program that included
English and French—a canny respect for the multinational character
of the region. Apart from commercial messages, music, and notices
of a general nature, the programming on Radio Emisora Bilbaina explicitly served as a public voice of regional concerns.[22] Independent
radio of this kind was stopped, however, by the Spanish civil war

(1936-39) when radio stations became outlets for military propaganda from both sides.

In the nationalist zones, Franco ordered the unification of radio stations under the direction of the new state. The technical network of transmitters that the Second Republic had established within a rather laissez-faire framework was thereafter integrated into a state-controlled network called Radio Nacional de España. Use of idioms distinct from Castilian (i.e., Basque, Catalan, Galician) was suppressed within the nationalist Spanish territory, and broadcasting became purposefully singular in its propagation of Francoist state-nationalism. New media laws gave the fascist Ministry of the Interior full power to silence communication that "directly, or indirectly, may tend to reduce the prestige of the Nation or Regime, to obstruct the work of the government of the new State, or sow pernicious ideas among the intellectually weak."[23] As with prior centralist regimes, all expressions of regionalism were immediately codified as treason.

Thus when the Basque government agreed to start Euskal Irrati Telebista in May of 1982 (followed by the Catalans a year later), their action constituted the most significant institutional change of broadcasting since the Spanish civil war.[24] It was, moreover, a direct assault on the national law that had regulated radiowave communication for over seventy years. The socialist government responded, with what is known as the Third Channel Law, months after the Basques had begun broadcasting (experiments started in December 1982). The Third Channel Law was meant to cause controlled denationalization of television by creating channels that responded to the plurality of cultures, languages, and communities within the Spanish territory—a radical multinationalism indeed when compared to the Francoist regime. However, the Basque Government (as well as the Catalan Generalitat and Galician Xunta) countered with a distinct interpretation of their rights to broadcast, arguing that they were not subject to the relevant decrees of the central government.[25]

The background to this battle over jurisdictional exclusivity is worth noting briefly. In 1979, the Basque and Catalan authorities negotiated the first full autonomy granted under article 151 of the new constitution; the Basque Country and Navarra later regained control over tax collection under a historical Charter, or *Fueros*.[26] Besides greater autonomous control over the regional economy, article

151, known as the immediate route to autonomy, also includes provisions that guarantee rights to an autonomous education system, to a separate police force, and to *an independent radio-television network*.[27] Paradoxically, the constitution also reserved for the central state *basic regulation of the press, radio, and television*.[28] This overlap of powers was complicated by a final clause in article 149 that gives the Autonomous Communities "exclusive" policy domains in which regional laws prevail over the national norms.[29] In other words, the Statutes of Autonomy can retain exclusivity in areas that obviously contravene the laws at the national level, which are also curiously granted "exclusivity." One significant area of contention is broadcasting—hence, Basque intransigence.

From the point of view of the regionalists, the Third Channel Law aimed to deny autonomy to new regional institutions. In contrast, absolute autonomy for Basque TV was simply de rigueur for the local authorities. Their self-determination rested on two crucial points: (1) using transmitters, relay-amplifiers, and interconnections of their own that literally ran parallel to those of Radiotelevisión Española (RTVE), the central state's national network; and (2) managing their own program purchasing. The only dependency of consequence would be the central state's control over universal frequency allocation within the Spanish territory.

Frequencies were assigned in bulk by the central government with regional allocations left to regional authorities. But the regional authorities ignored strict adherence to the central government's allocations. A sovereign state, after all, controls the spectrum of frequencies within its territory.[30] Despite their failure to gain international recognition in the club of electronic sovereigns, the Basques (Catalan and Galician communities too) had taken over parts of their electronic region. As the chief technician in charge of monitoring frequency use in Spain put it: "We know which frequencies we've assigned, but we don't know which ones they're using. It looks like they'll use whichever ones they find most convenient."[31]

Although they may have been a nation without a state, the Basques still had their own broadcast network. And in the territory of the electronic region, if nowhere else, the Basques enjoyed sovereign status—at least for the time being. Julián Pérez, once the manager of Euskal Irrati Telebista (EITB), explained in an interview that EITB's resistance held to "the traditional point of difference between the central government and the Basque government." To wit: the central government says Basque TV (Euskal Telebista) is merely a Third Channel like the other regions have, but Basques counter that *Euskadi* is unique among regions. As Pérez says, "The infrastructure here exists because of a mandate in the Statute of Autonomy and not because of the Third Channel Law, which, in any case, was promulgated after Euskal Telebista was constructed. The law here states that *Euskadi* has the right to construct and maintain its own television system." The central government's only responsibility was to perform its duties as a signatory of the conventions of the International Telecommunications Union, that is, they are obliged by law to provide frequency allocations once regional broadcasters decide to build new systems.

That was five years after EITB began broadcasting. What happened in those five years was that the central government failed to fulfill its obligation. "As a consequence," said Pérez, "our radio and television systems have to this day 'occupied' the frequencies." Thus "there is no legalization for Basque radio and TV from the point of view of the central government. From our point of view, Euskal Telebista functions 'alegally' since only the administrative concessions are lacking while the constitutional and statutory frameworks are active."[32] That was August 1988. The phone was ringing in Julián Pérez's office while I conducted the interview with him. His assistant answered and told him that an official from Madrid was on the line. That day EITB had started up a new radio channel but had not told the central authorities about it. From the Basque point of view, it was none of Madrid's business. Pérez smiled and instructed his assistant to tell them he was out. "Let them call. I know what they'll say and I don't care. We have another radio channel, and that's all that matters."[33] Julián Pérez was born in La Mancha, far from *Euskadi*, and was studying *euskera*. He wanted to become an euskaldun-berri, but he would always be Manchego—yet he was no less a Basque nationalist, as he told me, because of his love of the land.

In the zone of conflict where electronic and political regions converge, the political region sets decisive limits on the scale and use of electronic regions, yet not always in ways plotted by political intention. The political region is created by law, through constitutional and statutory order. Regional political authority is established to protect investments, the built environment, and cultural institutions within its territorial purview—this includes electronic media. An infringement on this legal authority can constitute the basis of political conflict, interregional rivalry, and negotiated exchanges. According to the law, regional broadcasters cannot establish relays outside of their borders. That is the logic of the political region. To do otherwise would constitute an infringement.

The signals of the electronic regions of Spain, however, trespass the borders of the political region, legal restrictions notwithstanding. Basically, there are three causes of this trespass. First, electromagnetic waves, by their nature, spill over borders—nowhere on this planet can radio signals be expected to stay within boundaries of political regions (but let us not anthropomorphize the signal: people exploit the possibility of technology, not the other way around). Second, felt alliances of viewers do not necessarily correspond to borders; regional sentiment anchored to same-language programming, for instance, might not share a political region. And finally, the commercial imperative of broadcasting seeks to maximize audience size; rarely does this inherent expansionism retreat from spatial containments of politics, sentiment, or technology.[34]

The first kind of trespass among political regions comes from radiowave spillover. Basque TV technicians report that beyond the three provinces of official *Euskadi*, signal coverage reaches north to the three provinces of the French Basque Country, that is, from Hendaya to Bayonne, Saint Palais, and Mauleon. It reaches south to Burgos (Castile-Leon), Logroño (La Rioja), and parts of La Ribera del Ebro in the south of Navarra; east into Navarra as far as Pamplona; and west to Santander (Cantabria). With this territorial claim, the engineers are able to reassert the medieval boundaries of *Euskal Herria*. Power amplification of the signal expands this electronic region, and its trespass becomes a kind of technological fetish standing in for the impossible object of the national fantasy, *Euskal Herria*. "Welcome to *Euskal Telebista*," hails the EITB brochure, "the youngest TV for the oldest country in Europe." Containment of this signal coverage is next to impossible, though no guarantee of broadcast quality exists beyond the ring of relays on the borders of official *Euskadi*. There have been reports, however, of signal jamming in the western reaches of Navarra, which has an old rivalry with its Basque cousins to the west.[35]

The second form of trespass across political boundaries, the transgression of the electronic region created by the felt alliance of user groups, has not been an important force in and around the Basque Country. Language seems to be the decisive motivation for such alliances outside the political region. Recall, however, that there is not a significant presence of *euskaldun,* that territory has been more decisive in the Basque national fantasy. This paradox has shadowed the nationalist desire from the time of Sabino de Arana's linguistic engineering to the present work of EITB's engineers.

Nevertheless, to clarify how felt alliances might encourage trespass, compare the cases of Galician TV and Catalan TV. Signals of TVG, Galician television, reach into northern Portugal and east into parts of Asturias and the provinces of Leon and Palencia (Castile-Leon). The border crossing into Portugal was caused by Portuguese user groups who put in the relays to get the signal of TVG. In the case of TV-3, the Catalan channel, a relatively significant number of viewers throughout southern Valencia and the north of Murcia were getting the signal beyond the "natural" electronic region (i.e., southern France, eastern Aragón, northern Valencia, and the Baleares Islands). In Valencia, as in the Portuguese example, the relays were set up by independent cultural groups who, in Valencia's case, desired Catalan language programming (Valencian and Catalan are linguistic cousins as are Galician and Portuguese). In both these cases, the electronic region was widened beyond the reach of the political region in order to fit a language zone of viewers.[36]

Nothing like this happened to Basque television. Language may have identified the race in nationalist jargon, but lack of significant numbers of *euskaldun* limited this identification on the reception side of nationalist technology. People who watched TV tended to watch more of the state television. Then as if to reiterate the old nationalist conundrum that confronted Sabino de Arana, administrators of Basque television started a second channel in Castilian.[37] A territory of Basques, more than a language of Basques, identified the electronic nation. Once again, *erdaldun* and *euskaldun* got merged into one identity; this time, however, they were crossbred as an *audience* in the electronic region. Thus an imperative to produce an *audience* from the electronic matrix reinterpreted and refetishized the territorial imperative once expressed by the nationalist desire to produce *Euskadi* from the vernacular matrix of *Euskal Herria.*[38]

The third trespass of political regions is the hardest to contain or control with political power. Commercial imperatives of communication require border crossings—it is an inherent, or (as Marx noted) extraordinary necessity of exchange. Of course, the most convenient way of expanding the commercial interpretation of trespass as exchange, and the rarest, is that furnished by user groups (in the jargon of the liberal communications model, this might be fancied as "consumer sovereignty"). Without user groups outside the political regions, however, there are few options for increasing the scale of viewership. One option has been to amplify the power of transmissions, which anyway seems to be the rule defining the nationalist play of trespass and containment among the regions (although figures for spillover reception are negligible). Another option was the multiplication of audience volume, which was achieved one way by starting second channels, especially the Castilian language channel in the Basque Country, which tripled the audience for Basque TV (to a little over 16 percent of official *Euskadi*'s population in 1990).

A third option has been production/organization innovations, such as the federation of regional companies initiated in meetings in the fall of 1988. The directors of seven regional "autonomous" systems agreed to merge into a national federation creating a network of public broadcasters to rival the national state's RTVE. The Federation of Autonomous Radio and Television Organizations (FORTA) enables them to pool resources for program purchases and coproductions. And as a de facto network linking diverse regional audiences, FORTA also exploits a unitary structure for advertising sales and contracts.[39] The objective rationale for FORTA is clear. Although programming strategies or signal spillover might be appealed to for increasing audience ratings, a basic spatial barrier to regional TV economies exists, namely, the political region. A federation helps overcome this barrier through transregional exchange aimed to defend the interests and investments of regional broadcasters stuck behind a political barrier.

In the porous heart of this electronic regionalization are conflicting interpretations of the value of the *audience*. For obvious reasons, when RTVE was the only television broadcaster, the private media promoters, regional broadcasters, advertisers, and their agencies understood the state's hold over the airwaves as a monopoly over audience attention—a monopoly with economic and political value.

When this (misnamed) monopoly was dismantled and confronted with pressures of decentralization, a battle over viewer attention commenced. In this "war of audiences," as it was called, TV broadcasters began to zero in on ways to sell more viewer attention to advertisers.[40] The state broadcast authorities reacted by pirating regional television's claim over regional audiences, offering their own brand of regional markets to advertisers. One year later, investment in TV advertising increased 156 percent, followed in consecutive years by jumps of 239 percent and 53 percent. (Compare average yearly global advertising billings of 10 percent.)[41] Impressed with this regionalized media market, the U.S. trade press called Spanish TV "Europe's sleeping giant." Spanish TV looked like a post–mass market fantasy of business as usual, an efficient way to communicate with culturally diverse consumers.[42]

A market interpretation of TV audiences valorizes attention paid to the commercial messages of advertisers. In market terms, the sale is always local. A desirable communication system from a market standpoint, therefore, positions advertisers equidistantly to a multiplicity of distinct sentiments and tastes among key customers.[43] From this institutional perspective, a regionalized television audience makes localization easier and transcends the limits of a mass market logic that elides difference. As Basque TV fantasized about a regionalized audience in a nationalist image, both state and private firms pressed with a counter-fantasy of regional audiences—of maximum commoditized attention within and across local markets.

To reiterate: the defense of investments in the political region constituted the material basis for the localization of audiences; at the same time it has led to the factional struggle over the interpretation of the value of audience attention. In this struggle, the values of maximization and exchange elided the value ascribed to *Euskal Herria* by the nationalist fantasy. One explanation for this is that difference is important in the commercial game of trespass, whereas sameness matters most in the nationalist game. In other words, maximization plus localization of audience volume favors transregional competitors, whereas purely localized audiences of regional TV end up supplying grist to transregional competition. This interpretation of audiences appears to disfavor broadcasters where the political limits to transregional electronic space are rigid. Put simply, for the regional firm, official political limits restrict audience volume to their politi-

cal region; for national firms, volume can expand to include all political regions in Spain; and for transnational firms, the sky seems to be
the only limit. Each expanded scale of audience space represents a
market closed off to some participants at a smaller, politically defined, spatial scale. Capital investors can participate at all spatial
scales and thereby duplicate their efforts to expand audience attention at their disposal—that is, holders of money-capital (e.g., banks
and private investors) can be local, national, and transnational all at
once—given lax trade and foreign investment protection, and the
fungibility of the currency in use.

Consider the premise that if an audience is not produced under
the commercial interpretation for a firm located in a political region
(say, for instance, in the Basque Country), then it is possible in a
transregional economy that it can be produced for a firm located
outside that region (say, for instance, a national network head-
quartered in Madrid). In theory, when this occurs, then it becomes
feasible for the advertising value ascribed to a regional audience to
be realized outside that audience's home region. In this scenario, a
regionalized audience does not necessarily contribute income to the
regional firm. Obviously, again, the nationwide broadcasts (public
and private) are the primary beneficiaries of the transregional system
in Spain. The Basques, to use the same example, are thus constrained
by the institutional logic of the political region, whereas private TV
and RTVE are less so.

At the national scale, then, an open *transregional* economy favors
the commercial interpretation of the audience. Restricted participation to a subnational scale would not only disfavor this interpretation
but would also allow for greater competition among more numerous
interpretations of the value of audiences. Although this last point
runs counter to the Basque case, not to mention the factual world of
deregulation, there is a residual presence of contending interpretations of the audience retained by the discourse of localization.[44]

Nevertheless, the rather simple point made here is that the desire
to capture transregional audiences is favored at the national scale
and thus favors institutions operating transregionally. Whereas the
desire to redeem the distinctly interpreted national identity (and irredenta) of a nation is not favored at the transregional scale, and so
neither are regionally confined institutions. The numbers bear this
out.[45] At the end of 1991, RTVE's two TV channels continued down-

ward but still topped the ratings with over 55 percent of the total national audience. Private broadcasters (all with controlling interests held by foreign investors and national banks) together came in a distant second (but still rising) at around 27 percent. Broadcasters in the regional federation were holding averages of about 15 percent throughout the national electronic space.[46] At the regional scale, the numbers reflect more clearly how transregional competition over audiences tends to disfavor regional firms.[47] In this politico-economic framework, it is clear that a regionalized audience does not necessarily offer a better money value to a regional firm, at least as long as there are transregional participants operating in the same electronic space and under the same commercial pressures. But who said the Basques were in it for the money?

In mid-year of 1992, the regional firms together registered a deficit of $2 billion, quadruple the figure of 1991.[48] Given the political and cultural importance of TV to the regional governments, financial problems are especially influential. In June of 1993, Euskal Telebista and Radio Televisión Española entered into a cooperation agreement as a result of these money pressures. That these two bitter rivals should come to a truce raises the specter of economic causes. The deal is designed to eliminate the duplication of resources, encourage joint production, share transmission rights (especially sports), and exchange information.[49] Ten years ago when Euskal Telebista was being created, many Basque politicians treated Spain as an external state, an imperial ruler. Rather than turn to that state for help, the Basques looked to Germany for expertise to create their new TV system.[50] For a decade, the tensions between RTVE and ETB persisted, reflecting historic conflicts between centralism and regionalism. The cooperation agreement of 1993 is perhaps a small sign that this conflict has lost some of its defining force. But if finance is superordinate, where does this leave regional TV?

Regional finance on the whole depends on resources from the central government. With the exception of the Basque Country and Navarra, which retain the right to collect taxes within their regions, all the remaining regions receive a percentage of public monies that reflect their contributions to the national tax base. Two state programs exist that are designed to redistribute a portion of this public funding to less developed regions to adjust for the inherent inequalities of the national tax base.[51] However, the redistributive aims of these projects have not been fulfilled, and some changes have been made to entitle only the poorest regions to these benefits. Nonetheless, the regions have a high degree of discretionary power, and are basically "free to dispose of more than 80 percent of their [tax] revenues as they wish."[52]

Given the spatial hierarchy of the tax base, the inadequacy of the redistributive programs, and the persistent economic geography of Spain, the poorest regions have accumulated the highest debt percentage of the regional gross debt per person. In other words, regional governments are better able to protect their investments in their political region if they are located within the core region of capital accumulation in Spain. More precisely, this means that Catalonia, Madrid, and Navarra (the last situated between the European Community and the rich Ebro River valley) are particularly well positioned to keep public projects from collapsing. Although the strength of the Basque economy once rested on industrial sectors that were very prominent during the "economic miracle" of the 1960s, these same sectors were hit hardest by the oil shocks of the 1970s (e.g., steel and shipbuilding). As a result, the northern Basque provinces, especially in the zone of Bilbao, fell back in their overall contribution to the national economy, while employment sunk, and general social well-being declined.[53]

Two outcomes affecting the regional TV industry can be noted. One is that capital flows continue to concentrate in Catalonia and Madrid.[54] For the public TV industry generally, this means that human and technical resources are anchored to the same old places. Madrid and Barcelona retain a privileged place in this industry. Their position within this infranational hierarchy helps offset the inherent spatial bias, discussed earlier, which favors broadcasters operating at the national scale. Thus in spite of the general decline throughout the public system, the Catalans have been bringing in between 60 and 100 percent of their budget in advertising revenues. Basques cannot make the same boast, as self-financing has barely reached 25 percent of the budget for Euskal Telebista. Julián Pérez of EITB put it simply: "The Catalans have been much more serious about making money than we have."[55]

The other outcome of the financial bust concerns the collapse of the national independent video and film production industry. Towns and villages throughout Vasconia typically had only one of two channels to choose from in 1982. By 1988, they had four. And by 1990 they could choose up to six or seven when the addition of private channels doubled the number of programming hours to nearly 60,000 a year. This multiplication of channels generally enhanced Spanish TV culture, to be sure, but at the same time it outpaced the production capacity of the Spanish TV economy. As it turned out, broadcasters could not fill the amplified schedule with independent or in-house (i.e., Spanish) productions. Without exception, all TV firms in Spain today depend on foreign production to meet demand. A negative consequence of this situation was the decline and bottoming out of production orders for independent film and video work, with most money going to cover reduced in-house production and increased foreign purchases or licensing. Indigenous production in Spain suffered from what has become known as the "European paradox of more television hours, but less work."[56]

In 1990, ETB-1 imported up to 39 percent of its programs, and ETB-2, the Castilian-language channel of *Euskadi,* 49 percent (i.e., imports from outside Spain).[57] So-called fictional programming— films, series, soaps, and telenovellas—takes up the majority of both broadcast time and the number of imports on all channels. In contrast, "entertainment, sports, and children's shows" hold the greatest share of in-house production. Entertainment programs like game shows and variety shows constitute the second most important category after fiction on all production schedules, followed by sports.[58] Dubbing has obviously been a minor (negligible) growth industry in *Euskadi.* But with the two channels of Euskal Telebista together attracting averages of only 15 percent to 16 percent of Basques, *euskera* continues to resist revival.[59]

Finally, transregional finance has been revealed as also always a transnational affair in the Spanish TV industry. "Our reference is not just Spain, it's Europe," said Francisco Virseda, director of social communication in Spain under the presidency. "It's logical that Berlusconi—and I believe that it is good—enters the Spanish market through the autonomous TV systems."[60] Virseda was referring to the advertising and program purchasing deals that the Italian media promoter made with the Catalans, Basques, and Galicians. The Catalans gained license to 180 episodes of *Dallas,* for which Berlusconi at that time owned the sole European rights. In Galicia and the Basque

Country, Berlusconi's advertising sales agency, Publitalia, became the international sales representative for TVG and ETB. Prior to the legalization of private channels, the regional systems were the most attractive entry point for investments like Berlusconi's (because to enter from the local grassroots offered him a way to achieve national dominance, as it had for him in Italy). FORTA would come to inherit this relation with Berlusconi, who eventually gained control of the private Spanish TV company Telecinco. Other than the state, who is left to step forward with the loans, hard cash investments, or partnerships if not those who already control private television businesses?

The nationalist desire transposed onto a commercial interpretation of audience value undergoes another transformation in the electronic space described here. The form it assumes in the electronic matrix cannot make claims of the sovereign—the economic borders are too porous, the political borders too weak, the electronic transgressions too numerous, the linguistic community too small. Moreover, this space sits in an inconstant geography of capitalism, where investment imperatives do not tend to value a place-immobilized public good unless, of course, such investment is a condition of capital mobility. Money engineers its own borders and alliances; it even seems to control the domain of technologies of national desire. In the Basque example, the threads of this desire interweave *euskaldun*, *Euskal Herria*, *Euskadi*, and Euskal Irrati Telebista—in other words, national desire is constituted by and constitutive of language, presence, politicized territory, and (linking these) an electronic communication network. However, like a cat with a ball of yarn, money value unravels this object of national desire; money dissolves Euskal Irrati Telebista and in doing so reinterprets and refetishizes *Euskal Herria*. Alas, a (rather globalized) money fetish stands in as a superordinate technology of national desire in the transregional electronic space.

It is this kind of *post*modern, *post*national interpretation of identity that has framed the emerging European television economy.[61] Three hundred sixty million consumers are hailed by claims of a unitary European identity and dozens of counterclaims for national identity and even more claims for a mosaic of contingent identities and disturbances. My own research has tended to focus on the manner in which the commercial interpretation of regionalized, or nationalized, or postmodernized audiences has come to dominate the

European electronic space of identity. It does not come to be this way by any "natural" course of events, however. In the specific case of the Basque Country of Spain, the nationalist desire mitigates the control of commercial interpretations. *Euskal Herria* actively remains the impossible object of *Euskadi*—and I suppose if the nationalist desire persists in action, then a time will come for that nation. Nevertheless, the problem has rested in the territorial definition of this nation, of this nationality. Whether its Sabino de Arana engineering a place-name, or Basque TV engineers rigging up an amplified relay system, the reach of the national technology relies on a desire to make territory a characteristic quality of a people whose linguistic presence in the world, or memory of it, used to be enough. It is possible for Euskal Irrati Telebista to retain the valorization of the vernacular matrix, even if the recipe is reduced to one part poetry and one part banality of a lingua franca. But in transferring this value onto territory, however, an *audience*—maximized and localized in commercial desire—displaces the *euskaldun* in the same manner that *Euskadi* once displaced *Euskal Herria*. The problem for the national culture is that this *audience* belongs to a discourse generated by a commercial interpretation that values attention as property, territory as markets, and money as communication. In the present struggle to own an *audience* for themselves, then, Basque nationalists are encouraged to dream of communication in a market imaginary, to dream, that is, without a nation.

In extending the metaphor of the nation as "an imagined political community"—as Benedict Anderson and others, including myself, have done—we are recognizing that some "thing," albeit as intangible and abstract as a community, is there for the imagining. Anderson prefers, with what he calls "the anthropological spirit," to interpret what is there as a cultural system that inhabits our "modes of apprehending the world, which, more than anything else, made it possible to think the 'nation.'"[62] Others, such as Miroslav Hroch, prefer a more strictly materialist interpretation of national consciousness in which what is there to be conscious of must be identified as a fundamental reality.[63] Hroch demonstrates, however, that national consciousness does not necessarily arise out of historically typical conditions (e.g., Wales did not, though according to archetypal experiences of nation building should have, emerge as a fully formed nation in the late nineteenth century); nor, he adds, is national consciousness necessarily awakened by a "spirit of the nation" or "will of a Subject."[64] For critical historians the problem has been one of explaining the combination of relations that made national existence more than a possibility, that made nations (like *Euskadi*) both "emotionally plausible and politically viable," as Anderson puts it.[65] In other words, and disregarding the arguments of narcissistic nationalist intellectuals, the problem is explaining how a group of people, sufficiently large to constitute a mass movement, recognize themselves as identical with a nation. As a starting point for understanding this national imaginary, Anderson, Hroch, and others suggest that an extensive, and extendable, realm of collective action must already have made routine such an identity with the imagined community.[66]

It is well known that Anderson placed communication among the realms of collective action that helped solidify national consciousness in the capitalist epoch; that is, following Hegel, he saw print providing a routinized communion of national readerships. Without printing technology, the optical illusion that fixed particular vernaculars in time and space and to power would not have been available to national consciousness. But print is a capitalist business, as Anderson points out early in his book, and as such "felt all of capitalism's restless search for markets."[67] Thus a kind of print-international developed in Europe that saturated literate (Latin) markets and redoubled its efforts by adapting first to a few diverse official vernaculars within the anciens régimes.[68] Unfortunately, Anderson shifts to a modular elaboration of this aspect of the nationalizing process and consequently splits off the nationalizing effect of the print technology from the capitalist structure in which it arose and to which it has been tied ever since. We are left to fend for ourselves if we want to understand more about the tension inherent in a technology that at once invites communicative action to be national while its owners are searching for ways to make it international. Anderson takes us brilliantly through the events and the issues—with seven-league boots as Fernand Braudel would say—that mark out the cultural transformations giving historical force to national identity. In the process, however, Anderson steps over much of the history of mass media, their ties to state power and capital, and the role of mass media in extending collective consciousness. This is unfortunate, for there are very few comparative studies of the nation and national identity that have sustained the link between capitalism and communication long enough to explain, beyond the social effects of Gutenberg technology, the development of the three interplayed elements stressed by Anderson (fatality of linguistic diversity, capitalism, and print technology).

Obviously, with radio and then television, the limitation imposed by literacy upon the diffusion of national imaginaries was significantly reduced. At the same time, however, the technology made the communicative barriers of territorial states much more porous. Thus the "language" of sounds and images, with its conventionalized assembly and diffusion, signaled changes in the communicative practices within and among national cultures. Like print, electronic communication is a technology with the potential to have an international presence and to involve its users in a temporal simultaneity of knowing the world. Yet unlike the story of print's nationalizing effects, electronic communication fell within the borders of particular national cultures because early scientific and technical knowledge limited the exploitation of its primary medium of diffusion, the electromagnetic spectrum. This scarcity of resource combined with both the capital-intensiveness and strategic uses of radiowave technology to confer upon national states decisive control over its use and expansion. The scarcity of spectrum would, of course, eventually become over the years less of a factor in keeping radio and television tied to state regulatory institutions. And though strategic-military uses of the spectrum expanded, the remaining, highly capitalized broadcast industry underwent a series of commercial ownership concentrations that resulted globally in regional monopolies and in a consolidation of a homogeneous market of audiovisual "goods." Nevertheless, a nationalist ethos pervaded much of the "public service" rhetoric that developed to defend the new media against the (eventually successful) commercial takeover of the national industries. Thus, as this technology manifested "all of capitalism's restless search for markets"— rapidly in some countries (e.g., the United States) but taking decades in others (e.g., in Europe)—the national interpretation of its value collided with that of capitalist valorizations.

It is in the context of these theoretical and structural problems that I want to summarize my arguments. The tensions between the ruling nation of Spain and the small nation of *Euskadi* permeated the techniques that regional political and intellectual elites mobilized to extend a national imaginary. For instance, the invention of the word *Euskadi* fixed in space an imagined political community— against but modeled on the ruling nation—that integrated populations of *euskaldun* and *erdaldun,* giving a new permanence to the desired object of *Euskal Herria.*[69] Using Euskal Irrati Telebista as a more recent, though no less modern, example, I argued that the electronic technology of communication refetishized *Euskal Herria* to produce a national imaginary for Basques in the post-Franco period. The analysis is, admittedly, focused on a top-down interpellation of Basque national identity and does not presume to explain the felt attachments of people in Vasconia with the national imaginary of *Euskal Herria.*[70] However, the focus on television as a commercial industry/technology retained a perspective on electronic communication that kept track of its capitalistic origins and imperatives. Such a perspective necessarily led this essay to a confrontation between transnational and national imaginaries; that is, to put it slightly differently, the contradiction in communication technology (indirectly posed by Anderson as a nationalizing/globalizing tendency) provided an analytical fulcrum for understanding the links between commercial electronic communication and national identity.

I have suggested that fiscal crises, transregional competition, and transnational capital combine to unravel the national fantasy of Euskal Irrati Telebista. Contradictory collective imaginaries can, in theory, be produced from this collision of institutional actions and desires. I focused on one such confrontation in terms of a contest between the regionalist desire to localize/nationalize TV viewer attention and the capitalist valorization of viewer attention as a commodity. The commodification of audiences is a transregional, and ultimately transnational, impulse of commercial television. In the Basque Country, as indeed throughout most market economies, the repertoire of symbols of national identity has been raided by commercial interests to sell goods and services. In Spain, this first took the form of regionalized audiences for advertisers produced by national-state TV, which proved to investors that selling difference can make a positive difference (at least within their version of margins). This exogenous regionalization undermined the self-financing of the regional TV industry, yet paradoxically made the project of producing national identity part of a transregional and transnational interpretation of an audience's value. Localization for global marketers is about making the sale local. And what we have seen is that the technology of electronic communication—fitted though it is to produce a national imaginary—sits Janus-faced within this nexus of global localization.

Anderson noted that one of the paradoxes that perplexes and irritates theorists of nationalism is that nationality is characterized at once by its "formal universality" and by the "irremediable particularity of its concrete manifestations."[71] If my analysis is correct, the merchants of commercial culture have found a business opportunity in this paradox by using electronic communication to absorb the "irremediable particularity" of a national imaginary into a parallel though imperious interpretation of its "formal universality" in the audience commodity. This transnational image market privileges the coordinating power of money, which, in relation to Basque radio-television, further encouraged the commercial valorization of the national imaginary. Nevertheless, although capitalist media owners and promoters intend, and mostly succeed, in imposing their own imperious coordination of cultural industries across the globe, it appears that a volatile torque of the national imaginary and the transnational market imaginary twists together competing interpretations over the value of electronic communication in the Basque Country. And whatever cultural system is "there" guiding the procedures for apprehending the world, the possibility of "thinking the nation" in the Basque Country is thoroughly wrapped up in supranational routines of collective thought and action (read Spain and "Europe" as providing the conditions for this). Finally, we can imagine that as social and economic crises worsen in *Euskal Herria,* collective identification with the nation will perhaps aid in administering collective succor; then again, the appeal to the "European Community" (via Spain) will perhaps attract a more decisive mass movement. In moments of such collective trauma, the role of the media will be decided. As it is, electronic communication for *Euskadi* is forced to become a rather promiscuous technology in order to survive, with loyalties to the nation only somewhat more predictable than a Basque banker's.

352 · RICHARD MAXWELL

NOTES

1. Pierre Vilar, *Spain: A Brief History* (Oxford: Pergamon Press, 1967); Robert P. Clark, *The Basques: The Franco Years and Beyond* (Reno: University of Nevada Press, 1979); Koldo Mitxelena, *La Lengua Vasca* (Durango [Vizcaya]: Leopoldo Zugaza, Editor, 1977).

2. Koldo Mitxelena, *La Lengua Vasca*, pp. 23-25, 51-52.

3. Robert P. Clark, *The Basques*, pp.131-35.

4. Eric J. Hobsbawm, *Nations and Nationalism since 1780: Programme, Myth, Reality*, 2d ed. (Cambridge: Cambridge University Press, 1992).

5. Fernand Braudel, *Civilization and Capitalism, 15th-18th Century: The Perspective of the World*, vol. 3, trans. Sian Reynolds (New York: Harper and Row, 1986), p. 288.

6. J. Nadal, *El Fracaso de la Revolución Industrial en España, 1814-1913*, 2d ed. (Barcelona: Editorial Ariel, 1977); J. Vicens Vives, *An Economic History of Spain* (Princeton: Princeton University Press, 1969).

7. Nevertheless, the northern industrial zones grew as European capitalism developed, while the south became a reservoir for additional capital for the north—siphoned out of agriculture through a process of northward labor migration combined with undervaluation of southern products. Ernest Mandel, "Capitalism and Regional Disparities," *Southeast Economy and Society* 1, no. 1 (1976) pp. 41-47; J. Naylon, *Andalusia*, Problem Regions of Europe series, D. I. Scargill, ed. (Oxford: Oxford University Press, 1975); Costis Hadjimichalis, *Uneven Development and Regionalism: State, Territory and Class in Southern Europe* (London: Croom Helm, 1987); Salvador Giner, "Political Economy, Legitimation and the State in Southern Europe," in R. Hudson and J. Lewis, eds., *Uneven Development in Southern Europe: Studies in Accumulation, Class, Migration and the State* (London: Methuen, 1985); and J. Nadal, *El Fracaso*.

8. Euskera lacked more than a linguistic familiarity with romance languages, however. There was no national grammar at the time that provided rules and unity for the multiple dialects. Written texts were largely confined to arcane religious translations, and the oral diffusion of euskera ran into as many barriers as there were villages. Apparently it still happens that two euskaldun from distinct zones meet each other and believe the other is speaking in some garbled code only to discover after a short time that they share the idiom. See Koldo Mitxelena, *La Lengua Vasca*, pp. 47-48.

9. Robert P. Clark, *The Basques*, pp. 34-40.

10. J. Hooper, *The Spaniards: A Portrait of the New Spain* (London: Penguin, 1987), pp. 216-18.

11. Ibid., pp. 225-26. In 1910, seven years after Sabino de Arana's

death, his followers founded the conservative Basque Nationalist Party (PNV), which nevertheless traces its origins to 1895.

12. Ien Ang, *Desperately Seeking the Audience* (London: Routledge, 1991).

13. This and related points are drawn from my book, *The Spectacle of Democracy: Spanish Television, Nationalism, and Political Transition* (Minneapolis: University of Minnesota Press, 1995).

14. Basque government estimates for 1986 put the figure for total non-Euskara speakers at 64 percent; of the remainder who understand Euskara, only 21 percent claimed to speak it. The total of nonspeakers of Basque varied among the provinces: Alava, 87 percent; Vizcaya, 73 percent; Guipuzcoa, 42 percent. Anuario Estadístico del Pais Vasco, Gobierno Vasco 1986.

15. Article 45, Law 5/1982, May 20.

16. Koldo Mitxelena, *La Lengua Vasca*, pp. 84-85.

17. Justino Sinova, *La Gran Mentira* (Madrid: Planeta, 1983), p. 30, emphasis in the original.

18. E. López Escobar and A. Faus-Belau, "Broadcasting in Spain: A History of Heavy-handed State Control," in R. Kuhn, ed., *Broadcasting and Politics in Western Europe* (London: Frank Cass & Co., 1985), p. 122.

19. Ibid., p. 124, emphasis in the original.

20. Lluis Bassets, ed., *De las Ondas Rojas a las Radios Libres* (Barcelona: Editorial Gustavo Gili, 1981), p. 266.

21. See Hooper, *The Spaniards*, pp. 204-51, for a general perspective on this period.

22. Alberto Díaz Mancisidor, *Historia de radio Bilbao: antecedentes y primeros años.* (Bilbao: Banco de Bilbao, 1983), pp. 75-93.

23. Article 18, Press Law of 22 April 1938, quoted in Henry F. Schulte, *The Spanish Press 1470-1966: Print, Power, Politics* (Urbana: University of Illinois Press, 1968), pp. 13-14.

24. Radio liberalizations had taken place in the 1960s, followed by further licensing to commercial stations in the late 1970s. However, the actions of the Basques and Catalans were to have more far-reaching consequences than the central government's radio reform.

25. Rather than abide by the letter of the Third Channel Law, which established the norm of one network within each autonomous region, the authorities in these three regions built independent networks that function, in their words, "alegally." The result is that the Basques and Catalans operate two channels but argue, along with the Galician parliament, which operates only one channel, that these are independent of existing law. Thus they maintain that they are still guaranteed one additional channel within the framework of the Third Channel Law. On a smaller scale, a similar battle developed over local, village-level television, which passed from a situation

characterized by "a-legal" broadcasts to one regulated by a posteriori legislation to normalize spectrum use and state regulation. Transmission for which there is no explicit law is considered alegal, rather than illegal, unregulated, or pirated. See also Clemencia Rodriguez, "Media for Participation and Social Change: Local Television in Catalonia," *Com Dev News,* fall 1990/winter 1991.

26. In the Basque Country, the recuperation of the historic fiscal privileges under the *Fueros*—the *concierto económico* as it is called—provided the right to collect all taxes within their territory (except custom duties and receipts of state-controlled businesses) and to make a lump sum payment to the central government for national services.

27. This is main difference of article 151, as the provisions related to articles 143 and 148 left education, police, and mass communication to the central state. Article 143 with exact provisions provided in article 148 of the Spanish constitution furnished what was known as the slow route to autonomy. Devolution under this article limited, during an initial five-year period, Statutes of Autonomy to administrative and legislative powers in the areas of "regional interest" such as local government, housing, small roads and rail, noncommercial ports and airport, forestry, and so on. Against these provisions for regional autonomy, the central state retained control of foreign affairs, constitutional enforcement, defense, industrial relations, and monetary policy. Ramón Tamames and T. Clegg, "Spain: Regional Autonomy and the Democratic Transition," in *Regionalization in France, Italy and Spain* (London: London School of Economics, International Centre for Economics and Related Disciplines, 1984), pp. 38-43.

28. Ibid., p. 40. This was included along with control over interregional flows of railway, roads, telecommunication, and post.

29. Ibid., p. 41.

30. Efforts were in fact made to act out this sovereignty over spectrum allocations, as the Basques and Catalans applied for independent status within the European Broadcasting Union (EBU).

31. Pasqual Menendez, phone interview by author. Madrid, July 11, 1988.

32. Interview by author with Julián Pérez Delgado, Managing Director of Basque Radio and Television. Durango, Vizcaya, August 4, 1988.

33. Interview with Julián Pérez Delgado, Managing Director of Basque Radio and Television. Durango, Vizcaya, August 4, 1988. The insistent ring disrupted the interview briefly but significantly.

34. Recall also the tension between centralism and regionalism, which can give rise to electronic trespass of political regions. In the discussion earlier, the central state was seen as trespassing beyond the statutory limits of its power. Centralism motivated a trespass in electromagnetic policy, region-

alism its containment through ungovernability. In this regard, I think it goes without saying that the values of containment and trespass can dress up whichever sovereign one wants to privilege. Again, in general, it is the play of trespass and containment that has defined the electronic turf wars over television in Spain.

35. Technical information provided by engineering staff at *Euskal Telebista,* to Julián Pérez, who provided me with access to it. Details for Galicia provided by Antonio Posse Peña, Director of Engineering for TVG, interview, August 3, 1988. Details for Catalonia provided by Lluís F. Grau i Bruni, Production and Transmission Engineer for TV-3; interview with Grau conducted July 26, 1988. Further information provided by Jaume Pérez i Santos, Director of Administration for TV-3; interview July 26, 1988.

36. The claim to a "right to antenna," as it was called in Spain, was not a good enough principle to keep these relays working. Containment of the electronic region, which had been extended to fit a language zone of viewers in Valencia, fell back into the hands of official politics. Under these circumstances, in the region of political and electronic conflicts, politics proved to be more decisive than viewer choice. Containment of TV-3's signal became the basis for a political trade-off between the Catalan government and central government. The story is that the conservative nationalist Catalan party, *Convergència i Unió* (CiU), bargained with the central government to let the Catalan radio-TV corporation have a second channel in exchange for the containment of TV-3 in Valencia. The Catalan government was said to have cooperated to garner political capital. Whatever the case, the result was that the control over interconnections in the Valencian Community was returned to the regional authorities and to Valencian television. The "alegal" system of relays was thereafter legalized within the framework of the Third Channel Law. Within a month of each other, the Catalan second channel and the Valencian channel began broadcasting. By 1990, the number of Valencian TV households still reporting regular viewing of TV-3 was about 3 percent, which was triple the next highest figure in any region for audiences of spillover TV.

37. In May 1986, Basque television set up their second channel, ETB-2, as a broadcast service in the Castilian language. ETB-2 was meant to attract a very significant portion of the regional population that did not speak Basque. See note 14.

38. This may overstate the presence of TV and radio in the Basque Country. As Juan Linz discovered in his analysis of the feelings of people (importantly) both outside and in *Euskadi,* territory more than any other variable lay at the heart of the general self-definition of Basqueness. The symbolism of Euskal Irrati Telebista, however, may in fact draw on this kind of sentiment, that is, its *thereness* matters more than how it speaks or if any-

body is watching or listening. See J. Linz, "From Primordialism to National-ism," in Edward A. Tiryakin and Ronald Rogowski, eds., *New Nation-alisms of the Developed West: Toward Explanation* (Boston: Allen and Unwin, 1985), pp. 203-53.

39. A committee meets once a month to decide on the program pur-chases to be made, and on who will participate in the deal. One of the buy-ers of one of the firms makes the acquisition and signs contracts that include licensing for the rest, who pay that firm their part of the purchase price once the deal is made. Dubbing is then done by local firms. In 1991, about 80 percent of acquisitions were shared by all FORTA firms, 10 percent by only some, and 10 percent was bought on an individual basis. Susan Eardley, "Spain: Increased Competition at Home is Forcing Broadcasters to Rethink Their International Strategy," *Broadcast*, April 19, 1991, p. 25.

40. David Nogueira, "Unrelated Diversity," *The Business of Film*, Janu-ary/February 1991, p. 9.

41. Total TV advertising in Spain was miniscule in comparison to global advertising revenues (less than 1 percent of the estimated 252 billion dollars of global ad trade in 1989). *Europe 2000*, July 1, 1991. Enrique Bustamante and Ramon Zallo, coordinators, *Las Industrias Culturales en España: Gru-pos Multimedia y transnacionales* (Madrid, Akal, 1988), pp. 155-56. José María Villagrasa, "Spain: the Emergence of Commercial Television," in Alessandro Silj, ed., *The New Television in Europe* (London: John Libbey, 1992), pp. 337-426 (p. 353), points out that TV revenues alone reached 0.49 percent of GNP.

42. *View Magazine* 9, no. 10, June 6, 1988. The Dow Jones publication *American Demographics* put it this way: "You'll know it's the 21st century when . . . everyone belongs to a minority group." *American Demographics,* a publication of Dow Jones & Co. Inc., promoted its 11th annual confer-ence on consumer trends and markets with such slogans.

43. Kevin Robins, "Global Times," *Marxism Today,* December 1989, p. 21.

44. In recognition of the limits of supralocal identity mobilizers (e.g., Coke, McDonald's, Sony, etc.), media and marketing research tries to differ-entiate among local identities within maximized audiences.

45. See José María Villagrasa, "Spain: The Emergence of Commercial Television," pp. 391-92. In 1989, TVE's share of the national audience was 87.6 percent, whereas the regionals together registered 12.4 percent. In 1990, after private TV reached into half of Spain's TV households, private television moved from 8 percent to about 23 percent of the audience, while the average share for TVE dropped to 66 percent. The regionals held their own within the four-fifths of the territory they reached, with registered to-tals surpassing 18 percent in some ratings periods.

46. Ibid., p. 425.

47. In 1990, Basque viewers preferred the two channels of the national state television almost 72 percent of the time, whereas they watched ETB's channels 16.4 percent and private TV 11.6 percent of the time. Catalans, in contrast, preferred to watch private TV 41 percent of the time, their own TV-3/Canal 33 about 25 percent, and TVE channels about 43 percent. Galicians only watched private TV 7 percent of their viewing time, whereas TVG enjoyed a regular audience of almost 20 percent, with TVE's channels reaching a high of over 73 percent. By far the most avid viewers of private TV are those in the region of Madrid, who claimed that over 41 percent of their viewing time was devoted to commercial TV and only 45 percent to TVE's two channels. Ibid., p. 392.

48. International TV and Video Almanac (New York: Quigley, 1993), p. 655.

49. El Pais, June 5, 1993, p. 65.

50. Although there are conflicting reports about who turned down whom, RTVE was not involved in the design of ETB; instead the Basque government called upon Media Consult International, a subsidiary of Studio Hamburg. See John Howkins, "Basques Use TV to Speak Their Own Language," Intermedia 11, no. 3 (1983), pp. 20-25; Jill Fickling, "Spain: From Broadcast Backwater to One of the Most Exciting Markets in Europe," Broadcast, April 19, 1991, p. 4.

51. One program is the Inter-territorial Compensation Fund, a Spanish government project, the other is the European Regional Development Fund, a creation of the European Community that is administered by the central state.

52. Organization for Economic Cooperation and Development, OECD Economic Surveys, Spain, 1993 (Paris: OECD, 1993), pp. 62-66.

53. Ibid., pp. 76-77. After the boom of 1985-90, Catalonia, Madrid, and Navarre (holding 30 percent of the population) had improved their economic position relative to the rest of Spain. Meanwhile, Extremadura, Galicia, and Andalusia (with another 30 percent of the population) suffered further impoverishment. Euskadi achieved some minor revenue growth before the most recent crisis set in in 1991.

54. Moreover, the OECD estimates that between one-half and two-thirds of all foreign investment into Spain went to Madrid and Catalonia (in 1992, foreign investment accounted for 20 percent of all private investment in Spain).

55. Interview with Julián Pérez Delgado, August 4, 1988.

56. Broadcast, April 16, 1993, p. 42.

57. José María Villagrasa, "Spain: The Emergence of Commercial Television," p. 382.

58. Game shows are often based on foreign shows, however, like *El precio justo* (*The Price is Right*) or *La rueda de la fortuna* (*The Wheel of Fortune*).

59. In both the Basque Country and Catalonia, children and adolescents taught in the regional schools were more fluent—indeed, mass education more than mass media seems to be the decisive element in language acquisition. But that is another story.

60. Interview by author with Francisco Virseda Barca, Director General of Social Communication under the executive branch of the presidency, July 18, 1988.

61. See Armand Mattelart, Xavier Delacourt, Michèle Mattelart, *International Image Markets* (London: Comedia Publishers, 1984); Armand Mattelart, *Advertising International: The Privatization of Public Space*, trans. Michael Chanan (London: Comedia/Routledge, 1991); and Armand and Michèle Mattelart, *Rethinking Media Theory* (Minneapolis: University of Minnesota Press, 1992).

62. Benedict Anderson, *Imagined Communities,* rev. ed. (London: Verso, 1991), p. 22.

63. Miroslav Hroch, *Social Preconditions of National Revival in Europe* (Cambridge University Press, 1985), p. 3.

64. Ibid., pp. 4-11.

65. Benedict Anderson, *Imagined Communities*, pp. 51-52.

66. This is clear in Eric J. Hobsbawm, *Nations and Nationalism.* We might also cite L. Althusser in this context.

67. Benedict Anderson, *Imagined Communities*, p. 38.

68. Ibid., pp. 42-45.

69. The political agitation that took place in the ensuing years would illustrate some of the most decisive features of collective action that characterized this particular national movement, which became differentiated into clerical, conservative, liberal-democratic, and other variants of sociopolitical nationalism under both constitutional and authoritarian regimes. That story is important, and its obvious absence in this essay results from a lack of space and expertise.

70. Nor do I presume to explain the transnational imaginary of Europe and a European market as an effective element of identification among Basques. This unruly aspect of identity is a crucially important and miserably understudied area of research. See Phillip Schlesinger, "On National Identity: Some Conceptions and Misconceptions Criticized," *Social Science Information*, 26 (2), June 1987, pp. 219-64.

71. Benedict Anderson, *Imagined Communities*, p. 5.

VI

Gay Diasporas

Introduction to Part VI

MICHAEL J. SHAPIRO

The sexualities and sexual identities of national populations have increasingly been objects of attention ever since the "governmentalities"[1] of nation-states have manifested an intensified interest in a "calculated management of life."[2] In particular, as a scrutiny of "peripheral sexualities" erupted throughout the nineteenth and twentieth centuries and became a significant part of the management of populations, social control agents in governments and in knowledge and care-oriented agencies and disciplines produced a complex grid of differentiated sexual identities.

At the same time that they were scrutinizing their population's sexualities, nation-states were also creating complex security apparatuses. Their outward gaze on global dangers complemented their inward attention to dangers originating in the social body. Not surprisingly, therefore, the global panic resulting from the discovery of transmissable AIDS viruses intensified a border policing on the one hand and a disparaging focus on contemporary sexualities, especially homosexualities.

What Cindy Patton calls a "travelogue version" of HIV's dispersal became the primary narrrative of AIDS transmission. The already-in-place security problematics and suspicions of "peripheral sexualities" combined to provide much of the frame that has since governed attempts at containing "queer peregrinations." In addition, as Patton points out, the discourse of epidemiology, which has been the primary "scientific" interpretation summoned by professionals and bureaucrats, has encouraged a focus on "the problematic mobile body," as opposed, for example, to "unethical blood-banking practices."

Epidemiology is sustained as the dominant explanatory frame in the United States not because it is the only scientifically viable model but because it accords with a preexisting set of social and global control ideologies. Similarly, responses in other nation-states operate less out of wholly scientific frames than they do out of historically developed discourses for locating dangerous forms of alterity, for example, "the licentious West" or permissive "European liberalism."

The tracking of the movements of those with "proscribed or persecuted sexual identities," as Benigno Sánchez-Eppler puts it, emerges out of a world of ideationally driven anxieties with considerable historical depth. As in the case of inquiry into interpretations of the AIDS issue, an analysis of the trajectories of homosexuals crossing borders provides, at the same time, a mapping of the institutional sites and rationales of global homophobia and its differentiated shaping across different nationally based political cultures.

In his account of the literary career and related travels of Reinaldo Arenas, Sánchez-Eppler provides an account of the identity investments surrounding "contested sexualities" and insight into the political regulation of "gender performance and sexual regulation." Migrating sexualities, like capital, labor, and technology flows, confront differentiated forms of resistance and regulation in a way that reveals a map of global political spaces. Moreover, this map of regulation and oppression is absent from the dominant cartographies that accompany mainstream discourses of international politics.

NOTES

1. Michel Foucault, "Governmentality," in Graham Burchell, Colin Gordon, and Peter Miller, eds., *The Foucault Effect* (Chicago: University of Chicago Press, 1991), pp. 87-104.

2. Michel Foucault, *The History of Sexuality*, trans. Robert Hurley. (New York: Pantheon, 1978), p. 140.

14

Queer Peregrinations

CINDY PATTON

> Researchers believe that the virus was present in isolated population
> groups years before the epidemic began. Then the situation changed:
> people moved more often and travelled more; they settled in big
> cities; and lifestyles changed, including patterns of sexual behaviour.
> It became easier for HIV to spread, through sexual intercourse and
> contaminated blood. As the virus spread, the isolated disease already
> existing became a new epidemic.[1]

Although this account has become commonplace, closer examination reveals complex, even incompatible ideas about disease and its
translocation. Crisscrossing temporal and geographic tropes, the account vacillates between the *story* of a virus and a *description* of
bodies who might disperse it. "The virus" is first described as lodged in
a timeless and immobile *place:* grounded in an "isolated population"
until modernity stepped in to inscribe time and a mania for travel.
People move and change, carrying with them the dangerous combination of their new sexual practices and their contaminated blood.
Miraculously (inevitably?), an epidemic ensued. Modernity catapulted
the virus that had once lived peacefully among unnamed "population groups" into an epidemic of history-changing proportions.

This travelogue version of HIV's dispersion was easier to swallow
than the part of the story we did not yet know, or could not bring
ourselves to believe: that arrogant and grotesquely unethical blood-
banking practices dispersed HIV-infected blood among hemophiliacs

in France and god knows where else.[2] It was preferable to blame modern sexuality than the equally modern capital interests in medicine that fueled the epidemic in places where no one went anywhere at all. I want to suggest here that this basic "explanation" is accepted as fact because it employs widely recognizable tropes that have woven their way through two medical disciplines and framed popular narratives about disease and migration for a century. The sketchiness of the account allows for a plethora of more detailed versions of the story. The central roles are anonymous, allowing reporters and international health policy analysts to enliven their accounts with "real people." Almost *anyone* can be implicated as the problematic mobile body. A Canadian airline steward or jet-setting gay tourist, an African truck driver or the rural woman who now sells him sex on the edges of the city, a male migrant laborer who crosses national borders to feed his family, the soldier who defends his country or invades another: these are the vivid characters who bring HIV from Africa, from Haiti, from anywhere but "here."

But despite the common tactic of placing infection in the body of an Other, the U.S. media and international policy discourse define the geography of disease differently and rely on structurally different concepts of how disease moves. These differences have a great deal in common with the narrative tropes of epidemiology and of tropical medicine, which, in turn, propose different solutions to pathology. The U.S. media and epidemiology share the fantasy of eradicating AIDS, while international policy and tropical medicine hold out hope for immunity. These disease teleologies enable and promote different, conflicting, and multiple institutional strategies of control that finally have enormous if unpredictable consequences for those subject to their regimes.

This essay is one of several in a project that contemplates the incoherences between three bodies of discourse about the HIV pandemic: (1) the national U.S. discourse about its own epidemic, as observed in the U.S. media, (2) the discourse about the pandemic as a global phenomenon, as exemplified by documents from the World Health Organization and other nongovernment, transnational organizations, and (3) the imperialist Euro-American discourse about the AIDS epidemic in so-called developing countries, evident in the media and in the general outline of international research projects.[3] The U.S. national discourse about AIDS is the apotheosis of what

Michel Foucault described as the hallmark of modernist knowledge, in which the "empirico-transcendental doublet" takes itself as both the object of inquiry and the subject of knowledge.[4] The discourse of the World Health Organization and other Euro-American transnational nongovernment organizations depends on a kinder, gentler form of knowledge. Territorially divested but very much nationally interested, postcolonial positivist science extracts "local knowledge" from those who become subject to "cooperative" policies and programs developed after translation into "scientific knowledge" and retranslation into local vernacular. Finally, the discourse *about* AIDS in the developing world covertly acknowledges places outside the first world authorial center. But these places become a projective screen or laboratory for performing ideological or real (vaccine trials?) procedures that solve the master countries' internal epidemic or absolve their responsibility for the devastation occurring *outside* the collective Euro-American borders.

Although the analysis here is somewhat abstract, my concerns are not disinvested. The ongoing and excessive influence of postcolonial powers over their former or current client states coupled with the reconsolidation of systems of medical control under the sign of the AIDS call for urgent but thoughtful intervention. AIDS science, as it trickles down through policy and media, substantially informs popular interpretations of the epidemic, shaping the experience of those directly affected and forming the moral logic that determines the popular acceptability of policing in fact or through resource distribution. In addition, the narratives of scientific progress, which emphasize the coherence and additive nature of scientific research, help rationalize discriminatory policy and continued pursuit of unwarrantedly narrow research questions. In relating specific documents of the AIDS epidemic to larger, abstract medical logics and suggesting that neither research paradigms nor the various levels of policy and representation are logically coherent, I hope to indicate the relations of power that several forms of AIDS discourse secure.

PARADIGMS OR THE NONPROBLEM OF EPISTEMIC COHERENCE

The issue of scientific coherence has been widely treated by sociologists, historians, and philosophers of science. Although most interrogators agree that scientific knowledge is at least heavily mediated if not socially constructed, they differ in the accounts they give for the apparent incoherences among contemporaneous research endeavors. The most popularly known account is Thomas Kuhn's description of sequential states of science: normal science and scientific revolution.[5] But neither of these seems to account for the current state of affairs in the sciences employed in the AIDS pandemic. Indeed, despite the heavily reported disputes about the cause of AIDS and the reliability of antibody testing, medical science proceeds with a united front, denying any conflict among research paradigms.[6]

Foucault also considered the issues of change and conflict in medical ideas, but he focused on the gradual and discontinuous constitution of sciences.[7] But what to make of a situation in which the objects under constitution by discourse and the relation between discourses and their administrative regimes are in extreme flux, but have no clear direction? Neither the Kuhnian nor the Foucauldian frame offers much solace or guidance to those faced with making decisions or lodging critiques during periods of scientific uncertainty.[8] What I want to provide here is a partial account of the specific confrontations between two contemporaneous but incompatible formations that provide the logic for policy and media representation concerning the HIV pandemic.

Eve Sedgwick has suggested that it may not be unusual for more than one discourse of a deeply fundamental sort—what I will call a "core logic"—to temporally coexist, constituting some of the same objects while relating these in different ways to some but not all of the same institutions and discourses. For her, concurrent discourses are mutually inscriptive and circumscribe each other's reach. The alternate modes of describing gay oppression, for example, as history's pressure on a minority versus culture's expulsion of a universal feature of human presence are not opposite but must imply each other in order to be legible themselves.[9]

The epistemologic coherence of concern to historians of science is only a problem if theories of paradigms assume that there must be a consistent logic across the domain chosen for study. The problem of conflicting but coincident formations is to some extent an artifact of privileging their temporal appearance and duration over their perspectival and spatial differences.

Kuhn's account treats inconsistencies as local deviations with only limited capacity *over time* to challenge the primacy of a paradigm. Foucault's archaeologies treat local deviations retrospectively, not as violations of a central logic, but as early signs of an emerging discursive formation.[10] Because he is concerned with knowledge formations and with the cartography of bodies, it may be possible to work outward from Foucault's formulations about discourse to describe partial or core logics linked to identifiable administrative centers that have a triple history, or rather, two genealogies and an archaeology. The logics and the administrative centers mutate, and they may converge and detach, marking the emergence and transformation of regimes. As a microperspective on the regulation of knowledge formations described as "archives" by Foucault,[11] "core logics" are describable sets of formally related assumptions and procedures that, together with concurrent apparatuses, form objects and perform organizing functions like policy or popular representation.

Fragments of logic collide and recombine at the margin of the domain effectively governed by a core logic, but without necessarily producing a new, hybrid logic. It is in these margins that "switching" between logics occurs. Certeau—for example, referring to the basic AIDS origin myth recounted earlier—extends logic to the margins, tying fragments into the core and increasing the reach of the institutions that interpenetrate the core logics. Spatial practices—for example, cutting the sutures between constitutive elements in a story—dislink fragments, loosening them up to be recruited to an alternate logic or to drift away.[12] Policy or representation may combine or switch between two or more core logics without apparently altering the formal principles internal to logics.

If the spatial descriptions of core logics are privileged, the current AIDS policy and media representation seem less illogical than disjunct. Like a *Star Trek* journey, coexistent, conflicting formations map bodies into different dimensions, altering the rules of object formation like the Worm Hole bends space. Imagining core logics as sectors in a hyperspace version of the child's board game, Chutes and Ladders, I want to mark the places where various accounts of the epidemic switch readers between core logics. Although I want to describe briefly the logical differences between the coincident medical formations that seem to underwrite accounts of AIDS, I am most interested in describing the shuttle between them. Although they share a primary concern with the relations between bodies and space, and especially with the identification of bodies moving through space, epidemiology and tropical medicine have distinct core logics.

The bulk of this essay will relate three categories that appear in the public health policy or media accounts to underlying tropes of divergent medical discourses. For example, in U.S. media, "bisexual men" are sometimes treated through epidemiology's notion of risk group, and sometimes treated as colonists who only visit a homosexual tropic. The Global Program on AIDS' term, "men who have sex with men" gets around the problem of self-definition but collapses when Eurocentric ideas of sexual vectors are introduced. Similarly, the idea of "sex workers" makes sense in economies that recognize domestic favors as value-equivalents of commodities that can be purchased in a sexual economy. But as "heterosexuality" (in high gear), the dramatic increase in HIV seropositivity reported among female sex workers, first in Africa and more recently in Asia, promises Euro-American researchers the bodies they need in order to construct a vaccine—which women like these research subjects will be the last to receive.

TROPICAL MEDICINE AND EPIDEMIOLOGY: COMPETING COLONIALISMS

Many of the concepts in what in the West are called tropical medicine and epidemiology developed as crucial parts of nineteenth-century and early twentieth-century colonial expansion. Tropical medicine, obviously, from its very name, dealt with the problems Euro-Americans encountered in their local occupations, merging empirical science with the fantasy of the colony. As Bruno Latour has suggested, the displacement of the scientific laboratory from the academy to the field was crucial to the "discovery" of etiologic agents.[13] Not only did the displacement literally produce the isolated research conditions necessary to finally establish germ theory, but it provided the colonial imaginary with a series of metonymically linked spaces: the colony of scientists in the client state colony studying the colony of germs on the surface of the agar plate. This cemented a homological turn of mind that could justify colonial power as an extension of the emerging modern will-to-control through positive science.

Tropical medicine wedded imperial notions of health and geography to the bourgeois notion of the domestic as a space within a space (the public). Colonial movement is bidirectional along a single axis; movement into the constructed domestic space of the colony is always accompanied by nostalgia for "going home." Tropical medicine relies on a diasporal imaginary of displacement and return that presumes that local diseases do not affect indigenous people in the same way that they affect the Euro-American occupier. A tropical disease is always proper to a place, to *there,* but only operates *as disease* when it afflicts people from *here.* Pathogens in a locale achieve historicity only when consolidated as disease in the colonist's body. The colonist's ailing body is heroic, not the victim of his or her dislocation but the most intimate site for domesticating the tropics. Tropical disease is contained by virtue of already being *there,* in the "tropics": even if he could not always get well, the colonist could always go home.

Critically, the very idea of tropical medicine rests on the ability to reliably separate an indigenous population perceived to be physically hearty but biologically inferior from a colonizing population believed to be biologically superior even while subject to the tropical illnesses. Sustaining this medical paradox requires perpetually refilling the category "exotic ailment." Tropical medicine grows out of and supports the idea that the first-world body is the proper gauge of health: the third world is the location of disease, even while its occupants are not the subjects of tropical medicine. Tropical medicine, then, is ostensive, a *pointing* that presupposes a map and a hierarchy of bodies.

Epidemiology, on the other hand, is performative. By separating pathogens from the body, epidemiology enables itself to declare "disease" from some but not all conjunctures of body/pathogen. Less concerned than tropical medicine to detail the diseases that may befall the Euro-American body in a place, epidemiology visualizes the place of the body in the temporal sequence called "epidemic." It is no longer the body fighting disease that is heroic, but epidemiology, the "disease detective," which alone has the power to visualize and disrupt the "natural history" of germs' vectorial movement.

An "epidemic" is more cases than expected, a deceptively simple definition that hides the messy truth that declaring an epidemic depends on cultural perceptions about who is likely to be sick and to what degree. Epidemiology reverses tropical medicine's concern with who may fall sick by removing disease from the natural environment and placing it in the body. Instead of viewing tropical inhabitants as more or less immune to the diseases that surround them, *indigenes* are now themselves the location of disease, reservoirs, carriers; poverty is no longer "natural" but an assault on the middle class. Epidemiology defines the boundaries of a disease by constituting a category of subject ("risk group"), an imagined community produced through vectors that epidemiology simulates as though discovered. Bodies are at once subject to and perpetrators of pathology, both "sick" and reservoirs or carriers in the larger network of disease.

Pathology is visualized against a background state of health, and this background definition of health becomes the ideologic lynch pin, the very condition of possibility for panoptic epidemiology. If the colonial homology could mask the medical crimes of transporting disease *to* the colony, epidemiology could hide the crimes of class-tiered health care delivery, not through naming disease, but by constituting the background definition of health in relation to the concerns of the enfranchised.

An "epidemic" is vectorial, movement is always outward from the center. Migratory sites of pathology can at any time be linked. Each new locale becomes a new center capable of projecting its vectorial links with yet more periphery, which in turn become new centers. Links are multidirectional; it makes no sense to speak of diaspora or return, but of vectorial logic.

If in theory anyone could be a vector, epidemiology's statistical procedures "discovered" that some bodies were more likely than others to carry (transport/harbor) disease. Bereft of a stable *place* of pathology, epidemiology must constantly construct and correlate populations and subpopulations in order to make epidemics visible, hence the interest in technologies of "surveillance" and of "sentinel studies."

VECTORS AS COMMUNITY

The recognition of a change that triggers the epidemiologic establishment is usually presumed to be a change in pathogens or in the interaction between disease pools. But the crucial, unspoken part of the AIDS story is the background change in social attitudes about expected health, critical not only in the initial identification of the epidemic but in setting the *terms* of subsequent discourse about HIV and AIDS. By 1981, when the new medical syndrome was identified, the decade-old gay liberation movement had gone a great distance in establishing itself as a civil entity ("minority") and had won increased tolerance from the mental and physical health care establishments. Health care providers were increasingly sensitive to both to the "normality" and to the special needs of gay clients. At least in large urban gay ghettos, openly gay people could come to the attention of openly gay or sympathetic health care professionals. The resistive visibility that enabled rapid collective response by gay men (and their lesbian collaborators) became a tool of epidemiologic surveillance: the idea of vectors was nestled into the protective perimeter of "community."

The concept of the "healthy homosexual," combined with the refiguration of gay people as a "community," turned gay men's collectivities into an agar plate. Intra-gay community transmission was viewed as multidirectional, pure vectors limited by the boundary of community. Unlike women and heterosexual men, gay men were not considered "partners of" other men: HIV circulated freely within the gay community. If such men had a female "partner," however, the media banished him from the gay community, now viewed as something like a colony. Bisexual men *went to* the dense spaces of homosexuality and returned to the heterosexual home infected with HIV.

Popular-press writers in the United States went to great lengths to simultaneously alert heterosexual women to their potential risk of contracting HIV, while denying a *place* within the space of heterosexuality for the man who had contracted HIV from another man. The bisexual man was variously described in the U.S. popular media as "a bogeyman . . . cloaked in myth and his own secretiveness";[14] "men [who] may be dangerous to your health";[15] "the invisible men . . . without a national organization or sexual agenda";[16] the man who might "live in towns, cities or suburbs and . . . look and dress like everybody else" while "playing straight with you."[17]

The authors set out with epidemiology's description of risk groups—homosexual men and female "partners of"—but they resort to tropical medical conceptions when faced with placing "the man in your life who has a man in his life."[18] The switch to tropical narratives enables the homosexual risk of these men to be contained in a specific local: "Bisexual men and male drug users do have one thing in common, besides their AIDS risk: geography."[19]

But literal geography only anchors the trope of displacement. Dorothy Rabinowitz's "The Secret Sharer: One Woman Confronts

Her Homosexual Husband's Death From AIDS" spatializes the Dr. Jekyll and Mr. Hyde narrative. The now-possibly-infected-wife says, "I married a very different person," and the writer takes pains to distinguish between the husband's localized homosexual life ("In the bathhouses, Alex marched around exhibiting himself") and his despatialized straight life ("everywhere else, he was the quintessential straight, sometimes homophobic male").[20] In relation to the "general population," who live in the generalized "everywhere else," homosexuality—and with it, HIV—is proper to, endemic in, the imagined place of gay community: bathhouses in cities like New York.

These switches occur because the writers refuse to follow through with the vectorial logic that would acknowledge straight men's risk of homosexual transmission, either directly, as when engaging in queer acts, or indirectly, through acknowledging that their women might have been engaging in straight acts with queer men. Instead, men who have sex with men, as the World Health Organization's Global Program on AIDS now calls them, are reinserted into the endocolonial version of the gay community.

QUEER BODIES, INVISIBLE SEX

The pressure to contain the AIDS epidemic and the hope that patterns of spread would be roughly the same worldwide legitimated epidemiologic inquiry into sex between men.[21] Although this work has extended the range of knowledge about same-sex affectional bonds, the underlying agenda of control and the obvious reluctance to let go of comfortable Eurocentric sexual categories and ideologies have resulted in confusion between "gay" "men" and same-sex practitioners who go under other names (or no name at all). Euro-American homosexualities are both implicated in and are the Other to homosexualities in other parts of the world. Colonial expansion mingled forms of same-sex union that operated with different symbolic meanings. But unlike homosexuality at home, which was thought to result from decadence in the upper classes—*over* civilization—homosexualities found in the colonies were perceived to be *un*civilized. Colonial administrators outlawed varieties of traditional homosexual marriage or legal partnership that got in the way of tidy management, and Christian missionaries turned special scorn on homosexual practices.[22]

It was unlikely, only a few decades later, that postcolonial governments were going to acknowledge that social patterns had once been used to demonstrate their inferiority. By the 1980s, disavowal of indigenous homosexualities was articulated *in terms of* the Euro-American "gay lifestyle" that had become increasingly visible in part because of media coverage about the AIDS epidemic and international scientific exchange during it. Implicating this already stereotyped Euro-American postindustrial homosexuality as the motor of the epidemic enabled developing countries' governments to ignore the potential for epidemics among other kinds of homosexual social-symbolic formations in their countries.

A representative of the South African Ministry of Mines[23] made a strange reading of an ethnography[24] of male relations in the mines, which suggested that although men formed long-lasting domestic and sexual bonds, sex between men had not usually included anal intercourse. Instead of promoting male miners' sexuality as a model of safe sex, the minister concluded that the miners were not appropriate subjects of prevention discourse aimed at homosexuals: they did not engage in "real sex."

Citing such work on miners and migratory sexual relations, social constructionists were able to get the WHO/GPA to choose and normalize the term "men who have sex with men," a conceptual move away from Euro-American notions that grounded homosexuality in psychic processes and made queer bodies amenable to organization into an identity and community. Although the term "men who have sex with men" made it possible for HIV educators to work closely and sensitively with local homosexualities, safe-sex discourse itself insists on a fixed link between sexual identity and practices of pleasure. To the extent that it tries to hail appropriate (if closeted) subjects to convert to condom use, safe-sex discourse collaborates in constructing intercourse as both the sine qua non and principal danger of sex. This has narrowed the (safe) sexual imaginary available to Euro-American gay men and produced a tendency, even in the most savvy projects, to accidentally produce Westernized, urbanized sexual subjects among men who have sex with men in other cultures.

Once men who have sex with men are located, it frequently turns out that they in fact do not, or only under some circumstances, engage in anal intercourse with other men: they *already* practice safe sex, but not as such. Thus, in order to promote maintenance of the already safe cultural norms, the Westernized notions of unsafe sex must be introduced. This is difficult to do in a colonial context without suggesting that intercourse, the now distinguishing preoccupation of urban Western gay discourse, is the "real" form of homosexuality. Paradoxically, at least in current practice, Western safe-sex programs directed toward "men who have sex with men" must introduce intercourse in order to discourage its practice. The inadequacy of a behavioral intervention designed with vectorial, *democratic* concepts of movement in mind and the practices and mores of the actual men who might be its "target" is nowhere clearer than when the men described by these different frameworks meet.

Western homosexuals are understood to be members of an epidemiologic category until they arrive in the developing world, where their activities are understood as quasi-domestic. To the extent that they are a vector between North and South, the possibility of HIV transmission is understood as operating in one direction. Thus, the "Western gay" arrives to constitute a "domestic relation" with the non-gay (heterosexually identified) man who has sex with men.

> Haitian researchers have accumulated evidence, through analysis of Haitian blood samples going back over a decade, which they believe shows that the AIDS virus arrived in Haiti with [gay] North American tourists . . .
>
> The neighboring country of the Dominican Republic, another favoured holiday destination for homosexual men from the United States, has seen a similar shift from homosexual to heterosexual transmission.[25]

This tourist version of colonial relations makes the American gay man (a deviant in his homeland) the bearer of disease to the colony, but, as I will detail in the last section, the epidemic produced is not among indigenous "homosexuals" but among *hetero*sexuals. The hurtling queer body goes ballistic in the tropics, producing abroad the heterosexual epidemic feared at home.

REAL WORK, STRAIGHT SEX

The semantic moves from homosexual to gay to men who have sex with men track sophisticated changes in concepts about male sexuality: from gender of object of affection to social identity to specificity of practice. The pressures of the epidemic did not produce a parallel reconsideration of bartered straight sex. But if the shifts in queer nomenclature kept relapsing to already inscribed notions about Western homosexuality, it was unclear whether or how the coexistence of terms prostitute/prostitution: sex worker/sex work was problematic. While deconstructing the traditional negative associations with prostitution and signaling the labor issues involved, the term *sex work* retains a Eurocentric bias. Rooted in a marxist feminism that attempts to shift debate about bartered sex away from issues of morality and onto issues of labor, the term sex work, at least as it is used in discussions of global HIV policy, promotes capitalist concepts of market and economy.

Like the versions of gay male community work in the West, which attempt to achieve safe-sex conformity by strengthening individual identity and identification with an oppositional community, organizing women as sex workers attempts to construct a notion of identity—as a worker—for individuals engaging in symbolically and practically disparate erotic episodes. Promoting the idea that bartering domestic services, including sex, is work requires introducing capitalist concepts of the split between domesticity and labor into cultures where such divisions of labor are not fully established or have resulted from the mixed motives of postcolonial development plans.

Like the hyperproduction of anal intercourse necessary to Western safe-sex ideology, using the term sex work requires introducing the very morality activists hoped to overcome. Sex must be *privatized* in order to make it public as formal work. Even if wages are due for housework,[26] paid-for sex appears to be a commodified substitute for what properly happens at home.

Sex work does not seem to reflect the experience of these informal sector traders in developing nations, and probably also misunderstands the role and nature of sex trade in Europe and the United States. Renegotiation of domestic and sexual relations in countries experiencing intensive economic reorganization and massive, gender-linked migrations is extremely complex. For most men and women, trading sex and domestic favors is not a profession but a transient activity that occurs alongside domestic relations, or a cyclical activity used to amass capital alongside economically sanctioned jobs. In the Cameroon and other parts of West Africa, for example, rural women migrated to the cities throughout the twentieth century and commonly own small beer houses or food stands that they capitalize through periodic sale of "sexual favors." Alternatively, especially in South Africa, where mining has resulted in massive and cyclical migration of men from the countryside, women, and sometimes men, who live near mining camps sell home-cooked meals and wash clothes, supplementing these cottage industries through trading sex with favorite customers. In the major cities of East Africa, where the massive migrations of the immediate postcolonial period have stabilized, a large class of "free" (unmarried) women work in clerical or other low-level nondomestic jobs. These women supplement their wages by trading companionship or sex for consumer goods, a practice known in Senegal as "going out."

The women who most clearly fit the Western model of professional sex work receive the most attention in global AIDS discourse, but largely to constitute them as the growing "reservoir" of HIV infection in an accelerating epidemic among heterosexual men and their families. Like gay communities in the West, geographic areas (parts of cities, sometimes whole countries) where prostitution is thought to occur are treated as colonies with an endemic disease to which single or migratory men go, only to bring HIV back to their proper or future wives.

IMAGINARY DIASPORAS

Policymakers and newspaper writers switch between logics when they describe the epidemic, not because they fail to recognize or understand the underlying medical logics (which they may not) but because the bodies they describe sometimes outrun the discourses that try to secure them, forcing those discourses back on themselves, indicting their own administrators. Switching is not capricious or illogical but symptomatic of the pressures power investments make on the activators of discourses. Observing switches from vectorial to diasporal logic helps make sense not only of confusing accounts of how HIV was transported to Asia by migratory homosexuals, but also of how HIV became endemic among heterosexuals once there, revealing the larger investments in maintaining the privileges that accrue from running the master discourse. Many of the first AIDS cases diagnosed in Asia were among hemophiliac men, but this did not challenge the travel narratives used to insist that Western homosexuals had imported HIV to Asia. The Director-General of the Department of Health of the Taiwan Provincial Government described the trajectory of HIV as it made its way to his tiny country:

> AIDS has been identified only within the past ten years in central Africa; from there it quickly spread to Haiti and then to the U.S. and to Europe. It came very late to Taiwan: in December 1984 an American transiting Taiwan was found to have full-blown AIDS. This triggered our first major concern over the fatal disease. However a rapid increase in the number of AIDS patients locally, the spread of the disease to other parts of Taiwan, development of AIDS among HIV carriers in hemophiliacs, the diversification of risk groups—all have followed the same pattern seen in Western countries and throughout the world.[27]

But although the director-general describes the epidemiologic pattern of HIV as identical to that in the rest of the world, colleagues provide considerable detail about indigenous homosexuality in order to construct even the "tabooed" practices in Taiwan as yet different from those in the more licentious West:

> According to the statements on the questionnaires, kissing was the most common sexual practice but, after extensive interviewing, male homosexuals often admitted anal intercourse as well. . . . None described practices of "fisting" . . . Low prevalence of HIV-1 was detected in several high risk groups. If the results of the questionnaire and interview are accepted as reliable, homosexual behavior in Taiwan appears to be much less promiscuous than in the western world.[28]

Although cases of HIV and AIDS were described among Asians in the early to mid-1980s, HIV only became visible as a problem *for* Asia when it appeared among sex workers, transforming sex workers from the sexual/tropical home-away-from-home for Westerners into a vector within Asia. Because Asian sexuality was stereotyped as passive, as capable largely of receiving but not passing on HIV, early low incidence figures were interpreted within the tropical medical framework as a kind of immunity rather than an artifact of HIV's late arrival per the epidemiologic model. But, by the 1992 International Conference on AIDS in Amsterdam, HIV was represented as a phenomenon now indigenous to Asia—being passed among members of the Asian migrant and underclasses. Once "Asian AIDS" was launched, blame concerning the diasporal relations of migrant Western homosexuals was subordinated to hysteria about heterosexual vectorial transmission. Asia's plight was compared to "African AIDS," not to the unmarked, but unmistakable queer AIDS of Anglo-America.

Similarly, a description of the "heterosexual" epidemic in Haiti separates both American homosexuality and heterosexuality from their cohorts' practices in the tropics:

> While large numbers of tourists visited briefly from cruise ships, the majority of those who stayed in Haiti were homosexual men, who paid for sex with local men who had wives or girlfriends and considered themselves heterosexual. First the bisexual men become infected, then their female partners, and now Haiti has a full-scale heterosexual AIDS epidemic on its hands.[29]

Western heterosexuals had the good sense to visit Haiti only briefly from the safety of their cruise ships, but the "homosexual men" stayed to bring both capitalism and HIV. Queer lucre engenders disease in the tropics because heterosexuality in the colony is premodern. As Ugandan president Yoweri Museveni described the inscription of two epochs of sexuality in his country: "[AIDS] is the result of European influences—European liberalism, which is good in some respects, has brought a lot of permissiveness, which in a backward society is dangerous."[30]

The Haitian denial of local homosexualities (the men only "consider themselves heterosexual") and the Ugandan infantilization of heterosexuality allow HIV to take root "there," to become endemic. From the local perspective, the epidemic *among* heterosexuals may be vectorial, but from the *global* perspective, HIV's arrival is diasporal. The libertine European or queer colonist *arrives* sick, but, as in the Taiwanese account of the "original" case of AIDS—a transiting American homosexual—his ailing body is simply "sent home."

COMPETING LOGICS, MASTER TROPES

I hope I have demonstrated both the solidity of two core logics and the ease with which writers move between them. The insistent use of concepts of movement and the construction and detachment of ideas of place enhance the legibility of the more general but "scientific" story of the epidemic, which in turn serves as the foundation for the more colorful descriptions of a global disaster. A key reason for switching between the two core logics, I suggested, was the desire to sustain larger cultural narratives about sexuality and secure broader national and transnational interests. In the details of producing a story, writers lose their grip on migrating body-objects that resist the codes scientific discourses try to impose on them.

I suggested, for example, that Euro-American homosexuals are a "risk group" as long as transmission is considered a "community" issue. But the very places gay men occupy are a colony for their bisexual cohorts, even if gay men are themselves colonists from the perspective of the developing countries' governments who wish to deny homosexualities in their own borders. Homosexuality must be kept out of the domestic space and heterosexualities-for-hire must be maintained as private: homosexuality must not count as real sex, and prostitution must not count as real work.

This peregrination of narrative tropes defies science's view of itself as coherent and belies policy and media writers' belief that they can "apply" objective knowledge. The AIDS epidemic is a particularly spectacular example of the switching, drifting, *bricoleur* use of supposed disinvested descriptive frames. Although tropical medicine's modes of thinking are clearly critical to understanding these multiple registers of AIDS discourse, the limiting metadiscursive logic is still that of epidemiology, though not because it has any greater scientific explanatory power. Rather, because it can describe place, and especially origin, in concrete spatiotemporal terms called "natural history," epidemiology meets the internal management and the external image needs of the United States, the country at greatest political risk of having to acknowledge its role in creating and sustaining the HIV pandemic.

NOTES

1. Global Program on AIDS, "Broadcasters' Questions and Answers on AIDS" (Geneva: World Health Organization, 1989), p. 6.

2. Jane Kramer, "Bad Blood," *The New Yorker,* October 11, 1993.

3. Cindy Patton, *Inventing AIDS* (New York: Routledge, 1990); "Containing African AIDS: The Bourgeois Family as 'Safe Sex,'" in *Nationalisms and Sexualities,* ed. Andrew Parker, Doris Somer, and Patricia Yaeger (New York: Routledge, 1992); "Ground Zero: AIDS Education and the Decline

of Epidemiology," in *Performance/Performativity,* ed. Eve Sedgwick and Andrew Parker (New York: Routledge, 1994).

4. "Man, in the analytic of finitude, is a strange empirico-transcendental doublet, since he is a being such that knowledge will be attained in him of what renders all knowledge possible. . . . For the threshold of our modernity is situated not by the attempt to apply objective methods to the study of man, but rather by the constitution of an empirico-transcendental doublet which was called *man.*" Michel Foucault, *The Order of Things* (New York: Vintage, 1973), pp. 318-19.

5. Thomas Kuhn, *The Structure of Scientific Revolutions,* 2d ed. (Chicago: University of Chicago Press, 1970).

6. The Robert Gallo-Luc Montagnier dispute served to displace concern about paradigm conflict onto concern about research ethics. Despite the important differences in their training and the institutions where they work, the battle was described as one of who found the virus first. Gallo and Montagnier were individual scientists vying for fame, not two instruments of incompatible medical research frames. Although Gallo's superior laboratory methods allowed him to describe—*to visualize*—the virus (which he may indeed have obtained from Montagnier's lab by deceit), Montagnier "won" in having his account of the emergence of the epidemic accepted (in fact, it is the one recounted, unattributed, in the WHO-GPA document discussed at the beginning of this essay). Securing the narrative tropes of the epidemic is surely a more impressive and ominous accomplishment, even if this form of authorship, if signed, is more likely to win a Pulitzer than a Nobel Prize.

7. Michel Foucault, *The Order of Things* (New York: Vintage, 1973); *The Birth of the Clinic* (New York: Vintage, 1975); "The Politics of Health in the Eighteenth Century," in Michel Foucault, *Power/Knowledge* (New York: Pantheon, 1980).

8. Indeed, the very idea of scientific uncertainty is symptomatic: uncertain to whom? with what effect? And when did we come to expect science to be certain? The idea that medicine knew best was only recently established and is now challenged by "patients" who want to choose between or mix treatment modalities that conceive the body quite differently — not only Western and Eastern systems but subdivisions within Western clinical medicine. As I have suggested elsewhere (*Inventing AIDS,* 1990), both virology and immunology are quite "certain" about the interaction between HIV and the human body, but they offer radically different accounts of the body in illness.

9. Eve Kosofsky Sedgwick, *Epistemology of the Closet* (Berkeley: University of California Press, 1990).

10. Accounts that treat the logical viability of a domain of knowledge as

a site of struggle for space rather than a development over time permit or even presuppose considerably more inconsistency among stated knowledge principles and technical practices: Karl Mannheim, *Man and Society in an Age of Reconstruction* (London: Routledge and Kegan Paul, 1940); Ludwig Fleck, *The Genesis and Development of a Scientific Fact,* trans. Fred Bradley and Thaddeus J. Trenn (Chicago: Chicago University Press, 1979); and more recently, Bruno Latour, *The Pasteurization of France,* trans. Alan Sheridan and John Law (Cambridge: Harvard University Press, 1988); Bruno Latour and Steve Woolgar, *Laboratory Life: The Construction of Scientific Facts* (Princeton, N.J.: Princeton University Press, 1986); Mary Douglas, *How Institutions Think* (Syracuse: Syracuse University Press, 1986); Donna J. Haraway, *Simians, Cyborgs, and Women: The Reinvention of Nature* (New York: Routledge, 1991); Sandra Harding, *The Science Question in Feminism* (Ithaca, N.Y.: Cornell University Press, 1986); and others I have not yet encountered. I focus on Kuhn and Foucault because these are probably the best known works on scientific knowledge outside the discipline of philosophy and history of science.

11. Michel Foucault, *Archaeology of Knowledge* (New York: Pantheon, 1972).

12. Michel de Certeau, *The Practice of Everyday Life* (Berkeley: University of California Press, 1988).

13. Bruno Latour, *The Pasteurization of France.*

14. Jon Nordheimer, "AIDS Specter for Women: The Bisexual Man," *New York Times,* April 3, 1987, p. A10.

15. Christopher Norwood, "AIDS Is Not for Men Only," *Mademoiselle,* September, 1985, pp. 198-99, 294-97.

16. Anne Conover Heller, "Is There a Man in Your Man's Life?" *Mademoiselle,* July, 1987, p. 135.

17. Heller, "Is There a Man in Your Man's Life?" p. 135.

18. Ibid.

19. Norwood, "AIDS is Not for Men Only," p. 199.

20. Dorothy Rabinowitz, "The Secret Sharer," *New York,* February 26, 1990, pp. 103-112.

21. Paul R. Abrahamson and Gilbert Herdt, "The Assessment of Sexual Practices Relevant to the Transmission of AIDS: A Global Perspective," *The Journal of Sex Research* 27/2 (May 1990).

22. Gil Shepard, "Rank, Gender, and Homosexuality: Mombasa as a Key to Understanding Sexual Options," in Pat Caplan, ed., *The Cultural Construction of Sexuality;* Gloria Wekker, "Matisma in Black Dykes," in *Homosexuality, Which Homosexuality?* Conference Papers, Social Science, vol. 2 (Amsterdam: Free University, 1987); Saskia Wieringa, "An Anthropological Critique of Constructionism: Berdache and Butches," in *Homosexu-*

ality, Which Homosexuality? Conference Papers, Social Science, vol. 2 (Amsterdam: Free University, 1987).

23. Alan Whitehead, "Migrant Labor and AIDS in South Africa," Global Impact of AIDS Conference, London, March 8-10, 1988.

24. Dunbar T. Moody, "Migrancy and Male Sexuality on South African Gold Mines," *Journal of South African Studies* 14:2 (January 1988).

25. Panos Institute, *AIDS in the Third World* (Philadelphia: New Society Publishers, 1989), p. 88.

26. The slogan "wages for housework" and "wages due lesbians" were used by marxist feminist organizers in Britain. They stem from a similar analysis, which attempts to signal the labor dimensions of women's activities.

27. Chun-Jean Lee, "Address," *Human Retroviruses and AIDS*, Proceedings of the Symposium, November 11-13, 1988, pp. xii-xiii, at p. xii.

28. Ho-Chin Lee et al., "Update: AIDS and HIV-I Infection in Taiwan, 1985-1988," *Human Retroviruses and AIDS*, Proceedings of the Symposium, November 11-13, 1988, pp. 61-70, at p. 65.

29. Panos Institute, *AIDS in the Third World*, p. 88.

30. Ibid., p. 91.

15

The Displacement of Cuban Homosexuality in the Fiction and Autobiography of Reinaldo Arenas

BENIGNO SÁNCHEZ-EPPLER

Taking as a point of departure that growing up hetero, bi, or homo-sexual in a so-called homeland of one's own is complex enough, I in-quire into the convolutions that accrue when that growing takes place while migrating across territories that are not ours at all, or while residing in places that come to be ours only after costly accom-modation and contestation. This essay begins to focus on the record of displaced homosexuality in the work of Reinaldo Arenas: Cuban and gay, anti-Castro dissident and anti-Miami malcontent, exile and writer, and someone brought to the United States during the 1980 Mariel exodus. In inter/national terms, his story is just another Cold War Cuban migration to the United States. Yet, although it may be just that, much that does not fit in the analysis of how border cross-ings affect state interactions is also at stake in this story, and all of that would continue to be left out of the picture unless we shift focus to concentrate on a preeminently nonstate or state-occluded phe-nomenon of those demographic displacements in which people move with or because of issues related to a proscribed or persecuted sexual identity or set of practices. Even if one of the states in question is as preoccupied with intensifying the criminalization of homosexuality as the Cuban Socialist state has been, and even if the other state in-volved has an explicitly articulated intent in excluding homosexuals from its pool of immigrants as does the United States, there is very little chance that either the foreign policy or the international relations analysts bound to the study of state interactions would ever focus on the issue of queer displacements across the borders in question. I have to confess that there is even some comfort in this structural lack of attention by disciplines that may actually inform future restrictive state policies of homophobic societies. So I proceed to discuss this story of a transnational and primarily nonstate phenomenon somehow reassured by the official lack of interest in this kind of analysis, and because I feel that those who are actually moving across state borders with their contested sexualities ought to start paying special atention to the global range of consequences—advantages and pitfalls—of their sexually marked displacements. These displacements will continue to look like so much traffic of people with or without passports across airports, seaports, border checkpoints, and borderlines. But under that façade of international migration, one finds the richness and peculiarities of postmodern geographies mapped out by the displacement from one home-national closet or gay ghetto to another host-national-space for their homosexuality.

There is not much room to deny that people in Cuba and in the U.S.–Cuban community live out gay lifestyles or practice homosexual acts, nor is it terribly controversial to assert that a pronounced compulsory heterosexuality—or proportionally pronounced homophobic compulsions—informs Cuban national or ethnic myths, normative prohibitions, and other means of regulating gender performance and sexual orientation. Although at times the definitive sanctions benignly miss this or that individual, and although there is much talk of recent liberalization, these sanctions do remain firmly installed in conventional ideology both in and out of the island: real Cubans are not homosexuals, or homosexuals are not real Cubans. In this regard Cubans are no major exception among so many other homophobic societies. This inquiry also takes as a point of departure that the more sharply articulated the homophobic investments of an identity—individual or communal—the more definitively homosexuality plays a role in the construction of that identity.[1]

Even if constitutive homophobia seems to be a constant of Cuban national life—as it may very well be of others—there is a period of Cuban history where it becomes most visible or most virulently symptomatic. In this period, through the combined effects of revolutionary political changes in the island and the subsequent waves of migrations, Cubans are also exposed to remarkable multiplications of situations in which to experience homosexuality and of subject positions from which to articulate the nature and consequence of such experiences. This period spans the 1960s, 1970s, and 1980s, and includes the triumph of the Cuban revolution, its initial campaigns to eradicate all practices of the commodification of sex in the early 1960, the subsequent internment in work camps of a long list of social undesirables prominently featuring homosexuals during the mid-1960s, the institutionalizing legal codification of the 1970s, the expulsion through Mariel in 1980 of people on lists very similar to those previously persecuted as social misfits and scum (*escoria*), and the need throughout the 1980s, both in Cuba and U.S.–Cuban communities, to respond to the onslaught of AIDS. These developments, generally described as the Stalinization of Cuban homophobia, coincide with the literary activity of Reinaldo Arenas (1943-90) and form the preeminent backdrop for his highly denunciatory autobiographic or testimonial narratives.

Throughout the 1980s and beyond, one major phenomenon to watch involves the repercussions of the AIDS epidemic among Cubans. The initial straightforward homophobic refusal to heterosexualize the epidemic in the U.S.–Cuban community somehow matches the symmetrically opposed initial rush of the Cuban government to gloss the disease as a heterosexual epidemic with its roots in Cuba's military intervention in Africa.[2] Those highly emblematic initial attempts have since yielded to the weight of the evidence, and lately both communities have moved to a more balanced way of looking at the makeup of the at-risk populations. In terms of policy and care, moreover, the differences prove to be quite emblematic. In the United States, Cuban AIDS victims suffer the generalized pattern of clinical neglect. In Cuba, relatively efficient centralized medical intervention makes blanket testing obligatory, surveillance possible. The very opposite of clinical neglect produces de facto terminal quarantine units where despite the availability of better food than one would find outside the sanatoriums, and despite the state's investment in the medical attention provided to all who have tested HIV positive, the whole no-exit arrangement is often experienced as quasi-penal.

Backing up to April 1980, 10,000 people, many gays among them broke into the Peruvian embassy in Havana asking for asylum, thus sparking a foreign policy nightmare, and the Mariel exodus of the next six months. Through Mariel, Cuba would—more systematically than ever before—purge itself of many who wanted to leave, and it would also expel, whether they wanted to go or not, those classified as worth excluding from Cuban territory and its revolutionary society. Among the 125,000 Mariel immigrants, a majority would have emigrated without much hoopla, yet this number included, by policy, a minority that the Cuban government was interested in documenting as the definitive portion of the lot: the criminal, the psychologically disturbed, and homosexuals. Immediately, one term came to be used in Cuban official statements and press releases for all refugees, "escoria," "scum," explicitly labeled refuse and in very clear ways, non-Cubans.[3]

The number of homosexuals among the 125,000 immigrants is impossible to ascertain. The U.S. National Gay Task Force, using State Department reports and refugee camps studies, estimates that between 2,000 and as many as 10,000 of the refugees were gay men and, in much lower numbers, lesbians.[4] The international attention attracted by Mariel, together with time-honored Cold War priorities that extended a generally unqualified welcome to Cuban refugees, for once protected the Mariel gays from being processed as "excludables," a U.S. immigration classification that would have applied to them otherwise. If in the past gay immigrants had left their countries of origin and entered the United States without leaving the closet, this time a group of immigrants had arrived as a consequence of a massive Cuban outing, and with little recourse to the closet. Interestingly enough, here is one of the few cases in which the foreign policy imperative of granting refuge to victims of an "enemy state" occluded the long-standing immigration restriction of excluding foreign homosexuals.

The predicament of so many Cubans, migrating not only with their homoeroticism but because of it, clarifies to what extent anyone who migrates or moves with his or her homosexuality is always faced with the need to negotiate the transformation in meaning of a set of sexual practices or axis of identity. These transformations and complications would always remain marginal to the concerns of state entities and their analysis. On the move through Mariel, and very quickly, the Cubans had to reposition their homosexuality, first, inside of yet another reassertion of Cuban State homophobia (whether that meant freedom for some or enforced banishment and separation from friends and family for others); second, inside the limbo of the provisional refugee camp culture; third, in relation to a tradition of Cuban homophobia still preeminent in Cuban Miami; and then finally, in relation to the real or imagined projections of gay liberationist options within the relative safety of U.S. gay enclaves, primarily in New York or San Francisco.

Mariel was not the first time the Cuban state had decreed exclusionary homophobic policies. In the 1970s in Cuba, homosexuality was not only criminalized explicitly as never before, but it was elevated to the rank of a politically undesirable or dangerous behavior.[5] The 1971 Declaration of the First Congress on Education and Culture stands as a key document from this period, uncannily resonant with recent recourse to HIV quarantine sanatoriums: "The social pathological character of homosexual deviations was recognized. It was resolved that all manifestations of homosexual deviations are to be firmly rejected and prevented from spreading."[6] After a point by point description of policies to further induce compliance with compulsory heterosexuality, the fragment concludes:

> It was resolved that for notorious homosexuals to have influence in the formation of our youth is not to be tolerated on the basis of their "artistic merit."
>
> Consequently, a study is called for to determine how best to tackle the problem of the presence of homosexuals in the various institutions of our cultural sector. . . .
>
> It was resolved that those whose morals do not correspond to the prestige of our revolution should be barred from any group of performers representing our country abroad.
>
> Finally, it was agreed to demand that severe penalties be applied to those who corrupt the morals of minors, depraved repeat offenders and irredeemable antisocial elements.
>
> Cultural institutions cannot serve as a platform for false intellectuals who try to make snobbery, extravagant conduct, homosexuality and other social aberrations into expressions of revolutionary spirit and art, isolated from the masses and the spirit of the revolution.[7]

Before the explicit legislative codification of the 1970s, the late 1960s had already witnessed the Stalinization of Cuban homophobia as it produced the UMAP work camps (Military Units for Aid to Production), where those charged with homosexuality or extravagant effeminacy were interned together with others classified as social threats, the chronically unemployed, gamblers, and antidraft Jehovah's Witnesses. The operation of these camps has been seen as an extension of the radical programs against corruption in general, and more particularly, radical policies to eradicate all practices of the commodification of sex, instituted with the triumph of the revolution since 1959.

For the picture in Cuba before 1959, before the revolution, I am persuaded by the following succint description of business as usual in Allen Young's *Gays under the Cuban Revolution*:

> legal persecution and other forms of official harassment were sporadic. Certainly [before 1959], there were no ideological grounds for such persecution: homosexuality was not politicized, because the *locas*, like the women, knew their place. As for religion, the Roman Catholic hierarchy in Cuba was weak, especially as compared to such other hispanic nations as Colombia or Spain. The church's negative attitude toward homosexuality did not have much meaning in the day-to-day life of a country whose economy was largely based on providing facilities for sinners of all sorts.[8]

Reinaldo Arenas (1943-90) carries his sexuality through the cultural-historical panorama I have just summarized, and his portage can be trailed in the gallery of representations he created primarily by deploying and deforming in fiction and poetry his fund of autobiographical material. Arenas's characters clarify how people carry their homoeroticism from one territory to another, from one cultural stage to another, from one politically saturated space to another, and from one linguistic register to another, from the margins of one mainstream to the eddies of another.

Arenas's life can be summarized roughly as a succession of decades lived in different cultural or social spaces, and with different levels of access or exclusion to social and/or political enfranchisement. Born in Cuba in 1943, the 1940s and 1950s include twelve years of childhood living with his mother and his grandparents in rural isolation and poverty, and, after 1955, six years of adolescence and poverty in the provincial city of Holguín. Although no writings from this period have survived, all of his representations of childhood have their roots in these years lived in rural or provincial Cuba. The 1950s end as Arenas reaches age seventeen, and as Cuba enters into its revolution.

After sharing in the revolutionary hopes and ferment, he goes to Havana, where he spends the 1960s entering into the life of the writer, passing through a world of university, National Library, and official literary periodicals, all substantially reinvigorated and politicized by revolutionary cultural activism. It is also during this period that he makes the transition from the world of hard to acknowledge and hardly labeled early rural or provincial homoerotic encounters into a set of practices clearly discernible as part of a Cuban urban gay culture. By the end of the 1960s and the beginning of the 1970s, the increasingly explicit dissonance of his writing, particularly with respect to his representations of homoeroticism and its discontents in an increasingly Stalinized socialist order, force him to bypass Cuban publishing restrictions. He starts to publish outside of Cuba without the requisite official imprimatur. By then both his own homosexuality and the nature of his writing make him the perfect target of surveillance and subsequent prosecution, imprisonment, alleged rehabilitation, and a postpenal return to a social limbo of unemployment, substandard housing, and homelessness, all accompanied by a continuous clandestine production of frankly antirevolutionary writing with homoeroticism and the accompanying denunciation of state homophobia as an important component. This limbo ends abruptly with the onset of another one.

The same criminal record that puts Arenas in jail in 1973 puts him in one of the boats leaving through Mariel in 1980: "counterrevolutionary activities" or "attitudes" that included "ideological diversionism" with reference to his writing, "public scandal" and "corruption of minors" with reference to his homosexuality. He enters into his last decade as a Cuban exile, very much ill at ease within the Cuban exiled community, and as a Cuban homosexual within the relative freedom and territorial unspecificity of U.S. gay culture. He becomes also the highly visible anticommunist cold-warrior capable of opening Reagan's Cuban gay front. The full record of the boundaries crossed over, under, or erased would certainly baffle those exclusively intent on recognizing as borders only those drawn between the territories controlled by states.

In 1990 Arenas commits suicide, a complication related to AIDS, another kind of supra/national passage related to his position in an extremely challeging supranational, map-defying epidemiological phenomenon. Never has a literary corpus better deserved the rubric of complete[d] works, for Reinaldo Arenas kills himself only after doggedly staying alive to bring to completion his autobiography and the two remaining novels of his promised *pentagonía,* all in the short years that followed his diagnosis.

The vantage point of the book Arenas publishes—posthumously— as a frank "Autobiografía," *Antes que anochezca,*[9] is framed as the final panoramic retrospective of a life and a writing career, truncated by AIDS. From the site of narration circa 1990, Arenas revisits the 1950s of his childhood. A three-page vignette under the rubric of "La escuela" (*Antes,* 27-29; *Before,* 9-12), takes up only one page to talk about school itself, and then two pages to document a rich catalog of sexual activities: the first looks at other boys, his relief discovering that others also masturbated, his individual forays with chickens, goats, and pigs, and the collective enterprise of making love to a mare, not ever quite knowing whether the pleasure was in the contact with the mare or in the sharing of group sexual spectacle (*Antes,* 28; *Before,* 10-11). He quickly glosses over his unpenetrative naked play with his cousin—*prima*—Dulce Ofelia (*Antes,* 28-29; *Before,* 11), and then pauses to relish in the page-long narration of his first proper intercourse with his cousin—*primo*—Orlando:

> The *consumated* act, in this case reciprocal penetration, was performed with my cousin Orlando. I was about eight years old, and he was twelve. Orlando's penis was a source of fascination to me, and he took pleasure in showing it to me whenever he had a chance. It was somewhat large and dark, and once erect, its foreskin would slide back and reveal a pink glans that demanded, with little jerks, to be caressed. One day, up on a plum tree, Orlando was showing me his beautiful glans, when his hat landed on the ground. (Out in the country we all wore hats.) I grabbed his hat and ran off to hide behind a bush in a secluded place. Right away he understood exactly what I wanted; we dropped our pants and began to masturbate. What happened then was that he stuck his penis into me and later, at his request, I stuck mine into him while flies and other insects kept buzzing around us, apparently wanting to participate in the feast.
>
> When it was all over I felt completely guilty, but not entirely satisfied; I could not help but feel very much afraid. It seemed to me that

we had done something terrible, that in some way I had condemned myself for the rest of my life. Orlando laid down on the grass to rest, and in a few minutes we were romping around again. "Now there is definitely no way out for me!" I thought or I believe I thought, when I crouched and felt Orlando grabbing me from behind. While he was sticking it into me, I was thinking of my mother [abandoned by my father], and all the things that during all those years she never did with a man, which I was doing right there in the bushes within earshot of her voice, already callling me for dinner. In a rush I separated from Orlando and ran home. Of course, neither of us had ejaculated (*Antes*, 29; *Before*, 11-12).

Arenas himself provides a very clear sign of his sense that memory is operating over a radical separation from a moment in which the narrated experience would have signified differently: to voice the double take he says "I thought or I believe I thought." I would argue that this double take remains applicable to the entire autobiography.

There is no reason to doubt the veracity of Arenas's report with respect to the reciprocity of the cousins' alternate penetrations. Yet it must be acknowledged that such specificity goes against the grain of the conventionally accepted modality of Cuban, or generally Latin, homosexual contact in which the so-called passive and active roles are not supposed to be interchangeable,[10] and with the grain of the ostensibly mainstreamed reciprocity of Anglo-American gayness. Despite the dark notes about the sense of guilt, the mother's tyrannical omnipresence, and the mock-Freudian detail of occupying her place while making love with the father, the vignette still comes through as a celebration of gayness spiced with its rural picaresque treatment of validated children's sex play. The children carouse inside a culture where their sexual play, if it actually led to adult homosexuality, would be attached to all the feelings of guilt the eight-year-old Reinaldo is reported to have felt. On the other hand, if this sexual encounter somehow led to nothing—that is, to heterosexuality—a related social logic would exonerate all guilt. Arenas goes on to report both the fear he remembers to have felt, and the certainty that none of those reasons to fear ever stuck to his cousin Orlando.

The spirits [who spoke at a seance his family attended] had not openly revealed my sin enough, a sin I was not, by the way, at all eager to give up. In time, Orlando grew into a handsome young man, and he even acquired a bicycle, something unusual in our neighborhood. He got married, and now has many children and grandchildren (*Antes*, 30; *Before*, 13).

Because of where he comes from, as Arenas articulates what he remembers, his text also proves quite capable of grating against the supposedly more enlightened sensibilities of his possibly homophile contemporary U.S. urban readership with the documentation of sexual practices with animals and vegetables that are regarded as relatively commonplace in his rural setting (*Antes*, 39; *Before*, 18-19). He proceeds to illustrate the profusion of Cuban rural pan-erotism with this account of his enjoyment of homosexual contact, right smack in the midst of the most comforting of familial heterosexist arrangements.

> An example of this is my uncle Rigoberto, the oldest of my uncles, a married, serious man. Sometimes I would go to town with him. I was just about eight years old and we would ride on the same saddle. As soon as we were both in the saddle, he would begin to have an erection. Perhaps in some way my uncle did not want this to happen, but he could not help it. He would put me in place, lift me up and set my butt on his penis [I propped myself as best I could, I lifted up a bit and placed my buttocks on top of his sex], and during that ride, which would take an hour or so, I was bouncing on that huge penis, riding, as it were, on two animals at the same time. I think eventually Rigoberto would ejaculate. The same thing happened on the way back from town [we repeated again the same ceremony]. Both of us, of course, acted as if we were not aware of what was happening. He would whistle and breathe hard while he trotted on. When he got back, Coralina, his wife, would welcome him with open arms and a kiss. At that moment we were all very happy (*Antes*, 40; *Before*, 19-20).

This vignette demands to be read as the tenderest lampooning of the ostensibly straightest male who enjoys sexual contact with another male and nevertheless refuses to recognize it as a homoerotic encounter or practice. There are other positions—subject positions—from which to arrive at a different reading, and Arenas leaves plenty of room for them with his careful attention to the articulation of the boy's, the uncle's, and—by extension—their society's willed or repressed, but at any rate, unquestioned lack of knowledge. Arenas, working from an authorial emplacement where he definitely knows, and from where he wants very much to include this "ceremony" among a set of practices unambiguously recognized as queer, still allows the boy, the uncle, and their society not to notice. The practice, the desire, and the achieved satisfaction remain fully enjoyed and socially untarnished because of the carefully reported lack of codes or vocabularies to label them queer. Arenas, in memory, is *framing* his straight uncle, but he is also reporting on a moment before language or social code come in to give name and label to a range of activities that since then have suffered both labeling and subsequent proscription. Many of the difficulties in mapping or accounting for nationally occluded sexual practices or whatever identities may be grounded on such practices have a great deal to do with the availability or unavailability of categories or vocabularies for their representation. The mapping problem is as pronounced when the societies operate as if they lacked these vocabularies as much as when the existing registers end up being different from those available at different cultural sites. When a story like the one Arenas tells to record his sexual contact with his uncle crosses the many borders he has crossed, such a story, together with the nature of the event it represents, is exposed to a transnational and transcultural multiplicity of value judgments very hard to control. But whatever the outcome of the unexpected and unmanageable readers' responses, the image has affected—transnationally—the unassailable straightness of the serious and ostensibly hetero-macho Cuban male, as much as it has brought to the U.S.-gay debates on intergenerational homosexuality one Cuban rural modality of the issue.

No one can really speculate to what extent this passage, and the autobiography as a whole, owes its intensity to the dynamics of remembrances at a distance, to the surplus energy in the testimony because the autobiographical subject is actually away from Cuba. Yet it is clear that the book as a whole, as suffused as it is with the sense of loss of the exile, does project its vision as re-membering in the service of an explicitly political retaliation. The barbs of retaliation homosexualize Cuba as a whole, its most male and its most heterosexist emblems, and all of this is enabled by that dual emplacement in the relative gay-affirming surrounding of New York City, and in the certainty of the threshold of his death sentence by a sexually transmitted disease. Arenas's displacements provide the altered focus for his remembered Cuban experiences, the historical-political frame for his condition as the exile who writes, and finally the social and med-

ical surroundings during the period of textual production. The displacements also provide a transborder tension between so many possible audiences he may be addressing in his book: on the North
American front, the substantial gay and gay-affirming U.S. post-
Stonewall readerships for whom his Cubaness will signify all sorts of
indexes of otherness; in the Latin American rearguard, the substantially left-wing intelligentsia of post-Boom readers with their residual
romantic attachments to Castro; and in the Cuban heartlands of the
island and Miami, all the politically irreconcilable parties who may
agree only in their homophobia, plus the full census of queer Cubans
both at home and abroad.

I do not have the space here to provide a full sociological profile
of probable readers' expectations within the variety of cultural and
political sites that Arenas's narratives engage. But I do want to argue
that readers would do well to retain or develop some awarenes of the
difference between the contexts operable in the moment and site
of the narrated scene—1950s rural Cuba—and the moment and site
of narration—late 1980s New York and its gay enclaves. The specificity of the latter, together with, say, the generic expectations created by the celebratory coming-out testimonial, resonates in much of
Arenas's tone of validation and openess. These images and tone, affirming and enjoyable, but hardly provocative or surprising in gay
New York, exert a substantially different index of provocation
among other readerships, among the other print communities,[11] inside which Arenas's work demands to be read: gay Cubans, closeted
or not, will read it differently from any other gays; straight Cuban
Miami will read it differently still; and inside of Cuba, it will be read
as equally proscribed ideologically deviant material by all, but differently by gay and homophobic or homophilic straight, or by state security personnel gay or straight, and by rural or urban, young or old.

In sharp contrast with the 1990 autobiography, Arenas's earliest
novel does not or cannot take up the representation of homosexuality with the same directness. *Celestino antes del alba*, already written
by 1964, is nationally recognized and institutionally sanctioned inside Cuba by a prestigious award and with its publication in 1967 by
the official Unión de Escritores y Artistas Cubanos (UNEAC).[12] This
is the story of a visionary boy, living with his tyrannical grandparents and his ambivalent mother, deep in the poverty and isolation of
an undated—but clearly prerevolutionary—Cuban rural setting.

This novel is also full of cousins. Celestino is sometimes a cousin of the nameless child narrator, and other times the narrator's alter ego. The two children, or the two modalities of the same child, are extremely close, they sleep together, and share the full spectrum of children's play, children's tenderness, and child abuse. The adults inflict the abuse for all sorts of reasons but most emblematically to discipline Celestino's recalcitrant insistance on writing an unending flow of what the adults around him see as dangerously weird signs, and what the readers of the novel soon recognize as poetry. Before the grandfather launches his campaign to chop down every tree on which Celestino has scratched out his poems, the narrative registers the following response from the narrator's mother:

> Writing. Writing. And when not a single yucca leaf is left to mess up—or a single palm leave husk, or Grandpa's ledger books—Celestino starts writing on the trunks of trees.

> "That's faggotry [mariconería]," said my mother, when she found out Celestino had started his writeries [escribideras]. And that was the first time she jumped down the well.

> "I'd rather die than have a son like that," and the water level in the well rose.[13]

In this text from the mid-1960s, the issue of homosexuality comes into the work as an exploration of that Cuban cultural truism that asserts that all or nearly all artists are queer, or that even if all Cuban artists are not queer, no one who knows, including the drafters of the Declaration of the Congress on Education and Culture, would disagree that a peculiarly large proportion happen to be. In *Celestino antes del alba* what can be read as a denunciation of homophobia can also, and much more safely in line with the expectations of the revolutionary cultural machinery, be read as a denunciation of pre-revolutionary boorish anti-intellectualism. On the political front, those in a position to emit official appraisals from the cultural institutions of the revolution during the mid-1960s can read the anti-intellectual, anticultural tyranny of the Grandpa-deforester, for instance, as a critique of the cultural wasteland in which many Cuban artists suffocated before revolutionary cultural policies provided much improved means for the production and dissemination of—ideologically instrumental—culture.[14] With all its references to "mariconería" *Celestino* remains substantially a closet text. Even so, we can see the barely-twenty-year-old Arenas looking back toward that childhood where cousins frolicked and got into trouble playing around trees—remember Orlando. Yet here he avoids sexual explicitness while still articulating that an artistic sensibility had started to develop under the label of queer.

Let me just highlight briefly that the relationship always evident between the closet and self-imposed or external censorship appears substantially complicated in the case of Arenas. During the second half of the 1960s and through the 1970s, as the Stalinization of Cuban homophobia intensifies, it could be argued that his writing becomes successively uncloseted as he himself progressively descends into invisibility inside of Cuba by a succession of retreats, imprisonment, flight, and internal exile. His border crossings in fact intensify right here, while he crosses many still inside of Cuban territory, and very much while he is not yet an object for the observation or analysis of interstate displacements. His Mariel outing is just the displacement that took him across the Florida Straits into the U.S., but a careful study of his displacements would have to look at the others.

Two major novels, *El palacio de las blanquísimas mofetas* and *Otra vez el mar* (both portraits of the artist as a young queer in pre- and postrevolutionary Cuba), and an epic poem, *El central* (collapsing nineteenth-century slaves and twentieth-century homosexuals as labor pool for Cuba's sugar plantation economy), are repeatedly rewritten, hidden, confiscated, or destroyed. Migration gives Arenas the opportunity, first of all, to rewrite many of the texts he had been working on in his underground days, and subsequently the opportunity to elaborate a set of texts fully conceived and developed *out* in the United States. The Mariel outing takes him out of invisibility of internal exile to allow him to work now inside of a new situation with the complications of being simultaneously out of the closet, out of his underground, out from under the threat of further imprisonment, but also out of Cuba. This fact of being out of Cuba has consequences for the kind of denunciation of Cuban homophobia he can now produce, and for the astounding fact that such denunciations can become, in an international forum, Cold War ammunition that a preeminently homophobic U.S. administration can use, together with whatever else might be of use, in its confrontations with the Cuban state.

In an essayistic exercise of literary history, Reinaldo Arenas asks about Cuba's romantic poets one of his often painfully evident self-referential questions: "¿Qué, que nunca tuve y he perdido, y sin lo cual no podré seguir viviendo, añoro?"[15] (What is it that I want? What is it that I long for? What is it that I hanker after? What is it that I mourn? "¿Qué . . . añoro?" This is the basic query, but the verb of desire comes separated from the interrogative relative pronoun by a long and telling qualifier: What is it, that I never had and have lost, and that I will not be able to continue to live without, that I . . . *añoro*? All this loss could be related to continued displacement that leaves behind something the fleeing subject once had, yet it could also refer more sharply to the headlong search for something the displaced always lacked and desired. One basic, definitive, identity-grounding thing that Arenas never had, and lost, and was not able to continue to live without was precisely a space, a territory, in which to be, with neither risk nor apology, both Cuban and gay. With homosexuality at the center of his project, Arenas provides one of those pronounced illustrations of what Timothy Brennan discusses as "the fictional uses of 'nation' and 'nationalism'. . . not simply an allegory or imaginative vision, but a gestative political structure which the Third World artist is consciously building or suffering the lack of."[16] There is no doubt that Arenas is gestating a political structure, one which, given the resounding failures of all the previously installed homophobic ones, deserves at least some chance in Cuba's political culture, one in which Cubanness would no longer definitionally deny, exclude, or reject gayness. As an author operating sequentially in and out of Cuba, in and out of a variety of homosexual arrangements with a variety of cultural mainstreams, Arenas expands the possibilities of Cuban homosexuality. His expansions, with all their risks, and with the pain of exile as their preeminent high cost, do amount to discursive practices with territorial consequences that state-bound models could never account for, and which state-bound critiques could never fully validate nor nurture as a supranational pattern of resistance, even for subjectivities as clearly rooted in nationalism as Reinaldo Arenas.

NOTES

1. Eve Kosofsky Sedgwick articulates what I take as one of my points of departure in the following terms: "The analytic move [deconstruction] makes is to demonstrate that categories presented in a culture as symmetrical binary oppositions—heterosexual/homosexual, in this case—actually subsist in a more unsettled and dynamic tacit relation according to which, first, term B is not symmetrical with but subordinated to term A; but, second, the ontologically valorized term A actually depends for its meaning on the simultaneous subsumption and exclusion of term B; hence, third, the question of priority between the supposed central and the supposed marginal category in each dyad is irresolvably unstable, an instability caused by the fact that term B is constituted as at once internal and external to term A." Eve Kosofsky Sedgwick, *Epistemology of the Closet* (Berkeley: University of California Press, 1990), pp. 9-10.

2. Eliseo Pérez-Stable, "Cuba's Response to the HIV Epidemic," *American Journal of Public Health* 81, no. 5 (1991), pp. 363-67.

3. The mass demonstrations of support for the Cuban government, denouncing those who were about to leave also came to be known by a resonant and highly symptomatic name: "actos de repudio," "acts of repudiation."

4. Allen Young, *Gays under the Cuban Revolution* (San Francisco: Gray Fox Press, 1981), pp. 34, 53.

5. *Mariel: Revista de literatura y arte* 5 [Sección especial] "Los cubanos y el homosexualismo" (spring 1984), p. 8.

6. Excerpt from *Granma Weekly Review*, May 9, 1971, p. 5; as quoted in Allen Young, *Gays under the Cuban Revolution*, pp. 32-33.

7. Ibid.

8. Allen Young, *Gays under the Cuban Revolution*. Carlos Franqui expresses his assessment of the prerevolutionary extent of homophobia more succinctly: "Cuban cruelty allows you to make fun of a homosexual, but not to imprison or harass him." Carlos Franqui, *Family Portrait with Fidel* (New York: Vintage, 1985), p. 140.

9. Reinaldo Arenas, *Antes que anochezca (Autobiografía)* (Barcelona: Tusquests, 1992); see also, Reinaldo Arenas, *Before Night Falls*, trans. Dolores M. Koch (New York: Viking, 1993).

10. See Tomás Almaguer, "Chicano Men: A Cartography of Homosexual Identity and Behavior," *differences* 3, no. 2 (1991), pp. 75–100; Ana María Alonso and Teresa Korek, "Silences: 'Hispanics,' AIDS, and Sexual Practices," *differences* 1, no. 1 (1989), pp. 101–24; Joseph M. Carrier, "Cultural Factors Affecting Urban Mexican Male Homosexual Behavior," *Archives of Sexual Behavior* 5, no. 2 (1976), pp. 103-24; Joseph M. Carrier, "Family Attitudes and Mexican Homosexuality," *Urban Life* 5, no. 3

(1976), pp. 359-75; and Roger Lancaster, "Subject Honor and Object Shame: The Construction of Male Homosexuality and Stigma in Nicaragua," *Ethnology* 27, no. 2 (1988), pp. 111–25.

11. Benedict Anderson, *Imagined Communities: Reflections on the Origins and Spread of Nationalism* (London: Verso, 1991).

12. Reinaldo Arenas, *Celestino antes del alba* (Caracas: Monte Avila, 1980).

13. Reinaldo Arenas, *Singing from the Well*, trans. Andrew Hurley (New York: Viking, 1987), pp. 4–5. Hurley's translation is slightly altered.

> Escribiendo. Escribiendo. Y cuando no queda ni una hoja de magüey por enmarañar. Ni el lomo de una y[a]gua. Ni las libretas de anotaciones del abuelo: Celestino comienza a escribir entonces en los troncos de las matas.
>
> "Eso es mariconería," dijo mi madre cuando se enteró de la escribidera de Celestino. Y esa fue la primera vez que se tiró al pozo.
>
> "Antes de tener un hijo así, prefiero la muerte." Y el agua del pozo subió de nivel (*Celestino*, 16).

14. Roberto Valero declares about *Celestino*: "Sería imposible esperar que una novela escrita dentro de Cuba fuese más directa. Quizás sea la primera novela seria que cuestione la ética del proceso revolucionario. El autor utiliza la situación del artista que por casualidad nace en una familia donde reinan la ignorancia y la brutalidad, tema perfectamente válido e interesante en sí, para aludir y condenar la otra tiranía, la que espera al artista una vez que se libere de su familia. . . . parte de la información sobre las posibles implicaciones anti-castristas me la ha dado el propio autor,—no estoy convencido del todo—, aunque sus comentarios parezcan lógicos." Roberto Valero, *El desamparado humor de Reinaldo Arenas* (Miami: Letras de Oro, 1991), pp. 75–76.

15. Reinaldo Arenas, "Desgarramiento y fatalidad en la poesía cubana, *Mariel 6* (summer 1984), p. 22b; or Reinaldo Arenas, *Necesidad de libertad: Mariel: testimonios de un intelectual disidente* (Mexico: Kosmos-Editorial, 1986).

16. Timothy Brennan, "The National Longing for Form," in Homi K. Bhabha, ed., *Nation and Narration* (London: Routledge, 1990), pp. 46-47.

VII

War and Identity

Introduction to Part VII

MICHAEL J. SHAPIRO

The three essays in this section issue from the state of Hawai'i, one of the planet's most intensely militarized venues. In addition to being the home of the U.S. "Pacific Command," a key nodality in military cartography, it is also, with its national military cemetery at Punch Bowl and its war memorial at Pearl Harbor, a tourist-oriented military history museum. In modernity, much of the history of warfare returns as film (as Anton Kaes has put it).[1] It is also the case that "tourisms of war,"[2] for example, tourist visits to military shrines, like films and other media representations, help create the narratives through which nations consolidate their identities and, more specifically, the identity investments that reproduce societal support for militarization.

The *Arizona* Memorial at Pearl Harbor provides an important intersection for global tourist traffic. It is a place where many U.S. and Japanese tourists go to re-create memories of World War II, re-create or dissolve grievances as the case may be, and help reproduce their respective national imaginaries in the context of a reading of that war.

The signs of war that the memorial dispenses, however, are packaged with the totality of other signs in Hawai'i, which tend to dissimulate and pacify the more violent aspects of war. The resulting mythologizing of war, read differently by the different national cultures who confront them, plays into the legitimating of state warfare or at least of the legitimacy of the state-as-actor in making the decision to put the lives of its citizens at risk. Like all such legitimations, the memorial, as Phyllis Turnbull points out, is "a pedagogy of state and personal identity" that reminds us of the intense ontological stakes of war, that is, of the self-other ideational commitments, which connect citizen bodies with their national body and give warfare an identity-affirming impetus.

Kathy Ferguson's kibbutz journal describes another highly militarized venue. In addition to its high level of militarization, Israel is a place where contending identities between Arab and Jew, women and men, and native-born and immigrant peoples complicate and intensify the issues surrounding Israel's warfare. Ferguson's analysis reveals how misleading it is to apply a state-oriented grammar in which "Israel" as a whole is the actor. All of the state's attempts to legitimate or celebrate its use of force operate within a set of centrifugal ideational forces that contest the state's rationales.

As a traveler from another political culture who is married to an Israeli, Ferguson reads Israel's political dynamic from a place partly inside and partly outside of its identity pressures. Her reading provides a gloss on militarization that contests state legitimations while, at the same time, foregrounding the differential identity stakes, which she has been in a position to experience, as they are elaborated through gender, ethnicity, generational, and place of origin identity problematics.

Finally, my essay on warring bodies seeks to reveal more generally the implications of seeing warfare ethnographically rather than strategically by focusing on the ontological or identity stakes rather than the strategic, means-ends implications of violence between peoples. By examining tribal warfare in cultures that do not overcode their ontological interests with strategic discourses, it becomes possible first to isolate the ontological impetus to warfare and then to examine its more fugitive existence in the warfare representations of modern state societies.

Because the ontological aspects of warfare violence encourage a preoccupation with dangerous Others, the current, post–Cold War situation of unstable global enmities has produced an incitement to discourses of danger. What must be examined more fully to understand the present, sometimes frantic production of dangerous Others is the internal logics within which the nonacceptance of forms of otherness within the order of the self or nation are implicated in the identification of global antagonists. I argue, in short, that the meanings of global dangers emerging from the interpretive activities of a given state must be read in the context of the complex identity economy operating within that state's society.

NOTES

1. Anton Kaes, *From Hitler to Heimat: The Return of History as Film* (Cambridge, Mass.: Harvard University Press, 1989).

2. Elizabeth Diller and Ricardo Scofidio, *Back to the Front: Tourisms of War* (New York: Princeton Architecture Press, 1994).

16

Remembering Pearl Harbor: *The Semiotics of the* Arizona *Memorial*

PHYLLIS TURNBULL

INTRODUCTION

Returning recently to Honolulu from the West Coast, I was struck anew by the eagerness with which many passengers struggled to glimpse Pearl Harbor as the plane came in to land. The interest was perceptibly different from that in other identified landmarks such as the volcanic mountain peaks of the island of Hawai'i or Diamond Head and Waikiki Beach. Because most travelers to Hawai'i[1] usually come seeking the carnival pleasures of sunny beaches, romance under the palm trees, and exotic drinks, the site of a major military disaster of fifty years ago would not seem to lie in the suntan and mai tai register of desire. Or would not seem to if the positivist account of the world and reality made the calls.

But from a perspective that emphasizes the contingent nature of reality, both are forms of desire[2] focused by the discourses and practices of the global economic system and nation-states. Instead of a contradiction, we can read them as multiple inscriptions of the ways that those forces mold and fortify identities. The tourist gaze is part of that process; it is a reading of self and space through taken-for-granted cultural boundaries that divide like from unlike, belonging from not belonging. It is the metes and bounds work that constitutes identity from and against difference.

Travel theoretically resists or is at least an unruly agency of the inscription processes because it involves encountering foreign-ness[3]

407

and persons moving across spatial and political borders, coming into contact with human difference and alternative ways of being. But modern air travel, itself part of the dynamics of global capitalism, international politics, and their mappings of the world, interdicts much of that implied negotiation and self-reflection. The pressurized, hermetically sealed jet airplane flying at 35,000 feet is both metaphor and reality here. Modern travelers have become passengers, a cargo needing special restraints and management; pacification technologies and technologists successfully and comfortably address the passengers as consumers. Consequently, when they leave the carousels as Arrivals, their expectations and understandings of human difference to be encountered are still relatively undisturbed, and they are prepared to be monarchs of all they survey, with mai tais to follow.[4]

This gaze of entitlement reveals an identity that rests upon and repeats historical patterns of dominance occluded by our political discourse. It defines states as discrete geo/political entities.[5] Enwreathed with a global economic/tourist discourse, the two dimensions of the discourse constitute the world, in the words of Jonathan Culler, as "more imperiously an array of places one might visit than it is a configuration of political or economic forces."[6] Americans arriving in Hawai'i to "see Pearl Harbor" may, in a perceptual sense, see it for the first time, but their reading of Pearl Harbor was framed long before they bought their airline tickets. As a national memory site, the *Arizona* Memorial releases identity-claiming narratives in which the passengers' self-recognitions are embedded.

In order to elaborate the connections between memory, identity, and discourse, this essay heeds the words of a popular song of 1942 to "[r]emember Pearl Harbor,"[7] and remembers Pearl Harbor through deconstructing it, for deconstruction is nothing if not remembering.[8] Constructed and reconstructed for nearly a century, Pearl Harbor is ripe for analysis as a site of historical appropriations and struggles, and a set of modern cultural practices and self-understandings. Its combinations of the submerged, hidden, obscured, subordinated, repressed, and engulfed with the visible, apparent, dominant, present, remembered, and buoyant are among the "boundary producing practices central to the production and reproduction" of the identity of the American national state.[9]

Remembering begins with a semiotic reading of the *Arizona*

Memorial through the frame of Pearl Harbor, revealing the domestication of war in the construction of national memory and identity. Doing this gives voice to some of the tongues stilled by such a memory and genealogically retrieves an erased history of Pearl Harbor. For access to the semiotics of Pearl Harbor and the *Arizona* Memorial, Roland Barthes's work on myth lays down a useful path because he saw myth as an active social practice, a form of speech ostensibly depoliticized, but in which political preferences are already embedded. Myth gives an eternal reading to the historically contingent sign, holding fast to the form of the sign while emptying or substituting its meaning.[10] Myth recruits phenomena to itself or has meanings that lie in wait for subjects and objects, just as a position in the family, and often a name, await an unborn child. At Pearl Harbor, myth is hard at work, weaving together narratives about the power of the United States in the world and victory in war and in the process transforming "history into nature."[11] Where the passengers eagerly look for a glimpse of "where it happened," Pearl Harbor semiotically summons them to its signs and terms.

PART ONE

Pearl Harbor's pull on visitors comes from their familiarity with a historical narrative that begins with the "sneak attack" by Japanese airplanes at eight o'clock on the sleepy Sunday morning of December 7, 1941. American losses, in both ships and men, were disastrous; over 3,000 people died.[12] All eight combat-status battleships of the Pacific Fleet were hit; four of them sank and the other four suffered serious damage. Luckily, high seas had delayed two aircraft carriers enroute to Pearl Harbor, or they also might have been among the losses. The USS *Arizona* sank at its moorings ten minutes after it took a bomb hit on an ammunition magazine, and carried with it 1,177 crewmen, most of whom were trapped below decks. The narrative closes when America's honor is vindicated with the unconditional surrender of Japan in 1945. The *Arizona* Memorial was dedicated seventeen years later in 1962.

This is not the only narrative possible or extant, and the relationship between Pearl Harbor and the *Arizona* Memorial is more complex than the simple chronology of attack, victory, and dedication suggests.[13] But it is the reigning narrative, one of war and victory, and it is escorted energetically along in the company of other major narratives of domination by our political and economic discourses. In order to shape the world as a boutique, as Jonathan Culler suggests is the case,[14] it is essential that the appropriations, struggles, and subjugations of its formation must have become invisible and lost to memory even though the subduing has meant the disappearance or marginalization of its floral and faunal indigenes through clearcutting, mining, dredging, smelting, tanning, bleaching, educating, improving, plowing, seeding, harvesting, culling, stamping, medicalizing, mapping, developing, and straightening. The world as boutique means that the remnants and reshaped residues are reframed within market relations as exotic and safe. It is this political/economic web that produces an "it" for the tourists to see.

A keenness to see new places makes tourists, in Culler's memorable phrase, the "unsung armies of semiotics";[15] as tourists, they fan out all over the world in quest of sites or places to visit. As semioticists, their work is to confront symbolic complexes "head on and explore . . . the relation of a sign to its markers," because a site must be marked in order to be apprehended as such.[16] The semiotic soldiers who fly in to Honolulu encounter and negotiate the array of symbolic complexes and sign codes of the pervasive tourism of Hawai'i. Many are greeted at the airport by exotic-looking young men or women wearing their workaday uniforms of "native dress" and are given leis (whose colors might have been enhanced by dyes or spray paint); they drink mai tais embellished with orchids and pineapple and stay in hotels built for tourists by international capital. They are taken in buses or vans to see the "sights." Those who want to escape the tour and its packages of the "inauthentic" rent cars to see more of the "real" Hawai'i; they swim at beaches other than Waikiki, they hike, they windsurf, they go to Pearl Harbor. But the troops' efforts are always doomed to defeat because the iron law of the floating signifier is there before them: the "authentic" must be marked to be properly read. The authenticity of the signs of Pearl Harbor is inscribed in an unremitting code of realism.

PART TWO

The framing of the real begins as visitors arrive by rental cars or tour buses, having taken the Pearl Harbor or *Arizona* Memorial exits from Interstate Freeway H-1. A federal interstate highway on a small island 2,500 miles from the nearest state is less an oxymoron than a territorial inscription by the nation-state and a sign that helps make the war narrative comfortable. With the completion of a long-contested[17] third highway, there will be about 50 miles of interstate highways in the state, all on O'ahu.

The interstate highway system was originally built for national defense, providing rapid ground transportation between U.S. military bases in case of enemy attack.[18] Although the need for "rapid ground transportation" between military bases is obsolete, the military's writing of the land is indelible. The system provides the main, usually only, transportation corridors, and at another everyday level, highway construction provides some temporary relief to an immense increase in auto traffic and provides jobs for residents, profits for construction companies, and contributions to politicians' campaigns.[19] Highway exits to military bases as everyday destinations are an additional practice that hides the militarization of O'ahu in plain sight by making them merely directional clues.

Just before coming to the large guarded gate, visitors who enter via the Pearl Harbor gate are shunted through Navy housing, a pleasant area of one- and two-storeied buildings with long sloping roofs and grassy lawns planted with monkeypod and palm trees. It is a trip through the suburbs, only with a difference. It is also public housing with a different difference. It is public housing in the same sense that the White House is. What is common about them is that the state peeks through these spatial inscriptions; the differences lie in its contrasting ways of constituting publics and persons and its relationships to them.

This tourist corridor continues on through to a large parking lot shared by the USS *Arizona* Memorial Visitor Center and the USS *Bowfin* Submarine Museum adjacent to it. Both buildings are at the water's edge, and it is at this point that the spatial coding of the area changes abruptly. The grass and trees of domesticity are replaced by other signs: sea water, buoys, ships, cranes, rectangular gray buildings, concrete ramps, chain-link fences, masts, uniformed personnel, antennae, military vehicles, flags, guards, rifles, stenciled acronyms.

What gives unity or an apparent coherence to this collection of signs is the Pearl Harbor narrative in which is embedded the concept of the nation-state as a "natural" political entity. The national security state is its modern dress, and at its center is the idea of "armies as the singular face of state power."[20] The signs signify both the might of the American state as well as its legitimacy, a power both threatening and reassuring. For visitors, it is an unusual sight of the material reality of state power. Neither Norfolk nor San Diego, for instance, offers such up-close-and-personal views of the implements of the national security state, signs that readily fortify the idea of the world as a place of dangerous foreign-ness and the need for the armed state to protect its boundaries and people against the menacing others. For visitors who have seen the armed guards at the gate and wound their way through Navy housing, it is like being permitted to see their father's gun collection that is normally kept locked, shown only to his friends. This is the point at which the narrative about American power in the world begins to pick up speed.

From an overhead semiotic infrared camera, the *Arizona* Memorial would appear as a very large vibrant red spot. A national monument operated by the U.S. Park Service, it is not coded as a recreational or leisure area but as a hallowed site. Despite the softening touches of trees, grass, and shrubs, its visitor center takes the realism code to the edge in its architecture and in an audiovisual program staged in a Park Service auditorium. As visitors approach the visitor center from the parking lot, their first sight is of an anchor from the *Arizona* and a piece of its chain leaning against an exterior wall. Evoking the nonexistent ship and lost men as well as the threat of chaos and destruction that other nations pose, this reminder of the real is an icon making the classic move of myth.[21] The myth picks the anchor's pockets and gives it only one history—a cowardly attack by a foreign Other on American *men* on American soil.

Ah, yes. *American* soil. Myth works overtime here. In constituting the United States as the innocent victim of Japanese aggression, it obliterates the history of decades of contending American and Japanese foreign policies and economic and military goals. The story becomes, in Bakhtin's words, a unitary language. Moreover, in representing Pearl Harbor as "American soil," it obliterates another long history, that of the appropriations and usurpations by which Hawai'i was annexed to the United States.

At the time of the raid, Hawai'i had been a territory of the United States for over forty years. At the time of the raid, Hawai'i had been continuously populated for about two thousand years by Polynesians who sailed up from the Marquesas against both doldrums and countervailing winds and currents to make landfall at the southern tip of the island of Hawai'i. Between then and when Hawai'i was "discovered" by English Captain James Cook in 1778, Hawai'i had grown into "one of the most sophisticated, complex, and developed of the . . . indigenous societies and cultures . . . [in] the Pacific." The "densely settled population"[22] was well nourished by a complex, interconnected system of agriculture and aquaculture.[23] But enormous cultural changes occurred after Cook's intrusion, as a flood of Others, principally Anglo-American entrepreneurs (spiritual, mercantile, political, and military) came to Hawai'i with their various imagined projects and (hitherto unimagined to Hawaiian bodies) diseases for Hawai'i.[24]

The ultimate subjugation of Hawai'i came through the overthrow in 1893 of the legitimate government of Queen Lili'uokalani by a small number of American businessmen with the support of the American consul as well as some marines stationed aboard the USS *Boston*. The Americans had been assured by the American consul prior to their actions of the likelihood of American annexation, which did occur in 1898.[25]

The subjugation of Pearl Harbor likewise began a century ago as one of the not at all obscure objects of American military desire; the forms of the desire ran from Pearl Harbor being the site of early hydrographic surveys, to serving as a coaling station, to becoming a simple naval station, to the dredging and construction of a major dry dock, to the increasingly fortified and complex fleet and command headquarters of today.

All points on desire's trajectory required vigorous pacification of indigenous people and culture, fauna and flora. In Hawaiian times, the body of water now called Pearl Harbor was a large irregularly shaped body scalloped along its edges with a number of inlets, each of which had specific geographic identities. In the very poetic Hawaiian language, there were a number of ways of referring to any or all of them. One was Pu'uloa (literally long hill), the larger land district in which they were located. It is now the name given to a nearby street.[26]

It is estimated that Pu'uloa was the site of 40 loko i'a, or fishponds, part of the 360 estimated to have been in existence in Hawai'i at the time of Cook's arrival. Fish was an important element in the diet of Hawaiians; the annual production of fish from all the ponds is estimated to have been about two million pounds.[27] The waters of

Pearl Harbor were a heteroglossia of sea life or, as a recent critique of the navy's stewardship wrote, "the stuff of legend," supporting enormous schools of mullet and nehu (baitfish), rich in oysters, clams, and mussels. In the pacification of Pearl Harbor, the fish have gone, the fishponds are nearly all filled in, now "part of the real estate occupied by the navy in connection with its activities at Pearl Harbor."[28]

The anchor, in other contexts, might well evoke the sunken ship and lost men but in a way that denaturalizes the national security state to show how it participates in constituting the kinds of dangers against which it ostensibly defends us. It could expose the nature of war in a way to make it look less desirable, in the fullest sense of the word, or inevitable, as the positivism of realpolitik would have it. Or it might implicate the military or political leaders more than foreign demons, questioning the politics of the promotion process that selects naval commanders. It might make an issue of the soundness of naval warfare tactics that anchored eight battleships in two tidy rows in such a vulnerable place and at a time when the probability of war seemed very high. But it is the practices of myth that contextualize the anchor and chain with the master narratives[29] of American might and victory that keep their meaning from wandering off or speaking to such strangers.

The visitor center is tourism discourse in full voice.[30] Built around a large open courtyard, it offers the expected tourist amenities of rest rooms, drinking fountains, benches, and soda machines. It is signed throughout in both English and Japanese. There is also a bookstore/gift shop reflecting the market constituted by battlefield tourism in its wealth of documents of the real: innumerable publications and forms of printed matter about December 7 and World War II (with special emphasis on the naval war in the Pacific). From the Barthean perspective, this is a history posing as History. This is the sly move that myth makes—to make one reading of an event appear to be the only one possible and to enfold it within a larger "inevitable" history of Western civilization. Beyond these signs of the real, there is a predictable stock of postcards, slides, T-shirts, flags, models, and replica newspapers. This material is a reminder of Culler's argument that the real must be marked by signs in order to be apprehended as "the real" and that the tourist quest is thus for the "experience of signs."[31] Surrounding the anchor of the *Arizona* with key chains with anchor replicas attached gives the anchor its authenticity.[32] For the tourist, the key chain is a sign of the real; it is also a sign that says "I was there," a demonstration of consumer skill and prowess in the scavenger hunt of tourism.

PART THREE

Myth continues its theft of meaning in a larger koa-paneled gallery. Koa (*Acacia koa*) is a rare wood that grows only in Hawai'i. It is not likely that very many of the visitors recognize it as such; its importance here is as a "natural" sign of authenticity in the same way that any wood paneling would be and a plastic surface would not. At the same time, the use of a native wood in this place domesticates the navy, codes it as native, not a colonizer, of this place. The use of koa also encodes economic power and prestige. It is used today for flooring, furniture, paneling, and, occasionally, outrigger canoes and ukuleles, but not for *most* floors, furniture, or wall panels; and only a few canoe clubs sport koa racing canoes, for it, like its users, commands a price.

Native Hawaiians used koa in making outrigger canoe hulls from trees selected for their size and straight trunks. Both the selection and cutting of a koa followed prescribed religious practices, and the canoes themselves were used by the chiefs.[33] Today koa has become a rare commodity, in part because of its vulnerability to a destructive pest and, even more, because of private and public land practices.[34]

Koa can also mean brave and bravery, fearless, valiant, and warrior. (The name of the military hotel at Fort DeRussy in Waikiki is Hale Koa, the "house of the warrior.") The gallery in which koa has such an active semiotic life features paintings and drawings of World War II sea battles, navy life, and marine landscapes, models of ships and bombs, and portraits of admirals and of ships both afloat and afire. Other installations are photo-essays on such male-bonding themes as "Battleship Life," "Hawaiian Liberty," and "Battleship Row." The theme of heroes and martyrs can be seen in one display of some personal memorabilia of survivors and victims of the raid, and in another of photos and a biography of a Medal of Honor recipient. It is choice, not the luck of the draw, that determines what is displayed in any gallery. The documentation of a particular historical narrative creates a reality, not mirrors it. At the visitor center, each gallery becomes a relay point of the Pearl Harbor story, as we can see in the exhibit of the personal effects of a seaman lost on the *Arizona*.

The memorabilia of Acting Paymaster Paxton Carter include his uniform, eyeglasses, wallet, high school diploma, Purple Heart, letters, Order of Neptune, and the telegram informing his wife of his death on the *Arizona*. These signs describe the trajectory of a martyr; we see Carter as the form of the sign that myth grasps tightly, emptying his life of all details except for those that save and relay the historical narrative. About Carter we know almost nothing except that he died with the *Arizona*, for the personal is captured but absent. The people and conditions that shaped his life—his parents, his boyhood friends and experiences, his education, the conditions leading to his enlistment, and whether his heart lifted at the sight of the ocean, the shrill of a bo'sun's pipe, or a puff of a Camel cigarette—are importantly absent and not needed. Myth makes Carter a public figure who enlisted "in the service of his country" for which he "gave" his life, rather than a man who, perhaps faced with bleak employment prospects in the American pre–World War II economy, joined the navy less to serve his country than to have a job or a place to live. The few signs of Carter in the case—his eyeglasses, his high school diploma, his medal—are myth's way of keeping him on active duty and forestalling his having had a life in which he loved, laughed, and lived. The master narrative of war has no need of such voices.[35] More than that, it insures that if they register at all, it is as the personal, the particular, or the anecdotal. As "subjugated knowledges . . . a whole set of knowledges that have been disqualified as inadequate to their task or insufficiently elaborated," they are seditious to the unanimity of the narrative and to the kind of legitimate knowledge that is required to make war rational.[36]

The hero myth skimps death as well as life. In other circumstances—as sailor or civilian during peacetime—the cause for Carter's death would have been closely scrutinized and the responsible agent identified and prosecuted, for his death, if not accidental, would have been a criminal act. In the case of the mass deaths on the *Arizona*, such a question could not arise, and the grisly deaths of the men have been enshrouded in the heroic language of "gave his life," "fell in action," or "died gallantly."

War and its deaths are a high-stakes legitimacy game for any state; myth's work is invaluable not only in transforming the deaths from the torn-flesh register to something ethereal, but also—in giving a coherence to war and its prosecutors—in solidifying the importance and naturalness of the state and its responses to the dangers that threaten. An example of this production and reproduction is the "we regret to inform you . . . " telegram announcing a death or casualty. The "we" gives organization and direction to war, suggesting that it consists of the unified and synchronized movements of an army or ensemble of men by those who are prosecuting it according to a pattern. The myth work of the telegram is difficult to transform or decode because it contains little or no information. The military's practice in the last several decades has been to send an official spokesman to break the news to the next of kin as a symbol of care and concern, but these men solidify the legitimating frame of war, for they have no voices of their own. Breaking death out of the grasp of myth's unitary language is difficult precisely because it is determinedly monoglossic.[37]

Another gallery display focuses on sailors/heroes decorated for bravery. Photos of one officer (a noncommissioned officer at the time of the raid), a recipient of the Medal of Honor, with accompanying descriptions of his gallantry, are displayed in the gallery. Next to this display is one focusing on an enlisted mess attendant whose courage and action won him the Navy Cross, a decoration slightly less valued than the Medal of Honor. Myth lurks in the photo captions that indicate that even mess attendants, who normally do not have combat duties, respond as heroes when their ship and comrades are attacked.

What myth casts aside here is the institutional racism of the navy at that time as it effortlessly reproduces both the color and hierarchy of navy command as normal. As the photos make clear, the Medal of Honor recipient was white and the mess attendant African American, but that racial discrimination was as much a naval practice as button flies and black shoes goes unremarked. The gaze is directed to the mess attendant's use of an automatic weapon to good effect against enemy planes, not to the naval practice of assigning black men to duties that precluded their contact with guns.[38]

The few females, other than ships, who appear in the gallery exhibitions do so in roles and activities predictably ancillary to the main business of both warrior and state. The gallery, indeed the whole center, is as much about the ship of state as it is a ship of the fleet, a white and masculine vessel propelled by the master myths of national preeminence and warrior heroes. [39]

Prior to taking the short boat ride to the memorial, visitors are moved along into an auditorium where a Park Service Ranger in a Smokey Bear hat makes a short speech before the movie. The content of the speech has varied over the years as the ages and nationalities of the visitors have changed. The current theme, addressed in large measure to persons born well after the raid and including a large number of Japanese nationals,[40] asks them to respect the memorial as the final resting place of "the men who still live beneath her decks" and to refrain from eating, drinking, and smoking while there.

The movie, using actual military footage from both American and Japanese sources, opens with questions that acknowledge the loss of life and the military disaster: What happened? Why was Pearl Harbor attacked? Why were so many killed? The answers, spelled out in the substance of the movie, renaturalize the state and its actions to secure its boundaries against dangerous and alien others. Japanese conquests in Asia are represented as leading in a direct line of military conquest from the actions of "extremist" elements of the army in Manchuria through Asia to Pearl Harbor, whose destruction was essential in order to "secure" the former European colonies in Southeast Asia.

Then the focus changes to footage of the *Arizona* on maneuvers and back in Pearl Harbor with the rest of the fleet "as the last night of peace slipped away." After five minutes of footage of the violence and extent of the raid, the camera pans slowly over the water to the serenity of the *Arizona* Memorial where "they will never be forgotten."

PART FOUR

Properly catechized and benumbed, the 150 visitors file out and board the navy launch, manned by navy personnel, for the ride to the memorial. It is a long and narrrow white concrete structure, hull-like in shape, built athwart the long axis of the sunken hull, the middle portion quite open to the air and sky. In profile, the structure dips down in the middle to just above the water and soars at both ends. Visitors alight from the launch at one end of the memorial and make a slow elongated U-shaped tour before reembarking as another group arrives. The signs of the memorial are a semiotic doppelgänger; at the entering end of the structure is the lost ship's bell, and at the other are carved the names of all the dead men. What can be seen of the ship is a rusted remnant of a large gun turret, some just-submerged supports for another turret, the stump of a leg of the main mast from which flies the American flag, and, under some conditions of tide and light, the dim outline of the *Arizona*'s coral-encrusted hull. This is in the middle low section of the memorial, where visitors are only several feet from both water and ship remnants.

The combination of the real of the movie footage and the real of the ship's wreckage is a powerful propellant of the war narrative and produces epiphanic moments in the tour. Visitors' voices are quite subdued; they pause a long time (given that they have about twenty minutes on the memorial) by the gun turret; some throw leis into the water and watch them slowly bob away.[41]

Throughout the memorial, myth has its semiotic work cut out for itself in marshaling fickle, unstable signs into domesticating ranks and order. Despite the anesthesia of the lecture and movie, there is a dangerous surplus of meaning. The rusted bits of the *Arizona* are potentially destabilizing; another place that has this effect is the "shrine room," the wall of Vermont marble at the end opposite the ship's bell; it is a site where the palimpsest of war's merciless violence nearly bleeds through, for on it are inscribed the names of the perished members of the ship's company. When the group comes to the wall where the names are carved, its members hesitate to approach closely. The wall, set back eight to ten feet from several low steps, is flanked by flags and roped off by the kind of velvet rope used for crowd control in places such as banks and post offices, only this rope is black. Sometimes there are leis draped over it. Although some visitors pose for photos in front of it, none violate its surface by touch or even approaching closely.

But these names, which threaten to signify war as torn humans, ruptured social fabric, and their kin's catastrophic sense of loss, are impressed into the service of the historic narrative and the structuring of a sentimental memory of war through the way they are framed, distanced, and ordered. This wall contrasts starkly with the wall of the Vietnam Veterans Memorial. This framing closes the narrative,[42] leaving war undisturbed, whereas the Vietnam memorial leaves the narrative open and challenges the waste of war. The never fully replaced loss that the death of someone close to us leaves is literally palpable at the Vietnam wall, but is abstract and abstracted by the *Arizona* Memorial. The names are untouchable because the wall itself is remote, guarded by two flags, several marble steps, and the (velvet) rope. Moreover, its height puts hundreds of names out of reach. Visitors would have to reach up (as well as act up), not out, to touch most. The palpability of the names on the Vietnam Veterans Memorial makes the history of individual persons recoverable because they are at and below the viewer's level; visitors walk among them having come upon the wall set down in the ground, not towering over it. It sabotages any hope of a single closed narrative. The chronological ordering of the names at the Vietnam memorial opens up reflective room to multiple histories; a visitor to the site has his or her own lived experience of the lost ones, their own histories, and ways of remembering where they were, what they were doing, when this person was lost, when they heard of the loss, and what kind of life was no longer possible. Trying to find a name within the chronology reproduces for the visitor some of the chaos of war.

Naming the dead men in the order of their deaths was impossible at the *Arizona* Memorial. Instead, the impersonal nature of modern wars and mass death that made it has molded the names into a bizarrely egalitarian order at the memorial; all men's names are listed alphabetically with rank listed after their names, as though it were a simple descriptor, and not a significant navy and political marker. The alphabetical listing is a domesticating move in that men killed in war become depoliticized data, adjuncts to the single chronological history and memory. Lists make war more orderly, as though there had been an underlying plan all along. Moreover, it is easier to locate the names of its victims if the *when* of the deaths is taken care of; then the alphabetical order seizes the gaze, averting it from the cruel realities of the *how*. If a visitor were to locate a name from looking at the list of 1,177 names carved on a single flat wall, outlined in black, there would be nothing else for him/her to do except to leave, because this is a *tour* of the memorial and the timetable requires it; the domesticating order doubles back upon the visitors. The wall is an image constructed for the visitors to participate in the experience of reverence, as Baudrillard's discussion of the political economy of the sign suggests. As tourists consume the sign, it comes to define them; they are at the memorial being reverent.[43]

If the shrine room wall represents one brisk way of sweeping signs into a normalized and predictable order, other aspects of the memorial work away differently at masking or, following George Mosse, "displac[ing] the reality of war" by reshaping its grisly character as a "meaningful and sacred experience."[44] Mosse is speaking here of the ways in which the reality of the World War I experience was reshaped as the Myth of the War Experience through such images as monuments, cemeteries, and other kinds of war memorials. To suppress the horror of the swift annihilation of American sailors, the themes of resurrection and reverence are promoted in several adroit ways. In the first instance, the location and architecture of the memorial cooperate by taking Nature firmly in their grasp, compelling it to frame the text in the same way that the koa paneling did in the gallery. The water of the harbor surrounding the immaculate white concrete memorial, the blue sky, and sunlight overhead are all signs of a tranquillity and an immutability completely at odds with the sudden and grisly deaths of the sailors. These are the "natural" signs of resurrection indicating that here is a place of eternal peace, the peace of an immutable and universal cycle of life where death is as abstract as life.

The Nature that speaks here is a severely regulated one, allowed to set the stage for memory but not to perform biochemical processes on ship or men. The wreckage of the *Arizona* has, over time, been transformed by marine creatures and processes into a reef where marine organisms live out their lives; some of the animals, like coral, significantly stabilize the wreck. The bodies of the sailors long ago underwent the sea changes effected by the ocean's tides, currents, and animals. There *is* a cycle of life here in these transformations. But the displacement of the reality of war requires resurrection's story of denial,[45] not a food chain story.

Wrapping Nature daintily in the dress whites of immutability also suppresses the violent crimes committed by the navy against the waters of the harbor. The habor has been used by the navy for over one hundred years, and the contamination of its waters is so extensive and concentrated that in July 1991, Pearl Harbor was nominated by the Environmental Protection Agency for inclusion on its Superfund list. A study of six sites in the harbor gave it a score of 70.82; a score of 28.5 is enough to qualify.[46]

Situating the memorial in order to span the midsection of the *Arizona* suggests the same kind of reverence for the dead as avoiding stepping on graves in churchyards does. The hush gently moves along the idea of the ship as a tomb and gathers reverence for the dead. Such signs as the ship's bell, the rusted gun turret remnant, and the leg stump of the main mast are essential to the narrative even though they are another moment that could overpower or undo myth's whole project. The water moves, the good and bad odors of a harbor are present, an occasional oil bubble still slowly leaking from the ship's tanks surfaces. The reality may not be all white marble and blue skies; the violence of the destruction of 1,177 men in a dozen minutes is just below the surface literally as well as metaphorically.

But it is these signs that allow the realist code and the myth to work together to solidify the narrative, for the literal meaning of the signifiers—rusted hull, ocean water, oil leaks—is but a foil for their intention.[47] The duplicity of the sign allows intention to hide in the "imperative, buttonholing" quality of myth[48] even as the signs appear to register simple facts. At the memorial, intention's shrill whistle hides just as it summons visitors to look at the rusted steel whose concrete details are supposed to denote a reality—"we are (the remants of) reality"—but they are props for the presentation of a different story. The preserved bits of wreckage are parts of the myth, not independent investigators.

The final semiotic gesture the memorial makes is in the ambiguous sign of the upward sweep at each of its ends capable of being read as either resurrective or triumphant. As resurrection, it continues the theme of war's redemption and an afterlife for the dead men. Triumph is about something else. Marita Sturken aids us here: "a memorial refers to the life or lives sacrificed for a particular set of values. Memorials embody grief, loss and tribute or obligation; in doing so, they serve to frame particular historical narratives."[49] The death memorialized here is, just as the name suggests, just as the rusted scraps suggest, just as the American flag flown from the mast leg suggests, that of the ship. And the ship, in its last suppression of war as bursting lungs and torn bodies, comes, in a strange synecdotal turn, to stand, however reverently for the 1,177 men. The upward sweep of the memorial is a metaphor of triumph that brings closure to the tensions of the scene so that war can become a "meaningful and sacred event."

CONCLUSION

Charles Griswold has written that a memorial is "a species of pedagogy . . . [that] seeks to instruct posterity about the past and, in so doing, necessarily reaches a decision about what is worth recovering."[50] The pedagogy of the *Arizona* Memorial can now be spelled out. For those forces constituting the American national security state, its silences and its vociferations normalize war and reproduce the legitimacy of the state.[51] It does not ask war to explain itself but, instead, points to the strangeness that lies beyond our borders and against which we must always be defended. In this respect, that the enemy was Japan is less important than that the memorial sings the important refrain that beyond these borders lie disorder and danger. The memorial and Pearl Harbor alibi each other in respect to war and in different ways. Pearl Harbor, as the frame through which the memorial is experienced, is simultaneously a sign of America's puissance in the world and a ghostly reminder of its vulnerability for which it must constantly compensate.

For its part, the memorial is the underwriter for the *sneak attack* narrative on which the state's legitimacy rides. War deaths are acceptable only if they represent a sacrifice for the country and not waste by its leaders. A *surprise attack* suggests such a possibility, for it involves a certain parity between the warring parties, a sharing of a universalized rationality; within this logic a "surprise" raid may be unexpected but rational, well within the realm of possibilities as understood by both parties. In the case of such an attack, the attacked party has to recognize itself and its *failures* to know, anticipate, and act. A "sneak" attack, however, locates the attacker in a space of irrationality where difference has run amok; motives and methods bear no correspondence to universalized human rationality but have become the bestial actions of radically alien Others. From the outset the sneak attack was the American myth of choice.[52] And although today there are no traces of the rabid dog rhetoric at the memorial where its story is played out in the open—rusted metal, ocean water, fresh air—the deaths are still unthinkable except as the result of a sneak attack.

For the American tourists who go to Pearl Harbor to "see where it happened," the memorial is a pedagogy of state and personal identity, and a dangerous one at that because of the orientations and dispositions toward human difference upon which the logic rests. John

Dower has recounted how the "exterminist rhetoric" that spawned the "sneak attack" continued throughout the war, making a negotiated conclusion to the war impossible.[53] The construed radical foreign-ness of the Japanese—sneaky, treacherous, inhuman—absolved the United States of responsibility for the ferocity of battle and the loss of life in the Pacific military campaigns that saw few prisoners taken, and it legitimated nuclear warfare on the people of Nagasaki and Hiroshima "in order to save American lives." Again, it is not that the memorial demonizes any given national group but that it keeps warm the rich broth of superior/inferior, safety/danger, interior/exterior distinctions that makes demonization possible.

The memorial can remember American soil only by a structured amnesia about its provenance. It can "remember Pearl Harbor" only by drawing an opaque screen between memory and the racism that made possible the firebombing of population centers and the dropping of atomic bombs on Others. This pedagogy submerges the dead. It does not recover them.

Finally, the memorial makes it possible to close the book on war, to tuck war into the master narrative about this country's dominance in the world and its ability to imprint its order on others.[54] The closure of the *Arizona* Memorial normalizes a particular war as well as war itself by giving it a completed (narrative) structure of beginning, middle, and end, leaving "cause and effect intact."[55] The effect is to reserve a place for war and victory in the nation's self-understanding.

NOTES

1. In 1990, approximately 6,700,000 tourists visited Hawai'i, while the population of the state itself was approximately 1,100,000. Hawai'i, Department of Business, Economic Development and Tourism, Research and Economic Analysis Division, Statistics Branch, *State of Hawaii Data Book: A Statistical Abstract* (Honolulu: 1991), pp. 11, 178.

2. Saussurean linguistics prized word apart from object by showing how meaning is produced by the relational structure of signifiers. See Ferdinand Saussure, *Course in General Linguistics*, trans. Wade Baskin (Fontana: Fontana, 1974). In Jacques Lacan's "The mirror stage . . . " is found his explication of how the infant's discovery of its existence within, rather than as, the world radically fractures its identity. Its subsequent lifelong attempt to

recapture the earlier whole and unbroken identity is termed *desire* by Lacan. See Jacques Lacan, *Ecrits: A Selection*, trans. Alan Sheridan (New York and London: W. W. Norton & Company, 1977), pp. 1-7.

3. Foreign-ness is David Campbell's term. See his *Writing Security: United States Foreign Policy and the Politics of Identity* (Minneapolis: University of Minnesota Press, 1992), p. vii.

4. I have borrowed Mary Louise Pratt's felicitous phrase and added company to its original first-person singular. See Mary Louise Pratt, *Imperial Eyes: Travel Writing and Transculturation* (London and New York: Routledge, 1992), p. 201.

5. This way of both reifying and naturalizing the nation-state is critiqued by Campbell. He opposes the conventional concept of this fixed nature of the state with an argument emphasizing its contingent nature whose identity is achieved performatively and discursively, rather than ontologically.

6. Jonathan Culler, *Framing the Sign* (Norman, Oklahoma: University of Oklahoma Press, 1988), p. 153.

7. "Let's Remember Pearl Harbor," words by Don Reid, music by Don Reid and Sammy Kaye. Republic Music Corporation, 1941.

8. When Jacques Derrida said in a recent interview that deconstruction was "a way of remembering what our culture is made of," he was talking about a way of disturbing the taken-for-grantedness of culture through recovering the usurpations, appropriations, and struggles of its formation. See *The Times of London*, June 13, 1992, p. 3.

9. Campbell, *Writing Security*, p. 75.

10. See Roland Barthes, *Mythologies* (New York: Hill and Wang, 1978), especially pp. 109-59.

11. Ibid., p. 129.

12. William P. Iles, "In Quest of Blame: Inquiries Conducted 1941-1946 into America's Involvement in the Pacific War," (Ph.D. diss., University of Iowa, 1978), p. 11.

13. Bakhtin's work on language addresses the first of these reservations. In "Discourse in the Novel" he fluffs up the flattened pillow of language conventionally viewed as a "system of abstract categories" into a plump cushion of activity replete with contending voices, opinions, and world views—an ongoing contest between centripetal forces aiming at a centralized language and centrifugal forces that foster a heteroglossia. The familiar story of Pearl Harbor is, to use his terms, a "unitary language," a unification and centralization of a verbal and ideological world. But his argument about language also alerts us that its victory over the contending voices is not the same thing as an unconditional surrender: "At any given moment of its evolution, language is stratified not only into linguistic dialects in the strict

sense of the word . . . but also—and for us this is the essential point—into languages that are socio-ideological: languages of social groups, 'professional and generic' languages, languages of generations, and so forth." See M. M. Bakhtin, *The Dialogic Imagination*, ed. Michael Holquist, trans. Caryl Emerson and Michael Holquist (Austin and London: University of Texas Press, 1981), pp. 271-72.

A small sample of other accounts of the war includes John Dower, *War without Mercy: Race and Power in the Pacific War* (New York: Pantheon Books, 1986), whose work deals with the intense racism on both sides that made the Pacific war a vicious and savage conflict that could only end through the unconditional surrender of Japan. Casualties were high on both sides, and few prisoners were taken on either side. Dower also discusses how this commitment to an all-out victory combined with the new technologies of war changed its nature and made possible the killing of masses of people (especially civilians) and at greater distances.

Gerald Wheeler's history of Japanese–United States relations in the two decades prior to the attack on Pearl Harbor argues both that war in the "Far East" was regarded as likely by naval officers during this time and that Japan was constituted as the likely enemy by the War Plans Division and the Naval War College. Gerald E. Wheeler, *Prelude to Pearl Harbor: The United States Navy and the Far East, 1921-1931* (Columbia, Missouri: University of Missouri Press, 1963).

In *Pacific Estrangement: Japanese and American Expansion, 1897-1911* (Cambridge, Massachusetts: Harvard University Press, 1972), Akira Iriye traces the estrangement of Japan and the United States during parallel periods of imperialism by both nations in a period earlier than Wheeler.

Other investigations and hearings focused on the attack and military vulnerability. Between 1941 and 1946, eight separate official investigations into the attack were held by various authorities including the president, the secretary of the navy, the secretary of war, a military court of inquiry, and assorted others, including a final Joint Congressional Committee on the Investigation of the Pearl Harbor Attack. For the complete record of the forty volumes of hearings, not indexed or cross-referenced until 1990, see Stanley H. Smith, compiler, *Investigations of the Attack on Pearl Harbor: Index to Government Hearings* (New York, Westport, Conn., London: Greenwood Press, 1990).

Some sense of the politics of military command is contained in the memoirs of Admiral James O. Richardson, *On the Treadmill to Pearl Harbor: The Memoirs of Admiral J. O. Richardson* (Washington, D.C.: Naval History Division, 1973). Richardson recounts his efforts to be appointed chief of naval operations, a position to which President Franklin Roosevelt appointed Admiral Harold Stark instead. Richardson comments, in respect to the appointment, "I do believe that the United States Fleet would not have been in Pearl Harbor on December 7, 1941, had I been Chief of Naval Operations at that time."

William Iles, in "In Quest of Blame," argues that for the authorities, it was important that blame for the attack, rather than responsibility, be quickly established, and this was the tack that President Franklin Roosevelt took when he instituted the first inquiry, which resulted in General Walter Short and Admiral Husband Kimmel being charged with poor judgment and dereliction of duty and retired from duty. Iles shows that subsequent investigations shied away from institutional explanations, for there the issue would have been responsibility.

14. Culler, *Framing the Sign*, p. 153.

15. Culler, *Framing the Sign*, p. 165.

16. Ibid.

17. Interstate Highway H-3 was first proposed twenty years ago as a fifteen-mile defense highway. Even then, the nuclear age had made it militarily obsolete, but economic considerations and the availability of 90 percent federal funding made it an attractive public works project for the state. Opponents, whose identities and reasons for opposing it changed over time, initially delayed it politically by arousing community opposition; they then went to court, where they successfully challenged the state's repeated irregularities in meeting environmental impact statement standards; they won there, too. Opposition then came from a U.S. Senate committee, which found its proposed cost exorbitant. This left H-3 dead until the senior senator from Hawai'i tacked a provision exempting H-3 from environmental laws onto a military appropriations bill. This bill passed. After H-3 was under construction, it was again held up for several months by native Hawaiians because the route was through an area heavily populated by ancient Hawaiians and not well investigated archaeologically. The route also takes motorists directly through an OMEGA antenna field in one valley; the signal is produced by 150,000 watt blasts of electricity, posing health hazards to motorists and workers alike. Finally, the cost of the fifteen-mile highway was estimated in 1968 at around $12 million. By 1987, estimates set it at $850 million, which a U.S. Senate Committee on Environment and Public Works chairman said was too low and that since his committee felt the cost was more likely to be $100 million dollars per mile, it also recommended rejection of H-3. H-3 proceeds under construction. See Steven Goldsberry, Clemence McClaren, Tamara Moan, "H-3, What price? What purpose?" *Honolulu*, March 1992, pp. 32-47.

18. H-1 connects Hickam Air Force Base (home of the Pacific Air Force) and Pearl Harbor (headquarters for the Commander in Chief of the Pacific, the Pacific Fleet, and the Navy Yard) with a disused army post at Diamond

Head; H-2 connects Hickam and Pearl Harbor with Schofield Barracks (home of the combat-ready 25th Infantry Division Light). The still-under-construction H-3 will connect the Kaneohe Marine Corps Air Station (which maintains the First Marine Brigade as a combat-ready force) with Pearl Harbor. Pearl Harbor is the military communication center of the Pacific, and headquarters for military operations that extend from the West Coast of the United States to the east coast of Africa, from polar region to polar region. Goldsberry, McClaren, Moan, "H-3, What price? What purpose?"

This number of major bases and their connections are situated on an island of about 620 square miles; on O'ahu the military owns or controls about 25 percent of the land. The total number of military installations in the whole state is about 100, and the military controls about 10 percent of land overall. See Mehmed Ali, Kathy Ferguson, and Phyllis Turnbull, "Gender, Land and Power: Reading the Military in Hawai'i," paper presented at the 15th World Congress of the International Political Science Association, 21-25 July 1991, Buenos Aires, Argentina.

19. See Tom Coffman, *Catch a Wave: A Case Study of Hawaii's New Politics* (Honolulu: University of Hawaii Press, 1973), Epilogue II n.p.; Ian Lind, "Architects, engineers provide bulk of Democratic funds," *Hawai'i Monitor*, December 1992, p. 1.

20. Bradley S. Klein, "The Textual Strategies of the Military: Or Have You Read Any Good Defense Manuals Lately?" in James Der Derian and Michael J. Shapiro, eds., *International/Intertextual Relations: Postmodern Readings of World Politics* (Lexington, Mass.: Lexington Books, 1989), p. 103.

21. An icon, as C. S. Peirce has written, is a sign that would "possess the character which renders it significant even though its object had no existence," in Mieke Bal and Norman Bryson, "Semiotics and Art History: The Semiotic Critique and Its Relevance for Art History," *Art Bulletin*, vol. 73, no. 2, June 1991, p. 16.

22. Patrick V. Kirch, *Feathered Gods and Fishhooks: An Introduction to Hawaiian Archaeology and Prehistory* (Honolulu: University of Hawaii Press, 1985), pp. 2-7.

23. An excellent description of the agricultural and aquacultural practices of the indigenous natives is found in Samuel Manaiakalani Kamakau, *The Works of the People of Old: Na Hana a ka Po'e Kamakau*, translated from the newspaper *Ke au 'Oko'a* by Mary Kawena Pukui, arranged and edited by Dorothy B. Barrere. Bernice P. Bishop Museum Special Publication 61 (Honolulu: Bishop Museum Press, 1976), parts 2 and 3.

24. For various interpretations of the impact of Western culture on Hawai'i, see: O. A. Bushnell, *The Gifts of Civilization: Germs and Genocide* (Honolulu: University of Hawaii Press, 1993). Bushnell, a microbiologist,

has written a series of essays on the impact of disease on the health of Hawaiians. David E. Stannard, *Before the Horror: The Population of Hawai'i on the Eve of Western Contact* (Honolulu: Social Science Research Institute, University of Hawaii, 1989). Stannard revises sharply upward the number of indigenous natives living in Hawai'i at the time of European contact from the long-accepted 250,000 or 300,000 to 800,000 or 1,000,000. Elizabeth Buck, *Paradise Remade: The Politics of Culture and History in Hawaii* (Philadelphia: Temple University Press, 1993). This is an analysis of the politics of culture as Hawai'i was colonized; the focus is on the transformations of the indigenous culture. Lilikala Kame'eleihiwa, *Native Land and Foreign Desires: Pehea La E Pono Ai?* (Honolulu: Bishop Museum Press, 1992). This is the first analysis of the effects of the imposition of an Anglo-American system of land law on a social system where land had use rather than exchange value. It is the first such work based on Hawaiian language documents.

25. The overthrow of the government of Queen Lili'uokalani is widely held to have been illegal. The thirteen men who engineered it and carried it off included no Hawaiians, and only seven were citizens of Hawai'i. By the time of the overthrow, the monarch's powers had been seriously truncated; in 1887 a larger group of (largely) Americans and Europeans had forced the king to sign the "Bayonet Constitution," which, through a property ownership requirement, largely disenfranchised the Hawaiians and allowed foreign nonresidents to vote provided they could understand the constitution translated into English. The "Bayonet Constitution" had been forced upon the king because, among other things, he refused to grant Pearl Harbor to the United States when the Reciprocity Treaty was due for renewal. The treaty allowed local sugar grown mostly by Americans to enter the United States without tariff. The Bayonet Constitution satisfied both the sugar growers' desires and those of the American government. See Liliuokalani, *Hawaii's Story by Hawaii's Queen* (Rutland, Vt., Tokyo, Japan: Charles E. Tuttle Company, 1964). *Blount Report*, U.S. 53rd Congress, 3rd session, 1894-1895, Affairs in Hawaii, House of Representatives (Washington, D.C.: Government Printing Office, 1895). Ninety-Eighth Congress, 2nd session, Committee on Energy and Natural Resources, U.S. Senate, Hearings on the Report of the Native Hawaiians Study Commission, Honolulu, Hawaii, April 16, 1981, parts 1 and 2.

H. K. Bruss Keppeler, Esq., "Native Hawaiian Claims," in Randall W. Roth, ed., *The Price of Paradise: Lucky We Live Hawaii?* (Honolulu: Mutual Publishing, 1992), pp. 196-200.

Grover Cleveland. Executive Document no. 47, 72nd Congress, 2nd session, House of Representatives, 1893.

26. Among the lost names are Ka-awa-lau-o-Pu'uloa (the many harbors

of Pu'uloa) and Awaawa-lei (the garland of harbors). See Pat Tummons, "Remember Pearl Harbor: A Call to Arms for Environmentalists," *Environment Hawai'i* 2 (December 1991), p. 1.

27. Mehmed Ali, "Loko I'a and Modern Aquaculture," unpublished manuscript, Honolulu, Hawai'i, 1992, n.p.

28. Pat Tummons, "Bay of Infamy," *Honolulu Weekly*, 4 December 1991, p. 4

29. See Marita Sturken, "The Wall, the Screen and the Image: The Vietnam Veterans Memorial," *Representations*, 35 (summer 1991), footnote 2, p. 138.

30. Copies of the free brochure "Official Map Guide to Oahu's Premier Attractions," published by the Oahu Attraction Associations, are on display at the center. The *Arizona* Memorial is one of the twenty "premier attractions."

31. Culler, *Framing the Sign*, p. 159.

32. As Culler writes, a "marker is any kind of information or representation that constitutes a sight as a sight: by giving information about it, representing it, making it recognizable." Ibid., p. 159.

33. Kamakau, *The Works of the People of Old*, pp. 118-22.

34. At one time, koa covered about 200,000 acres on the island of Hawai'i. See Jay Hartwell, "Battle over koas of Kilauea," *Honolulu Advertiser*, March 4, 1985, p. A-3. In 1985, there was only one healthy, virgin koa forest left in Hawai'i. Present-day landowners want to "farm" koa rather than selectively log-off mature trees, the difference being that between a monocrop plantation and an ecosystem containing a number of indigenous fauna and flora. Present-day people of Hawaiian ancestry explain that their ancestors planted a single tree at a time and amidst a diverse ecosystem. Letter to editor, *Honolulu Star-Bulletin*, 11 July 1985, p. 12.

35. See Bakhtin, *The Dialogic Imagination*.

36. James W. Gibson, *The Perfect War: Technowar in Vietnam* (Boston, New York: Atlantic Monthly Press, 1986), pp. 462-63.

37. C. D. B. Bryant's *Friendly Fire* is an account of the experiences of the Iowa farm parents of Sgt. Michael Mullen in determinedly breaking up the unitary story surrounding their son's death in Vietnam by "friendly fire." The experience of being long stonewalled by the Department of Defense when they sought to know more of the circumstances surrounding such a death jarred loose legitimacy's hold on them. Not only was their own resistance to the war increasing but that of many other Americans as well. The Mullens spent the gratuity payment from the Army (meant to cover the cost of his funeral) on a half-page ad in the Sunday edition of the main newspaper in Iowa; its half-inch-high black headline read "A SILENT message to fathers and mothers of Iowa" and beneath that ran fourteen rows of forty-

nine crosses each and a fifteenth row with twenty-seven, leaving space for more. Each cross represented the death of an Iowa soldier in the Vietnam War. Courtland D. B. Bryant, *Friendly Fire* (New York: Putnam, 1976), p. 129.

38. A total of 469 Medals of Honor were awarded for heroic acts during World War II; none was awarded during that time to African American men, although they were awarded the medals in all the wars prior to World War II and all those since. Irvin H. Lee, *Negro Medal of Honor Men* (New York: Dodd, Mead & Company, 1969), p. 110.

39. There is little about the Pearl Harbor–*Arizona* Memorial relationship that would escape a feminist critique, beginning with the warrior myth and the state itself, as a number of feminist writers have interpreted the state as essentially masculine in origins and practices. See Carole Pateman, *The Sexual Contract* (Cambridge: Polity, 1988); Nancy Hartsock, *Money, Sex, and Power: Toward a Feminist Historical Materialism* (New York: Longman's, 1983); Wendy Brown, *Manhood and Politics: A Feminist Reading in Political Theory* (Totowa, N.J.: Rowman & Littlefield, 1988). Others such as Judith Stiehm have argued that the exclusion of women from military combat is necessary in order to insure the turf and boundaries of the masculine category. See Judith Hicks Stiehm, *Bring Me Men and Women: Mandated Change at the U.S. Air Force Academy* (Berkeley: University of California Press, 1981).

40. The number of Japanese nationals who visit the memorial annually is estimated at around 150,000 to 200,000. Approximately one-half of the 1,500,000 annual visitors are foreign nationals. Don McGee, Superintendent of the *Arizona* Memorial, interview by author, telephone conversation, Honolulu, 21 January 1994.

41. Lei giving is a social practice in Hawai'i with many meanings. Giving them can be personal, as when they are given by family or friends to graduates, lovers, birthday boys and girls, and others, marking other big events in their lives. Leis can also have a sacred use when they drape coffins, ashes urns, and photos of mourned persons. On other occasions, they are part of the commodity flow of aloha: politicians, public officials, ranking military officers, and corporate executives wear them as an expected part of their clothing on such occasions as campaigns, television appearances, news conferences, ground-breaking ceremonies, building dedications, openings of conferences, changes of command, opening malls, being seen around town, and so on. Tourists are given leis by exotically dressed greeters hired for the purpose; newly introduced models of autos and refrigerators sport them. Navy ships returning to Pearl Harbor after lengthy but routine deployment in the western Pacific are hung with big plastic leis. When passenger ships used to call regularly at Honolulu, departing tourists would throw their leis overboard as the ship rounded Diamond Head. If a lei drifted back toward

the harbor, it was a sign that the person throwing the lei would return. In the *Arizona* Memorial context, the focused gaze on reverence for the dead claims the gesture from these other possibilities.

42. Sturken, "The Wall, the Screen and the Image," p. 122, writes that traditional war memorials invoke closure on the conflict and that "this closure can by its very nature serve to sanctify future wars by offering a completed narrative with cause and effect intact."

43. Jean Baudrillard, *For a Critique of the Political Economy of the Sign* (St. Louis, Mo.: Telos Press, 1981).

44. George Mosse, *Fallen Soldiers: Reshaping the Memory of the World Wars* (New York, Oxford: Oxford University Press, 1980), p. 7.

45. The following words are taken from the dedication by Admiral A. W. Radford, USN, March 1950: "Dedicated to the eternal memory of our gallant shipmates in the USS *Arizona* who gave their lives in action 7 December 1941. . . . From today on the USS *Arizona* will again fly our country's flag just as proudly as she did on the morning of 7 December 1941. I am sure the *Arizona*'s crew will know and appreciate what we are doing."

46. Not only were the fishponds and fish lost but so was a large freshwater lake into which were dumped "metal scrap, engine parts, empty ammunition casings, and airplane and ship parts." Military equipment being returned to the mainland from wartime use sank in marshy areas. "Petroleum pipelines were laid and abandoned almost at will. Unlined pits that drained straight into the harbor received everything from petroleum sludges to paint to battery acid. Storm drains provided a convenient means of disposing of everything from mercury to chromium." U.S. Navy report quoted in Pat Tummons, "Bay of Infamy," p. 4.

47. Barthes's explanation is that "myth is a type of speech defined by its intentions . . . more than its literal sense." Barthes, *Mythologies*, p. 124.

48. Ibid.

49. Marita Sturken, "The Wall, the Screen, and the Image," p. 120.

50. Charles Griswold, "The Vietnam Veterans Memorial and the Washington Mall: Philosophical Thoughts on Political Iconography," *Critical Inquiry*, 12 (summer 1986), p. 689.

51. Forty volumes of hearings on Pearl Harbor speak eloquently to this crisis and anxiety. See notes 5 and 7. The fortieth volume is not always cataloged with the thirty-nine volumes of the hearings because it is a report. United States. 79th Congress, 2nd sess. Report of the Joint Committee on the Investigation of the Pearl Harbor Attack. Including the Minority report. Reprint (New York: Da Capo Press, 1976).

52. Dower, *War Without Mercy*. See esp. pp. 35-38.

53. Ibid., p. 37.

54. "Because acts of closure represent the particular interests of those empowered to commemorate, narrative is selective and distortive; it privileges and advances certain world views over alternative ones." Peter Ehrenhaus, "Commemorating the Unwon War: On *Not* Remembering Vietnam," *Journal of Communication* 39(1) winter 1989, p. 98.

55. Sturken, "The Wall, the Screen, and the Image," p. 122.

17

From a Kibbutz Journal: Reflections on Gender, Race, and Militarism in Israel

KATHY FERGUSON

BORDERS, VOICES, AND THE TRAFFIC IN BETWEEN

Life in Israel brings one into intimate contact with a variety of borders and an intense set of claims about identity. There are the obvious physical borders, the ones between disputed territories and hostile states, where people cross between contested places in search of work, or in the line of duty, or for renewal or revenge. Then there are the seemingly obvious cultural borders between contending identities, between Arab and Jew, women and men, immigrant and native-born, religious and secular, dove and hawk. These too turn out to be contested spaces, hosting their own, often clandestine, border crossings. And then there are the furtive borders, woven into language practices and written onto bodies, which demarcate that which can be spoken from that which lies in silence.

This journal is an effort to engage these borders, to map their inclusions and exclusions, to chart the migrations they sustain and to attend to the utterances they authorize or forbid. These efforts are both informed and complicated, perhaps sometimes derailed, by the borders of my own inhabitations—a U.S. academic living on a kibbutz, a *goya* (non-Jew) marrying into an Israeli Jewish family, a feminist in the place that may well have invented patriarchy. These deceptively straightforward traits seem to confirm my outsider status. But I cannot stay comfortably outside Israeli Jewish life, because my children have one set of roots, one cherished link with family,

435

one opening to language and memory, in this troubled and troubling place. This journal has become my forum for negotiating a peaceful identity space for my sons, a kind of belonging that is living and livable for them and for myself. Constructing these terms for Oren and Ari requires mapping the available practices of identity construction in Israeli life. I find them to be complex, disturbing, appealing, in some ways unacceptable. I want to close the distance between us and Israel, but not always on Israel's terms.

But of course there is no one Israel. There is more than one discernable voice, more than one detectable construction of who lives here and what they are about. A state or a society is never a simple or static thing; it is always a process of becoming. Global politics tends to be understood as monoglossic—that is, we say "Israel" acts in a certain way on the world stage—but that common, unitary way of speaking conceals great turbulence. One of the tasks of the Israeli state has been to mask this turbulence by defending its borders— geographic, cultural, linguistic—in ways that co-opt or delegitimize these subversions. The less common views are hard to hear when the hegemonic voices are turned up to full volume. The dominant perspective becomes deafening, but the less legitimized views continue to intersect the identity practices in complex ways. They do their work on the slant, so to speak, uncaptured by the prevailing orthodoxy, but not unaffected by it.

Bakhtin is helpful in unraveling these complex intersections of language and identity. He distinguishes between centripetal and centrifugal forces in genres, language, and politics. Centripetal forces "serve to unify and centralize the verbal-ideological world."[1] The centripetal forces make themselves felt through corralling the diversity within a social field, struggling to reinforce the reigning claims to meaning. Centrifugal forces, in contrast, are those enabling the manyness of things to find expression. Centrifugal forces are the carriers of Bakhtin's heteroglossia, the differences in language, ideology, and identity that constantly put pressure on the prevailing truth claims and self-understandings. This journal aims to enable a heteroglossia similar to that which Bakhtin finds in the novel, a space where many voices can be heard.

The landscape of Israeli political and cultural life is both ruthlessly centripetal and heteroglot to the max. There are the frictions among/between the many languages of the immigrants and the official Hebrew; between *sabra* (Israeli-born) Hebrew and the Yiddish of the *shtetl*; between Hebrew and the widespread use of English in commerce, tourism, and diaspora fund-raising; between Hebrew (the first language in the schools) and the subterranean Arabic of the nearly one million Israeli Arabs (not counting the population of the occupied territories). There are also the discrepancies and antagonisms within the Hebrew-speaking population: between Ashkenazi (European) and Sephardic (Mediterranean) Jews, secular and religious Jews, conservative and radical Jews, Jewish women and Jewish men. There are the subtle contests between the available linguistic registers within which self-understanding can be constituted: between the images of globalism and nationalism, victims and warriors, remembrance and forgetting, nostalgia and irony. The self-understandings that people can articulate within Israeli society always hum with the energies of these interacting interpretive moments; the words they can speak are always already half someone else's.

Set against this unruly heteroglossia are the agents of centripetalization—the state, the rabbinate, the media, the schools—and the relentless unifying drone of the discourse of "national security." Further harnessing the dominant self-understanding is a particularly strident masculinity, a gendered underwriting of the central order. The centripetal forces attempt to tame the fractious dialogues, to marshall the (selective) resources of history, geography, and culture around a single understanding of what it means to be Israeli.

Mapping the spaces upon which these forces interrupt and reinforce one another requires detecting the resonances and incompatibilities among various ways of representing the world, and between ways of representing the world and ways of being in the world. One looks for the symbolic markers by which people establish and assess their sense of themselves. This way of looking at global politics seeks the locations in language that constitute people's sense of pride or shame, their fears and expectations, their resistances and resignations. It looks at the practices of power involved in struggles to maintain, and to reformulate, identities. One attends to the recurrent images anchoring the available understandings people have of themselves and others. One looks at how identities travel, contrasting their reception in different contexts in order more fully to chart their relations. Encounters among different languages—what Bakhtin calls intertextuality—offer a space for reflection on the requirements of each. Identities on the move highlight the construction of the cultural categories they encounter, and might even occasion their reconstruction.

April 19, 1992

Yesterday we went with Gili (my husband) and his family to Yad Mordechai, a nearby kibbutz where the kibbutzniks held off the invading Egyptian army in 1948 for several days. Their actions gave the towns farther north, including Tel Aviv, time to prepare for the invasion. There is a field containing statues of Egyptian soldiers charging up the hill, with their tanks and heavy artillery. The trenches at the top of the hill hold reproductions of the scant kibbutz armaments. There is also a museum there to the memory of the Holocaust and the Yad Mordechai fighters. The claims on memory are heavy: defending the new state from the invading Arab armies is all intertwined with the Holocaust and the struggle in the Polish ghettos against the Nazis. In each case the story features the underdog Jewish fighters who have some temporary successes against a larger and very evil enemy, and in each case their immediate defeat paves the way for a long-term victory. The setting for memory at Yad Mordechai contributes to maintenance of the Israeli understanding of themselves as beleaguered underdogs, victims constantly threatened. It allows them to dislocate this identity from its moorings in 1942 or 1948 and float it into place in 1992, so that the Palestinians (and their supporters, and anyone who ever criticizes Israel) become the feared enemy and the Jews are still the victims.

An oppressive state gives its dominant classes many alibis for their superior position. State censorship and economic segregation make the Palestinians invisible to most Israeli Jews. For some, the Bible (and not the Koran) is taken to be a land-granting institution. Evocations of biblical legends shore up contemporary claims to land and power. What to do with a people who remember events from 3,000 years ago as though they happened last week? A recent *Jerusalem Post* article sees Hebron as a likely place for Jews and Arabs to make peace because Abraham's sons Isaac (Jewish) and Ismael (Arab) both buried him near there. (I think I have gotten that story right.) Similarly, the last stand of the ancient Zealots against the Romans at Masada becomes intertwined in imagery and legend with the contemporary Israeli army, the old heroism helping to produce the new.

Oren and I found some fascinating productions of militarized Israeli identities on postcards for sale at the Soreq caves in the Absolom Reserve. In among the wide-angle landscape shots of the Sea of Galilee and Masada were two cards also evidently deemed by the Israeli state and its tourist industry to be fitting mementos for visitors and the folks back home. One shows a close-up of a *sabra*, a cactus with large flat leaves and round orange fruit. The caption states, "The renowned Israeli *sabra* cactus, symbol of the Israeli temperament: prickly on the outside, sweet on the inside." Behind the cactus stand two young, attractive women in military uniform; wearing red flowers on their shirts, they stride forward with confidence and exchange friendly smiles. The cloudless blue sky shines brightly behind them. The card radiates reassurance. The military trappings on the cheerful young women are quintessentially Israeli, the prickly "outside" hiding the sweet feminine "inside." The women, like the cactus, are "in bloom," sporting flowers, promising new life. The young women smile at each other, happy with life; their military presence is folded into that contentment; all is well with the Israeli army, where beautiful young women serve their country with a smile. There is no mention of women's second-class status in the military, their obligatory presence there in perpetual subordination to men. No sign of what these charming, attractive soldiers might actually be doing, which is probably staffing the clerical ranks of the Israeli war machine. Do they, perhaps, call up the reserve soldiers who police the territories? Do they keep the files on suspected "terrorists"? Do they consider their hands to be clean? They wear their jaunty red caps at a dashing angle; they are proud and strong. Their beauty and boldness reside robustly in their military uniforms; the military presence is unremarkable in itself, imbricated thoroughly into what it means to be an Israeli.

A second postcard reproduces a reassuring militarized identity from a different angle. It shows three men, each wearing green military fatigues and sporting a different colored beret—purple, red, brown. They stand with arms clasped around one another, backs to the camera, their faces hidden against a wall. Not "a wall"—"*The* Wall." The caption reads, "Meeting of fighters at the Western Wall." Their faces are pressed up against the white-gold Jerusalem stone, which gleams hot in the sun. Their weapons hang from their shoulders; they appear to be weeping. Their bodies are slim and strong, their arms well muscled; they are strong enough to cry, perhaps for a fallen comrade, perhaps even for a slain enemy. Again, Israeli strength and youth, this time marked masculine, are interwoven with fatigues and weapons; to be a real Israeli *is* to be a soldier. In Israeli postcard iconography, the women soldiers are strong enough to serve their country, to *be* Israeli, with a smile; the men soldiers are strong enough to grieve at the costs of their military service while continuing to provide it. Serve, serve, serve; little room here to recognize young people with a different dream, a different strength. Little room for some other kind of Israeli.

The second postcard represents a line of Israeli kitsch going back at least to the creation of Zionism. In "The Kitsch of Israel" Avishai Margalit tells about a "bizarre controversy" in 1988 over the question, "Should soldiers be allowed to cry at the funerals of their comrades?"

> The general who opposed crying—or, more exactly, being seen crying—was a *sabra* born on a kibbutz; the one in favor of showing soldiers crying was a Polish-born survivor of the Holocaust . . . The argument about the soldiers' tears goes to the heart of a fundamental issue about sentimentality in the Zionist revolution, the revolution that took it upon itself to mold a "New Jew." The New Jew was not supposed to shed tears.[2]

For the *sabra* general, tears recall the helpless Jews of the ghettos and pogroms, history's victims. His rejection of public vulnerability aligns Jewish victimization with a no-nonsense, "stop whining and do something about it" revision. The Polish-born general is more representative of immigrant and diaspora Jews, the archetype of a righteous sentimentality that can sometimes take a universal turn (as in the *mensch*-ideal, one sensitive to the suffering of others) but more often is channeled by state-orchestrated ideological production lines into an insular tribalism (as in the "we-love-Israel, the-world-is-against-us" form of self-justification).[3]

No one in this debate suggests that the military does not need a policy about soldiers crying or not crying, that such matters are private and none of the state's business. The production and deployment of images of young people in uniform is so central to Israeli self-understanding, and so critical to its marketing of itself abroad, not to mention to its ideological and commercial tourism, that the constitution of the phenomenon as a public issue was self-evident. The postcard Oren and I secured along with our M&Ms is the heir of countless photographs, poems, songs, books, legends. Margalit writes:

> The quasi-official symbol [of soldiers and sentiment] became the photograph by the veteran *Time* photographer David Rubinger which shows a group of unshaven helmeted paratroopers at the wall, in the middle of which one sees—*ecce homo*—a young, blond, lean-featured fighter with his eyes lifted upward and holding his helmet next to his heart. This altogether non-Jewish gesture of taking off one's hat at a holy place became the symbol of the return of the New Jew to the site of his holy temple.[4]

Margalit also indicates some of the sources of resistance to the practices of kitsch. A popular rock song by female performer Sy Hyman criticizes the saccharine, sanctimonious tone of the "Shooting and Crying" literature, as does poet Dennis Silk in "On the Way to the Territories." Hyman's song is banned on the army radio station in Israel.[5] I remember some of Gili's stories about his days in the military, his indifference to patriotic exhortations and his small gestures of defiance. It is crucial to keep evidence of these resistances in mind, both to help explain the continuous onslaught of the prevailing identity practices and to marshal some resources against them.

In Israeli military kitsch, as in most state-produced excuses for killing people in war, the actual soldiers, their particular lives, and concrete characteristics are only important to the extent that they can be recruited into legitimacy-sustaining discourses. Margalit notes that Israel boasts "a thriving industry of books dedicated to the memory of fallen soldiers. It was almost invariably pointed out that they secretly read the poetry of Rachel ("the Israeli Anna Akhmatova") or Alterman ("the Israeli Gumilov"). These soldiers never got much credit for their love of poetry while alive, only after their premature deaths."[6]

I am reminded of James William Gibson's comment on the production of the image of the unknown soldier in the Vietnam War. In *The Perfect War* he writes: "The Pentagon, which waved its informal rules that 80% of a body must be recovered for it to be designated an Unknown, has now *intentionally destroyed all identification records related to the Unknown* to prevent inadvertent disclosure of information that might provide clues to the identity of the man intended to be a universal symbol of Vietnam battle dead."[7]

The Israeli government is certainly not alone in marshaling the resources of kitsch-in-uniform to deflect criticism, to forestall unpalatable questions from grieving families, to paste over the recurrent cracks in hegemonic, militarized, national identities. But they have raised kitsch-craft to new depths. Milan Kundera gives a wonderful explanation of kitsch in *The Unbearable Lightness of Being*:

> Kitsch causes two tears to flow in quick succession. The first tear says: How nice to see children running on the grass! The second tear says: How nice to be moved, together with all mankind, by children running on the grass!
>
> It is the second tear that makes kitsch kitsch.[8]

Margalit calls the second tear a "meta tear"[9]—the glue holding together a state-orchestrated collective identity. The Israeli military/state apparatus cannot refrain from politicizing and administering the grief of soldiers, because they want to control that second tear, the watershed that can either lubricate or dissolve a national identity.

April 27

Yesterday was *Yom HaShoa*, Holocaust Day. At 10:00 A.M. the sirens blew. The entire country came to a halt (at least, so they say; I am not sure what the Palestinians and Israeli Arabs were doing). For two long minutes everyone stands still and remembers: remember the six million, one million children killed, gassed, burned, tortured; remember the indifference of the world to the horror; remember, remember, never again. I was in my *ulpan* (Hebrew school for immigrants), and I saw the tears in my friend Rosa's eyes matching my own. The wrenching photographs from the Yad Mordechai museum seemed imprinted on my retina, activated by the sirens and the silence. I knew that I was having exactly the response that I was supposed to have, but no political critique could short-circuit the searing imagery.

Yesterday's *Jerusalem Post* is filled with stories of Holocaust Day. There are memorials, marches, ceremonies, dedications, publications, interviews. On the nightly news, Holocaust memorial ceremonies are interrupted by an old man walking slowly down the street, leaning on a cane. He is wearing the striped camp uniform, including the small bowl-shaped hat. The on-the-scene television cameras zoom in on his face. He looks dazed, uncertain. His steps are slow. The announcer's voice identifies him as a survivor. He does not speak. A curious crowd gathers, a few tentative gestures are made to include the man, then he is wisked away. His is an unstaged presence, too raw, too ambiguous; it unsettles the careful orchestration of memory produced for public display. Within Holocaust kitsch, the specter of the Holocaust itself confuses and disturbs.

Bakhtin's words about the working of authority in language are helping me make my way through the cultural barrage of Holocaust Week. He writes:

> The authoritative word demands that we acknowledge it, that we make it our own; it binds us, quite independent of any power it might have to persuade us internally; we encounter it with its authority already fused to it. The authoritative word is located in a distanced zone, organically connected with a past that is felt to be hierarchically higher. It is, so to speak, the word of the fathers. Its authority was already *acknowledged* in the past. It is a *prior* discourse. It is therefore not a question of choosing it from among other possible discourses that are its equal. It is given (it sounds) in lofty spheres, not those of familiar contact. Its language is a special (as it were, hieratic) language. It can be profaned. It is akin to taboo, i.e., a name that must not be taken in vain.[10]

The authoritative word in Israel is *Shoa*, Holocaust. It is the symbolic anchor of Zionism, a shorthand for the weight of world anti-Semitism, and the litmus test for political loyalty—peace demonstrators are frequently accused by hostile passersby of forgetting the Holocaust. From it radiate a series of powerful demands: Never criticize a war while it is being fought. Always rally behind the cry of national security and accept it as the excuse for nearly any government policy. Never compare any act of Israel's with the Holocaust, but always equate Israel's opponents with the Nazis. Always emphasize the relative benevolence of the occupation, not the fact of it.

The authoritative word hosts numerous contradictions on its terrain. It shores up a siege mentality that justifies the investment of enormous national resources in the military, at the expense of schools, hospitals, and culture, while claiming the title "civilized" for itself and attributing barbarism to its enemies. The authoritative word provides the moral underpinnings for the Israeli authorities to represent themselves as omnipotent victors to the Palestinians in the territories, and as besieged victims to the rest of the world and to themselves.

Bakhtin talks about how difficult it is to reorient the authoritative word:

> It is not a free appropriation and assimilation of the word itself that authoritative discourse seeks to elicit from us; rather, it demands our unconditional allegiance. Therefore authoritative discourse permits no play with the context framing it, no play with its borders, no gradual and flexible transitions, no spontaneously creative stylizing variants on it. It enters our verbal consciousness as a compact and indivisible mass; one must either totally affirm it or totally reject it.[11]

Some Israelis approach the authoritative demands of the Holocaust by withholding rather than offering their fealty: a caustic saying in Israel is "There's no business like *Shoa* business." My father-in-law responded to my questions about Holocaust Day with a shrug, commenting ambiguously, "We Jews love to remember." A close friend confessed with considerable irony that he found himself in the bathroom taking a shit during the two minutes of national silence; he found it inconvenient to stand. One can either acknowledge or turn away from the claims on memory of the authoritative word, but it is difficult to rework those claims. Where in Israel is the effort to redefine the discourse, to revise its practices, and put it into circulation differently? The challenge to state-sponsored Holocaust kitsch is not cynicism, but redefinition; the challenge to official memories is not in forgetting, but in remembering differently.

Art Spiegelman's *Maus*, a set of comic books about the Holocaust, suggests ways to remember differently. He tells the story of his father's life in Poland before the war, his increasingly desperate efforts to protect himself and his family, his deportation to Auschwitz, his survival. The Jews are portrayed as mice, the Nazis as cats, the Poles as pigs. The juxtaposition of the usual associations of comics with the trivial, and the Holocaust with the epic, provides the space within which he does his work. While he tells his father's story, he also tells about the telling, bringing the act of representation into the story. He locates his own resentments and obsessions alongside those of his father, sometimes imagining himself the victim and his parents the murderers, while highlighting the irony of such self-preoccupation. Spiegelman portrays the horrors starkly but does not cannonize the victims—his father turns out to be manipulative, domineering, rather unlikable. The author's own relation to the Holocaust, as a Jewish writer making a living from the onslaught on the Jews, occasions ironic comment: at one point he draws himself writing on a desk supported by piles of little mice skulls.

Maus remembers, but it insists on attention to *how* one remembers. I wonder what would happen if each locality in Israel were left to make Holocaust Day in its own way, to come to active terms with it, not just be carried by state definitions of history? Bakhtin says that the authoritative word is always calcified, offering no space for play, no contradictory emotions or cacophonous dialogic space.[12] But perhaps the agents of the central order work so hard at maintaining the official definition precisely to ward off pending recalibrations of the demands of memory on life.

May 6

Today is *Yom Zikaren*, Memorial Day, dedicated to the memory of the over 17,000 soldiers killed in Israel's wars since the founding. Memorial Day looks backwards, mourning the fallen. Last night there was a ceremony on the kibbutz, today one at the *ulpan*, both accompanied by the nationwide sirens signaling a minute of silence, remembering. I stood last night with my arms around Oren, thinking please, no more wars, not for my sons, not for these children, no more killing. Would Israel's self-understanding shift if it could redefine the remembering more toward the future, toward a determination to avoid more death rather than a commitment to avenge past deaths? Did anyone else perform a silent revision, warding off future loss instead of acknowledging that from the past?

What selective memories are honored in this country of heroes and martyrs, knit together with blood and history. Everywhere there are memorials, ceremonies, official and unofficial rituals that define the past, capture it within the cruel and tragic boundaries of Israeli kitsch. Israel's kitsch, their catagorical agreement with being, underwrites a militarized self-understanding. Heroes, martyrs, victims; suffering, persecution, survival. It is a gendered kitsch, with heroes and warriors occupying the masculine pole while victims carry the feminine. The hegemonic Israeli self-understanding is thoroughly masculine, the proud and manly warrior prepared to die for his country.

In Margalit's discussion of the "should soldiers cry" debate, he misses the gendered dimension of its kitsch. Everything about tears that he disdains is coded feminine: helplessness, vulnerability, passivity, openness to others, grief in the face of loss. The prized "take-charge" mentality of the *sabra* is both a gung-ho masculinity and a strong-man resignation. The archetypal *sabra* soldier is eager to do what is necessary, regretful of its costs, yet proud to pay the price exacted. Marcia Freedman comments that in the schools Israeli children learn, as a maxim, the words of a famous Israeli warrior, "It is good to die for one's country." Aaron Wolf's account of his time in the Israeli army stresses the hero status accorded to soldiers by schoolchildren; he and his friends all wanted to be pilots or paratroopers. (The girls cannot become pilots or paratroopers; do they dream instead of marrying them?) Gili says that as children they referred to Jews who would not defend themselves, contemptuously, as "soap." It is not a discourse that fields many openings for critical reflections on patriarchy, war, or racism.

The military writes itself on physical, social and bodily landscapes in myriad ways. The ubiquitous brown uniforms on young bodies, machine guns swinging from shoulders, seem to inhabit every street, bus stop, restaurant. Military training writes itself on bodies, on their carriage and musculature, in a particularly public way in a society in which nearly every Jew has been or will be a soldier. Wolf recalls the identifiable bodily markings left by paratrooper training:

> Repeated jumps from the Eichmann [a training tower] leave a paratroop trainee with burn scars along his neck that give me a certain amount of prestige in Israel, where everyone knows what they mean. When I hitchhike to the kibbutz on weekends, people who pick me up, seeing the burn marks, say respectfully, "Oh. Paratoop training, eh?!" I am supposed to think of the burn marks as a badge of honor.[13]

The symbolic significance of the characteristic burn marks has completely replaced their functional meaning because the Israeli military no longer uses parachute jumps in combat. (They have been replaced by the more precise operations of transport helicopters.)[14] But the bodily markings of military prowess continue to provoke the admiration of schoolchildren and the respect of adults, and to underwrite a militarized, implicitly masculinized, notion of citizenship.

Both "Arabs" and "women" are folded neatly into the metaphoric apparatus privileging Jewish, military, masculinity. "Women" (that is, Jewish women) take up necessary supporting roles: the plucky female officer, the loving wife back home, the devoted mother raising her children to be soldiers. They are coded feminine, positive; lesser than men, but crucial and highly valued in their place. Not so dissimilarly, the representational practices creating "Arabs" also work the feminine side of the street. "The Arabs" are weak, stupid, not a worthy enemy but a sneaky and therefore dangerous one. The Arabs play the woman to Israel's man, a deadly affair. They are coded feminine, negative; lesser than Jews, stirring both fear and contempt, yet in their own way necessary to the maintenance of hegemonic Jewish self-understanding. Could the widespread contempt for "the Arabs," manifested frequently and casually even among my Labor party friends who support "land for peace," be a kind of self-contempt, a disdain for those who allow themselves to lose?

In *Keepers of the History* Elise Young finds a consistent intertwining of "Arab" and "feminine." She recounts a terrible incident on May 20, 1990: a group of Palestinians from Gaza are waiting at Rishon Lezion, a place outside Tel Aviv from which day labor can be arranged (commonly known as a slave market). A young Israeli man in army fatigues, carrying an automatic weapon, asks to see their identity cards. As the men offer the required cards, the Israeli opens fire, killing seven and wounding ten more. The media reports: "one Israeli driving by stops his car, jumps out, and dances around their bodies."[15] The media further reports "that the murderer is himself a victim—of unrequited love. He told his girlfriend that if she would not take him back, he would go out and kill. Palestinians and women became confused in his mind."[16]

Young goes on to analyze women as an occupied territory, conflating Palestinian and feminine from the opposite political direction, with the intent of valorizing them as parallel victims. It is hard to know precisely what to make of this semiotic intersection of race and sex (Jew is to masculine as Arab is to feminine) when it is put to work by the killers as well as the defenders of the weak. The metaphors become even more slippery when complicated by the history of anti-Semitism, where it is the Jew who is feminized, othered, construed as irrational, dirty, and sinful, while the Christian passes as the implicitly masculine universal norm, the fully human "man."

May 15

I am reading Jacobo Timerman's *The Longest War*, his searing, self-searching analysis of Israel's invasion of Lebanon. As his own son leaves for the front, and eventually serves time in a military prison for refusing to return, Timerman examines the crises of moral and political life occasioned by this war. In no other war had Israelis understood themselves to be aggressors. Certainly not in 1948, when the Zionist enterprise protected against any infusion of the Arab perspective. It was a War of Independence, not a colonial migration; the Arabs did not flee real or imagined terrors; they simply "left." Not in 1956, the war in the Sinai; not in 1967, when Jerusalem was liberated (not occupied); not in 1973, the nearly disastrous Yom Kippur War (not the Ramadan war). Of course there were always calls for peace and warnings about the malevolent consequences of occupation for Jewish identity and security. But these reservations were marginal to what passed as a national consensus.

Nineteen eighty-two was different; the war in Lebanon drew widespread protest from soldiers as well as citizens. Dissenting soldiers interviewed after the Lebanon war speak with bitterness about waste, stupidity, immorality, deceit. A marked contrast with the memories of necessity and collective destiny recorded after the Six-Day War. Israel has had its Vietnam.

Israeli soldiers sometimes speak of their army in terms of purity. One frequently hears reference to *tahor neshek*, a purity of arms. The ethic of the noble soldier using the minimal necessary force to defend his community against an implacable enemy clashed painfully with the experience of an aggressive war against a largely civilian population. The friction generated what Bakhtin might call a double-voiced discourse in Israel. A double-voiced discourse accommodates two different kinds of speech at the same time. It contains a potential dialogue of opposing worldviews, reflecting the diversity and tumult within what seems to be a shared language. Begin and Sharon called on the ethic of the purity of arms to define the war as inevitable, necessary, as part of a quest for peace. Many of their supporters took refuge in the standard Israeli discipline surrounding war: don't criticize the war while it is happening; stand by your men. Of course Israel is not unique in this regard; I am reminded of the nauseating yellow ribbons and "support our boys" rhetoric in the United States during the Gulf War. But in a nation with a citizen army, this mandate to loyalty via silence is overwhelming.

The ethic of the purity of arms also generated a critique of the Lebanon war, and subsequently of the occupation. This second voice takes the purity of arms not as an excuse but as a standard, a moral imperative. This voice put hundreds of thousands of Israelis into the streets to protest the war, and created the category of conscientious objector for the first time in Israeli military life.

This voice also prevents critics who are grounded in it from assessing the limits of their animating ethos, limits that stem from the hidden dependencies of the two voices upon one another. Both the opponents and the defenders of the Lebanon War share the same identity terrain, where militarism and masculinity intertwine. They differ over how to apply the ethos, how to fulfill the demands of that identity. These are not small differences; they often seem to be tearing Israel apart. But they do not make a space for other, perhaps more fundamental, questions, such as: Is it ever possible for arms to be pure? What self-deceit is likely to ensue from the pretense that a military can be synonymous with virtue? The identity practices embedded in the ethos of purity of arms produce the kinds of people who are prepared for, or resigned to, military solutions, rather than searching for political ones.

June 1

This week marks yet another heavily freighted holiday: Jerusalem Day, marking twenty-five years since the "reunification" of the city. Today at the *ulpan* we had a lecture about the Battle of Jerusalem by a soldier who fought there twenty-five years ago. An unassuming personable man in his mid-forties spoke about the battle, showing us the shifting borders on the map and describing the battle strategies. Israelis savor the memory of their wars—this man described the sounds of the different weapons, the intimate proximities of the armies, the view from Jerusalem's hills. His account of the street fighting conveyed the soldiers' fears, the actions of the medics. It is a kind of heroism of the ordinary; Israelis democratize their militarism, offering the image of soldier/hero to every man in uniform, which means nearly every man. The papers are also full of stories of every man's heroism in the reunification battles. I thought about Nicaragua when I was there, only six years after the revolution—there was little worship of soldiers and battles there; their excitement was about their literacy campaign, their health programs, their poetry workshops. Their predominant self-understanding was anchored in revolutionary hopes; here it is planted firmly in an identity of martyrs and survivors, heroes and victims. During class we had to write a story to go with a picture of a young white man, smiling, holding a dark-skinned infant in front of a very dilapidated set of shacks. We all dutifully made up stories about generous white men coming from the West to help needy black children in Africa. Our limited, highly conventionalized vocabularies confined us to this story—we have not learned the words to tell any other story. I do not know how to talk about indigenous people driven from their land by multinational corporations and greedy local elites. I suppose that would be the case with most introductory language courses—when I first studied Spanish and French, I do not remember learning the vocabulary of political critique. On the other hand, I also do not remember learning the words for "soldier," "border," "war," or "battle," which were early acquisitions in the language arsenals of the *olim hadashim* (new immigrants) in our *ulpan*.

June 8

We have just returned from a trip to Jerusalem, where I met with several women involved in peace issues, and participated in another demonstration of Women in Black. Several times during my interviews and conversations I have heard someone say, about some other group perceived as a bit farther to the left, they have "gone too far." Dov says that the organizers of the Givat Haviva conference have "gone too far." Galia Golan, a Peace Now activist, says that Women in Black have "gone too far." My friends Tamar and Sarit say that *Challenge* magazine, an English-language publication of the Israeli Left, has "gone too far." What does this mean? It could mean that the offenders have, from the speaker's point of view, become too sympathetic to the Palestinians, to the point of identifying completely with them and forgetting that there is a legitimate Jewish point of view. But what is it, exactly, that is endangered? Is this a sexual anxiety, a fear of intimacy with the Other? Perhaps the offender has gone too far the way teenagers in the back seat of a Plymouth might go too far, committing an irrevocable act, somehow destroying their innocence and purity. Is this why the epithet "whores of Arafat" is so frequently flung at Women in Black? Or is it more generally about acceptance, a fear of accepting the other so they are not so Other any more, and you, then, are not so special, so unique, so separate? Maybe "whores of Arafat" is similar to the white epithet "nigger-lover," designating not primarily a sexual connection but a general, and illegitimate, acceptance of the other. And because acceptance of the other might be the first step toward the forbidden intimacy, perhaps the two are wound up together. I wonder what "going too far" means from the Palestinian point of view.

The phrase "going too far" connects identity with a spatial metaphor and suggests a link with the territorial dimensions of identity practices in Israel, and in most modern nation-states. Each people has/demands its proper place, its state. Jonathan Boyarin points out that the creation of the state of Israel was a convenient solution to Europe's "Jewish problem"; it got rid of the Jews without having to examine the state policies in Europe and North America that helped create the crises of Jewry.[17] Presumably the state of Israel will someday figure out that the creation of a Palestinian state could perform a similar clearing operation. Meanwhile, the territorialization of identity gives it a sharp either/or component: either our land or their land. Palestinians and Israelis both struggle to delineate their collective identities by establishing/maintaining themselves as nation-states. Identity collapses into (existing or sought for) state power.

Jonathan Boyarin gives a particularly striking example of the conflation of identity and territory: he cites "the recent arrest of an Israeli Jewish educator named Arna Mer on charges of 'identifying with the enemy.' The specific act she was censured for was going to the Palestinian town of Jenin to provide educational materials to school children."[18] Collective identity based on control of territory sponsors a zero-sum calculation: either we belong here or they do. One can imagine collective identities that are deterritorialized, knit together in some other ways, perhaps from shared memories, daily practices, concrete needs, specific relationships to people, locations, and histories. Such productions would be more narrative than territorial; they might not be so exclusive because they are not so relentlessly spatial. Connection to a particular place could still be honored as one dimension of identity, but its intensities could be leavened by less competitive claims. Participation in such identities could be self-consciously partial, constructed, mobile; something one does and re-does every day, not a docile space one simply occupies and controls. Empathy across collective identities constructed as fluid and open could enrich, rather than endanger, one's sense of who one is. In that sort of world, Arna Mer's act would not need to be one either of a traitor or a hero. It could simply be a life.

July 10
Today's *Jerusalem Post* carried a fascinating article on the current "national craze" of courses preparing high school boys for the army and improving their chances of being selected for an "elite unit."[19] Those electing not to take the course can instead purchase the video, a "'Jane Fonda Workout' for future soldiers," promoted as "ideal viewing for the entire family." Course-creator Yuval Eliam, "army preparation guru," stresses that he is "an educational figure, not some kind of macho man." He is striving to create a "prepared gen-eration," "ready and informed about what's going to happen." There is, of course, no companion article detailing any national craze for, say, conflict resolution courses, no large-scale efforts to prepare a generation for the hard work of peace.

Women soldiers are present in this happy account of budding young soldiers only indirectly and through denial. Although Israeli girls also face compulsory military service, these prep courses are, it seems, only for boys. "Eliam even brings in the students' girlfriends, so that both sides know what to expect from the relationship once one of them enters the army." There is a remarkable slippage in this sentence: it recognizes that the "girlfriends" too will enter the army, yet reserves the position of student-preparing-for-the-army for males. The obligatory academic observor is brought in to comment on these procedings: Hannah Herzog, lecturer on Israeli society at Tel Aviv University, points out that the high price of these prepara-tion courses works against the poor and undermines the opportuni-ties for upward mobility traditionally made available to the disad-vantaged through the military. No one thinks to regret the lack of upward mobility via military service for women, or for the Israeli Arabs who are barred from military service altogether. Nor does anyone comment on the lesser forms of citizenship implicitly bestowed upon Jewish women and Israeli Arabs in a society in which to be a citizen is to be a fighter is to be a man.

IN LIEU OF A CONCLUSION: MEMORY AND FORGETTING

Growing up in a society whose founding heritage is Anglo-American liberalism gives one an abiding faith in knowledge and remembering. Perhaps it is indicative of our continued affiliation with Hegel, our implicit dismissal of Nietzsche. At any rate, such a person wants to believe that, if adversaries would only get to know each other, perhaps work together at shared tasks, common memories would be created and trust would be built.

There are those in Israel who share this faith, Jews and Arabs who defy state-drawn borders to meet together in search of peace. Their efforts are admirable, even heroic. But they are so few. Another way into the dangerous terrain housing adversarial identities might be to cultivate a selective forgetting, a partial disengagement from historical investments and authoritative words. This distancing gesture might lead toward uncoupling identity from its territorial obsessions, making room to create stories less dependent on antagonism toward otherness.

It is hard to imagine how the heritage of the Holocaust, or of three generations of Palestinians living in the dismal camps in Gaza, could allow for such a recalibration of memory and identity. Nor is it easy to see such perspectives competing successfully with the hegemonic identity practices produced and circulated so vigorously by the Israeli state and society. Still, perhaps, in this region of passions and counterpassions, of blood and grief and history, in indifference to otherness and refusal of inheritance may lie the possibility of peace.

NOTES

1. M. M. Bakhtin, *The Dialogic Imagination* (Austin: University of Texas Press, 1981), p. 270.

2. Avishai Margalit, "The Kitsch of Israel," *New York Review of Books,* November 24, 1988, p. 20.

3. Ibid., p. 21.

4. Ibid., p. 20.

5. Ibid., pp. 20, 22.

6. Ibid., p. 20.

7. James William Gibson, *The Perfect War* (Boston, New York: Atlantic Monthly Press, 1986), p. 8, quoting *New York Times*, May 29, 1984.

8. Milan Kundera, *The Unbearable Lightness of Being* (New York: Harper and Row, 1984), p. 251.

9. Margalit, "The Kitsch of Israel," p. 20.

10. M. M. Bakhtin, *The Dialogic Imagination*, p. 342.

11. Ibid., p. 343.

12. Ibid., p. 344.

13. Aaron Wolf, *A Purity of Arms* (New York: Doubleday, 1989), p. 191.

14. Ibid., p. 201.

15. Elise Young, *Keepers of the History* (New York: Teachers College Press, 1992), p. 1.

16. Ibid., p. 2.

17. Jonathan Boyarin, *Storm from Paradise: The Politics of Jewish Memory* (Minneapolis: University of Minnesota Press, 1992), p. 121.

18. Ibid., p. 123.

19. Yigal Schleifer, "The Few, the Proud," *Jerusalem Post Magazine* (July 19, 1992), pp. 16-17.

Warring Bodies and Bodies Politic: Tribal Warriors versus State Soldiers

MICHAEL J. SHAPIRO

THE INDIVIDUAL BODY AND THE WARRING BODY

Within the Hegelian construction of human consciousness, self-other relations are framed within the individual's striving for unity and coherence. The unity of the individual body results from the dynamics of negation. Because other bodies are non-selves, the stuff against which the self establishes coherence, the human subject emerges as a result of an "ontological rift."[1] The desire for a unified, coherent body thus requires both confrontation and radical separation from alterity, and this drama is played out in a multitude of arenas. When the arena of interest is contemporary warfare, the focus must be on the symbolic connections between individual bodies and the body politic as represented by the state. While various strategically aimed considerations energize state warfare, identity interests at individual and collective levels are also involved. Because of this dimension of the involvement, the state's warfare serves as a form of identity affirmation. Enemy/others in the case of warfare as in the case of less violent forms of self-other confrontation are to be dominated or destroyed in the interest of the constitution of the self.

Although the analysis that follows departs in important respects from the Hegelian construction of the ontological stakes involved in the confrontation of warring bodies, the focus is nevertheless inspired by the Hegelian construction of desire as an ontological rather than psychological phenomenon. If we entertain the suspicion that an important impetus in modern warfare, at least in the case of the modern state-dominated society, is the human body's drive toward unity and coherence, there must be a way to subject this suspicion to a provisional historical test.

The "test" that follows is not rigorous. It is an interpretive thought experiment rather than an exercise in hypothesis testing. As is the case with all thought experiments aimed at understanding the dominant institutions of the present, it is necessary to achieve some institutional and historical distance as a first step. Therefore, in order to examine the implications of how the drive for unity of the modern body relates to warfare it is useful to recover different institutional and historical bodies. To do this, the analysis turns to various non- and prestate societies in which ontological aims are more clearly in evidence. In addition, much of this part of the analysis focuses especially on a particular historical body, one that was more divided and ambiguated and did not make the same coherence demands that many have discerned as characteristic of the modern self.

Not long ago, the novelist Brian Moore restaged a confrontation between the Western European body and one that functioned within a remarkably different self-understanding, that of the Huron tribes of North America (or New France) in the seventeenth century.[2] Moore focused on the clash of cosmologies in which "the Indian belief in a world of night and in the power of dreams clashed with the Jesuit's preachments of Christianity and a paradise after death."[3] His restaging of the confrontation can be elaborated by going back to the same sources, the Jesuits' writings, which provide both an ethnography of the Hurons and a set of historical biographies of the Jesuits doing missionary work in the New France.

Later, therefore, the Jesuit-Huron confrontation is staged again within a special interest in the articulation between the Huron body and the warring tribal body. However, because the primary concern remains with the contemporary versions of this articulation, it is necessary first to elaborate some contemporary ontologies of warfare.

THE FACES OF WARFARE

A concern with strategy dominates contemporary representations of warfare. This representational practice is relatively recent in the broad sweep of history, however, and it is associated with a structural change that Michel Foucault has noted: Whereas prestate societies were "entirely permeated by war relations," the modern state is "equipped with military institutions."[4] This rupture between civic and military modes, along with the international delegitimation of warfare, has encouraged states to represent peace and security as their characteristic concerns, even as international violence grows. But although the state does not see itself as a primarily warring body, signs of warfare, although dispersed and often dissimulated, remain visible. Currently, the warfare of the modern state reveals two different faces. Its most prominent face is turned toward the light of official, public recognition, for its features are described primarily in official releases (and in those journalistic and academic discourses that slavishly reproduce official articulations). This is warfare as an instrument of state policy, and as such, the physiognomy of warfare represents itself as expressive of a deeper logistical truth: the need for the state to approach a dangerously disordered world with force. Instrumental and rationalistic talk links the features of war with enduring projects of the state: maintaining security, clearing spaces for effective and vital functioning, meeting obligations to friends, and so on.

In time of war, this face is almost continually bathed in light. In time of peace, it is illuminated only on occasion. Being temporarily out of work, it is unveiled at fleeting moments (e.g., the Memorial Day parade) to wink at us as a reminder that although now largely unseen, it remains watchful and ready. If one takes the long historical view, however, this face is rarely out of work. Its nose is almost always to the grindstone. That many think otherwise is largely a function of the contemporary tendency to construe hostilities as temporary readjustments, as aberrations from the norm of peacefulness in policy as well as in fact. This tendency has been expressed as a historical narrative in which humanity's warlike tendencies, from tribal societies through imperial dynasties to the international system of states, have been mitigated by the rule of law.

The other face of warfare is ontological rather than strategic; it is focused more on the affirmation of identity than the instrumental effects of the use of deadly force. In the modern period, this face has been less prominent than the strategic one; its features have been more difficult to discern because they are reflected in the nooks and crannies of daily life, tending to achieve only local forms of recognition—for example, the National Guard uniform hanging in Dad's closet. Although it is the face whose expressions are not always discerned, the features are nevertheless deeply imprinted. To get a glimpse of this face, one has to look obliquely. Rather than to operate within the regard of the dominant, state-oriented modes of political expression, it is better to treat this aspect of warfare ethnographically, that is, to examine its imprint on society as it is inscribed in mentalities and, more broadly, in the social system of signification.

The signifying practices associated with this face of warfare are also episodic. For example, in the United States in recent years, the visibility it has achieved has been affected by changes in the symbolic status system. For example, in the post–Vietnam War years, combat veterans became increasingly invisible. Having fought in a war that many wanted to forget, these veterans, and to some extent, war veterans in general moved to the periphery of the societal system of sign exchange. Their chairs became vacant on the podiums of public festivities as warfare lost its prestige. This second face of warfare had, for a time, to remain largely in the shadows.

More recently, however, the markedly decisive military victory for the United States and its partners in the Gulf War has coaxed this face out of hiding. Without reviewing all the features, it should suffice to note the proliferation of license plate insignia on motor vehicles. Throughout the nation, those stranded in lines of traffic going to and from work can read while they wait. Emblazoned directly on some plates are the words "wounded combat veteran," or on the license plate bracket, "combat veteran."

To say that military signs have become a pervasive part of contemporary social life would be an exaggeration. It is the case, however, that they have recently increased their visibility. They are now more a significant part of the national identity economy. The national mood in reaction to recent warfare has encouraged military signs to reenter the sign exchange process. Taken as a whole, the signs' reemergence serves as a reminder that despite the prominence of the strategic face of warfare—its outward-reaching role as a projection of the state, its ontological face—its inward reaching role as part of the constitution of identity remains significant.

TRIBAL SOCIETIES AND MILITARY SIGNS

To place this dimension of warfare in perspective, it is instructive to examine a society in which military signs played a more continuously prominent role. In sharp contrast with the modern state, for whom warfare, however chronic it remains, has been delegitimated—it is represented as a last resort rather than a ready-to-hand option—are those prestate or tribal societies for whom warfare was recognized as intimately constitutive of the body politic. Given the prestige and ontological depth of warfare and accordingly the prestige of the warrior, these societies have tended to make the signs of warfare a continuous, pervasive, and legitimate part of everyday life.

The Aztecs provide one of the more extreme cases of the unabashed celebration of war, which they represented as a complex system of adornment. Not all men were warriors, but a high percentage of the society's able-bodied men participated in war, and each one who did wore dramatic, easily read signs of their personal warring history. The war-society relationship was both vocational and extensively semiotic/ontological. Parents who wanted their male children to be warriors struck a deal with a military instructor early in the child's infancy, and when, at the age of fifteen, training began, the inchoate warrior's body became a bearer of warring signs. "The hair on his head was shorn, but at the age of ten a tuft of hair was allowed to grow on the back of his head, and by the age of fifteen, it was long, signifying that he had not yet taken captives in war."[5]

When that inchoate warrior had become an adult fighter and had taken two captives, he went to the palace to receive a mantle with red trim from the king. For three captives he got a richly worked garment, and for four, a special war garment as well as a complete haircut.[6] As a result, Aztec public space was dense with military signs, for "status achieved in war was marked by the honors one received, the way one's hair was worn, the jewelry one was entitled to wear, the clothing one wore in peace, and the arms, armor, and insignia one wore in war."[7] In short, there was nothing esoteric about the warring body; it was perpetually visible within the social body, displaying its combat history.

For the Aztecs, then, it is hardly metaphorical to say that they wore their warfare on their sleeves. More importantly for conceptual purposes is that along with this exoteric representation of combat biographies, Aztec society also wore its ontology on its sleeve. Although it was certainly the case that some of Aztec warfare was strategic and predatory, inasmuch as it involved territorial conquest, the taking of captives, which provided the basis for the society's paramount military sign system, was primarily ontological. The enemy/other seemed to have been there less to provide a managed space to be taken over than to provide bodies as a resource for collective ritual as well as individual status striving. Captured enemy soldiers became slaves who served not only as workers but also as iconic tributes to their particular captors. In addition, after rendering labor service and symbolic capital, they became the sacrifices for feast days and other religious observances. Accordingly, they were the adversaries against which the Aztecs could develop not only their individual martial skills and prestige but also their collective identity, their location in a cosmos occupied by the spirits nourished by the sacrifices.

This ontological service the enemy provided was most evident in a particular, specifically demarcated form of war. These wars the Aztecs called "flower wars," which were distinguished from wars of territorial conquest by having the primary function of demonstrating martial skills and serving the subsequent prestige structure. Although at times these wars developed into territorial wars, flower wars were also used to secure captives as well as to supply combat training.[8] In particular the securing and sacrificing of captives and the role played by their sacrifice makes clear the ultimately inward, ontological aim of Aztec warfare. As the historical scholarship has shown:

> Whatever else it may have been human sacrifice was a symbolic expression of political domination and economic appropriation and, at the same time, a means to their social reproduction . . . The sacrificing of slaves and captives and the offering of their hearts and blood to the sun thus encoded the essential character of social hierarchy and imperial order and provided a suitable instrument for intimidating and punishing insubordination.[9]

Aztec as well as enemy death was part of the ontological impetus of war. To die in a flower war "was called xochimiquizli—flowery death, blissful death, fortunate death."[10] The flower wars therefore represented the ontological part of the Aztec military repertoire. That they were not strategic as in the case of wars meant to appropriate someone else's wealth or to expand territory is evidenced by the formality surrounding these wars—a set day, a sacred place, and accompanying religious ritual such as the burning of incense between the two armies before they engaged. It would therefore be inapposite to approach this dimension of tribal warfare with the traditional political apprehension that links violence with reasons of state, which are understood rationalistically and strategically. But it is equally important to avoid assigning a wholly rationalistic structure to the warfare of the modern state.

STATE SOCIETIES: AN ONTOLOGICAL CLUE

In the case of the modern state, the ontological dimension of warfare is more fugitive, for generally most of the state's explicit articulations represent war as rational or instrumental policy, and, as was noted earlier, the warfare-related identity markers are usually less prominent. Nevertheless, even in those rational/instrumental articulations, the ontological can be discerned, seeping through the discursive cracks. This is even the case in the writings of Carl von Clausewitz, who is often credited with fashioning the purely strategic/utilitarian discourse on warfare that still dominates the military thinking of the modern state.[11]

In his explicit arguments and propositions, Clausewitz lived up to his reputation as the cool, calculating rationalist who treated war as instrumental. As is well known, he claimed that "war is nothing but the continuation of politics by other means,"[12] and in general he argued explicitly in many places that military considerations must be subordinated to political deliberation. A focus on this aspect of his discourse must therefore necessarily locate him as an instrumentalist/utilitarian rationalist who supported an enlightened view of state sovereignty, a political community of consent based upon citizen control over policy in war as well as in peace.[13]

These impressions derive primarily from Clausewitz's grammar, which constructs a military actor in pursuit of "objectives" that issue from the separate domain of political deliberation. In Clausewitzian grammar, military action is instrumental. It is aimed only outward at an external enemy/other. Time and again, Clausewitz turns our attention outward, for all action is organized by the epistemological trope of the object as he refers to the "political objectives of war."[14]

However, there is a very different Clausewitz, but his discovery requires that we ignore the grammatical dimensions of his texts. It is the rhetorical Clausewitz that allows us to discern an alternative construction of war. A passionate, ontological commitment emerges from the way Clausewitz figures war. Whereas epistemologically, as revealed in Clausewitzian grammar, war is a form of *acting* in behalf of externally perceived threats in order to achieve politically educed objectives, ontologically, as revealed in Clausewitzian rhetoric, war creates the conditions under which selfhood can be achieved.

War, it would seem, creates the conditions of possibility for the production, maintenance, and reproduction of the virtuous self. It is a way (for men) to achieve an ideal form of individual moral fulfillment and civic virtue.At one point, for example, Clausewitz suggests that war is "nothing but a duel on a larger scale."[15] This perspective harks back to the aristocratic warrior ethos in ancient Greece. There, military action was "a mosaic of face-to-face duels" between *promachoi* (champions), with the purpose of producing "a wholly personal superiority."[16]

In his more rationalistic moments, Clausewitz emphasized the importance of the soldier acting en masse, which is reminiscent of the subsequent Greek development in which hoplites—citizen soldiers fighting in close formation—displaced the old aristocratic warfare. But the dueling and, more generally, contest mentality (Clausewitz also likens war to a gentleman's game of cards)[17] that emerges in much of Clausewitz's rhetoric harks back to the forms of warfare in Greece, when warfare was not conducted by armies that were, as in modernity, a "specialized body with its own particular techniques."[18] Rather, war was oriented primarily toward the ontological task of allowing men to realize their "natures" and to achieve virtue, for fighting involves "a trial of moral and physical forces."[19] Clausewitz kept his nostalgia for this form of warfare under control in parts of his text, but it showed nevertheless in others.

In effect, the linguistic twists and turns through which Clausewitz identifies actions and objectives obscure the subjectivity-constructing aims resident in much of his figuration of warfare. His grammar is therefore an aggressive misrecognition. One can agree with him that war is "policy" only by recognizing that policy is to be understood not within a simple grammar of subjects acting on the external world to achieve objectives but as the process within which subjects are producing and reproducing themselves.

This disjuncture, evident in Clausewitz's formulations, suggests that so-called "objectives" represent different kinds of investments. In the domain of policy talk, objectives have a legitimating significance. Insofar as they can be evoked as collective goals, they serve as the end point of a narrative or strategic calculus and help to summon collective efforts. However, the story of objectives is clearly not exhausted by this model. This becomes especially evident when the particular objects on which rationalized justifications for action are based become unstable as they have, for example, in the post–Cold War world in which some traditional enmities have dissolved while others have been reasserted. The interpretive activities through which national bodies have located themselves and projected dangers no longer enjoy the stability they had during the recent East-West, bipolar power configuration.

A THEORETICAL DETOUR

Whereas Clausewitzian grammar mediates relations between warring bodies with rational calculations involving disembodied objectives and means toward them, what Clausewitzian rhetoric reveals is a dependency of bodies on other bodies for the development and coherence of their identities. When this dimension of Clausewitz is heeded, the antagonistic other can be viewed not simply as something to be out-played but as a resource, an object whose dangerous existence supplies the meanings against which the warring body maintains unity and consistency. To pursue this aspect of the relationship between warring bodies, it is appropriate to summon once again a domain of theory that elaborates the ontological significance of encounters with alterity rather than one providing a syntax for strategic calculations and analyses.

Although as noted earlier, Hegel provides the initial relevant theorization, nowhere is this ontological dependency of bodies on other bodies better elaborated than in the approach to subjectivity of Jacques Lacan, who discerns this dependency very early in a person's transactions with the world. Psychoanalytic experience, asserts Lacan, shows that the child constructs its initial coherence as an autonomous body by seeing itself in a mirror (or by viewing an-other). Because one's own bodily existence provides only fragmentary experience, it is the sight of a whole autonomous other that provides the basis for a sense of unity, coherence, and stable identity.[20] This construction of subjectivity as a function of contacts with alterity has obvious debts to Hegel's notion that objects and other subjects serve the developing coherence of the subject. In Lacan's psychoanalytic mediation of the Hegelian view, however, the particular objects toward which the subject strives become the arbitrary and often unstable substitutes for interests that do not achieve clear recognition for the subject.

Combining the Freudian and Hegelian emphasis on the problem of the subject, Lacan helps us to understand what I have called Clausewitz's aggressive misrecognition. Like the Hegelian subject, the Lacanian subject seeks a coherent selfhood and uses alterity in the service of that aim. Unlike Hegel, however, who posited a wholly successful narrative of the development of a continuously more self-conscious and coherent subject, Lacan emphasized the Freudian dissimulating mechanisms whereby the subject dwells in misapprehensions, projecting meanings on objects as a result of irreconcilable incoherences within its aims.

The turn to Lacan to investigate the ontological dimension of warfare is appropriate, then, because what are at issue are the various displacements and projections through which objects of violence are interpretively selected, and because this interpretive dynamic operates in relation to the identity interests of the subject.

As it is emphasized here, the point is not to ascribe the impetus to violence to individual psychology but to employ it to break down the facile, subject-object separation, which dissimulates the complexities and stakes involved in producing violent aims, both individual and collective, and their target/objectives. The combination of Freudian and Hegelian emphases on the dynamics of subjectivity that constructs Lacan's approach to the formulation of aims and their objects helps to elucidate what I have called Clausewitz's aggressive misrecognition. In the case of the public discourses associated with the warfare of the state, at both individual and collective levels, the identity stakes of relations with alterity (other nations and nationalities) are overcoded with strategic, means-ends rhetoric. It is therefore difficult to recognize the ontological, identity-serving function of those relations.

However, a Lacanian approach to subjectivity points to another barrier to the recognition of the ontological impetus involved in foreign relations. Whereas the Hegelian subject moves toward coherence and self-understanding, the Lacanian subject dwells in misapprehensions, projecting meanings on objects as a result of irreconcilable incoherences within its aims. Most significant in the structures of misrecognition are the lack of appreciation that individual and collective forms of identity have for the other's roles in their self-recognitions. The debts to otherness remain unrecognized at the level of explicit discourse and produce an incoherence within the coherence in the subject's sense of unity. This incoherence within the coherence or disorder within the order of the self creates an impulse to aggressivity toward alterity, an aggressivity whose rationales are displaced through a complex chain of signifiers. What the subject represents as a hostile object of an aggressive aim is a stand-in for an inward aim; it is a scapegoat, produced by the drive for inner coherence for those elements of the self that defy this coherence.[21]

This detour into the psychic supports of a violent orientation toward alterity is meant to provide a model rather than an explanation, for warfare is a collective rather than an individual enterprise. As a result the objects of violence in warfare take on their meaning in the critical articulation between coherence problems at the level of individual subjectivity and those at the level of cultural and national discourses. To treat collective effects it is therefore necessary to recognize the symbolic dependencies of the individual body on the collective body. For each individual or self, the group—tribe, culture, state, or village, as the case may be—is a symbolic projection. Moreover, given that the media of self-recognition—signs, languages, discourses, and so on—are undeniably public and collective, the conditions of possibility for locating the individual self must operate within the discursive frame of the order to which that self belongs.

The dynamics through which objects of violence are recruited are therefore not exhausted by the psychodynamics of individual actors, or even by the way in which individuals project or displace their psychic demands onto the group. For example, to appreciate the interpretive impositions on those who become targets in the case of relatively complex tribal societies, one must recognize the level of cultural interpretation involved. For example, ethnographic evidence suggests that for the Huron tribes of the Great Lakes in the seventeenth century, for some of the American Indian tribes of the U.S. plains at the same time, and, more recently, for the Anggor of New Guinea, cosmological commitments and other dimensions of the cultural or group ontology provide the collective coherence that determines the peaceful versus militant or violent apprehension of others.

In the case of the modern state, a complex clash of interpretive positions, driven by interests and bureaucratic and institutional complexities as well as ideological positions, plays a major role in the selection of dangers in general and foes in particular. As a result, the ontological aims, which are forthrightly expressed in tribal societies, are overcoded by official and bureaucratic discourses in modern states. Nevertheless, although warfare in the modern state is legitimated on the basis of a discourse of security interests, to which a variety of security-related agencies contribute, the ontological aims seep through the cracks of the policy-oriented face, very much the way they did in Clausewitz's discourse. The identity stakes driving hostilities go unarticulated, however, when a policy grammar commands attention, and the rationale for violence emerges as something like suppressing or destroying external threats.

Once the ontological aims can be discerned beneath the strategic discourse, tribal and state warfare become less dissimilar. Both rely on a discourse of danger based on a radical separation of a domestic order versus a disordered world. But in the case of the former, the agents of disorder tend to remain historically stable—the traditional enemy tribe, the other village, and so on—whereas for the latter, particularly of late, the map of danger is unstable, and identity-related violence or the preparation for it must operate in a climate of uncertainty.

TRIBAL WARFARE AND STABLE SYSTEMS OF ENMITY

The Anggor of New Guinea provide an exemplary case of the tribal approach to warfare. For them, intervillage violence is a stable and "central feature of social life."[22] To locate this violence within their meaning system, one needs to appreciate their historically stable, imagined cartography. As Peter Huber has said,

> Each Anggor village can be considered a cosmos in itself, an autonomous and essentially harmonious moral system confronted by a uniformly hostile, dangerous, and chaotic outside world. Violence between these villages is consequently not a form of policy or a distinct kind of political situation, but an inescapable feature of man's existential condition.[23]

It is clear by this account that Anggor warfare has a markedly ontological orientation, based on the contrast between the inside and outside of the village order. This orientation is highlighted further in Huber's observation that "the integrity and solidarity of the village is further manifest in its contrast with the surrounding world . . . beyond the village boundaries, social and spatial safety gives way to danger, order to chaos, and peace to violence."[24] Therefore, central to the Anggor self-understanding is that the village is a "cosmos," that is, an autonomous order, one that does not recognize its debts to alterity. As a result, the relations between the village and the outside involve "dangerous and ambivalent manipulations of the very boundaries of the cosmos."[25]

Perhaps the most appropriate contrast in this tribe-state comparison is between the Anggor and the United States during the Cold War period and subsequently. What constituted the cosmos for the United States during the Cold War was what was called "the free world." The outside, represented primarily by the Soviet Union, was the domain of danger and disorder. Although the Soviet Union or, more generally, the East Bloc was represented in the strategic discourse as a "military threat," ontologically, the world of danger and disorder served as a stable identity support. David Campbell, in a remark that effectively locates U.S. cartography in the camp of the Anggor, has put it well: "The cold war was an important moment in the (re)production of American identity animated by a concern for the ethical boundaries of identity rather than the territorial borders of the state."[26]

What then can one make of the post–Cold War situation for the United States. At a minimum, instabilities abound. The traditional enemy is absent, but the necessity for having one, which is ontological rather than strategic, has produced an anxious search for a stable ethical map. The articulations from various branches of the enemy-producing establishment bear witness to this ontological angst. Before elaborating this new, unstable discourse on danger, however, it is propitious to stage again the Huron-Jesuit confrontation that interested Brian Moore, this time both to elaborate a different period of ontological angst and to examine its effects in the context of a different construction of the body. By examining this confrontation of bodies at a moment near the beginning of the modern state system, we are in a better position to elaborate with more detail the ontological basis of violence.

JESUITS AND HURONS

Without elaborating all the elements that drove French Jesuits to "New France," I will simply say that they represented an aspect of

French foreign policy. They were involved in domesticating the New World, and although in some ways they were a sideshow to the acquisitiveness of political and commercial authorities, they also represented a more general ontological concern. They sought to confirm the truth of their way of life and the spiritual commitments in which it was anchored. Unlike their Latin American counterparts, the missionaries who accompanied the Spanish and Portuguese conquistadors, the Jesuits in New France two centuries later expended considerable effort to learn native languages. However, this effort was not a comprehending regard and respect for alterity. These Jesuits wished to make the Other the same, to deepen the certainty of their own spiritual practices, and to confirm the view that they were on the right trajectory from this life into the next. Confirmation would come from convincing the "savages" that they had to accept the true God.

The words of the Jesuit Le Jeune leave little doubt that their aim was to deepen their own moral certainty:

> There is some pleasure in taming the souls of the Savages and preparing them to receive the seed of Christianity. And then experience makes us feel certain that God, who shows his goodness and power to all, has nevertheless, for those who expose themselves freely and suffer willingly in his service, and succors them in the midst of their dangers with so prompt and paternal assistance, that often they do not feel their trials, but their pain is turned to pleasure and their perils to peculiar consolation.[27]

What is this "pleasure" but the inward-oriented, ontological communion of those whose confrontation with alterity serves only a project of self-confirmation of a deepening of the identity coherences that are their major project? And, more generally, what is the relationship of this kind of pleasure to "foreign policy?" If one recognizes the debts to otherness that identity both requires and abjures as part of what constitutes foreign policy, one can discern a similar pleasure in some recent, violent aspects of U.S. foreign policy.

The role of this kind of pleasure is shown in a recent treatment of U.S. participation in the Gulf War, which emphasizes the symbolic connection between the coherence of individual body or identity and the satisfaction derived from a "unified national body."[28] Given this projection from individual to state, the appeal of the war lay in its ability to provide the state's subjects with "the illusion of being masterful agents of history."[29] In prestate, tribal societies, it was through participation in rituals that individuals derived their ontological connection between their individual bodies and the social body. In modern society, it is through consuming media representations rather than participating in festivals that the connection is established. The fixing on an enemy other, in either case, is a major aspect of this ontological connection. In general "both external and internal enemies, or more precisely, enemy images that can be attached to 'alien' bodies within and without, are indispensible to the armament of the body politic and to the pleasurable experience of community."[30]

And this provided the ontological enjoyment of the U.S. public that watched the war on television. The Jesuits' pleasure in confronting an alien other was similar, but in their case the pleasurable experience was one of deepening their attachment with the divine rather than a secular, state-based community.

Ironically, it was often the "savages," for whose reasoning the Jesuits had such contempt, who had a more critical comprehension of and respect for cultural difference. Perhaps the Hurons were exemplary in this respect. Because they were deeply attuned to comprehending others, they were, in the words of one who has studied their epistemology, able to "receive the revelation of insights about the other in an objective fashion, that is, in terms of the other and not merely in terms of subjective claims and needs."[31]

A conversation between a Jesuit and Huron that took place in 1637 is notable in this regard. A tribal leader named Onaconchiaronk was cooperating with the Jesuits along with his tribesmen in the building of a chapel. They labored with the expectation of being paid in tobacco. On hearing that he and his tribe were expected to renounce their spiritual beliefs and worship in the chapel, he spoke as follows:

> We have our own way of doing things, and you yours, as well as other nations. When you speak to us about obeying and acknowledging him who you say has made Heaven and earth, I imagine you are talking of overthrowing the country. Your ancestors assembled in earlier times, and held a council where they resolved to take as their God him whom you honor, and ordained all the ceremonies that you observe; as for us, we have learned others from our Fathers.[32]

This view was of course unacceptable to the Jesuits, and as the commentary continues:

> The Father rejoined that he was altogether mistaken in his opinion,—
> that it was not through a mere choice that we had taken God for our
> God, that nature herself had taught us to acknowledge as God him
> who has given us being and life: that, as for what concerns our cere-
> monies, they are not a human invention, but divine; that God himself
> had prescribed them to us, that they were strictly observed all over
> the earth.[33]

Exaggeration about the comprehensiveness of the observance of
Christian ceremonies aside, what the rejoinder reveals is the persistence of a unitary and exclusively vertical view of space as well as an
uncritical reading of history. This privileging of a single version of
the sacred is intimately connected with a failure to countenance the
ethical integrity and worth of the practices of exotic others. For the
Jesuits, the Hurons were not eligible to negotiate a code of conduct;
they had to succumb to the Jesuits coding of the world and of the
propriety of sanctioned actions within it.

At the same time, however, that the Jesuits were imposing this
particular vertical universe and mythic reading of history, it was
under extreme competitive pressure back in France. Two years before this Jesuit-Huron conversation took place, Richelieu had committed French forces to the Thirty Years' War, and at its end, the
Treaty of Westphalia helped establish the dominance of a horizontal,
geostrategic version of space as well as a decisive erosion of ecclesi-
astical authority. The dissolving of the old Hapsburg empire, along
with a more general end of attempts at maintaining religiously oriented empires, helped to consolidate a system of nation-states. And
as reasons of state subsequently supplanted what remained of the
power of spiritual proprieties, all codes based on personal commitments and/or group affiliations paled in comparison with the proliferating norms of the order of states and their interrelationships.

However, as reasons of state have overcoded the personal and
collective spiritual commitments behind violence, they have also monopolized the historical narratives within which warfare is currently
understood. Most significantly, as was noted earlier, the tendency
has been to represent modern war as solely an extension of state policy and as a less and less frequent resort.

Why the dominance of this interpretation, when a relatively dis-
passionate, historical overview reveals that (1) "the twentieth century has already established itself as the most bellicose in human

history," and (2) "the nuclear age has not slowed the centuries-old trend toward more frequent, deadlier wars?"[34] One answer is that the contemporary account sheet privileges Great Power wars and classifies other deadly quarrels as nonwarfare. The answer needs elaboration in terms of practices as well as discourse, however. First, the historical trend whereby the state has increasingly monopolized violence must be recognized:

> Since the seventeenth century . . . rulers have managed to shift the balance decisively against both individual citizens and rival power holders within their own states. They have made it criminal, unpopular, and impractical for most of their citizens to bear arms, have outlawed private armies, and have made it seem normal for armed agents of the state to confront unarmed civilians.[35]

Thus, within the state, the rivalrous and violent struggles have lost their warfare-oriented coding as state social control and policing discourses dominate historical narratives. Then, as the international system came to be dominated by powerful states and their allies, the international discourse on warfare became dominated by their narratives. And, most importantly, discourses that have dominated in the modern era are *political* discourses.

With the development of the modern state and along with it of specifically military institutions and the legal, bureaucratic, and political interfaces (and their relating primary, secondary, etc. discourses), the ontological dimension of warfare becomes dissimulated by a web of practical and discursive relations. The violent arm of the state is not directly connected with the state's articulations. In short, we are thrown off the trail of the ontological engine of warfare by the dominance of legal, political, and bureaucratic discourses through which the state represents the harmony of its order. Along with this institutional obfuscation has been one at the center of modern political orientations. Since Hobbes raised nonwar to the privileged position in the order of the state, warfare has been treated as an aberration, a failure of politics rather than a result of the individual and collective identity drives that constitute the domain of the political.

Nevertheless, warfare in the modern state remains constitutive of its self-understanding. Enemy/others are ontologically just as important to the state society as they were to the prestate society. The primary difference is that the prestate society did not segregate its military operations in the same way as the state society. It is necessary, therefore, to overcome the dissimulating political discourse of the modern state with an ethnographic one that will show the ways in which individual and collective modern bodies constitute themselves through war. To recognize this relationship, however, it is important to look at it within a context in which the individual body is differently constituted. For this purpose, the Hurons serve admirably.

What is dramatically significant by way of comparison is that unlike the case of the modern state, the Hurons manifested a remarkably straightforward understanding of the economies of their peaceful and violent proclivities and the relationships of these tendencies to their ways of constituting self and other.

HURON USES OF ALTERITY

It was noted earlier that the Hurons seemed to be better able than the French Jesuits to accept cultural difference. Perhaps this stemmed in part from their lack of pretention. The Hurons had only a local map of the world. Their spiritual life had a delegating effect on their practical existence, but Huron self-confirmation did not require an external validation of the kind involved in universalizing one's particular commitments. A remark by Aimé Césaire is apropos here. In a lament about the many societies in the Americas that were effaced in the process of colonization, he states, "They were the fact, they did not pretend to be the idea."[36] Others were not there to serve as confirmation of their transcendent and universal significance.

In addition, because they did not have a fictitious entity, the state, their extratribal relations did not have to be located vis-à-vis this particular symbolic entity, which serves in modernity as the general equivalent for what can be threatened in each individual. More generally, Huron-other relations did not partake of any of the mediations at the level of the psyche or collective identity familiar in modern state societies. Although they had traditional enemies, whom they often treated with ferocious violence, they did not locate others in a lesser moral space. Indeed, they believed that confrontations with the power and integrity of their enemies strengthened them. In various ways, they strove to incorporate others—sometimes by consuming them as food and sometimes adopting them as members of their tribe to replace their warfare loses.

The Hurons did not therefore represent their violence as "defense" or "peacekeeping." Like the Aztecs, they wore the ontological dimension of the violence on their sleeves. Warfare was an important, even vital activity, an activity through which they completed, reproduced, and enhanced the self. To understand this ontological connection between warfare and the self or body, one must know how that body was assembled.

The Huron had two "souls," an intellectual soul and an emotive soul. The former predominated during periods of deliberation and slumber, and the latter, a sensitive-animating soul, was part of conscious life.[37] This dualistic approach to the body, a recognition of different, often opposing orientations and forces, which the French Jesuits found perplexing, translated into the body-warfare relationship. Specifically, the Hurons' intellectual and emotive souls operated respectively as peace and war souls: "Corresponding to the intellectual soul are the chiefs and councils of peace; corresponding to the emotive soul are the chiefs and councils of war."[38]

Whatever else such a divided body and its correspondingly divided practices might imply, warfare for the Hurons could not be totalizing, for the whole identity was not involved. And, perhaps more important for purposes of comparison with modern state warfare, there was a relative absence of collective stakes. Specifically, in contrast modern states have decidedly collective stakes, which have a peculiarly modern character. What makes the contemporary state-oriented war animus peculiar, when placed in historical perspective, is the structure of its rationale. The stakes of war are bound up with the survival of a kind of collective body that did not exist in the seventeenth century, the "population." Speaking of modern warfare, Foucault isolates the relationship of this new body to violence:

> Wars are no longer waged in the name of a sovereign who must be defended; they are waged in behalf of the existence of everyone; entire populations are mobilized for purposes of wholesale slaughter in the name of life necessity . . . The principle underlying the tactics of battle—that one has to be capable of killing to go on living—has become the principle that defines the strategy of states.[39]

"Strategy" here does not mean the instrumental rationale through which violence is a policy to achieve various ends. It is meant ontologically, for it refers to the modern self-understanding that provides the predicates through which the globe is mapped and dangers are discerned. By contrast, warfare for the Hurons was very individual-istic; it involved the exercise of bravery and anger (parts of the emotive soul, for revenge was always involved), and the torture and cannibalism, described with horror and distaste by the Jesuits, practiced on their captives stemmed from their notion that they needed the other to nourish their soul: "To procure and deepen their courage, young men were encouraged to torture the flesh and minds of their victims, tear out their hearts and then partake of their roasted flesh and intermingle their blood with that of their victims."[40] The body to body relation here was literally one of incorporation.

Moreover, the symbolic meaning of this "nourishment" is under-scored by the metonymical character of the eating of flesh. High-status members of the tribe such as chiefs ate the head, while those in lower position got fingers or toes. The consumed body had parts with differential relations to parts of the Huron social body. Although the postwar canibalism of the Hurons has deep symbolic and ontological resonances, it represents, at the same time, a relative absence of symbolic mediation in the Huron-Other relationship. The differences between Huron transactions with human alterity and those of moderns in the context of warfare would seem to operate at two different levels.

First, at the interpersonal level, Huron epistemology did not function within the modern frames of interpersonal perception and interpersonal communication. The relationship of one body to another emphasized "excursive" rather than discursive activities.[41] For them, the mind and body did not accrue data in an abstract way on the other, but moved toward it, even to the point of consuming it. The second level is that at which self-other relations animate warfare relations. The Huron model of dealing with alterity is coherent with their tendency to either eat or adopt captives, to incorporate them. The ontological significance of warfare thus was experienced primarily at an individual level; each person who partook in the incorporation experienced a spiritual nourishment. There remained, of course, a level of group recognition as well. Warfare for the Hurons as for moderns had the collective ontological function of producing group self-recognition through radical difference with the enemy. What differed was the Huron practice of incorporation to overcome difference once actual contact was made.

In the case of the modern state, the individual does not consume the enemy in a bodily sense. Because of the distancing technology associated with modern weapons and the separation between civil and military institutions, which dematerializes enemy/others, modern citizens consume codes. The self-enemy relationship in the case of most members of the body politic is a highly mediated symbolic form of consumption. It is enemy images rather than enemies that must operate for a culture that is discursive rather than excursive. In the case of the ontological investments associated with modern warfare, they involve, as was noted earlier, "enemy images that can be attached to 'alien' bodies" and provide "the pleasurable experience of community."[42]

Moreover, it is a stability in these images that provides the coherence in the body politic along with a stable structure of symbolic identifications for its citizens. In this context, the end of the Cold War has produced a frantic attempt in the United States to reestablish a coherence that is threatened by the lack of a stable enemy, a stable orientation toward potential warfare to construct the order on the basis of what is dangerous and disordered outside. A brief review of some recent, post–Cold War articulations is therefore in order, for it demonstrates that the ontological stakes are presently very much in view. When instability reigns, as in the post–Cold War circumstance in which the map and the distribution of subjectivities is in flux, the ontological begins to assert itself because the problem of coherence and the unity of the national body recommends itself.

CONCLUSION: THE SEARCH FOR NEW ENEMIES AND DANGERS

The current problem is well represented in a recent essay by the U.S. Commander in Chief Colin Powell in *Foreign Affairs*.[43] In his opening gesture, he locates "America's armed forces" in an ontological rather than a strategic space, "as part of the fabric of U.S. values."[44] Thereafter, much of his discourse is strategic and Clausewitzian—he even specifically invokes his name—and he maps the world geostrategically while speaking in a means-ends, policy-oriented grammar. The ontological is the prime predicate, however, for all the policy talk is based on an ontology not unlike that of the Anggor villagers elaborated earlier. First there is the domain of order, which Powell designates as "the free world," then there is the domain of disorder. However, the map of the disordered world of dangers is undergoing alteration; the threat is now "regional" rather than global—and an even more alert and active posture with the expectation of enmity is appropriate.

That the "free world" is a cosmology rather than a specific set of institutional practices is evident from how it functions conceptually. It does not get elaborated as a way of life but as a thing to protect against the nonfree world. Regions are as close as Powell gets to designating the more dangerous forms of alterity against which the U.S. national body can define its virtue.

Recently, however, General Lee Butler, whose approach is more immediately instrumental, provided some fine-tuning. Butler, who heads the U.S. nuclear command, has a vocation organized around specific targeting. Rather than to speculate about enemies, his job is to aim nuclear weapons at them. Having been deprived of his primary "target," the Soviet Union, he and the like-minded, have evoked a new world of disorder; it is filled with "terrorist states" and "rogue leaders."[45] History has not yet been able to provide the stability that logistical functionaries would like, but their rush to aim their weapons seems often to run ahead of the process of political deliberation. While national political leaders express uncertainties about the future of danger and the addresses of friends and foes, those with the more specific responsibilities for violence are promoting a view of an increasingly dangerous world and are rapidly designating potential foes.

Butler has therefore many fellow travelers. For example, President Clinton's nominee to head the CIA "described the world as an even more dangerous place for the United States than it was in the days of the Soviet Union,"[46] and after saying we had slain the large dragon, noted that there still exists "a jungle filled with a bewildering variety of poisonous snakes."[47] Enemy bodies turn out to resemble a threatening bestiary. His list of specifics included third-world nations with sophisticated weapons, ethnic and national conflicts such as the one in the former Yugoslavia, drug trading, and terrorism.

No doubt this is still an insufficient degree of specificity for those manifesting the higher levels of ontological angst. Happily Charles Krauthammer can be relied on as a spokesperson for those who need a more specifically dangerous world to constitute the symbolic pleasure deriving from being in the virtuous part of the world. Without a hint of irony, Krauthammer has designated Iran as "The New Evil

Empire."[48] He has overcome his ontological angst by finding Iran as an unambiguous substitute for the old world of disorder:

> Iran is the center of the world's new Comintern. It is similarly messianic and ideological, ruthless and disciplined, implacably hostile to Western Liberalism (though for different reasons) and thus exempt from its conventional morality. Hence, for example, that common thread, terrorism.[49]

Here is someone who needs an implacable foe, one who is unambiguously evil or at least an unambiguous threat to the order. To situate this radically antagonistic position, it is useful to recall again the Hurons' accepting reaction to a culture that was also outside of what Krauthammer calls "conventional morality." Without going into an exhaustive analysis of the Huron self-understanding, it should be noted that the Huron acceptance of a pluralistic moral universe was complemented by their recognition of a divided body, of different, opposing forces within the self (that is, the peace and war souls).

To put the matter within the discourse of order, which emerged in the discussion of Anggor cosmology, a sensitivity to the ontological dimensions of warfare should lead one to expect a complementarity between the orders of the self and those discerned in the world. Those who regard any aspect of disorder within the self as intolerable, that is, who demand a totally coherent and unified body, must necessarily engage in a denial of the forces of disorder, within the ordered self. Insofar as this is the case, external disorder, that is, practices in the world that do not comport with the system of order within which one resides, will be particularly threatening.

When one recognizes in addition that the collectivity or nation serves as a symbolic extension—the individual body connects to the national body—the same structural logic linking self and other at the level of individual selves also applies to the link between the domestic and foreign order. Denial of disorder within the order for the collective body as a whole should lead to an intolerance of an external order that fails to validate, by imitation, the domestic order. Thus a nonimitative order will be interpreted as disordered and, accordingly, as a threat. Moreover, the "threat" is dissimulated because of the misrecognition involved in the very constitution of the self, a failure to recognize dimensions of incoherence and otherness within the self. Accordingly, the threat is treated as a danger to the general survival of the order rather than as an affront to the order's interpretive coherence.

What we are left with beyond the recognition that the modern nation-state, like the prestate society, contains an ontological impetus to warfare are some speculations about the variable intensity of that ontological drive and its selection of dangerous objects. Perhaps the next step is a comparative ethnology of modern societies in search of differing levels of acceptance of inner disorder. As modern bodies collide with increasing intensity, we need to know more about what generates extraordinary demands for coherence within both the orders of the self and the collectivity, for the suspicion deepens that these demands are responsible for the interpretations that map international or external dangers and overdetermine belligerence.

NOTES

1. For an elaboration of a neo-Hegelian approach to war and an explicit focus on the concept of the "ontological rift," in this connection see Janine Chanteur, *From War to Peace*, trans. Shirley Ann Weisz (Boulder, Colo.: Westview, 1992), pp. 195-211.

2. Brian Moore, *Black Robe* (New York: Dutton, 1985).

3. Ibid., p. ix.

4. Michel Foucault, "War in the Filagree of Peace," *Oxford Literary Review* 4 (1979), p. 16.

5. Ross Hassig, *Aztec Warfare* (Norman: University of Oklahoma Press, 1988), p. 39.

6. Ibid.

7. Ibid., p. 41.

8. Ibid., p. 128.

9. John Ingham, "Human Sacrifice at Tenochtitlan," *Comparative Studies in Society and History* 26 (1984), p. 379.

10. Hassig, *Aztec Warfare*, p. 10.

11. See Michael J. Shapiro, "That Obscure Object of Violence: Logistics, Desire, War," *Alternatives* 17 (1992), pp. 453-77, for a more elaborate treatment of Clausewitz's discourse.

12. Carl von Clausewitz, *On War*, ed. and trans. Michael Howard and Peter Paret (Princeton, N.J.: Princeton University Press, 1976), p. 69.

13. See, for example, Michael Howard, "Introduction," in Clausewitz, *On War*.

14. For example, ibid., p. 80.

15. Clausewitz, *On War*, p. 75.

16. Jean-Pierre Vernant, *The Origins of Greek Thought* (Ithaca, N.Y.: Cornell University Press, 1982), pp. 62-63.

17. Clausewitz, *On War*, p. 86.

18. Jean-Pierre Vernant, *Myth and Society in Ancient Greece,* trans. Janet Lloyd (Atlantic Highlands, N.J.: Humanities Press, 1980).

19. Clausewitz, *On War*, p. 127.

20. See Jacques Lacan, "The Mirror Stage as Formative of the Function of the I as Revealed in Psychoanalytic Experience," in *Ecrits*, trans. Alan Sheridan (New York: Norton, 1977), pp. 1-7.

21. See, in particular, Lacan's, "Aggressivity in Psychoanalysis," in *Ecrits*, pp. 8-29.

22. Peter Birkett Huber, "Violence and Social Order among the Anggor of New Guinea," pp. 619-61, in Martin A. Nettleship, R. Dale Givens, Anderson Nettleship, *War, Its Causes and Correlates* (The Hague: Mouton, 1975), p. 619.

23. Ibid., p. 620.

24. Ibid., p. 626.

25. Ibid., p. 630.

26. David Campbell, *Writing Security* (Minneapolis, University of Minnesota Press, 1992), pp. 186-87.

27. *The Jesuit Relations and Allied Documents*, vol. 6 (Cleveland: Burrows Brothers, 1898), p. 153.

28. The expression is in Jochen Schulte-Sasse and Linda Schulte-Sasse, "War, Otherness, and Illusionary Identifications with the State," *Cultural Critique* no. 19 (fall 1991), p. 68.

29. Ibid., p. 70.

30. Ibid., p. 79.

31. Michael M. Pomedli, *Ethnophilosophical and Ethnolinguistic Perspectives on the Huron Indian Soul* (Lewiston, N.Y.: Edwin Mellen, 1991), p. 70.

32. *The Jesuit Relations and Allied Documents*, vol. 13, pp. 171-73.

33. Ibid.

34. Charles Tilly, *Coercion, Capital, and European States, AD 990–1990* (Cambridge, Mass.: Basil Blackwell), p. 67.

35. Ibid., p. 69.

36. Aimé Césaire, *Discourse on Colonialism*, trans. Joan Pinkham (New York: Monthly Review Press, 1972), p. 23.

37. This commentary on the Huron souls is taken from Pomedli, *Ethnophilosophical and Ethnolinguistic Perspectives on the Huron Soul*, p. 59.

38. Ibid., p. 62.

39. Michel Foucault, *The History of Sexuality,* trans. Robert Hurley (New York: Pantheon, 1978), p. 137.

40. Pomedli, *Ethnophilosophical and Ethnolinguistic Perspectives on the Huron Soul,* p. 64.

41. Ibid., p. 68.

42. Schulte-Sasse and Schulte-Sasse, "War, Otherness, and Illusionary Identifications with the State," p. 79.

43. Colin L. Powell, "U.S. Forces: Challenges Ahead," *Foreign Affairs* 71 (Winter, 92/93), pp. 32-45.

44. Ibid., p. 32.

45. Eric Schmitt, "Head of U.S. Nuclear Forces Plans for World of New Foes," *New York Times,* February 25, 1993, p. A-1.

46. *Honolulu Advertiser,* February 3, 1993, p. D-1.

47. Ibid.

48. Charles Krauthammer, "The New Evil Empire," *Washington Post,* January 1, 1993, p. A-19.

49. Ibid.

Contributors

HAYWARD R. ALKER received his Ph.D. in political science from Yale University in 1963 after graduating from MIT in mathematics in 1959. He taught at Yale for five years and at MIT for twenty-six years before recently joining the School of International Relations at the University of Southern California as John A. McCone Professor of International Relations. He has been a visiting professor at the Universities of Michigan, Geneva, FLACSO (Chile), Stockholm, and Uppsala (where he was the first Olof Palme Professor). Professor Alker is a former president of the International Studies Association, and former member of the executive committee of the International Social Science Council, for which he now coordinates a research program on Conflict Early Warnings Systems. A collection of his essays, *Rediscoveries and Reformulations: Humanistic Methodologies for International Studies*, is being published. He is completing a collaborative study of the dialectics of world order, focused on the development of international relations theories in the twentieth century.

BRUNO BOSTEELS is a member of the Department of Romance Languages and Literatures at Harvard University. A graduate from the Katholieke Universiteit Leuven, Belgium, and from the University of Pennsylvania, he is preparing a study of the theoretical and philosophical legacy of Jorge Luis Borges. He has published articles in the fields of Spanish-American literature and critical theory, and has co-translated Gianni Vattimo's *The Secularization of Philosophy* (1995).

DAVID CAMPBELL teaches international politics at Keele University. He is the author of *Writing Security: United States Foreign Policy and the Politics of Identity* (1992) and *Politics without Principle*, and is coeditor with Mick Dillon of *The Political Subject of Violence*.

WILLIAM E. CONNOLLY teaches political theory at the Johns Hopkins University, where he is a professor of political science. He has served as the editor of *Political Theory* and is now the editor of *Contestations: Cornell Studies in Political Theory*. He has been a fellow at Nuffield College, Oxford, the Institute for Advanced Study, Princeton (1986-87), the European University Institute, Florence (1990), and the Center for Advanced Study in the Behavioral Sciences, Stanford (1993-94). His publications include *The Terms of Political Discourse* (1993), *Politics and Ambiguity* (1987), *Political Theory and Modernity* (1993), *Identity/Difference: Democratic Negotiations of Political Paradox* (1991), and *The Augustinian Imperative* (1993). His essays have been published in *Political Theory, Millennium, Theory, Culture and Society*, and *Polity*.

KATHY FERGUSON is professor of political science and women's studies at the University of Hawai'i at Manoa. She teaches courses in feminist theory, historical and contemporary political theory, and organizational theory. She is currently writing a book, with co-author Phyllis Turnbull, on the semiotics of the military in Hawai'i. Her publications include *Kibbutz Journal: Reflections on Gender, Race, and Militarism in Israel* (1995) and *The Man Question: Visions of Subjectivity in Feminist Theory* (1993).

KENNAN FERGUSON is a graduate student in political science at the University of Hawai'i. He is currently working on a dissertation concerning aesthetics and political identity.

JONATHAN FRIEDMAN has degrees from the École Pratique des Hautes Études (now École des Hautes Études en Sciences Sociales) in Paris and the University of Paris in sociology and social anthropology. He obtained his Ph.D. from Columbia University in 1972. Since then he has taught at the École des Hautes en Sciences Sociales, University College London, University of Copenhagen, and currently the University of Lund, where he is professor of social anthropology. He has specialized in Southeast Asia, Oceania primarily, and has written on questions of long-term historical social transformation, global systemic processes, the relation between global social and cultural processes, and cultural movements. His most recent publications include *Cultural Identity and Global Process* (1994), and an edited volume, *Consumption and Identity* (1994).

JIM GEORGE is senior lecturer in international relations in the Department of Political Science (Faculties) at the Australian National University, Canberra, Australia. He is the author of *Discourses of Global Politics: A Critical (Re)Introduction to International Relations* (1994) and has written extensively on issues of contemporary global politics for journals in the United States, Britain, and Australia.

SANKARAN KRISHNA received his Ph.D. from Syracuse University in 1989 and teaches comparative politics and international relations at the University of Hawai'i at Manoa. He is especially interested in critical theory in international relations, postcolonial studies, and Indian politics.

FOLKE LINDAHL is associate professor in political theory at James Madison College at Michigan State University. He received his B.A. from Reed College and his Ph.D. in political science from the University of Hawai'i. He is the author of a monograph on Tocqueville's political theory, titled *Tocqueville's Civil Discourse: A Postmodernist Reading*. His current research and teaching interests are in modern political philosophy, liberal democratic theory, postmodernism, and Caribbean politics and literature. He is also the director of the Caribbean Summer Program of Michigan State University.

RICHARD MAXWELL teaches international communication and political economy of media and culture in the Department of Radio-Film-TV at Northwestern University. He is author of *The Spectacle of Democracy: Spanish Television, Nationalism, and Political Transition* (1995).

ABBAS MILANI is professor and head of the Department of History/ Political Science at College of Notre Dame. A collection of his essays on Iran's encounter with modernity was just published in Europe. He has also published a translation of *King of the Benighted*.

LORIS MIRELLA received his Ph.D. from Duke University in 1991. He has taught for the past three years as a lecturer at the University of Pennsylvania.

CINDY PATTON is an assistant professor in the School of Theater and Communication at Temple University, Philadelphia. She has written extensively on the AIDS epidemic and its medical and popular representation, including *Inventing AIDS* (1990).

JAN JINDY PETTMAN is senior lecturer in political science at Australian National University. She has written extensively on gender and the politics of identity, including *Living in the Margins: Racism, Sexism and Feminism in Australia*. She now teaches and researches in feminist international relations, especially issues to do with women and nationalism, the gender of war, and the international political economy of sex. Her book *Worlding Women: A Feminist International Politics* is forthcoming.

BENIGNO SÁNCHEZ-EPPLER has been teaching and doing research in Latin American studies and comparative literature at Brandeis University since 1989. His published work includes a monograph (1986) on the reception young Cuban poets provided for the exiled Spanish poet Juan Ramón Jiménez and his work during the 1930s. His current work on Reinaldo Arenas, the Cuban gay anti-Castro exile writer, has also led to wider exploration of gay diasporas and queer transnational studies.

PETER A. SCHILLING received his doctorate in English literature from Columbia University in 1994. His published work is in the area of British and American literary and intellectual culture of the late-modern period. He has also begun work with cultural and academic institutions in the development of multimedia educational resources.

MICHAEL J. SHAPIRO is professor of political science at the University of Hawai'i. His recent publications include *Reading the Postmodern Polity: Political Theory as Textual Practice* (1992) and *Reading "Adam Smith": Desire, History and Value.*

NEVZAT SOGUK is an assistant professor of political science at the University of Hawai'i. Most broadly, his research is guided by an interest in international relations theory, especially those aspects centering on global and transnational processes of institution building, economic, political, and cultural identity constructions, and human migrations. Pursuant to these interests, his work examines the practices of global political/cultural economy as they bear upon changing conceptualizations and practices of state sovereignty. He has published on related issues in *Alternatives*, *New Political Science*, and *International Issues.*

PHYLLIS TURNBULL is an assistant professor of political science at the University of Hawai'i. She teaches courses in the politics of Hawai'i. Her research interests include the politics of land, language, and militarism.

NICHOLAS XENOS teaches political theory at the University of Massachusetts at Amherst. He is the author of *Scarcity and Modernity* and is currently completing a book on the idea of a homeland.

Index